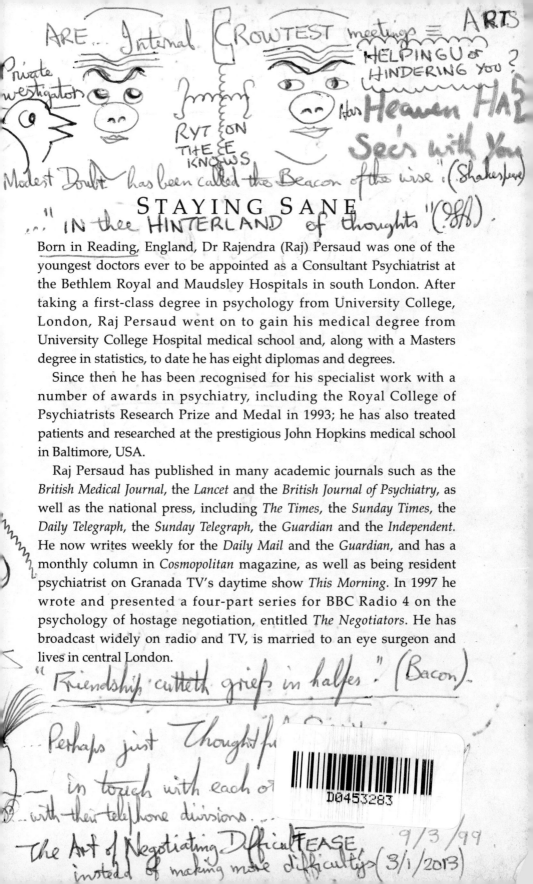

ARE... Internal CROWTEST meetings = ARTS

Private investigators

HELPING U or HINDERING you ?

RYT EON THE CE KNOWS

Has Heaven HA? Sec's with You " (Shakespeare)

Modest Doubt has been called the Beacon of the wise : (Shakespere)

STAYING SANE

... " IN thee HINTERLAND of thoughts " (RP).

Born in Reading, England, Dr Rajendra (Raj) Persaud was one of the youngest doctors ever to be appointed as a Consultant Psychiatrist at the Bethlem Royal and Maudsley Hospitals in south London. After taking a first-class degree in psychology from University College, London, Raj Persaud went on to gain his medical degree from University College Hospital medical school and, along with a Masters degree in statistics, to date he has eight diplomas and degrees.

Since then he has been recognised for his specialist work with a number of awards in psychiatry, including the Royal College of Psychiatrists Research Prize and Medal in 1993; he has also treated patients and researched at the prestigious John Hopkins medical school in Baltimore, USA.

Raj Persaud has published in many academic journals such as the *British Medical Journal*, the *Lancet* and the *British Journal of Psychiatry*, as well as the national press, including *The Times*, the *Sunday Times*, the *Daily Telegraph*, the *Sunday Telegraph*, the *Guardian* and the *Independent*. He now writes weekly for the *Daily Mail* and the *Guardian*, and has a monthly column in *Cosmopolitan* magazine, as well as being resident psychiatrist on Granada TV's daytime show *This Morning*. In 1997 he wrote and presented a four-part series for BBC Radio 4 on the psychology of hostage negotiation, entitled *The Negotiators*. He has broadcast widely on radio and TV, is married to an eye surgeon and lives in central London.

" Friendship cutteth grief in halfes " (Bacon).

... Perhaps just thoughtfu ... ... in touch with each o ... with their telephone divisions.

The Art of Negotiating DifficulfEASE, 9/3/99 instead of making more difficulty (3/1/2013)

DUMBARTON
HISTORACLE ACCOUNTS

HEAR' S'HE NORTON

THINK...

YOU SIGNAL WHO

THOUGHTS

HOSTING

THINK

A REMINDING
THOUGHTS

2013

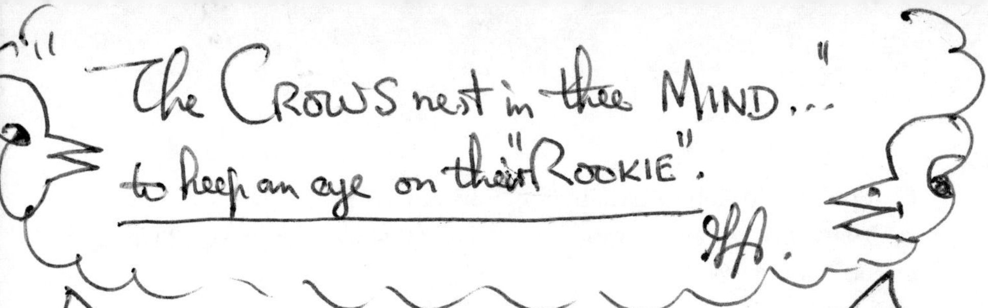

"The CROWS nest in thee MIND..."
"to keep an eye on their "ROOKIE".

STAYING SANE

CATS ERES
CATECHISMS

How to make your mind work for you

THOSE...

I HAVE A GOAT
THATASSESES... ME THEM
ASSES
ASSESS MENTALLY.

FORSIBYL ACCOUNTS

HINTERCOM
2 WAY
Dr Raj Persaud

ACCOUNTS FOR SI3YL

FORSIWYL
ACCOUNTS

metro

2012

First published in hardback in Great Britain in 1997
by Metro Books (an imprint of Metro Publishing Limited), 19 Gerrard
Street, London W1V 7LA

This paperback edition first published in 1998 by Metro Books

Raj Persaud is hereby identified as the author of this work in accordance
with Section 77 of the Copyright, Designs and Patents Act 1988.

British Library Cataloguing in Publication Data. A CIP record of this
book is available on request from the British Library.

ISBN 1 900512 38 6

10 9 8 7 6 5 4 3 2 1

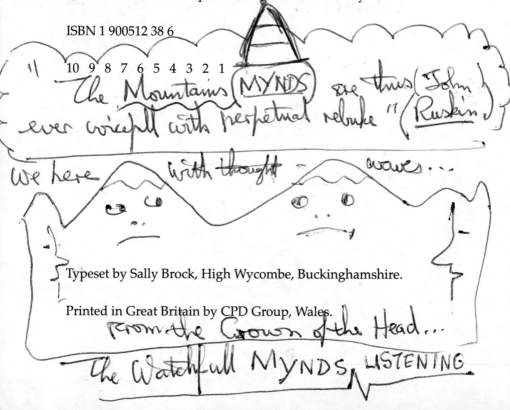

Typeset by Sally Brock, High Wycombe, Buckinghamshire.

Printed in Great Britain by CPD Group, Wales.

The { OPinyon POLLS } thought.. (JA) 2012
     { Opinion Poll is }

[MIN>RUM THOUGHT } MESSAGES on a →
[MIN>EN THOUGHT   }
                              ←2 Way Train of
                                 thoughts ....
                                      (2012)

listening for BRAYINS..

If I am sane, it is entirely because of my lovely wife Francesca.
This book is dedicated to her.

With   MYN>ONKEY   Thoughts—

Show me a sane man and I will cure him for you.
                              C. G. Jung
                         Observer, 19 July 1975

" My mind to me a kingdom ys ...
such present joys therein in find;
That it excells all other bliss
That Earth affords, or grows by kind :
Though much I want; which most would have
Yet still my mynd forbids to crave ..."

Sir Edward Dyer
(1545 — 1607)

AUTHOR'S NOTE

Therapeutic work with patients often hinges on the precise form of words used in a session. Yet in this book I communicate ideas in a way so candid as to risk unnerving some people. I do this not because I wish to provoke, but to cut through jargon and go for the essence of what needs to be done to maintain mental health. We can only act when our options are clear, so I believe that the value of words in therapeutic practice lies in their ability to lead to action and change. If in trying to set out the possibilities available to us I risk upsetting some, I hope that the benefit in stimulating debate of this neglected subject may compensate for this.

The questionnaires in this book have been carefully designed and are an authentic representation of the tests psychologists use to assess personality. However, because of space requirements, they are shortened versions. The scoring analysis should not be taken as a definitive judgement, but as a rough guide to help improve your self-understanding.

The case histories used throughout this book have had significant personal and clinical details changed to protect the identities of those concerned. In addition, as well as cases I have dealt with personally, I have also used situations which commonly occur in my NHS clinic, and have amalgamated disparate aspects into each case. Any apparent resemblance to a specific person is accidental and unintended.

The superscript numbers in the text refer to referenced research publications which are detailed at the back of the book. The interested reader is invited to pursue these references if they would like to take their study of this fascinating subject further. I hope I will be forgiven for not detailing the methodology involved in the several hundred academic papers I have drawn on, as this would have distracted the general reader from the main thrust of my arguments.

I hope my academic colleagues will not be suspicious of my attempt to communicate these ideas to a wider audience. Psychiatry is suffused with uncertainty, but I believe that although precise data is absent or – in many cases – the necessary experiments have simply not been done, this does not mean that an informed opinion is devoid of value.

The public need to know now what they can do to preserve and enhance their mental health. While we wait for the much-needed research to be done (and given the dearth of academic work in the area of preventive psychiatry, we might be waiting for decades) this book attempts to provide as comprehensive a guide as possible to the current state of scientific knowledge on the subject.

A note about the organisation of the book. Every chapter, with the exception of Chapters 2 and 10, deals with a particular issue central to mental health. Chapter 2 ('Am I Insane – or is it Everyone Else?') in contrast reviews the philosophical and academic issues central to defining mental health; however, the non-clinician or non-academic reader can safely skip this chapter without missing the essential advice on how to preserve mental health.

I hope therefore that the book will be appraised in the spirit with which it is offered – as an attempt to help people help themselves.

ACKNOWLEDGEMENTS

Without the support of my wife, parents, sister and brother, the prospect of writing a book based on an original and controversial idea would have proved too daunting. My mother and father-in-law as well as two sisters-in-law also gave me much-needed encouragement to keep going.

I am grateful, too, to my secretary at the Bethlem and Maudsley Hospitals, Sheila Banks – a much better psychiatrist than I ever will be! Sheila keeps me sane by ensuring that the stressful working conditions of practising adult and community psychiatry as a Consultant in the British National Health Service do not discourage me.

While a lecturer at the Institute of Psychiatry at the University of London, I have had the privilege of working with some of the most eminent psychiatrists in the world. Professor Sir David Goldberg introduced me to the fact most mental illness never reaches the attention of psychiatrists; Professor Isaac Marks acquainted me with the idea that patients could learn to treat themselves even for serious psychiatric illness; Professor Robin Murray stimulated my interest in prevention by suggesting the possible importance of good obstetric care in averting adult psychiatric illness caused by subtle brain damage; Professor Gerald Russell, who first properly described Bulimia Nervosa, taught me to scrutinise how research might actually benefit our patients; Jim Birley, past President of the Royal College of Psychiatrists, encouraged me to communicate complex psychiatric ideas to a wider audience, while Professor Stuart Checkley gave me the opportunity to see patients too afraid of visiting a psychiatric hospital, by arranging for me to consult at ground-breaking psychiatric clinics in General Practice.

Judy Finnigan and Richard Madeley, who kindly pilot me through our demanding live TV phone-ins, showed me that saying the truth about mental health is what that public still wants, no matter how unpalatable that might be; Rory Clements, Health Editor of the *Daily Mail*, and Mandi Norwood and Louise Atkinson of *Cosmopolitan* magazine guided my writing for the national press to focus on what the community really needs to know and not what professionals deign to tell them; Sally Flatman and Hilary McLennan of BBC Radio 4 persevered in teaching me how to popularise academic ideas.

I am particularly grateful to the team at Metro Books – Becke Parker, Sally Harding, Emma Bryant, Alan Brooke, Anne Askwith, Jane Robertson, Sally Brock, and Susanne McDadd – for their support and belief in the project.

The community psychiatric nurses in my team – Asha, Theresa, Farid, Iqbal, Mandy and Sandra – have taught me more than any textbook.

But I owe most to my patients, who on a daily basis tolerantly continue my education in mental health.

"I lay awake, distraught with aching thoughts..." (L. Morris)

"The Association of ... thoughts, form Cues for thee Mind) (Eff)

He who is not free, is not an Agent but a Patient

(Charles (Wesley) preacher man.

"The Dimensions of this mercy are above my thoughts... It is, for aught I know, a crowning mercy.
(Oliver Cromwell)

5025

HEAR 2 HELP
THOUGHTS
WALSINGHAM
THINKUSAID
THOUGHTRADER
INSIDELINES . . . .

Contents

"The Hearer on the Speakers mouth depends" (J. Dryden)

"Remember...

$\left\{\begin{array}{l} \text{Inside/Out} \\ \text{Inside/Doubt} \end{array}\right\}$

" Hearken to ...
" The lovers say; and Happy is the love" (A.E. Housman)

" Thinks K⟩ ..
(always the Child of Thought)
is having a GOAT it " (SfA)

" The Logic has not left the building (-Bill ding thing) the old -
(IT IS the BillDing.) RYTON DUNS MORE

" Logic contrives to knit true arguments
... and unknit false ones!' (J. Locke)

" The Mind is always the Dupe of the heart".
(French Proverb)
(La Rochfoucald)

" ITS INCONCLUESIEVE ..
WITH THOUGHTS..
WINKING WITH INKLINGS " (SfA) 2015

INTRODUCTION

"To clense houses of dust." (Trevisa). (T'Revisa)

"To clense MINDS of interfearance;" 25/12/2013

'Know your limits, and then destroy them'

MINDONKEY

'I'm losing it', 'I can't cope', 'I'm going round the bend' – how often have any of us cried out such words to ourselves?

Nearly everyone I have met has admitted to feelings like these. Indeed, many of the famous and apparently self-assured people I have come into contact with as a result of my press column and broadcasting have confessed to me privately fears about their sanity and about how difficult it seems to maintain positive mental health in the face of pressure.

As with anyone, these feelings may have been triggered by a specific event – a divorce or job loss, for example – or simply have crystallised over time, because of some long-term difficult situation, or even the cumulative effect of daily irritations. *Thought PA Troth*

Worries about mental health are widespread, and yet, even nowadays, there is still a stigma attached to mental ill-health. While sharing misgivings about your physical state of health is socially acceptable, it is virtually taboo to discuss apprehensions about sliding into mental illness. Just imagine what the reaction would be if you responded to a conversational *'How are you?'* with *'Feeling extremely pressurised, thanks, but the doctor's given me pills to cope with my aggression'*. Time after time I come across the belief that the sufferer is alone in his or her concern – precisely because of the stigma attached to discussing these issues.

In my book I want to break down the taboo on this subject and put maintaining and improving mental health as prominently on the public agenda as public health campaigns have put preserving physical health. I aim to make getting into shape apply as much to your mental as your physical well-being; in fact, I believe that once you know how, it is in many respects easier to stay sane than it is to remain in physical shape.

'...Telepathy' is A New Sense of thee Mynd . 2014

17/9/2013

1

Unlike many other self-help books, *Staying Sane* focuses on prevention and is aimed at people who would think of themselves as well – people like you or me. It explains to a general audience the tactics most likely to help you prevent the onset of psychological problems. In writing this book I have drawn on the latest international research in preventive mental health care, as well as lessons learned from my ten years working as a psychiatrist at the Bethlem Royal and Maudsley Hospitals in South London.

I should say now that the very belief that you can prevent mental illness is extremely controversial. Perhaps one reason for my unusual perspective lies in the nature of my academic background. I gained a degree in psychology before going on to qualify as a medical doctor and then eventually attained membership of the Royal College of Psychiatrists. Few doctors or psychiatrists have qualifications in psychology, and fewer still psychologists have formally trained in medicine or psychiatry.

As a rough generalisation, psychology is the study of the 'normal' mind, while psychiatry is more interested in an 'abnormal' mental state. Unfortunately, having carved up the world in this way, neither psychiatrists nor psychologists appear interested in the group of people who are moving from one category to the other. Instead, general psychologists largely study those who are mentally healthy while psychiatrists investigate those who are already mentally ill. But it seems to me that it is vitally important to predict who is going to change before it happens. We should focus on processes rather than states.

My training in both psychology and psychiatry is relevant here as it has exposed me to the academic study of both the normal and abnormal mind.

The starting point of preventing psychological problems is to be armed with information. While it is virtually impossible not to come across details about staying physically healthy – in everything from your daily newspaper to the labelling on supermarket foods – reliable facts on maintaining mental health tend to be buried in textbooks and academic journals.

There may appear to be numerous books available to the general reader – publications of the 'ten tips to deal with stress' variety. Advice from these sources may offer short-term solutions for the mildly

*The GOODS TRAIN of thought...
Stays on Track and picks up the GooDS on its way*

distressed or contain information not tested in clinical practice. As a source of guidance on prevention of serious problems, however, these books do not offer a way to achieve long-term mental health.

On the physical side, most of us know that if you eat a balanced diet, watch your weight, exercise regularly, don't smoke, drink moderately, get vaccinated, drive carefully and avoid fights and dare-devil sports, your bodily health is likely to remain good and you should be robust enough to ward off many illnesses.

If you are not as physically robust as you would like to be, this is rarely because you do not know what to do. You may plead lack of time, but you cannot plead ignorance. In this age of wall-to-wall advice from media doctors, women's magazines and health programmes, the problem is escaping from high-quality health advice, not getting it.

But how easy is it to get guidance on what really influences mental health? By this I don't mean tips on relaxation or the catch-all direction to go and see a counsellor or psychotherapist. I mean advice you can follow yourself and which really can make a difference to your long-term mental health.

A few years ago I presented a national BBC radio programme which involved asking members of the public: 'What should you do to maintain your mental health?' I went to a well-known London gym and interviewed a number of the health enthusiasts busily working out there. First, I asked them what they did on a daily basis to maintain their bodily health. Without exception they enthusiastically detailed their combination of physical work-outs and diet programmes (these descriptions were invariably so long they had to be severely edited before being broadcast).

Then I asked the same question with regard to their mental health. The response was usually a blank look. Falteringly, a few people came up with things like: get a good night's sleep; read a lot; try to take things easy – and that was about it.

I drew three conclusions from this. First, the obvious one, that mental health is the poor relation of physical health as far as public awareness is concerned, even though psychological health is at least as important as physical health to a person's well-being, if not more so. Secondly, even when people had ideas about how to stay mentally

3

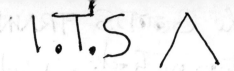

healthy, they were much more tentative as to whether these proposals worked in practice than they were about ways to keep physically fit. And thirdly, most of the notions they had, such as punching a pillow to release aggression, were ineffective and, in some cases, counterproductive.

There is a deep irony in this imbalance of knowledge. Young to middle-aged people in the western world are in many cases far more at risk of deteriorating mental than physical health. In other words, the young, fit group I met in that London gym, who devote so much energy to perfecting their sit-ups, are in many cases statistically more vulnerable to suffering from psychiatric than physical illness.

Here are just a few statistics:

- Two-thirds of suicides are under 35 years of age.[1]

- Young men are particularly vulnerable to suicide. The suicide rate among men aged between 25 and 44 years in England and Wales rose by 33 per cent between 1980 and 1990[2] and by 85 per cent for men aged between 15 and 24 years. This dramatic rise of suicide rates in young men means that suicide is now one of the leading causes of loss of expected years of life through death. That is to say, an illness that leads to death in an older person shortens their expected life-span by much less than death by suicide in a young person, who should normally have had many more years to live.

- The average age when clinical depression begins is 30 years,[3] with particularly high rates in younger married women with children.

- More than one in five of the people reading this book will at some time in their lives suffer from an episode of clinical depression[4] of the kind requiring psychiatric intervention.

- 20 per cent of adults suffer from psychiatric problems at any one time.[5]

- 48 per cent of adults will suffer from a psychiatric disorder at some time in their lives.[6]

HAUNTED HOUSE... A
UNIVERSE OF

- At least 40 per cent of general practice consultations involve mental health problems.[7]

PERPETUALLY

- In any one week 10 per cent of adults are depressed.[8]

EXPANDING ... ON

- In Britain there are 5,000 deaths annually through suicide and more than 100,000 suicide attempts.[9]

THOUGHTS AHEAD...

- At any one moment, one in ten young adults suffers from long-term personality problems.[10] A personality problem is a troublesome aspect of your character which causes suffering in others or yourself.

(WAVERLY ..., THOUGHT)

- At some time in their lives, one in four adults suffers from alcohol dependence and/or other drug abuse problems.[11]

- One in five adults suffered from serious anxiety symptoms in the previous year.[12]

These figures are in themselves a shocking testament to the prevalence of psychiatric problems. But it is perhaps even more sobering to realise that these disorders tend to strike young, fit adults. In contrast, the majority of the physical illnesses that account for most disability tend to be the preserve of older people.

Another irony, given the lack of preventive mental health care, is that while most mental illnesses are treatable, recovery is less certain and more problematic than from most common physical illnesses. The term 'disability-adjusted year' has been coined to measure just how much disability is caused by one illness as compared to another, i.e. for how long the illness and its effects occupy your time. According to a recent World Development Report, mental disorders exceed cancer and heart disease as a leading cause of such disability-adjusted life-years, accounting for 10.5 per cent of all such lost years in men and 8.3 per cent in women.[13]

Unlike physical illnesses, in which the process of prevention is often straightforward – even intuitively obvious – avoidance and management of psychological problems often require strategies which are not so apparent – indeed, what most people would instinctively do to preserve mental health is often counterproductive. For example, the healing process for one of the most common psychological symptoms, anxiety, often requires you to use a strategy which seems unnatural: to stay with the thing or situation making you anxious and not avoid the problem, in other words to face your fear. One reason this is not the approach favoured by most people is that it invariably makes you feel worse in the short run, despite being better for you long term.

Or take stress, where the natural response is again to withdraw. As I demonstrate later in this book, withdrawal and avoidance strategies have been shown to worsen mental health rather than improve or preserve it.

Most people's instinctive response when asked what they should do to stay sane is to suggest they should do less, avoid stress and relax more. The kernel of this advice is basically not to do what you are doing at the moment. But it is very difficult to change your routine like this. If we could only withdraw from the problems life throws at us, we might indeed feel better. Yet we are often so caught up in the web of demands upon us so that suggestions like taking more time off are simply impracticable. Instead, the key to positive mental health and staying sane is how to deal actively with crisis, stress and difficulty.

Given all those facts, one would think that prevention would be given higher priority in mental health care. Yet, whereas modern physical medicine has, since the 1940s, expended huge resources on preventive measures such as vaccination and public health campaigns, mental health care is still in the Dark Ages as far as prevention is concerned. For example, the distinguished British medical epidemiologist, Sir Richard Doll, whose work helped establish the link between lung cancer and smoking and who therefore has a deep interest in preventive health, has stated '...it will, I suspect, be many years before we can design a programme for the prevention of mental illness'.[14]

One reason for this is that, whereas physical health is usually obvious to everyone, mental good health remains an unfamiliar entity – to experts as much as to the layman. Even one of the definitive textbooks on the subject, *Prevention in Psychiatry*, edited by a Professor of Psychiatry at the University of Cambridge and Principal Medical Officer at the British Government's Department of Health, states in its introduction, 'In general, this volume does not deal with direct issues of positive mental health'.[15]

The lay person's confusion as to what mental good health is became clear during my interviews for the radio programme. For example, it was clear that people tended to view mental fitness, health and happiness as a single concept.

In fact the three are quite different, mental fitness being something like IQ or cleverness, mental health being the ability to ward off mental illness, and happiness being a state of long-lasting, overall contentedness (although it is frequently confused with pleasure, a temporary sensation which results from a good thing happening in your life).

There are many other misconceptions about mental health. One is that intelligence is more likely to lead to mental health. While there is some association between intelligence (or intellectual ability) and mental health, it is only moderate, and some studies suggest the reverse. For example, there is some evidence that those with a higher IQ are more prone to worry excessively.

Dr Felix Post, a Consultant Psychiatrist formerly at the Maudsley Hospital, has studied world-famous men including scientists, composers, politicians, artists, intellectuals and writers, and concludes that anxiety and depressive psychiatric disorders (or, as he terms them, 'neurotic characteristics') were more common in some groups of highly creative people than in the population as a whole.[16] Other research has borne this out, leading to the suggestion that creativity and psychiatric abnormalities can be linked.[17, 18, 19]

Post[20] also found that in a study of 100 of the most eminent writers in recent centuries, 72 per cent suffered from depression, a similar figure to the 80 per cent which has been found for more recent prominent American writers.[21] What is particular intriguing about these findings is that they suggest that the most verbally expressive people in the world are prone to psychological problems. This is not what you would expect if you accepted the prevailing counselling/psychotherapeutic model of mental health that the ability to verbalise your problems is good for you.

Post went on to ask whether psychiatric treatment to cure writers' psychological problems would make them less creative. This raises the wider issue of trade-offs: preserving your mental health often requires trade-offs with other priorities in your life. It may be, for example, that the relentless ambition needed to become a top business executive

To SHEW HOW INCREDIBLE THOUGHT

produces, as a by-product, symptoms likely to weaken mental health. A less obvious trade-off is the ability to lose an argument, as compromise is vital in maintaining relationships. Sometimes you can't be both right and happy.

One of the issues I discuss in a later chapter is that because many successful or high-achieving people (not just in terms of career or material gain, but also those who successfully raise a family) tend to get positive feedback for their achievements, they are likely to become preoccupied with that area of their lives, to the neglect of other aspects. You are, in fact, increasing your vulnerability to psychological distress by allowing your life to revolve around one issue.

Given that much psychological distress follows a loss – particularly if the lost person, event, thing or activity is central to your life – if you were suddenly to lose that job, career, family, or relationship, you would be unlikely to survive unscathed mentally. The better positive mental health strategy is to ensure your life is complex, not simple. I will explain this in detail later in the book.

If, for example, you have five interests rather than one – say, work, family, a sport such as tennis, a leisure activity such as the cinema, and a spiritual activity such as meditation or religion – losing one of the five is less likely to precipitate mental illness than if you had devoted yourself just to work, for example.

Imagine losing something very important to you right now. Sometimes simply imagining your life without something you have come to take for granted helps you work harder to ensure you don't lose it. Do you have other things in your life which would help compensate for the loss? If you don't, beware – you have adopted a life path which leaves you particularly vulnerable to psychological problems.

All too often I see in my NHS practice at the Maudsley people whose mental health has suffered because they have failed to adopt the simple preventive mental health strategy of seeking a balance in their lives. Of course, this doesn't mean you should cram your life so full as to cause excessive stress!

The fact that there only seems to be a moderate association between intelligence and mental health suggests that while intelligent people are clever enough to avoid some things which cause mental illness – they are perhaps less likely to lose their jobs or suffer the problems of low

"Perpetual Motion"

By the —

incomes – they are still not aware of the full picture, particularly the need to keep a balance to stay sane.

Given that intelligence as measured by IQ tests is often not a good predictor of success in life and emotional health, psychologists have recently suggested that emotional intelligence (EQ rather than IQ) may be more relevant. Emotional intelligence is a measure of your ability to perceive correctly your own and others' emotions, and to use this information shrewdly.[22] Because the more emotionally intelligent person is better able to regulate their and others' moods they are superior at understanding and managing themselves as well as others. Mental health is probably more closely determined by the kind of social intelligence as measured by the EQ scale below, than the intelligence measured by IQ tests.[23]

To see how you score, try this quiz.[24, 25, 26]

INTERACTIVITY of MINDS

ARE YOU EMOTIONALLY INTELLIGENT? THE EQ SCALE

Each statement is followed by two possible responses: agree or disagree. Read each statement carefully and decide which response best describes how you feel. Then put a tick over the corresponding response. Please respond to every statement. If you are not completely sure which response is more accurate, put the response which you feel is most appropriate. Do not read the scoring explanation before filling out the questionnaire. Do not spend too long on each statement. It is important that you answer each question as honestly as possible.

COVARIANT GHOSTS THAT INTERACT WITH THOUGHTS

		AGREE	DISAGREE
1	When I am emotionally hurt I can disguise it well from others	A	✓ B
2	I might never get over things which upset me	B	✓ A
3	I usually know how someone is feeling before they tell me	A	✓ B

TELL TALE TWISTERS

(2016) △ (#6)

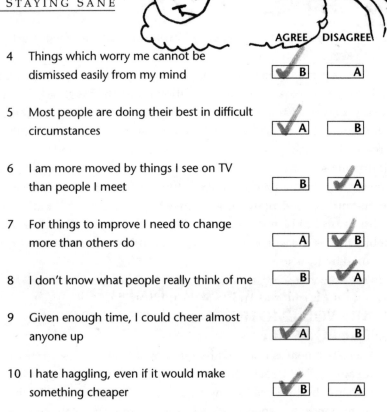

4   Things which worry me cannot be dismissed easily from my mind   ☑ **B**   ☐ **A**

5   Most people are doing their best in difficult circumstances   ☑ **A**   ☐ **B**

6   I am more moved by things I see on TV than people I meet   ☐ **B**   ☑ **A**

7   For things to improve I need to change more than others do   ☐ **A**   ☑ **B**

8   I don't know what people really think of me   ☐ **B**   ☑ **A**

9   Given enough time, I could cheer almost anyone up   ☑ **A**   ☐ **B**

10 I hate haggling, even if it would make something cheaper   ☑ **B**   ☐ **A**

Add up your score from summing the numbers of As and Bs in each box you have ticked. Your score and the interpretation given below should be treated with caution – this short test is by no means definitive, but may offer a guide to where you stand compared to others around you.

SCORE

8 or more As. You are scoring very highly indeed in emotional intelligence and this may explain your ability to continue functioning fairly well even in the grip of strong emotions. Your superior control over your emotions means that even when angry you are often able to remain fairly civil, while lower scorers resort to rudeness and aggression. Your understanding of the emotions others invoke in you, and your ability to control these feelings, explain why you may be able to get on with a much wider variety of people than lower scorers, and this skill of co-operation will explain the greater likelihood of career and relationship success in your life compared to lower scorers.

5A'S

Between 5 and 7 As. You are scoring above average for emotional intelligence and this may explain your superior ability (compared to lower scorers) to understand quickly what others are feeling, before they manage to express their feelings. One possible problem you may encounter is that your skills in handling your own and others' emotions lead you to focus too much on getting on with others, and to neglect other important ingredients to success in life, like hard work and having good ideas. One of the reasons others may turn to you for advice is your ability to act wisely in human relations.

Between 3 and 5 As. You are scoring around average for social intelligence and this means your understanding of your own current emotional state might not be quite as insightful as higher scorers. Certain goals, perhaps like financial success, take priority in your life over getting on with others, and yet no matter how many of these goals you attain, you remain relatively unhappy. This means you may not yet have understood what emotions in your own life are really important to you, or what causes them. Your happiness may be linked to your chronic need for praise from certain significant others in your life, like your parents, siblings or your partner. Only when you understand what you really need can your EQ score go up.

Between 0 and 2 As. You are scoring very low in emotional intelligence and this is probably explained by your inability to divert your attention from concern with your own emotions to being more sensitive to how others are feeling. You may feel there is already too much emphasis on etiquette and politeness as you like to break social rules and are not afraid of alienating others to get what you want in life. The more emotionally intelligent way is to get others to enjoy giving you what you want. You are perhaps too impatient with others to be in control of your emotional state, and only when you gain more control over your emotions will the impulsive and temperamental side of your nature improve, with consequent gains in EQ.

There are KNOWALLS on MY MYND ...TO DETERMINE THOUGHTS!

But even EQ is not the complete answer to mental health. Another common belief is that happiness is the key. While happiness has a stronger link than intelligence, it is still not a predominant factor. Those who are deeply unhappy are clearly prone to poor mental health, and many who are only moderately happy seem to be more mentally healthy than those who rate themselves as very happy indeed.

Why this apparent contradiction? It seems that those prone to intense happiness are also prone to more intense unhappiness, suffering from spectacular 'highs' and 'lows'.[27] Some people seem deliriously happy one morning, greeting you as though you are a long-lost friend, and yet totally dejected a week later, hardly looking you in the eye.[28]

One explanation for the randomness of feeling happy and unhappy is that these feelings are caused by events, triggered by whether good or bad things have happened to you. Happiness based on the pleasure which follows from external events is always likely to be fragile, as pleasure is usually fleeting.[29]

Moreover, happiness is a misleading standard by which to judge mental health. The big indicator of mental health lies not in our reaction to good events but in our response to bad ones. Research has shown that one of the distinguishing features of mentally healthy people is that they are not set back so much by negative life events. So while mentally fragile people may feel temporarily happier than the mentally healthy because of recent good news, a few negative events will drive them towards mental ill-health. In contrast, the mentally healthy person reacts more positively – or less negatively – to these same bad events.

Happiness itself is made up of two different parts (which psychologists call dimensions): a pleasure component – simply a measure of how good people feel at a given moment – and an intellectual or cognitive aspect termed satisfaction,[30] which is a more thoughtful state. The latter occurs when we think about our lives and how satisfied we are about how things are going. This process supports the subsequent emotional mood of happiness.

Maintaining and improving mental health seems more strongly linked to this satisfaction component of happiness than to that of momentary pleasure. Trying to get 'happy' by, say, using drugs or turning to a leisure pursuit, may succeed in the short term. However, if

AUDIBABBLE INCREDIBUBBLE ORONSAY

dab audio BROADCASTS

OUTSIDE

it does nothing to alter your overall contentment with yourself or your life it will have done nothing for your mental health.

Ways of influencing your life satisfaction might range from examining the important goals in your life and reviewing whether your day-to-day activities are going to move you any closer to them, to the realisation that what you thought was important cannot really be, because even when you get it, you remain unhappy.

I would go further than saying that the pleasure part of happiness is not synonymous with positive mental health and argue that many people's rather desperate pursuit of happiness is symptomatic of poor mental health. The relentless pursuit of pleasure as manifested by excessive spending, taking drugs, sexual promiscuity, alcohol abuse, or the addiction to falling in love as opposed to experiencing long-term relationships is linked to future poor mental health.

I would say the key component of mental health is the ability to withstand events or situations known to precipitate mental illness. Some have called this 'psychological hardiness' or 'resilience'. The mentally healthy person doesn't necessarily sail through their divorce, sacking or bereavement, but is less prone to a nervous breakdown on such occasions.

The resilient person may appear at first glance just to be a hardened case. After all, a psychopath – someone devoid of the capacity to enjoy close affiliations – would sail through relationship losses just as easily, perhaps even more easily, than the mentally healthy person. But psychopaths, unlike the positively mentally healthy, are so bad at relationships they do not usually have healthy ones, in the sense of having someone to confide in, seek advice from or get practical assistance from at times of need.

Even when the more mentally unhealthy do not actually suffer a breakdown at times of stress, they are likely to be severely weakened, and a combination or sequence of negative events is more likely to push them over the edge into breakdown. In contrast, mentally healthy people often find themselves strengthened by negative events and are less, rather than more, likely to suffer a breakdown should another crisis follow on the heels of the last. In other words, mentally healthy people are able to learn emotionally from whatever life throws at them.

My view is that there is a spectrum of mental health. I have a dimensional view of mental health as opposed to a categorical one, in which you are either sane or insane. (The other classic categorical entity is pregnancy – you are either pregnant or you are not – you cannot be a little bit pregnant).[31] According to my idea, even if you are not suffering from actual symptoms, there is still much you can do to shift yourself in the right direction along the spectrum of mental health and away from illness.

This concept of a spectrum is deeply controversial in medicine and psychiatry. Most doctors today still diagnose on the basis that people are either mentally ill or healthy. They give no thought to the idea that while many do not have enough symptoms to be diagnosed, there are enough signs to indicate that without intervention they will become unwell in the near future. The idea that you can predict who will become unwell before it happens is considered by most doctors implausible; they argue that as we cannot yet be certain about the causes of psychological problems, how can it be possible to determine who will become unwell?

My particular interest is in defining and measuring positive mental health in those with no symptoms of mental illness, with a view to predicting who will be resilient and who the more vulnerable to psychiatric problems. I believe it is possible to measure where a person lies on the spectrum ranging from mental ill-health to good health to predict with a fair degree of accuracy who is likely to become ill. I believe we all fit in somewhere along this spectrum of mental health, and the aim of this book and, I hope, preventive mental health programmes in general, is to move us all a little in the right direction. The main advantage of being further from the mental illness end of the spectrum, of course, is that it gives you a kind of mental credit – a buffer zone – should you begin to suffer strain on your mental health.

Think of a few people you know well. While most don't suffer from mental illness, you could probably rank those you consider most mentally healthy and those less blessed with positive mental health. Don't look for actual symptoms – these often don't manifest themselves until a person is virtually off the scale already, in the same way that an alcoholic's morning drinking doesn't occur until virtually the final stage of the problem. Instead, judge by how you have seen them behave in stressful situations.

Then try to put yourself somewhere on the spectrum. Where would you place yourself in comparison to your friends? After reading this book you should be able to judge fairly accurately who is most likely to develop psychological problems. Also, think of this book as the mental equivalent of regular exercise and a healthy diet. Physically healthy people won't be afraid of taking on a new activity because they are confident of their physical fitness, and, similarly, mentally healthy people will not shy away from a challenge to their mental health.

Be prepared, though, for some of the prevention strategies explained in this book to take time and effort. Others, such as what to do immediately when facing a crisis, should enable you to see mental health benefits almost straight away.

Just as when you first take up exercise, you may initially feel uncomfortable as those unused muscles spring into action, the same will happen when you start your mental exercises. They may feel a little awkward to begin with, but the long-term benefits will soon become clear. You will begin to feel more confident of your ability to look after yourself in mentally tough or stressful situations.

Prevention is an investment in your future health, but the modern tactic in physical illness prevention is to emphasise its immediate returns – for example, the positive benefit in feeling good NOW if you exercise or diet. This is because most people find it difficult to make personal sacrifices for a future benefit.

There are any number of reasons why we might benefit from working on our mental health. One is our ability to handle new challenges. For example, a common habit we get into is assuming – almost unconsciously – that we cannot handle certain situations. These may range from chatting up a stranger to public speaking, asking for a rise at work or generally asserting ourselves. How many times have you avoided doing something because you thought the strain would be too great, that it might make you feel bad about yourself, or lower your mood?

You choose to stay in and watch a soap opera rather than going out to a drinks party where you might have to meet new people, or you back out of giving a speech or presentation. We have all restricted our lives like this at some time or other. Gradually, you adapt your lifestyle to avoid these scenarios and, inevitably, the less practice you have, the more your fears about failing in certain situations are realised.

Taking on new challenges involves facing up to your fears about the stress involved. The more mentally healthy you are, the more you will embrace these situations. This is because even if you are rebuffed when you chat up that stranger, you will be able to take the setback in your stride and try again.

Imagine putting yourself in a situation you might be afraid to tackle now and remaining relatively unaffected by it – even benefiting from it in some way. This might be asking somebody for a date, applying for a new job, finally telling your parents something you have never been able to say to them or trying a completely new career.

You may worry whether, by putting yourself in a stressful situation, you will crack under the pressure. And this is not surprising given that people are so pessimistic about treatment – even doctors doubt their ability to prevent mental illness. In a book review in the *British Medical Journal*, Christopher Dowrick, Senior Lecturer in General Practice at the University of Liverpool, commented, 'The prevention of mental illness has much in common with the prevention of terrorism – it is a goal that is worth pursuing, to use T. S. Eliot's words, "Not for the good that it will do, but that nothing may be left undone on the margins of the impossible."'[32] This explains the kid-glove approach to our mental health, based on a fear that our own actions might push us over the edge.

However, as I emphasise throughout this book, I do not share the belief that it is almost impossible to prevent mental illness. I have a number of reasons for my view. As a Consultant Psychiatrist working in the community, I am the first person to whom doctors refer patients when they are just beginning to experience what are called clinically significant psychiatric symptoms. In many of these cases the factors are apparent many months, if not years, before the patient's visit to the doctor. When I explain this to my patients they can usually recognise for themselves these early signs, and see with hindsight what they should have done to prevent things from getting so bad.

While my psychiatrist colleagues are usually good at spotting where things begin to go wrong for people, they are less accustomed to alerting mentally healthy people to these issues in the first place.

This is partly because psychiatrists, overwhelmed with the demands of the mentally ill, obviously have less time for those not yet mentally unwell. But it is also because many of my colleagues are pessimistic about the ability of lay people to develop enough insight into the intricacies of how their minds and personalities work to be able to help themselves.

Through my work in the media, I have had contact with hundreds of mentally healthy people who are nevertheless worried about becoming unwell. Contrary to the fears of my colleagues, I have found them eminently capable of following positive mental health advice, as long as it is explained with a minimum of jargon and a maximum of common sense.

Moreover most mental health problems relate to events which are very much part of everyday life, and which are very difficult to avoid, or legislate against (unlike poor sanitation or food hygiene in relation to physical health). To quote Michael Harris, writing in the *Los Angeles Times*, 'Human problems are simply that: problems. Problems are life, not just occasions for therapy. If things happen to get better, that's life too.'[33] So the great need is for good advice on how to lessen the impact of these events on our mental health, rather than simply to turn to therapy to remedy their consequences. For all these reasons I am a passionate advocate of ordinary people not being kept in the dark about what psychologists and psychiatrists know concerning how to lessen the impact of 'negative life events'.

Another way in which my view differs is that I do not share the belief of many psychiatrists and psychologists that much mental illness is entirely due to disturbances in the brain's biochemistry. This view implies that the causes of psychiatric problems lie in your genes or your physical make-up. Therefore, by implication, using psychological strategies is virtually useless.

I find this kind of reasoning flawed for several reasons. First, take the most biological kind of illness possible – lung cancer, for example. While scientists beaver away trying to uncover the precise biochemical causes of lung cancer, we already know enough to be certain that if you give up smoking cigarettes you will have helped your health much more than any doctor could by treating you after you developed the cancer. So, even if an illness has a biological root, our behaviour can still sometimes prevent some problems. The same is true in the case of heart disease, for example, or cirrhosis of the liver.

Even some of the most definitively biological of psychiatric problems like dementia (particularly Alzheimer's disease, which causes severe intellectual decline in the elderly due to apparently irreversible brain cell changes) might still be preventable via self-help strategies.[34]

There is accumulating evidence that the amount of constant intellectual stimulation you receive during your life might influence your likelihood of getting Alzheimer's. The lesson appears to be 'use it or lose it' when it comes to your brain. Even if your daily job isn't very intellectually stimulating, taking up activities where you have to use your intellect might help prevent you getting Alzheimer's in later life – activities such as chess, bridge, and puzzle solving.[35]

Another argument against the biochemical view is that although some biological causes of psychiatric problems have been found, these have not usually proved to be sufficient in themselves to bring on the mental illness.[36, 37] Usually some other factor, social or psychological, is also involved, and this, together with the genetic predisposition, causes the illness.

For example, you are most likely to develop serious clinical depression following a 'negative life event' such as a divorce or being robbed. These odds approximately double again if you are genetically susceptible to depression because it runs in your family.[38] The genes seem to work by altering an individual's sensitivity to the depression-inducing effect of stressful life events. The positive mental health strategies discussed in this book will reduce the sensitivity to negative life events of even the genetically vulnerable.

People genetically predisposed to mental illness might have been helped by preventive mental health strategies, rendering their genetic predisposition less important in determining their future mental health.

Preventive strategies work best when started early. Perhaps the major stumbling block is that people developing mental illnesses put off visiting the doctor for as long as possible. One British survey[39] found that, despite the fact that one third of the general population reported clinically significant psychiatric symptoms, 71 per cent of these did nothing about them, 12 per cent talked to friends and relations, and only 17 per cent saw a doctor.

In the case of your body, a doctor uses instruments like stethoscopes and X-rays and so is likely to develop greater knowledge of your body than you have yourself. However, the same cannot be said for your mind – you ought to be able to tap into the state of your mind at any given moment. So whereas you could suffer from a hidden brain tumour and have no symptoms until it reached a certain size, yet still be suffering from a disease, even if it doesn't visibly affect you, with mental health the situation is very different. Psychological problems are always linked to our behaviour, causing suffering either to ourselves or to others. The notion that there could be a hidden disturbance of our mind of which we are unaware, which then develops into a clinically significant illness, is much less likely than with a physical disturbance.

While self-deception may reduce our ability to see ourselves as others do, it is possible to learn greater objectivity with regard to the way we think about ourselves. This search for objectivity is often why some people turn to therapists, whereas those with superior mental health have learnt to acquire this themselves.

You have more direct access to your internal consciousness than anyone else can ever hope to gain. You may not realise the clinical significance of what you experience, but you alone encounter it, no matter how clever your psychiatrist. For this reason *you* are the best placed to detect aspects of your mental life which might predispose you to psychological difficulties – as long as you learn what to look out for. For example, there is evidence that your own rating of your level of emotional arousal is more accurate than any test doctors might use.[40]

The reason ill people seek help from psychiatrists and psychologists is to understand and change themselves. These professionals can assist because they have seen thousands with similar problems, and become aware of patterns and links. But mental illness is such a taboo that few pluck up the courage to see a specialist unless things become so bad they are forced to go. I am convinced that it would be much better if it were socially acceptable – even the norm – to gain understanding of ourselves and our predisposition to mental illness, long before a disease develops.

The stigma, fear and taboo surrounding psychiatric problems means that few people think seriously about their predisposition to mental illness while still well. I am not advocating that everyone should go for regular mental health checks. In the first place, unlike most therapists, I believe in a self-help philosophy and that the first step to positive mental health is for all of us to start taking personal responsibility for our sanity – just as we do with our physical health.

Why is psychiatric and psychological information so rarely consulted by people who are well? One reason is that professionals are seen as ineffective and their advice has little currency amongst those well enough not to be in immediate need of them. There is some confusion over terms like psychiatrist, psychologist and psychotherapist, so clients might not realise when they are being treated by a non-academically trained, minimally qualified counsellor or therapist. This of course debases the professional status of those who work in the Health Service treating the seriously mentally ill. Another reason psychologists and psychiatrists might appear ineffective is that by the time they get to see many illnesses, they have progressed to a very serious stage indeed. Recovery is then very difficult, precisely because of the fear of stigmatisation and the belief that treatment is ineffective; a Catch-22 situation. Public suspicion of the profession spills over into uncertainty about the value of its ideas. Despite this common misgiving, good psychiatrists and psychologists can be as effective as most other doctors.

One of the problems with implementing positive mental health is that it means anticipating mental ill-health, which, naturally, is something no one likes to do. This reluctance is compounded with uncertainty over how to do it.

I will draw on this experience to argue that any such short-term embarrassment in examining your sanity is more than compensated for by the long-term results. Just as physical fitness allows you to experiment with your body's capabilities, so mental fitness allows you to try out aspects of life the mentally unfit shy away from. When sports stars celebrate on the field after scoring a spectacular goal, try or run, they are partly demonstrating their surprise and delight at their physical ability. If you follow positive mental health strategies you will create a resilience which will enable you to survive stress you never thought it possible to cope with. You, too, will be surprised and exhilarated at your own facility.

Unlike any other book on mental health written by a qualified psychiatrist and psychologist, the emphasis of this volume is on what you can do to help yourself, rather than turning to professionals, clinicians or therapists. I believe that true mental health cannot be achieved by relying on consulting experts whenever we hit problems in our lives.

This central thesis caused much controversy upon the publication of the first edition of *Staying Sane*. One of the main criticisms was that it is difficult people or problems in life, like poor housing and disturbed family environments, that cause poor mental health, and I seemed to be advocating strategies which suggested you could maintain your sanity, whatever stress you were under. This, many critics argued, belittled the problems people face in life and put the onus back on their shoulders to maintain their own mental health rather than blaming the situation they found themselves in.

What is interesting to me about this criticism is how it reflects our perennial and deep need to blame other people, events or situations outside ourselves for our poor mental health. In fact, our real enemy is often ourselves, not others. One of the catchphrases it is useful to remember on your journey to improved mental health is 'we have seen the enemy, and it is ourselves'. There is much evidence that having an adversity or another issue in our lives on which to heap the blame for our troubles seems profoundly therapeutic, but this is so only in the short term. When our enemies disappear or are defeated, and many of our problems remain, we are left wrestling with the inescapable conclusion that the source of our difficulties is most often within ourselves.

True and profound mental health starts with the courage to confront this thorny reality. Poor mental health stems from the constant and extreme attempts people make to avoid accepting this issue and starting to deal with it positively.

An example of how having an enemy affects mental health is recent research, published just as the second edition of this book goes to press in 1998, which has found a surprising 'peace dividend' of the new relative harmony in Northern Ireland, following decades of terrorist violence: that suicide rates have suddenly risen dramatically. The *British Medical Journal* reported recently that on average sixteen people in Northern Ireland were attempting suicide every day in the middle of 1998, and that the rate of completed suicide appears to have risen by 20 per cent compared to that in 1997.[41] Public health physician specialists in

Northern Ireland suggest there appears to have been a cluster, or doubling, of male suicide rates in 1994 and again in 1997, two years that were particularly peaceful in terms of terrorist activity.

Another peculiarity about the spate of suicides is that despite their occurrence in a community where guns are readily available, there is a very low rate of firearm use for suicide. In every other place where guns are widely available they become one of the preferred methods for suicide. For example, in the USA more people commit suicide by shooting themselves than are killed by acts of homicide with guns.[42] In Northern Ireland, however, hanging is the overwhelmingly preferred option. The precise method – hanging from the attic beams and using the loft trap door as the mechanism to create the drop – is copied in such detail so often, in Belfast particularly, that this technique appears to almost be almost part of local Northern Ireland culture. The only group who use guns on themselves are members of the armed forces. One public health doctor commented that these do it usually immediately after enjoying a laugh and a drink with friends.

The avoidance of guns in the community tells us something about their particular cultural significance in Northern Ireland. Perhaps they have a particular symbolic meaning linked to the defence of the community, and not the individual.

The victims in Northern Ireland are most often young men, described as 'unemployable' by the public health doctors investigating the current epidemic. Some have suggested these men would previously have seen their role as defending their communities from the enemy outside, and, now peace is beckoning, envisage losing their only role in life.[43] Perhaps the reconciliation might accelerate a breakdown in the divisions between communities, rendering previous territoriality more difficult to defend, again leading to a loss in role for many young men. Maybe, too, peace is rendered possible only by a loosening of the significance of faith in the community's life, therefore reducing the religious disapproval of suicide and making it a more acceptable option for the hopeless.

In response to the epidemic, the Samaritans in Northern Ireland launched an suicide prevention advertising campaign in cinemas, bars and on buses, targeting young men, thought to be most at risk. But previous research into the strong association between suicide rate increases and the reduction of conflict in a community, which has been found repeatedly worldwide, suggests that the social forces at work are too strong to react to such an individualistic response. Instead what is needed is probably more attention to what the conflict is replaced with, rather than just striving for peace as an end in itself, for the evidence is that the removal of antagonism in fact leaves a vacuum, which then releases self-destructive forces. The government has worked hard to ensure the leaders of the various opposing movements in Northern Ireland develop a personal stake in peace. The next step is to render this equally so for the marginalised.

Traditionally Northern Ireland has had relatively low rates of suicide compared to other European countries,[44] and in the early years of civil disturbance following 1969, a fall in the suicide rate occurred.[45] This was explained by psychiatrists then as being because aggression was externalised. Freud's theory is that suicide, being at its core an act of aggression, is in fact very similar to homicide.

If suicide and homicide are alternate ways of expressing hostility, during war, in which homicide (in the form of killing the enemy) increases drastically, so encouraging the homicidal expression of aggression, suicide naturally declines. Public health specialists in Northern Ireland have suggested the recent rise in Northern Ireland suicide rates represents a 'catching up' of the province with the rest of Europe, now the 'troubles' are over.

This finding in Northern Ireland reflects one of the most intriguing ironies of sociological research, the repeated observation that the horror and disruption of war lower the rate at which people kill themselves.[46] Durkheim, the father of modern sociology, first discovered this by studying data from the Denmark–Saxony war of 1894, the Austria–Italy war of 1866 and the Franco–Germany war of 1870–71.[47]

Since then the phenomenon of war lowering national suicide rates is one of the most robust sociological findings, holding true for Britain[48] and the USA,[49] as well as every other country where the effect was looked for, throughout this century. Durkheim's explanation was that a clear external enemy causes a society to bond together in the face of this threat, so increasing social ties and networking. Thus external conflict produces enhanced internal social integration, which reduces the individual alienation from society that leads to suicide.

The ability of war to arouse collective sentiments like partisan, religious and patriotic spirits, and concentrate personal activity towards a single community end, must be a profound effect, because the lowering of suicide rates during war occurs in both winners and losers of conflicts. Although one might have thought that women are more likely to be suicidal during wartime, because they experience bereavement for lost male partners at the front, the lowering of the suicide rate during war also applies to women. [50]

Recently other sociologists have argued that there is a more prosaic explanation for war's positive benefit on the suicidal: in all wars national economic activity increases to service the military effort, and so unemployment rates fall. It may simply be that war produces not so much social solidarity as therapy for the otherwise suicidal, but is ironically still the most effective way of integrating even the most marginalised into the economy. [51]

But this theory does not explain the Northern Ireland phenomenon. There the 'troubles' reduced levels of investment, producing job losses which led to rising unemployment. The demise of the troubles should bring with it greater economic prosperity in the future and so should be a source of hope rather than despair. This should have produced fewer suicides, not more.

The theory for the positive effect of a wartime economy on the suicidal received a further blow from a study on the Australian suicide rate during the Second World War. [52] This found that suicide rates went up or down depending on the year-to-year fortunes of the Allies in the war, regardless of the economic activity of the country. When the Allies were doing badly the suicide rate went down, and when they began winning the war, the suicide rate crept back up. Another study examining the Tamil conflict in Sri Lanka found that even just a few months of peace were associated with rises in the suicide rate, which dipped again immediately the conflict resumed. [53]

That an improvement in fortunes leads to more suicides while a distressing circumstance reduces them has been widely reported in sociological and medical research. Concentration camp residents have a surprisingly low suicide rate, [54] while a startling tendency to commit suicide has been found in those patients whose hearing and sight have been restored by operations after long periods of profound disability. Prisoners of war have been noted to become more suicidal after release.[55]

Perhaps an amelioration of suffering may facilitate suicidal behaviour because the loss of suffering removes an external apparent cause of an individual's distress and suffering. If this cause is in fact a crutch, once it is eliminated, you are forced to confront the internal causes of distress. Your unhappiness must therefore have its source in your own personality. When there is no clearly definable source of frustration other than yourself, suicide becomes a more viable option.

This theory suggests that armed conflicts are therapeutic because we need enemies upon whose heads we can heap blame for the source of our misery. Once our opponents disappear we find that the convenient explanations do as well, and the hope evaporates that once we defeat our enemies our problems will be over.

But this doesn't necessarily mean we have to go to war to bring down suicide rates. A recent study by David Lester, of the Centre for the Study of Suicide in the USA, found a relationship between the annual suicide rates there and the number of war movies produced each year between the 1940s and the 1980s.[56] Annual war film production was taken as a rough measure of patriotism levels. Certainly Hollywood expected war movies to be more profitable during particular periods, probably based on an assessment of how receptive society was at the time to being stirred by stories of military success and glory. An increase in the number of war films produced in a year strongly predicted a decline in suicide rates at that time, and fewer war movies were associated with higher suicide rates.

This finding appears to take us back to Durkheim's and Freud's original ideas. Real or even imaginary enemies, serve a fundamentally useful social unifying function. Having an external object for our aggressive tendencies saves us from turning them inwards on ourselves. This can produce such profound effects as inhibiting suicide. It seems we need something to hate and blame, be it an enemy or a disability, and if what we are used to hating is taken away, we start hating ourselves. And for some, it's the hatred which is all that they are living for, and so is all that is keeping them alive. Maybe that is why so many seem less than pleased by peace.

A better long-term mental health strategy than finding others to blame for our misfortune is to learn how to deal positively and

constructively with the personal issues that conspire to produce problems in our lives. The first step to achieving this is to accept more personal responsibility for the stress we experience in life. This may sound daunting at first, and not as easy or convenient as finding someone or something else outside ourselves on which to blame our problems. But it is worth attempting because in the long run blaming others never gets us anywhere fundamentally. When our enemies eventually disappear, our problems don't seem to cease – instead they merely continue, or are replaced by other problems.

In my daily clinical practice I see over and over again my patients blaming their stress and problems on others. The implication of this strategy is that others must change for us to feel better, not that we need to transform ourselves – an approach that suggests 'everyone else needs treatment by a psychiatrist, not me'. I often try to get my patients to see the short-sighted nature of this tactic by offering to treat whoever in their lives they believe is the true source of their distress.

I could treat anyone and everyone you ever met, so they no longer caused you problems; this seems to be what many people believe is the only way to stay sane. Even if this appears a tempting prospect, it is impossible in practice to achieve! Therefore there is no option but to fall back on yourself, and in particular your own resilience to get you through life. That is what this book is about: how to help yourself.

Most people start health-prevention techniques out of desperation, having experienced an episode of illness. They may continue because they want to avoid getting ill again. The best prevention strategies, however, are those you continue with because you enjoy them in themselves. I hope that achieving, maintaining and constantly improving your positive mental health becomes an enterprise not only of benefit, but also an interesting and delightful pursuit in itself.

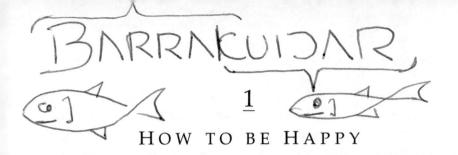

1

HOW TO BE HAPPY

'Pain is inevitable. Suffering is optional.'

M. Kathleen Casey

Since the first edition of this book appeared, the most dramatic event to have raised questions about the state of the nation's psyche has been the death of Diana, Princess of Wales, in August 1997 and the immense outpouring of public grief that followed. This led many academics to rethink their views on the precise state of the public mood and its causes.

Experimentally speaking, the only way to assess whether the extensive mourning for Diana signalled a shift in public mood would be if a death of a similar matching British public figure had occurred a few years before, and it was possible to compare the public consequences. However, there was no such figure, and Diana's death was a unique event, and singular incidents usually produce uncommon consequences.

The debate in academic journals after Diana's death was complicated by the difficulty in measuring exactly what the emotional temperature of the population is,[1] for a baffling paradox is emerging. Evidence from medical research indicates that the incidence of depression is increasing, whilst sociological research suggests that levels of happiness have not fallen.

In this chapter I shall explore the fascinating scientific research that has been conducted into happiness and depression and suggest some possible explanations; and in doing so I shall illuminate some surprising but important conclusions:

- happiness is not the opposite of depression, and therefore the pursuit of happiness is not the same as the avoidance of depression;
- the chase for happiness, in particular intense happiness, will in all probability render depression more likely;
- the attempt to enhance mood in some permanent way is usually doomed to failure because of intrinsic mechanisms built into our

27

mood systems which lead eventually to us getting used to improvements in our lives, with the effect that they no longer make us as happy as they did at the beginning;

- improvements in our living conditions not only fail to make us happy in the long term, as we get used to them, but they also contribute to our future unhappiness as we end up feeling worse if we eventually lose these improvements than we did before they ever arrived;
- contentment is possible, but only by employing some strategies that do not always include the avoidance of personal difficulties;
- mental health is best established by aiming for mood stability rather than extreme happiness.

To start our exploration of the issues of happiness and depression, let us look at the evidence that we are more depressed today than previous generations were in the past.

Several recent studies suggest that the likelihood of having depression in your lifetime has increased in the West during the twentieth century, and also that the age of first onset has been dropping for successive generations.[2, 3, 4, 5] Evidence from medical records going back to the beginning of the century suggests that, even allowing for an increased detection rate, each successive generation has doubled its susceptibility to depression.[6]

It appears that the 'baby boomers'– the short-term bulge of those born in the years after the Second World War – have had increased rates of depression and other related illnesses, including drug abuse and alcoholism.[7] For example, data from the American Epidemiologic Catchment Area studies suggest that the probability of experiencing an episode of major depressive disorder before reaching the age of 34 was ten times greater if you were born between 1945 and 1954 than if you were born between 1905 and 1914.[8] Those born after 1950 are now estimated to have a 30 per cent lifetime prevalence rate of depression by the time they reach the age of 20.[9]

The increase in the lifetime rate of depression, with more recent birth groups at increased risk, is largely replicated worldwide, though the rates of increase vary by country.[10]

For example, in what remains a unique longitudinal study[11] psychiatrists interviewed the entire population of the town of Lundby,

Sweden, three times in 1947, 1957 and 1972. There was an overall marked increase in depression among the more recent birth groups. Rates of mild and moderate depression increased with age starting at ages 20 to 29. Moreover, the cumulative probability of depression more than doubled between the first and second survey (1947 and 1957), and more than tripled between the 30 and 50 year-old age groups.

Previously it was thought that depression increased with age. As individuals grow older, the theory was, they experience more losses such as deaths of relatives and friends; the growing independence and departure of children; increased likelihood of medical illness, infirmity and disability; and lowered income and economic resources brought about by retirement.[12]

Lifetime prevalence rates for any disease should increase with age since the time of exposure to risk increases.[13] But peculiarly, the lifetime rate for depression now seems to decline with age. For example, one recent study found for men and women respectively, the lifetime rates were 6.6 and 15.3 per cent for those aged 30–44, but 1.6 and 3.3 per cent among those aged over 64.[14] And the recent dramatic rise in rates of depression, paralleled by increases in suicide attempts and death by suicide, is in the young to middle-aged.

In contrast to the apparent improvement in the economic, physical and mental health status of the elderly are the trends among the young in the West. For example, a comparison of post-mortems of suicides occurring in two cities in the USA in 1956–7 compared with 1981–2, found that in the 1950s 43 per cent of all suicides were aged over 61, but this had dropped to only 27 per cent of the total by the 1980s. Whilst there were no suicides at all under the age of 24 in the 1950s example, there were nine in the 1980s sample.[15]

The increase of depression, particularly in younger people, is of major importance since the 'baby boom' generation now comprises almost one third of the population.

The findings seem to be fairly specific to the industrialised countries and are often not replicated in developing[16] or Third World countries over the same period.[17] Also, immigrants living in western countries do not seem vulnerable to the same trends.[18]

Some academic psychiatrists have gone as far as asking whether we are entering a new age of melancholy,[19, 20] while others have described a

29

'depression epidemic'.[21] There have been a number of theories attempting to explain these findings.

For instance, it has been suggested that older generations have a social desirability bias (a tendency to pretend to feel better than you do because you are embarrassed to admit to depression) in responding to questionnaires, forget and underreport episodes of depression, and have a tendency to label psychiatric symptoms as arising from physical illness in the past, which might explain why there appears to be more depression amongst younger generations. But this and other similar attempts to explain away the apparent rise in reported depression as methodology artefacts (problems with the way the experiments were conducted) have all largely failed.[22, 23, 24, 25, 26] The increase cannot just be due to greater psychological-mindedness, as there has been a parallel increase in the serious consequences of depression such as suicide, hospitalisation and seeking medical treatment.[27]

The inescapable conclusion appears to be that we are witnessing a genuine increase in the occurrence of depression and other neurotic mental disorders like panic disorder, obsessive-compulsive disorder, alcoholism, substance abuse and suicide in adolescents and young adults. The rise does not apply to major mental illnesses such as schizophrenia and organic brain disorders (those due to biological brain dysfunction like epilepsy).[28] This increase is despite the fact that cohorts, or groups, born since the Second World War are physically healthier than their predecessors.[29] In most European countries there was a sharp and persistent decline in death rates between around 1915 and 1955, which was the period of the greatest improvement in physical health. These facts were not accompanied by a decline in psychiatric problems. Conversely, as our physical health has improved, it seems our mental health has deteriorated.

The evidence is that this increase in psychiatric problems is not a period effect: it is not the case that everyone is similarly at elevated risk today. Rather, it appears to be a combination of an age effect – younger people are at greater risk – and a cohort or group effect – those born after the 1950s and before the 1980s seem at greatest risk.[30] A study showed that recent cohorts (in this case, those born in 1972–5) have lower age at first onset of depression than only slightly earlier birth cohorts (1971–2 and 1969–70).[31] This increase over a period of a generation and less (even siblings born more recently in the same family have significantly higher risks for depression) is occurring too rapidly to be explained by genetic changes in the population.[32] It seems that environmental factors must be involved, but if a period effect has been operating since the Second World War to increase rates of depression, the nature of a so-called 'agent blue' is not yet properly established.

Social disadvantage, like poverty and deprivation, is associated with many psychiatric disorders, and it has been suggested that worsening living conditions account for these rising levels of disorder. However, when mental illnesses were increasing in frequency, living conditions were on the whole improving.[33] Living conditions in the first half of this century were also improving (with concomitant benefits for physical health) but it seems that this was not accompanied by any marked increase in psychiatric disorder. It is therefore unlikely that living conditions affected the rise.

Increasing affluence in itself probably does not account for the overall increase in psychiatric disorders, although it is likely to play a role in increasing opportunities for crime, and for alcohol and drug abuse, but it seems that increases in the documented incidence of depressive disorders occurred in the most industrialised countries during a period of increasing wealth. The economies of developed countries grew by a factor of six between 1900 and 1987, including a golden era between 1950 and 1973 when economies grew at an unprecedented rate, and accompanying this golden era was also a rise in rates of common psychiatric problems.[34]

Economic links with poor mental health may be apparent in other ways. The status and mental health of the unemployed might vary depending on the context of the unemployment. For example the Depression of the 1930s hit whole communities at one time. The fact that unemployment affected a whole reference group (the group of people with whom you might compare yourself and derive your sense of self-esteem from the comparison) could have lessened the psychological consequences on individuals: you are likely to feel less upset at being out of work if everyone on your street is as well than if you are the only one. Today the different pattern of unemployment could produce more detrimental effects on individual self-esteem because the unemployed are more likely to live alongside the employed.[35, 36]

Other hypotheses include the bulge in the labour force leading to increased competition between this particular generation,[37] and increased geographic mobility with resultant loss of relationship attachments.[38]

'Attachment theory' proposes that depression is a response to the loss of an attachment figure, such as a parent or a lover, which causes the depressed person to conceive of him- or herself as unlovable.[39] Since divorce leads to loss of attachments between adults and also between children and carers, this perspective would lay the blame of rising rates of depression on escalating divorce rates in the Western world.

Increasing levels of family discord and break-up may well have played a role in the rise in psychiatric disorders; an association with poor mental health and these factors has been confirmed at both individual and community levels. The main risk of disorder stems from discord and lack of parental support and involvement, rather than the break-up of the family as such. But while it is clear that divorce rates have risen substantially in most Western countries in the last fifty years, the extent to which this reflects an increase in family discord rather than an increasing tendency to resort to divorce when there are marital difficulties, is uncertain.[40]

A high divorce rate is therefore not necessarily a reflection of rising levels of family conflict – indeed it may even be that there is now less family friction around if marriages which in the past would have continued at the expense of a fraught home atmosphere are now dissolved by divorce. Given that we therefore have little evidence that family discord really has increased over the century, it is difficult to lay the blame for 'agent blue' at this particular door.

Where attachment theory may have some bearing is in the fact that it is certainly true that an increasing number of people live alone for a greater proportion of their lives (either before uniting with their partner or in their extended old age) and people who live alone are known to be prone to depression. But attachment theory does not account for the many depressed people who have not lost an important attachment figure, but are still low nonetheless.

Another theory rapidly gaining ground in modern psychology and psychiatry suggests that depression is closely tied up with our perception of our status in our community. This lays the blame for rising rates of depression on increased competition between group members.

Of the children born in the years immediately following the Second World War, in the West the large cohorts were aged 5–19 in 1970 and 25–39 by 1990. Perhaps this bulge led to greater competition between individuals in these groups, so producing elevated rates of depression.

Humans, the rank theory argues, are fundamentally social animals and the evolutionary advantage of living in groups is the protection they provide from predators and other rival groups of hominids. Living in a group became crucial for safety, and also facilitated access to resources, thanks to cooperative hunting of large game and sharing the tasks of farming. Associating with a group also made it more likely you would meet a mate and therefore increased your chances of reproductive success.

So over millions of years of evolution a sense of belonging to a group has become vital to our physical and emotional security. Therefore to be popular and hold high rank within a group are immensely desirable accomplishments; to perceive oneself as unpopular and so of low rank will therefore cause misery. Unpopularity or a lowering of rank might presage rejection from the group altogether – one of life's greatest disasters.

The main problem of living in a group is that competition, rivalry and aggression between members are rendered more likely than if we lived more solitary existences and so hardly encountered each other. Therefore some mechanism evolved to ensure that aggression between rival members was curtailed. This, the rank theory proposes, is the function of depression. Without depression, two rival members of a group might have continued to fight each other to a point which was dangerous for the survival of each other and the group, particularly if the group needed its leaders for more useful purposes other than simply beating off personal rivals. Depression therefore emerged as a 'yielding subroutine'[41] to prevent too much overt conflict in a group. The function of the depression is twofold: first it ensures that the yielder truly yields and does not attempt to make a comeback, and, second, it reassures the winner that yielding has truly taken place, so that the conflict ends, with no further damage to the yielder. Relative social harmony is then restored.

So the rank theory proposes that depression is an adaptive response to losing rank and conceiving oneself as a loser. It facilitates losing and promotes accommodation of the fact that one has lost. In other words, according to this theory, the depressive state evolved to promote the acceptance of a subordinate role and the loss of resources that can only be secured by holding higher rank in the dominance hierarchy. The function of the depressive adaptation is to prevent the loser in a status conflict from suffering further injury and to preserve the stability and competitive efficiency of the group by maintaining social stability.

In circumstances of defeat and enforced subordination, an internal inhibitory process comes into operation which causes the individual to cease competing and reduce his level of aspiration.[42] This inhibitory process is involuntary and results in the loss of energy, depressed mood, sleep disturbance, poor appetite, retarded movements and loss of confidence which are the typical characteristics of clinical depression.

Because he or she is perceived as being ill, the depressed person gains group nurturance and care, which might go some way to stabilising the loss of status. The function of depression is thus damage limitation – a strategy to prevent further loss of reputation and to prevent the ultimate disaster of banishment from the group.[43]

Hundreds of thousands of years ago, when we lived in a closely knit society of kin-based bands of 20 to 100 hunter-gatherers, a depressed individual could depend on the altruism and generosity of the group. The depression indicated that allowances should be made for him – he could not be expected to contribute to the group's economy with the same efficiency as if he were well. However in modern conditions, in the relative isolation of contemporary society, which has seen the 'waxing of the individual and the waning of the commons',[44] depression no longer elicits group caring in the same way. In these circumstances, the depressive reaction can more readily enter a vicious downward spiral of deepening helplessness and despair. This might explain the increase in the incidence of depression over the past century.

Those trying to explain the rising rate of depression have only rarely looked at happiness surveys for confirmation of their findings from illness surveys, and when they have, the apparent contradictions they present and the lack of a fall in happiness during the 1970s have not been remarked upon.[45, 46] However, the findings of survey research by the fields of sociology and social psychology into happiness, apparently contradicting the increase in depression, are vital to our understanding of depression. While medical research focuses on asking people questions about how depressed they are, sociologists tend to perform surveys where the question of interest is how happy people are.

Life satisfaction is defined as the degree to which an individual judges the overall quality of his life as a whole to be favourable: in other words, how well he likes the life he leads. The more common term 'happiness' is often used as a synonym.[47]

'Quality of life' researchers consistently find that most people give themselves high to very high ratings on happiness scales. In all developed countries in which 'quality of life' studies have been conducted, almost all sections of the community rate themselves above the mid-point of scales.[48]

The stability of happiness levels over time is astonishing. Despite the waves of recession and unemployment experienced since the first European surveys back in 1973, the result in 1994 is exactly the same as it was twenty years ago – 79 per cent are satisfied with their lives.

Professor Veenhoven from the Netherlands, the world's leading authority on happiness, describes it as a common myth that modern Western society is a sink of unhappiness. He declares that inhabitants of Western democracies appear quite satisfied with life for the greater part, and typically more than half of them identify themselves as very happy, while generally less than 10 per cent claim to be unhappy.[49]

Time-trend data for Western countries shows a 'striking stability in average happiness',[50] for example in the US between 1946 and 1977[51] and for Western Germany between 1954 and 1976.[52]

The public opinion journal *Eurobarometer* publishes annual population surveys, conducted throughout Europe, which investigate the average happiness of the average person. A recent summary of these surveys, covering a period of twenty-four years, found that eight out of ten European Community citizens are on the whole satisfied with the life they lead.

UK scores have been consistently above average over time, compared to those of other European countries, ahead of France, Italy and Germany; indeed surveys worldwide repeatedly find Britain one of the happiest countries of all (a result that I shall examine later in this chapter).

Academics hotly debate the significance of the rival sets of findings. For one thing, there are important political implications. If most people feel happy under the current political regime, why change it? For that reason, conservatives tend to claim that we are happy, while revolutionaries try to prove we are not.[53]

One attempt to explain how high levels of happiness can be reconciled with evidence of social pathology – divorce, delinquency and neurosis – is to invoke the notion there is a general human tendency towards a sense of relative superiority. That is to say, a large majority of people explicitly believe that they rate 'above average' in most major roles and domains of life. For example, it transpires that most people believe that they are better than others at judging the length of objects, that they are healthier, will live longer and are more considerate, honest and creative than others.[54]

How can over 50 per cent of the population feel above average? One suggestion is that all major roles in life, such as parenting or being a marriage partner or a worker, are usually exceedingly complex and can readily be divided into many sub-roles. Usually if we look hard enough we can find at least one sub-role in which we can judge our performance to be above average compared to that of others we know. We then tend to attach greatest importance to that sub-role and give it a high priority when arriving at our overall perception of whether we are above average or not in life, and whether we are satisfied with our own overall performance or not.

A curious corollary of the tendency of most people to filter out adverse information is the finding that depressed persons are more realistic than others in appraising their own performance.[55] The implications of this for mental health, and the necessity for positive illusions about ourselves, are explored in greater depth in the chapter 'I Will Survive'.

The prevalence of satisfaction with life as a whole does not wash away the multitude of suffering and laments. Even the happy are not without complaints. The German Welfare Survey conducted in 1978 found that half of the 'highly satisfied' report frequent worries.[56]

Further evidence of investigations of positive mood producing results independent of negative mood findings is the verdict from research into sex differences in depression. Women report being depressed on average at twice the rate men do, yet 'well-being' investigators find women are just as happy as men.[57]

A similar paradox is that suicide rates seem to correlate poorly with happiness rates. For example, Scandinavian countries traditionally score high in national comparisons for happiness – indeed they came top in one of the largest cross-national surveys on happiness ever conducted – yet they also traditionally have one of the highest national suicide rates.[58] Oddly there is a small positive association between suicide rates and happiness across nations, even when the tendency for suicide rates to be higher in affluent countries is taken into consideration;[59] in other words having a higher suicide rate in a country often predicts that the population will also score higher on happiness. The paradox is exemplified by the finding that India has a lower suicide rate than the USA, indeed at 12.2 per 100,000 the suicide rate in the USA is almost twice that of India's (6.5 per 100,000),[60] but also scores lower on happiness. But, it is argued, suicide rates probably tell us more about how people cope with unhappiness than about their level of happiness.

These findings seem incongruous if happiness and unhappiness are assumed to be opposite ends of the same dimension. This assumption is based on the idea that emotions tend to occur singly, with mixtures being rare. If emotions function to make ready a small set of action plans – for example, anger prepares us for a fight – it would be dysfunctional for several such sets of differing action plans to be made ready at the same time, since conflict and indecision could occur. So psychologists postulate there is some mutual inhibition between emotions: it is impossible, say, to feel say relaxed when anxious. According to this theory, it should therefore be hard to feel sad when happy. What has been found, however, is that mixtures of emotions occur commonly – for instance, on average in more than a third of emotional incidents.[61]

The possibility that depression is not the opposite of happiness would explain why the increase in depression is not matched by a decrease in happiness. Indeed, research into the psychology of happiness has abandoned the notion that happiness is simply the opposite of depression for at least thirty years now, in particular since the 1969 publication by the American National Opinion Research Centre of a famous psychology text entitled *The Structure of Psychological Well-Being* by Norman Bradburn. This reported a series of questionnaire experiments into the happiness of normal populations, which found, unexpectedly, that feeling bad and feeling good are in fact independent of each other.[62]

Further support for the idea that happiness and depression are not the opposite of each other comes from brain-scanning research into moods of transient sadness and happiness. One study in healthy volunteer women found that these moods are accompanied by significant changes in regional brain activity, but transient sadness and happiness affect different brain regions in divergent directions, and are not merely opposite activity in identical brain regions.[63]

None of this work suggests that positive and negative emotions occur together at the same moment,[64] or that we move from positive to negative feelings and back again in a regular or periodic cyclical fashion. Instead it seems within any period of time we experience many different emotions, both positive and negative, but there is no tendency for the two types of emotion to be experienced in any particular simple relation to one another. This lack of association means information about the extent of positive feelings a person has experienced in the recent past does not give us any information on the level of their negative feelings.[65, 66, 67, 68, 69, 70]

This parallels research which compared scales measuring general well-being with those focusing on 'ill-being' and found that these states are independent of each other, having separate associations and causes.[71] A cursory scan of recent work using PsycLIT – the database containing most published psychological research – discovered no fewer than 193 research studies between 1987 and 1991 that found positive and negative mood to be not the inverse of each other, but instead distinct from each other.[72]

But surely, one might ask, the more a person experiences pleasant emotions, the less time is available to experience negative ones? Certainly this is borne out if the time period sampled is momentary, but in a period of a few weeks or longer in a person's life, the amount of positive and negative emotion one experiences is independent, even though experiencing the two emotions simultaneously is unlikely.[73] In other words an inverse association between positive and negative effect emerges most strongly the shorter the time period sampled. On a second-by-second basis being happy means you are not sad, but it seems that in a sample of your mood over a longer time how happy you are tells us little about how sad you are as well.

A part of the solution to this enigma is to include an intensity dimension in our understanding of our mood. The mean level of mood sampled over an extended period is determined not only by the independent contributions of frequency (how often) but also by intensity (how extreme). It seems that how intensely you experience emotions is an important part of your personality,[74] so low- and high-intensity people experience happiness and unhappiness in very different ways.

People who experience strong positive emotions are also probably those who endure forceful negative feelings as well – and this proposal has been supported by numerous studies.[75, 76] When intensity of emotion is taken into account with average positive and negative emotion, they seem to become the inverse of each other.[77] In other words, the reason why a population who score high on positive mood may also score high on negative mood is because of those individuals in that population who tend to experience emotions intensely. They get very low moods whenever they feel depressed and are also the ones who get much more euphoric when they feel good.

Many studies of daily mood have strong associations between positive emotional intensity and negative emotional intensity, strongly suggesting that those who experience intense negative emotions over time will also be the ones most likely to experience intense positive emotions.[78] The issue for depressed people, then, is not how to feel happy rather than depressed, but how to feel emotions less intensely.

More emotional people would be located nearer the extremes of a happiness continuum than calmer people; and they experience both pleasurable and aversive events more acutely.[79] So stable people often appear less happy than these more intense individuals, but on other occasions would also be less depressed, when the intense group would swing wildly down.

The fact that people differ in the typical intensity with which they experience their emotions[80] suggests that, perhaps contrary to expectations, the magnitude of a mood response is not related to the strength of the event which prompts the change in mood.

Even when exposed to identical emotional stimulation, the more mood-intense subjects consistently exhibit stronger emotional reactions.[81] This suggests that perhaps these subjects think about or perceive the world in a manner that results in a stronger emotional reaction.

Those prone to intense depression tend to interpret bad events as internal (caused by themselves), global (will happen in other spheres of life) and stable (will continue to occur).[82] For example, such a person would interpret being rebuffed when asking someone for a date as meaning they are unpleasant to be with, rather than simply not being to the other person's taste, or the other person not being interested in dating in general. They would also interpret this as meaning they will always get rebuffed in the future, and that they will be rejected in other spheres of life. Those prone to intense happiness, on the other hand, do not make these internal, global and stable interpretations for bad events, while they make precisely these assumptions for good happenings.[83] So people prone to positive mood interpret getting accepted for a date as meaning they are devastatingly attractive, and a sign they will always get their way in life.

Personalisation refers to the process when an individual interprets events in a self-referential manner. Emotionally intense individuals tend to personalise, overestimating the degree to which events are related to them, and being excessively absorbed in the personal meanings of particular happenings.[84] Such people often have another habit called 'selective abstraction', of focusing attention on specific emotion-provoking aspects of events: you ignore the fact that the person you approached for a date also rebuffed everyone else in your focus on the fact they rebuffed you. A third habit is over-generalisation, or the construing of a single event as representative of the general state of affairs.[85] Those prone to intense moods also have more difficulty distracting themselves from negative experiences.[86]

Since emotional intensity seems to go hand in hand with these habits of reasoning, to become less prone to intense moods you need to alter the way you intellectually react to the world. So if someone behaves negatively towards you – for instance, gives you the sack – instead of imagining this has happened to you because of your own personal qualities (the boss is picking on you) the more impersonal explanation (the firm is downsizing and had to lose some people anyway)[87] will lead to a less intense emotional reaction. (These concepts are gone into in more detail in the chapter 'So, You Think You are Sane?')

Since emotional intensity explains why some people experience both positive and negative emotions strongly, the various survey findings that women appear more depressed but just as happy as men can be accounted for by the finding that women experience more strong emotions or greater mood intensity than men.[88]

The way women respond to a low mood appears to cause the gender differences in clinical depression.[89] Women tend to ruminate about the cause of their low mood, but men distract themselves when they experience a similar unhappy event. This tendency makes the probability of clinical depression greater for women.

A disposition to use these ways of thinking about the world distinguishes individuals with high mood intensity from those with low mood intensity, and does so regardless of the hedonic tone of the emotional stimuli, positive or negative. So individuals who report strong positive emotions when good events happen also report potent negative effect when bad things happen.

All this lends some credence to the folk notion that the higher you go up when you are up, the lower you'll go down when you are down.[90] It seems there are emotional costs to having very intense positive emotions – one of which is the inevitable experiencing of more intense negative emotions.

Psychologists now argue[91] that the key to overall contentment is simply the total amount of time a person experiences pleasant emotions versus the amount of time they feel unpleasant emotions, regardless of the peak intensity of emotions experienced. This is an important difference from the general lay approach which is to seek as intense a positive experience as possible (such as the pursuit of heady romance, passionate sex, wild parties, meteoric careers, instant lottery jackpots, love at first sight) as the key to happiness. In fact the resulting intense positive emotion provides a person with only momentary happiness. Research suggests intense positive emotions are not as strongly related to general well-being or increase of long-term contentment as frequent but non-intense positive experiences.

One reason for the failure of intense positive emotions to increase well-being is that they occur only infrequently. For example, in one study on daily mood in which a total of 5,586 subject days were assessed,[92] psychologists found that their subjects experienced intense positive emotion on only 2.6 per cent of the days. Therefore it is unlikely that overall contentment could be influenced by such an uncommon occurrence.

Secondly, and most importantly for an understanding of how to preserve and enhance your mental health, there appear to be costs associated with experiencing intense positive emotions that counterbalance the positive effects of these experiences in relation to long-term contentment. It seems that the processes resulting in intense positive emotions will also intensify negative effect, leading to the possibility of the experience of intense negative emotions. If you are deliriously happy to be accepted on a date, you are also likely to be deeply upset when rejected, precisely because of your tendency to personalise and render the event overly meaningful. Likewise when people compete in sports, a win will be much more positive for those who desperately feared losing than for those who were less concerned about failure. So a particular goal regarded as very important will be associated with intense satisfaction after a success in that direction is achieved, but similarly will be associated with heightened sorrow after a setback. In other words, intense positive emotions often depend on psychological conditions which would have resulted in intense negative emotions had circumstances not turned out favourably.[93]

Also, an extremely positive event – for example, a perfect score in an exam – when contrasted with a future event judged as moderately positive – merely a good score in an exam – renders the future event less satisfying. Thus extremely positive events, when compared with moderately good ones, can lower the value of and make less pleasurable mildly positive experiences. When milder levels of positive emotion are compared with high levels of intense positive feeling, the net effect may be to lower the value of the moderately positive experiences.

Freud[94] had some sense of this problem when he wrote that extreme cravings, when satisfied, can lead to more intense enjoyment than moderate yearnings, but extreme cravings left unsatisfied can similarly cause greater displeasure. Freud therefore believed we are psychologically disposed to experience intense positive emotions only in contrast to intense negative emotions.

But some psychologists have actually promoted intense experiences. The famous psychotherapist Carl R. Rogers[95] encouraged people to experience intense positive emotions by being open to experience, by which he meant that people should not defend against or repress their moods, so blunting their emotional experience of life. He believed it necessary to experience the full range of emotion, from extreme, positive intense mood to negative, intense spirit as a part of the journey to becoming a fully functioning person. While it sounds great from a libertarian standpoint to advocate that people should try to experience all that life has to offer, I do not believe Rogers was fully aware of the negative consequences of pursuing intense moods.

In stark contrast the Greek Stoic philosophers believed that extreme emotional experiences should be avoided. Indeed they attached so much importance to this they even suggested that the experience of extreme positive emotions should be moderated by thinking about a negative experience at the same time. This would tend to make future negative events less extreme and therefore less emotionally arousing.

In the ascetic tradition of the Christians and Buddhists, a philosophy of self-denial and non-attachment is advocated, partly in recognition that a strong attachment to worldly objects can lead to emotional despair when those same objects are lost or removed. Implicit in these philosophies is the idea that the experience of intense positive emotions will increase the probability of experiencing intense negative ones. (More about these Buddhist techniques can be found in the chapter 'Crisis, What Crisis?')

The concept of depression as a factor plotted against happiness and producing a U-shaped curve, whereby those who score at the extremes on happiness (very happy or unhappy) are also prone to score high on depression, and those who score low on depression are those who score at the midpoint in happiness scales, is like that of the ancient Greek physician Galen. In Galen's scheme, in which four temperaments are based on the four humours,[96] a choleric person feels strongly or intensely, whereas the phlegmatic is relatively unemotional and therefore does not experience emotions intensely.

Intense moods are probably the consequence of investing too much of one's sense of well-being in too few spheres of life. So, for example if getting a date is what the whole meaning and purpose of life hinges on for you, then you will tend to be deliriously happy if the person you ask out accepts, or deeply upset if you get rebuffed. On the other hand, the phlegmatic tend to be protected from extreme mood swings because they have more roles in life that are important to them, for instance not just a chaser of the one-night-stand or career, or not just a spouse or parent. They have more complex self-concepts (this will be expanded in the chapter 'Me, Me, Me') and so are buffered against emotional incidents by the fact that other areas of their lives remain unaffected by emotionally significant events.[97]

HOW COMPLICATED ARE YOU?

Psychologists have termed the way we look at ourselves our self-concept; it includes our own view of whether we consider ourselves to be attractive, ethical, intelligent and so on in any number of different ways of comparing ourselves to others. An important factor in the nature of our self-concept is how complicated we are. This is measured by looking at whether we think we tend to be better than most people at most things, or worse than most people at most things – in either of which case our view of ourselves is simple; and whether our thinking that we are better or worse than most people varies a lot depending on the particular characteristic we are discussing (how good we are at tennis, in bed or at work) – in which case we have more complicated personalities.

Another way of looking at this is how we think of our roles. We have roles as workers, lovers and friends, and if our performance in one of these roles is likely to dominate our view of ourselves and hence colour what we think of ourselves globally, then again we are simple. If instead we think of ourselves as different in each role – for instance, as poor lovers but good at work – then we have a more complicated self-concept. Whether we are complicated or simple appears to have important implications for how we react to stress and whether we have a tendency to extreme mood swings. To find out how complicated you are, and the implications, try the simple quiz below.

COMPLICATED SCALE

Each statement is followed by two possible responses: agree or disagree. Read each statement carefully and decide which response best describes how you feel. Then put a tick over the corresponding response. Please respond to every statement. If you are not completely sure which response is more accurate, put the response which you feel is most appropriate. Do not read the scoring explanation before filling out the questionnaire. Do not spend too long on each statement. It is important that you answer each question as honestly as possible.

		AGREE	DISAGREE
1	How much I am liked by a stranger depends more on me than them	A	B
2	I am above average on few aspects of my daily work	B	A
3	Failure knocks me back less than most others I know	A	B
4	It is possible for me to compensate for my worst mistakes	B	A
5	My past determines my future	A	B
6	I have few alternative ways of using my leisure time	B	A
7	I would be willing to try very different work to what I do now	A	B
8	My hobbies are the same as when I was much younger	B	A
9	I have skills I have not discovered for myself yet	A	B
10	I do not appear a different person to different people	B	A

SCORE

Add up your score from summing the numbers of As and Bs in each box you have ticked. Your score and the interpretation given below should be treated with caution – this short test is by no means definitive, but may offer a guide to where you stand compared to others around you.

8 or more Bs. You are scoring well above average for simplicity of personality, which means that you are prone to quite extreme mood swings, depending on your successes or failures. This is because your view of yourself is linked very strongly to only a few of your roles – for instance, your role as a worker or your role as a partner in a relationship; hence if these go badly they easily affect the rest of your life. You need to learn that just because someone does not like you it does not mean you are a useless person. Perhaps you have not experimented enough with different lifestyles since your youth, and hence there are hidden depths to your personality that will surprise you when you discover them.

Between 5 and 7 Bs. You are scoring above average on simplicity of personality and this means you are not doing enough widely different things with your life so as to discover all aspects of yourself. On the positive side you tend to be more delighted by good news than many others you know; hence on good days you are the life and soul of the party, but on bad days you tend to let bad news, or a poor performance, affect you too adversely. Your tendency to believe that the past determines the future or that bad things come in runs means you see bad events as symptomatic of something you are doing wrong with your life. You need to learn that there is much you cannot control, and if things go badly it is not always your fault.

Between 3 and 5 Bs. You are scoring around average to above average in complexity, which means that, as a more complicated person than higher scorers, you are less perturbable by good or bad news, because such information does not tend to affect your overall view of yourself. On the other hand, this also means that when things go well for you, you are less likely to feel overjoyed that your life is about to take off for the better. You need to realise that it is very important you hang on to your wide variety of friends, who are often very different from each other. If you let lack of time constrain your social circle, you will tend to move away from your complexity and become more simple.

Between 0 and 2 Bs. You are scoring very high indeed for complexity and this means the dramatic differences in your behaviour depending on who you are with sometimes even surprise you. Unlike higher scorers in simplicity, the multiple roles you have in life mean that one role – for instance, work or love – is not the only thing important to your sense of self-esteem; and this has a protective effect against the adverse effects of stress, particularly if something goes wrong in any of these fields. The fact that you are more complicated means that it is more difficult for you to gain a sense of the general direction in which your life is going. Successes in one sphere are usually offset in your mind by failure in others. You need to take a step back and try to get a feel for the big picture, otherwise you may find some of your decisions are not taking you towards goals that are really important to you.

Interestingly, older people, who are likely to have learnt from bitter experience the short-sightedness of investing too much meaning in too narrow a part of life, experience both positive and negative emotions less intensely than younger people.[98, 99] This may go some way perhaps to explaining the tendency to find poorer mental health in younger people recently. In comparison with adults, adolescents' moods swing more widely with more intense highs and lows.[100]

Although we have now explained why surveys can find high rates of depression and happiness in the same samples, what is the relevance of this to mental health? After all, the pursuit of happiness is not the same as the quest for mental health – an important distinction made in the introduction of this book. Well, we have already seen the importance of aiming not for intense positive moods, but simply an increased frequency of moderately positive ones as the pathway to overall better well-being.

But when a person's level of depression is under control, they still experience significant variation in life satisfaction – in other words, people who are not clinically depressed still differ widely in their levels of well-being. For example, if we looked at all of the people who are not formally depressed, there would still be significant differences between them in life satisfaction and associated variables such as self-esteem and self-confidence.[101]

It seems that low life satisfaction tends to precede the onset of depression. In other words, individuals with low life satisfaction ratings are more likely to become depressed in the future than those with higher reported life satisfaction. This is important because it provides a potential method of identifying people at risk of impending clinical depression.[102]

Therefore one way of interpreting these findings is to suggest that decreased life satisfaction may be prodromal, or an early manifestation of clinical depression's onset.

For those who already have some risk factors for major depressive disorder, experiencing two or more weeks of sad mood in one year raises the likelihood 5.5 times of a first onset of major depressive disorder in the next year.[103] This has led some to suggest that if an efficient screening device, such as a questionnaire, could be found, for doctors this would be a useful way of identifying those amongst a population suffering this two-week period of sad mood who would urgently need preventive interventions in order to stave off a high likelihood of succumbing to the depression syndrome.[104]

It seems loss of pleasurable engagement with life, or anhedonia, or the inability to derive pleasure from things which previously cheered us up for at least a few weeks is a distinctive predictor of future depression.[105] Becoming more aware of a lowered sense of ability to derive pleasure from life aids us in identifying at the earliest opportunity the possibility of future mental ill-health.[106]

So there is a connection between happiness and positive mental health, even though it is not so, as we have seen, that the more intense happiness is better for you – quite the contrary. Generally positive self-attitudes work as a buffer to stress. A positive view of the world means that stressful life events are perceived as challenges rather than as threats (more about this in the chapter 'I Will Survive'). Bad luck hurts less when one can draw on some emotional reserve. Protective effects of this kind are associated with a positive appreciation of life as a whole, or with mood level. The more one enjoys life (non-intensely), the better one can take knocks.[107]

But it seems that raising levels of happiness in a community is surprisingly difficult.

Since the beginning of the nineteenth century when British utilitarians proclaimed the enjoyment of life to be of the highest value, it became the duty of governments to promote the greatest happiness of the largest number of people. Hence this is one of the ideological ingredients of the current Western welfare states. The US constitution even defends 'the right to pursue happiness'.

The first basic theory as to the cause of happiness is the idea that it is based on the quality of living conditions – people who have improved housing, transport, food, leisure time and consumer goods will be happier. Better living conditions lead to better resources for the fulfilment of needs, therefore, it logically follows, they should lead to improvements in happiness. This is the theory which most lay people subscribe to and at first glance seems to make common sense.

Yet it is surprisingly difficult to find evidence that improved living conditions lead to enduring enhancements in people's mood. For example, while the Gross National Product, or wealth of a country, doubled in the USA between 1946 and 1970, the average level of happiness remained unchanged during that period.[108]

If countries of differing wealth are assessed for happiness, a pattern emerges that suggests that wealth is subject to a law of diminishing happiness returns.[109] The improvement in living conditions between those in the very poorest countries and those in countries that are slightly more prosperous is indeed associated with dramatic increases in happiness. However, in wealthier countries happiness is less connected to improved living conditions: the difference in happiness between rich and poor tends to be smaller. The higher the Gross National Product, the lower the association between individual happiness and relative income.[110]

One reason why there is a link between improved living conditions and happiness in poorer countries is the very strong association between average happiness and sufficiency of food consumption, based on estimates about what calories per day are biologically required.[111] Happiness is typically lowest in nations where malnutrition is most frequent. Since happiness depends to some extent on health, poverty is thus a detriment to it when the privation is so bad as to endanger physical fitness. This effect is demonstrated by a dramatically strong association between average happiness and average life expectancy across countries throughout the world. Also there is a close relationship between economic development and life expectancy until a threshold is reached at a Gross Domestic Product of $5,000 per head of population (at 1984 values). Beyond that threshold, further economic growth bears little or no relationship to improvements in life expectancy or happiness.[112]

How to explain why improvements in living conditions do not lead to improved happiness once certain basic nutritional requirements are satisfied? It seems that in fact once we get past this threshold, happiness is largely unrelated to objective conditions of life. Instead, changes for the better tend to raise expectations and thus do not result in greater happiness. If anything, over-stressing of progress by the mass-media and politicians may even cause an inflation of aspirations and result in a decline of happiness.

So the theory most psychologists subscribe to now is that happiness results from the perception of being relatively well off rather than the actual quality of living conditions. The important implication of this theory is that happiness depends on mental constructs, or the way we think about our situation, rather than on the realities of life. Therefore people can be unhappy in almost perfect conditions because they want more, and be happy in tough circumstances because they resign themselves and acquiesce to their situation.

In particular, psychologists now stress that happiness depends on how small a gap there is between what a person hopes to achieve, and what he or she is actually achieving.[113] The evaluation of life is a more or less conscious mental process and involves assessment of the degree to which perceptions of 'life as it is' meets the individual's standards of 'what life should be'. The better the fit, the happier the person. Satisfaction is greater when achievements are close to aspirations and lower when they fall short. Aspirations are based largely on comparisons with other people and our own past experience. To predict how happy someone is, simply ask them about the gap between their aspirations and achievements.

High aspirations, which are harder to achieve, can be a threat to happiness. Therefore 'happiness therapy' sometimes includes persuading clients to lower their aspirations.[114]

The most comprehensive view of the series of comparisons people indulge in is encapsulated by what is technically known as 'multiple discrepancy theory'. This holds that people use several standards in evaluating their life.[115] It distinguishes seven main discrepancies perceived in this evaluation, between where one is now in one's life and (1) what one wants (2) what other people have (3) the best personal experience in the past (4) expectations for the next few years (5) personal progress (6) what one thinks one deserves and (7) what one thinks one needs.

Perceptions of success in these matters predict happiness better when combined than separately, but the perceived gap between what one has and what one wants is the best simple predictor of happiness.[116] The vital point is that discrepancies in these seven areas predict happiness much better than an objective appreciation of an individual's living conditions.[117]

For example, to take one of the seven discrepancies, in which people compare their present situation with their own past, there is evidence that people brought up in poverty during the 1930s Depression evaluate later periods of their life positively.[118] Hence there may be an advantage to having had an unhappy childhood in terms of being a happy adult. Also, when people are asked to think about events in their past, reminiscing about a negative event in the past produces higher ratings of present happiness than recalling a positive event.[119]

It seems, therefore, that happiness builds on hardship. Because standards of comparisons anchor in earlier experience, people tend to be happier after hard times. The worse life was earlier, the lower one's standards are for what one requires now to be happy, and the more favourable the judgement of present life.

This theory provides an interesting possible explanation for the lower mood of 'baby boomers', alluded to earlier. These people were brought up at a time of wealth and stability unprecedented in history. Multiple discrepancy theory would predict that as they grow, they will be prone to unhappiness because they will compare their current state with their relatively wonderful childhoods, and so feel bad about the present.

The theory also provides an explanation as to why satisfaction with life tends to increase with age: as people become older their achievements increase and their aspirations decline, until eventually the gap closes.[120]

But if it is so that people compare themselves to others to determine their happiness, and it is differences vis-à-vis others that make us happy or unhappy rather than the actual quality of our life, the implications for society at large are sobering. This means that collective changes in society for better or worse will not affect general happiness. If everyone improves their living conditions together, it is not possible to feel better in comparison to others. Therefore general social progress can never raise happiness and happiness for everyone is impossible.

For example, if most satisfaction with income arises from an individual disproportionate increase, the disproportionate decrease for others which unavoidably accompanies this will result in dissatisfaction over the comparison. As long as social comparisons are strongly important for subjective well-being, never will it be possible for everyone to be capable of maximising their satisfaction at the same time.[121]

Who you choose to compare yourself with is significant. A famous study found that manual workers in the top third of all salaries were more satisfied with their pay than non-manual workers at the same salary level.[122] Note that these manual and non-manual workers were earning the same. The explanation was that the manual workers compared themselves with other manual workers, who usually earned less, and not with better-paid non-manual workers. The non-manual workers were comparing themselves with other non-manual workers who tended to earn the same or more. Other studies have confirmed that satisfaction with pay and housing depends more on comparisons with what other people have, and on comparisons with own past experience, rather than on the actual amount of pay received. The most likely comparison is with people in the neighbourhood, relatives and those who went to the same school and college.[123]

The effect of comparison on happiness is well illustrated by William James, a famous American nineteenth-century psychologist who was perhaps the first to recognise this psychological principle: '... so we have the paradox of a man shamed to death because he is only the second pugilist or the second oarsman in the world. That he is able to beat the whole population of the globe minus one is nothing; he has pitted himself to beat that one; and as long as he doesn't do that, nothing else counts.'[124]

William James's observation represents an early statement of a fundamental principle of psychology: a person's objective achievements often matter less than how those accomplishments are subjectively construed. In this example, being one of the best in the world means little if it is seen not as a triumph over many but as a loss to one; being second best is therefore not as gratifying as perhaps it should be.[125]

Another mental activity linked to this comparison process, which seems to greatly affect people, is comparing objective outcomes to imagined outcomes – in other words, contrasting the reality of your situation with what might have been.

The intensity of people's reactions to events appears to be proportional to how easy it is for them to conjure up greater or lesser outcomes that almost happened. For example, compare the reactions of two travellers who both missed their scheduled trains, the first by five minutes and the second by thirty minutes. The outcome is the same – both must wait for the next train. But it is easier to imagine the first traveller arriving on time than the second arriving on time,[126] so the first traveller feels more intensely upset than the one whose train left much earlier, even though the objective situation of both travellers is exactly the same – they are both stranded on the platform for the same reason.

This dwelling on 'what might have been' is termed 'counterfactual' thinking by psychologists. The effects of counterfactual comparisons can even be sufficiently strong to cause people who are objectively worse off sometimes to feel better than those in a superior state. For example, researchers at Cornell University in the USA studying athletes at the 1992 summer Olympics at Barcelona concluded there was evidence that silver medallists were less happy than bronze medallists.[127] The theory that explains this depends on counterfactual thinking and comparisons going on in the medallists' minds. The silver medallist, according to this theory, focuses on the fact that he almost won the gold medal, because there is a qualitative difference between coming in first and any other outcome. The bronze medallist tends to compare himself with fourth place. Third place merits a medal whereas the fourth place finisher is just one of the field. By this process the person who is objectively worse off (the bronze medallist) nonetheless feels more gratified than the person who is objectively better off (the silver medallist). Like William James's pugilist, silver medallists probably torment themselves with counterfactual thoughts of 'if only' or 'why didn't I?', whereas bronze medallists may be soothed by the thought that 'at least I won a medal'. It seems that there may be times when less is more.

The Cornell University research focused on the emotional reactions of athletes shortly after their events. What do we know of how people adjust over longer periods of time to the objective reality of their situation?

Perhaps the most dramatic demonstration of the power of the comparison effect in determining happiness was a famous comparison study of 22 major lottery winners, 22 normal controls and 29 paralysed accident victims.[128] Rating themselves on a 6-point scale of feeling happiness, ranging from 0 for not at all to 5 for very much, lottery winners, controls and quadriplegics were surprisingly close in their ratings of present happiness (winners: 4.00, controls: 3.82, quadriplegics: 2.96). They were not significantly different in how happy they rated themselves likely to be in the future, although the quadriplegics scored higher. After a time the quadriplegic become nearly as satisfied as the general population, though never quite as much.[128]

The researchers suggest these findings can be explained by actual happiness being largely determined by the pleasure you take from mundane everyday events. The problem with winning the lottery is that your expectations of the pleasure life should bring you are instantly revised upwards, which, with the intense joy of winning, renders everyday events less likely to give you the same pleasure that they did before you won. The quadriplegics, on the other hand, took greater pleasure in everyday events[129] because in a sense they didn't have much other choice. It seems from this study that, again, lasting happiness is unlikely because any improvement is overshadowed by, among other things, a rise in aspirations. Standards of comparison adjust and follow the perception of reality.

According to this view experiences of happiness and unhappiness alternate and largely outbalance each other. Comparing ourselves with others we are either happy or unhappy because we are better or worse off relatively, and this mood is only short-lived because we soon adjust our standards of comparison. If our lives improve we feel happy for some time, but soon we get used to that level, and feel neutral again, or even unhappy because we come to expect continuous progress. The same applies to comparisons with expectations and aspirations. If all this is true, we can expect that happy and unhappy periods will alternate through our life and that in the general population the number of happy and unhappy people will tend to match each other. This implication is known as the 'zero sum theory'.[130]

According to Freud, unhappiness is caused by unmet needs, such as the need to be free to do what we really want regardless of social rules. Therefore it follows that happiness results from the meeting of needs. The problem is that if you need a need to be met before you can be happy, then you have to have had an unmet need before you can be happy. So needs are required to provide a reservoir for the release of happiness, by the meeting of these needs. Happiness is therefore inevitably related to unhappiness:[131] paradoxically unhappiness appears to be the cause of happiness.

Without needs there can be no satisfactions. Furthermore if we did not experience unhappiness, we would not be motivated to pursue happiness. Interestingly taking the most direct route to satisfaction results in the most rapid extinction of motivation. Drug use, for instance, results in lessened motivation over the long term, because drugs act immediately to produce gratification and so take away all other drives.[132] So, Freud argued, humans must learn from infancy to curb their drive to attain immediate gratification. Freud labelled this process learning self-restraint, or the reality principle. It is self-restraint which achieves mental balance, health, personal order and civilisation.

This view is often termed the 'opponent-process theory of motivation',[133] which argues that psychological mechanisms exist for the automatic control of emotions. For example, repeated pleasures lose a lot of their pleasantness and this automatic adjustment to a good thing means we do not lose our sense of motivation, therefore making us potentially capable of finding new sources of pleasure.

After a while, when we have got used to a good thing happening to us, if we lose that good thing, we are more upset than we were before the improvement occurred in the first place. The tendency to get used to improvements, and to get more upset by their loss than we were before we received their benefit, means, according to opponent-process theory, that it is very difficult for mere objective improvements in our lives to produce long-term enhancements in our mood.

An example of this process in action is when marriages end. Marriage has been found to make us happy: although research has found that marriage is the greatest source of conflict as well as being the greatest source of satisfaction, the married, including the happily and unhappily married, are overall much happier than those who are not. This is probably because spouses are major sources of all kinds of satisfaction, instrumental, emotional support and companionship.[134] The main cost of marriage for happiness is when it ends: bereavement and divorce are major sources of unhappiness.[135] The divorced are the least happy, being even less happy than the widowed.[136]

So marriage is an improvement in our lives, but after a while we take this improvement for granted – so much so that if our spouse leaves us or dies, we feel worse than we were before we met them. By arguing that wired into our brains is a mechanism whereby over time we get used to improved conditions in our lives, the opponent-process theory suggests that long-term improvements do not lead to prolonged changes above or below the norm in our mood. Instead the most dramatic changes in mood occur in response to changes in our lives which perturb the equilibrium. Bereavement and divorce should not be the major causes of unhappiness they appear to be if we, more logically, took into account at least all those years of benefit we received from having been with our spouses. Instead we get so used to marriage that we cannot cope when we are left alone. Before we were married we were single, but the effect of marriage appears to be to make us feel worse about being single again – worse off returning to being single than being single all along. In other words, sometimes the net achievement of receiving a benefit in our lives is that we end up feeling much worse when it is taken away than if we had never been given it in the first place.

As the opponent-process theory suggests, the most intensely happy times in people's lives are often preceded by negative events.[137] Mood is significantly better on the day following a stressful event than on other stress-free days, suggesting that the termination of an negative event appears to function as a positive experience. Also potentially linking intense negative and positive states is a process called 'arousal'.[138] It has been demonstrated experimentally that the excitation or arousal associated with a distressing event can lead to intensified satisfaction or appreciation when the event is over and replaced by a positive one. For example, the extreme distress that a husband and wife experience during the birth of a child is often replaced by overwhelming positive emotions once the child is born.

Although the evidence all suggests that there is a complicated and close link between unhappiness and happiness, those who make simplistic attempts to enhance mood ignore such a link. Some psychotherapists today seem to feel that suffering is unnecessary, and that mental health will be promoted by the removal of life's stresses and strains[139] – a kind of 'living-conditions-improvement' approach to enhancing our mood, which, as we have seen is doomed to failure. In fact, what we need in life is not fewer problems, but more solutions.

Deep satisfaction is produced by the combination of challenges, and skills with which we meet them.[140] What contributes to the experience of happiness is a person's perception of the extent to which their capacities to act (or skills) correspond to the available opportunities for action (or challenges). So being a parent, for instance, becomes most satisfying when you feel you have the necessary parenting skills to help your child through a difficult time. When skills are perceived to be greater than challenges, people tend to feel bored. When challenges are seen as being higher than skills, they tend to feel anxious. When both challenges and skills are low, the person tends to feel apathetic. It is when high challenges are perceived to be matched with high skills – a subjective condition that psychologists have come to call a state of 'flow'– that a person experiences the highest levels of well-being.[141]

So one strategy to the long-term enhancement of your quality of life is to seek to improve your skills, perhaps in particular your skills at dealing with stress. You will feel at your best when you find a match between high challenge in your life and these improved skills.

We can also conclude that happiness may be maximised by minimising the impact of our previous positive experiences in any comparison with our lives today. To achieve this goal one should find ways to treat positive experiences of the past as different from the present and so not strictly comparable. This will help to avoid comparisons with a glorious past. By the same token, one should make strenuous efforts to compare present conditions to worse situations in the past, to enjoy the benefits of a positive contrast.[142]

The bottom line of this chapter is that it is best not to pursue bliss as this is usually a doomed endeavour. Instead, since the pursuit of intense positive emotions is inevitably accompanied by profound negative moods, the pathway to positive mental health is to seek emotional stability, not intense moods.

Given that it is difficult to elevate moods in any society, how may we account for the fact that the happiness of one nation may be greater than that of another – and that in particular, as mentioned earlier, over time the UK scores for happiness have been consistently above average compared to other European countries?[143]

This appears to be contrary to the theory that contentment results from the comparison we make between our lives as they are now and how we feel they could – or should – be. According to this, the British should be gloomier than other nations. The media constantly provides us with evidence that we have been in economic and world status decline over the last few decades, and shows us that nations elsewhere in the world are catching up and overtaking us, particularly America, and the nations over which we were victorious in the last war.

In terms of happiness there is a striking north-south split across the European Union, with the proportions of those satisfied with their lives above average in Denmark, Benelux countries, the United Kingdom, Ireland and Germany. All the countries below average are to the south, including Portugal and all the countries bordering the Mediterranean. This is at first glance surprising, as you might have thought the pleasanter weather of the southern European countries might predispose to a sunnier disposition.

The most popular theory among academic psychologists[144] which attempts to explain these consistent national differences is that climate patterns over thousands of generations have shaped the particular personality of a country. In colder countries there is a huge seasonal variation in the availability of food: you have to harvest in the summer and store for the harsh winter. To survive these difficult circumstances requires long-term planning and careful regulation of resources. This meant people facing these climates had to learn to do without, even when there was plenty, in order to survive times of scarcity. In other words, they had to learn to control their impulses and plan ahead. People in warmer countries, with the year-round abundance of food, never had to discipline themselves as much as the Northerners had to.

The famous stiff upper lip and reserve of the British perhaps originates from this self-control and stability. This might make us stoical in the face of adversity (as in the Blitz, when we showed the 'Bulldog spirit') and so protect us from a plunging mood when things are bad. Over thousands of years of evolution we may have got used to putting a brave face on things as the weather often let us down.

Britain also tends to score very low on neuroticism, or a tendency to over-react emotionally to negative life events; in world surveys only the Irish population scores lower than the British for neuroticism, while the most neurotic are the Austrians (interestingly where Freud originated his theories). Another way of looking at neuroticism is to see it as analogous to a tendency to sudden intense moods.

The traditional British suspicion of extremes of emotion may be attributable to the fact that they suggest an inability to control yourself, which in turn may have had poor survival value in the past. It may also explain why we are likely to rate ourselves as happy in the privacy of a survey, yet tend not to display a great deal of happiness to each other, leading to the erroneous conclusion that we are an unhappy people.

Our continued happiness over the last few decades in the face of relative economic decline seems remarkable, but could they in fact be linked?

It is intriguing to note that in 1948 West Germany had one of the unhappiest populations in Europe, with six times fewer Germans than English rating themselves as very satisfied with the way they were getting on. Yet West Germany's economic performance was to outstrip the UK's in the next forty years. Indeed all the countries in Western Europe which were generally unhappier than Britain then went on to economically out perform us over the next few decades. Is it possible, then, that, conversely, high levels of happiness in a country might predict future economic decline? Perhaps one of the dangers of happiness is that it leads to complacency.

But recent research has found substantially less happiness in the population of Pacific Rim countries like Japan and South Korea compared to Western countries like America and the UK, even after allowing for differences in income. One suggested explanation from the University of Illinois Psychology Department, which discovered the finding in 1995, was that the tremendously high growth rates of the Pacific Rim countries may mean that the people suffer from the stress of having such high expectations for achievement placed on them.

It may be that the British opt for happiness rather than the stress of the kind of competitiveness demanded to maintain a top world ranking in economic performance. Perhaps the solution to having it all – relative contentment despite the strain of striving – lies not in happiness but in resilience, which psychologists term hardiness: the ability to withstand pressure without extremely negative emotional reactions and not to let stress get to you. There appears to be very little correlation between happiness and resilience. Recall the fact that while America scores higher on happiness than India, its suicide rate is almost double. Resilience may prove a more important quality than simple happiness, which remains a media preoccupation. But until psychologists study hardiness as much as they have investigated happiness, how to achieve it will remain controversial.

Now that we have established that extreme happiness is not necessarily the goal we should be striving towards, in the next chapter we discuss how to achieve positive mental health.

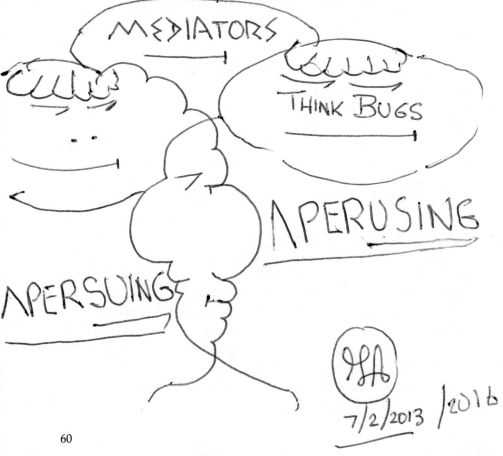

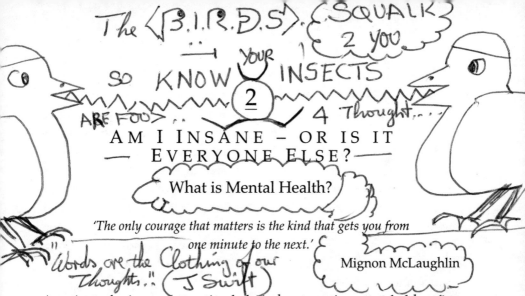

AM I INSANE – OR IS IT EVERYONE ELSE?

What is Mental Health?

'The only courage that matters is the kind that gets you from one minute to the next.'

Mignon McLaughlin

A patient of mine, an attractive lady in her twenties, attended her first appointment with me following severe symptoms of depression. These had been precipitated by three male bosses in separate organisations trying to have sex with her. The behaviour of her bosses had been outrageous: one pestered her with phonecalls laden with sexual innuendo and kept inviting her into his office whenever the building was relatively empty; he tried to touch her inappropriately despite all her protestations of lack of interest in him. Another even came into her office during a lunch hour, when others were out, and dropped his trousers to show her his penis, suggesting she might have been rejecting him because of doubts over the size of his organ. He wanted to reassure her that everything was OK in that department.

Whenever a manager started to make sexual advances she changed jobs, traumatised by the fact that wherever she moved, soon afterwards, the same problem began again. By the time of her appointment with me she had largely recovered of her own accord. She had found a job well below her capabilities but with no male bosses. Now that she was beginning to feel better and her self-confidence was returning, she felt ready to think about looking for a more senior position.

This case raises several of the factors involved in trying to define mental health. For example, the fact that my patient had recovered by herself despite the lack of psychiatric help – not an uncommon occurrence – suggests that simply experiencing symptoms of mental illness may not be a good indicator of the lack of sanity. In my view, the better measure of mental health is your ability to bring yourself back from the brink – not just the fact you were there in the first place.

I do not believe in prescribing treatment or intervening in others' lives simply because they display psychiatric symptoms. Symptoms of what might be considered quite severe mental illness may be more common than we realise in those who seem to live quite happily without the need of a psychiatrist. Surveys suggest that hallucinations (hearing voices or seeing things which really are not there) have been experienced by between 10–25 per cent of people at least once in their lifetime,[1] while 39 per cent of college students have experienced hearing their own thoughts spoken aloud – in other words, more like a voice than a thought – and 5 per cent have held conversations with their own hallucinations or 'voices'.[2,3,4]

All these findings suggest that a psychiatric symptom should only generate concern if it prevents individuals from conducting their lives as they would like, or leads to suffering in others. Indeed, there is a shift in view among some psychologists that the key issue is not the symptom itself, but your ability to retain control over it,[5,6] and I concur with this approach. So if you are happy talking to your voices that's fine, but if it interferes with your ability to concentrate on work, perhaps you do require treatment. This ability to prevent the symptoms from interfering with your important life tasks suggests the issue of control is central to mental health.

A shift of view has led to the development of treatments designed to help patients manage their symptoms rather than to get rid of them entirely. But this then produces results which may lead to improvements in quality of life very similar to eliminating a symptom altogether.[7,8] I have been involved in research focusing on helping patients whose hallucinations or voices do not respond to high doses of medication. This shows that, once they learn psychological techniques to help regulate their voices, they feel a lot better.[9] Sometimes gaining control is the prelude to dismissing a symptom.

I believe that control is a cornerstone of mental health – being able to manage your mood, temper or attitude is a key component of staying sane. If, for example, you get your bad temper under control, so that it no longer corrodes your relationship with your spouse or gets in the way of promotion at work – in other words, if your bad temper is no longer an obstacle to you getting what you want from life – do you really still need professional treatment for it?

What, then, gets in the way of control? I discuss this issue in more detail later in the book, in the chapter on the self ('Me, Me, Me'). But briefly, those better able to manage themselves are those who are able to be as responsive to the external environment (their spouse or their boss) as to their internal environment (their feelings and thoughts). A cardinal sign of poor mental health is that your internal state takes precedence over whatever is happening in the external environment. For example, take the situation where you do not feel like going to work because you feel low, but your boss desperately needs you to finish a vital project. The more mentally healthy person is able to de-prioritise his internal demands for an external one, and will be more likely to get to work even though not feeling like it.

Or take the situation of being at a party when a colleague of your spouse keeps making irritating comments. You would like to retaliate with some cutting put-down but you know it is important to your spouse that you make an effort to get on with this person. Again, the mentally healthy would be able to respond more to the demands of their spouse's happiness (assuming that is important to them) than to their internal state of annoyance. Clearly this does not mean you should always suppress your internal needs and put external ones first, but it does mean you should be able to do so if the situation requires it. The less mentally healthy cannot.

If control and the ability to retain a balance between the demands of your internal and external worlds are the foundations of mental health, does that mean that mental illness symptoms are irrelevant? Of course not. But if you share my view that such symptoms – by the time they are seen by a psychiatrist – are the culmination of a long-term inability to control oneself or to suppress internal issues for external ones, it is clear that preventing mental illness must centre on aiming to improve such control as well as the ability to distract oneself from internal states and focus on external ones. Simply concentrating on symptoms isn't a long-term cure.

Obviously professional intervention is needed when people cannot help themselves, and they should be encouraged to seek assistance in these situations. But anything which can help us help ourselves is clearly useful, and I hope my book will contribute to this process.

As was the case with my sexually harassed female patient, the tendency for large numbers of people to get better without help, but with the passage of time, is so well known that some psychiatrists have suggested[10, 11] that the waiting list to see a psychiatrist could be seen as a form of treatment in itself. Sometimes if you managed to see a clinician too soon after an upset, when you were in a terrible state, he or she might prescribe treatment which in the end could prove unnecessary because recovery was possible without it – given enough time.

I am always arguing that the health benefits of the passage of time need to be studied more by researchers as so little is really known about them. In the next chapter, on counselling and psychology, I briefly explore how much mental health improvement may simply be due to this factor and that this improvement is sometimes ascribed to the counselling process.

The healing process works in many different ways. For example, the elapse of time could help you change the way you think about your problem; mobilise personal resources like support from friends; give rise to positive life events which make you feel better in the short run; permit solutions to suggest themselves or be volunteered by others; allow time for the problem either to get better by itself or be reassessed and shown to be not as bad as it first seemed, and so on. How to take conscious control of all the things which help people solve their problems, without needing to see a therapist, is also a major focus of this book.

Time worked in the case of my young lady patient. However, although she now felt much better, she was still unsure enough of herself to need to keep her appointment with me. She had symptoms of depression, like loss of weight, sleep problems and feeling miserable, and so thought her mental health had deteriorated. Yet here is a central paradox in defining what mental health is: she was very upset – many would say understandably given what she had experienced – yet the boss who dropped his trousers in front of her probably did not feel the need to see a psychiatrist, even though his behaviour was clearly more questionable than hers.

This manager may never volunteer to see a doctor or (given his seniority) be asked to. Does this therefore mean he is mentally healthy while my patient is not? I believe any coherent definition of mental health has to accommodate both people and their behaviour. Certainly a central component of poor mental health has to be suffering – both your own and that of other people. My patient certainly experienced this, and her boss was the cause. A definition of mental health should be broad enough to include people who consistently produce unnecessary suffering in others as a result of their behaviour as well as people who experience suffering themselves.

One reason for this is that your inability to get on positively with others will eventually rebound when you need them to help you out. This is because all rewards in life, without exception, are either social ones, or linked to relationships in some way. Even if your ambition appears to be extremely anti-social – to live alone on a desert island – you still have to get to your desert island somehow and make sure you have picked one where you will not be disturbed. These tasks will inevitably require you to interact with others. All these goals cannot be accomplished unless you have basic abilities to interact with others in order to get from them what you need.

Mental illness is usually linked to a breakdown in relationships, often to the extent that the people in the immediate environment of a severely insane person take the initiative themselves to arrange for psychiatric intervention, as they are affected so negatively by the behaviour of the mentally ill person. If you are sensitive to the needs of others and have relationship skills, you will find yourself helped towards your life goals by other people, and not impeded by them.

So, I have broadened the concept of mental ill-health to include a lifestyle, attitude or behaviour which produces personal suffering or distress in others as well as in yourself. But should the criteria for mental health and illness not also include a person's state of being *before* illness or symptoms start to show, where action now might prevent them starting? For example, even though my patient's bosses may not be in immediate need of psychiatric help, would it be possible to predict whether they will develop problems in the future? Would it not be helpful for them to change now?

Since they seem unable to control themselves, allow their internal states to dominate the needs of others, and are insensitive to the upset they cause, I would argue that while my patient recovers from her distress, her bosses are vulnerable to future psychological problems.

Given that mental health is such a popular and professional concern, with important implications for the individual and society, it is surprising how little serious attention is given to defining precisely what we mean by the words 'mental health' – even amongst professionals and specialists. There is no single accepted definition of mental health in any one country, let alone throughout the world.

Some people argue that trying to define psychological health is a bit like trying to define what love or consciousness is and that some concepts or ideas may simply be too complex to be defined pithily. Perhaps sanity also means contrasting things to different people, hence your own opinion of mental health may differ from mine because it diverges from my ideals or values. Furthermore, normal behaviour in one country might be considered abnormal in another, and the same problem applies to historical epochs. For example, years ago in the West, and still to this day in some countries, giving birth to an illegitimate child raised questions about the mother's mental health.

In some Arabic countries during the Middle Ages there was a disease known as love. The symptoms were really rather severe. The sufferer lost appetite, couldn't sleep, lost interest in life, had difficulty concentrating and lost weight. The physician established the diagnosis by listing the names of all the eligible members of the opposite sex who lived in the village, while taking the patient's pulse. At the sound of a name where the patient's pulse quickened, the illness was confirmed. The treatment was marriage.[12]

In the North American deep south, before slavery was abolished, doctors recognised and listed diagnoses in their textbooks, such as the mental illness which caused slaves to run away from their masters, and the illness which caused them to fail to learn from their wrongdoing even after being whipped.[13]

Now, you and I might not consider these behaviours to be symptoms of ill-health (nor the 'symptoms' of love for that matter), but these examples illustrate why health in general, not just mental health, is difficult to define. Your values – what you think life ought to be about – always intrude. This explains why, decades ago, USSR psychiatrists were sometimes involved in diagnosing political opposition as a sign of mental illness, and why homosexuality only stopped being described in North American psychiatry textbooks as a mental illness in the 1970s.

Advances in medical science also influence what gets defined as an illness. For example, the menopause is an entirely normal biological event, which every woman who lives beyond a certain age will experience. But in the West, women going through the menopause regularly receive treatment by doctors in the form of Hormone Replacement Therapy (HRT). Some could argue that this is a step on the way to defining the menopause as a disease. While the unpleasant 'symptoms' of the menopause should undoubtedly be treated if doctors have the capacity to help alleviate them, doctors' ability to relieve all kinds of misery leads to the medicalisation of distress.

Another example is that the disturbed sleep and unpleasant emotions following the shock of bereavement now regularly receive treatment by doctors in the form of sleeping tablets and anti-depressants. This has led to the suggestion that grief[14] has begun to fit the definition of a disease and could soon be categorised as one. It is clear that if new disorders keep appearing like this,[15] we are in danger of reflecting the belief that the normal experience of life should never include distress, and that such experiences require professional or medical assistance. In the chapter on counselling I go into greater detail on one aspect of this – how counselling is in danger of psychotherapising unhappiness. This process perhaps also explains why so many people confuse mental health with simple happiness.

I believe that what has happened recently is that, although doctors continue to define ill-health in terms of a deviation from biological or statistical norms, the way the profession behaves towards patients, and prescribes medication, reflects an altogether different view: that disease has simply become a state we consider undesirable, and for which there is a possible medical solution. Given enough detailed understanding of our biology, doctors should be able to transform many of our states – even normal ones – into ones we might prefer.

For example, at times we prefer to be infertile (temporarily) and doctors prescribe the contraceptive pill to produce this effect. This is an abnormal state produced by doctors because, more importantly, many people also find it desirable.

I am emphasising the problem using the concept of 'norms' or 'the normal' because whenever people – even doctors – define health and, in particular, mental health, the word 'normal' is never far from their lips. Yet I believe norms or being normal have very little to do with health at all. For example, a doctor[16] recently explained that while acne affects 85 per cent of people and starts in the teenage years, as it causes considerable psychological distress, 'it is no longer thought of as just a *normal* part of growing up'. Clearly if it affects 85 per cent of people, acne *is* a normal part of growing up. However, this does not mean it should not receive treatment if that will allay unnecessary suffering.

Another good example of this confusion between normality and health is IQ scores. These are designed so that the average IQ is 100 and the same number of people in the population have IQs higher than the average as those who have a lower score. Yet, while those with an IQ far below normal receive professional attention because of their disability or learning difficulties, those with an equally abnormal score – but which just happens to be above 100 – do not. To illustrate the example with some extreme score results – someone with an IQ of 150 is just as abnormal, statistically speaking, as someone with an IQ of 50, but we tend to believe that the person with an IQ of 50 should receive help, while the person with an IQ of 150 receives no similar assistance to reduce their score! Why is this, if it is simply abnormality that determines disease?

The answer must be that aberration alone does not resolve whether we believe an experience or phenomenon is a disease. Instead, what we consider undesirable becomes the crucial issue. So an IQ of 50 is undesirable, but one of 150 is possibly not.

The point here is that, for us to pursue it, good health must be considered a desirable state of being. What we consider preferable also has something to do with our priorities in life, which it is (to some extent) down to the individual to decide. One person, for example, might like to socialise, and if they find themselves alone more than they would like, their resulting feeling of loneliness is likely to be a more worrying development in their mental state than it would be for those who prefer solitude.

So, anyone striving to define health or disease must take this individual variation into account. It is best to try to take a view of health which fits in with the kind of life most people would consider agreeable. The best advice on preserving your mental health should remain pertinent even if your values depart radically from those of the psychiatrist who is advising you how to stay sane. For this reason I will set out the different ways specialists have thought about mental health, so you can decide for yourself what you consider mental health to be.

Many people's view of sanity is determined more by their individual preferences for the kind of life they want to lead than would be the case for physical health. But I hope to persuade you in this book that, although everyone values certain qualities and lifestyles differently, there *are* various components of mental health which, if adopted and maintained, will keep you from ever having to see a psychiatrist.

Whatever the difficulties of defining health and disease, it is important to try to define the concepts as clearly as possible. As a psychiatrist, I am particularly interested in defining what *mental* health is. If you can arrive at a sensible definition, you might then realise that some aspects of your behaviour may have more significance than you realised in terms of your sanity – whether good or bad. For example, it is highly likely you have selected your social circle with a view to those whose company you enjoy. But your choice of friends can also influence your long-term mental health. Will they be supportive when you are in a crisis? Another aspect of behaviour which has more significance than you may realise is your coping strategy (dealt with in detail in the chapter 'Crisis, What Crisis?'). Have you been using coping strategies which are the most effective in preserving your mental health regardless of the stress under which you find yourself or are you simply using measures which only make you feel better in the short term, such as losing your temper or drinking heavily?

One of the most satisfying aspects of my job as a consultant psychiatrist working in the British National Health Service is being able to tell people categorically that they are not suffering from the illness they are desperately worried they have. I see a lot of people terrified of going severely insane, and the diagnosis which seems to strike the most terror is schizophrenia. The person referred by their family doctor may have no mental illness at all, or may simply be suffering from anxiety or depression, and is usually extremely relieved to hear me tell them that their symptoms, experiences or behaviour are not indications that they are heading for schizophrenia.

So a paradox now emerges: how is it doctors can agree on whether or not you have something like schizophrenia, but cannot agree on what mental health is?

Perhaps the most straightforward conception of mental health used by professionals is that it is simply the absence of mental illness. This is the legal definition pretty much throughout the world. For example, if someone exhibits none of the identifiable symptoms of psychiatric disorder listed in the *Diagnostic and Statistical Manual of the American Psychiatric Association*, or the International Classification of Diseases, published by the World Health Organisation (WHO), according to the present state of thinking in psychiatry, they are considered by doctors to be mentally healthy or 'normal'.

It is important to remember that physical as well as mental health is usually referred to by doctors in negative terms as the absence of disease, illness and sickness. All measures of health status tend to take health as a baseline and then assess deviations from this. Thus, what those interested in health end up really measuring is ill-health, because it appears easier to measure departures from health than to find signifiers of health itself. But reliance on such a negative definition provides scanty information about the health of the remaining large numbers of the general public.

The reason doctors find it easier to recognise and agree on illness than on health is that, by the time you have got so ill as to think about seeing a doctor, you are in a state which is so unpleasant that there is little doubt that this is undesirable and should be reversed. However, milder degrees of disease are more controversial, and the variability in people's reactions to these discomforts begins to have more to do with their individual tolerance than the illness itself. For example, a mild headache or cold may keep some people away from work more because they do not really like their job than because of the degree of pain. In contrast, virtually no one would agree to go in while suffering a severe epileptic attack, no matter how dedicated to work they may be.

And is the boss who seems to be performing well at work, has no symptoms like depression or hallucinations, and who appears at first glance to have a happy married life – but who also drops his trousers to show his penis to a new employee – mentally healthy or not?

If you have no symptoms at all, but display characteristics which will increase the likelihood of illness in the future, such as taking a long time to recover from a relatively mild psychological upset, such a state is even more controversial. This is because predicting who will become ill before they do so is always tricky. It is made more difficult when complex diseases whose causes are still not fully understood, like many mental illnesses, are involved.

Yet trying to determine what leads to illness before symptoms become apparent is extremely useful. It allows you to target vulnerable individuals and change their risk factors *before* they start to suffer from a disease. With common illnesses, such as psychiatric illness, if everyone were to adopt simple preventive health strategies, the rewards to the Health Service as well as an individual's well-being would be enormous.

The idea behind physical illness prevention strategies – like getting people to take up regular exercise, give up smoking and excessive alcohol consumption, and eat healthily – is that by so doing you will reduce your chances of physical disease. People who do not do these things may not yet suffer the ill effects of a definite disease, and are probably not yet sick. However, they are likely to become unwell in the future, and it is possible to describe them, if not as diseased, certainly as less healthy than those who have these health-promoting habits.

A huge amount of medical time today is spent targeting people who have not yet developed any disease, but who are thought likely to. GPs expend great effort identifying those on their lists who have high blood pressure, or hypertension, with the aim of reducing it. People with elevated blood pressure are not yet ill, but just have a marker which indicates future illness if the present state goes unchecked. I am advocating a kind of blood pressure check for your mental health.

As mentioned, I will attempt to set out the characteristics of those who are not yet formally psychiatrically ill, but who are likely to become mentally ill in the future. I will also suggest that there are simple strategies you can use to prevent yourself developing significant psychological problems. If you accept the possibility of preventive action, then defining health, and in particular mental health, as simply the absence of mental illness will no longer seem very satisfactory.

There have been previous attempts at a more positive approach to defining health. The World Health Organisation (WHO) has recommended the development of measures of positive health[17] and, in its 1946 constitution,[18] emphasised that health is a state of complete physical, mental and social well-being, and not merely the absence of disease and infirmity. Yet beyond this there are no descriptions which would allow people to determine how healthy they are or permit doctors to measure health as opposed to disease.

Despite the controversy provoked by the WHO's Utopian definition, it has generated interest in a broader, more positive concept of health, rather than a narrow, negative, disease-based focus. The WHO 1985 ideal of health for all by the year 2000, and the 1986 Ottawa Charter for Health Promotion,[19] with its emphasis on assisting us to increase control over and improve our health, both employ broader definitions of health than those traditionally employed by physicians.

But in a classic essay in the *British Journal of Sociology* in 1953, the eminent British psychiatrist who was instrumental in establishing psychiatric research in Britain, Sir Aubrey Lewis, commenting on the WHO's definition of health as 'a state of physical, mental and *social* well-being', noted that a proposition could hardly be more 'comprehensive than that, or more meaningless'.[20]

The thrust of Sir Aubrey's argument was that disease cannot be assessed in terms of *social* standards – the idea that you are mentally healthy if you get on with others and they get on with you; or even that you are well because you are regarded by others as well. My young lady patient may have fitted in better with what sounds like a very disturbed office environment by agreeing to have sex. Yet is conforming with the demands of those around you always the most mentally healthy response?

The WHO view that mental health is also equated with appropriate social behaviour is popular among some psychologists, especially those who call themselves behaviour therapists.[21] After all, people usually become candidates for psychiatric help only because of some inappropriate behaviour. This may range from holding up the traffic because you believe you are the next Messiah to wearying your spouse with accounts of your depression. But this perspective seems to hinge on conformity to an arbitrarily defined set of social rules. Why should who you get on with determine your mental health? At one extreme this defines mental health as simply the ability to fraternise with your psychiatrist.

Moreover, this view of mental health is also 'culture-bound', and what is appropriate in one culture may not be so in another. It also ignores the fact that sometimes conforming would be an unhealthy thing to do – for example, if one was in a drug or alcohol sub-culture, or a member of a cult. Cults appear attractive to young otherwise intelligent people who may be having problems fitting into mainstream society, a society they may reject because of its materialist and competitive values. Although they find a group they get on well with when they join a cult, their parents argue that what has really happened is a retreat from mainstream society. They would say that the real solution is to make your way through life without having to retire to a camp in the desert, wear only purple or have group sex with your guru. The parents and children clearly disagree on what is desirable and therefore mentally healthy behaviour. But who is right?

Many psychologically unhealthy people do indeed get on fairly well with others – but those who are all equally psychologically unhealthy themselves. In fact, the only mentally healthy person in a group of unhealthy people probably gets a hard time from the others. Sometimes the 'black sheep' of the family when brought to family therapists turns out to be the most healthy person amongst dysfunctional relatives.

Sir Aubrey Lewis argued against fitting in with others as the measure of mental health, in his famous account. Instead, he claimed that ill-health must be judged by evidence of pathological function or abnormality. So, yet again, the notion of health was equated to the absence of disease.

Instead, my view is that positive mental health should be defined as states of mind which experts tend to agree are desirable, and which in their experience are likely to protect us from psychiatric problems in the future. When psychologists and psychiatrists with an interest in mental health (as opposed to just illness) are asked,[22] certain themes recur in the different definitions of positive mental health over the last few decades. These themes are 'constructive attitudes towards the self', 'integration of personality', 'autonomy', 'accurate perception of reality' and 'environmental mastery'.

I shall go through these concepts one by one below, and indicate the ones I see as true signposts of mental health.

'Constructive attitudes towards the self' includes ideas like self-acceptance – you have learned to accept your capabilities and limitations. Self-confidence, self-esteem and self-respect suggest a more positive attitude to yourself than mere acceptance – you like yourself, and feel you are basically good. Self-reliance suggests you are independent from others and take your initiative from within. I discuss these ideas in greater depth in chapter 4 ('Me, Me, Me') because I agree your attitude to your self is such an important aspect of staying sane.

'Integration of personality' means, broadly speaking, that you do not hold attitudes to the world which are in abrasive conflict with each other. For example, if you want to get on with people but at the same time feel a deep disdain for most of them, you would appear to be in the grip of a conflict which could produce psychological problems for you later. As a lot of poor mental health is attributed to internal conflicts which tear us apart, it makes sense that the positively mentally healthy person should be relatively free of conflict. A good example of an almost universal clash was Freud's suggestion that, driven by our animal urges and instincts, we are all caught in a contest between what we would really like to do or say to those around us (e.g. something pretty unpleasant to a boss who drops his trousers in front of you) and what is deemed appropriate by civilisation or society (e.g. forcing yourself to keep quiet in order to keep your job).[23]

Freud's solution to this conflict was his famous dictum 'Where Id was, let Ego be'. The Id is our dark instinctual animal-like self which wants to be gratified immediately, while the Ego is our more rational calculating self. In other words, Freud was saying that the solution to this struggle, which we are burdened with by civilisation and which animals are free from, is that we should suppress our animal instincts and replace them with more civilising responses, thus banishing the urge to behave impulsively or extremely.

However, some therapists take issue with this as the avenue to mental health[24] and suggest that if we do away with our baser urges altogether and are super-rational all the time we also become rather passionless. The real solution is probably some kind of balance between our internal forces; leaving us with the flexibility to be aggressive or passionate as the need arises, and to be in control and calm when required.[25] I agree with this latter view.

There are alternative opinions to Freud's view of the basic conflicts in life we all face. Existential therapists, for example, suggest that the four basic conflicts we all confront are those of death, freedom, isolation and meaninglessness.[26]

According to this perspective, mental ill-health is the product of an inability to come to terms with at least one of these four conflicts. For example, we know that one day we must die and yet in our daily lives we behave in a way which appears to take little account of this. We claim we value freedom, and yet our lives exist within narrow boundaries we appear to have chosen for ourselves. We also fail to face our fundamental aloneness or the apparent meaninglessness of life. Existential therapists argue that the pathway to mental health involves proper if not painful confrontation with these inescapable givens of existence. This theory could be used to explain why bereavement may precipitate severe mental illness in some, yet leave others relatively psychologically unscathed – it is those who have not come to terms with these conflicts who will be most badly affected, as death forces us to confront all four conflicts at once.

The problem with this view of mental health is that there are probably as many fundamental conflicts one could postulate as there are mental health experts. That said, while being entirely conflict-free might be an impossible aspiration, certainly reducing our conflicts is good for our mental health.

The third state of mind experts agree is desirable is 'autonomy'. This refers to personal independence, where you feel free to do and think what you like without being too dependent on others or restricted by fears or other incapacities. Some have referred to this as a kind of self-containment which suggests the autonomous are not dependent for their main satisfactions upon the external world or other people, but are more dependent on their own personal resources.[27] So one obvious measure of this would be the ability to be alone without undue distress, and this has been described by some psychoanalysts as one of the most important signs of maturity in emotional development.

Autonomous people will not react in the same way to an event as the crowd. Instead the autonomous take time to make up their minds independently, and often have no trouble coming out against the majority viewpoint. They do not mind not conforming.

The obvious advantage of being more wrapped up in yourself rather than the external world is that this should give you relative immunity to negative changes in your external circumstances. However, one disadvantage, as mentioned earlier, is that it suggests a relative indifference to those around you. Herein lies a paradox with positive mental health. If you care about others you leave yourself open to be hurt by them. But if you do not care for them you cannot be so hurt, while on the other hand you are unlikely to have built the kind of social support found to be helpful in withstanding stress.

So the sensitivity of my lady patient left her open to being so upset by the behaviour of her boss, while his indifference might preserve him from feeling upset when others do not like him. This difference between them explains why, in the short term, she was visiting a psychiatrist and he was not. Yet her social sensitivity probably means she will end up with more social support from friends in the long run than her boss, who might find himself isolated when his divorce comes through. To achieve long-term mental health you need to strike a balance and develop the ability to be both sensitive and insensitive as required.

The fourth state of mind is an accurate perception of reality, which has long been popular with psychologists and psychiatrists as a requirement of mental health – partly because they are used to seeing people who hear voices and believe they must go to Buckingham Palace to claim their rightful place on the throne. This clear inability to comprehend actuality as the rest of us agree on it is such a cardinal sign of severe mental illness it seems only logical that an accurate perception of fact is important to mental health. However, as I demonstrate in the chapter on resilience ('I Will Survive') this is not quite as straightforward as it sounds. There is new evidence that those most resilient to the impact of negative life events often have an overly positive view of themselves compared to what is strictly true.

It is also in any case very difficult to decide upon the correct perception of reality – after all, opposing political parties and different religions cannot seem to agree on this. Instead, the characteristic of the truly mentally healthy is the ability to take in the world as it is, particularly when this state of affairs is different from the way you wish it was. You may need to believe you have done enough revision for your exam – and can therefore take yet another break – but the mentally healthy can see the distinction between what they wish to be the case, and what really is. This has been described as a 'relative freedom from need-distortion'.[28]

So, for instance, those who become stalkers keep following their victims even though their quarry make it crystal-clear they have no romantic interest in their pursuers. The stalkers are genuinely unable to perceive reality accurately because their strong need not to be rebuffed grossly distorts their perception of what is going on. The importance of not letting your needs contaminate your appraisal of reality is discussed in greater detail in chapter 5 ('Crying Is Good For You') and chapter 6 ('So, You Think You Are Sane?').

Finally, 'environmental mastery' refers to having a sense of control over your life and destiny and, in particular, to the feeling that you are more in control of your environment than it is of you. One measure of environmental mastery is some sense of personal achievement in the significant areas of life, like relationships, work and solving your problems. The difficulty with this view is that it sometimes seems to oversimplify mental health. As one psychologist put it, 'My co-workers and I have settled for some such simple criteria as these: the ability to hold a job, have a family, keep out of trouble with the law, and enjoy the usual opportunities for pleasure.'[29]

However, it is possible to see that success in even these relatively few different areas in life often comes down to mastery of relationships. You are unlikely to progress far in your career if you cannot get on well with bosses or perform well at interviews – all relationship skills, which I deal with in chapter 3 ('Hell Is Other People'). Conflict with others, like your spouse, the in-laws, an aggressive drunk in the street, the person who sold you a duff motor-car, are all important sources of psychological distress, and the social skills necessary to handle these disparate situations so as to produce a positive outcome are an essential component of staying sane.

The world is full of people who we require to meet our needs: love from a spouse, reward from a boss, respect from a colleague, co-operation from a potential adversary. Getting what we need from all these different people requires careful negotiation, which is achieved through social skills. Some people have superior social skills and they are likely to get their needs more easily met by others than those with a tendency to poor mental health, who have more difficulty in this area.

The popular view is that you are either born with social skills or not. Some people seem to have innate charm, poise and grace in social situations, while others can never think of anything witty to say. Yet the current view among psychologists is that social skills can be learnt, in precisely the same way as a competence such as driving a car. I devote a section to acquiring social skills in the chapter on relationships.

The environment is not just composed of people but is also made up of difficult situations, such as facing an extremely important exam or trying to decide which job offer to accept. Negotiating our way effectively through these difficult situations is another key way of staying sane. The method suggested for this by psychologists is called 'problem-solving', with these situations referred to as problems. I discuss these techniques in chapter 8, on coping skills ('Crisis, What Crisis?') and chapter 6 ('So, You Think You Are Sane?').

The difficulty with all these criteria for mental health was summed up in a report published in 1958 to the Joint Commission on Mental Illness and Health in the USA as part of an attempt to prepare recommendations for a national mental health programme: 'there is hardly a term in current psychological thought as vague, elusive, and ambiguous as the term "mental health"'.[30]

At the beginning of this chapter I pointed out that the insane are too dominated by their internal states and feelings and ignore the environment as a result. This seems at first glance in direct contradiction of the idea of autonomy, where what everyone else is up to gets put to one side while the autonomous go their own way. The danger here is that concepts like 'environmental mastery' and 'accurate perception of reality' are selected by psychologists as determinants of mental health without a really clear idea of why they are important. Instead, they get chosen just because they seem desirable and sensible components of sanity.

For me, a slightly more practical perspective comes from René Dubos, a microbiologist and the discoverer of the source of the first commercially produced antibiotics. He was engaged in the study of disease and environment, and in so doing noted the extraordinary adaptiveness of organisms to changing conditions. The important implication of this is that health cannot always be determined by the same features, so the suggestion, for example, that 'accurate perception of reality' or 'environmental mastery' will always be linked to health should be rejected. Instead, Dubos suggested, 'Biological success in all its manifestations is a measure of fitness, and fitness requires never-ending efforts of adaption to the total environment, which is ever-changing'.[31]

A key issue in positive mental health therefore appears to be adaptability to the environment in which you find yourself. I would like to argue that disease occurs when you are clearly poorly adapted to the situation in which you find yourself, while health is a measure of your adaptability to a wide variety of possible situations you might find yourself inhabiting in the future. Less healthy people, though not yet formally ill, are currently in an environment they are adapted to. However, should there be only minor changes in that environment, they would be unable to cope or adapt, and that would produce ill-health. The more adaptable you are to a wide range of environments, situations, people and predicaments, the more mentally healthy you are.

In a fast-changing world, the need for adaptability increases, whereas in a static world where there's not much change, or changes happen with plenty of warning or very slowly, adaptability is clearly not of so much benefit. Given that the world is being transformed at a faster and faster pace, the need for adaptable people has never been more imperative. This perhaps helps to explain the rise in rates of mental illness, despite the simultaneous rise in standards of living.[32]

Evidence for such a rise in mental illness includes one historical study in Sweden which found the rate of depression in women over the age of 30 born before 1910 was about 3 per cent, while for this same age group born after 1950 the rate had risen to 60 per cent.[33]

My views on the importance of adaptability to mental health have been confirmed in my clinical practice where I see much mental illness in people who appear perfectly well for many years, yet whose problems are precipitated by small changes foisted upon them – a change in manager at work, a partner taking up evening classes, for example. There is an important paradox here. You may be very well adapted to your particular situation – your spouse, your job, your circle of friends and your neighbourhood – but if you are not flexible, changes may cause illness. Another person who may not be quite so well adapted to his or her particular situation, if they are more adaptable than you, would be – in my terms – still more mentally healthy.

So, appearing sane is not a necessary pointer to mental health and even the most normal-seeming person could be at risk. Lack of adaptability often becomes apparent only after a change occurs which people have particular difficulty accepting, and it is hard to anticipate in advance which changes will cause us most problems. I should stress that my view, that those who appear well but not adaptable are still suffering from poor mental health, is not shared by the majority of my colleagues, and will be resisted furiously by the mainstream.

However, I emphasise the need to be flexible because I have seen many clients who appear to be much healthier than they really are simply because they have developed a lifestyle which accommodates their particular problems.

For example, I knew a patient once who had a form of anxiety disorder – she developed a phobic avoidance of any floor above ground level. Because she carefully planned her day and anticipated cleverly, she made sure she never found herself in a situation where she had to leave the ground floor. If invited somewhere where there was the possibility of going on to a higher floor, she would make up some excuse not to go.

Her avoidance strategy meant that most people had no idea she was so ill. However, if the need suddenly arose for her to climb some stairs she would be in deep trouble, so she was very limited in her pliability to the demands of her environment. For example, if there was an accident, or a fire, or a door which did not open properly, she would be unable to climb a set of stairs to find another way out of a building.

This person was clearly not trying to change to become more adaptable; instead, her motivation was just to adapt her situation to herself as she was. She was not going to modify herself to become less fearful of higher floors. The approach of not changing yourself but simply making your environment fit you, may seem to hold immediate benefits, particularly if you feel personal change is difficult or frightening. Aiming to adapt to whatever situation you find yourself in is much harder at the time, and only pays dividends later when you discover that changes in your environment do not produce the problems for you that they would for the less mentally healthy.

But despite the difficulties, it is much more healthy to aspire to adaptability, as this makes it easier to fend off future mental illness.

While most other psychiatrists do not accept my view of health as centring around adaptability, they do agree that the concept of positive health is more than the absence of disease or disability and, instead, that it implies completeness, full functioning and efficiency of mind and body, together with social adjustment. Beyond this there is no universally accepted definition.

Positive health is widely accepted among doctors as the ability to cope with stressful situations, the maintenance of a strong social support system, integration in the community, high morale and life satisfaction, psychological well-being and even possessing levels of physical fitness, as well as physical health.[34] These are all laudable aims, but unless they lead to adaptability, I do not believe they are necessarily key components to staying sane. Positive mental health is not just about coping with stress, but also about surviving, adapting and then thriving no matter how your life circumstances change. The key question is how to achieve this.

However you define mental health, the crucial point is that you cannot improve it unless you know clearly what you are trying to achieve. You need a clear idea of the goal to which you are aspiring. Indeed I believe that, although most people will not have so precise or clear a view of what positive mental health is, they already have some intuitive sense of how likely they are to make successful adaptations to future possible life changes. For example, my young lady patient who had already made a recovery from her depression following her bosses' sexual harassment, despite being now well, still kept her appointment to see me rather than cancelling it, because she was worried about her ability to cope should the same problem recur in a new work situation. She now felt better but lacked confidence in her ability to adapt in the future, and was really asking for advice on how to do this.

Research backs up the notion that this intuitive sense of our own level of health exists and may even be surprisingly accurate. Personal judgements of own health status, or subjective health assessments are among the best general predictors of future ill-health and use of medical care services,[35-43] often superior to objective medical assessments.

A good place to start unravelling this enigma might be to see how clinicians judge the concept of mental health.[44]

These appear to be 'the patient's need to be protected and supported by the therapist or hospital versus the patient's ability to function autonomously', 'seriousness of symptoms', 'degree of discomfort and distress', 'effect on the environment', 'degree to which the patient can utilise his abilities, especially in work', 'the quality of interpersonal relationships – warmth, intimacy, impulse control', and 'breadth and depth of interests'.

The problem with this approach is that recording no clinical symptoms at all still leads to a rating as healthy. Even if you are filled with tension, anxiety and guilt, if you keep these hidden from the outside world you will still meet the criteria. I believe this is more appropriately a view of mental illness rather than health.

Another problem with most doctors' view of mental health is that it leads to what is known as a 'categorical' approach – you fall into the category of health if you are not ill. This black-and-white approach is the opposite of what is termed a 'dimensional approach' – where some people appear healthier than others, although none of them would be termed ill. One advantage of a dimensional approach to health is that you can identify that some people are healthier than others, and therefore pinpoint those who would benefit from some health-improving manoeuvres. It also lends itself to the idea of a popular wish to improve personal mental health, even if not actually ill.

The idea that even apparently symptom-free individuals could improve their mental health is similar to the psychoanalytic view. Psychoanalysis is a branch of psychiatry particularly interested in hidden emotions, motivations and the unconscious. Psychoanalysts typically conceive mental health as freedom from psychological conflict, anxiety and guilt. Freud,[45] writing in 1933, specified the ability to love and work as the hallmark of mental health and devoted most of his energies to unearthing factors that inhibit this ability. For health to flower, the choking weeds of guilt and anxiety must be removed.

However, not feeling guilt or anxiety in many situations would definitely be unhealthy – for example, after committing murder. So the complete removal of guilt or anxiety would seem undesirable; it is only its absence in certain contexts which is useful. In other words, feeling only *appropriate* guilt or anxiety would seem to be the key here. My view of adaptability as the key to mental health would suggest that in some situations being able to adapt to not feeling excessive guilt after killing someone might be useful – for example, if you found yourself having to fight as a soldier in a war.

Unfortunately, Freud made no attempt to define more precisely his view of health – and after all, to love and to work seems a rather broad definition! This was partly because he did not believe anything other than a fellow human being could measure health. He believed the assessment of health could arise only from a personal feeling which developed between a client and a psychoanalyst over many years.

This is clearly of limited use for most individuals. Freud argued that everyone would benefit from psychoanalysis and that therefore the understanding of your mental health by anyone other than your analyst was likely to be incomplete. But even assuming the limited objective of assessing who needs psychoanalysis most urgently, or comparing how good different therapists are, some more precise view of mental health would seem desirable.

Other psychoanalysts[46] suggest that neurotic conflicts, or the precursors to mental ill-health, usually arise from the adoption by an individual of an idealised view of what he or she should be (the ideal self) – one that makes what the individual knows that he or she actually is seem horribly inadequate. A wide or unbridgeable gap between how we would like to be and how we see ourselves results inevitably in self-hate and produces poor mental health.

One problem with this view is that some notion of an idealised self would seem necessary for any self-development. If you decided there was no difference between who you wanted to be and what you already were, you would have no need to improve yourself and this would lead to complacency. Self-satisfaction seems to be the danger here.[47] Other psychologists have even suggested a key component of positive mental health are the aims you devote yourself to in the interest of personal growth.[48] They suggest[49] there are two kinds of goals people set themselves – mentally unhealthy goals are simply those that aim to correct a deficiency in our everyday needs. We all need safety, a feeling of belonging, love, respect and self-esteem, and the mentally unhealthy are struggling to attain these goals, and so have to devote themselves to achieving them.

The mentally healthy on the other hand achieve these goals without having to work so hard, and so have personal resources and time left over to devote to higher-order or more mentally healthy long-range goals, like trying to realise fully their potential. If you are not confident in your ability to meet your own basic needs, like those for safety and self-esteem, you will tend to be self-centred in pursuing these, and so have few resources to give to others. But because you cannot be generous and concerned for others, as your energies are taken up with yourself, problems will develop, for example, your ability to foster good relationships will be impaired, which will lead to relative social isolation or a lack of social support, which, as mentioned, is a useful buffer when dealing with stress.

I do not agree with the psychologists from the 1950s and 1960s who saw these higher-order goals or 'self-actualising' as the key to positive mental health. Instead I believe that if you are pursuing goals beyond those of just fulfilling your basic needs, these longer-term aspirations are simply a marker of the fact that you must be meeting your basic needs easily, and this is the real sign of positive mental health. But those goals which are not basic need goals are also useful, because they usually mean you are focusing on problems outside of your immediate needs, and so you are not so self-preoccupied – a sign of positive mental health.

The freedom to pursue ambitions beyond basic needs also allows you to develop quite a complicated life. You might be pursuing being good at your job, as well as trying to be good at tennis and learning to play the piano. This complicated self is in fact a sign of positive mental health and I explain why further in the chapter on looking after your self.

More recently, psychoanalysts[50] have argued that 'coherence' is the key feature of a healthy internal world, based on the capacity for self-reflection. This ties in with an old idea[51] that mental health is the ability to see yourself realistically (to 'objectively self-inspect') and so control the wishes and fears which colour your view of yourself. The mature person is able to see themselves as they are seen by others. This ability is crucial in enabling us to change the way we are perceived so as to get on better with others.

Another view of mental health is that of Victor Frankl, a psychiatrist who survived Nazi concentration camps. He saw mental health as deriving from spiritual values or the ultimate meaning pursued in life. To this end he constructed a scale termed the 'Purpose In Life' (PIL)[52] scale which he claimed differentiates the purposeful from the purposeless, the latter being assumed either to suffer from poor mental health already, or to be vulnerable to it in the near future.

Interestingly, a low association between the 'PIL' and educational level implies, on the one hand, that purposeful, meaningful lives are not limited to those with educational opportunity and, on the other, that education alone by no means assures the attainment of meaning in life.

Frankl's PIL scale and views of mental health remained largely idiosyncratic to him and were not taken up by mainstream psychology or psychiatry. However, I do believe Frankl was getting at something important which is relevant to any view of positive mental health. In my clinic, one of the issues which separates those who seem to be more mentally healthy – who recover quickly from psychological problems – is whether they have something they desperately want to do, which the mental illness prevents them from doing.

To take one example, I have seen people who develop a motorway phobia, which often follows on from a panic or an accident while driving. The only truly effective treatment of any such anxiety disorder is to face your fear and expose yourself to it.

Given this principle, if you have a motorway phobia, you need to get back to driving, perhaps first around the block, then gradually exposing yourself to B roads, A roads and then, finally, to motorways. What seems to determine who gets better and who doesn't is whether they have a strong reason to get back on to motorways. Those whose jobs depend on motorway driving inevitably get better faster than those who have no powerful reason for driving on them.

Similarly, agoraphobics who want to recover because they have to leave their homes to earn a living do much better in treatment than those who do not have any burning desire to leave the house, but just 'want to feel better'. Often, recovery from, or treatment of, a psychological problem, in particular a phobia, involves having to do something you do not want to do, and which might make you feel worse in the short term. The fact that treatment makes you feel worse to begin with reduces your incentive to get better. At the other extreme are those whose problem actually helps them achieve a major life goal – like not working – and these people almost never recover.

My belief is that you are much more vulnerable to future mental illness if you have no goals which you are desperate to achieve, and which psychological problems might hinder. I believe this is a form of Frankl's 'purpose in life' concept. Those who have little or no purpose in life are most vulnerable to future illness, and the more reasons you have for not getting ill, the less likely you are to. By 'goals' I do not mean that you simply want to feel well – we would all like to stay feeling well – but goals like performing a certain activity. Perhaps you really enjoy playing golf, or you are highly motivated to rise up the ladder in your career? The more different reasons you have for needing to stay well, the better for your mental health.

Another key aspect of having many purposes, or a deep purpose, in life is that this means there are things for which you are prepared to endure personal sacrifice. Learning to tolerate and endure negative experience for ends you consider worthwhile is also a vital part of positive mental health.

This view may be at odds with the psychoanalytic view, which, as mentioned earlier, conceives mental health as freedom from psychological conflict, anxiety and guilt. This view, I believe, neglects the positive aspects of negative emotions like anxiety, for it is often anxiety which forces us to improve and change. In other words, there can be no motivation (a positive thing) without some anxiety. Indeed, personal positive change occurs only when our problematic behaviour gets into conflict with a really important goal. So we may begin to learn to control our temper, not when our family complains about it, but only when we realise our tantrums are putting our pay-rise at work in jeopardy.

Previously psychologists believed there were only a few basic drives, like the drive for sex, food or sleep, and you were biologically driven to appease these needs, so until you did so you were filled with tension. If mental health is simply tension reduction then sanity begins to look like the sort of torpor you might feel after a massive meal, lots of sleep or plenty of sex. This view has been shaken by research on curiosity and puzzle-solving which found that well-fed, contented animals would work at puzzles for long hours without any extrinsic reward, and would even expend considerable energy just to have a look at a different environment, thus proving that they were highly motivated.[53, 54] This reinforces the point that once our more basic needs are met we can usually afford to be more experimental and exploratory in life and experience personal growth as a result.

Reflecting on the implications of such research, psychologists have postulated this means we may have another basic need beyond those for sex, food and sleep, a need for what they term 'competence', a sense that we can deal effectively with the environment and are in control. Although this concept is intuitively appealing, control in some contexts would be inappropriate and would stifle spontaneity. The need to stay in control could easily lead to people avoiding new situations, which carry with them the risk of being out of control.[55] The problem of control is discussed in the chapter on coping. But the vital point here is that putting yourself in new situations as a way of learning to be adaptable, and so improve your mental health, will enhance your basic need to feel competence, but only if you do this only in an incremental way. We gradually acquire competence through step-by-step learning in a new situation. Trying to learn too much too fast will take away our feeling of competence and not be helpful.

But a common problem with all these views of mental health is that they ignore the fact that responses do not occur in a vacuum. Evaluation of an emotion or behaviour depends largely on its context, so suggesting that more or less of something leads to mental health, while ignoring its context, is clearly far too simplistic. Our evaluation of our sanity must hinge on our assessment of the requirements of our environment.

Taking part in a rowdy drinking session, which may be healthy behaviour in terms of promoting integration into our workplace, would be inappropriate at the in-laws. Similarly, spontaneity and curiosity might be appropriate at a tutorial but not at a funeral. This, again, goes back to the concept of adaptability, which appears to underlie mental health and will rear its head on numerous occasions throughout this book.

One of the fascinating implications of this view of positive mental health is that it means different people, in contrasting situations, with alternative aims in life, could all behave in different ways and yet be equally mentally healthy, because they are adapting to the situation they find themselves in.

Appropriateness is also to some extent dependent on the goals you set yourself in life. If one of your goals is not to conform, then spontaneity and curiosity at a funeral might not be so inappropriate.

But is having one overriding goal the secret, or is it better to have a multiplicity of goals? Some psychologists have argued[56] that the healthy personality has a unifying philosophy of life, even though it may not be articulated in words, or entirely complete, and that it need not necessarily be religious in type.

I discuss the important and surprising implications of religious belief on mental health as well as alternatives for the non-religious in the final chapter 'Is Prevention Possible?'. Briefly, what psychologists are suggesting here is that a unifying philosophy of life, like religion, provides you with a clear purpose and guidance as to your goal, no matter how unexpected the situation you find yourself in.

So, for example, if you find yourself in an upturned boat, alone in the middle of the Southern Ocean not knowing whether rescue is on the way, a strong desire to survive because of your attachment to your family and a belief you need to look after them or that they will be devastated by your demise should probably help you hang on. However, the problem with this kind of single goal is that if you make it back to dry land only to find a little while later that your spouse is leaving you for another, your whole purpose in life might then collapse, producing poor mental health.[57]

The advantage of religion is that it seems to provide some kind of meaning or purpose to whatever terrible thing happens to disrupt your goals, and so faith is helpful in offering some kind of guidance as to what to do no matter what trouble you find yourself in.[58]

This unifying theme of a healthy personality might simply be a way of saying that the mentally healthy have a set of goals, including some overriding aspirations, such as 'to leave the world a better place than you found it'. The specific nature of the goals might not be so important as having goals which are compatible. A set of incompatible goals would be to devote yourself entirely to the relentless pursuit of wealth, and still believe you could also have a healthy family life.

A wide set of goals or one over-arching goal which provides guidance whatever the situation you find yourself in will ensure you feel driven to adapt successfully. So if one of your goals is to get on with your in-laws, or an over-arching goal is to always try to get on with everyone, you will make the effort to adapt to difficult in-laws.

As I discuss in more detail in the chapter on coping, disturbing events produce different reactions in people, so that some people can handle the loss of a job but cannot cope when their spouse leaves them, while others cannot survive the first but can the latter. As I hope to show in this book, if you can acquire adaptability you will learn how to cope with a wide variety of life changes.

Each chapter in this book has tips on how to achieve this but one general principle is to expose yourself in small gradual steps to a wider variety of situations than the ones you currently experience. Don't avoid new situations and in particular try and focus on those scenarios you suspect you would be particularly bad at dealing with, and which you are probably very good at avoiding. This is undoubtedly a stressful thing to ask you to do, because we naturally evolve lives which protect us from areas in which we feel we would cope less well, and stick to the familiar rather than the unknown.

I appreciate I am suggesting you undertake something you would not normally do, and which might make you feel worse in the short run. However, I should like to emphasise that you must do this in a gradual and controlled manner. I am not suggesting, for example, that those who avoid flying because this makes them anxious, should start parachute-jumping!

What you are training yourself to do, by exposing yourself to a wider variety of life situations than you would normally let yourself encounter, is to become accustomed to adapting. People usually ask me if there is any way of becoming more adaptable without having to deal with new situations, which they know they will find uncomfortable. I am afraid there is not. The point of the exercise is to get used to the temporary mild discomfort of adapting as by doing this you enhance your ability to cope with these feelings, and thereby strengthen yourself.

If you can do this, you will find over a surprisingly short period of time you will gain confidence in your ability to adapt to new situations and so ensure that you will react more positively to a wide range of negative events you might encounter in the future. Those who will find this pathway to improved mental health most terrifying and who therefore will now be busy thinking up reasons this tactic will not work are the nervous.

ARE YOU TOO NERVOUS?
The word *fear* comes from the Old English 'faer' meaning sudden calamity or danger; *anxiety* has its etymological origin in a Greek root meaning to press tight or to strangle; and *panic* is derived from the Greek god Pan, who was said to produce

abrupt and inexplicable terror. In the fearful, panic and anxiety are never far away.

Fear is a vital emotion that leads us to avoid threat, and has obvious survival value – fear helps us drive carefully and keep a foothold when climbing a mountain. Without fear our ancestors would not have survived long enough to pass on those fear genes to us. Fear can also be enjoyable; the thrill of suspense films or roller-coasters partly derives from the experience of fear. But the problem is that nervous people, labelled neurotics by psychiatrists and psychologists, just experience too much fear – out of all proportion to the actual danger they are in. Their fear cannot be assuaged by explanation or reasoning, and is largely beyond their voluntary control. Their fear leads to avoidance of many feared situations and so restricts their lives dramatically.

You can get some idea of where you rank in terms of nervousness by looking at your relatives – there is some genetic component to fearfulness. Anxiety disorder among close relatives of the overly fearful is 15 to 18 per cent, two to three times as much as in the general population.

The problem with fear is that we need an optimal amount of it for good performance: too little and we are careless, too much and we react clumsily – 'choke' in the parlance of the tennis player. To find out if you have too much or too little fear, complete the quiz below.

NERVOUS SCALE

Each statement is followed by two possible responses: agree or disagree. Read each statement carefully and decide which response best describes how you feel. Then put a tick over the corresponding response. Please respond to every statement. If you are not completely sure which response is more accurate, put the response which you feel is most appropriate. Do not read the scoring explanation before filling out the questionnaire. Do not spend too long on each statement. It is important that you answer each question as honestly as possible.

		AGREE	DISAGREE
1	I avoid talking to people in authority	A	B
2	Criticism of myself is easily forgotten	B	A
3	I dislike large open spaces	A	B
4	I enjoy crowded parties	B	A
5	I detest being watched or stared at	A	B
6	I sometimes like travelling alone	B	A
7	The sight of blood makes me feel very faint	A	B
8	I enjoy being the centre of attention of a large group	B	A
9	I am not relaxed if alone far from home	A	B
10	I have a good dentist	B	A

Add up your score from summing the numbers of As and Bs in each box you have ticked. Your score and the interpretation given below should be treated with caution – this short test is by no means definitive, but may offer a guide to where you stand compared to others around you.

SCORE

8 or more As. You are scoring high on fear which means that you are likely to have become paralysed with anxiety on several occasions, including perhaps even fainting, or being so afraid that you might faint or do something similarly socially embarrassing, so you avoid certain situations. The problem is the more you avoid, the more you are preserving your fear of the avoided situation or object. You need to expose yourself gradually to things which frighten you if you are going to conquer your fear.

Between 5 and 7 As. You are possibly not quite as nervous as higher scorers but when you feel your heart beating loudly, or perspire heavily, or have difficulty breathing or swallowing, these symptoms may have made you worried about your health, when in fact these are the physical signs of your excessive anxiety. You have a tendency to fear the worst whenever things are not going your way and this compounds your anxiety. Although a calamitous real-life experience, where things went badly wrong may be at the back of your mind, reminding you that the worst can actually happen, your evaluation of the likelihood of danger is usually overly pessimistic.

Between 3 and 5 As. While your anxiety levels are not as high as those who are more nervous, you do not tolerate so well many situations that others enjoy, like horror films or dangerous sports. Very subtly you may be narrowing your horizons by some of your avoidances and hence may be missing out on foreign travel or situations where you would meet many new people. You could consider following the lead of your more reckless friends more often than you do now.

Between 0 and 2 As. You are scoring low in fear which means you are less anxious than higher scorers and probably even enjoy fear. You may like risk-taking activities such as mountaineering or sky-diving. The danger for you is that, because your fearlessness leads you to underestimate the danger you face, you could become careless in situations which would make most people behave very cautiously. Beware your recklessness will land you in trouble! If you can keep this problem at bay you should consider applying to become a bomb-disposal expert!

If you are feeling a bit nervous about this suggested path to improving mental health, remember that all the skills you acquired and all the most profound growth experiences in your life probably occurred only after you had placed yourself in situations you found – at the very least – mildly uncomfortable to begin with, but which with practice you got used to and even began to enjoy. These might range from learning to drive (do you remember how badly you felt the first time behind the wheel?) to going on your first date (all those pre-date nerves).

During childhood your attempts to avoid discomfort (like having to go to school for the first time, or do homework, or a whole set of other activities you would rather not have done because they felt unpleasant at first) were unsuccessful because your parents or other adults forced you to do these things against your will. Having been forced, you learned to cope, adapt and even possibly enjoy endeavours you would have avoided if left to your own devices. The problem is that as adults we often have no one other than ourselves to push us into such scenarios.

However, if you do force yourself into areas you previously avoided, an interesting change occurs in your relationship with yourself: you gain a lot more respect for yourself.

This exposure approach works and I will expand on this in the chapter on moods.

In the next chapter I look at the long-term as well as the short-term effects of therapy or counselling, and highlight some intriguing facts about the whole industry. Seeing a counsellor or therapist is the main avenue most people take in trying to improve their mental health. That surely seems a lot easier than some of the tactics I have suggested so far – or does it?

ANYONE WHO GOES TO SEE A THERAPIST NEEDS HIS HEAD EXAMINED

Therapy

'To know the road ahead, ask those who are coming back.'

Chinese proverb

Counselling has been described as the growth industry of the 1990s.[1,2] There has been such an expansion of counselling services in British general practice that, currently, one third of practices in England and Wales have a counsellor *with no other task* within the practice.[3] The British Association of Counselling (BAC) has around 13,000[4] members (compared to only 600 in 1977). One estimate is that there are at present 30,000 people earning their living from counselling, while a further 270,000 in the voluntary sector also deliver counselling services. Research conducted on behalf of the Department of Employment suggests that over 2.5 million people use counselling as a major component of their jobs – including nurses, social workers, careers guidance workers and GPs.

Internationally, counselling is big business too. According to the first ever national survey of counselling, recently published in Rome, there were nearly 32,000 psychotherapists with a diploma of some sort working in Italy, or 55 per 100,000 people.[5] Italians, out of their own pockets, spend a billion pounds per annum on psychotherapy – not that much less than the amount spent on sport and entertainments.[6]

For many people, being chic now means being in treatment. Isobel Palmer for the BAC says that, while their own helpline attracts several thousand calls annually, others receive over 60,000 calls a year. And the media bombard us daily with advice to go for counselling or therapy.

Before scaling these dizzying heights, counselling developed in Britain very gradually, starting with the foundation of the London Psychoanalytical Society on 30 October 1913. However, the word counselling was used as early as 1386 in Chaucer's *Wife of Bath's Tale*.

Things moved slowly because of the dominance of the medical profession, which was suspicious of psychotherapists because they were not medically qualified. Even up to the 1950s, the Institute of Psycho-Analysis and the Society of Analytic Psychology remained the only training bodies and they were both closely guarded, esoteric and secretive organisations.

There then followed an explosion in therapy during the 1960s, fostered by the burgeoning experimentation with lifestyles, and today there are over 30 large rival schools and institutes of psychotherapy in Britain, including the British Association of Psychotherapists, the British Psycho-Analytic Society and the Institute of Group Analysis, and numerous smaller groups.

So what exactly is the difference between counselling and psychiatry and psychology.

A commonly accepted definition of counselling is that it 'aims to promote healthy functioning as well as having a problem-solving focus'.[7] In the words of the British Association of Counselling:[8] '...the task of counselling is to give the client an opportunity to explore, discover and clarify ways of living more resourcefully and towards greater well being...'

Psychotherapy, which could be viewed as a slightly more long-term form of counselling, is described in terms of a conversation which involves listening to and talking with those in trouble with the aim of helping them understand and resolve their predicament.[9] Another definition is 'guided introspection'.[10]

The above definitions make 'counselling' sound safer and 'therapy' more daring – and the choice of these words may be largely a marketing exercise.[11] One social work dictionary wryly comments, 'Counselling is hard to define but there is a great deal of it about'.[12] It is perhaps the very vagueness of technique and purpose which separates counselling or therapy from the academic disciplines of psychology and psychiatry, which are based on an attempt formally and scientifically to study human behaviour. Only a small number of people are considered to have the symptoms which warrant psychological or psychiatric help. Patient selection is an important part of this treatment process.

Psychologists, for example, use treatments where progress to a clearly defined aim can be agreed with the client. For example, a goal for an agoraphobic might be to go outside. Psychiatrists use treatments which have been designed for mental illnesses where the presence of certain symptoms has established a diagnosis. This may be, for instance, the prescription of an antidepressant to someone so depressed they cannot sleep and are losing weight. In both cases, a definite and recent change has occurred in a client, and treatment is aimed at reversing that change.

One common denominator of all counselling is the confidentiality which underpins this talking treatment. This may inadvertently add to the confusion over precisely what it is, as the secrecy inevitably encourages speculation and misinformation. The safest definition might be that counselling is a 'talking treatment', comprising advice, insight, and the offering of a 'therapeutic' relationship. This definition suggests that counselling by a 'professional' may not be so different from counselling by someone who is not officially qualified.

All forms of counselling attempt to offer emotional support. This has been described as a second attempt at parenting,[13] while some even suggest that all therapies are really forms of mothering.[14]

Several of my patients see counsellors or therapists (often in the private or voluntary sector) as well as seeing me. While I don't mind my patients seeing other professionals – this can even relieve pressure on the under-funded British Health Service – I have seen many examples where counselling or therapy does anything but promote mental health. Often people go into counselling or take therapy to help with a particular problem – let's say a problematic spouse or low mood. A few months later they feel better and stop the therapy. However, after a short while the problem returns and back they go into therapy, so establishing a pattern which will often last for decades. No amount of therapy seems to be enough.

A large amount of time and money can be invested in therapy but no one seems to question whether or not any real long-term benefit is occurring. Nor do they question the fostering of a dependency on therapy, whereby over time these clients seem less able to handle their problems by themselves without help. Once in therapy, it seems very difficult to get out.

This may seem an odd position for a psychiatrist to take and when people hear of my criticisms, they query, 'but isn't counselling what you do yourself?' It is true that a large part of my work involves talking to patients. One great advantage of working in the NHS is that I am not dependent for my income on luring patients into long-term therapy, so I can tell people more dispassionately whether they have problems they can resolve themselves, or whether they have mental health difficulties which are so severe as to require professional help. So there is a sense in which as a psychiatrist I do some counselling. However, I carefully select the small number of clients for whom this is appropriate, and I also use counselling as a means to an end – resolving symptoms or promoting mental health. The big problem with the current counselling model is that it seems to suggest that just getting counselling in itself is a mentally healthy activity, whereas in fact counselling is merely a possible means of promoting mental health.

To take one example, I have several patients suffering from bulimia, where they vomit several times a day after meals in an attempt to avoid gaining weight. Many of these clients have been in weekly therapy for years, discussing with the private therapist how their early childhood sexual abuse is connected with their bulimia.

But such discussions often do not help these clients to stop throwing up, or even reduce the frequency of such potentially life-threatening behaviour (if you throw up enough you will lose vital minerals in your vomit which your heart needs to beat regularly). This does not seem to concern either the therapists or their clients, who persist in thinking that mental health is being promoted, despite the fact that no change often occurs in the client during year after year of 'treatment'.

Anyone who questions the efficacy of such treatment is viewed as needing psychological help themselves! The notion that counselling must be good for you is deeply embedded in our culture.

One of the dangerous things happening here, and this is common to much therapy, is that the therapist persists with an agenda related to his own view of what causes psychological problems, even where it bears little relation to the client's 'real-world' needs. Therapists decide in some cases, for example, that early sexual abuse is the cause of bulimia, and persist in getting patients to understand why being sexually abused makes them feel bad. The patient's need is to stop throwing up – and quickly – but the therapist argues that this can only happen once the patient understands why it is happening.

I believe that persisting with such misguided assumptions is extremely damaging. Many people change their behaviour without understanding why they behaved that way in the first place. In fact, the treatment which has the best scientific evidence of its effectiveness is a behavioural approach, where the therapist is not at all interested in why a behaviour started, and doesn't even need to know this to bring about a change in the client. Why we do what we do is explained in different ways by Freudians, Jungians, Adlerians, Laingians and so on. The plethora of different schools of psychology, psychiatry and psychotherapy multiply because they all come up with a different explanation for the causes of our behaviour.

It may be rather shocking to hear it put so bluntly, but no one really knows why we do what we do. There are loads of theories but very few definitively established.

This means that spending much therapeutic time endeavouring to determine the reasons behind a behaviour is always going to be highly speculative and there is little scientific evidence that this helps the process of change in any way. And let us not forget that what clients want from treatment is change. But the worthwhile agenda of change usually gets set aside in counselling and talking therapies and is replaced by an agenda of exploring causes, so change gets neglected, which explains why it is only rarely achieved.

By telling patients they can change only after understanding their past therapists are often hampering change, because why people do what they do remains one of the hardest questions of all.

I remember when I attended group therapy as a client as part of my psychiatric training at a group analytic practice in London, meeting several group members who had been there for years. I asked them what their goal was from being in group therapy, only to receive exceedingly blank looks. The concept of a goal seemed not to have occurred to them – therapy seemed to be an end in itself! This, perhaps, explains why so much therapy can go on for so long and achieve so little.

The inertia of such therapy – where therapist and client believe tremendous progress is being achieved in gaining 'insight' and 'understanding of self', yet no change is observable to anyone else – troubles me greatly. I believe change is the essence of positive mental health, and am concerned that so much therapy seems, if anything, suspicious of change – declaring, 'change is difficult' – or that people may need 'containing' rather than changing.

One contributing factor is that the differences in counselling practice are probably wider that in any other profession.[15] The different backgrounds of counsellors, whether from medicine, psychology, social work, theology, nursing or education, mean that when someone says they are 'getting therapy' or 'seeing a counsellor', we still do not know what is really going on between the two parties.

So I believe therapists are failing to address a client's real needs. And seeing a therapist often removes the client's impetus to change. If clients believe they are doing all they can to promote their mental health simply by seeing a therapist, of course this erodes their motivation to change themselves. If, by turning up to the sessions they are doing all they can for positive mental health, why do any more?

One of the key themes of this chapter, therefore, is that therapy and counselling and all the other related treatments should be repositioned as only part of a means to an end, the end being positive mental health. Counselling in itself does not constitute positive mental health and, as I hope to demonstrate further in this chapter, we should be constantly questioning whether it is even moving people towards improved sanity, for often it is not. This leads to the conclusion that the growth in the consumption of counselling does not signify that more people are taking care of their mental health (though it does, perhaps, show that they are *concerned* about improving their mental health). Why, then, does the expansion of counselling continue?

One theory – given that many of the problems which lead us to seek therapy seem to stem from interpersonal crisis – is that, with greater geographical and social mobility and the breakdown of racial and class stereotypes, we are exposed to more relationships than ever before. In addition we have fewer rules and less guidance regarding our relationships, which we make and break all the time. This produces stress. Problems with relationships did not occur to this degree when people were born, lived and died in the same small community, when roles were defined and they had years in which to get to know and understand those around them.

Certainly, we seem to have problematic relationships with others. We crave intimacy and yet we need space. This may explain why so many people find the idea of talking to a professional appealing – at last we can say what we really feel about our relationships, which are not strong enough themselves to sustain plain talking.

Despite the predominance of counsellors and therapists and other professionals involved in mental health, there is still a taboo about seeking therapeutic help for mental health problems, so most people avoid seeing a professional. Whenever I meet people socially, as soon as they find out I am a psychiatrist, many lie in wait for me to move out of earshot of the party, then confide some personal mental health problem for which they are too scared to seek proper help.

So how do most people who do not go for professional help try to sort out their personal troubles? The most common techniques are distraction (to try to cheer themselves up), avoidance (in the hope it will go away or get better; or it's just too painful to confront), or suffering in silence.[16]

A number of counsellors and therapists encourage those who seek to improve their mental health to come to them, rather than to others – psychiatrists, etc – who may be better able to help them.

It is only because so many people with mental health problems are suffering in silence that senior members of the psychology and psychiatry professions have refrained from voicing their concerns about the lack of regulation within counselling and therapy. They feel that any form of counselling is better than suffering in silence. Given my belief in the negative effect of counselling, I differ from my colleagues on this point. In many instances I believe therapy could be damaging.

The problem of the lack of regulation within the counselling and therapy industries is one which is becoming increasingly acute as the industry grows. It is now the norm for counselling and therapy to be conducted by many without formal qualifications in psychology or psychiatry. One survey of 586 counsellors working in British general practices found that only 95 had formal training in theories of the mind, in the form of degrees in psychology – the largest untrained group being almost 200 community psychiatric nurses.[17]

There is also no umbrella organisation to register and regulate the industry, and dissension between these cliques over what comprises suitable training means we continue to lack a proper national register of counselling. This produces the alarming situation where literally anyone is able to set up practice as a counsellor without possessing any credentials at all.

In addition, the current qualifications in counselling and psychotherapy are insufficient to cover all sources of emotional distress. It is easy to forget that psychiatrists are doctors and one reason why this lack of psychiatric qualification in counsellors is disturbing is that physical problems can manifest themselves as psychological disturbance, and a counsellor is unqualified to diagnose a physical medical problem. Sometimes medical illnesses can also produce psychological symptoms. I have sometimes had referred to me patients suffering from problems such as brain tumours, which have gone undiagnosed for many months by private therapists. Even Freud, who agreed that clients did not need to see a doctor to receive good therapy, did concede that only physicians are able to screen for physical disorders.

However, getting professional advice is not always straightforward. According to the Royal College of Psychiatrists, there are only around 6,500 medical doctors specialising in psychiatry in Britain and the Republic of Ireland, while non-medical graduates, typically with a three-year psychology university degree, who then specialise in clinical psychology, number only 3,000. The small number of properly qualified professionals in the NHS means long waiting lists and, inevitably, NHS therapists tend to concentrate on the very ill – those who hear voices or are suicidal, relinquishing millions of non-psychotics to private practice.

Freud, although medically qualified himself and a practising neurologist, did not advocate medical qualifications for psychotherapists. When one of Freud's colleagues was reprimanded by the Austrian authorities for practising as a psychoanalyst as he was not medically qualified, Freud pointed out that since analysts used no medicines but only talked and exchanged information, they could not really be forbidden by any authority to do this.[18] This certainly emphasises an important point – nobody has the right to dictate where personal salvation might be sought – and people have the right to seek help from wherever they choose.

Nevertheless, the better-informed mental health consumers are, the higher the quality of service they are likely to receive and the less room there will be for abuse and exploitation. There is an important need to distinguish between receiving therapy and getting better. Though some therapy can be effective, if you are using a therapy but not getting better the treatment must come into question.

At present, consumers have no way of appraising their counsellor or therapist and, while psychiatrist and psychologists assess and select their patients, counsellors often do not, accepting all-comers. Potential therapy clients are therefore left to make uninformed choices about whether they really need to seek a therapist; what kind they should see, how to choose a good one, and how to tell if the treatment is not working and it is time to leave. I believe this lack of information is potentially disastrous.

In the early 1990s I hosted part of a BBC Radio 4 phone-in programme in the 'Against the Grain' series, in which the host questioned some deeply held beliefs that are widespread in society. In my case, as you may have guessed, I was questioned about whether counselling was as good a thing as everyone thought. It has to be said that the producer probably overemphasised the point I was making by choosing as a title for the programme – 'Counselling Screws You Up'. Or maybe, being a good producer, she could read my mind...

During the show numerous people rang up saying they had been in distress, had sought counselling and now felt better, proving, they thought, that counselling must have helped them. In fact, research has demonstrated repeatedly that if you divide those who might seek counselling into two groups and give one counselling and another nothing at all, the difference between the two groups a few months later is often hard to distinguish.[19] This suggests either that getting better is part of the natural progression of the distress and may have nothing to do with counselling, or that it can be attributed to other therapeutic things which happen to people and not to the counselling.

What was particularly fascinating about my callers was how resistant they were to the suggestion that they could have got better without professional help. They almost seemed to worship therapy. I wondered how they might cope in the future with personal distress, so convinced were they now of their inability to cope without professional help.

The debate over clinical trials of counselling has been long and acrimonious, starting when the eminent psychologist Hans Eysenck charged that counselling produced no greater changes in emotionally incapacitated individuals than naturally occurring life experiences would.[20] Despite 40 years of clinical research since, the effectiveness of counselling remains controversial, with three recent reviews failing to find it superior to placebo treatment.[21]

Not only do academic psychologists dispute whether counselling is of any more benefit to many clients than the natural healing of the passage of time, they also dispute whether any specific therapy offers advantages over any other. This is an important issue, given the plethora of new therapies which offer a cure on the condition that you follow their tenets and no others.

What distinguishes all forms of analytic or Freudian therapy and counselling from others is the belief that obvious personal problems are invariably underpinned by hidden, powerful forces which require expert identification, interpretation and resolution. Simply dealing with the symptoms, Freudian-type therapists argue, will not radically help the client to alter the balance of conscious management and unconscious conflict in his or her life.

This approach may seem justified when trying to understand why people persist in self-defeating behaviour. But other therapies, based on philosophies diametrically opposed to these, can also seem reasonable. In person-centred counselling, for example, therapists are trained to believe that only a person knows herself and what is really right for her. In other words, this therapy is definitely not about using interpretation to tell a patient what is really going on.

If person-centred therapy was more effective than analysis, or vice versa, we might have a basis for determining which therapy came closer to a real appreciation of human problems. But despite their respective claims, there is no evidence that any one therapy is more effective than the other. The British Psychology Society,[22] includes the following comment in its statement on the statutory registration of psychotherapists, published in 1980: 'Existing psychotherapeutic techniques are insufficiently grounded in formal evaluative research... until this is done, the claims of the different psychotherapeutic methods rest on the clinical experience of practitioners rather than on public evidence capable of withstanding critical scrutiny.' So the claims on which they base their argument for superior efficacy must be questioned.

One area of debate between rival schools, for example, is how many times a week a client should be seen. Some schools still insist on the old Freudian 50-minute sessions five days a week. If that sounds like excessive navel-gazing, bear in mind many therapies are described as 'open-ended' which means there is no clear end foreseen at all. Some clients stay in therapy for many years – a few for decades – and, for a handful, therapy ends only when the therapist dies. In other schools of therapy treatment might be once a week for only eight sessions.

Just as therapists work in hundreds of different ways, people seek therapy for any number of reasons. Some will be suffering from bereavement, marital disharmony, or excessive stress at work. Many are lonely. Some seek therapy because their behaviour and feelings are inexplicable to themselves. And some have nothing they can pinpoint as wrong; they just don't feel anything is particularly right. These people are really seeking some meaning to life so, in a sense, therapists have replaced the role of priests today.

The chance to talk things over in confidence with an understanding and objective outsider is the only way many people claim they can resolve personal problems. Friends don't possess the objectivity, patience, tolerance and therapeutic skills needed on a regular basis. In therapy, patients are encouraged to examine closely their past and even their childhood and relationships with parents, because persistent ways of seeing the world and relating to others develop out of these early experiences. Clients believe that the large amount of time spent carefully listening to them and the development of a trusting relationship enables them to gain insight slowly into underlying mental processes, which had previously eluded understanding. So convinced of its effectiveness are they that they are sometimes prepared to take out loans the size of the average mortgage to pay for therapy.

But does this make psychotherapy simply the ultimate purchase for those who have everything? Is being in therapy a perfect solution to the new demands of the 'caring, sharing' nineties, the best way for the 1980s 'me' generation to obtain instant sensitivity, while quietly taking self-obsession to new heights? After the designer house, the designer car and the designer clothes, why not the designer personality?

One psychoanalyst reports that he was once told by a client at the end of several years of therapy that he had not heard anything which he could not have heard from his mates at the local pub[23]. And another[24] claims that his own part-time psychoanalytic training took eight years, but could probably have been condensed into just a few hours of pertinent reading. He suggests that the real reason for a protracted training period is to indoctrinate therapists and produce professionals who will have a great stake in remaining loyal.

Yet despite the prevalence of counselling there is absolutely no evidence that counselling has anything which clients with mental health problems cannot acquire by other means, whether through self-help books, self-help groups or simply through experience. Certainly, there is crucial information which those interested in preserving their mental health need to acquire, but it can be obtained in other ways than by seeing a counsellor. Although the advantage of seeing a counsellor might be that they can personalise the advice to your particular situation, that depends on finding a good counsellor who doesn't simply end up giving the same advice to everyone.

There are plenty of examples of therapy occurring outside the consulting room. Some people argue that you do not need to see a therapist to get therapy. The power of the confessional in the Catholic religion, for example, has been likened to that of psychoanalysis: both persuade people that they have deep, hidden, inner secrets to express and that the sanctioned listeners have the power to absolve. One famous anecdote tells of a therapist who undertook research with a group of women experiencing premenstrual problems. They may have derived most benefit, as they later claimed, not from the advice the therapist gave them, but from chatting to each other in the waiting room while waiting to see him![25]

Another woman, having found formal counselling of little use, took a friend out for dinner at regular intervals, paying for the meal herself and in return asking her friend to listen to and advise on her problems. She seems to have benefited more from this arrangement than from seeing the professional counsellor, which might suggest that friendship can be controlled in such a way as to perform the same roles as a professional counsellor.[26]

In one description of psychotherapy, an academic pointed out that, 'although the definition of psychotherapy customarily refers to what transpires within the consulting room, a broader view of psychotherapy would include the fact that life in itself may be, and is often, psychotherapeutic... many fortunate people trained in courage and social interest, do it for themselves without therapeutic assistance'.[27]

I mentioned earlier that, unlike in psychiatry, where there is a process of client selection, in counselling clients need only to be 'in distress' and to accept the structure of the counselling sessions in order to be taken on. This provides counsellors with a very wide catchment area, as even the notion of a client being in distress has an elastic definition. On page iii of the British Association for Counselling's *Directory of Counselling*, those who might need counselling are described as 'suffering the death of a loved one, or not getting on with their partner, they may have lost a job or be worrying about coping with a new one, they may be finding the strain of work or exams too much, they may be at the end of their tether, anxious about the kids, their parents, or themselves, or simply down in the dumps.'

Firstly, all these experiences are part of everyday life and, as I discuss in more detail in chapter 8 ('Crisis, What Crisis?'), relying on counselling to help you cope in the short term could reduce your confidence in your own ability to do so in the long term.

Secondly, even the textbooks on counselling and counsellors do not identify when unpleasant mental states end and definable psychological problems or medical illnesses begin,[28] i.e. where counselling's remit ends. Titles like *The Psychotherapy of Everyday Life*[29] reinforce this impression. This seems part of a clandestine conspiracy to extend indefinitely the boundaries of mental illness[30] so that anyone suffering from life's problems needs expert intervention, so creating the notion of a 'therapeutic state'.[31] Every problem gets reduced to one requiring a therapist.

While this may put the argument rather brutally, it raises the question of whether there are any conditions or situations when seeking counselling is inappropriate. I believe it is a great indictment of the whole counselling industry that, while different types of counselling may be specified for contrasting situations, the industry has failed to specify the occasions when counselling would be unsuitable. A treatment which is advocated as 'good for anything and bad for nothing', at the very least fails to recognise alternative approaches which may be just as useful in many situations. At worst, it appears to reduce complex problems to mere examples of 'counselling deficiency'. Everything would be solved by a good enough counsellor.

For example, counselling is frequently sought by those who are not formally medically or psychiatrically ill, but who are simply unhappy, people sometimes described as the 'worried well'.[32] But should unhappiness be treated? Attempting to do away with unpleasant mental states, regardless of their medical status, involves extending the ethics of health. If we ought to be healthy and have rights to health, professionals have obligations to restore us to health.[33] However, ought we always to be happy, and do professionals have an obligation to restore happiness on demand?

I see many clients whose unhappiness has been directly caused by their own behaviour but who nevertheless turn to therapists for help. But if we turn to therapists whenever we are unhappy and do not take personal responsibility for our unhappiness, we are only creating a vicious circle. In many situations it is appropriate to be unhappy and it would even be ethically questionable not to be so. If we have behaved in an immoral or antisocial way, such as bullying a partner or colleague, then feeling unhappy about our behaviour is the more healthy reaction. Rights to happiness are different to rights to health, yet those who seek counselling appear to be equating the rights of these two different states. Different forms of counselling might produce separate ethical problems.[34] For example, 'non-directive' counselling, where the therapist does not tell the client what to do but merely listens non-judgementally to whatever the client says, may provide a sense of guiltlessness in clients, freeing them from moral judgements about behaviour, which is actually what they most need, while 'supportive counselling' may inadvertently reinforce undesirable behaviour patterns by providing emotional support whenever problematic behaviour is indulged in, as well as rationalising rather than judging ruinous attitudes.

Another complication is that people who are genuinely unhealthy as well as those who are simply excessively worried about their health turn to therapists for help. The latter merely need to be shown that the problem is not an illness but an anxiety that they *may* have an illness. These people do not need treatment, but instead reassurance that no treatment is necessary,[35] yet counsellors seem only rarely to reassure their clients no help is required.

A paradox about people receiving counselling is that the evidence suggests that those who are offered counselling after traumatic experiences really value such help, even though no benefit to them can be measured objectively and, according to some studies, these people sometimes do worse than control groups who do not receive counselling.[36] While clients may value or choose counselling, it seems obvious that counselling should not be endorsed if controlled trials, using objective measures, demonstrate that people may even get worse as a result of it.[37, 38]

Yet therapists persist in such endorsement. The idea that counselling is implicitly 'a good thing' is now so strong in our society that its dangers are being ignored.

Most people would agree in principle that it is ethically desirable to assume some responsibility for their own physical and mental health. But at what point should we stop taking moral responsibility for our mental states and seek help? Again, this question of moral responsibility for our mental life is ignored by the counselling industry, and there are no explicit criteria setting out which problems of living we are responsible for, and when we can abrogate responsibility to a counsellor and ask for help.[39]

Critics have argued that many of those who seek counselling have unrealistic expectations of what life should offer them.[40] One study, for example, found that only patients with sufficient psychological resources to become involved in interpersonal relationships, and who can 'tolerate the anxiety of insight-oriented techniques', can benefit from counselling.[41] In other words, the 'worried well' who seek counselling have to be fairly well indeed to tolerate the demands of counselling!

Another way to put this is that those who have the courage to seek therapy, the intellectual resources to find a good therapist, the emotional resources to withstand the stress of establishing a relationship with a therapist, and the financial resources to pay for it, have too many resources not to be able to solve their problems themselves. They simply lack confidence. Because of the current fashion for counselling it is counsellors themselves who have undermined our belief in our ability to solve our problems on our own.

So, who are these counsellors who are so influential in the realm of managing our mental health, as we perceive it?

The existence of a profession implies a boundary which separates it from other professions and from non-professional activities.[42] This boundary is usually drawn using notions of expertise, so that those within a profession should be expert in a sense that members outside a profession are not. While it may not be possible for the public to detect or rate this expertise, the profession's regulatory bodies ought to be able to do so.

If counselling is a service provided by members skilled in the provision of that service, a profession of counselling is well on the way to being delineated. The multiplicity of courses and qualifications available[43] support the view that this is a skill which can be distinguished from informal counselling between friends and relatives.

Up till now, attempts to distinguish between 'friendly' and 'professional' counselling have been based on notions of what constitutes basic training. These training requirements include an age limit for candidates, the observation of counselling in action, a certain amount of counselling experience, and receiving a certain amount of counselling yourself.[44]

However, clinical studies throw doubt on whether professional counsellors possess special expertise, any more than lay people using basic common sense or minimal training.[45] Research has also found no relation between the experience and training of the counsellor and the outcome of treatment; and in several studies untrained non-professionals were perceived by clients as better therapists than professionals.[46]

For example, in 1995, researchers[47] at the University of Rhode Island, USA, reviewed all previous research comparing the therapeutic skills of non- or para-professionals (like community volunteers) with those of professional therapists. Their aim was to investigate whether therapists with formal training delivered better therapy than those without.

The overwhelming conclusion was that non-professionals were just as able to produce significant behavioural changes in clients, without formal training or supervision by a senior therapist. Some of the experimenters even concluded that para-professionals achieved clinical outcomes significantly better than those of professionals!

And a recent review also concluded that there was little evidence that training improves trainees' skill levels sufficiently to guarantee that they can deliver therapy effectively.[48]

As might be expected, these studies produce heated debate as to whether their findings can be trusted. After all, you do not embark on a long, personally demanding and often expensive training unless you believe that learning about the causes of psychological problems and their various treatments will improve the quality of care you will be able to deliver. The professionals voiced several criticisms, including that they produce 'deep' change, which is difficult to measure, while para-professionals produce only easy-to-measure, superficial change; and that professionals tend to see more seriously unwell people than non-professionals. These criticisms are discussed and eliminated one by one by the authors of the aforementioned research review.

I agree with many of the criticisms of the research. For instance, I find the idea that a long training period is unnecessary belittles patients' problems, which are often deeply complex. Another interpretation of the research, with which I do agree, is that the research is not saying that training doesn't help, but that it is important to focus on the *right kind* of training. For example, the report highlighted one important flaw of professional training programmes: that they focus on a scientist-practitioner approach (using knowledge of the scientific literature and research to inform clinical practice) rather than, for example, interpersonal skills. If the professionals listened to the 'news' the report was telling them, rather than reacting defensively, they might be able to improve their training programmes by incorporating client, or service-user feedback in the assessment of trainees at the end of a course.

Another drawback the report highlighted is that there is little attempt in training programmes to assess the practical competence of therapists.

Some have argued that the reason counselling is difficult to define is that the particular counsellor is so critical to the treatment that, as with acting or singing, an evaluation of the activity is impossible without an evaluation of the person.[49] If this is true, then a crucial counselling concept such as 'developing insight' can be redefined as *you* basically agreeing with your therapist's understanding of you, which then becomes therapeutically meaningless. Research into the ways in which counselling achieves change suggests that clients simply identify with healthy aspects of the therapist's personality.[50] I believe this could be extremely dangerous for the client, given that the selection of trainee counsellors is rarely done using standardised and validated measures of mental health.[51] In fact, most discussions of psychotherapy training and supervision ignore the issue of improving the mental health screening of counsellors altogether.[52-55]

The most striking difference between counselling training and other training, such as university degrees in medicine or psychology, is the lack of a standardised assessment at the end of the course. All university selective courses use external examiners who have been trained or who practise elsewhere to evaluate the acceptability of candidates. Most degree courses also have a failure rate; often the more rigorous the training, the higher such a rate. In contrast, counselling courses do not appear regularly to use external examiners to check on the standard of their graduates and also publish no data on failure rates.

I find this lack of rigour in training all the more disturbing given counselling's emphasis on the importance of the intellectually demanding 'detective work' of the counselling mission. Counsellors tend to see observable symptoms not as the real problem but as something overlaid upon a deeper, more important issue[56] – as with the case of bulimia and sexual abuse.

Although I would agree that counsellors need to be skilled to take part in such detective work, I disagree with this model of mind, for is it not equally likely that the underlying problem is itself an overlay on something else even more deep and important. The issue is not merely what to look for, but when to stop looking. If there are levels of problems, working backwards step by step logically introduces the danger of what has been called 'infinite regress'. Infinite regress also besets explanations founded on critical moments in a person's past – why should events prior to that not be even more important? In the history of academic psychology no personal historical event has ever been found reliably to produce distress years later.[57] Although many colleagues will disagree with this statement, quoting, for example, their various clients having nightmares about previous trauma. I would argue that the wide degree of individual variations in personal reactions to negative events show there are factors other than the event at work here.

For example, I mentioned earlier the therapist who insists that early childhood sexual abuse needs to be dealt with before the specific problem of bulimia can be cured. But how do you explain, for example, all those people who were abused but who do not develop bulimia? Or all those with bulimia who were never sexually abused? As well as objecting to this model of mind on philosophical grounds, I also object to it for pragmatic reasons. After all, even if an event can be proved to cause a certain type of behaviour, what can we do about our past? To emphasise the past is implicitly to suggest that we are trapped by it. And I believe nothing could be further from the truth. Given these problems with the counselling models of behaviour and mind, it should come as no surprise that training these counselling approaches is also problematic.

Another issue with the whole counselling industry to which surprisingly little attention has been given is that of payment. Counselling has been dogged by ethical questions over business considerations since its inception, with counsellors often declaring that free therapy is devalued by patients as being worthless.[58] A recent survey found that, predictably, counsellors who felt most strongly that paying fees was essential for effective psychotherapy, were also most heavily dependent on fee-paying for their livelihood.[59, 60]

Even therapists who agree that there are ethical problems with the current business considerations advocate little change. For example, some therapists accept that therapy can be expensive and time-consuming, but merely suggest – 'one should not underestimate the capacity of a patient who has had therapy for several months to be able to form a rational assessment of whether or not it is doing any good'.[61] My own view is rather that one should be just as careful not to overestimate it.

One ethical dilemma occurs when a patient commences therapy and is then unable to pay for it.[62] The issue is made more acute in that counselling can induce dependence on the counsellor.[63]

Today's economics of health-care require a cost-benefit analysis be undertaken of any treatment, so that health services and individuals can determine whether to invest in it. Again, this does not appear to have been completed convincingly with counselling.[64] What evidence there is suggests that counselling represents a relatively poor return on resources. For example, a survey in Australia in 1993 found that the long period of counselling required by each patient meant that only 0.5 per cent of patients who needed treatment could possibly receive it with available counselling manpower.[65, 66]

LISTENINGHOST ♪♭ ♪♭ ♪♭ NOTINGHOSTS
with the LANGUAGE ..

The limitations of the training of counsellors and organisation of the profession are such that the exploitation of clients is a real possibility; and whereas in most professions this danger is limited by regulatory bodies and consumer rights organisations, counselling has virtually none of these safeguards,[67] despite its consumers being particularly vulnerable.

According to past legal decisions, clients' complaints about therapists' activities are not always believed because the very fact that they are psychotherapy patients is seen as evidence of mental instability.[68] Clients are made even more vulnerable by their fear of public humiliation due to the stigma surrounding psychiatric problems, so abused patients are reluctant to present their claims publicly.[69]

With such an imbalance of power between counsellor and client, the danger is that the unscrupulous will take advantage, and unfortunately this has been demonstrated repeatedly.[70] For example, surveys in the US have found that up to 10 per cent of therapists admit sexual impropriety with clients.[71] The real figure could be very much higher, as these statistics represent only those willing to admit such misconduct.[72] This was the major cause of successful malpractice cases against US therapists from 1976 to 1986 in terms of costs involved, representing 44.8 per cent of the total paid for all claims.[73] In fact, therapists in North America are the only professionals dropped by their insurance carrier because of the frequency of malpractice suits involving sexual molestation.[74, 75]

This is all the more shocking since, in counselling, the quality of the relationship with the client is fundamental; counselling has been described as *hingeing* on the provision of a 'safe environment' in which 'relationships between self and the world can be explored'.[76] Despite this, and the fact that this safety and intimacy is supposed to demarcate the counselling relationship from other professional relationships you could choose, the evidence suggests that you take pot luck when you contact someone calling himself a counsellor in much the same way as you do in contacting a friend. But at least we know something about our friends.

If, for example, you take the perspective of a consumer with no background information trying to find a good counsellor, perhaps starting with small ads in the back of a magazine, the search might well resemble the proverbial hunt for a needle in a haystack. The few investigations available do not portray a positive picture of the experience for clients.[77] While professional counsellors might be aware of many good fellow practitioners, their perspective remains that of insiders.

Furthermore, providing a 'safe environment' is a deeply problematic issue, not only in terms of the ability of either therapist or client to assess safety objectively, but also for this to be guaranteed without regulation and supervision by a third party. Therapist supervision by other therapists is a significant part of the counselling industry, but it is by no means universal. And even where such supervision exists, there is usually little or no attempt to obtain the client's perspective of the relationship. This, perhaps, highlights an unresolvable conflict between the need for privacy and the requirement for regulation. When clients go to medical clinics for counselling, they may be resigned to their notes being accessible to other professionals there, but the tension between regulation and privacy becomes particularly acute in single-handed, private-practice counselling.

No other relationship in modern society, not even the most intimate ones, such as marriage, rests on the notion that the quality of that relationship can be regulated purely between the two consenting parties. Marriage, for example, is governed by laws and often by recourse to third-party intervention, like mediation or solicitors, when serious problems develop. No married couple would ever seek to judge the quality of their marriage solely by reference to their relationship. They would compare it with other relationships as well as discussing it with outside parties. However, none of these informal mechanisms are usually available to clients or counsellors. Given the taboo surrounding psychological problems it is more difficult for someone in therapy to compare notes with another person in therapy.

It is interesting to note that none of the mechanisms which regulate the safety of the doctor–patient relationship and involve a third party, such as patients bringing friends or relatives to the consultation, asking for second opinions, seeing more than one doctor at a time, or using bodies like the General Medical Council, are thought to threaten the practice of medicine. Such involvement is seen as a threat to counselling because the privacy of the consultation between client and counsellor must not be violated by third parties.

This complacency about guaranteeing and regulating a safe relationship may derive from the assumption that most counsellors are ethically motivated. This assumption is rarely challenged, despite the fact that the whole question of why people want to become counsellors has largely been neglected. It has been argued that[78] the vocation of counsellor is an avenue of fulfilment for eight personality types: those with an uncertain sense of their own identity; the socially inhibited or withdrawn; the dependent; those who like others to be dependent on them; the rigidly intellectual; the sadistic; those who have difficulty expressing hostility; and the masochistic.

But even such less sound personality types who become counsellors could be countenanced provided that counselling *worked*. But as mentioned earlier, studies have not found it superior to a placebo treatment.

Crucially, from an ethical perspective, counsellors seem largely unconcerned about testing their claims or altering their behaviour in the face of opposing evidence.[79]

Inevitably, debate on this issue is heated, with the argument often revolving around the accuracy of particular research. Criticisms of clinical trials of counselling increasingly focus on how representative a trial is.[80] For example, critics argue that counselling is a deep experience that occurs between two people and that this can only be communicated very inadequately to another person.[81] The counter-argument is that other research shows that counsellors are the poorest evaluators of client change when compared to assessors such as the patients themselves and outside judges.[82] They often do not agree with non-counsellors on the amount of change the patient has manifested.[83]

To complicate matters further, there is even widespread disagreement over what constitutes a positive outcome. The measures used include social functioning, sense of personal satisfaction or well-being, and personality integration.[84] Jung[85] was similarly vague on this point, declaring '...it is commonly supposed that the therapist has an aim. But in psychotherapy it seems to me positively advisable for the doctor not to have too fixed an aim... '. I believe it is ethically questionable to supply a treatment without a clear idea of what it is meant to do, given that it may do no good at all, and involves costs to clients.

From an ethical standpoint, much less important than whether counselling is effective is whether the aim is in itself worthwhile. Healing practices throughout the world seem to have eight basic aspirations: symptom removal, attitude change, behaviour change, insight, improved interpersonal relationships, improved personal efficiency, improved social efficiency, prevention and education.[86]

Given this limited number of aspirations, a more basic question than 'Which therapies work?' is, 'Why should there be so many in Western culture in the first place?' One survey conducted in 1986[87] found that there are more than 460 psychotherapies in the West. In the light of this huge variety, the counsellor's choice of therapeutic orientation cannot be based on any commonly accepted method of validation. One possible reason for a proliferation in therapies is that most new treatments are established by a particular personality who splits off from an accepted therapeutic school or starts a new one. One[88] interpretation of this process, as a drive to 'go into business for oneself', may be cynical, but it does raise questions over the motivations of such 'new' therapies.

One standard counselling rejoinder to anti-counsellor sentiment is, 'if it can do no good, then surely it can do no harm'.[89] The evidence suggests otherwise.

Several contraindications to counselling exist including that of becoming over-dependent on the therapist and too comfortable with receiving counselling.[90] Yet no reliable method of monitoring such contraindications has been taken up.

Other known negative effects of therapy on the client include:[91] 'decompensation' or breakdown, in which the patient's sense of reality is impaired; exacerbation of depression, with suicidal or other self-destructive features and loss of hope about future prospects for recovery; lowered self-esteem, with feelings of humiliation and shame; a decrease in self-control and acting out of sexual or aggressive impulses; prolonged dependency on the therapy and therapist, with abdication of responsibility and self-direction. Clinical research has documented clients' confused and impulsive actions involving family, work; or other significant obligations and commitments.[92]

One patient of mine indicated that she had finally got over her dependence on therapists, having, over several decades, jumped from one counsellor to another. I enquired how she had achieved this. 'Well,' she said brightly, 'I have found this new person who isn't a therapist. He is a healer who I see once a week and that has finally helped.'

Like my patient, many people believe that they have broken free from dependency, whereas all that has really happened is that they have substituted one form for another.

To see if you are in danger of falling into the dependency trap, try this quiz.

ARE YOU INDEPENDENT?

One of the major causes of low mood is now thought to arise in people whose personalities are marked by strong feelings of dependency on others. Dependent people feel helpless when not in a relationship, but when they are in relationships they constantly fear being abandoned by others. These people are likely to have problems trying to leave counselling once in it. More independent people are not bothered so much by threats of loss of relationships, instead their low mood is accounted for by achievement issues – feelings of inferiority, guilt, worthlessness and by a sense that they have failed to live up to expectations and standards. Exactly why people should vary along a spectrum of dependency and independence is still not clear but some think it's something to do with childhood experiences. Perhaps dependent people as children experienced relationships with parents characterised by little certainty over closeness, while independent people had parents whose love appeared conditional on achievement. However, what is particularly important about the dependency–independent classification is that it may allow psychiatrists to predict what kind of life event is most likely to cause low mood in different people. Those characterised by marked dependency are less likely to be made depressed by losing a job, and more likely to get upset by a problem in a close relationship, whereas independent people survive remarkably well the loss of close relationships but react badly to the vaguest threat to their achievements.

DEPENDENCY SCALE

Each statement is followed by two possible responses: agree or disagree. Read each statement carefully and decide which response best describes how you feel. Then put a tick over the corresponding response. Please respond to every statement. If you are not completely sure which response is more accurate, put the response which you feel is most appropriate. Do not read the scoring explanation before filling out the questionnaire. Do not spend too long on each statement. It is important to answer each question as honestly as possible.

		AGREE	DISAGREE
1	Breaking off relationships that make me unhappy is easy	A	B
2	After fights with friends, I need to make amends quickly	B	A
3	People leaving me is not a danger I worry about	A	B
4	After an argument I feel lonely	B	A
5	Losing close friends is not like losing a part of yourself	A	B
6	Anger in those close to me, worries me, in case they leave me	B	A
7	When I get very angry with others it is usually justified	A	B
8	My problems are better solved discussing them with others	B	A
9	Other people trying to be friendly distract me from my goals	A	B

	AGREE	DISAGREE
10. I often wonder about signs of rejection of me in others	B	A

Add up your score from summing the numbers of As and Bs in each box you have ticked. Your score and the interpretation given below should be treated with caution – this short test is by no means definitive, but may offer a guide to where you stand compared to others around you.

SCORE

8 or more Bs. You are scoring very highly indeed for feelings of dependency, hence you do not seem to feel at all independent and are prone to low moods characterised by fears of abandonment and helplessness. You may often get secretly angry with others for not showing the same commitment to relationships as yourself, in fact you often go out of your way to perform extraordinary acts of generosity to those you like. You may not realise, however, that these acts simply mean you do not feel you are a very lovable person, and hence you have to compensate for this by doing wonderful things to make others like you.

Between 5 and 7 Bs. You are scoring above average for dependency on others and this explains your occasional feelings of being weak, lonely, depleted and unloved. When threatened with the loss of a relationship you sometimes can respond by clinging desperately to others, or you urgently search for a substitute, which may take the form of an addiction of some kind. You may not realise that your dependent behaviour is often not interpreted by others as a sign of closeness, more as a sign that you put yourself and your needs above theirs. You need to rely on others needing you a little more and you needing them a little less to form the basis of your relationships in the future.

Between 3 and 5 Bs. You are scoring around average to below average for dependency and this explains your ability not to be exploited in relationships by others, unlike those with higher scores. If someone begins to take advantage of you, you can walk away without as much pain as those who are more dependent. Having said that, you are vulnerable to strong feelings of dependency arising under conditions of stress, when you may find you cannot cope without clinging to those whom you may not have bothered to contact when things were going well. This see-saw approach to relationships is probably found a little irritating by those around you, so you need to decide not only how much you need others, but also how much they might need you, and so you need to be available for others as much as they are for you.

Between 0 and 2 Bs. You are scoring very highly indeed for feelings of independence from others. While this may make you less prone to low mood due to feelings of dependency, your independence is characterised by self-criticism, a sense of failure to live up to standard and concerns about approval and recognition. In other words, your independence from others also cuts you off from the emotional side of relationships. Perhaps you fear dependency on others too much, leaving you to rely on your accomplishments as the only way to engage with others. You have to ask yourself if you really just want an audience, or would you prefer genuine friendships?

The prevalence of these negative effects like dependency is not really known, but studies have suggested that 10 per cent of clients experience deterioration and even psychotic reactions.[93] Yet counsellors have given this problem little attention[94] and have been reluctant to publish research that casts colleagues in an unfavourable light.[95] This is, of course, ethically questionable given the age-old dictum for health service providers – 'above all, do no harm'. The research findings conclude that the two most important causes of negative effects are inadequate training and the effects of the counsellor's personality but, as discussed earlier, little has been done to address these issues.[96] Negative effects also affect the client's friends, relations or even acquaintances. Very little is done to monitor whether counsellors maintain certain basic standards in clinical practice.

I have come across repeated examples of people who use their psychotherapeutic experience to rationalise feelings of smugness and superiority over others, and utilise their insights to comment aggressively on other people's behaviour.[97]

For example, if you are critical of counselling, this elicits responses which simply interpret legitimate criticism as indicating emotional problems in the critic. Phrases such as 'You seem overly angry about counselling' or 'You seem frightened of dependency – maybe that's why you are suspicious of the therapeutic relationship' are typical.

For some clients, counselling becomes an end in itself, taking priority over other tasks and goals; being a good patient comes to assume precedence over that of living life to the fullest.[98] Some become so focused on the wonders of their psyche and its internal connections, that they begin to ignore their commitments to others. They constantly interpret what they think is really going on in a relationship rather than actually having one.

One of the limitations of counselling and its evaluation of itself as a profession is that it ignores the effects on the client's other relationships, and even the impact on society in general.[99]

On various phone-ins about counselling, many callers have told me of instances where their spouses followed the advice of therapists, often to the detriment of family life.[100] Families have broken up, wives have left husbands, children have left to stay with another relative, all at the advice of counsellors who did not see any other member of the family but the client before proffering such advice.

At the simplest level, counselling might affect a client in a way that alters family or work relationships but which may not constitute a positive outcome for the whole community.[101-103]

I believe counselling must recognise the duality of human existence[104] – in other words that we have both needs and obligations. Not only must we acknowledge the self-gratifying aspects of life, but also the need to belong and the mutual obligations that bind humans in society.[105-107] Yet therapists only ever listen to one side of the case – the client's side. So these wider ethical questions, regarding the occasions when clients may have to sacrifice their own interests for others in their lives, are largely ignored.

Counsellors help adjust people to the effects of many questionable state policies, thus diverting attention away from the political, social and economic causes of distress. For example, counselling treatment programmes were developed for black refugees in South African townships who suffered from policies of apartheid and police brutality.[108-111]

According to political economic theorists, widespread human misery is inescapable within societies which ordain particular power relations between people[112] and the issue then sometimes becomes whether we work to change ourselves or to change society. The danger of counselling is that it obfuscates this issue.

Political, social and economic reforms are largely responsible for improving relationships between people, not piecemeal counselling. But instead, counselling creates a conflict between mental contentedness and altruism, as mental health is achieved through introspection, and not social action.[113-115] People turn into themselves for happiness rather than finding contentment from their action or the world.

I believe that counselling encourages dissociation from society, by claiming that there is a 'real' self which is forever hidden from society – the 'mental iceberg' Freud describes.[116] This leaves people free not to feel a part of, or responsible towards society. In addition, if we only think and act in certain ways because of our background and upbringing, we cannot be blamed for our current attitudes and actions. It is not our fault we are the way we are. But if we are blameless, we are also impotent.

The paradoxical concept that to gain self-knowledge we must ask others about ourselves has never been more exploited by professionals, alternative therapists and mystics than it is today. But it leaves people feeling alienated from themselves.

Psychologists and psychiatrists, on the other hand, work with a model that is close to that of counselling but has a crucial difference. They believe that you need to seek professional help for your psychological disorder or illness, but it is not always necessary to spend years in treatment to comprehend yourself.[117] This explains why psychiatrists and psychologists are likely to recommend the same treatments for the same mental health problems, regardless of who you are. So, for example, regardless of how you developed your fear of spiders and what this may tell us about your unconscious, the treatment will always be the same – to expose yourself to the thing you fear and to stop avoiding it.

Psychologists and psychiatrists rarely require clients to consider their whole self, or their past, as a fundamental part of treatment. This is in contrast to most non-academically trained counsellors who focus on links between the past and present and in so doing implicitly suggest that the change required is going to be difficult to achieve, as the maladaptive behaviour is such a fundamental part of the person.

Existentialists argue that it is characteristic of our society that we seek to provide a professional response to personal and intimate issues – the professionalisation of personal problems.[118, 119]

In my view, counselling attempts to provide consolation for the messy, awkward, personal nature of distress by forcing complex experience into a handful of psycho-social generalities.[120] This prevents people experiencing their own difficult, unmanageable emotions, and the absurd, often sheer pointlessness of life is replaced by textbook generalisations which attempt to impose meaning and pattern on the meaningless and chaotic.[121]

All attempts to manipulate or influence behaviour – which is what therapists do – raise ethical questions: how ought people to behave, how ought they to feel, what ought they to want? These questions involve value judgements and, as such, enter the remit of ethics. Perhaps counsellors are treating a group of people who could be better served by priests and philosophers, not therapists.[122] In an attempt to avoid being too interventionist, the counselling model tries to avoid prescriptive practice, yet the decision over who needs counselling, when, and from whom it can be withheld, inevitably involves implicit judgements of what is acceptable or desirable behaviour and emotions.

Therapists might argue that they are not moral agents, but research has demonstrated that, inevitably, they communicate their personal value system to patients.[123] Studies have also found that patients who do change in counselling tend to revise their moral values in the direction of their therapist's.[124] In other words, we tend to take our therapist's view of right and wrong. Yet, while our therapists may be skilled in many ways, can they really determine right from wrong?

Are they in a position to advise a client directly or indirectly whether or not to leave an unhappy marriage, and to assess the possible adverse consequences on their children? Is this issue really one for a therapist to help resolve, or rather a moral dilemma for the client?

A person's duty to relieve other people's suffering depends on the perceptions of the cause. For example, if a doctor who can cure blindness fails to provide such treatment, he will be held partly responsible for the continued disability. The same applies to counselling. If counselling is perceived to relieve a particular form of suffering, the cause of suffering will gradually be seen as a lack of counselling. If there was no other way an individual could prevent or alleviate his suffering this would be unproblematic, but is this really the case?

Another criticism is that, although a large part of counselling's 'success' is attributed to the provision of a relationship, it may be that the accessibility of such a relationship prevents people from negotiating and developing similar relationships in their own lives, which would then be therapeutic. It may even be that the availability of counselling is beginning to alter the structure of personal relationships, as serious discussion of one's emotional troubles is increasingly seen as inappropriate for discussion among non-professionals. The recommendation to 'see a professional' becomes a convenient way of pre-empting any entanglement with another's emotions.

Most people who experience distress and have no access to professional help are not bereft of alternatives, and will usually pursue a variety of other choices. These include introspection, speaking to friends or relatives, self-help techniques, distraction and other activities. One study found that 86 per cent of those who used self-help books reported benefit.[125] One question to ask is whether the availability of counselling prevents people from developing their own solutions to problems by ensuring they do not struggle with the issues for long enough by themselves.

All psychologically therapeutic procedures, whatever their format, act to create and strengthen expectations of one's personal effectiveness.[126] There has been a growing awareness among therapists of the importance of self-regulation, or self-control, as a factor influencing change in therapy.[127] Indeed, self-regulation or control may be a goal of therapy in its own right[128] – and if this is the case it leads naturally to the view of self-administered procedures as being 'the therapy of choice' in many situations, bypassing the therapist altogether.[129]

I mentioned earlier a definition of psychotherapy as 'guided introspection'. I believe a much more efficient approach than paying someone to guide your introspection would be to learn to guide it yourself. I believe it is vital that the public realises that there are many ways of improving your mental health besides going to see a therapist and that – even more crucially – we should focus our efforts on prevention so that we never get into the state where we need to consider professional help.

Prevention is clearly never going to eliminate all mental illness, but it could stop many seeking therapy unnecessarily. You can try this using the scientifically proven techniques given later in this book, also derived from my own clinical experience. Only when these have failed need you seek help from a professional. This approach is not the norm amongst counsellors or therapists, who believe that seeing a professional should be the starting point, rather than a last resort. Psychologists and psychiatrists are sympathetic to the idea that people should first try to solve their problems using established techniques, before seeking an encounter with a professional.

In cases where people do derive some benefit from counselling, the issue then becomes whether this is sufficient to outweigh the problems which inevitably accompany it.

Another important question to ask when considering the role of counselling in society is whether counselling benefits clients because it alleviates suffering or because it enhances happiness.[130] Ethicists have argued that there is an important difference between the two, and that we have different moral obligations to alleviate the suffering of others as opposed to enhancing another's happiness.[131] Human suffering makes a direct moral appeal, the appeal to help, but there is no similar call to increase the happiness of those who are not suffering.

Distinguishing whether one is alleviating suffering as opposed to enhancing happiness is difficult, and a reliable method has yet to be formulated, However, any such approach would need to form a judgement of whether one's actions are returning a human being to a notion of a 'par state' or taking him or her from a 'par state' and helping them go above it[132].

The idea of 'par' is the level at which a recognisably human life is possible: where one is free from great pain and insecurity and where one has the materials available to improve one's life.[133] This definition begs as many questions as it answers, such as what the materials are, and to what level we should expect to improve our life. Even those who have suggested the concept accept that it is too vague, but argue for the need to form a view of what constitutes an acceptable life, given that professional intervention will at some point progress beyond a relief of suffering towards an increase in happiness.

The notion of a par state, with its implied states of above and below par, is also important because it reminds us that, although suffering is perhaps an eradicable part of human life,[134] it is also a defining characteristic of life. A life without any suffering would be unlike any kind of life we could recognise or relate to. In other words, if it succeeded in eradicating suffering at some point, counselling may threaten our normal experience of life.

People will obviously differ as to where they place 'par', but the crucial issue is that this depends on expectations of what life ought to be like and, in particular, how much of life's problems we should be expected to take responsibility for dealing with ourselves. Given that upsetting things inevitably happen to people, rather than try to eradicate all suffering, we should try to distinguish between whether people are facing difficulties which are out of the ordinary but do not need help, or difficulties that have provoked reactions too extreme for the individual to cope with.

I believe a view of the par state is one in which, although possibly deeply distressed, you are able to carry on with the roles you have chosen in life. For example, you can still get to work and perform in a way which does not raise alarm amongst colleagues; still care for your children or other relatives and/or still look after yourself in terms of food, housing, hygiene, warmth and so on. You are sinking below the par state when you can no longer carry out your previous roles; when you forget to eat or wash, or can't carry out the routine tasks at work. It is at this point that you probably need the intervention or expertise of mental health services.

In the context of the par state, it is worth going back to the British Association of Counselling's 1979 declaration that: '...the task of counselling is to give the client an opportunity to explore, discover and clarify ways of living more resourcefully and towards greater well-being...' This statement appears less concerned with relieving suffering and more with enhancing happiness. According to the BAC declaration, a person might appear to function at 'par', yet still need counselling.

It is also worth reminding ourselves of the British Association for Counselling's *Directory of Counselling*, where those who might need counselling are described as 'suffering the death of a loved one, or not getting on with their partner, they may have lost a job or be worrying about coping with a new one, they may be finding the strain of work or exams too much, they may be at the end of their tether, anxious about the kids, their parents, or themselves, or simply down in the dumps.' As I said before, what is so striking is that all these issues are part of everyday life. While it is true that people experiencing any of the above problems may benefit in some way from seeing a counsellor, this benefit is certainly not in the form of relieving suffering that is out of the ordinary for anyone to experience during a lifetime.

The issue of whether counselling enhances happiness or relieves suffering goes to the heart of unease over the growth of counselling's availability to all. An analogy might be another industry, such as alcohol. Most people feel better after a drink following a stressful day, but does that mean that alcohol is a healthcare enterprise, or is it in fact closer to a leisure industry? These considerations are crucial in determining the way alcohol is regarded and regulated. Much disquiet might disappear if counselling was similarly re-classified as a leisure pursuit, something which enhanced the enjoyment of many people's lives, rather than which relieved their suffering. With such a definition, the important contribution of counselling to many people's happiness would not be denied, but access would not be a right.

In other words, if people want to purchase counselling because it might enhance their quality of life, they should be free to do so. The state, however, should not be under an obligation to provide counselling on demand, and no one should be encouraged to expect to be counselled if they cannot arrange such provision themselves. Rights to counselling should not be equated with rights to health.

In this chapter I have attempted to suggest that counselling, now an accepted part of health-care, has problems that are multiple and complex, and profound enough to call into question whether – no matter how and well-meaning in aim or spirit – it is the most useful approach to enhancing our mental health.

The BBC TV programme, *Watchdog*, approached me for help during their preparation for an investigation of the counselling industry. Some of my concerns over counselling were tested by covertly filming a journalist posing as a client answering advertisements for private practice counselling services in general interest magazines. This method caused great controversy after the programme was broadcast. The journalist was briefed to present a recent history which was typical of a normal everyday life experience. His girlfriend, with whom he had been in a stable and meaningful relationship for some months, had left on a business trip for a week and he was missing her a little. He had a job he enjoyed, a supportive social network, a normal sleep pattern and a good appetite. Perhaps most importantly, his girlfriend was definitely returning to him in a few days' time and they were even still in contact on the phone. He was instructed to display no symptoms of formal psychiatric problems.

Two out of the three counsellors he approached did not suggest the obvious – that the client wait to see how things were after his girlfriend had returned – but instead stated, purely on what they had so far heard, that more (private practice) sessions were required, even *after* the girlfriend had returned (our 'client' indicated he had too active a social life to allow a return visit to the counsellor until after his girlfriend had come back). In one case the number of further sessions suggested would have incurred a cost of over £100. None of the counsellors asked screening questions to try to detect suicidality, psychosis, serious depression, medical illness or non-illness, or even real distress. After all, 'missing her a little' was his only 'symptom'. On a positive note, all the counsellors did appear to be good listeners and were clearly interested in what the client had to say.[135]

To eliminate the argument that any of the counsellors could just have been having a 'bad day' – after all, it is doubtful that secret filming of GPs or psychiatrists would always uncover wonderful practice! – each counsellor was approached by other journalists telling very similar stories within around a week of each other. Sure enough, each counsellor gave exactly the same response on each occasion. This massive diversion of private practice therapeutic resources in the wealthy West to helping people who will get better anyway may go one way to explaining why the prognosis for psychological problems in societies less blessed with counselling services appears, in fact, to be better than in 'counselled' countries.[136]

What those poorer cultures do offer, instead of a professional relationship, are other connections which are perhaps as, if not more, therapeutic.[137] How to build good personally therapeutic relationships is the subject of the next chapter.

Perhaps the fundamental problem with counselling is that its encouragement of talking about problems, as a solution in itself, neglects the fact that talk often becomes a replacement for action.

Talking may convince us that we are doing something about our problems, when in reality all we are achieving is self-obsession – or 'self-focus'. Indeed, client improvement in talking treatments is associated with a decline over time in the use of self-references (these usually start with pronouns like 'I', 'me', 'my') during the session. Improvement in mental health coincides with an increase in the content of client talk about things other than themselves.[138]

Given that the evidence suggests that self-focus is counterproductive in improving mental health,[139] in other chapters I explore alternatives to counselling which have been proved to enhance mental health. In particular I emphasise the importance of action rather than talk. For it is only when we act that we genuinely make changes.

The psychoanalyst Karen Horney herself once said, 'Fortunately, analysis is not the only way to resolve inner conflicts. Life itself remains a very effective therapist.'

A recent MORI nationwide survey of 2,003 people,[140] sampled to be representative of the general UK population, found that 91 per cent thought that people suffering from depression should be offered counselling, while a mere 16 per cent thought they should be given antidepressants. Less than half thought antidepressants were effective and 78 per cent considered them addictive. Even though the research evidence is to the contrary, considerably in favour of the efficacy of antidepressants and their non-addictive nature, and despite a dearth of evidence for either clinical efficacy or cost-effectiveness of counselling,[141] a rapid growth of provision of counsellors in British NHS general practices has occurred.

The most recent study attempting to resolve the issue was published in the prestigious medical journal the *Lancet* at the end of 1997.[142] This found no significant differences in psychological or social outcomes between patients receiving brief psychotherapy or routine GP care, though patients allocated to the psychotherapists were more satisfied with the help they received.

Despite what may be inferred, 'brief' in the term 'brief psychotherapy' usually refers to the number of sessions offered, not the length of time per individual session, which often remains a standard fifty minutes, as it was for the *Lancet* study. While the psychotherapists had fifty minutes per session with each patient, the description of the GP care – 'routine general-practitioner care' and 'see their GP as usual' – suggests the GPs probably spent around a fifth of the time per patient than the psychotherapists. This surely is the explanation why patient satisfaction was greater for the brief psychotherapy group than for those seeing their GPs. Remember, though, that in the *Lancet* study there was still no difference between the two groups in objectively measured changes to the clinical condition of the patient.

Psychiatrists working in community mental health teams find busy GPs often refer on to other services simply because they feel patients with milder emotional problems need more time to be listened to than they can provide. But this issue of time per session is becoming confounded with the content of a session, by research that attempts to compare counselling with GP care. The accompanying discussion papers in the same issue of the *Lancet* considered the reasons behind the astonishing recent growth of demand for counselling in general practice, but neglected to mention the time spent per patient consultation. This suggests a disregard of this important variable in explaining patient dissatisfaction with routine GP care for psychological problems.

In fact, despite all the interest in different therapies expressed by researchers, all that psychotherapists may really offer over sensible GPs is simply more time. The recent growth of interest by the public in counselling and alternative therapies despite a lack of evidence for their superior efficacy is not that mysterious – it coincides exactly with the era when doctors, squeezed by an under-funded NHS, have never had less time to give their patients.

Perhaps the next step in this kind of research programme should be to allocate patients with emotional problems to just ten minutes per session of psychotherapy, or even alternative therapies like aromatherapy and homeopathy, and give the GP-allocated group fifty minutes per session with their doctors. One wonders which approach would patients be more satisfied with then? If academics do not become more aware of how important time is in explaining outcome, doctors are in danger of being discriminated against unfairly by research comparing what physicians do for their patients with what psychotherapists or alternative therapists offer.

If more time is simply all that most counsellors have to offer over GPs, are there any alternatives the busy GP can offer his or her patients to the expense of hiring in a counsellor?

Counselling training appears to concentrate on developing non-judgemental supportive listening skills,[143] and usually trainees are cautioned against giving information and directives. So the emphasis on counselling tends to be on listening well, rather than advising skilfully. But very little research has been conducted into what the precise characteristics are of a counselling session most likely to benefit patients. A 1997 study published in the *British Journal of Guidance and Counselling* from researchers in Australia[144] is one of the few to investigate directly this issue. It found that more effective counsellors were not (contrary to therapy folklore) the ones who listened a lot with minimal responses such as 'I see'. The most dubious experiences of patients were with counsellors who allowed lengthy quiet periods in the session. The most negatively rated counsellor in this study commented she had been trained to 'listen for the significance of the patient's silences'.[145]

In fact, the impressive counsellors tended to be more verbally active in the session, took the initiative in structuring the interview and systematically explored all aspects of the problem situation, rather than simply letting the patient dictate what happened and responding only to the issues they raised. Overall, what the most effective counsellors appeared to be doing was altering patients' perspectives on their circumstances, in particular assisting the development of more optimistic viewpoints.[146]

Effectual counsellors summarised their understanding of the problem situation with frequent use of complete sentences such as 'Let me just check, you're worried about ...', 'You're also concerned that ...', and 'As we've been talking you've realised that... '. They also differentiated between more immediate and less pressing practical concerns, saying things like: 'So for the moment you have enough money to keep going, but if you were not able to keep working full time at your job, that would be really serious'.[147] This could be termed 'active listening'.

This kind of evidence suggests time-constrained GPs, or even members of the public, can help patients with emotional problems effectively, once the principles of truly effective listening are grasped. These do not include leaving long periods of time for the client to fill, but do entail actively taking charge of and intervening in the session. Alternatively, the GP could try to get those people already in the patient's life to listen better, perhaps by asking the patient to bring such a person to an appointment. While effective listening and responding might help patients reframe an event, altering an overly negative appraisal of their situation, beyond this, exactly why simply talking about one's problems should be beneficial is less clear. But talking productively about one's problems usually involves confronting a personal trauma, and this may be beneficial because ventilating emotions means by definition there is no longer a need to actively inhibit or hold back thoughts and feelings from others. This may be useful because, as several studies have found, actively preventing yourself from doing something, like keeping a sentiment from someone, leads to increased physiological stress and psychosomatic disease.[148] Thus confronting a trauma may reduce the long-term work of inhibition.

If the benefit of talking about your problems simply arises from anything which stops your inhibition, it follows you do not actually need to have someone to talk to in order to benefit. This theory was tested by a famous USA study conducted in 1988 where fifty healthy undergraduates were assigned to write about either traumatic and upsetting experiences, or superficial topics, for four consecutive days.[149] At a six-week follow-up, those who had written about traumatic experiences had made not only significantly fewer visits to their doctor, but also notable improvements on two measures of cellular immune-system function. The students who seemed to benefit most from writing about upsetting things which had happened to them in their lives were those who said they had written about events they had previously actively held back in discussing with others.

Clearly 'writing therapy' is tremendously cost-effective, it allows people to confront traumas at their own rates, and encourages them to devise their own meaning and solutions to their problems. Because of these possible advantages 'writing therapy' has been suggested as an alternative to counselling.[150] A GP could therefore help the patient ventilate previously inhibited feelings by suggesting they write some notes on their trauma. But 'writing therapy' does not allow for emotional support from others, and may therefore be most effective when used in conjunction with brief counselling. Suggesting a client writes down their thoughts and feelings and brings the results to sessions, or even mails them in, may assist a client to benefit from disclosure, without a GP having to provide someone for the patient to disclose to.

In my experience, many of the public who write to me about their personal and emotional problems as a result of an article of mine they have read in the national press, often add at the end of their letter that they already feel a bit better simply for having put down their thoughts and feelings for the first time on paper. It seems I have unwittingly started to help before I even get round to responding!

How does the MIND work?

by Gathering Thoughts Together..

by IMPerceptible amounts..

IMPerfectly...

133

HELL IS OTHER PEOPLE

Relationships

'Trouble is a part of your life, and if you don't share it, you don't give the person who loves you a chance to love you enough.'

Dinah Shore

As well as seeing the seriously ill, one aspect of my job, both at the Maudsley and through my media work, is to advise couples with relationship difficulties.

Rachel and Peter, around thirty with no children, were one such couple. When they walked into my consulting room, Rachel looked drawn and ill. 'She's making my life unbearable,' complained Peter.

'Whose fault is that?' demanded Rachel. And within seconds they were demonstrating why they needed help.

Peter had had an affair two years previously. It was over now and he had on his own initiative accomplished the tasks therapists believe are the only way back from an affair: he had apologised, accepted responsibility for his wrong-doing and tried to make amends. Yet for Rachel the incident had become an obsession. Two years after Peter had stopped seeing the other woman, Rachel was still quizzing him about it. He was losing patience.

Like many couples, they had a long catalogue of complaints about each other and were perfectly happy to spend the session comparing lists. 'Stop, both of you!' I said. 'Trying to work out who is to blame is just going to slow us down.'

They stopped glaring at each other and glared at me instead. Rachel said, 'It's not me who needs help, it's him. He's a liar and a cheat, he won't admit he's done wrong.'

'That's not true. I know I was wrong, but it's over now,' Peter retorted.

An early step in couple therapy is to get each partner to break the cycle of saying negative things (or insults) to each other and instead encourage them to try saying something positive (or a compliment). Indeed research suggests that the ratio of positive statements to negative statements between successful couples is around five to one, i.e. in an average day a happy couple will say five positive things to each other for every one negative statement which passes between them.[1] So I tried to get the ball rolling by asking Peter and Rachel to say just one nice thing about each other.

There was a stony silence.

From Rachel's medical record I saw that the problem went deeper than jealousy. Finding out about Peter's casual affair had shattered her fragile self-confidence and she had needed sedation, prescribed by her GP. She had also started waiting around outside the other woman's flat, had written her letters and followed her about until the police were called.

Rachel had told her GP that she couldn't stop herself, and that was why she had been referred to me. As is usual with all my first appointments, I had asked her to bring someone who knew her well, which explained why Peter was there. The fact that he had come was a hopeful sign. I often see people whose psychiatric problems are closely linked with someone in their lives, but who cannot get that person to accompany them to the clinic, signalling their inability to obtain co-operation from precisely those they need it from.

'So how are things now?' I asked.

'I have to account for every minute of my time,' replied Peter. 'She even follows me to the pub.' Rachel said, 'I don't see why he shouldn't suffer for what he did.'

'But it's you who is suffering,' I said. 'You've had to give up your job and take antidepressants.'

'Don't worry, doctor, she's making me suffer too,' said Peter.

But I wasn't going to act as umpire. I said, 'Well, I don't understand why you're still together. You don't trust each other and neither of you is prepared to make allowances for how the other feels.'

'I don't want to live on my own !' snapped Rachel.

Peter said, 'We've been married for nearly ten years – this woman wasn't important.'

I realised the only thing they agreed on was that – strangely enough given their apparent mutual hatred – they wanted to stay together, or at least could not consider living apart. I decided to play devil's advocate.

At the next appointment I said, 'Being married is making Rachel ill. I think you would be better off apart.'

They were both shocked that the doctor had pronounced there was no future in their relationship. Shock dissolved into anger. How dare a relative stranger tell them their marriage was over?

'I thought you were meant to be helping us,' snapped Peter.

'I will decide when it's over with Peter, not you!' said Rachel.

What had at last managed to bring them together was their mutual annoyance with me. And although you can't base a relationship simply on the fear of being on your own, by drawing their attention to the alternative – splitting up – I seemed to focus their attention on their mutual dependency. Once you admit that you need the other person, you are in with a chance.

The next stage was to ask each of them to nominate a change they would like from the other. Most couples ask for changes like, 'I would like you to become more kind and considerate' while the other says, 'I would like you to give me more attention'. Such requests are too vague and abstract and therefore difficult to act upon. They are also a veiled way of getting a few more complaints on the agenda. So couple therapists instead request that such complaints are turned into wishes which can be acted upon. Any changes need to be specific and concrete. In Peter's case, giving Rachel more attention meant, when she was asked to give a specific example, talking to her for half an hour when he came home from work and not immediately sitting down to dinner in front of the television. In Rachel's case, being more kind and considerate meant, from Peter's perspective, not talking about the affair. So in exchange for Peter chatting to Rachel for half an hour in the evening, Rachel would not mention the affair for the whole of that same night.

Next time we met Peter had apologised for making Rachel so unhappy, while Rachel had promised to stop harping on about the other woman. After being on the brink of severe mental illness, Rachel was back to normal. But I'm sure she would tell you her psychiatrist had been really unhelpful!

This case illustrates some of the principles of couple therapy, in particular the importance of the 'change for a change' principle which is a very powerful way of breaking couples out of a downward cycle. Couples agree to make one change their partner would like, in exchange for a change they would appreciate. Clearly the alterations have to be roughly equivalent in terms of their ease of doing and impact. It would be unfair, for example, for Peter to expect Rachel never to mention the affair again in exchange for one evening's chat. But most couples are sensible enough to see the principle of equity here, that one change can only occur in exchange for another. And once couples get into the swing of it, there is nothing to say one cannot nominate three changes in exchange for three from the other.

Although this technique is a powerful therapeutic tool, it seems a crude way of improving relationships. Shouldn't relationships be above trade-offs? Yet it embodies perhaps the most important principle of how to better human association, namely the idea of exchange. People tend to get on when they feel mutually rewarded by each other. These 'social rewards' need not be abstract or ephemeral, indeed concrete specific dividends are best.

People who are successful at relationships are those who are generally most rewarding to be with. They also tend to be those who are skilled at analysing which social rewards are valued most by the individuals they would like to get on with. Clearly some of the social rewards valued by a Nobel Laureate physicist might be different from those of a building labourer, yet they also have some desires in common.

Social rewards are usually mediated through positive talk, and psychologists have defined these as the following: showing approval (for example, compliments), agreeing, offering support, encouraging, giving reassurance, attending (for example, listening, concentrating and paying attention to the other person and what they are saying), facilitating (helping in some concrete way) and empathising (demonstrating you know how the other person feels).[2]

People tend to like those who give social rewards in the above way.[3] Just how powerful a model this is of human relationships can be seen by research into which factor most powerfully determines career success at work. The evidence is that doing a good job, or even just appearing to do a good job (only working hard when the boss is around, or being skilled at drawing the boss's attention to your good work) are both inferior career success strategies compared to the most powerful factor of all – ingratiating yourself with the boss.[4] When your boss comes to decide who to promote, they are likely to choose whoever they have found most rewarding to work with, and this is likely to be the ingratiator rather than the hard worker.

The problem with this model of relationships – reward others to get on with them – is that it seems a little manipulative and insincere. But this needn't be the case. Although many manipulators use these techniques to get on in life, because they see people as means to an end, it is still possible to be interested in rewarding others because this is a pleasant and positive way of establishing and maintaining relationships. The opposite side of the coin to reward is of course punishment, which I discuss on page 103.

Relationships – whether with our boss, partner, family or friends – are one of the most important aspects of mental health. When they are going well we may take them for granted. On the other hand, if they are going badly, they become a major source of distress. If you are facing crisis, not having anyone to turn to exacerbates psychological problems. The absence of a relationship to buffer us against stressful times can lead to disaster, but having a bad one may be even worse. The wrong kinds of friends can lead you into problems like drugs while disorders as varied as alcoholism, psychosis and psychosomatic illnesses are often attributable to the stress of living in troubled marital relationships.[5]

In addition, the loss of those close to us is one of the major predictors of future psychiatric disorder. Indeed, I would go so far as to say that there is *no one* I see in my NHS clinical practice who is not partially psychologically disabled by relationship issues. For example, a woman who appears to have an eating disorder might really be suffering from a poor relationship with a spouse who is not supportive in helping her towards healthy weight loss, and who subtly belittles her appearance. A gay man who is alcoholic and depressed will not be helped by antidepressants and Alcoholics Anonymous until his insecurities over his promiscuous boyfriend are also dealt with.

Yet loneliness is also a growing problem in wealthy societies, particularly with the breakdown of the extended family. If people resolve to abandon relationships altogether (a common decision – for example, those women who decide never to date again after a bad marriage followed by a traumatic divorce), they may discover what psychiatrists already know – that those with no, or few, relationships also seem to be prone to psychological problems.

HELP IS OTHER PEOPLE

Think of your own social network, the people you are drawn to and those you shy away from. Who wants to be friends with people dominated by conflicts and personal problems? If you don't have many friends it could be an early sign of poor sanity. There is such a powerful link between relationship difficulty and psychological problems that one crude marker of your mental health is the extent and depth of your social network – in other words, how many friends you have and how close you are to them.

Even if you are one of the lucky ones who has a network of good relationships, losing one of them might still precipitate psychiatric disorder. As changes in relationships are inevitable, and are critical crossroads in your mental health, the purpose of this chapter is to help you pick your way through the minefield of affiliations.

One of the conundrums perplexing psychologists and psychiatrists is why psychological problems are on the increase, given that we do not have many of the stresses our ancestors – or even grandparents – faced. Most of us do not need to worry about having enough to eat or finding shelter, for example. Problems over romantic/intimate relationships may be one of the reasons for our distress. For example, never before in history in the West have we entered and left so many romantic/sexual involvements, with people beginning to date the opposite sex at a younger age than previously, even starting to have boyfriends and girlfriends in primary school. Marriage is also being postponed to a later age than ever before; the divorce rate is rising and extramarital affairs are increasing. All this means that even marriage does not signal the end of our romantic relationship history.[6] This continuing stress of breaking and entering so many more intimate relationships than our predecessors may be one of the reasons why, despite being better off materially, we are still subject to so many psychological problems. Our greater freedom to leave and start relationships as the opportunity arises may have caused us greater stress.

Yet most of us believe that relationships are not something we can control, and that we tend, by sheer luck, to bump into people we find sustaining or otherwise. One of the commonest beliefs of the people I speak to, either on television or radio phone-ins, and who write to me via national newspapers and magazines is a fatalistic view of relationships.

Moreover, even with relatives and friends, most of us feel powerless to improve the quality of those transactions, and difficulties with all these relationships account for much psychological distress. A common reason for women phoning me on my TV shows is to complain bitterly about the poor relationship quality they have with their husbands. But underlying the complaint is a feeling of helplessness over their ability to improve their relationship. They feel this is solely down to the whim of their partner. They also feel bleak about entering any other relationship which would be any better.

This goes to the heart of much human suffering because it explains why so many tolerate such poor-quality relationships – they are pessimistic about their ability to influence who they might meet in the future, so they prefer the devil they know to the uncertainty of re-entering the search for a new romantic relationship.

I do not believe relationships are beyond our management, and will show in this chapter how we have a lot more control over them than we realise. I want to show you how to develop the skills to initiate and sustain relationships, which will then help buffer you from poor mental health. For example, the 'change for a change' technique usually helps give us back the power to regulate a relationship going wrong. A basic error is expecting your partner to change without offering a change in yourself in return. You do this because you believe that the change you want from your partner is a reasonable expectation. Yet if you have tried reason and this has failed, continuing with a floundering strategy is bound to make you feel helpless.

The first step in improving your relationships is to assess your own network as objectively as you can. Do you have a wide circle of friends? Do you see relations regularly? But most importantly, how many people can you depend on in a crisis?

A lot of people think they are at the centre of a large and complex social circle, and only discover just how lonely they really are when they are faced with an emergency and no one appears willing to help. They learn the hard way that the quality of their relationships is really quite superficial. Indeed, some therapists have gone as far as suggesting this is one of the hidden benefits of a personal failure – you discover who your true friends are! Loneliness is not just an unpleasant emotion, but also a predictor of future poor mental health, particularly at times of stress. A high-quality social circle helps to buffer us against the events which would otherwise make us vulnerable to emotional crisis.

Paradoxically, some people who appear to have few friends may be less lonely than those who seem very popular, if the former can turn to their friends at times of crisis and confide things which would be socially unacceptable to reveal to mere acquaintances. Perhaps that is one of the tests of a strong friendship – the capacity to make emotional demands on a relationship without incurring guilt or the irritation of the other person. Such 'emotional demands' may include, for example, ringing somebody up late at night, expecting them to listen to the horrors of your forthcoming divorce. Another issue is whether we feel optimistic about the possibility of making new, deep friendships in the future, or whether we feel this opportunity has passed us by in our youth. This view may determine how lonely we feel.

In my NHS practice I frequently see people whose mental health problems arise directly from poor relationships or the loss of a relationship. Invariably, these clients blame the other party for the problems in the relationship. However, usually by the end of our encounter, it becomes only too apparent why the patient has had a series of fraught relationships. He or she is doing something which contributes to poor-quality relationships, which in turn leads to poor mental health.

People at my clinic also often complain that their husband or wife has left them and that this has plunged them into severe mental illness. On closer analysis, it is often possible to see the choice of partner was inappropriate in the first place and destined to failure. The relationship events which lead to illness could be prevented with 'social skills training'. These are skills which it is possible to learn and which help build high-quality relationships. These skills include the social rewards mentioned earlier and the ability to make a better choice of partner in the first place. The care taken with any other major commitment in your life – like buying a house or moving country – forms a stark contrast to the way people make marriage choices. The errors people make when incautiously choosing a marriage partner are so common psychologists call them 'marriage paradoxes'. The paradox is that despite marriage being such an important decision, people decide hastily, before meeting the other person's family and social circle and without taking account of the advice of family and close friends.[7]

Another classic is when patients bring a partner to the clinic and effectively demand that we change the partner. Some of my patients have even become extremely angry with me when I explain that I cannot magically change their partner for them, even though I may agree that the partner's unacceptable behaviour is contributing to their mental illness. In reality, those patients who demand we change their partners do so because they feel unable to bring about the needed change themselves – they feel powerless in their relationships and therefore turn to us in the hope that we in the clinic will have more power.

The real problem these patients have is in accepting that they are faced with a dilemma. Their partner may be behaving in an unpleasant manner which causes severe stress, but they have no motivation to change. The partner has long ago worked out that my patient will not leave and has therefore effectively resigned himself or herself to putting up with the distressing behaviour.

The only way to change such consistently distressing behaviour, other than leaving, is to change the pattern of consequences which currently occurs within the relationship. This means implementing some negative consequence whenever the person behaves in an unacceptable manner, and a positive consequence whenever they behave in a way we like. The examination of motivation – why we do what we do – is one of the most controversial areas in psychology and psychiatry. The simplest and most powerful analysis is that we always do what we do because we receive some benefit or reward for this behaviour, and avoid some less pleasant consequence by not behaving in the alternative way.

So if your husband comes home from work and refuses to do the dishes despite being asked repeatedly, this is because he is being rewarded by his current behaviour pattern (he gets to watch sport on TV instead). To change him you need to alter the current reward structure of his environment (stand in front of the TV until he does the dishes or be extra pleasant to him after he has finished them).

There are several important points to be borne in mind when trying to change reward structures. To start with, you need to alter the reward structure consistently, not intermittently. If you stand in front of the TV on only a few occasions, your husband will work out that if he holds out for long enough you will eventually give up and he gets to watch sport on TV again. So reward structures have to be transformed to produce a permanent change in behaviour. Sometimes people also confuse where the rewards are. If you get annoyed over the dishes not being done, your husband may feel he has already been punished and that watching TV is his only escape, so why change? If he is annoyed with you for going on about the dishes, getting you upset may even be rewarding for him.

If you believe the reward arrangement of your partner's environment is such that his current behaviour shouldn't continue but it does, this usually means you have failed fully to understand the benefit structure from his standpoint.

It is obviously much easier for an outsider to talk about change than for someone in such a relationship to implement it, especially if they feel powerless. If you have no power in your relationship, particularly if this is the most significant relationship in your life, ask yourself how that situation evolved in the first place. The most basic power we have over those who care for us is that they are concerned when we are upset, and do their best to heal our distress.

The ideal situation would be if people would change in response to reasoning. Psychologists term the most powerful form of reasoning 'humanistic reasoning'[8] and this is communication which emphasises the human happiness or suffering produced by any type of behaviour.

Assertive humanistic statements are usually of the type, 'When you do X, this makes me feel Y because of Z'. An example would be, 'When you come home and don't do the dishes, this makes me feel upset and angry because it seems you don't care about the housework'. This is the first thing which should be tried to improve a relationship.

Yet what happens when, as is sometimes the case, the person we are reasoning with no longer cares about our happiness? If they no longer care, they are not going to change in response to our upset, and it may be time to consider that the relationship has long been washed away by battering over time.

The important lesson here is that we often cannot change other people directly. However, we can change the way we react and behave towards other people, and once others experience our changed response, they often also adapt and change as a result – but only if we are able to sustain our own changes.

A good tip, as I put it when discussing relationships with my patients, is to treat people as pets. In an ideal world you should not have to treat people as pets, as you should be able to reason with them. However, in my experience, much of the time people do not respond or listen when we speak to them, however reasonably, about something they are doing which upsets us. So, one of the most frequently quoted pieces of advice – to communicate – is flawed from the outset. Once you have given one strategy a good try and it is no longer working, *change strategy*. The next step is to *abandon talking*. At least you will have learned from the failure of reasoning that whoever you are dealing with is clearly not able to respond to your concerns on the same level and you will not waste your time in future.

However, instead of changing strategy, most people continue to try to effect change by talking, pleading for those close to them to change, and merely succeeding in getting more and more upset. Instead, stop exasperating yourself in this way and realise that the time for words is over, and the time for action is nigh.

The media encourages people to talk; communication is perceived as a way of increasing understanding. And yet, if you have *tried* to achieve understanding and, despite your best efforts, you have failed, then what?

Now you have to begin to treat them as a pet. How do you get your dog to change? You would not try pleading with it but would rather reward it when it does the right thing – a bone when it sits, for example – and invoke a negative consequence when it behaves in a way not helpful to you – a stern reprimand and no treats or dinner. Soon the pet learns to behave correctly, simply because life is not as pleasant if it doesn't. The feature which unites us all, and links us with pets, is that we would all prefer a pleasant life. So, treat people you cannot reason with in precisely the same way: reward them whenever they do what you want and ignore or invoke a negative consequence whenever they behave in a way you find unhelpful. The 'treat people as pets' approach is what is more technically known as 'behaviourism'.

The process is, of course, more gradual than the example suggests. To begin with, you may find people do not behave precisely in the way you would like, so start off by rewarding them when they come close to the desired goal, then change the reward structure so as to encourage even more movement in the right direction. Then, as they get closer and

144

"ITS NOT AN AGENDA bender."

ITS THOUGHTS—URCHIN—

RAINING THOUGHT
STRNNING THOUGHT
HELL IS OTHER PEOPLE
JUST
You
Can
Hear !

closer to the desired state of affairs, change the reward structure so that movement towards the desired goal is always encouraged. This is what psychologists call 'shaping'.

For example, if your children never help with the washing up, reward them when they clear away plates and put them in the sink. Then, as they get used to that, change the system so they get rewarded for doing some of the washing up, and finally reward them when they complete the washing up.

A reward need not be a material item but could be something as simple as praise. The best kind of reward is merely to make someone's life more pleasant and to withdraw your co-operation when they do not co-operate with you. It is also best if you link your co-operation with the thing they are not co-operating with. So, going back to your unco-operative children, if they refuse to help with the washing up, suggest they eat off paper plates, or even not be served dinner at all.

The problem most people have with the 'treat people as pets' programme is that they feel unable to withdraw their co-operation, let alone go so far as to implement a negative consequence, when dealing with those close to them. This may be because they fear negative consequences for themselves in the form of personal repercussions or they feel unable to bring themselves to be 'nasty' to those who are close to them.

As I try to point out, you are not being asked to be nasty, merely to reflect the lack of co-operation you experience back on to the other person, so they get some feeling for what it is like from your perspective of the relationship. You have felt that your children not assisting with the dishes is deeply unhelpful and upsetting, so you are merely making them feel what you have been feeling by a similar withdrawal of your co-operation at mealtimes. Why should that be unfair or nasty? After all, if they have been doing it to you, they should not feel it is unfair to have the same thing done to them. I should stress that the 'treat people as pets' programme should be tried only after communication has clearly failed. Sometimes treating people as pets is inappropriate or dangerous but only because direct communication wasn't tried first.

Another problem is that my patients are fearful of what others might do to them in terms of getting angry or upset if they implement the 'treat people as pets' policy. If you do not feel free to behave as you

ITS AHEAD STRAINER (FILTER)

146

(A hunter-gathering thoughts in to the Mynd)

would like in a relationship, if you are so much under the control of the other person that you are fearful of doing anything other than what they want, then they have you exactly where they want you. First, you are in a master–slave relationship, where they are the master and you the slave, and they will be able to get you to do anything they want, like put away the dishes. Secondly, how can you expect them to pay any regard to your wishes? Why should they, for what benefit will they gain from paying attention to your needs over their own?

You will notice I have avoided using the term punishment and instead referred to negative consequence. Punishment is certainly a popular method of discouraging undesirable behaviour and often produces rapid change – but punishment has problems.[9]

The first problem is that punishment is usually an aggressive act and even if it works it often teaches the recipient that aggression works, so raising the aggressive atmosphere in a relationship. Punishment also tends to heighten people's arousal levels and this increases the vigour of their response to your intervention, again elevating the tension in a relationship. Another problem is that, though punishment may lead to avoidance of the undesirable behaviour, it will also produce an attempt to escape the punishing person. Finally, punishment can produce a general tendency not to try doing anything, such as taking the initiative, in case one gets punished. VOICE OVA MOLE...

The most positive kind of punishment is to let people face the natural consequences of their actions. So if your husband does not help with the laundry, let him experience wearing dirty clothes. The more constructive alternatives to punishment include withdrawing something good one does for the other person – you are not actively doing something unpleasant to them, but stopping doing something pleasant instead. Also reward the preferred behaviour, particularly if this is in contrast to the undesired one. So, for example, if someone racks up large phone bills talking to friends, yet doesn't speak with you enough, reward them for activities which get them away from the phone, like taking you out for dinner. The schemes which work best are when you change the reward structure so that the reward or negative consequence follows *immediately* the action you are trying to change.

In any relationship there is a balance of power and the 'treat people as pets' perspective merely illuminates and tests the power structure. The

with 146 INDESCRIBABBLE thoughts

balance of power lies in favour of the one in the relationship who is less dependent on the other. The more dependent you are on the other person, the less likely it is that you will be able to get them to do what you want, because all they have to do is withdraw their co-operation and you will be the loser.

A central paradox of relationships, therefore, is that the more independent you are of those you are in a relationship with, and the more dependent they are on you, the more power you will have to get them to co-operate with you in a way which makes your life more pleasant. Yet when we fall in love, or feel deeply attached to others, we become dependent on them for our feeling of well-being. The ideal balance for positive mental health is to ensure that you never get so dependent on someone that you cannot begin to 'pet' them into co-operation with you to make your life more pleasant, should negotiation begin to fail.

A good example of the 'treat people as pets' policy occurred with a patient of mine, a mother in her late forties, who had become suicidally depressed because of the behaviour of her two unemployed sons. The two sons, in their early twenties, would swear at her and refused point-blank to do any housework, not even putting their dirty clothes in the laundry basket. MONI TO RING... THOUGHTS

My patient appealed to them *ad nauseam* over this but they would ignore all pleas and verbally abuse her whenever she brought up the subject. I instructed her to refuse to wash any clothes not in the laundry basket. She implemented this plan with grave reluctance, terrified of how upset the boys would become. Sure enough, the boys tried bullying her into picking up their clothes wherever they had left them. But, as she resolutely stuck to her guns, they soon learnt how uncomfortable it is to walk around in unwashed clothes and eventually learnt to put the washing in the basket.

The point here is that these boys would never have changed their behaviour because they were asked to, or because they did not want to upset their mother. They only did it because it had negative repercussions on their own lives if they did not co-operate. *For those who will not listen to reason, the only way they will ever do what you ask is if they can see a personal advantage in co-operating with you, or a disadvantage in not co-operating with you.*

REPETITIONS

147

LEND AN EAR!
STAYING SANE (Lender Near)

The interdependency between people – what they gain from each other – is the vital foundation on which co-operation is based. Negotiations in politics, industry, or terrorist sieges always start by analysing what the two opposing parties really depend on each other for. Who is most dependent determines where the balance of power lies. So, for example, if a wife is dependent on her husband for her financial welfare and the husband quite likes the way she keeps house but is not dependent on that for his well-being, it is fairly clear where the balance of power lies and who will tend to gain co-operation. But even in such situations there are ways of changing the balance of dependency in your favour. For example, you could start doing extra special favours for the person you want to gain power over, get them used to and dependent on your favours, and then threaten (subtly!) to withdraw them if they do not co-operate with you in the way you want.

If you have nothing to offer which will make another person's life more pleasant, or a way of making their life more unpleasant, you have few real ways of eliciting co-operation from them. Those who are most powerful in relationships have things which others need; it might be something as simple as being seen with an attractive person, being witty, or being warm.

Others are unlikely to find association with you rewarding if you have nothing to offer in your relationships in terms of basic human needs, for example, the need to feel valued, the need for intimacy, the need for sex, the need to be listened to, the need to be cheered up, the need to be distracted, or the need to feel attractive. This means you will find it more difficult to initiate relationships or keep them.

Another important point is that people's needs differ. For example, if you are able to make someone feel attractive by complimenting them, yet that is not one of their needs, you are not really meshing with them.

One way of thinking about needs is to consider the kind of emotional state another person might favour. Some people might like to feel dominant in a relationship, in which case supplying that feeling to them by being submissive will fill a basic need of theirs. If you are doing this better than anyone else they will become dependent, if not even addicted, to you.

Another good example would be that psychiatrists like to feel insightful. So if you want a psychiatrist (God forbid!) to fall in love with

148

you, make them feel more insightful when they are with you than they experience elsewhere in their lives. They will find you irresistible!

It is important to get on with people for an entirely different reason if you want to stay out of a psychiatric hospital. Those who are so mentally ill that we have to admit them to the hospital compulsorily have reached a stage where those around them also believe them to be mentally ill – I am often called out by the family or friends to 'take away' the patient. The person concerned will be beyond responding to the advice or pleas of those around them.

I have found a distinguishing factor of these seriously ill people to be that not only do they not respond to the concerns of those around them, but they do not care much about what others think. This inability to respond to the concerns of others or the feedback they give you, and the de-prioritising of others' perspectives is a major factor in all mental illness. For example, obsessives are unconcerned about why it is that everyone else gets through the day without washing their hands at least 50 times – they do not give enough attention to the way their behaviour and beliefs diverge from most other people's. If you are responsive to the opinions and feelings of those around you, you will never encounter men like me in white coats bearing legal documents.

However, as conflicts are unavoidable in relationships, maintaining them requires conflict management skills. These involve being able to suppress criticism and disagreements with others, or to restore them without endangering the relationship. A central difference between those who are good – and bad – at relationships is the difference in conflict management skills.[10]

The capacity to respond to, select, initiate, maintain, deepen, end and simply survive relationships are key skills in enhancing positive mental health. These skills prevent us from entering into a relationship which will not be good for us, and also stop a particularly bad relationship from dominating our lives. They ensure a sensitivity to feedback – no matter how subtle – so you are responsive to it and act upon it immediately, thus preventing a situation developing when everyone around you becomes concerned about your mental health, while you ignore them.

I have mentioned that being lonely is not down to the number of friends you have, but rather to their qualities. Psychologists now realise

... HAS A COMMENTATOR
... RETURN ! "

2016

there is no absolute figure for how many friends or relationships you should have as a marker of positive mental health. Instead, they now suggest the crucial issue is how satisfied you are with the quality of your relationships.

The two particular qualities important for maintaining mental health are: first, to have relationships in which you perceive that you are cared for, esteemed, or otherwise closely involved with other people,[11] and second, to have relationships in which you can talk about yourself and your problems.[12] More of this second quality later.

The very best preservers of positive mental health are those relationships where you feel cared for and esteemed even when you are at your lowest ebb and can give little positive of yourself. There is nothing quite so reassuring for your self-esteem than the thought that when you have hit rock-bottom there are those around you who still like you and feel you have things to offer the world.

Many people continue to invest in relationships which quite clearly offer little or no support at times of distress and need. Emotional investment in these relationships is counterproductive, as they are likely to exacerbate your problems. If maintaining your mental health is your priority, do not invest emotionally in those who cannot sustain your mental health and concentrate on building those relationships which can.

Another factor which separates the mentally fragile from the healthy is their inability to detect that the person they have committed themselves to is actually incapable of emotional support, or to reject the company of those who are capable of such assistance.

I remember being called during one of my television phone-ins by a woman whose husband had left her a few days after the birth of her child. He now wanted to come back into her life. He had been good to her, she claimed, most of the time, but just happened to have a habit of deserting her at times of crisis. In terms of her mental health, the advice would be clear: this man is of no help in maintaining her sanity at all. He might be good in bed or a witty companion, but these characteristics have nothing to do with the kind of relationship which contributes to positive mental health.

Another example: in my *Cosmopolitan* column I counselled a woman who stayed in a relationship with an alcoholic because she felt he was very caring towards her. Her definition of caring seemed to be that the man was not aggressive to her even when blind drunk. In other words, she felt he was caring because he did not make demands on her, while in fact he was so fragile that she could not make any calls on him.

As she was fairly mentally healthy at the time, this was not an issue. However, were she to hit some kind of crisis, such as a job loss or a problem with her children, he simply was not the kind of person who could provide any emotional, financial or physical support. I believe that because of this she was in grave risk of poor mental health at such a hypothetical time in the future.

This relationship follows a common and predictable pattern in that we fall in love and attach ourselves to another when at the peak of physical or mental health. A partner's ability to provide support in times of crisis is never an issue when we are choosing our life partner or friends, even though this may be crucial in the future. Because of this, I tend to advise those trying to decide on the suitability of future partners to generate some kind of personal crisis to test the supportiveness of their intended. By generate I do not mean make one up if your life is running smoothly, but perhaps be a lot franker and emphasise a problem in your life you might otherwise ignore.

The big mistake most couples make is to seek to commit themselves after a period of courting during which they have carefully presented only the best aspects of themselves to each other. But you will only know whether someone is really right for you when you still feel you want a relationship after you have seen them at their worst, or find they can still support you when you are at your lowest. The acid test of a relationship is its ability to survive when one partner is going through a crisis.

We often seek out friends or lovers according to a certain set of criteria: how physically attractive they are, how wealthy, how witty, how popular, and so on. But the best way to preserve and enhance your mental health is to put at the top of your list of priorities the quality of being emotionally supportive. Once you have understood the importance of this goal, the ability to detect the capacity to give emotional support becomes a crucial skill.

Professor Michael Argyle, one of Britain's most eminent social psychologists, suggests from his research[13] into friendship that there are three key areas which determine our satisfaction with it. These are: how helpful (materially and tangibly) that friend is; how emotionally supportive; and how many of our interests are shared.

The quality of a relationship is also determined by how intimate and confiding you can be in that relationship. If you can divulge potentially damaging information, yet know your confidant will not ridicule you or divulge it to anyone else, you know you have the essence of genuine friendship.

One measure of how rare such intimate, confiding relationships in our society have become is the growth of the counselling and psychotherapy industry. We have seen that many psychologists and psychiatrists now wonder whether, essentially, what therapists provide is simply the kind of confiding, intimate relationship their clients need but for various reasons are unable to obtain. The advantage of seeing a counsellor over building your own such relationships is that you can start divulging information about yourself immediately, safe in the knowledge that your counsellor is bound by professional and ethical rules which prevent him using such information against you. A therapist is unlikely to be shocked or judgmental – again, qualities difficult to find in many relationships. Perhaps one reason for the rise of the counselling industry is simply the increasing poverty of our relationships. Higher quality affiliations would probably render much counselling redundant.

Perhaps the biggest advantage of a therapist over a friend is that the obligations of professional relationships are more clearly defined. You hopefully enter, explicitly or implicitly, into a contract with a therapist, whereby you agree to pay a certain amount and the therapist agrees to be available to you at certain times. Mutual obligations are a source of great discontent in non-professional relationships because there is much more difficulty establishing what our obligations to our friends are. We often grumble if they ring us late at night or if they ask to borrow money, as we feel these favours cross the boundary of friendship.

There is, perhaps, for many people who are poor at relationship skills, less chance of feeling taken advantage of or neglected in a relationship with a therapist. Therapists frequently encounter clients who are reluctant to leave when the session is over, or who try to make contact outside the session. These people are trying to extend their relationship with their therapist because of the poverty of their relationships outside therapy. But a good therapist will be able to maintain the boundaries of the professional relationship and restrict the important work to a session, usually without endangering the actual relationship itself.

Yet what a good therapist provides is often simply being a good confidant – which is actually what a good relationship or friendship should also supply.[14] A good confidant is someone who is discreet and who will keep your confidential information to themselves and not share it with your social circle. They will also not be judgmental when you divulge negative information about yourself or your behaviour (after all, that is what most secrets are). Finally, a good confidant should be able to offer some new perspective or insight into your problems.

How should you set about finding a good, non-professional confidant?

Perhaps the first step to test your friends with a small confidence and see what happens, as well as also being a good confidant to them. Women are much better at this kind of deep friendship with each other, where they mutually confide, than men are.

Closely related to friendship is the notion of social support. Research has found that social support is so important to health that it helps you live longer. It is a predictor of lower rates of mortality.[15]

Social support falls into two categories: 'appraisal support' and 'belonging support'. Appraisal support is a useful stress buffer, and it refers to having other people available who can help you comprehend what is really going on during a stressful incident. Appraisal support is crucial for maintaining mental health at times of stress.

It is helpful because you cannot react to a problem unless you fully understand it, and appraisal support from friends helps you to understand the problems at a time when your stress, or your particular prejudices, stop you from objectively appreciating what is really going on.

Appraisal support is also useful in assessing just how serious a problem really is. Those who are excessively prone to depression or anxiety, or are facing a problem for the first time, may tend to exaggerate its seriousness, and friends can be more objective at this time.

Belonging support refers to having people with whom one can spend and enjoy time – and this appears to be helpful in maintaining positive mental health, whether or not you are experiencing stress.

One way to get others to be good friends to us is to be a good friend to them first. Offering help beyond the norm is one way of deepening a friendship. But most of us tend to wait for another to volunteer help before we offer to reciprocate, and this is why many of our friendships remain relatively superficial. As our pace of life increases, we are often too busy for our friends, putting them second to our families and our workmates, even though good friends are an important foundation for positive mental health, and well worth the investment of our time and effort.

However, psychologists and psychiatrists are not simply saying that being sociable protects against poor mental health. Sociability can be a sign of psychological problems in which people seek relationships compulsively. Some people are too dependent on certain relationships and find it difficult to oppose the decisions of friends or partners, or even to make decisions at all, without seeking guidance from others. We can all think of examples of this. The father-in-law of a friend of mine, for example, will never agree to meeting up with his only grandchild in the park without effectively seeking permission from his wife. So, being too enmeshed in relationships can be as bad as being too distant from others.

The central paradox in handling relationships in a healthy way is that the mentally robust have many relationships, some of them deep and firm, yet they can also do without relationships if needs be, i.e. if they lose someone close, they will survive. Psychologists term this ability 'the capacity to be alone'.[16] Mental health is both being able to be alone and also to be with others.

Another way of looking at this paradox is that the mentally healthy are able to utilise social resources when people are accessible, but can also fall back on their own resources if no one is available, even if they may have to do without social contact or support for quite some time. This leads to another key concept fundamental to mental health: as well as being resilient, the mentally healthy are also socially resourceful and, the final quality, they are also self-reliant.

One study found that adolescents who spent at least some regular amount of time alone (between 20 and 40 per cent of their waking hours) were better adjusted than those who were never alone.[17]

Rousseau wrote, 'The habit of retiring into myself eventually made me immune to the ills that beset me',[18] while a famous British psychiatrist once declared, 'The capacity to be alone is one of the most important signs of maturity in emotional development'.[19] Some have even advocated solitude as an opportunity for self-appraisal, healing and emotional renewal, and certainly those able to use it in this way should be more resilient to stress, given that loneliness is a major issue in everyone's life. The average adult in the Western world is estimated to spend about 30 per cent of the day alone, and this amount increases in old age.[20]

A great many symptoms the mentally ill display only manifest themselves when they are alone, because while they are with others their symptoms do not arise. Some treatments even involve the prescription of company during danger periods, when a relapse is likely. A good example is bulimia. Most bulimic episodes tend to occur when sufferers are alone,[21] and this may mean bulimia and other psychiatric symptoms are the consequence of feelings which only come to the surface when alone. There are many other problems which seem to get worse when people are alone, including depression, alcoholism and excessive spending. Spending large amounts of time alone is linked with psychiatric depression.[22]

Since being alone sometimes is unavoidable, it makes sense to learn how to cope positively with this experience. If we have been using social support as a way of escaping from ourselves or from uncomfortable personal issues, these become much more salient when we are alone. If you can be comfortable with only your own company, it is unlikely that you need to escape from some painful aspect of yourself or your situation.

Being alone is important to adapt to. While only 7 per cent of adults report having no friends at all, this rises to 12 per cent for women and 22 per cent for men over 65.[23]

Another positive aspect of being alone is that it allows you to examine yourself and your life uninterruptedly, which may help clarify your current situation. It also highlights the fact that we all have an inner dialogue with ourselves. In effect, we have a relationship with ourselves, the quality of which is crucial to our mental health.

We establish this relationship with ourselves through self-talk, i.e. what we say to ourselves during our incessant internal conversations. This is such an important aspect of mental health that a whole chapter of this book is devoted to it, on thinking your way to sanity (chapter 6).

Certainly, whatever the reason, a person's reported comfort when alone is an indicator of well-being,[24] with those who report greater comfort when alone being significantly less depressed and more satisfied with their lives. However, the average person reports feeling somewhat less happy and aroused when alone.[25]

There is a group of people who prefer to be alone, or who retreat into themselves when under stress. They prefer to deal with emotional turmoil by themselves rather than by sharing their troubles with others. In fact, there is now evidence that those who react to stress by seeking social support are better adjusted than those whose typical reaction is to avoid social contact.[26]

One explanation is that, since much mental distress comes from relationships which are working badly, seeking out other relationships for support – talking to a girlfriend if your boyfriend upsets you, for example – first of all gives you a temporary replacement for the lack of support in your unsuccessful relationship. Secondly, you can use your social support to help you understand the association that is not working out. You need relationships to help you understand relationships. And, thirdly, you can try out different solutions to a relationship problem by discussing them with others.

Such relationships can be a huge resource in providing information and advice based on previous experience, as well as simple encouragement, which all helps you to deal with the minefield of unsuccessful relationships.

In chapter 8, on coping with crisis ('Crisis, What Crisis?'), I explain how to cope with upsetting events. But I will focus here on one major method of coping – help-seeking – as this concerns relationships. We tend to turn to two kinds of social support when in crisis. The first is 'formal' support, in other words, GPs, social workers, therapists, crisis phone lines, priests, pharmacists and so on. And the second is 'informal', that is, friends or people we know socially.

As explained in chapter 2, 'Anyone Who Goes To See A Therapist Needs His Head Examined', I believe we have started to over-emphasise the benefits of seeking help from formal sources of support. Supposed advantages of professionals include notions that they are more objective and that we can be franker with them than with our family or friends. But there are also disadvantages to professional sources of help, which I feel do not get emphasised. I discuss these in detail in the chapter on counselling, but here are just a few problems with such professional sources of help.

On the whole, professionals rarely know us as well as our friends and relatives (though this, unfortunately, is changing in our increasingly anonymous world). So when we turn to professionals for help, they have to spend time getting to know us before being able to offer constructive help. Many professionals – harassed family doctors, for example – simply haven't the time to get to know us well enough on the first consultation to be able to offer high-quality help. Even those who have more time, like private-practice therapists, are reluctant to offer much help until they have seen us over several sessions. So, while professionals may be experienced as to patterns of behaviour in that they have usually seen similar problems in others before, they often lack knowledge about our particular situation. In contrast, friends and relatives will usually be strong (hopefully) on in-depth knowledge about us, but weak on general knowledge about problems.

Another problem with seeking help from professionals is that they are rarely that accessible; you cannot simply make an appointment at will, but may need to wait a few days. Even when you are in treatment, professionals are not easily available between appointments. Friends and relatives are usually available (almost) immediately. This is a huge advantage which is often overlooked.

Another positive aspect of friends and relatives is that the information you tell them is genuinely off the record; they do not keep records or medical notes, whereas your family doctor does. So, she will have recorded that time you went to her many years ago feeling particularly low, and when your insurance company or employers contact her for her opinion on your mental fitness, that record may come back to haunt you.

A possible problem with obtaining help from friends and relatives is a tendency for the 'principle of reciprocity' to put us off. You may want to obtain help without feeling obligated in return. I suspect this is a major, albeit unconscious, reason that people turn to counsellors rather than friends for emotional support. In purchasing that form of help you have repaid your obligation to the helper instantly. Indeed, research has found a connection between formal help-seeking and the kind of social milieu in which people find themselves in terms of reciprocity, where low levels of reciprocation are associated with a tendency to seek help from professionals rather than from each other.[27]

There is also the fact that if friends or relatives tell us they believe we need professional help for our problems, we are more likely to seek such help, as well as follow the advice of the professional. So informal support can be useful in telling us when formal support might be required.

Another possible explanation for why some turn to professionals rather than friends for help might be to avoid 'losing face'. We may fear the loss in self-esteem or feelings of personal inadequacy in turning for help to a friend rather than the more anonymous consultation with a professional.[28] An increasingly competitive society, in which revealing our vulnerabilities could be interpreted as a sign of weakness, may be partially responsible for the rise in professional counselling where we can more safely display our vulnerabilities.

However, this also implies that if our personal relationships were of a quality that did not make us feel so inadequate when seeking help, we might need less professional help. This, therefore, suggests another criterion for measuring the quality of our personal relationships: whether we feel able to seek help from them without feeling a loss of self-esteem, or personal inadequacy.

So, there are pros and cons of both formal and informal methods of support. Research suggests that the majority of people in distress turn to informal rather than formal methods of help and that these are probably effective, as the majority of those who use them do not seem to go on to seek professional assistance.[29] One way of thinking about seeking aid from professionals is not that this demarcates those whose symptoms have become severe, but that it marks out those whose informal sources of succour are ineffective or have dried up.

The kind of help we seek from others varies from information or clarification of our problems and solutions, to self-esteem bolstering and practical help, such as money or help with day-to-day functions like childcare or housekeeping. Such assistance (known in the jargon as 'instrumental support') may reduce distress because of the direct effects it has on depleted resources, whether financial aid to supplement lost income or by reducing the overload of the stressed person.

If you need further persuading of the benefits of deepening and widening your friendships, remember how expensive and difficult it is to find a good therapist, and bear in mind that a strong friendship will often negate the need to see a therapist. One disadvantage of a good friend over a therapist, however, is the fact that those therapists who have gone through a rigorous training will be able to appraise objectively a client's problems. They (hopefully!) learn to dissociate their own personal prejudices and histories from their reaction to the client's situation. In contrast, a friend will probably give you a highly personal reaction to your issue, deeply contaminated by their own prejudices and personal history. To overcome this problem, you need first to be aware of it, and second to cultivate friends who can dissociate themselves from their prejudices and listen objectively to you. Finally, having more than one friend you can confide in to give a consensus view from friends of widely differing backgrounds probably comes close to what a good therapist would say.

In fact, what makes a mental health professional able to produce therapeutic change in clients may have less to do with specific technical skills and more to do with general social skills. Indeed, empathy and warmth have been found to be the two qualities in a therapist which most often accounts for positive change in clients. Warmth is the valuing of another person and the communication of that attitude both verbally and non-verbally so that genuine interest in him or her has been conveyed. Empathy is the ability to understand the way another is feeling and to communicate that understanding of feelings to them. Empathy and warmth appear to be the most positive rewards we get from social interaction, so to be rewarding we need to generate empathy and warmth, while if we have social contacts who are empathetic and warm to us this is good for our mental health.[30]

Incidentally, you may find that many – if not most – of your friendships do not meet the criteria set out in this chapter. This does not mean you should dispense with them, but rather that you should be aware of which relationships will help mental health and nurture those in particular.

You may need to consider starting new relationships that will help your mental health. Either you are simply not meeting appropriate people – in other words your problem is one of opportunity – or you are meeting people all the time but you can't seem to take the relationship beyond the superficial. The problem of opportunity can be divided into two kinds: either you are not meeting people at all, or you are meeting people but not usually of the right type for you.

Start with a bit of self-analysis. In my experience, those who tend to be bad at meeting the right people have not fully understood what kind of person they are themselves and therefore what their needs are. Although we often speak of the attraction of opposites, we tend to respond best to people who are like us. This is not to dispel the idea of opposites attracting – in fact, we may well like people who are a bit different from us – but if you take the really big issues into account, such as social class, attitudes and interests, we tend to gravitate more towards people who are like us than different from us.

So, once you have understood what kind of person you are, you need to start finding yourself in places or following activities where people like you will tend to congregate. It is best to do this through a hobby or interest, as such activity acts as a distraction and takes the pressure off you to be particularly socially skilled in getting the person you are trying to get to know to stay in your company. The major disadvantage of social events like parties is that the only way to keep someone whose company you are interested in close to you is to be socially skilled enough to give them reasons to stay and talk to you. Showing interest in others so they'll respond to you may help break the ice, but maintaining the conversation requires levels of wit and charm in circumstances – the presence of someone you really do not know enough about – which are difficult for even the most polished conversationalist.

So, take control of your social life and do not leave it to chance. On one phone-in programme I was rung up by a woman who loved dangerous sports and who complained to me that she frightened off most men. How could she ever meet the right man? I recommended she joined clubs which specialised in dangerous sports like mountain climbing or parachuting. Meeting fellow risk-taking individuals increased the chances of her finding the kind of man she might like.

Her needs may have been somewhat specialised, but the general principle is the same. Think, 'Where do people like me hang out so I can be there to meet them?', rather than 'People like me seem very thin on the ground'.

Another aid to developing relationships is the use of small talk. Small talk is anything but small. It is, in fact, a deadly serious activity because it sets the emotional atmosphere in which more serious talk might occur, as well as helping to relax people so they do not find you threatening. When relaxed, people are more open both to your ideas and to you as a person, making the task of getting people to like you easier. It also makes the stressful business of dealing with different people more enjoyable. First, it subtly communicates important information about someone's state of mind; from people's opening small talk you can tell things like whether they have the time to talk about more serious things now. Because it appears unimportant, it frees people to tell you if something is on their mind, which they might not share with you, if you were talking about something more serious.

Radio DJs, hairdressers, taxi-drivers and bartenders are the street-smart experts when it comes to small talk. During World War II, governments checked the small talk of people like this in an attempt to monitor rumours!

The small-talk experts suggest a number of factors contributing to successful small talk. Being good at small talk means being exquisitely sensitive to the earliest sign of lack of interest in what is being said, and changing the subject at once. Small talk is more about keeping the other person engaged than deeply meaningful content. If you find you are doing all the talking, then something has gone wrong.

Secondly, you need a broad range of subjects to talk about. Small-talk bores stick only to the one subject they are interested in, whereas the small-talk king can talk about literally anything. This is why a broad range of interests is crucial to the ability to make small talk.

Thirdly, you need to find ways of uncovering what the other person wants to talk about. Asking people what they do for a living is not about extracting their CV, but a means to get clues about their interests. The best small talk is about finding things you both have in common. Self-disclosure is therefore an important part of small talk; revealing things about yourself helps the other person either to discover things they have in common with you, or to ask questions about you as a way of continuing the conversation.

Another rule is to ask 'open-ended' rather than closed questions. These are questions that cannot be answered by a simple yes or no. So, for example, instead of asking, 'Do you come here often?', a better bet would be, 'What do you think about this place?' Asking questions 'how' and 'why' is useful because they are difficult to answer briefly. 'How did you get here?' 'How did you come to be in that job?' 'Why do you think they do that?'

Praising people is an important part of small talk; people feel warmly towards those who give them compliments and are more likely to want to stay and talk to someone who gives them positive feedback. The classic small-talk initiator is the 'compliment and question' technique: you start by complimenting someone on some aspect of themselves, like their appearance, and then ask them something about themselves. For example, 'That's a lovely brooch you are wearing, wherever did you get it?'

Having a sense of humour is crucial to small talk, as humour stops things from getting too serious, which usually causes discomfort.

But, above all, don't think of yourself as making small talk; think, instead, of trying to get to know someone and of making their time with you a little more pleasant. The best small talk occurs because of your concern for the other person, not because you want to get something off your chest. This also helps avoid self-consciousness, the killer of small talk. If your small talk has a definite aim, like getting a bigger tip, or taking someone home for the evening, the goal usually becomes transparent and spoils the small talk for the other person.

Finally, even small-talk experts know that not everyone is always willing to make small talk, so you should also know when to give up and shut up. Forcing small talk on those who would rather be left alone is just as poor a social skill as not being able to make small talk at all. Taxi-drivers take note!

The best way of improving your small-talk skills is to start noticing when you are in the hands of an expert small-talker and to observe precisely what they talk about, and how they captivate the other party. You will need to be especially vigilant because good small talk is so engaging that you don't have time to notice you have been taking part in it at all!

Small talk and the use of charm are both ways of getting to know people in the first place. Once you have reached this stage, the next step is to deepen relationships.

One characteristic of people who are better able to develop a wide range of deep relationships is that they are less critical or condemnatory about the variety of ways of experiencing and living; some might term this being open-minded. A good test is the ability to sustain friendships, or at least entertain the possibility of deep relationships, with those who hold differing, or even diametrically opposite, political or religious convictions. The crucial point here is to take a non-judgmental view of human behaviour.

Another trait is that of good communication. For example, just as there is a recognised set of table manners – not speaking with your mouth full and so on – which offend people if broken, so there is a recognised, unspoken set of interaction skills. We are closest to those with whom we find communication easiest and who, as a result, we feel best understand us. Good conversationalists are good listeners; they encourage us to talk by not interrupting, appearing interested in what we are saying and asking clarifying questions to ensure they have truly understood us: 'So you mean...', 'Why was that...' and so on. When they are talking they monitor our reactions to check they are discussing a subject in which we really are interested, and if they detect a lack of interest they change the subject to something more likely to involve us. Good communicators therefore have a wide repertoire of conversation and are interested in your opinion, not just in letting you know theirs. Many people are poor conversationalists simply because communication skills are not formally taught.

Some of these skills sound very false when you first use them, as they seem to detract from the spontaneity of conversation. However, a magical thing happens if you persist in focusing on the quality of the communication, rather than just the content. After a while, you find people opening up to you, being more warm to you, and actively seeking out your company. Soon, these skills become habits and second nature to the way you communicate.

The best way to deepen a relationship is to become 'involved' with the other person. To become involved with others, their opinions and what happens to them in life has to matter to you. You have to share and feel their disappointments and triumphs; by this I mean that their feelings or actions have an impact on you. Research into predictors of long-term marital stability suggests that those marriages doomed to terminate early are those where one partner has little impact on the other person. By this I mean that the other person's feelings or views are of little consequence to you.

Once you've deepened a relationship, you'll need to develop ways of sustaining it. Relationships can only be sustained through some kind of contact, even if this is just letters between geographically distant people. So if you want to maintain your relationships, it is important to devote time to regular contact. However, in addition to contact you should also share an interest or some leisure pursuit. To paraphrase a famous saying of family and marital therapy, 'People who play together stay together'.

Relationships are often most in danger when people you are close to move away or do something you find unacceptable. When people move away, make a conscious effort to stay in touch; develop the patience to persist with geographically distant relationships. When they do something that upsets you, rather than terminate the relationship, let them know you have been hurt or distressed and also learn to forgive. If you insist that everyone conforms to your demands on a relationship, you will be left with very few good relationships indeed. The easiest people to stay close to are those who are the most forgiving of your transgressions. But there is also a paradox: it is often the people we are closest to whom we argue with the most.

Couples, even those who stay together successfully, spend more time arguing than doing practically anything else; in fact, arguing could be described as the favourite activity of couples. This means that sometimes it is not the arguments themselves that are the problem – indeed it is healthier to argue than resentfully to put up with something you do not like without raising the issue – rather it is the way couples argue which can be destructive and unhealthy.

Arguing is inevitable for a number of reasons. First, when two individuals live together, or share some aspect of their lives, compromise is inevitable, as you cannot both expect to get your own way all the time. Sometimes giving up freedom is likely to produce disagreements.

Your partner is the nearest person when you are disgruntled and so will be more exposed to your bad moods than anyone else. This, in turn, creates more opportunity to argue.

Because you are tied together in some way, even if you offend your partner they are unlikely to storm out of the house never to be seen again. Therefore, arguing with a partner can sometimes seem safe; no terrible consequences should flow from it immediately. Interestingly, we do not usually treat others in our lives, such as people at work, in quite such a cavalier way. We are usually more worried about offending them, so we hold back from arguing with them. Likewise, in the early stages of a relationship we hold back from quarrels.

Often we feel our partner is not listening to us carefully enough and believe we are being taken for granted. Having a row sometimes becomes a way of ensuring you get their attention. All couples argue, but what differentiates the healthy relationship from the unhealthy one is the intensity, destructiveness and frequency of arguments. Arguing can be positive, as long as you follow certain guidelines. Think of it as a way of introducing changes.

Phrasing is important and one well-known piece of advice is to turn a complaint into a wish. Instead of focusing on what your partner does to annoy you and so complaining about them, concentrate on what you would like them to do.

The more concrete and practical the things you want your partner to change the better. Rather than wishing for him to be 'a better husband', try and be specific: 'Take out the rubbish and occupy the kids while I make dinner.'

Instead of listing all the things they do which are bad, as in, 'you're late from work again', talk more about how what they are doing is affecting you. 'I worry about you when you're late home from work, perhaps you could ring me!'

Choose the time to have a discussion carefully. Arguments between couples tend to happen at particular times, such as when you return from work or are in a car driving somewhere. Observe these patterns and make a special effort to avoid issues likely to inflame the other at those flash-points.

When your partner does something annoying, mention it immediately, do not just put up with it and let your resentment fester. If you delay mentioning things, this will strain your relationship and lower its general quality. It also makes it difficult for your partner to address the problem when you eventually bring it up long after he or she was actually doing the thing that was wrong.

When you are having an argument, stick to the one issue. Do not indulge in what is known as 'kitchen-sinking', throwing everything else that annoys you into the argument at the same time (i.e. even the kitchen sink). Try to ensure that the argument does not get out of hand and become deeply personal and attacking. The point of an argument is to introduce change, not entrench positions. Couples who are not good at arguing do not have a way of de-escalating an argument once it happens. Keep in mind what your goal is – to achieve change or hurt?

Focus on the behaviour of the other person not on them personally. If you attack the actual person rather than what they are doing they will get defensive and find it difficult to respond.

Relationships commonly end over disputes, particularly ones which make us angry, and so dealing with confrontations is a crucial skill in relationship preservation. But sometimes couples break up because they never confront the conflict between them by not arguing. So how can you tell how close you really are?

HOW CLOSE ARE YOU?

How close or distant couples are seems fundamental in determining whether they will be able to resolve their problems without breaking up or seeking couple therapy. In fact, there are many different kinds of closeness, from sexual closeness – being comfortable with sex – to what is known among psychologists as 'operational closeness' – where daily tasks are shared – to how much of your life you organise together. But the most important closeness is emotional closeness, where you are able to understand and appreciate the feelings and experiences of your partner. In close relationships, your words and actions affect your partner in numerous ways. It is possible to be close in all the other ways mentioned and yet not really be emotionally close. The longer a relationship goes on, the less impact both partners' thoughts and feelings may have on each other, a sure sign of growing distance. To see if you have emotional closeness, try the following quiz. All the questions can also be used to determine how close you are to particular friends and family members as well as partners. Although our closest relationships are with intimate partners, the group of people we feel closest to next are friends, followed by family. The answers will probably differ depending on who you have in mind as you do the quiz.

CLOSENESS SCALE

Each statement is followed by two possible responses: agree or disagree. Read each statement carefully and decide which response best describes how you feel. Then put a tick over the corresponding response. Please respond to every statement. If you are not completely sure which response is more accurate, put the response which you feel is most appropriate. Do not read the scoring explanation before filling out the questionnaire. Do not spend too long on each statement. It is important that you answer each question as honestly as possible.

		AGREE	DISAGREE
1	If we argue, I am right almost always	A	B
2	My favours are always returned	B	A
3	The relationship takes a lot of energy	A	B
4	The relationship affects my moods a lot	B	A
5	Much that I do goes unnoticed	A	B
6	No one else influences my ideas as much	B	A
7	I cannot confide parts of my past	A	B
8	Parts of me are not easy to live with	B	A
9	We usually do not find arguing useful	A	B
10	Our generosity is best with each other	B	A

Add up your score from summing the numbers of As and Bs in each box you have ticked. Your score and the interpretation given below should be treated with caution – this short test is by no means definitive, but may offer a guide to where you stand compared to others around you.

SCORE

8 or more Bs. You are scoring high on closeness, which means, unlike many relationships, you can probably communicate emotionally as well as factually with each other. However, it may be that you are still in the stage of a relationship where there are many rewards for closeness (like giving each other a lot of pleasure) and as yet few costs (like the in-laws or children). Close relationships endure times of pressure only if you feel your complaints about your partner will be heeded.

Between 5 and 7 Bs. Although your relationship is quite close, you may be overestimating your own understanding of exactly how your partner feels in many day-to-day situations. Why not try asking more often, you could be surprised! This may also help break that cycle in which some of your arguments take on a rather repetitive sequence where old grudges are brought up yet again with no hope of constructive resolution.

Between 3 and 5 Bs. There are some problems between yourselves that you may have to agree to live with. The main problem you may find in trying to resolve your problems together is that you both cannot agree on what a close relationship actually means.

Between 0 and 2 Bs. Your relationship is scoring low on closeness and it may be that you prefer a more distant partner, as you find too much closeness stifling. However, if you are dissatisfied with this emotional distance, it is likely that you are both going to have to change a little, rather than continue to argue over which of you should take all the blame for your problems, which may have been happening until now.

The personal freedom people in the West now enjoy to enter and leave sexual/romantic relationships without stigma has many advantages. Playing the field gives the benefit of experience, which may help you to find the 'right' person for you.

But many have forgotten that it also brings with it a host of problems, in that for every new or additional relationship we choose to join, there is usually another we have chosen to leave. And it is the leaving which many cannot cope with, or not easily. Most of us find break-ups difficult and, if you are feeling vulnerable, a break-up may precipitate extreme psychological difficulties, to the extent of suicidal and homicidal behaviour.

Many are aware of the pitfalls of relationships and may choose to avoid entering them, not because they would not enjoy another's company, but because they are aware that the choices currently available mean that any relationship would be relatively short term and would not be worth the trauma of a break-up. In a way, they have worked out for themselves some of the principles of preventive mental health care – taking steps to prevent future distress.

The contemporary view of people who choose to stay single, while all around are making the sexual and romantic hay, is that there must be something wrong with them. Having a partner is seen as some kind of validation of your worthiness as a person. But current research about the consequences of relationship break-down suggests that those who have some kind of life separate from their partner are better able to cope when a partner leaves,[31] yet developing a life of one's own can only be done while alone. The modern prescription for the unhappiness of coping when a partner leaves – to find another partner – seems designed to create greater dependency in the long run, and greater unhappiness when you are left.

By a life of one's own, I mean developing the ability to provide for all your practical and emotional needs without a partner. Those who are independent financially and emotionally from their partner are better able to cope when their partner leaves them. This, alone, is a strong argument for women, in particular, to develop financial independence and maintain it before and during their relationships.

This may seem paradoxical. We are encouraged to see good relationships as those where we become interdependent, but psychologists tell us that the more we can survive without our partner the better for our long-term mental health. The distinction here is that, while sharing our lives with another is a measure of how deep our relationship is, this should not be interpreted as giving up our ability to do things for ourselves if necessary.

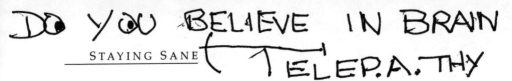

The preventive mental health strategy is to ensure that, while you share your life with someone else, you also maintain your ability to undertake all, or most, of the activities for which you depend on your partner. For many women this means retaining some financial independence, and for many men this means developing some skills of maintaining a home. There is research evidence that those who are less dependent on their partner's assistance in things like household tasks, transport, leisure activities, friends, emotional sharing and future plans are better able to survive relationship breakdown without great stress.[32]

For many women reading this, the thought of trying to maintain financial independence as well as run a home and family may seem impossible and likely to add to their stress levels rather than be a positive mental health strategy. Yet, in my clinical experience, women who cannot cope independently tend to put up with more and more in a relationship. They feel unable to insist that their partner changes, because of the fear that if they annoy him enough he might leave, and they cannot see how they would cope on their own.

This gradually produces unsatisfactory relationships. The best insurance policy for a good relationship is therefore to ensure that you are financially independent enough to leave if you had to, not because you want to but because that knowledge enables you to be stronger when negotiating changes with your partner.

Again, this may seem at first glance to be a rather morbid view of relationships. Maintain your independence and your distance from your partner to help your emotional survival just in case you break up. But do remember that even if you or your partner do not leave each other for another person, inevitably one of you will leave the other because of the certainty of death. The ability to cope with bereavement over the loss of a partner is similarly linked to some form of independence.

Another equally vital thing couples can share is their world view, or their perspective over everything from politics, opinions on friends, values and so on. It seems that the more dependent you are on your partner for sharing your world view, the more distress you will experience after a break-up.[33] Again, the positive mental health strategy is not to get into the situation where your partner appears to be the only one who shares your view of the world.

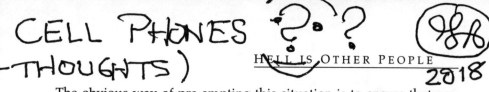
The obvious way of pre-empting this situation is to ensure that you still maintain a strong and wide network of friends and relatives. Having others who make us feel positive about ourselves is crucial when it comes to a break-up as, clearly, if we have lost the only person who made us feel we were worthy of others' love, this loss is going to be all the more devastating.

Another predictor of distress after a break-up is how unexpected the parting is. The more unanticipated it is, the greater the upset and the greater the difficulty of recovering. It may be that the best way not to be surprised by your partner leaving you is to ensure that you maintain emotional and intellectual closeness, so that any small change in their attitude to you becomes immediately apparent.[34]

Once more, the difficult balancing act of positive mental health care becomes apparent. You must be close enough so that any possibility of break-up is signalled far in advance, and yet independent so that if you do break up you can survive after the relationship is over.

One possible advantage of being able to anticipate a break-up is that this gives you time to work out why the relationship isn't working, which may help you cope after the break-up. Not knowing why the two of you are not compatible may take away your confidence to know what kind of person is appropriate for you, which is bound to make you uncertain about new relationships.

Research has shown that a key factor in adjusting to break-up is attributing the break-up to the interaction between the two of you rather than simply putting it down to your partner's deficiencies.[35] Blaming your partner, although doubtless satisfying in the short term, is unlikely to do you any good in the long run. One reason is simply that if they really were so terrible, more fool you for opting for a relationship with them in the first place. Another is if you simply blame them for the break-up, this makes it unlikely you will be able to maintain some kind of relationship or friendship with them afterwards. This makes the loss more complete, and possibly increases the chances that you will end up losing more permanently whatever characteristics you valued in them in the first place.

Finally, I believe that blaming the relationship rather than the other person is simply more realistic and, as I have mentioned before, realism, particularly in terms of your assessment of others, is a cornerstone of positive mental health.

171

To sum up, you will need several things to ensure you survive a relationship break-up. First is financial independence from your partner, then enough life skills to ensure that you can perform most of the tasks of daily life, and then a social network that is independent of your partner. Finally, don't go for the easy option of designating blame.

Since any relationship can theoretically turn negative on us at any time, a key aspect of positive mental health is to build and maintain relationships which are positive, where it would take a lot for the relationship to turn sour. In other words, you need to ensure that people are extensively well-disposed towards you. A key measure of the strength of a friendship is loyalty and a good test of this is whether such people are willing to defend you against attacks when you are out of earshot. This does not mean you should go around trying to please everyone; what it does mean is that building positive relationships is a bit like putting credits in the bank to be drawn on at a time of need when your mental health is not at its best.

This view of relationships is radically different to how we usually try to get on with others, which is to try and get on with those we like, and to ignore those we don't. We make little effort to build relationships with those we find difficult, but with whom a minimal relationship is possible.

This attitude to relationships is partly a product of an age where increasing mobility and communications mean we are not stuck with having to negotiate relationships with those geographically close to us. Our greater choice means we feel more able to dispense with people who appear at first glance to have little in common with us. This is in contrast with earlier times when you really were stuck with whoever your neighbour was. As you knew you might have to rely on him or her in the future, self-interest meant, at the very least, it was wise not to alienate them.

While our greater wealth means we no longer feel this way about our neighbours or relationships in general, in terms of mental health the interdependent approach of the past is actually better for us. When there was less choice, we learnt the skill of getting on with people with whom we might have little in common, or who leave us with a bad first impression, but who also might improve on better acquaintance. The modern tendency is to see time spent trying to build positive relationships with those who don't respond immediately as wasting your time, and obviously as we get busier, we do have less time for those who are clearly not of primary importance to us.

However, one of the things people with poor mental health share is a difficulty in getting on with a wide variety of people. Indeed, the more severe the mental health problems, the more constrained the social circle becomes. So I do believe there is a relationship between our tolerance for getting on with a wide variety of different people and our mental health. Trying to get on with lots of different people makes you more tolerant of others' differences and that tolerance is crucial both to positive mental health, and to deepening your own relationships with those very close to you (like a spouse, parent or relative). This tolerance is also fundamental to the relationship you develop with yourself.

If you look around your social circle and everyone you know well appears to be very much of a type – say, all friends from college, many more men than women, everyone from a particular social class, or colleagues from work – look on this as the earliest signal of some kind of defect in your ability to get on with a wide variety of people. I believe the mentally healthier person is interested in most people and does not dismiss anyone out of hand as being unworthy of getting to know.

Another common theme among those prone to severe clinical depression is a tendency to be unforgiving of their own behaviour or attitudes. The relationship you have to others is a kind of mirror image of the relationship you develop with yourself. This is perhaps why people who like themselves are easier to be with than those who do not.

I need to emphasise that I am not suggesting we should all go out and try to form deep, meaningful relationships with everyone we meet! If you go to this extreme, you fall into the category of a type of mental illness characterised by elation and increased sociability, where patients have a very low threshold for becoming intimate much too quickly with complete strangers. What I am saying is that we should be open to trying to get on as well as possible with as many people who enter our lives as is feasible, without adversely affecting our jobs or our other relationships. I am also suggesting that we should be more open to entertaining relationships with those who might appear very different from us.

The key point is not so much that those who score highly on positive mental health are simply more sociable than those who do not – more that the mentally healthy are more at ease with building relationships. They can do so if they want to and, as with most things in life, this is a skill which takes practice. The mentally healthy are more confident at initiating and deepening relationships with a wide variety of people and in a wide variety of situations. This also means that when things go wrong in a relationship they have a clearer idea of where the problem lies, and are less likely to try over-hard to please someone who is being unreasonable. They are also able to detach themselves from unyielding people with less guilt.

Developing this sense of where the issue really lies in a deteriorating relationship is a crucial part of positive mental health, and this only comes with the confidence that you can get on and have relationships with a wide group of people.

ARE YOU SOCIABLE?

Despite the emphasis on IQ and hard work, social skills are an underestimated cause of success in life and love. Social skills can be learnt by those whose answering machines never use up much tape, but how do you know if you need a top-up? Try this quiz and find out.

How well people get on with others is an important part of mental health; those with a good social support network cope better with stress from jobs, partnerships and families. Perhaps increasingly important in today's fragmenting society, they are also more likely to participate in community activities. Lack of social support has been linked to depression and slower recovery from physical illness. Social support is the availability of people whom we trust, on whom we can rely, and who make us feel cared for and valued. Some people are fortunate to have stumbled on to a good partnership and a group of close friends, while others' charm brings them a social network which helps them find the right marriage and career promotion.

SOCIABLE SCALE

Each statement is followed by two possible responses: agree or disagree. Read each statement carefully and decide which response best describes how you feel. Then put a tick over the corresponding response. Please respond to every statement. If you are not completely sure which response is more accurate, put the response which you feel is most appropriate. Do not read the scoring explanation before filling out the questionnaire. Do not spend too long on each statement. It is important that you answer each question as honestly as possible.

		AGREE	DISAGREE
1	I have someone in whom I confide totally	A	✓ B
2	I feel somewhat apart even among friends	✓ B	A
3	I am a lot of fun to be with	A	✓ B
4	I wish I could be more like other people	B	✓ A
5	Friends come to me for emotional support	✓ A	B
6	I am not important to many others	✓ B	A
7	I find it easy to make new friends	A	✓ B
8	I dislike many people whom I see daily	B	✓ A
9	People who have met me remember me	✓ A	B
10	My close friendships began years ago	✓ B	A

Add up your score from summing the numbers of As and Bs in each box you have ticked. Your score and the interpretation given below should be treated with caution – this short test is by no means definitive, but may offer a guide to where you stand compared to others around you.

4 A's

SCORE

8 or more As. You are very sociable and probably have always been someone near the centre of a social group, hence your charm is probably part of your personality and comes naturally. However, it may be that you pursue your social life a little relentlessly, driven by a fear of being alone, as this is a particularly empty experience for you. Remember that you are vulnerable to ending up in poor-quality relationships, as you might be too afraid of the possible alternative – having to be alone for a while.

Between 5 and 7 As. You are socially confident and have several sources of social support. You have the social skills to know the value of a well-timed compliment, but perhaps this is sometimes a little too well timed to be completely sincere. You have a dilemma between continuing to expand your social network or deepen the relationships you have already. You are perhaps jealous of some other people's ability effortlessly to charm their way into others' affections, though you could probably gain equal ability from a social skills course.

Between 3 and 5 As. Although you would like to be more socially skilled, do remember that the existence of a single confidant is of greater value in meeting emotional needs than having a larger number of more superficial friendships. There is possibly some aspect of your social life which dissatisfies you and it may be worth analysing this in terms of frequency of contact with others, strength of ties, degree of intimacy, expectation of durability, availability, or emotional intensity. One of these aspects is not quite right for you at the moment, and knowing which will help clarify the problem.

Between 0 and 2 As. You are scoring low in sociability and this could be for one of two main reasons: you would rather be left alone and enjoy your own company, or you lack the social skills to get on with others. If the latter is true, this is relatively easily remedied; social skills can be learnt like any other skill, they just require guidance and confidence in yourself. If the first reason for a low score applies to you, remember you are in good company, few truly gifted people created their best work in committees.

I hope what I've explained in this chapter will encourage you to feel that, by understanding how relationships work and how important they are for our mental health, there are plenty of things we can do to improve them.

Relationships are important for mental health for several reasons. First, they develop sensitivity to the feelings of others. Being termed mentally ill is often a social judgement brought about by an unresponsiveness to the feelings of those around us, and the easiest way to stay out of a psychiatric hospital is to learn how to be sensitive to other people.

Second, at times of distress, the company and help of others provides an important buffer. This is partly for emotional support but also for the financial, informational or personal resources others can provide when we need them.

Third, although much mental distress comes from relationships which produce problems, it is usually easier to deal with these if you have other more positive relationships.

Finally, people who end up needing counselling or psychotherapy are usually those who do not have relationships where they can confide intimacies, thus their need for a professional with whom to do this. The surest way to end up needing to see a mental health professional is to have things in your life you need to share, confess or discuss, but not to have anyone with whom you can do it.

So, if you want to immunise yourself against poor mental health you need to protect yourself from bad relationships, as well as feel confident about your ability to build good ones.

The key missing ingredient which helps build relationships is time. Middle-aged adults spend only 7 per cent of their time interacting with friends while teenagers spend around of a third of their waking hours doing so. This is one reason why teenagers have more friends than adults.[36]

But if you spend more time on your friends, what will happen to the time you spend on yourself? I examine the crucial relationship with your self in the next chapter.

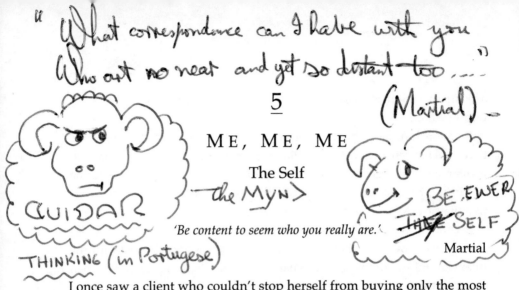

5   (Martial)

ME, ME, ME

The Self

the MYN>

'Be content to seem who you really are.'

Martial

I once saw a client who couldn't stop herself from buying only the most expensive objects – despite her inability to afford them. She soon got into massive debt. However, even though she was married to a wealthy man, she could not bear to tell him about her problem. So, despite the fact he could have bailed her out of her financial difficulties, she just went on spending.

It transpired that her need for designer labels and to entertain her friends at the most pricey restaurants, despite being poorer than all of them, may have been linked to a need to show off.

Perhaps the fact that her family went bankrupt while she was young, and she experienced the transition from being in a wealthy family to being in a poor one, left her with a profound sense of shame at being impoverished. Because her sense of self was closely tied up with material goods, this may have led her to need to display wealth, even when she hadn't any. Just how close this connection was can be deduced from the fact that even the most trivial items she bought – tea towels or toothpicks – had to be the most expensive ones.

> The self lies at the very centre of mental health. Psychologists have studied its various aspects from numerous perspectives, ranging from the notion of self-esteem or how high your personal morale is, to identity or how you determine your individuality. A simple way of understanding this concept is to think about what you would say if asked to describe your make-up. What characteristics would you single out if you introduced yourself to other people? The things you define yourself by – your occupation, your age, or your marital status – are important components of your identity. For example, my client would have chosen objects she owned, where she lived and how big the house was.

MONITORING

Self Esteem

ME, ME, ME

What constitutes your identity and how you view yourself in terms of self-esteem is a crucial aspect of mental health. This is because mental illness is invariably linked to disturbances in your relationship with yourself. The depressed tend to have a very negative view of themselves (low self-esteem), illustrated by their tendency to be overly self-critical.[1] For example, if they fail a job interview they would deduce that this is because they are stupid, rather than because their interview performance might need honing. Maintaining your self-esteem, particularly against criticism from others or in the face of personal failure, may help prevent mental health problems such as clinical depression.

If you are self-punitive, as perfectionists are, berating yourself for not coming up to your own high standards is likely to lead to a negative attitude towards yourself. There are three kinds of perfectionism: 'other-oriented perfectionism', 'self-directed perfectionism' and 'other-imposed perfectionism', and many people who are negative about themselves or suffer from low mood, suffer from at least one form.[2]

The first type, 'other-oriented perfectionism', refers to the tendency to expect other people to be perfect. Inevitably, this leads to stringent evaluations of others' performance, but because the standards you have set are unrealistic they will not attain them. As a result you will feel anger and hostility towards them, and frequently blame them for their failure. 'Self-directed perfectionism' involves a strong motivation to be perfect yourself, which produces compulsive striving towards unrealistic standards and a tendency to be preoccupied with past failures and current flaws. There is also 'other-imposed perfectionism' where you believe, erroneously, that others have unrealistic standards for you and are constantly evaluating you and pressurising you to be perfect. All three forms of perfectionism are commonly found in the same person.

The treatment for perfectionism is to learn to accept fallibility in yourself and others, and to become more flexible, replacing a constant striving for perfection with what is merely good enough. Good self-esteem has nothing to do with being perfect, rather it is feeling good about yourself despite your mistakes.[3] One of the best ways of doing this is to reframe a mistake into something more positive. By 'reframe' psychologists mean changing the way you view something.

To speak without thinking, is to shoot without taking aim. "

Mistakes litter the path to low self-esteem because of the prevailing view of them as negative, an indictment of your self. The more positive reframe would view them instead as teachers or as warnings.

Mistakes are teachers because every error you make also tells you what needs to be corrected to achieve your goal. Mistakes provide valuable information about what works and what does not. Indeed, they are the inevitable consequence of learning new skills. This explains why those most fearful of making mistakes have most trouble learning. There is a grand term from the psychology of learning – 'successive approximation'– which makes mistakes sound very wise indeed. This simply means getting nearer and nearer to triumphant achievement through the information provided by mistakes.

When you first learn to drive, all the mistakes you make are simply successive approximations to driving skilfully. The same is true with learning to read and write. Just as a good teacher is patient with a learner's errors, so you need to be patient with yourself and your mistakes.

Anthony Robbins, the American self-help guru, puts the most positive spin on mistakes and failure by pointing out a close link between success and failure. Success, he argues, usually can only follow from the kind of valuable experience gained from failure. Successful people are not those who have never experienced failure. Rather it is how they responded to failure, what they took away from it, and how they changed their performance as a result, which produced success.[4]

Mistakes are also useful as warnings – indicators that you may need to give more attention to an area of life you had been ignoring. If you find you have annoyed someone a surprising amount, this may be an indicator you have become a little less sensitive to others'feelings recently, and you may need to be more sympathetic in the future.

Reframe mistakes as warnings and lessons or the fear of error will stifle your self-expression and spontaneity. You cannot be relaxed if you are always focused on avoiding disappointing others, or not being awkward or appearing stupid.

That is why therapists frequently urge patients to be kinder to themselves. Excessively high standards also point to another potential problem, for if there is a major discrepancy between your real self and your ideal self, you are more likely to suffer poor mental health.[5] If the gap is large enough, it is likely to contribute to self-loathing, which underpins much mental illness.

Those who have most difficulty with this are termed self-critical – people who constantly judge and scrutinise themselves in negative ways.[6] Attacking yourself is bound to lead to low self-esteem which, as mentioned, has been found to be at the centre of poor mental health.[7] Research into which women will be predisposed to get a serious depressive illness has found four key factors: lack of an intimate confiding partner or husband, no employment outside the home, three or more young children at home and the loss of a mother while the woman was a child. All of these could cause depression because of their effects on self-esteem.[8]

If your partner does not want to talk to you about yourself, this will make you feel less valued. If you are not working outside the home and have three children to look after, you will have no opportunity to experience alternative roles (other than being a mother) in which you might gain a sense of importance. And losing a parent at an early age may have left you feeling uncherished, also diminishing your sense of worth.

This sense of consequence is vital to mental health. For example, the degree to which you rate yourself in a globally negative way, using terms like 'pathetic' or 'inadequate', predicts future chronic low mood.[9]

Researchers following up a group of children who started out normal, found that those who tended to be more self-critical at the age of 12 ended up by the age of 31 having completed fewer years of education, with lower occupational status, more dissatisfaction with relationships and deeper psychological problems.[10]

You might have thought that being self-critical could have a positive side – in striving to impress others the self-critical could reassure themselves of their own self-worth. But if you are too self-critical this can be very painful, as self-criticism is activated by experiencing failure, so you would probably avoid situations where you might fail or be criticised. As the possibility of failure usually coincides with the opportunity for success, avoidance of the first also removes the possibility of the second.

DO YOU LIKE YOURSELF?

Over time we develop fairly clear-cut views about ourselves, for example, whether we consider ourselves good at our work or whether we are good listeners. These judgements usually involve a process whereby we compare ourselves to others. Depending on how we compare, we usually come to a basic decision about whether we like ourselves or not. The strength of this feeling of affection for ourselves has a huge bearing on our self-esteem, or morale, and may be a major factor in our mental health.

Psychologists have known for a long time that painfully negative thoughts and feelings about the self are one of the strongest predictors of depression in people. One reason for this is that those who like themselves are kinder to themselves and regard their failures as indicators of circumstance, not character. People who hate themselves regard failures as evidence of how awful they are, and expect only failure in the future. A crucial part of treatment for psychiatric problems is often simply learning how to like yourself again. To check how much you like yourself, try the following quiz.

SELF-LIKING SCALE

Each statement is followed by two possible responses: agree or disagree. Read each statement carefully and decide which response best describes how you feel. Then put a tick over the corresponding response. Please respond to every statement. If you are not completely sure which response is more accurate, put the response which you feel is most appropriate. Do not read the scoring explanation before filling out the questionnaire. Do not spend too long on each statement. It is important that you answer each question as honestly as possible.

		AGREE	DISAGREE
1	I can do most things, not just my work, as well as most others	✓ A	B
2	If others knew more about me, they would like me less	B	✓ A

HEARS
HELPING
TO THINK..

LISTEN
WITH
MUTTER
ERDE..

182

30 MPG. 3L SUBARU OUTBACK
H6 Petrol 2004

BUILDING PRESERVATIONS

		AGREE	DISAGREE
3	If others do not like me, that is usually due to them, not me	✓ A	B

RENOVATIONS.

| 4 | There are many things about me I dare not tell anyone | B | ✓ A |

INFORMATIONS

| 5 | I have very few regrets about things I did in the past | ✓ A | B |

CONFIRMATIONS

| 6 | When I think about myself, I focus on what needs to change | ✓ B | A |

COMMUNICATIONS

| 7 | My parents think of themselves as lucky to have had me | ✓ A | B |

DETERMINATIONS

| 8 | Most people do not like themselves most of the time | B | ✓ A |

SOLUTIONS

| 9 | I was born with several talents few others have | A | ✓ B |

COGITATIONS

| 10 | I swear as much at myself as others | B | ✓ A |

CONSIDERATIONS

Add up your score from summing the numbers of As and Bs in each box you have ticked. Your score and the interpretation given below should be treated with caution – this short test is by no means definitive, but may offer a guide to where you stand compared to others around you.

SCORE   *8 A's*

8 or more As. You are scoring very high indeed on self-liking and this could explain your confidence in getting on with others; because you like yourself you expect others to as well. However, one problem with the extent to which you compare yourself favourably with others is that it can lead to complacency and you could be less interested in changing yourself, or improving

47·4 MPG   2 L SUBARU OUTBACK 183
F.4.   DIESEL 2016

aspects of your character, than most. It may also come as a bit of a shock to realise that the high regard in which you hold yourself is unlikely to be shared by quite as many of your acquaintances as you might imagine. One reason you may like yourself so much is your tendency not be brutally honest with yourself when you have not lived up to your own expectations.

Between 5 and 7 As. You are scoring just above average for self-liking and it appears either your self-esteem is particularly high at the moment because you are basking in the glow of some recent positive event in your life, or you could have a long-term tendency to feel good about yourself. What you may not realise is that your feelings about yourself largely account for how much you enjoy life, and those times when things are going badly coincide with times when your liking for yourself dips. At these times you may need to be kinder to yourself.

Between 3 and 5 As. You are scoring around average to just below average for self-liking and this may mean that while there are many aspects of your character that you like, there are also several that you find unacceptable, and which you suspect are also unacceptable to many you know. Since what others think about us is crucial in determining how we feel about ourselves, it is likely that people who are important in your life have communicated very negative messages about some aspect of your character. You may need to realise that their disapproval may actually say much more about them than about you; maybe you need to find people whom you can trust to tell you things about yourself which actually say more about you than about them.

Between 0 and 2 As. You are scoring very low indeed on self-liking, which could mean that for a lot of the time you actively dislike yourself, perhaps even hating many aspects of yourself. It may be that your parents did not provide much support during your childhood or adolescence, or an intimate relationship later in life was responsible for making you feel bad about yourself. You need to seek out those who make you feel good about yourself and build on those relationships; perhaps you even have a tendency to stay for too long with those who end up making you feel bad about yourself.

One of the key themes of this book is to learn how to accept yourself and not be plagued by constant internal criticism: in other words, to feel at ease with yourself. A key factor in doing this is to put your mistakes into perspective. Dwelling in an unproductive way on our mistakes can dominate our thoughts or memories when we are feeling low, perpetuating the mood. Our mistakes are one of the most corrosive agents, capable of eating away at our self-esteem.

In my experience of trying to help the mentally ill improve their mental state, getting them to change their attitude to their mistakes is one of the most difficult areas in treatment.

The definition of a mistake is an occasion in the past where, looking back, you believe you would have made a different decision, knowing what you know now.[11] You would not have accepted that promotion which led to such stress, or taken on that huge bank loan. In other words, mistakes become apparent only with hindsight. However, excessively self-critical people castigate themselves for their errors, which means that life for them is excessively painful (for, despite our best efforts, it is impossible to avoid making mistakes). Making mistakes does not mean that you are a terrible person, though that is what those with poor mental health tend to believe.

People with low self-esteem because of excessive self-criticism need to recall that, at the time they made the decision which led to the error, they were probably making the best choice, given all the information available to them. Logically, then, the only way to avoid ever making mistakes is always to have perfect and complete knowledge about the outcome, which is, of course, impossible.

It is also important to forgive yourself for mistakes. You have already been punished once by the natural consequences of your error, do not punish yourself twice by hating yourself for being fallible. Try, instead, to learn what this mistake tells you about yourself and your decision-making, and before making similar decisions in the future, pay more attention to the possible consequences. However, do not let your upset about your mistake prevent you from trying new projects. The only way to avoid ever making errors is always to stick to what you already do and never try anything new. Unfortunately, if you do that, you will experience no personal growth at all.

185

One mentally unhealthy response to mistakes is to try to avoid them by forever delaying making decisions. The tendency to procrastinate is a feature of obsession which is linked to mental ill-health. Obsessionals are often dominated by a perfectionistic streak which means they are terrified of getting things wrong. This leads to indecision, as their terror renders them impotent, locking them into delaying action until they can be absolutely certain they have made the right decision. Yet, since this is certainly impossible, it is better to act and accept errors for what they are – judgements which only hindsight has shown to be mistakes – rather than personal incompetence.

You can certainly use errors as a way of improving your decision-making and this becomes especially important when you notice you have made the same kind of mistake on more than one occasion. One of the best ways to improve is to examine why you made the wrong decision. Think back to your mental state at the time: what were the concerns which dominated your thinking? Were they the appropriate concerns? In particular, were you focusing on all the possible consequences of your options, and did you take into account the likely negative implications of your choice? If not, then when you find yourself in a similar position again, remember to place more emphasis on these.

The kind of repeated errors those caught in a bad pattern tend to make usually involve habits like addictions to alcohol or other dependency-forming substances, or vicious cycles like the diet-binge cycle of the bulimic. The alcoholic resolves not to drink again because alcohol is destroying his life. However, one day he passes a pub and needs to decide whether to go in for a quick drink or not. He almost inevitably goes in and, after his first drink, finds himself back on the treadmill of alcoholism.

He may bitterly regret his decision later. However, in order not to repeat it, once he has become sober again he must examine what was going through his mind at the time of his decision whether to drink, and see what was uppermost and what was suppressed. He needs to ensure that when he finds himself in the same position again, he does not make the same choice. He will have a different set of priorities and be more aware of the negative consequences of his decision to have a 'harmless' drink. For every action we take there are costs and benefits.

Actions we later regret are usually those where we did not take enough account of the costs. Often this is because the potential benefits divert our attention away from unpalatable costs.

It is not reasonable to blame yourself the first time you make an error, but if you repeat your mistakes, it is appropriate to call into question your decision-making skills, and decide that you need to improve them.

If you would like to minimise your mistake-making capacity, try to consider as much as possible the negative consequences of your decisions before you make your choice.

One of the reasons people repeat errors is that they have failed to understand themselves fully. The alcoholic fails to appreciate his inability to control himself and the extent of his need for alcohol, and perhaps what role it plays in his life. This is why he has difficulty comprehending that everyone else seems to know he will go in for a drink if he walks past his favourite pub, while he believes he has the willpower not to.

Those with addictions, or habit problems, or who find it difficult to resist temptation, tend to have a misplaced faith in the concept of 'willpower'. They may believe they can just will themselves not to drink if they simply put their mind to it. Psychologists, in contrast, believe it is wisest to assume willpower does not exist, as it is such an unreliable entity. Better instead not to go anywhere near a pub, or the scene of any temptation, so that your willpower does not get tested. Indeed, the further you are from the source of temptation, the longer you give yourself to change your mind as you start the journey towards the object of your desire and weakness. It is easier to turn down an invitation to go to a pub in the first place than to sit in a bar refusing drinks all evening.

Psychologists point out that there are two kinds of self-control being exercised here. In 'decisional self-control' you make the single choice to turn down the invitation to the pub, whereas in 'protracted self-control' you have to resist temptation continually over a long period of time (for example, sitting in the pub trying to avoid looking at the bottles behind the bar). Decisional self-control is clearly the better one to go for.

Another example of this is the compulsion to use credit cards. Some people have difficulty controlling their excessive spending but still carry credit cards, relying on willpower to curb their spendthrift tendency. Instead, they need to tear up their credit cards and take only as much cash as they need for basic necessities. The only sure way to start breaking a habit is to assume that willpower does not exist and that if you face temptation you will succumb. Then to avoid enticement. I discuss how to gain self-control, an important part of self-management, later in this chapter.

But even though the alcoholic who goes back for a drink has undoubtedly made an error, this does not mean he is a terrible person with no self-worth whatsoever. This is the kind of conclusion those who are vulnerable to low self-esteem get caught up in. The link they make is that if, for example, they fail an exam, or experience personal set-back or failure, they must be an appalling person. Therapists call this tendency 'self-rating'. You are rating how worthwhile you are by your achievements or failures.[12]

This is a major error. It is impossible, logically or reasonably, to rate yourself. The self is too complex an entity to be evaluated by performance in one or two areas. However, there does seem to be an inevitable tendency to make overall, or global, judgements about ourselves from individual, limited acts. Even if you keep failing a particular exam, the conclusion that you are fundamentally stupid is still unwarranted. However, this is the conclusion to which people with low self-esteem are prone. All it could logically mean is that your performance at exams needs to improve if you are to attain your goal of passing them. It may even mean that the subject you are studying is not something for which you have much aptitude. But notice that the words I am using to interpret what repetitive failure might mean are less likely to produce low self-esteem than the statement, 'This means I must be stupid'.

If you conclude that you are dumb, you make a global judgement about your fundamental intelligence and take a fixed view about what the future holds. This is simply jumping to conclusions following limited evidence.

Poor performance is just that, an aspect of your behaviour that needs improvement. So to draw the conclusion that the inability to attain your goals in one area has implications for your whole personality or self is simply illogical, as well as being dangerous for your mental health. If you do decide you are stupid you will be less likely to persevere in the face of failure, or even apply for testing situations, thus getting locked into a self-fulfilling prophecy of failure.

Why, then, do we tend to make overall judgements about people based on small aspects of their behaviour? A friend forgets a birthday and our irritation with their carelessness spills over, so that we feel they aren't really a good enough friend. There are several possible reasons for this tendency. One is that whenever we did something wrong our parents might have scolded us by declaring we were 'bad children'. This statement implicitly makes a global inference from one small piece of behaviour. So, for example, if we broke something we would be told off with words like, 'You're always breaking things; you are such a bad child!', when a more accurate assessment of the situation is that you may be careless when holding objects, but this does not mean you are a bad person.

Parents say this kind of thing either because the particular behaviour they are exasperated by is important to them or they are just not thinking about the implications of their words. What they may not realise is that they could be setting the stage for self-esteem problems later in their child's life, if, for example, that child digests the idea that being bad in one way (at exams, for instance) means they are a hopeless person. A better way to criticise people is to comment on the precise way in which their performance has displeased you and not make global inferences.

Clearly this is difficult to do in the heat of the moment. However, you can do it with practice. Criticising others by referring only to the specific problem, and not generalising the criticism to an attack on them as people, is an important life and assertiveness skill. So, for example, instead of saying to your partner, 'You were late for our date, you are inconsiderate, feckless and irresponsible', try being more strictly accurate (and helpful) by saying, 'Late again! I'm certainly going to have to do something about your time-keeping'.

The more you get used to criticising other people's specific behaviour and not their whole self, the more you will also get into the habit of doing this to yourself when you use 'internal self-talk'. As I will mention in more detail in a later chapter, 'So, You Think You are Sane?', internal self-talk is now thought by psychologists and psychiatrists to be crucial to improving your mental health.

Another reason we leap to global judgements is to motivate ourselves to perform well at certain times, like in exams or interviews. We have to tell ourselves how important these things are and how terrible it would be if we were not successful. Parents often use this technique to try to get their children to perform better at certain tasks. However, just because it is important to pass an exam, it still does not mean you are a terrible person if you fail.

Even if you are lazy and do not try at exams, fritter away your parents'money and commit adultery, none of these things mean you are a terrible person. You may be unpunctual and lazy, which may not help you with your relationships; but you may also be good with children and a creative painter. The conclusion that you are a terrible person because of your deficiencies implies a value judgement that being lazy is a more important attribute than kindness to children.

Society is certainly based on a shared acceptance of certain judgements and you're not doing your mental health any good if you don't recognise this; it would certainly be unhelpful for your relationships if you did not feel concerned about poor time-keeping of appointments, for example. However, the mentally healthy approach is to seek such an improvement because punctuality is helpful to yourself and others, not because being a poor time-keeper means you are a worthless person. We all have to make value judgements, but they are just that – our opinion, based on what we think is important in life. No single poor performance in one aspect of life should condemn us to feeling that we are worthless. The phrase to remember is 'rate the behaviour, not the person'.

To gain control over our self-esteem we need to give up rating ourselves altogether. Instead of judging whether we are intrinsically good or bad, we have to learn self-acceptance – we just are; we merely exist. But this does not mean you should not rate your *performance* whether at time-keeping or being a good parent or being thrifty with the intention of improving your skills in areas where you perceive yourself to be deficient.

But what happens when we decide that performing a particular task will determine whether we are intrinsically worthwhile? For example, many women stay locked into loveless, and even abusive, marriages because they believe seeking a divorce means they are a failure. Splitting up may mean your performance in the arena of matrimony needs improvement, but it does not mean you are worthless. If only such women could see this, they would be freer to take the step towards freedom.

Another good example is a person caught in a vicious cycle: the bulimic starts the day resolving not to eat as a way of losing weight (she already believes not being her ideal weight means she is an entirely worthless person, which is why so much of her day is devoted to weight reduction) but by the end of the day she is so hungry she has a binge. Then she feels so completely useless that she has to correct the problem immediately by throwing up or getting rid of the food in some equally drastic manner such as laxative abuse.

In each of these examples, as in much of poor mental health, self-worth has become too centred on one particular aspect of life. If everything – your self-esteem and whether you feel life is worth living – is focused on only one element of your existence, this will justify putting so much at stake to keep this part of your life as you would like it. Extreme behaviour then becomes justified, either in tolerating an untenable situation (the woman who should seek a divorce) or in pursuing a goal (the bulimic who desires weight-reduction).

Many women want to lose weight, and a healthy attitude would be that, while that goal may be desirable, and failures regrettable, it is not reasonable to pivot your whole self-worth on this aspect of being. If you do decide to found all your self-worth on one aspect of yourself, your weight, for example, that is your choice; you have elevated weight into a central aspect of your self and must be prepared to accept the poor mental health which will invariably follow. While people are free to make these decisions, the mentally unhealthy strategy is to fail to realise that they are individual choices. In my experience, the bulimic, for example, fails to understand that it is she who has chosen to centre her whole life around weight. Many people consider their weight important, but not so significant they are willing to risk death (which is a chance if you regularly throw up after meals, and so destabilise your body's minerals, which affects the heart). If you do decide weight is more important than your life, at least understand that you have made this choice and that it is by no means an inevitable one.

We all have a cluster of attributes, some of which need improving more than others, but none of them can lead to any logical conclusion about ourselves as total entities; the self is just too multifarious to allow such a simplistic judgement.

Another reason why drawing conclusions about ourselves is so commonplace and tempting is that forming such a judgement is intellectually a lot easier than trying to reconcile the mass of contradictions we all appear to be. We are often good in one area and bad in another, and the human mind tries to simplify things by lumping everything together and coming to some final summary. We pigeonhole people; if we do not like one aspect of them, we tend to assume we will not like any other aspect. And, of course, trying not to rate or judge ourselves and accepting that a failure relates to one specific instance involves more intellectual work than just drawing a simple, hasty conclusion.

For example, if you are rebuffed trying to chat someone up at a party, a natural (but illogical) conclusion is that you are not attractive to members of the opposite sex. If you deduce this, you also conclude that you should give up trying to chat people up. This makes life easier, as it protects you from further failures. But the more reasonable conclusion is that your chat-up performance needs improvement, or that a particular person did not find you attractive, but others may. This deduction logically means that you should keep on chatting people up. That's hard, because I suspect we would all prefer to simplify our lives and protect ourselves from potentially unpleasant situations. So, negative global deductions about ourselves appear an intellectually economical way of dealing with the world, which protects us from going down avenues which only seem to lead to more pain.

Another reason for making such sweeping judgements about ourselves is that, if we didn't, the truly random and chaotic nature of the world would become more apparent. Assuming that we are doomed to be no good at relationships explains our poor performance and protects us from the more difficult realisation that life is more random than that; if we keep trying to socialise we may get on with some people, but we may still fail with others, often for reasons beyond our control. Giving up rating yourself leads to the next step, again important in mental health, which is self-acceptance, or even feeling good about yourself.

Many find that no matter how much they achieve, it never seems to be enough to bring them happiness. Their life always seems to be about the next thing; how the next pay rise, or the next material acquisition, will finally bring them contentment.[13] But when they finally get the next thing, this happiness never seems to last long.

Psychologists believe those who constantly strive for success are really driven by a need for recognition and praise from others. Once the recognition they receive for their latest achievement begins to die away, they become restless for yet more success. The need for praise from others is really about a deep desire to be accepted. However, only when you accept yourself as good enough will you stop needing recognition from others, and only then will you finally be happy.

Religion may be a short-cut to such self-acceptance for various reasons. One possible explanation is that religious people do not believe that anyone, other than God or some kind of deity, can judge self-worth. If you believe this then, obviously, as long as you stick to the tenets of your religious faith, your self-worth is not at risk from the kind of everyday failures in life that endanger the non-religious.

No one really knows why, but there is a general consensus that religion or some kind of religious belief protects people from mental illness, and perhaps this could be one of the explanations. But if you are not religious, taking up religion simply to help protect your mental health may not be successful and is clearly not your local priest's idea of a religious conversion. So is there a way for the less religious to benefit from this 'self-worth-protecting' aspect of religion?

One possibility is suggested by a relatively new concept termed 'self-complexity' by psychologists, which explains one of the great puzzles in mental health – why people react in contrasting ways to various negative life events. One way of explaining this is to suppose that the events most likely to effect your mental health seriously are those that are most tied up with your self-identity or self-esteem.

If, for example, you lose your job as a journalist, and you had your whole heart set on journalism, this will cause more distress than if you lost the same job, but your self-identity and self-esteem were linked to other aspects of your life, such as being a good parent. In other words, failures in activities which do not matter so much to us are less problematic than those in areas which do.

According to this perspective, losses such as a partner leaving or dying, or the loss of an object or a job, are more potent the more closely they relate to our view and understanding of ourselves.[14] So if, whenever you talk about yourself, you find you mention your partner a lot, it is likely that being married is an important part of your self-

FALLAR (To Speak) SEM CUIDAR (Without) (Portugese Proverb).

identity and perhaps even your self-esteem. For you, the loss of your partner is likely to cause more mental health problems than for someone whose identity or self-esteem is more tied up in other areas.

It also seems that the number of different sources people have for their self-esteem and self-identity varies. Some people's self-esteem is tied up entirely with one aspect of their lives, their career, for example. If this is going well, almost everything else in their lives could be in ruins and they would still be happy. However, should their career begin to falter, they would be more at risk of suffering a serious deterioration in mental health than those whose self-esteem is more widely invested.[15]

The stockbroker whose job and earnings are her only source of self-esteem is storing up trouble for her mental health. Even if her career is going well, at some time she will have to retire, and then she will lose her only source of self-esteem. According to my theory, she will then suffer poor mental health. Even if things are going well, from time to time threats to her earnings or career will arise, and she is likely to respond with much greater anxiety than if her self-esteem was invested in other aspects of life, such as being good at tennis and having a good relationship with her children. Similarly, the mother who invests all her emotional energy in her children will suffer problems when they leave home or go through the inevitable teenage rebellion.

The obvious conclusion is that positive mental health strategies should include ensuring that your self-esteem is not focused in only one or two areas of life.[16]

The stability of those areas from which you derive your self-esteem is also important. A rapidly changing or unstable part of your life in which you have invested your self-esteem is likely to lead to precarious mental health. In this context, psychologists have speculated that one reason some religious people seem so resilient in terms of mental health is that they have invested their self-esteem and self-identity in a source (God) which is not only unchanging, but also never likely to leave them.[17] For example, one study[18] has calculated that adults' feelings of well-being can be predicted just as much by how religious they are as by their marital or economic status. However, even religious people suffer crises of faith and are more likely to experience poor mental health if their self-identity and self-esteem are solely tied up with their religion.

Thinking/Caring) ... É Atirar sem Apontar (1st to Shoot
without taking Aim) ...

The implication is therefore that having a complicated self, not a simple one is more likely to preserve mental health. The interesting thing about this concept is that it is slightly counterintuitive, in that when the public are asked how to preserve mental health, their opinion veers on the side of simplifying their life. While it might be quite stressful to develop a complex self, it would seem this investment pays off in the long run.

Now, suppose you have noticed that you need to increase your complexity by involving yourself in more spheres in life. You have decided to change. But how do you achieve it? Outside assistance, such as a therapist, is the usual way we think about achieving change, but the trend is for psychologists to encourage patients to change without too much interference from professionals.

The techniques involved are part of an approach called 'self-management'.[19] Central to self-management is the idea of self-control, a fundamental principle of mental health. Conversely, pivotal to mental illness is an inability to control the self. For example, depressed people cannot control their mood so that they do not feel bad all the time, and those who suffer from obsessive compulsive disorders would dearly like to stop washing their hands repeatedly, for example, but cannot. I would go as far as saying that it is not, in fact, the low mood or excessive washing of hands which are the central problems in these mental illnesses, but more that depressed people fear, and are frustrated by, their inability to lift their mood at all. I suspect they would be willing to tolerate the low mood a lot more easily if they felt they had some control over the situation.

Similarly, if my excessive hand-washers were able to wash their hands as much as they liked in the privacy of their own homes, the disorder would not cause them that many problems, and they may never come to the notice of a psychiatrist or even seek help themselves. It is their inability to control their hand-washing, so they may have to wash excessively at work, or that their hand-washing makes them late for the office, which draws them to public attention.

Lack of control means being unable to de-prioritise one set of needs (the need to hand-wash) because another set is more important (not annoying the boss). As mentioned, I believe that at the cornerstone of all mental illness lies an inability to exert self-control. The mentally ill

195

cannot integrate themselves into society, or get on with others, or pursue their life goals, because they cannot control a part of their lives they wish they could.

Lack of self-control is more obviously at the centre of a group of illnesses termed 'disorders of impulse-control'. These range from people who cannot control their tempers to people who cannot control their drinking, eating, smoking, drug-taking or spending. There is even some evidence that impulse-control disorders may have been on the increase over the last two to three decades in the West, which could account for the puzzling perceived increase in mental disorder, even in a time of greater prosperity.

One possible explanation for the increase in the numbers of people unable to control their impulses may lie in our child-rearing practices. Because of our greater wealth we are in a better position than ever before to give our children the things they demand. However, this may work to their disadvantage, in that in the past when we told them they could not have the toy they wanted because we could not afford it, we were inadvertently teaching them self-control.

But control does not just mean learning to stop doing something. It also means being able to start doing something you have put off, such as work, a new project, the redecorating, revising for an exam or regular exercise. Common to both scenarios is that a current behaviour needs to be stopped or decreased because it causes suffering and replaced by another action. Usually, the reason change is difficult is because the present behaviour produces some positive consequences, albeit short-term ones (for example, a smoker gets pleasure from inhalation) while the behaviour the person would like to change to might be beneficial in the long term (stopping smoking will help prevent lung cancer). Often, the short-term reward proves more alluring and powerful than the long-term benefit.

When we change our behaviour in a way we would like we are exerting self-control. So if we can stop ourselves spending less, give up unhealthy foods or take up jogging – simply because we want to – we are demonstrating self-control.

The key to change is to start with what psychologists call an 'ABC analysis'. ABC stands for Antecedents, Behaviour and Consequences. This illustrates the fundamental principle that all behaviour occurs as a result of events that have already taken place – the antecedent (the shopaholic finding herself in a shopping mall) and has consequences (the thrill of the purchase). To change behaviour you have to alter either the antecedents or the consequences, and often both.

It may not even be that the behaviour you are stuck with gives any apparent immediate benefits. The battered wife stays, not because she enjoys being beaten up, but more often because she fears the consequences of leaving immediately (not being able to cope alone and possibly never finding another partner) more than she fears the repercussions of staying with an abusive partner. She puts off leaving in the hope that things will change.

But why do we find it so easy to put off until tomorrow things we would be better doing today? Or why do we tend to have difficulty resisting the temptation to do something which gives us immediate pleasure but holds long-term negative consequences?

One theory is that these are universal human weaknesses. We evolved as animals in a rapidly changing and uncertain world. In such situations, where the future is difficult to foresee, immediate pleasures are at least certain, but the future less so, in which case a sacrifice for long-term benefit may be wasted effort.[20] However, the world we now inhabit is very different from the haphazard one of the jungle we evolved in. The long-term benefit of giving up smoking or drinking is one we are much more likely to experience if only we could overcome our natural, perhaps even almost biological, tendency to grab the short-term benefit at the expense of the long-term gain.

In spite of this natural tendency, we can increase our self-control by using self-management techniques. The first step therapists take when teaching clients self-control is to check whether the patient believes the particular behaviour under question is actually under their command in the first place. Addiction models, which help clients to believe that they, for example, smoke because they are 'addicted', tend to erode the belief that they can learn to control themselves and so stop smoking. Clearly it is more difficult to feel that you can gain discipline if you believe you are out of control, than if you believe the behaviour is under your power but that you just need some help to improve your self-management.

To avoid arguments with those in favour of the addiction model, I prefer to suggest that the real issue is whether it is possible to gain control of yourself. There is much research to suggest you can, and the group of people who successfully learn to control themselves without seeking help have a stronger belief that it is feasible than those who are less successful in learning to control themselves.[21] So, for example, one of the most powerful predictors of who will end a stop-smoking programme by dropping out is how strongly the smoker believes he can gain control over his smoking. Those who do not have much faith in their ability to give up before they start a programme tend to be much less successful in the attempt.

Psychologists have termed this 'self-efficacy', a belief in your self's ability to succeed. So, before you can start gaining self-control, you have to be convinced of your ability to do so. You can do this by focusing on previous similar successes in the past, as well as by checking with those who have achieved what you would like to, and seeing that they are not dramatically different from yourself.

The next step in self-management is to start monitoring the behaviour or aspect of self you would like to change. This may sound like an obvious thing to do, but it is surprising exactly how much of our everyday behaviour is routine and goes on below the level of conscious awareness, for example, driving after you have been doing it for many years. Given that the behaviour you may want to change displeases you, one way of defending yourself against your upset is to pay less attention to yourself when you are doing it. So, if you suddenly decided that you wanted to change the way you drive, your first step would be to pay more attention to exactly how you drive now.

Simply becoming more aware of the behaviour – 'self-monitoring', as psychologists term it – is a very powerful self-management technique, and often produces change by itself. One common self-monitoring strategy is to keep a diary of when and how you perform the behaviour you would like to change. For example, you might keep a diary of every cigarette you have during the day if you want to give up, or every item of food if you want to reach a more healthy weight. Keeping a record of a habit you wish to change has been found, in itself, to produce a modification. This may be because the diary raises your awareness of the aspect of yourself you are unhappy about, which raises your general unhappiness. You then seek to resolve this by making more effort to change.

As a general point, part of any long-term positive mental health strategy is to become more aware of self generally and, in particular, those aspects of your behaviour which may need to change.

Increased self-monitoring is particularly useful if you make a note of the ABCs as well (antecedents, behaviours and consequences). Awareness of the precise antecedents and consequences helps you to change them to bring about change in yourself.

Once you have completed your self-monitoring exercise the next step is to implement change. A big mistake people make here is simply to try to stop what they have been doing, for example, to cease smoking. This produces a vacuum and they usually end up by returning to the thing they were trying to stop doing, because that behaviour filled a gap in their life in the first place. Instead, never think of simply stopping a behaviour but always try to replace it with something else, so you are not taking anything away from yourself, but merely substituting it.

So, instead of simply stopping smoking, replace cigarettes with chewing gum, or go for a short walk whenever the urge to smoke comes upon you, and so on. Obviously, whatever you use as a substitute has to be more or less as easy to do, as the behaviour you are trying to stop, and should also serve the same function. So if you smoke because it cheers you up, replace it with something else which also pleases you.

The other reason why the replacement technique is so much more powerful than simply stopping is that an important part of self-management is to give yourself some short-term rewards for your sacrifice to keep you going until the long-term benefits start to be felt. Short-term rewards could be as simple as self-praise. If you are trying to give up smoking and go a day without a cigarette your self-praise might be 'Well done, you are stronger than you thought.'Or, for example, if you tend to overspend whenever you go down the high street, when you successfully return without spending, reward yourself with an indulgence you do not normally allow yourself (but obviously make it one that doesn't mean spending money). Involving a partner can be helpful; he or she could reward you in some pre-arranged way if you steer clear of overspending.

Receiving benefits from partners or others for successfully avoiding problem behaviour is an important part of self-management, as what usually tends to happen is that you get no reward for good behaviour but a telling-off when you indulge in the problem activity. A tense atmosphere at home means that the only pleasant refuge becomes the very setting in which to compound your problem – the bar, the drug dealer's den, or the shopping mall.

Considering the difficulty of short-term gains over long-term ones, another important aspect is to increase your motivation by staying conscious of all your reasons for change. Keep a list of the positive benefits of making your short-term sacrifice and an inventory of the negative consequences of your continued inability to change. For example, a practical way of reminding yourself of the consequences of unhelpful behaviour of overeating is to put a mirror on the fridge door. A graph is also a powerful tool, particularly if drawn on a large scale, using daily weighings, so the positive impact of the short-term sacrifice becomes more immediately apparent.

Any attempt to change is unlikely to be successful straight away and relapses are likely. Gradualism is a keynote to self-management, together with the acceptance that set-backs are inevitable and do not mean the programme is not working, more that the causes of failure need to be investigated and planned for.

Another tip is altering your consequences so you reward yourself for a behaviour you want to take up – let's say jogging. You promise yourself a new item of clothing for every extra mile you add to your daily run. The sophisticated psychological technique is to start with big rewards for small positive changes at the very beginning of a new programme to alter your behaviour. But as you do alter and the new behaviour you want to establish becomes a habit, change the reward structure so you have to do just a bit more to get the same reward.

Needless to say, if no antecedents change (for example, the triggers for the behaviour still remain) and no consequences alter, behaviour will not usually change. There has been a recent resurgence of interest in the manipulation of antecedents as a tool to changing behaviour because psychologists recognise they may have over-emphasised the importance of consequences at the expense of antecedents.[22]

Put simply, if you are a shopaholic you cannot shop unless you have money and are in a store: these are antecedents to purchasing. To reduce your spending behaviour, travel with only just enough for your immediate journey and avoid going anywhere near shops – change your route to and from work if necessary.

A good example of changing a consequence would be, for example, if you wanted to cure your temper tantrums – ask your girlfriend to not speak to you for an hour every time you lose your temper.

Another good example is an otherwise well-controlled lady who rang in for advice on one of my *This Morning* TV phone-ins. She wanted to help to gain control over the terrific swearing and upset with other drivers she indulged in while driving.

She was a staunch Labour Party supporter and so I instructed her to make sure her passengers (usually her children and husband) made certain whenever she swore she had to make a donation to the Conservative Party. She agreed to the programme and my understanding is that her swearing has stopped!

Other sophisticated approaches to self-control include taking account of the problem of delay. Saving up for a special treat means doing without now. Learning to deal with delay and the ensuing frustration is pivotal to self-control.

Distraction seems a vital technique here, occupying yourself with another pleasurable activity so your mind doesn't keep focusing on the short-term benefit you would rather be enjoying right now. Even the way you think about the activity you are trying to put off through self-control – for example, eating ice-cream if you are on a diet – can influence your ability to stay out of the freezer. The evidence is that if you keep thinking about the taste and pleasure of the ice-cream (so-called 'hot'thoughts as opposed to other aspects) this diminishes self-control whereas focusing on negative features such as the calories or the expense (so-called 'cool'thoughts) would not.[23]

Simply trying to anticipate the problems of resisting temptation and taking a few practical steps to limit your ability to respond when in the grip of strong emotions, while you have a chance to plan coolly, is probably the biggest contribution to self-control. This is called pre-commitment. Perhaps the earliest example in recorded history of this principle appears in the *Odyssey*, in which Odysseus had to sail past the sirens. Because the sound of their voices was so alluring other sailors had always rowed towards them and foundered on rocks. Odysseus had to pre-commit to stop this from happening to him. Before he was near the sirens, and therefore under their influence, Odysseus planned how to resist temptation when he heard them. He asked his crew to tie him to the mast and ordered them not to untie him until they had reached their goal. Meanwhile his crew had to be free to row, so he stopped their ears with wax to prevent them from hearing the sirens' calls.[24]

You may have a sneaking suspicion from the above examples that, in some instances (the alcoholic who forever seems to be 'just passing' his favourite pub) people not only verge on having poor self-management, but seem almost to go out of their way to create situations (or antecedents) which will endanger their resolve. I discuss self-sabotage, which is one possible explanation of what is going on here, later in this chapter. Another theory is that these people are deceiving themselves, or have poor insight into whether they really want to give up their bad habit, despite their claims to be motivated to do so.

The kind of behaviours addicts indulge in, such as while off drugs offering to post a letter which takes them near their favourite dealer and so increases the likelihood of relapse, are so frequent that a term has been created to describe them: Seemingly Irrelevant Behaviours, or SIBs. The beauty of SIBs is that they seem, at first glance, irrelevant to whether the addict steers clear of temptation, which is why long-suffering spouses or friends innocently allow them to post the letter. But, sure enough, this behaviour does make relapse more likely.

We have all indulged in SIBs. You just happen to glance through the paper, just happen to see what is on TV, which merely seems to be an important programme, which means that the planned evening's revision for your exam goes pear-shaped. Looking through the papers and not doing revision do not, at first glance, appear connected, but by a chain of events a relapse is thus engineered. Effective self-management means learning from past SIBs and avoiding the first event in the chain. Once the sequence begins it is more difficult to stop than it is to prevent it starting in the first place.

A good way to avoid SIBs is to examine them carefully. Start with the final behaviour, which you now regret doing, and work backwards through the sequence of events which led you there. Examine at which stages you could have decided to do something else, which would have prevented the undesirable behaviour occurring. In particular, look for the moment at which choosing another more helpful path would have been easiest, and aim to ensure that you do not find yourself at the early part of the progression again. The mentally unhealthy tend to focus only on the final episode in the chain of behaviour and wonder how to stop it happening when they get to this end stage. The mentally healthy go back further and anticipate which behaviours will lead to unhelpful actions in the future.

For example, I often see women alcoholics who can clearly identify that being alone at home precipitates their drinking. They try to fight the urge to drink alcohol under these conditions when they should instead prevent themselves from being alone at home in the first place. Being alone at home is the antecedent which needs to change.

But suppose, despite the best self-management advice, that people continue to insist that they really are trying to give up their habit, yet always seem to be alone at home, or out posting letters. In other words, they often find themselves in situations where relapse appears to everyone else to be inevitable?

Self-deception is another important aspect of poor mental health. The opposite of this might be termed insight – the ability to examine yourself dispassionately – and this is highly valued amongst psychiatrists as predicting a good prognosis from treatment. Many clinicians find that it is extremely difficult to help people gain insight if they have none already.

Self-deception is shored up by rationalisations and explanations we give to ourselves and others about why we do what we do, and which protect us from the real truth about ourselves. They hide the real reason why we did what we did.[25] Jeff Goldblum, in the film *The Big Chill*, points out that rationalisations are more important than sex. When his friends scoff, he asks them when was the last time they had a day without rationalisations?

Rationalisations tend to become epidemic when we are trying to protect a view we have developed of ourselves. For example, if I have decided that I am good at my job, any evidence to the contrary (mistakes I make) will be rationalised away by alternative explanations. The fault lies with colleagues or my manager, for example, which serve to protect me from the realisation that I may not be as good at my work as I had thought. Hence, the way to exterminate rationalisations, stop self-deception and encourage insight is to try to remain as open-minded as possible about yourself. Aim to draw conclusions from the evidence, rather than trying to accommodate the evidence to your view of yourself. The more you get attached to an opinion of yourself, the more prone to rationalisation you will be whenever evidence to the contrary comes along.

The problem with this suggestion is that it appears to run slightly counter to the advice given in the later chapter on resilience and hardiness ('I Will Survive'), which points out the mental health benefits of positive illusions about the self. As in all aspects of mental health, balance is important, and while I believe you should err on the side of being positive about yourself, you should also strive to be open-minded and avoid rationalisations. This is because, if your drive to hold a positive self-image leads you to being over-protective of your self, you will not lead a very healthy life in terms of exploring the self and the world.

Much of our behaviour has a hidden purpose, so hidden we often forget it's there. In addition to the goals we have every day (getting to work, doing the shopping), we also have more clandestine aspirations which determine our behaviour. In any encounter with another person, we try to behave in ways that reflect our desire to be viewed as reasonable, competent, attractive and moral people.

In reality, almost all our behaviour in the presence of others is designed to generate a positive view of ourselves, and severe discomfort occurs when our ability to do this is undermined. For instance, people who avoid parties and clubs, despite the desire to meet others, are simply avoiding the mortification which accompanies threats to their ability to project a positive identity.

If you stay at home alone, no matter how isolated you are, you are still in your comfort zone. The fear of going out is more that being alone at a crowded party will be humiliating. *Public* social rejection undermines our self-esteem much more than being alone at home, although in fact staying in is also a form of social rejection, *but one we do to ourselves in secret*. It is better to be alone but unseen, rather than alone *and seen to be alone*.

Embarrassment also results from the flustered uncertainty that follows not knowing how to behave in unfamiliar situations. Since we are accustomed to most of the people we encounter, we have evolved a set of rules and expectations about what to do and when – something psychologists call a 'script'. This governs most of our usual dealings with others. So another border between our comfort and discomfort zones can now be mapped: new situations where our scripts are inadequate to cope with the need to show ourselves in a positive light.

The couple who never talk frankly about sex, or those who avoid new social encounters, do so because they do not feel they know what to say or when to speak. They have no script on which to rely, precisely because these are confrontations they rarely have to contend with. But there will be many occasions when people do *not* have a script, such as when new situations occur. There is a difference between simply being exposed to a situation and having to develop a new script and not being prepared to change the old script you are using for an existing situation.

The only way to evolve an adequate script is to expose yourself to these situations more frequently. However, the necessary loss of poise which accompanies learning new scripts is something people are so averse to that they retreat to their comfort zone instead.

In fact, whenever we present ourselves to others we risk rejection of some kind. The form this takes may be flagrant, but it is more frequently quite subtle, perhaps only a missed beat in the rhythm of conversation. Just how negative an experience this is can be seen by our anxiety whenever we have misplaced our 'scripts'. If you are already worried about what the boss thinks of you, having to be with her in an unfamiliar situation outside the office is an even more anxiety-laden experience. Your evolved script for dealing with her at work may not stretch to the new social situation, while your usual social scripts may not be appropriate for your boss.

An interesting paradox of the comfort zone thus emerges, in that an individual's psychological strength lies not in avoiding negative judgements by others, but in a willingness to confront the risk of appraisal. Independence requires the ability to accept others' opposition to yourself, such as rejection, without a lowered sense of personal worth. The independent person often does things which might end in rejection, but is not deterred, because she does not see rejection as a reflection of her own value.

Many people avoid seeking professional help for their emotional problems, precisely because talking about themselves enters discomfort territory. Publicly owning up to our vulnerabilities is often just too discordant with the way we like to appear, so these avoiders never make it into treatment. For others, psychiatric treatment plays a valuable role because the professional insists on confronting and staying in discomfort zone territory, something the client would otherwise resist, and which friends are unlikely to persist with.

Many people in therapy, particularly those in treatment for a long time, cleverly avoid confronting those areas of life which lie outside their comfort zone. For them, therapy is really an indulgence because it has become too comfortable. Even if you are not in therapy beware, if you are feeling too comfortable about life, it may be because you are really not exploring it, or yourself, at all.

It seems that it requires a certain basic confidence in yourself, or perhaps self-acceptance, before you can feel safe putting yourself in situations where your sense of self might be threatened. People with a basic feeling of inferiority are the ones prone to rationalisation and self-deception. Self-acceptance allows you to contemplate possible negative aspects of your self without feeling you completely lack self-worth.

Despite some people's apparent best efforts at self-management to help achieve their goals, they still seem perpetually to fail. This raises the vexed question of motivation. Many people believe they dearly would like what they seem unable to achieve. They really believe they want to pass the exam, yet seem unable to revise properly.

We can all think of ways we would like to be more successful – in relationships, at work, with money, in our ability to attract others – and a vast industry has grown up selling the idea that if you want success all you have to do is buy this cosmetic, attend that seminar, or go to that therapy.

All these products and services are based on a simple premise: that you are not succeeding because there is something you have not got, even if it's just confidence. However, research psychologists have in recent years begun to wonder if the best way to understand success is to turn the question upside down; that instead, we should focus on why we fail.

The startling conclusion of asking the question in this way is that we often fail *because we decide to*. Not consciously, psychologists hasten to add, but unconsciously, yet still deliberately, we set about trying to succeed in ways that actually guarantee failure. This extremely common behaviour is termed self-defeating, self-handicapping or self-sabotage in a new field of study, which is little-known now but is likely to become the dominant self-help ideology of the nineties.

The exciting new message is: if you want to succeed at whatever goal you set yourself, be it career or relationships, the major obstacles you need to remove are not those erected by others, but the impediments you have placed in your own way!

Before these new developments in psychology, those who self-sabotaged were thought to be a small group labelled 'masochists'. Masochists are brought up by critical, rejecting parents whom they were forever trying to please. They tend to seek out critical and rejecting partners, from whom they similarly try desperately to get approval. When these relationships fail, masochists suppress their anger and blame themselves.

Again, because of their upbringing, masochists feel they are entitled to their pleasures only as long as they suffer for them first, and they further believe that if they suffer now, they will be rewarded in the future.

But there really are very few people who enjoy suffering (and therefore failure), so the old-fashioned idea of masochism has largely been replaced by the concept of the self-defeating personality, which experts now think is much more common.

There are several ways we deliberately choose self-destructive strategies. One way we defeat ourselves is by using approaches or responses that are ineffective; these are called *counterproductive* strategies. Sometimes people don't realise, even subconsciously, that their strategies are counterproductive because they really do want to succeed. They may not understand this, but what is really happening is that other goals, which probably have a greater priority, get in the way of the goals which they believe are their highest priority but which are not really.

So, for example, some who are obese may claim that weight reduction is their dearest wish, yet they may really be eating to cheer themselves up, in which case their dearest wish is really to be cheerful. It may be they would have to give up on cheerfulness for a while to achieve weight reduction. Certainly, it might be impossible to keep both goals and expect to achieve them together.

An example comes from a patient of mine, Joan, 32, a successful manager in a large company, whose relationships never lasted long. She began to fear being 'left on the shelf'. Increasingly desperate, she came to see me after trying innumerable dating agencies, eager to know what else she should be doing. In fact, she was attractive and charming, but whenever she met someone the relationship never lasted because she was so ingratiating and tried to get too close too soon. Her boyfriend would feel smothered and would soon abandon her. Her behaviour produced exactly the opposite outcome to what she wanted. While she was not necessarily deliberately or consciously sabotaging her chances, she was using a counterproductive strategy.

We often use counterproductive strategies like this because we have been taught (particularly as children) that failure occurs because we do not try hard enough. Fear of failure leads us to work even more strenuously. In fact, our escalating effort is self-defeating because we are working hard with an ineffective strategy, channelling all our energy away from capable behaviour. Sometimes we need to work less hard to get what we want. When Joan began to see that the real obstacle in her way was her own neediness, she was then paradoxically able to stand a chance of getting what she wanted. The appeal of such a counterproductive strategy is that we can always console ourselves with, 'Well, it's not my fault, look how hard I work, it must be their fault.'

Sometimes failure has benefits as well, and we choose failure, again unconsciously, because it has some positive consequences, and success may have some negative repercussions. This category of self-defeating behaviour is designated a *trade-off*. Many trade-off situations involve an immediate and a distant goal, and we often make poor choices by focusing on the short-term consequences at the expense of the long-term ones.

For example, another client of mine, Mary, 25, a primary school teacher, came to me complaining of severe shyness. Like all shy people, Mary was painfully aware of how she might be perceived by others, and her fear of making a bad impression caused her to avoid social encounters rather than risk embarrassment and rejection. Whenever she was thrust into meeting men, for example at work, Mary would nod and smile but would not disclose much about herself. As a result, developing any intimacy was out of the question.

Mary's shy behaviour was self-destructive in the context of her desire to be liked and to have friends. Her social anxiety caused her to avoid meeting others, so her chances of making friends or experiencing intimacy were diminished. In fact, Mary's shyness had become self-perpetuating, for social isolation prevented her from developing the social skills and contacts that could enable her to overcome her isolation. Once Mary could recognise her self-defeating behaviour – that avoiding the short-term discomfort of meeting people was perpetuating her shyness – she could break the vicious cycle which linked her shyness to loneliness.

Another trade-off we all make is the fact that failure produces sympathy from our friends and lovers, while success can often induce jealousy. We may choose failure so as not to disrupt the status quo in our relationships, or simply to preserve sympathy.

A deeper problem with success is that, once we start being successful, it generates the expectation of future success among friends and even in ourselves. Poor performance means we escape such expectations, and therefore anxiety and pressure. Success may also have unsettling consequences, for example, a promotion may move us away from the part of the office where our friends are. This means success could have long-term negative consequences, which is why we may opt to avoid it.

But perhaps the most startling reason for self-handicapping is that by doing this we cloud the issue of whether success or failure tells us anything about ourselves. Given that discovering how attractive or intelligent we *really* are might be deeply painful, particularly if we don't feel we could do anything about it, the advantage of a self-defeating strategy is that it provides a ready excuse if we fail.

A good example of this is a patient, John, 29, referred to me by his GP for impotence. It turned out that John had not really managed to get satisfactory erections for several years and was getting increasingly desperate, particularly as he had just embarked on a new relationship with a woman he was very much in love with. I reassured him that if he followed the techniques I taught him he would recover his erections. However, despite scrupulously sticking to the advice, his impotence remained stubbornly resistant to treatment.

I soon discovered that John had started drinking heavily prior to sex and that this was inhibiting his erections. He claimed this was due to his increased anxiety about sex. On deeper therapeutic exploration, he began to see he had also actually begun to harbour a deep fear that if he used the fail-safe treatment I had prescribed and still failed to get an erection, this would have serious implications for his manhood.

Drinking in this context provided a neat excuse whenever he failed to get an erection and did not jeopardise his own view of his masculinity.

Success and failure have powerful implications for our view of ourselves and our self-esteem, yet self-esteem is something we instinctively act to protect at all times. Sabotaging a forthcoming performance provides an external explanation for failure ('It was the drink', 'I didn't have enough time to revise'), other than our own ineptitude, where an internal explanation would be much more damaging to our view of ourselves.

If success occurs despite the obstacles we place in its way, we can always claim even more ability for ourselves. We can say to ourselves, 'I succeeded despite all I had to drink, so I must really be very good.'

Creating obstacles to one's success that can carry the blame for anticipated failure is called a *discounting principle*, where failure under extenuating circumstances is not taken as proof of incompetence. The contrasting *augmentation principle* is when success despite obstacles is seen as evidence of especially high ability.

The beauty of self-handicapping is that it has benefits regardless of whether we succeed or fail; we can preserve our sense of self-esteem whatever happens. However, the huge drawback is that self-handicapping inherently increases the probability of failure. Self-handicapping is thus the ultimate trade-off that sacrifices your chances for success in exchange for protection from the implications of failure, and extra credit for success.

People most likely to use self-handicapping unconsciously are those trying to avoid finding out the truth about their abilities. Thus we must ask ourselves the painful question, are we really ready to face the excruciating reality about our proficiencies? Because it is only if we can face the fact that we might be less good than we think that we can begin to tackle our problems effectively and do something about our abilities.

Ultimately, you cannot genuinely desire success in anything and not also desire challenge, as the chapter on resilience discusses. If you do not question your personal beliefs about your own ability, there is no personal challenge; and with no personal challenge, there is no personal growth. Any success that does not require personal growth is probably a success born of setting our sights too low.

But what about those who appear to have surely conquered self-sabotaging, the famous? Psychologists and psychiatrists have tended to neglect the formal study of fame, possibly because it is difficult to recruit celebrities into experiments. Can they teach us anything about our relationship with ourselves which might assist our understanding of mental health?

A recent list of the famous who die young from suicide or suicidal behaviour includes (with their age at death in brackets) River Phoenix (23), Jimi Hendrix (27), Kurt Cobain (27), Jim Morrison (27), Janis Joplin (27), Sylvia Plath (30) and Marilyn Monroe (36), has been added to most recently by Michael Hutchence, the Australian rock star, rekindling the issue of the psychopathology of fame.

Michael Hutchence's death remains a puzzle – the lead singer of the phenomenally successful Australian pop group INXS was described by close friends as happy only days before his death. He had just begun working on a solo album, he was hailed as an international sex symbol, his pop group INXS had the rare distinction in the fraught rock world of containing the six original members who put the band together in the late 1970s, and they had sold more than twenty-five million albums. But antidepressants were found scattered on the floor of his hotel bedroom and his death was apparently suicide.

Yet some recent psychological research into the link between self-obsession, fame and suicide suggests that becoming well known could be a psychological hazard.

The previous view in psychiatry had been that the kind of personality which pursues and finally attains fame may be one already predisposed to psychological problems, even before suffering the stress of celebrity. This personality type, the narcissist, was first described by Freud in 1914.

The psychoanalytic writer Michael Beldoch has since eloquently summarised what has happened in psychoanalysis:

What hysteria and the obsessive neuroses were to Freud and his early colleagues ... at the beginning of the century, the narcissistic disorders are to the workaday analyst in the last few decades before the next millenium. Today's patients by and large do not suffer from hysterical paralyses of the legs or hand-washing compulsions; instead it is their very psychic

selves that have gone numb or that they must scrub and
rescrub in an exhausting and unending effort to come clean.

According to the latest edition of the diagnostic bible of the American
Psychiatric Association – the *Diagnostic and Statistical Manual of Mental
Disorders* – narcissists exhibit extreme self-absorption and egocentrism,
display self-aggrandisement and self-importance, and fantasise of
unlimited ability, power, wealth and beauty. Narcissists tend to be
exhibitionistic and they frequently express a need for attention and
admiration. In relationships narcissists communicate a sense of
entitlement and tend toward exploitativeness, while failing to empathise
with the feelings of others.

The paradox for the self-absorbed is they are more reliant on others as a
source of self-esteem support than the rest of us, and herein lies the
narcissist's dilemma: the narcissist holds in contempt the very individuals
upon whom he or she is dependent for positive regard and affirmation.

The Freudian explanation for the origins of narcissism focuses on the
fact that all infants start out narcissists – completely self-absorbed – and
eventually learn as they grow that love and praise must be earned
through socially responsive behaviour. But adult narcissists never learn
this principle of reciprocation. Freudians join with Marxists in
suggesting that modern society might be particularly prone to
producing narcissists because making our children happy has become
the major theme of contemporary family life. Our alienation from the
world of work and society outside the home means we have turned
inwards to our children – now depending on them overmuch for our
own reassurance as to our lovableness and worth. This puts children in
the driving seat of the relationship.

However, the recent psychological research has contradicted these
ideas by suggesting it is the effect of becoming well known that is the
real psychological hazard, not the personality type seeking fame. The
research by Mark Schaller,[26] a Psychologist at the University of British
Columbia, analysed the lyrics of Kurt Cobain, the rock star who
committed suicide, Cole Porter (one of the most prolific songwriters of
the twentieth century) and the short stories of writer John Cheever (who
won the Putlitzer Prize in 1978), to investigate whether there was an
increase in self-referential statements (for example use of pronouns like

I, me, myself, mine) in their writings, between before and after they became famous.

Narcissists have been shown to use more self-reference than others in the form of personal pronouns in their speech, possibly signifying greater self-absorption and egocentrism, but his hypothesis was that famous people might become more self-conscious and therefore self-obsessed as a result of the increased public attention they face, and this may be reflected in increased self-reference in their work.

Psychologists argue that heightened self-consciousness and introspection may lead to mental illness or depression because increased self-consciousness makes you more aware of your failings, weaknesses and things you do not like about yourself. Psychologists even suggest prolonged self-focus will inevitably always uncover some perceived personal shortcomings, causing disquiet.

Schaller argues that famous people are prone to self-focus because other people are aware of them, and the well known are more likely to be aware that other people are aware of them, leading to enhanced self-consciousness. Most people feel self-conscious entering a room if everyone turns to look at them, and famous people experience that all the time. Other procedures used by psychologists in experiments to elevate self-consciousness and self-awareness in their subjects include pointing cameras at them, tape-recording them or making them stand out in a crowd – all of which are the inevitable accompaniments of fame.

When ordinary people become self-conscious they can usually retreat from such situations, ensuring this experience does not become too aversive. The well known usually have less control over this – and it is this problem of fame which may make the consequence of celebrity particularly unpleasant and enduring, so increasing the likelihood of self-destruction in this group.

When we find a mismatch between the self we would like to be and the self we in fact find ourselves, a disjunction we are more aware of when self-conscious, we can often lower our ideals. Schaller argues famous people have more difficulty reducing their expectations for themselves because of their ambition. Also their ideals might be imposed upon celebrities by fans, which they then feel a pressure to live up to.

Backing up this theory, Mark Schaller did indeed find an increase in self-reference in lyrics and writings of these famous three people. This increase was particularly significant in the case of John Cheever and Cole Porter.

Schaller's paper was published in the *Journal of Personality* before Michael Hutchence's death. Had he included Hutchence's lyrics in his analysis, would the theory apply to his situation? Indeed the ratio of personal pronouns increased from 0.47 in his first album's lyrics to 0.51 in his last, but this is too small an increase to be attributable to anything other than chance or random variation.

What is most interesting about this analysis is how high the ratio of personal pronouns to all pronouns is for Michael Hutchence (0.47) even before fame, a similarly high ratio as found for Kurt Cobain (0.506). This contrasts with the much lower ratios found before fame for John Cheever (0.200) and Cole Porter (0.247). It suggests the smaller increase in self-obsession in Kurt Cobain and Michael Hutchence from before to after fame is explained by what in statistics is called a 'ceiling effect': it might be that in some people self-obsession is already so high that it would have been difficult for it to get any higher.

Therefore it may be that Schaller's theory is pertinent to other forms of fame, but does not apply to the particular celebrity of the rock star, who, from this research, already seems self-absorbed before the onset of fame. One possible explanation might be the relative youth of rock stars compared to most other professions, where success is more likely to follow some gestation period of training and productivity before fame supervenes. The bottom line case is that excessive attention when you are too young might not be good for you.

In this chapter, I have concentrated on the self and tried to show that your relationship with your self is crucial to positive mental health.

The first step in building a healthy relationship is to stop self-rating; do not judge your entire self-worth solely on one or two aspects of personal performance. Instead, you need to accept yourself as someone who just exists and about whom global negative judgements are illogical and unhelpful.

You need to insulate yourself against poor mental health by ensuring greater self-complexity so that poor performances, untoward events or losses in one sphere of life, do not produce catastrophic collapses in feelings of self-worth.

You need to learn self-management, whereby you control yourself and orient yourself towards positive, long-term goals and avoid the trap of falling for short-term benefits instead.

You need to develop greater self-understanding of your hierarchy of goals so you can more easily see why some goals seem to elude you, despite your best efforts. Self-deception needs to be avoided by declining to accept rationalisations, and insight promoted by not being afraid to examine dispassionately whatever evidence there might be that a previously treasured view of yourself should be given up.

Self-sabotage needs to be circumvented by ensuring that your failures are not something you collude in because of the kind of hidden agenda discussed in this chapter.

The real self encompasses your views on your standing in comparison with others over things like physical appearance, athletic ability and acceptance by others. Your ideal self reflects your desire for improvements in these areas. Your 'ought-to-be'self is what you think other people, society, your parents or your peers want you to be. The fantasy self is what you would be if absolutely anything was possible, and often reflects a desire for celebrity, wealth, power and magical abilities. A large discrepancy between how you think you are and how others would like you to be seems to be associated with chronic elevated levels of anxiety, while a big gap between your real and ideal selves seems linked with depression. A preoccupation with the chasm between your fantasy self and your real self is connected to distracting day-dreams and anger over unfulfilled imaginings.[27]

So it seems there is a strong bond between poor mood and discrepancies in your view of your self. While in this chapter I have looked at how to correct these gaps between your real self and ideal self, in the next I will turn to what other techniques are available for managing moods, and also seek to explain the differences between moods like anxiety and depression.

6

CRYING IS GOOD FOR YOU

Moods

'Happiness is not a state to arrive at, but a manner of travelling.'
Margaret Lee Runbeck

A mood is a kind of response to what is happening to us, and uncontrolled emotions can produce retorts which we later bitterly regret. Research which sheds light on factors affecting mood has been conducted into how people in extreme predicaments (such as hostages) behave.

One organisation at the forefront of this research is the psychological department at the FBI Training Division at Quantico, Virginia, whose psychologists study situations, such as terrorist hostage-taking incidents, which FBI operatives commonly wrestle with. Their findings can then be used to advise flight crews, for example, at risk of encountering these problems.

To gain insight into how human behaviour changes under extreme circumstances the Special Operations and Research Staff (SOARS) from this division conduct field training exercises (FTXs) where the SOARS team play terrorists, abduct a number of people and negotiate with the authorities.[1]

These simulations use members of the public who have volunteered for the exercise and consented to become hostages. To add to the realism, 'terrorists' make the abduction unexpectedly while the 'hostages' believe they are being driven elsewhere. The terrorists have automatic weapons (containing blanks), cover their faces with ski masks or *kaffiyeh* (a Middle Eastern headpiece), and explode hand grenades. The bus driver and his assistant, who are in collusion with the exercise, break concealed blood bags to simulate the effects of being shot. So realistic is the exercise that a number of the hostages commented during the debriefings that they really thought during the four days they were held that they were actually being abducted.

Amongst other issues, the FBI psychologists investigate which hostages cope best with this extremely stressful situation. Their findings suggest that there are two different strategies in stress-management situations: those that are problem-focused and those that are emotion-focused.[2]

I deal with problem-focused techniques in greater detail in the next chapter, 'So, You Think You Are Sane?'. They can be summarised as action-oriented and problem-solving approaches, where you take steps to modify the stressor. In the case of being kept hostage, such a technique might be to try to escape or disarm the terrorists. Or in the case of builders botching the kitchen extension they were contracted to carry out, it might be to sack or complain to them, withhold payment until their performance improved, or write about them to their professional association.

Problem-solving or being action-oriented, seems to work well in situations where there really is something you can do to improve your lot, but not in other situations. For example, a different approach is required if you are being held hostage by heavily armed gunmen. In such an instance the problem-solver who attempts to escape usually ends up being shot! Problem-solvers who are vigorous and optimistic about their ability to change their circumstances, and in the case of work who rise up their career ladder as a result, can come a bit unstuck here.

The harsh lesson is that some problems *cannot* be solved. Instead, a more effective approach is to adopt a strategy where you try not be too upset by what is happening to you while waiting for others to change the situation. In the case of being taken hostage you would sit tight, try not to annoy the gunmen, and wait to be rescued. This is what is known as an emotion-focused strategy.

A vital aspect of stress management therefore appears to be the ability to appraise your problem accurately and decide whether or not it is solvable. For example, if you chose the emotion-focused strategy and made friends with the gunmen while your colleagues chose a problem-solving approach and successfully escaped, you would not have judged the situation correctly. On other occasions of course the terrorists might appear fairly competent, and you would be wise to discard problem-solving in favour of emotion-focused strategies. These are described in detail later in this chapter.

In the FBI research the hostages taught to use emotion-focused techniques reported the lowest anxiety, emotional distress levels and behavioural disturbance during captivity, while those trained in problem-focused preparation responded the most poorly of all.[3]

Unlike problem-focused strategies, emotion-focused techniques are designed not to change your environment, but to make you feel less upset about whatever is causing your distress. This involves not thinking too much about the problem – or even positively avoiding dwelling on it – and is termed an avoidance strategy. Particular techniques would include learning to relax when you are feeling tense, redirecting your attention to the most pleasant aspect of your environment, 'wishful thinking' and 'minimisation of threat' (constructing an overly positive interpretation of what is going on).

So, if you are taken hostage, wishful thinking might involve imagining landing a lucrative book deal about your experiences once you get out; minimisation of threat means believing help is on its way and that the terrorists do not really want to kill you; while attention redirection might involve trying to make friends with those around you.

This research therefore suggests that part of the art of staying sane is learning when to use the appropriate strategy. Another element is learning to manipulate your moods so that you are as little distressed as possible by negative events. My experience certainly supports this view. Often, when patients first start seeing me at the Maudsley, they pursue a particular approach regardless of the situation, which of course makes them feel worse. They then have no means of influencing their resulting poor mood. Once they learn to use different strategies, their control over their moods improves dramatically.

This is because people differ in their expectations of being able to regulate their moods. People who do not expect to be able to control their moods tend, in general, to feel worse.[4] This is because if you believe you can regulate your emotions you try to do so, and usually succeed, but if you don't think you can alter your feelings you don't try and so your mood remains for longer. Some people react to their moods with helplessness and tend to wallow in a low mood, listening to downbeat songs, for example, or looking miserable. Others, in contrast, fight low moods by doing something upbeat or exhilarating.

Our emotions are a major part of human experience, and responsible for much of our behaviour. Sometimes people explain their actions by saying that they make them feel good, or stop them from feeling bad. How you feel from moment to moment, i.e. the mood you are in, is a major factor in your quality of life. But perhaps even more fundamental is that simply being in a good mood can make unpleasant tasks seem nicer, while being in a foul mood can dampen the most agreeable experiences.

Despite their importance in determining mental health, moods remain largely ignored in academic debate. Even the best-known philosophers and psychologists seem to find them too difficult to study, and tend to avoid attempting to understand them.[5]

However, they are vital because true personal freedom and positive mental health require you to control your emotions, not be at their mercy. In other words, people who are put in a bad mood or affected for days by something relatively trivial, such as a train being delayed or by a quarrel with a partner, will be unable to attend to other tasks properly. Their bad mood will harm performance.

If you can learn to regulate your moods, you will help prevent long periods or extremes of unpleasant emotions. You may still feel low or depressed on occasion but this is likely to be just for a few hours rather than for days at a time. Most importantly, your emotional response to the situation will also be more appropriate. We all attempt to regulate our mood in one way or another, but our most frequently used methods are often unhealthy ones – drug-taking, cigarette-smoking or dependence on alcohol, for example.

People can go to extremes to improve their moods. For example, some of my patients say they can release tension by cutting themselves. The minute they see blood oozing from a self-inflicted wound they claim they feel a tremendous sense of relief, even euphoria.

A more common method of distracting you from an unpleasant mood is something less extreme, such as going shopping. Buying something may give you a short-term boost but in the long term proves expensive and works only for a short time. Moreover, the guilt over expensive, needless purchases ends up making retail therapy an unhealthy means of mood regulation. Yet much of advertising, and the presentation of shops and stores is designed to manipulate our moods as a way of getting us to spend: if you own this car it will increase the excitement in your life; if you wear that make-up you will be more attractive and less lonely, are the subliminal messages we are bombarded with. Improved mood management is therefore not only good for your mental health, but will also save you money!

Perhaps the most fundamental reason we act on our environment is that producing changes in the world around us is one of the most effective ways of altering our mood. When someone buys a Ferrari, it is not so much simply in order to possess a quantity of metal; it is rather that owning a Ferrari makes them feel good. We produce change in the world around us so that those changes in turn will alter our mood for the better.

But before you can regulate your moods, you need to become aware of them. Strange as it sounds, people are often not sufficiently in tune with their moods to realise when they are feeling bad-tempered, depressed or overexcited. This is partly because our moods are personal experiences which are difficult to compare with what others are going through. This also explains why empathy – the attempt to feed back to someone that you understand how they are feeling – is one of most personally rewarding aspects of relationships. We feel closest to those who we think understand our feelings best.

A mother once brought a teenager to see me because he appeared to be getting uncharacteristically tired during the morning at school, and would then wake up later on in the day. Was this sudden increased tiredness a sign of mental illness? I managed to get the teenager to tell me that the start of the term coincided with a new subject, which he hated, first thing in the morning, while his favourite lessons took place in the afternoon. The tiredness was merely a sign of boredom, but the teenager had genuine difficulty in identifying it as such.

Labelling a mood correctly is vital because only when you know what your mood is will you know how to change it. Boredom will obviously require a different approach from fatigue, although both may feel similar.

The obvious way of improving your ability to label your moods correctly is to think about them. Research indicates that, as might be expected, this helps to increase mood awareness.[6] One question it is helpful to ask, for instance, is, 'Exactly what am I feeling? '

This sounds simple in theory. In practice analysing your emotions is more difficult. First, the fact that there are so many different words for emotions, the meanings of which are not always clear, makes expressing how we are feeling fairly complicated. And without being able to express what you are feeling it is difficult to develop good mood awareness. Another aspect is that, in my clinical experience, this kind of introspection is simply too painful for most people. Thinking about yourself in a concentrated manner may bring on bad memories or regrets, which in turn lowers your mood and, inevitably, leads to your avoiding doing it again.

It is not just the general public who have difficulty thinking about mood. You can appreciate just how little we have advanced in our scientific appreciation of emotions by the fact that the Ancient Greek philosopher Plato's view of mind is still influential today. He divided the mind into three components, those of reason, desire and emotion. According to him, the best way of understanding why you experience the emotions you do, and of trying to change them, was to refer to the desiring and reasoning parts of your mind.

People often get confused by the idea that reasoning underlies emotions, as the two seem diametrically opposed. The best way to understand this idea is to appreciate that whatever emotion you feel cannot be experienced in a vacuum. For example, you cannot just feel pure anger and nothing else, you have to be angry with someone or about something; in other words, it has to have a target. Similarly you will never feel just love, but always a love for someone or something. Further, not only will there be a destination for your affections (they will be directed at something), but there will also be a set of reasons which explain why you feel that way about that object.

For example, you may feel anger towards someone or something – whether at your husband or at the poor quality of the goods sold in your local supermarket – but not everyone will necessarily feel the same way. The same objects evoke quite opposing emotions in different people. Politics and religion are the obvious examples – some people loved and worshipped Hitler, while others abhorred him – but it applies to every other aspect of life. Owning a Ferrari may make one person feel great while another is more moved by learning tennis. So your attitude towards these objects, or the way you think or reason about them, is in fact the cause of your anger or love. In this way, reasoning underpins emotions. I explain these ideas in greater depth in the next chapter, 'So, You Think You Are Sane?'.

The difficulty with this argument, which philosophers still debate, is that angry people get angrier about situations that only mildly irritate others, just as loving people seem to feel more love towards others than the average. So we have a tendency to feel certain emotions even before we encounter the objects that cause them. There is a sense in which this is the nature of what personality is – a predisposition to react with certain emotions to given situations. So a cantankerous person tends to react to events extremely irritably. If you want to change your personality you have to alter the way you tend to respond to the world.

Many psychiatrists are understandably deeply pessimistic about whether it is possible to change personality. There is a saying in the field that there are only two things which can change your character: one is psychoanalysis for an hour a day, five days a week for twenty years; the other is a severe blow to the head.

The conundrum is: where do these habitual responses, which are often so difficult to change, come from in the first place? Did we learn them or are some people biologically programmed by their genes to be more happy or sad than others?

Perhaps in the past we were rewarded for displaying such emotions. In some cases we have learned them. Maybe the parents of cantankerous adults ran around appeasing their irritability when these adults were younger, and so in effect obtained a reward for this display, which is why they now overuse this emotion.

In the previous chapter on looking after your self, I explained some of the techniques involved in altering the reward structure of your environment. These would help you to learn new ways of responding to and unlearn negative habitual responses which produce poor mood in the long term.

Some argue that in this sense reasoning does not exclusively underpin emotions. Yet it may still be that we have inherited a way of reasoning about the world or have learnt a reasoning style which explains our moods. Whatever the final answer is as to how our moods are as they are now, psychologists and psychiatrists still agree that changing your reasoning about objects is a vital part of altering your mood.

The best evidence[7] for this theory is you do not inherit your relatives' tendency towards depression or anxiety, instead they pass on their genetic predisposition to react in extreme ways. The particular mood you take to excess is more down to the situation in which you find yourself.[8] Genes determine a generalised vulnerability to emotional problems because they predispose towards emotionality (which is otherwise termed 'emotional reactivity', 'a tendency to over-react', or the most famous expression of all, 'being neurotic').

Later in this chapter I look at how it is possible to increase your emotional stability and reduce your tendency to extreme reactions to negative events – a vital part of staying sane. However, what determines the reaction you adopt, and the most common mood problems linked to mental illness (such as anxiety or depression), seem to be more down to the particular kind of negative event you experience than to genetic factors.

Anxiety tends to be precipitated by threat or danger in events, or changes in your environment which lead you to believe something terrible could happen to you in the future. For example, a change in management in your office followed by rumours of alterations in your job description might precipitate severe anxiety in the neurotic.[9] Depression, in contrast, seems to follow more from losses or what are termed 'exit events'. A bereavement, a break-up in a relationship, or being given the sack at work, will make the neurotic extremely depressed.[10]

This suggests there are two components to successful mood management. First of all, once you have experienced a negative event you should try to ensure your induced mood is not extreme, but also try to do whatever you can about the predicament that is positive. While this is difficult enough, how can anyone do anything about the second component, i.e. minimise the bad event itself? I discuss this in more detail in the chapters on thinking and coping, 'So, You Think You Are Sane?' and 'Crisis, What Crisis?'.

Oddly enough, the evidence is that negative life events are not randomly distributed throughout the population. Research[11, 12] has found that the relatives of depressives are not only prone to more depression, but also seem to experience more contrary life events as well. One study found that 41.8 per cent of depressives' relatives had experienced recent unfavourable life events while this was the case in only 7.3 per cent of a normal control group.[13, 14] By implication this suggests that the way you manage your life, and so the likelihood of negative life experiences, runs in families.

For example, choosing your husband may seem a random event. If you choose badly this produces its own stress, and it may well lead to a lack of support from someone close to you when you are in crisis. This has been found to be an important cause of depression.[15, 16] As mentioned in the chapter 'Hell is Other People', supportive relationships have an important stress-buffering effect.

An important feature of those who had very negative experiences during their childhood, but who seemed to transcend their early difficulties and not develop later mental illnesses during adulthood is the ability to plan their lives and take care over important choices, like marital partners and work.[17]

But what can you do more specifically to avoid anxiety, or loss, in order to prevent depression? I deal in more detail with anxiety and the technique of exposure treatment later in this chapter, while the importance of correct appraisal of threat is considered in the chapter on resilience ('I Will Survive').

One way of explaining why losses cause depression is to see positive mood as a secondary benefit of being rewarded, while low mood follows from a lack of rewards in one's life. It therefore follows that depression is produced by the loss of important sources of reward.[18] For example, losing a marital partner causes depression because all the dividends you got from them are no longer available to you. Similarly, losing a job causes depression because the benefits you obtained from work – perhaps your self-esteem and financial gains – are now also lost.

One of the best ways of preventing depression is to ensure that important rewards come from more than one source. If your only source of self-esteem is from your job, unemployment will hit your mood harder than if you obtain self-esteem from your children, your tennis prowess and your painting hobby. This is tied in with the notion of self-complexity which I explored in the previous chapter. The other approach is to look after your major sources of reward (for example, your husband!) very carefully and not to lose them through cavalier behaviour.

This probably explains why, after their divorce, so many men do worse than women in terms of mental health. More women than men initiate divorce in Britain, often because they are fed up with the intransigence of their husbands. Yet it is often only after they have left that the husbands realise what an important source of reward in their lives their wives were.

Another simple yet effective way of enhancing your mood, but one which is often neglected, is to make sure you receive rewards at regular intervals. Rewarding activities are acts and events you find pleasant, for example, leisure pursuits, seeing friends and dining out.[19] Certainly, depressed people report fewer of these positive events in their daily lives than the non-depressed.[20] A prevention strategy for depression called 'pleasant-activity' training involves keeping a daily record for around a month of what you do and which events seem to give you pleasure. Analyse which events enhance your mood the most, and simply increase the frequency of these activities.[21] Several experiments have found this simple technique is a helpful antidote to depression.[22, 23, 24]

Rewarding yourself, or ensuring your life contains regular rewards, may seem a little self-centred or hedonistic, and might explain why more people do not attempt consciously to take control of the reward structure in their lives. Yet as long as the pleasant activities are innocent and not incompatible with other major life goals or inconsiderate to other people, there is no reason, other than excessive puritanism, not to adopt this technique.

An important caveat is that the wisest positive mental health strategy is to build into your life a series of different kinds of rewards. Simply eating out and playing tennis more, even if those activities give you pleasure, is unlikely to form the basis of a long-term depression-prevention strategy. One simple reason for this is that if you do more of something you like doing you eventually get used to it – the psychological principle of habituation kicks in – and your increased pleasure diminishes over time. If you drink champagne and eat caviar every day, even these pleasures will start to lose their piquancy.

So it seems that rewards have to be of a slightly more sophisticated nature to maintain our mood in the long run. To explain the kind of reward structure you need, think of TV soap operas. Media experts have long speculated as to why soap operas are so popular. The storylines and the acting are looked down upon, yet TV channels increasingly use soap operas to achieve a regular high audience share. One possible explanation is that the nature of the plotting in a long-running soap opera means that in any one episode some storylines are just starting, some are developing, others are reaching maturity, while some are finally getting resolved.

This means the soap opera fan gets a multitude of rewards from following a soap over a long time; the dividends of following long-running plots intermingle with the pleasure of shorter storylines' denouement. My 'life as a soap-opera theory' suggests that to maintain positive mood over long periods of time, you will need both long-running goals (learning a language, for example), intermingled with short-term ones (going to see a film) which reach fruition at varying times.

Achieving an objective is a major source of reward in life. Indeed, just feeling you are getting closer to achieving a goal can be a reward in itself. A long-term intention might be a distant career aspiration, a medium-term goal might be to save enough for your holiday, while a short-term aim might be to win at tennis tonight. Another way of looking at goals is that these provide a purpose to life, and in the chapter on mental health I stressed how crucial to maintaining mental health having purpose in life is.

If you have only long-term goals you may receive little immediate reward from their pursuit, while set-backs will be even more likely to precipitate depression as they will arrive in the context of few recent rewards. On the other hand, having only short-term aims could leave you achieving all your goals relatively quickly, again with few rewards to look forward to in the future. Goal-setting is an important form of treatment for depression as a major component of low mood is a feeling of having failed to attain goals.[25] This is often because the goals were unrealistic or few and far between, or inappropriate for the skills and background of the person involved.

For example, the socially phobic avoid socialising because they often have unrealistically high goals for social encounters – that everyone they come across should be enthralled by meeting them. If that is your goal,

no wonder social encounters hold little prospect for reward, and this would explain why you might start to feel despondent about mingling. A more realistic goal might simply be to enter a brief conversation with a stranger, and to reward yourself for achieving this.

The depressed are taught to set a series of minor realistic goals, the accomplishment of which acts as a reward.[26] Learning to reward yourself by positive self-talk – like complimenting yourself, or giving yourself a treat – after achieving a goal is another way of remotivating those who feel pessimistic about ever accomplishing anything again. This approach has also been found effective in preserving and enhancing the positive mood of those not yet depressed.[27]

Often people make decisions without taking into account how the reward structure of their environment might change as a result. They believe leaving their spouse or job is a wise decision because of some irritant, yet fail to take into account the important benefits they may have been receiving which they now no longer obtain, and the lack of which will produce depression as a result.

Along with being aware of emotions, another crucial aspect which will help you to control them is to be aware of their self-perpetuating nature. If you are in a depressed mood, your view of the world will be negative too. You will recall only bad things about your past, selectively finding evidence in favour of your gloomy view of the world, and thereby staying in your low mood. The cycle at work here (becoming aware of cycles and breaking them are important in managing moods) is that feeling low produces a view of the world which makes it likely that you will remain low, and thereby makes it more difficult consciously to take control of your emotions and change your mood.

Whatever the original cause of this cycle, be it your genes or learning from your experiences, psychologists and psychiatrists alike agree that in order to break it you need to change the way you reason or think about the world. This will in turn change the way you feel about it.

So, while specific events, such as a late train or a fight with your partner, may appear to be the catalyst for your moods, your attitude, or the way you think about these events is also relevant. One reason so many people have difficulty controlling their passions is that they focus on trying to get a handle on an emotion, which is extremely difficult. The key instead is to take the counterintuitive step of focusing on your thoughts, which seem an unemotional and therefore irrelevant part of your mind at that time.

'But what about moods that seem to come out of nowhere?', some of you may be thinking, and it is certainly true that some of our emotions seem to come out of the blue. You may simply wake up feeling low one day and be unable to account for it. Later in the chapter I give some possible reasons for this.

Plato did not just mention reasoning but also emphasised the importance of the desire part of your mind. We feel positive emotions when our desires are realised, or are likely to be fulfilled, and negative emotions when our desires are frustrated, or we feel they will be. To change your emotions, you need either to change your desires, or to alter your chances of fulfilling them.

Plato's model of the mind is simple yet powerful. I believe trying to break down complicated subjects into simple components is the best problem-solving technique. You may have noticed that I tend to simplify psychiatry and psychology, which are traditionally seen as complicated subjects. They *are* complicated, but if you regard yourself and your problems as too complicated, you will never be able to change yourself or move in the direction of positive mental health.

To simplify the complicated world of emotions further, when trying to analyse your moods I suggest you adopt the perspective of researchers who have found that only six basic emotions are genuinely shared by all cultures of the world: happiness, sadness, anger, fear, surprise and disgust.[28] All other emotions – frustration and shame, for example – can be effectively explained as combinations or particular aspects of this basic six.

Being aware of these moods within ourselves and how they influence our behaviour, together with learning to control them is an important part of mental health. Of them all, in my clinical experience, anger is probably the one people have most difficulty acknowledging.

ANGER

Everyone gets angry if provoked sufficiently, but we all have different thresholds for erupting, depending on our personalities. While we often try to hide our anger, it is in fact a very important emotion. Medical research suggests that angry people are more prone to high blood pressure and heart attacks, so if you can learn to reduce the amount of anger in yourself, and in the way you see the world, you may actually live longer. Although men express their anger more often than women, either physically or verbally, research has found that anger is fairly equally distributed between the sexes. Women may turn their anger inwards, which could explain their higher rates of depression and self-harm compared to those for men.

This highlights another important point about anger. While some may express only a little anger, this does not mean they are not still very angry, and their hostility will emerge in more covert ways than simple aggression, such as withdrawal. While anger appears to have a strong genetic component (Mr Angry has angry parents), it is also partly caused by growing up in chaotic family environments that are full of conflict. However, it is still possible, no matter how angry we have become, to modulate anger by therapeutic techniques, for example, anger management courses. While some of these courses are good, unfortunately many of them are based on the mistaken belief that the only way of managing anger is by expressing it in copious amounts. This is pure psychobabble. Far better to recognise anger within, understand where it is coming from and devise alternative ways of resolving whatever is at its root. Evidence that few people do this comes from the rising tide of hostility in society, suggesting we are plagued by escalating levels of anger.

ANGER SCALE

Each statement is followed by two possible responses: agree or disagree. Read each statement carefully and decide which response best describes how you feel. Then put a tick over the corresponding response. Please respond to every statement. If you are not completely sure which response is more accurate, put the response which you feel is most appropriate. Don't read the scoring explanation before filling out the questionnaire and don't spend too long on each statement. It is important that you answer each question as honestly as possible!

	AGREE	DISAGREE
1 Getting angry rarely solves problems	A	B
2 I like playing practical jokes on others	B	A
3 I am rarely critical of others	A	B
4 People are often jealous of me	B	A
5 I am generally a cautious person	A	B
6 Some people have it in for me	B	A
7 Most people do not disappoint me	A	B
8 Our country is too soft on other nations	B	A
9 Revenge is no solution to injustice	A	B
10 I nearly always stick to my principles in an argument	B	A

Add up your score from summing the numbers of As and Bs in each box you have ticked. Your score and the interpretation given below should be treated with caution – this short test is by no means definitive, but may offer a guide to where you stand compared to others around you.

SCORE

8 or more Bs. It is possible you are so angry you are putting your cardiovascular system and your relationships at risk if you do not calm down. Even people who are close to you are probably a bit frightened of you, and your temper may put you in danger of losing an important client in business. Your anger is likely to have spilt over into verbal aggression and possibly even assault, and you are probably at grave risk from a physical attack on yourself from someone who won't tolerate your hostility or irritability. On the other hand, the very fact that you may be a little feared means many could give you a wide berth, so you often get your way. This may be the reward for your emotional display.

Between 5 and 7 Bs. Your hostility is possibly only rarely manifested in verbal or physical aggression, unlike the higher scorers above. Instead, your anger may come out in resentment of others who you feel have got in the way of your progress; in occasional suspicion that those who appear less angry and kinder than you only do so in order to get their own way; and day-dreams about getting revenge. In the short term you may not need anger management help but, in the long run anger could corrode the quality of your work relationships. In the meantime, it might be helpful if you could develop the insight to see your criticism of others as sometimes thinly veiled hostility.

Between 2 and 5 Bs. You are probably fairly unflappable and may even find yourself frequently having to calm down those who scored between 5 and 7. If you are ruffled, you could become angry, but this occurs only under provocation and you tend not to be as explosive as higher scorers. Instead, your anger usually takes a little while to develop. You will often try all sorts of alternatives to getting angry, but in so doing you may let higher anger scorers get their way rather than risk confrontation. You could be a little embarrassed by anger, which possibly prevents you from using it to your advantage on occasion.

Between 0 and 2 Bs. Very few have probably ever seen a temper tantrum from you, and most would be deeply shocked if they did. When you get angry you also tend to cry at the same time so your vexation is more one of despair than aggression. Although you have many more friends than higher scorers, you also might get pushed around a bit by them. For example, in an argument you are perhaps less likely to stick to your principles regardless (unlike high anger scorers), so you will tend to cave in to preserve a pleasant atmosphere. You usually see the good side of most people, but this means you often don't get either angry or even, although it might be helpful to express your frustration more.

Apart from trying to become more aware of your moods – happiness, sadness, anger, fear, surprise and disgust – chatting through what you are really feeling with friends (or, if your problems are very serious, a professional) is a good way of managing your mood. Talking helps to clarify precisely what you are feeling as well as being a basis for the examination of the thoughts underpinning your mood, and the target of your emotions.

Anxiety (a clinical term which is a synonym for fear) and depression are two moods most frequently associated with psychiatric disorder, so if you can control these, you will have eliminated at one stroke the reasons most people seek psychiatric help. But linked to anxiety and depression are a whole host of other undesirable or negative emotional states for which people seek therapeutic help, like anger, hatred and envy. These can sometimes go unrecognised.

A patient of mine described recently an incident in a restaurant where her reaction took her by surprise. It was her wedding anniversary and her husband had taken her out for supper. Also in the restaurant was a rowdy group of two couples whom my patient described as loudly showing off their wealth and success throughout the evening. My patient became increasingly angry with them and finally lost her temper, shouting at one of them to shut up. Her husband, not to mention the waiters, were clearly shocked at my patient's outburst, and the evening was ruined.

My patient's account of the incident was that she and her husband had been enjoying a quiet evening and that the group's noise intruded on their frequently silent meal. She regretted the incident afterwards and was nonplussed that she should lose her temper over such a relatively trivial event. I suggested to her (since I already knew her and her background well) that she was already in a negative mood because her relationship with her husband was not going well, but that this was something she had been denying because it was such an upsetting thought. I suggested the frequent silences during the meal were because they did not have much to talk about and that she was at some level aware of this. The fact that it was their anniversary had also brought on thoughts about their marriage, all producing a profoundly negative emotional state. Rather than confronting her husband she had displaced her anger and upset with him on to the others in the restaurant.

A R⊙UND

Whether or not my hypothesis was correct (and at first it did not go down at all well), I believe we are often in certain emotional states without realising it, and because our mood goes unrecognised, the resulting behaviour surprises us. It would be impossible to monitor perfectly our emotional condition all the time, and, while it is not healthy to suppress all our feelings, it is vital to have some ability to control ourselves. We are of course least in control when in the grip of strong emotion.

For example, many clinically depressed patients do not complain of serious depression but instead say they are irritable, bored or tired all the time. Only when the underlying depression has been identified and treated, does the boredom, tiredness or hostility disappear.[29]

Severe anxiety, in particular, is an emotion which most members of the general public would not recognise for what it is. Instead they mistake it for mental illness or serious physical problems. My patients experiencing their first panic attack think they are about to go fundamentally insane and many people experiencing acute panic are convinced they are having a heart attack and are taken by ambulance to hospital where they receive a full cardiac screening. Even some doctors, particularly if they are not well trained in psychiatry, fail to recognise the physical manifestations of anxiety and investigate patients exhaustively for heart disease.

If anxiety starts up suddenly and severely it can leave you utterly confused and frightened, so much so that you even mistake your own thoughts for alien experiences. You may believe the thoughts come from somewhere other than your mind; I have seen countless patients who, in the grip of acute anxiety, falsely assumed that some strange thought was a 'voice' or hallucination, which merely made them even more anxious.

A common symptom of acute and severe anxiety is to feel suddenly that you are not real any more, or that the world around you is no longer genuine. These symptoms are called depersonalisation and derealisation and are a way the mind tries to avoid the situation it finds itself in, by supposing that this terrible predicament is not even real. I explain later the intimate link between avoidance and anxiety.

When you are anxious you breathe more rapidly. This shifts the oxygen balance in your body, bringing about physical changes like tingling and pins and needles in your hands and feet. These physical

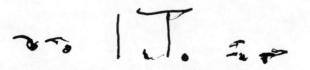

sensations are then often felt by the patient to be an ominous sign of some illness, and this makes them even more anxious, causing them to breathe ever more rapidly, producing more physical changes in their body, which ensures more panic and so on.

These vicious cycles of anxiety, physical sensations and panicky thoughts, produce severe states of anxiety, which can be treated only once the cycle producing the anxiety and physical symptoms is recognised and broken. Techniques include learning to slow your breathing, relax muscles and calm down. Some patients find that techniques such as yoga, self-hypnosis or meditation help in this. Although these different ways of relaxing have quite separate origins, like eastern religion or hypnosis, they have been found to retain the same basic components and so achieve calm by more or less the same means.[30]

They all usually involve taking control and slowing breathing, loosening muscles, and filling the mind with calming images or thoughts. Relaxation techniques are a crucial life-skill, because however mentally healthy, we will all experience severe anxiety from time to time, perhaps before a crucial interview or major exam. If I were in charge of the school curriculum, one of the first things I would do would be make sure those essential skills are taught at school.

Below are details of some proven relaxation techniques. First practise them when you are not feeling particularly anxious. It takes time and patience to learn how to relax, but eventually you will be able to apply these strategies in any situation.

Learning to relax, which ought to be easy, is actually a skill which requires much practice. The best techniques use a combination of visualisation and muscle relaxation. Visualise the most restful and pleasant scene you can. (Mine is a tropical sandy coast at the side of an extremely calm lake which reflects several beautiful mountains on its glassy surface.) Then focus on each part of your body in turn, shaking it and then relaxing it. I start with my toes and gradually move upwards. It is sometimes useful to wriggle the part of the body, or tense it first and then relax it. Slow your breathing down, concentrating especially on exhaling as slowly as possible. Become more aware of the sound of your breathing and of your environment. Be aware of your posture and try to move to a more relaxed one. My problem with my own relaxation ritual is I get so relaxed I always fall asleep!

However, before you can know when to apply relaxation, first you have to learn how to recognise anxiety.

Physical symptoms to look out for are: increased fidgeting, nervous habits like jiggling limbs, biting nails, inability to sit still, restlessness, fast breathing, dry mouth, tightness across the chest, awareness of heart beating (producing fear that you are about to die or have some cardiac problem), tingling or pins and needles, sweating, tremor, abdominal pain, butterfly feeling in the stomach, diarrhoea, increased need to urinate, nausea, retching, throwing-up, coughing and feeling that you are not real or the world around is not real in some way. Of course, we all experience the odd symptom from time to time and may just be mildly nervous, not anxious. But you will be able to recognise the difference between a mild butterfly feeling in the stomach and the more severe feelings of nausea or tightness across the chest.

Anxiety may not just manifest itself by sensations which occur once in a while. Sometimes our regular habits, which appear to be part of our character, may simply be symptoms of anxiety. For example, do you do any of the following things: bite your fingernails, pull out hair, twirl hair, pull or tug ears, stroke your face, tap your fingers or foot, swing your legs, cough or clear your throat, put your fingers in your mouth, bite pens or pencils, suck your thumb, chew objects, grind your teeth, scratch in places that don't itch, or rub your hands together? Psychological researchers have yet to find anyone who *doesn't* have at least one of the twitches on the above list! They are all habits, that is, defined as repeated actions that appear to serve no useful function, but which we regularly indulge in for no apparent reason.

The greater the number of habits you have, the more prone you might be to excessive anxiety,[31] so understanding your tendencies could help predict whether you will develop serious psychiatric problems in the future. The most widespread habits are biting fingernails, twisting necks, moving, clicking or grinding teeth and touching the face. Surveys suggest that the average number of different habits per normal person is seven though these will not all be indulged at the same time! The average length of time for continuing a habit is eight years.[32]

It seems, however, that contrasting habits have alternative implications; for example, neck twisting is a relatively uncommon habit compared to the others, but, of all habits, seems to be associated with the most tension.

The most common habit of all appears to be stroking or playing with hair (including eyelashes, beard or head hair); some 70 per cent of people do this.[33] We do it most often when alone and trying to concentrate on something, but it is not a habit which bothers most people at all. However, chronic hair-pulling, resulting in bald patches, is a serious psychiatric illness, called trichotillomania, and afflicts 5 per cent of people.[34] (It can be effectively treated with psychiatric medicines, and also a technique called 'habit reversal' which is explained below.)

More innocuously, 63 per cent of the population play with pens, pencils etc, 56 per cent manipulate jewellery and 45 per cent report touching their faces as a habit. The very latest psychological research, just published by scientists at North Dakota State University, USA, has found that hair and face play increases when we are feeling anxious, whereas we handle objects more when we are bored.[35]

The reason for this seems to be that anxiety causes muscle tension which may be relieved by habits involving repeated movement of muscles. Other habits help us to maintain our level of interest when we are not receiving enough arousal to keep our attention on what is going on around us.

Habits most frequently requiring treatment by doctors are hair-pulling, clenching and grinding of teeth, finger-sucking, nail-biting and body-rocking. Any habit which gives distress by causing embarrassment, disfigurement, or where the person can't seem to stop when they want to, requires treatment.

The technique used to treat a bad habit is called 'habit reversal'.[36] The sufferer learns to replace the habit with another activity which is incompatible with the bad habit. For example, if the habit is thumb-sucking, the sufferer is taught to sit on their hands or clasp them together as soon as they feel the urge.

Habits are not all bad, and some even help us concentrate in situations requiring close attention but not much physical activity. For example, studying a difficult problem may cause muscle tension that becomes unpleasant because sitting at a desk means being still. The only way to relieve this tension momentarily is to shake your leg or twist your neck.

The biggest problem with habits is that we do them so often that we have usually become totally unaware of them. The starting point of any treatment is simply to make you aware of what you are doing – for example, which of your habits are you performing right now?

The list of habits I have given is far from exhaustive and patients still surprise me by the novel ways they manifest anxiety. Patients can assess whether their bad habits are due to anxiety or not by looking at the situations when the symptoms come on. If this is only when the patient is under some stress or pressure, or in any way not completely relaxed, they are likely to be symptoms of anxiety. Another good clue is if the symptoms make the patient want to leave the situation he is in immediately, and feels this will somehow make him feel better. This is one sign of an acute anxiety attack.

The short-term treatment for anxiety could be to flee (for example, get up and leave the exam hall) or, more constructively, to learn relaxation techniques. At a more sophisticated level, a solution is to analyse dispassionately the fearful thoughts which are causing the anxiety and examine the evidence to see whether the extreme emotion is really warranted by the circumstances. But this, of course, is easier said than done.

Unlike depression, anxiety is always temporary. It is impossible to feel very anxious for a very long time. This may seem a surprising statement as many of us might recall feeling states of anxiety which went on for several months as we prepared for exams, interviews or our wedding day. But while we appeared to be feeling anxious for days on end, what in fact was happening was that we felt waves of anxiety which came and went, often just over a period of a few minutes.

Unlike other moods such as depression which seem more sustained, anxiety comes in waves. No one knows for certain why this should be but one explanation is that anxiety symptoms have a physical basis caused by the release of adrenaline-like chemicals from our nerve endings. Once our body has released all its adrenaline-like chemicals, which often takes only a short while, there is a period when the body has to replace these chemicals when we experience a reduction in our anxiety even though the feared situation continues to be present. You get a feel for this when public-speaking; after the first few minutes, which are the worst, most people feel a slow decline in how nervous they are.

Yet this law, that anxiety will go away of its own accord if you stay long enough in the feared situation, is one few discover for themselves. What tends to happen instead is that anxiety builds up and creates a strong urge to get away from whatever is feared, whether speaking in public (one of the commonest fears), travelling by air, or being in a room with a spider. Anxiety leads to avoidance; in fact, that is the purpose of anxiety, to make you escape from something. Within that simple statement is embodied the most powerful treatment for anxiety.

Nature built anxiety into us as a protective mechanism, to keep us away from cliff edges or lions. Our anxiety whenever we are near these things makes us want to get away. Once you escape the thing you fear, your anxiety disappears. However, my personal theory is that nature also had to come up with a mechanism whereby we could cope when our environment changed and we no longer needed to avoid a particular thing. If, say, a particularly dangerous species of animal had changed in some way and was no longer a threat, yet we still kept avoiding that animal because of anxiety, we would never realise that avoidance was no longer necessary.

So nature built in a mechanism whereby anxiety is always temporary. If you are prevented from fleeing, and instead stay near a fearful object for long enough, and if, despite the acute anxiety, nothing terrible happens to you, your anxiety will dissipate of its own accord. Nature reasons that since nothing bad has happened, maybe there is no longer any need to continue using avoidance tactics.

Thus, the way to treat any anxiety is to stop avoiding the feared object or situation. You will find that your anxiety begins to go away of its own accord. This is encapsulated in the catchphrase 'face your fear'. People experience the truth of this in everyday life. For example, when you are learning to drive, you are doubtless very anxious when you first sit behind the wheel. But the longer you drive, the less anxious you become. If you abandoned the car the first time you felt acute anxiety, and on every subsequent occasion, you would never lose your fear of driving.

Yet avoidance is exactly how most people respond to their anxiety. They then wonder why they still feel anxious. It is impossible to lose your anxiety through avoidance, as it will only do what psychologists term 'insulate your anxiety', in other words, preserve it.

Anxiety is probably the most commonly experienced psychiatric symptom and its influence on behaviour is enormous. One very common source of anxiety is fear of exams. The 'cognitive' or rational approach to tackling exam anxiety is to examine the fundamental fear. As it's usually a fear of failing, the most constructive approach is to see what you can do right now to reduce the chance of failure – usually a bit of revision.

However, thoughts of a future exam which come on during revision time create anxiety, and possibly the commonest approach to getting rid of this is to avoid thinking about the exam, or avoid doing anything relating to the exam. This usually leads to abandoning revision and doing something more pleasant instead.

This avoidance or distraction technique leads to another vicious circle. Because you are not revising, and you know it, you realise you are even more likely to fail and you get even more anxious. You deal with this by even more avoidance – no revision – which raises anxiety further, and so on.

In the chapter on coping ('Crisis, What Crisis?') I argue that distraction is not a bad coping mechanism, but must be applied only when there is nothing you really can do to change your situation (such as revising in the example above). The reason people use avoidance as a solution is not only because of their tendency to avoid unpleasant emotions but also as they fear that acute anxiety might damage them mentally in some permanent way. This last fear is unfounded, but is usually based on the assumption that when psychiatrists say you must face your fear you must do so all in one go.

The non-avoidance approach to anxiety doesn't mean facing a fear of driving by taking on a Formula 1 race, or facing a fear of public speaking by lecturing to an audience of 1,000. Instead, the keynote is gradualism, often extreme gradualism. As long as you continue moving in the right direction, this approach always works. So, if you are afraid of flying, facing your fear does not mean getting on an aeroplane, but means doing things which raise your anxiety levels but by only a small amount. This might be watching films which feature plane trips, or playing with flight simulator games on computers, or simply going near an airport. The key feature is to try doing something which you would ordinarily avoid, which raises your anxiety, but only does so to a small extent, and which means you can stay in the situation long enough to feel the anxiety go away by itself.

After you have conquered situations lower down the hierarchy of fear, the next step is to move up the hierarchy. But don't do this until you have completely conquered your fear of the lesser anxiety-provoking situation. Doing this can jeopardise the whole treatment, and is another key point which is often misunderstood.

As anxiety underpins a whole gamut of psychiatric problems, the principle of exposure to the object which raises anxiety is a useful tool for a wide variety of apparently disparate problems. For example, exposure to a feared object even applies to the psychiatric problem of obsessiveness.

Obsession and compulsion are much misused words; the media abounds with stories of fans' 'obsessions' or the 'compulsion' which drives the famous. Yet the psychiatric illness of Obsessive Compulsive Disorder (OCD) is one of a group of disorders, like phobias and panics, where the fundamental problem is an excess of anxiety. Hence the common situations of being obsessed with a pop star or a hobby (unless this is accompanied by severe anxiety) do not fall into the category of OCD. At any one time 10 per cent of the public display obsessive-compulsive symptoms while only about 2 per cent will have clinical OCD.[37]

The definition of OCD rests on two different but related concepts: the obsession and the compulsion. Obsessions are recurrent, persistent ideas, thoughts, images or impulses, experienced by the patient as intrusive and senseless. In other words, the patient would rather not have these thoughts and will go to extraordinary lengths to try and avoid them.

A compulsion is a repetitive, purposeful and intentional behaviour, often termed a ritual, performed in response to an obsession, designed to neutralise the dreaded obsession or to prevent the consequent discomfort. If prevented from carrying out their rituals sufferers become extremely anxious.

OCD appears more in those above average in social class and intelligence.[38] A good example of this was the billionaire Howard

Hughes. He became preoccupied with dirt and germs and started taking various complicated precautionary measures, like excessively washing his hands, using a tissue to avoid touching door handles and not shaking other people's hands. But as his OCD worsened, his rituals eventually became so time-consuming they could not be carried out, and Hughes then dealt with the problem of contact with dirt or germs simply by avoiding the outside world. Thus he became a hermit, but his OCD fear of doctors (and catching something from one of them) meant one was called too late to save him when he became physically ill. Hence the richest man in the world died a recluse, killed by his OCD.

Hughes' story is a good example of how easy it is to forget that OCD is among the most terrible psychiatric disturbances. Patients macerate their skin from repeated scrubbing or spend countless hours repeating meaningless calculations. One patient I knew had to spend hours repeatedly checking that the knobs on her video recorder really were four and not some other number. I have seen patients who spend eight hours in the shower every day, because of a fear that if they are not completely clean, something terrible will happen to them.

One psychiatrist described a patient who had a compulsion to pull nails out of walls. No one had any idea of the number of random tacks, bolts, screws and pegs which could be found on the vertical surfaces of a room until this patient arrived. During one out-patient appointment he managed to strip the doctor's office of pictures, diplomas and certificates, in order to pluck out the supporting nails.

Since orderliness, cleanliness, fastidiousness, meticulousness, parsimony, pedantry, persistence, endurance and unemotionality – all aspects of the OCD universe – can also be viewed as desirable qualities, sociobiologists have observed that the deep sense of responsibility, vigilance and attention to detail, which are all symptoms of OCD, are also virtues. Hence OCD survives in the human species because it also bestows a competitive advantage.

The best treatment for OCD is behaviour therapy, which entails the patient's repeated exposure to the feared stimulus. The exposure principle means the only cure is to face the fear of this event by gradually reducing the length of time spent in the shower. For example, if a patient is compelled to wash 20 to 30 times a day, one approach is deliberately to make him dirty, after which he is prevented from

" HEAR ...

washing. Such treatment may sound cruel, but it is important to remember that patients are only very gradually exposed to their fears. So before they are exposed to the most frightening stimuli they will have started with things that only cause a little anxiety. This treatment has proved to be effective in even the most severe cases, and research has definitively shown that exposure to the feared situation is crucial for recovery from OCD.

But it is possible for severe anxiety to lead to extreme attempts at avoidance.

A recent report prepared on behalf of the charity Childline[39] found that 79 per cent of children worried about exams more than anything and that this kind of exam stress led several to contemplate suicide; one girl even tried to hang herself because of pressure of GCSEs before ringing Childline last year.

Psychologists who study stress have long known that exams produce more strain than any other life pressure. One study found that one fifth of medical students were so stressed during exams that the high levels of stress hormones their bodies pumped out made them temporarily diabetic during an exam.[40]

Since achieving educational, professional and many other goals in life often depends on performance during a test of some kind (even interview nerves are basically a kind of test anxiety), the failure of able students means that society loses many talents. The solution may be more complicated than just trying to stay calm; American psychologists found that letting students take textbooks into exams, or even giving them take-home tests, still did not help those prone to exam stress, who performed poorly even under these supposedly less stressful conditions.[41]

The problem is difficult to treat because exam nerves cause many people to fall into the distraction/anxiety/more distraction cycle described above. Perhaps the most surprising finding from research into exam stress is that it is this cycle which accounts for so much poor performance, as opposed to the physical symptoms of anxiety – butterflies in the stomach, palpitations, tremulous hands, a dry mouth, and so on. In fact, psychologists found that those who have few physical symptoms of anxiety tend not to do so well. An adrenaline surge makes us perform better than those who are too relaxed, hence the recent

" METAPSYCHOSIS

finding that Scotland's failure in European football competitions was due to their players not getting anxious enough.

The problem for those whose performance is inhibited by too much anxiety is that they mentally plunge inwards, while less test-anxious people dive into the task itself. For example, instead of focusing on answering questions, those with high test-anxiety become preoccupied with thoughts that they are lagging behind others, rebuke themselves for forgetting answers, and recall in panic previous tests that ended in disaster. It is this distracting worry, not the physical symptoms of anxiety, that need to be addressed for test performance to improve.

Successful treatment of exam stress centres not so much on relaxation techniques, but more on getting candidates to replace their self-centred and self-derogatory concerns with more positive thoughts before and during a test. These might be thoughts of the 'just take one question at a time', or 'don't worry, worry won't help anything' variety. Most importantly of all, they need to develop the habit of instructing themselves to concentrate on the task at hand, and not be distracted by irrelevant and self-fulfilling fears of failure.

A more intriguing explanation for the difficulty of getting rid of exam nerves is the one I raised in the previous chapter on self. Some psychologists have begun to wonder if, for a minority of candidates, exam nerves play a useful role in helping them deal with failure. It seems that some prepare less well than they could – albeit unconsciously – because poor preparation provides a useful scapegoat for poor results. We all need excuses, often unconsciously prepared, to protect our egos in the face of failure. After all, if you prepare thoroughly, have no nerves in the test, and still fail, what conclusion is left other than that you are actually pretty stupid, a much worse deduction than failing because you were too nervous. So some people self-sabotage, which is precisely what exam nerves amount to.

One of the benefits of the mood of anxiety is that it leads to vigilance, as we monitor our environment more acutely for the presence of threat. Unfortunately too much vigilance makes it difficult to do anything else. The opposite mood might be boredom which often produces very low vigilance indeed.

Boredom has been implicated in the causes of clinical depression, alcoholism, over-eating, obesity and drug abuse; and beyond the clinic,

TELEPATAY "

243

in vandalism and crime.[42] Research on long-distance lorry drivers and airline pilots, for example, suggests that many of the most spectacular motorway pile-ups, air crashes and even oil tanker accidents are directly attributable to boredom.[43] In 1989 an entire cockpit crew of a commercial airline fell asleep and over-flew their destination by more than 100 miles, before being awakened by air traffic controllers.[44]

Complaints of feeling bored are common. Up to 56 per cent of British employees report they find their entire job boring, while up to 87 per cent maintain they feel bored on the job on some occasions.[45]

Medical research has found bored workers have three to five times the incidence of cardiovascular disease, four to seven times the incidence of neurological disorders, twice the incidence of gastrointestinal disorders, two to three times the incidence of musculoskeletal disorders, and were absent for medical reasons 3 to 5 times as often as their non-bored colleagues. As many as 60 per cent of Swedish mill workers doing one particularly boring task received treatment for peptic ulcers. Some in this study even complained of hallucinations during periods of boredom.[46]

Adrenaline levels are twice as high as normal during boring work, so incumbents of boring jobs paradoxically experience a great deal of stress. They even have more heart attacks, so it is possible literally to be bored to death.[47]

Boredom is not just restricted to work. One of the major uses of leisure time is watching TV, but surveys find that most only do this because they are bored. Despite its importance, psychologists and psychiatrists have neglected this 'boring' area, with an average of only one study per year having been published on boredom since World War II.[48]

However, interest in boredom has recently burgeoned with the development of the concept of 'pathological boredom', which may explain many current social problems, including youth violence and other dangerous risk-taking behaviour. Recent studies of school pupils show that while many are bored with at least one subject they are studying, a sizeable group finds all subjects boring, and are also largely bored during their spare time. These results suggest that some people may suffer from *pathological* boredom, boredom which is not task-linked but is centred on particular people. The same research also found that boredom runs in families, with bored pupils having bored parents.[49]

Boredom research really took off in Britain during World War II when RAF authorities were astonished to find that contacts of hostile aircraft and U-boats reported by radar operators dropped substantially as time on a duty wore on. As 50 per cent of targets were being missed, RAF Coastal Command immediately commissioned psychologists to study boredom.[50]

Early findings of research bodies like the Industrial Fatigue Research Board in England, included the startling finding that: '...boring tasks are those which are repetitive with little variability, but also needing much attention continually...'[51]

But research also suggests that the causes of boredom are not always that predictable. Many studies, for example, find that industrial workers who might be expected to suffer from boredom, actually claim to enjoy repetitive work. This worrying finding may be explained by an even more ominous discovery. A study of female Swiss watch-makers who worked for various periods at repetitive tasks found that tenure at monotonous jobs itself lowered the workers' intelligence scores.[52]

The most recent research has found that there may be many different kinds of boredom which permeate all aspects of life. For example, one sub-type noted is 'Sunday boredom' which is experienced only on Sundays and other vacations, and is peculiar to a subgroup who only succeed in diverting themselves while at work. When distraction is unavailable, the latent boredom they have been warding off all week finally becomes manifest.[53]

These people often require a lot of constant stimulation to avoid boredom. Psychopaths (ruthless, self-centred individuals) fall into this category. They have poor tolerance of routine work and rapidly become blasé about novelty.

Others prone to boredom include those with higher abilities who find most tasks relatively easy, less challenging and therefore not as stimulating as the rest of us. So, again paradoxically, more intelligent people are likely to feel bored. Surprisingly, extroverts, the more socially outgoing and lively, also suffer more from boredom than introverts. Their high spirits are actually attempts to generate the intense levels of stimulation they require to stave off boredom. Another counterintuitive finding is that boredom seems to decrease with age.[54]

It is interesting that adolescence is the time we are most prone to boredom; this is precisely when we are learning to focus our attention in ways younger children are unable to. At around 11 to 12 years of age the brain-wave patterns characteristic of selective attention, which is the first step towards an adult ability to concentrate, first emerge.[55] It may be that those teenagers who fail to make the transition to an adult ability to concentrate will suffer from boredom, and will therefore turn to crime and drug abuse.

Further evidence for the biological underpinning of boredom is the fact that our brains' frontal lobes seemed designed so that our attention can be focused on selective events (they send descending nerve fibres to the rest of the nervous system to inhibit widespread activity, producing concentrated activity in specific areas of the brain). The ability to focus and concentrate mitigates against boredom.[56] In those who are easily distracted this ability is less developed; they are more likely to be bored.

One reason understanding boredom has been so difficult for researchers is that it can even be difficult to recognise when you are bored. Boredom may be manifested by anxiety, hostility, difficulty concentrating, sleepiness, irritation, risk-taking and the experience of time slowing down.

This subjective experience of time is an important indication of boredom. In one experiment psychologists asked people to complete a task in a set time, using clocks that had been tampered with to run fast or slow. This showed that the subjective experience of time in itself altered interest in the work. Interest was increased when the clocks were speeded up, and boredom experienced when they were slowed down. One solution to boredom is thus simply to allocate less time, insufficient time, to boring tasks. In fact, many of us may already unconsciously be doing this; we find ourselves rushing to complete what we have put off because it's boring.[57]

Another reason why boredom might be difficult to identify is that it can be more profound than simply a lack of stimulation. Sometimes it is the experience of a complete lack of any impulse. The problem then is no longer that of finding something to do, but of finding a reason for doing anything at all. This explains the hopeless task of trying to interest some bored people in anything, despite the most riveting suggestions.

The following are attempts by different experts to define boredom:

'... an unpleasant transient emotional state in which the individual feels a pervasive lack of interest in, and difficulty concentrating on current activity...'[58]

'...occurs when an individual decides that an activity has no personal significance, they say to themselves – there is nothing in this for me...'[59]

'...boredom is the state which provokes a search for diversion...'[60]

'...when we must not do what we want to do, or must do what we do not want to do...'[61]

'...a tendency to revert to sleep due to inadequate motivation to stay awake...'[62]

Another sub-type of boredom was first described by Field Marshal Ligne, who said: 'I am not bored, it is others who bore me.'[63] Research into what we find boring about each other has uncovered that this is largely due to the quality of our conversation. The contents of speech from boring people was found to be self-centred and trivial, while their speech style was slow and low on emotional fervour.

Since being boring is a huge social disadvantage, as it causes extreme loneliness, are there treatments for the excessively or chronically boring? Given all the social and medical ills which result from boredom, anti-boredom strategies would seem more urgent today than ever before.

Remedies for boring work and people centre around the study of what makes things interesting. In fact, research into what determines our interests is meagre, which is surprising, especially given that discovering the root cause of 'interestingness' has huge commercial implications for all those in pursuit of our interest and attention – advertisers, broadcasters and publishers, for example.

Scientists have long looked to their own activities to explain what determines our interests; new ideas in science are only engrossing when they negate accepted theories, so researchers argue it is the unexpected and unlikely which are fundamentally absorbing.[64] This fact alone doesn't provide the complete answer, as can be illustrated by this simple example: suppose you are told that there are 26 prime numbers less than 100, but then subsequently learn that, in fact, there are only 25 prime numbers less than 100. This new information presumably should be interesting, as something unexpected has occurred, but it is rarely found to be so.

In fact, to be found interesting, things also have to bear on current personal concerns as well as being unexpected. The problem then is that theorists simply end up saying that we are concerned (and therefore interested) in those things which we are already concerned or interested in.

However, if the 'unexpectedness' theory of interest is correct, uncertainty becomes a desirable feature of our environment yet concern over a possible threat is at the root of anxiety. There is conflict here. By definition uncertainty involves not knowing whether an outcome might be positive or negative, so it seems that one of the prices we might pay for reducing uncertainty in our lives, and therefore danger, might be boredom.

Going back to the point about goal-setting and the reward structure in our environment, if we choose goals which are always easily within our capability, we will be certain of the outcome and will therefore become bored. Therefore a little bit of anxiety appears to be the consequence of setting aspirations which it is not certain we will achieve. Yet failure to accomplish goals seems to lead to depression. So a positive mental health strategy will always involve a balancing act between anxiety, boredom and depression. Small quantities of these are therefore an inevitable part of life.

But how are you able to tell when the amounts of anxiety, depression or boredom you are experiencing go beyond what is healthy? In my clinical experience, examining the techniques people evolve as ways of managing their moods is crucial to diagnosing serious psychiatric illnesses such as depression. Junior doctors and psychiatrists, whom I teach at the Bethlem Royal and Maudsley Hospitals, often ask me at what point does the normal, everyday depression or low mood we all experience from time to time differ from a clinical depression. Knowing the difference is important, not just for junior psychiatrists, but for ordinary people trying to maintain their mental health. Most of my patients worry that they are wasting the doctor's time because they are unsure whether or not they are formally ill. Often, because of this uncertainty, they postpone seeking help for far too long.

I have seen patients who have been seriously psychiatrically ill for years before seeking help. And, as I stress throughout this book, the longer you delay treatment for a treatable psychiatric illness, the less likely you are to make a full recovery. A cornerstone of preventive mental health care is to know with confidence when you are just low and when you have slipped into the kind of depression which needs more specialised treatment. Once you know this you can make arrangements to see a specialist immediately, or stay away with confidence.

Official manuals like the *Diagnostic and Statistical Manual* used by American psychiatrists opt for criteria such as a time limit to mark the line between illness and mere low mood. In some cases if you are depressed for longer than two weeks you have officially become psychiatrically ill, while thirteen days of continuous low mood does not qualify. I think you can see immediately the inherent problems of such a method.

I prefer to check whether the strategies a patient has always used when feeling low, such as talking to others, still work or not. If your own attempts to cheer yourself up are failing, so that nothing at all seems to give you pleasure or lifts your mood, it is likely you need to see a specialist.

I have already mentioned that our moods often seem impenetrable, even to ourselves. One way of simplifying thinking about our moods is to analyse them by breaking them down into the six basic emotions I described on page 182. Another model worth considering describes all the emotions as being formed from four basic components. And even four seems a bit complicated to some psychologists who believe they can be reduced further to two elements.[65]

Before considering the states which underpin mood an important question is why bad moods seem so difficult to get rid of and good ones so fleeting? This is such a common experience it has been crystallised into a psychological law of hedonistic asymmetry.[66] The law states: 'Pleasure is always contingent upon change and disappears with continuous satisfaction. Pain may persist under persisting adverse conditions.'

This law exists because of the postulated purpose of good and bad moods. Good mood tells the brain that things in the environment are OK and that no corrective action is needed. Bad mood informs our minds that something is amiss and needs attention – this emotion will therefore persist until all concerns have been met so bad mood becomes the emotion that prompts us to attend to or change something while good mood means we can stop for a while.

It may be that a good mood is the more fleeting because the mere possibility of something not being right and needing attention – like a worry – will replace a good mood by a bad one. Everything has to be in order to result in a good mood, while only one thing needs to be wrong to produce a bad one.

Our capacity to experience mood is passed on to us through evolution and can be seen as preparing the body for action or inaction. Animals have to devote most of their waking moments to eating and surviving – and are driven by their moods. When they are hungry, they seek food; when they are afraid, they retreat from an enemy.

Translating this into human terms, the philosophers have, perhaps cynically, boiled emotions down to drives which seek pleasure or avoid pain.

But if you accept the basic thesis that our moods tell us when to be active and expend energy and also when to rest, it follows that feelings of vigour and tiredness must underpin all emotions.

To seek pleasure or avoid pain you have to have the energy to do so, and when you are too tired you cannot react to the environment in a way that allows you to pursue your needs or avoid your fears. Research which has tried to induce the human mood of depression in animals has centred on giving an animal electric shocks, no matter what it does, so it soon learns it is impossible, whatever it tries, to avoid pain.[67] The animal falls into a state of what psychologists have called 'learned helplessness', which they feel comes closest to the essence of depression.

If feelings of high or low stamina underpin all our emotions, you could view depression as a state of low energy. After all, it makes sense for evolution to have programmed us into learning that if no matter what we do we get knocked back, it's time to stop doing anything. In this way nature presents us with a mood of low energy to save us from doing ourselves further damage.

In order to analyse and define our moods, it is useful to think of all emotions as falling somewhere along the spectrum of energy: when we are deeply and passionately in love we feel energised; when we feel hostility we experience vigour; when we feel sad we have little strength. But, while our energy level might determine how active we are it does not tell us whether we will be actively pursuing someone or something – like a date – or running away from it – our boss, for instance. Moods don't just have an energy level, they also have a direction – away from or towards something.

Given that some situations involving fear or anxiety might involve dangers, like predators and edges of cliffs, a major component of our emotional state in such anxiety situations must be to get the hell out of them, or to be so fearful of some that we avoid going near them and so stay out of trouble. Fear, or anxiety, may be defined as another fundamental mood, which may manifest itself as anything from mild nervousness and tension to sheer terror.

The emotion of anxiety is about detecting and protecting ourselves from danger. Anxious humans are very like fearful animals, in that both will be hyper-vigilant of their environment and interpret even innocuous signals in a negative way. In threatening situations their heart and respiration rate and blood pressure will go up, and they will be unable to carry out normal activities until the thing making them fearful has gone. The biological changes the body experiences when in the grip of fear help prepare it for immediate action – fight or flight.

The opposite of fear or anxiety is calmness, an emotional state which allows us to feel certain we are not in danger and are confident things will be OK. When we feel calm we know we can proceed without concern.[68]

It is possible therefore to think of all emotions as made up of only two basic types: negative and positive moods. Positive moods are underpinned by a state of high energy combined with feelings of low tension or anxiety. In contrast, negative moods are an amalgamation of high anxiety or tension plus low energy.[69] The other possible permutations, then, are low energy plus low tension, which probably most resembles sleepiness, while high energy/high tension is probably how most of us feel when experiencing an agitated anxiety.

In general, having high energy tends to lower tension while having high tension tends to lower energy: so depression is a state underpinned by high tension and low energy. Anxiety and depression so often co-exist that it is difficult to distinguish one from the other. Anxiety revolves around fear of the future and is imbued with uncertainty, whereas depression is characterised by hopelessness and is founded on certainty. So those who are anxiously depressed oscillate from uncertainty to certainty about how bad their future is going to be. The essence of mood management becomes regulating your energy and tension levels.

When you are full of energy, you are more liable to feel able to solve your problems; when you feel low in energy, your difficulties are likely to feel more onerous or even unsolvable and this pessimism is bound to increase your tension. The swing from anxiety to depression may reflect swings in energy level, while tension stays high.

Elite athletes are calm but full of energy, a state termed the iceberg profile.[70] This seems to be the ideal condition in which to face challenges, yet most of us, when facing tough situations like exams or interviews, are instead in a state of low energy and high tension.

As mentioned earlier, your analysis of a problem is determined by your mood, so either choose times when you're in a good mood to think about problems, particularly difficult ones, in other words wait until you are in a high energy/low tension state before making important decisions, as you are likely to be at your least vulnerable then. People too often try to tackle their problems when in a low energy/high tension state because they believe the only way to remove these uncomfortable feelings is to solve the problem there and then.

But our moods are altered not only by events, but also circumstances like the weather, our standard daily mood cycle and the season.[71] Although we may not be aware of it, our feelings of energy and tension have a fairly repetitive daily pattern which indicates that there are rhythms (often biological) at work in our bodies. These help to determine our mood, so how we feel from moment to moment is a product of these background factors as well as of specific events. For most people, energy is low first thing in the morning, and gradually rises to a high point at around midday, when it begins to decline.

Tension, in contrast, starts low first thing in the morning, gradually rises throughout the day and hits a high point around the time we are coming home from work. It then diminishes for the rest of the day, but probably at a slower rate than energy. So we are often feeling our best around mid to late morning when our energy is higher than earlier in the day, and tension has not yet hit the late afternoon peak.

This regular variation of mood during the day is easy to see when you monitor it. However, we usually put our mood down to what has just happened to us, without realising that even if we had a brilliant day at the office, our tension would still peak at around the time we leave it. In addition to these daily mood cycles, there are also weekly, monthly, and possibly even seasonal cycles. Understanding these cycles may be helpful, particularly if there is no event to which we can attribute our mood.

On the other hand, we can do something about some aspects of our biology. Psychologists have found one of the most productive techniques for encouraging a more positive mood is exercise. Moderate exercise, like 10 minutes of brisk walking, seems to enhance feelings of energy for up to 90 minutes afterwards.[72] The fact that research has found that exercise can so reliably make our mood more positive means we do not necessarily need to reverse a negative event to feel more positive.

There are several reasons why exercise is good for our mood, both in the short and long term. Physical activity is in fact the final phase of the process our bodies go through when we are in a stressful situation. This is because our bodies evolved to cope with anything causing tension – predominantly predators – by 'fight or flight' reaction. So any hormones, glucose and fats released into the bloodstream in response to stress are never dissipated without the expected exercise. Regular exercise provides a replacement to fighting or 'flying', and so restores our bodies to their natural balance.

Exercise is also a mental diversion, an outlet for emotions and physical tensions. So exercises benefit people because it means we produce lower levels of stress when under pressure, which improves our work performance. When under pressure at work, physically fit individuals show less muscular activity, a lower resting heart rate, and less accumulation of blood acid by-products, than unfit individuals.

Moderate exercise also boosts the immune function, which in turn lowers the risk of illness, because it releases natural body steroids. So the businessman who exercises regularly is literally competing on steroids! Exercise also improves mental functioning by increasing blood circulation to the brain. It releases the brain's natural opiates producing calmness and a happier state. Blood levels of noradrenaline are also elevated, which may help to cure depression (the chemical used in antidepressant tablets).

As well as affecting these physical changes, exercise also improves your emotional state. Exercise increases our feelings of self-mastery and self-efficiency which help reduce negative emotions. Our lifestyle patterns may change as a result of fitting regular exercise into a schedule, and new relationships may also start, leading to improved social support. Finally, more appropriate role models are often found in the gym than in the pub!

Exercise is just one way of influencing our mood. Other biological influences we have some control over include sleep and food. Skipping a meal, for example, can have a significant impact on mood. When a serious depression has taken a grip, sufferers tend to lose their appetite, lose weight, and suffer from a disrupted sleep pattern. They either have more difficulty getting to sleep in the first place or wake up in the early hours and find it difficult to get back to sleep. Depressed people certainly feel more tired and are less inclined to exercise.

An important aspect of mood management is to monitor closely your sleep pattern, appetite and weight and amount of exercise. If you notice deviations in your usual routine, this should suggest that important changes may be afoot in your emotional state. The received wisdom is that a certain number of hours of sleep is ideal. However, psychiatrists are more interested in any change to your routine, rather than what the normal routine is, as an indicator of a change in your mood.

Clearly, if your usual routine does not give you enough sleep, food or exercise, it would be difficult for psychiatric treatment to help your moods, and you should try to adjust these aspects to help your mental health. So although sleep, a good diet and adequate exercise are usually associated with preserving physical health, these are also useful things to get right in developing good mental health.

When members of the public are asked by researchers what they do to lift their mood they report strategies like seeing friends, going for walks, busying themselves with work, spending time on a hobby, watching TV, reading, listening to music and eating more or eating less.

Intriguingly, what works for some does the precise opposite for others. Some seek company to cheer themselves up; others avoid it. Some think through the problem that is causing them to be upset; others try to distract themselves from it – even making a conscious effort to avoid thinking about anything which might prolong or exacerbate their bad mood, like recalling previous negative experiences.

Social interaction is the most popular strategy for changing a mood because being with others changes our focus from inwards to outwards. We are less likely to think about ourselves, our problems and our low mood by having something else to focus on, and the presence of another person is one of the most powerful stimuli known to psychologists for diverting us from our internal state. Even if we are talking to others about our problems, the process helps to put them in perspective.

Talking to others could be classified as a distraction technique. Whatever the kind of distraction – devoting yourself to a hobby, busying yourself at work or talking to friends – the principle remains the same: being able to divert yourself from the cause of your bad mood (or the mood itself), is a crucial mental health skill. Psychologists often call this 'emotional management'.

But distraction techniques will be effective only if they occupy you convincingly. My patients often become ill, or stay unwell, because they employ distraction techniques which do not work properly for them. For example, if you watch TV because it distracts you, but you find you are worrying about your problem again in the ad breaks or even during the programme, your distraction is ineffective. For a distraction to work you have to be so absorbed by it that you really do forget all about your negative mood.

A particular mood management strategy may work by more than one means. Another important by-product of talking to others is that it energises us. We feel less tired, partly because talking or being with others arouses us. Even if it is only because it is rude to fall asleep, look bored, or appear tired in the presence of others, we make an effort to show some kind of interest in what is going on. As negative moods are usually associated with low energy,[73] the energising effect of social interaction is obviously beneficial.

Another distraction technique which has surprised psychologists by its effectiveness is listening to music.[74] Although there have been some rather fanciful theories as to why music is so able to affect mood, distraction remains the simplest and most plausible explanation for its effectiveness.

An even more sophisticated mood management technique is 'anticipating mood regulation' where people try to look forward to the mood they want to be in at a certain time and start preparing for it. For example, on a Saturday night before going out clubbing young people listen to club music to get them in the mood and radio stations play this kind of music at that time for this express purpose.

Anticipating future negative moods and planning to elevate mood is one of the most positive mentally healthy approaches and often means setting up a distraction in advance.[75] Perhaps many feel that diversion is a slightly trivial or cowardly way of dealing with their problems. I am not arguing that you should distract yourself from a low mood or a problem whenever you encounter one, but rather that the ability to distract yourself *should you need to* is an important mental health skill. If you do not practise distraction, your ability to distract yourself will atrophy.

Surveys have found that relaxation techniques, seeking pleasurable activities, watching TV, going shopping and seeking social support, are all common things to do to improve a negative mood, which may all have at their core the mechanism of distraction. Other mood management techniques are what psychologists call 'cognitive manoeuvres', which means trying to think about the cause of your poor mood in a way which improves your mood. I cover these techniques in the next chapter, on thinking yourself to sanity.

The third type of approach to improve negative mood is called direct tension mood reduction.[76] This refers to attempts to alter, directly and physically, our brain chemistry so that the negative mood is almost literally dissolved away. This category of mood management includes taking drugs and alcohol.

When the public is asked which of these different strategies they find the most effective, they tend to reply,[77] in descending order of effectiveness: exercise, relaxation techniques, listening to music, social interaction, and busying yourself with work. Cognitive strategies are also found to be pretty effective, not just by the people in general but also by psychiatrists and psychologists. That is why a whole chapter is devoted to them in this book.

The least successful strategies, even though they are very common, people quote are avoiding the person or problem that caused the low mood, being alone, or using drugs or alcohol. Why are drugs and alcohol unsuccessful strategies for mood regulation? One reason is that they are habit-forming and you can soon become driven to take them not to cheer yourself up, but to stave off withdrawal symptoms. Furthermore, excessive alcohol and drug intake, over time, seem to cause low moods themselves. An implication of these surveys is that people who drift towards drugs and alcohol may do so because they are not good at mood management.

It remains a puzzle as to why some can drink in moderation while others go on to depend on it. Perhaps the reason *why* you drink or take drugs comes into play here. If you do so because they have become the only way you can regulate your mood, you are likely to become dependent because you have no alternative strategies in your armoury. This supports the common advice that it's OK to drink in moderation, but beware if you begin to see a drink as the only way to cheer yourself up or calm yourself down – you are possibly at the top of a slippery slope, at the bottom of which lie dependency and poor mental health. Another possibility is that your moods have reached such an intensity of unpleasantness that you believe you need a quick method of dealing with them and drink and drugs are fairly effective. This hints at a certain impatience or intolerance of some moods – again, a sure sign of poor mental health.

BE A MUG

It is intriguing that exercise and music are so high up on the list of effective strategies. Exercise and music (as well as social interaction) are all combined in dance, so there does appear to be some basis to the notion that regular dancing may enhance happiness.

Exercise is evidently an effective and healthy method of mood regulation. Research has demonstrated that even a brief spurt of exercise is so useful in terms of managing our moods that it helps people whose dips in mood might lead them to relapse into smoking or eating when they are trying to give up or diet.[78, 79, 80, 81]

257

If you are beginning to think that your psychiatrist is suggesting that positive mental health is to be found only at discos, another finding is that some surveys of religious groups have found that prayer, meditation and reading religious works are also effective means of mood management.[82] You will find more about mental health and religion in the final chapter 'Is Prevention Possible?'.

Just in case I haven't convinced you of the benefits of distraction, bear in mind that some psychologists have put the persistently high rates of depression in women compared with men (women are about twice to three times as likely as men to be depressed) down to the fact that men tend to distract themselves when they are low (by turning to a hobby, for example), while women are inclined to ponder their negative condition.[83] While it is true that women use social interaction more than men as a mood-regulating strategy, it may be that they are not using it effectively. If you socialise to gain perspective on your problem or to distract yourself and improve mood, it can work well. But if you use social interaction merely to dwell on your problems, it will not have a positive effect. So if women talk to others when they are low merely 'to have a good moan', it will not be beneficial.

The way that even talking to friends can have such different effects illustrates yet again the subtle differences between a positive and negative mental health strategy in maintaining control over your mood.

There are several reasons why some may not make much effort to dispel a low mood in the first place. You may not want to get yourself too excited about an anticipated pleasant event to protect yourself from disappointment should things not turn out as well as expected. You may suppress excitement when a protracted and difficult task is nearly finished in case joy distracts from what still needs to be done. You may prefer a low mood because a more positive emotion may distract you from the kind of calm thinking you need to do. You may not desire a more upbeat mood because this would then put you out of emotional step with those aroud you.[84]

Even so, as I have argued in this chapter, the ability to regulate mood, or be in control of your moods, rather than allowing them to control you, is a crucial mental health skill. I explained that anxiety and depression are the two main moods you need to gain control over in order to avoid most of the common mental illnesses. The key to pathological anxiety is the way you overreact to threat. If you cannot easily avoid the object which you fear and which produces anxiety, exposing yourself to this in a gradual way – facing your fear – is the best way of overcoming anxiety. The key to clinical depression, in contrast, is the way you overreact to a lack of rewards in your life. Building more rewards into your life seems to be a solution to depression. Finally, boredom is due to too much predictability and a lack of uncertainty or the unexpected in your life, and may be the result of an attempt to avoid anxiety altogether.

I have explained the various methods of mood regulation, and that it is better to have more than one method in your armoury. I have highlighted distraction as a key mood management tool which underpins many of the other common methods, and that it is important to use distraction which works fully, not just partially. Distraction is part of an emotion-focused strategy which is in contrast to problem-focused approaches. I have also stressed that distraction should not be used indiscriminately. It may be better to solve your problems rather than distract yourself from them, and solving problems may require being focused on them for sustained periods. But distraction is crucial to mental health because it is important to be able to distract yourself when focusing on the problem or when staying in a certain mood ceases to help your mental health.

While controlling and reducing negative mood has been the focus of this chapter, I have touched on how to enhance positive mood through 'pleasant activity training'. One psychological research programme into how to increase personal happiness effectively – and which even eighteen months after the programme produced improvements in the long-term happiness of 72 per cent of participants – is the Fourteen Fundamentals Program designed by psychologist Michael Fordyce.[85]

Each of the fourteen fundamentals is an objective found by research to be a feature of people who score high on psychologist's measures of happiness.

Twelve of the fourteen fundamentals are: (a) Keep busy and be more active, (b) spend more time socialising, (c) be productive at meaningful work, (d) get better organised and plan things, (e) lower your expectations and aspirations, (f) become present-oriented, (g) work on a healthy personality, (h) develop an outgoing, social personality, (i) be yourself, (j) eliminate negative feelings and problems, (k) close relationships are the number one source of happiness, and (l) put happiness as your most important priority.

I have touched on these twelve fundamentals of happiness in this and earlier chapters. The last two, (m) stop worrying and (n) develop positive optimistic thinking, are the subject of the next chapter.

THOUGHTS SHARE

MYND THEM ON KEY

TELEPATHY

THOUGHTS

MIND THE MONKEYS.

2018

SO, YOU THINK YOU ARE SANE?

Thinking

'The only true thing one can say about the past is that it no longer exists.'
Kay Pollack (1994)

To the public, a psychiatrist is someone with a Viennese accent who puts you on a couch and remains silent as you spill out your concerns, apart from interjecting the occasional 'How do you feel about that?' This image is beloved by Hollywood and repeated endlessly in films, television and books. This media portrayal has undoubtedly shaped the public's attitude to the profession. It may, therefore, surprise you to know that it is a totally outdated concept, and unrepresentative of the modern practice of psychiatry.

This popular image is extremely frustrating to modern psychiatrists, as they feel that many who would benefit from treatment are put off by such stereotypes. Speculating as to why Hollywood has disseminated these out-of-date images for so long, some have wondered whether the largely Jewish psychoanalysts in Freud's Vienna circle, who fled the Nazis in the 1930s and 40s and headed for California in large numbers because of its tolerant climate and welcoming of new ideas, may have unduly influenced the intellectual climate there, and shaped the subsequent treatment of the profession by many film directors.

Psychoanalysis is a small and specialised part of the vast field of psychiatry, where the psychiatrist maintains distance during the therapeutic encounter and 'interprets' the hidden meanings of the client's dreams and statements. This is based on the assumption that understanding why your personality is as it is will produce insight into your problems, and that this will lead to change. If you believe there is a hidden meaning behind your everyday actions and statements because your unconscious is repressing memories from your conscious mind and keeping you from understanding what is really going on, it's easy to progress logically to believing that you need to see a trained

"You are as you were then .. but you are a bit older now."

STAYING SANE

psychoanalyst to further your mental health, rather than helping yourself.

But today the focus of the new generation of psychologists and psychiatrists has moved away from this approach. The emphasis is no longer on encouraging the client to express feelings and explore the past. Instead, they focus on the 'here and now' and your immediate thoughts, which underpin your current emotions. From the 1960s onwards, there has been what some call a 'cognitive revolution' in treatment, where cognitions or thoughts (not emotions) take centre stage. The most common form of non-drug psychological treatment offered by academically trained clinicians is now thought-centred, or what is known as 'cognitive' therapy.

Cognitive therapists have abandoned the previous preoccupation with delving into people's past lives as a way of understanding why they currently feel as they do. They are also much more actively involved in the session; they may even appear argumentative in that they persistently challenge clients' statements instead of speaking rarely, as a Freudian psychoanalyst might. The reason they are much more directive is because they believe that if you can be helped to see that your way of thinking about yourself and your predicament is irrational or unrealistic, that simple realisation will enable you to change your emotional state. So, the modern, academically trained therapist spends much time during the session arguing with you about whether your beliefs about yourself and the world are reasonable or justified in light of the evidence.

As with psychotherapy, there are several different approaches to cognitive therapy. The pioneer of one of the approaches, known as Rational-Emotive-Therapy (RET), Albert Ellis, promotes a forceful, confrontational therapeutic style, stating, '…therapists are too namby-pamby, or unforceful, in encouraging clients to surrender their irrational thinking'.[1]

Unlike the Freudian psychotherapy methods, this new cognitive outlook lends itself to self-help as, with a grasp of its fundamental principles, anyone can start doing it for themselves, in a way that simply was not possible with psychoanalysis. A key message is that change might be a lot simpler than previously suspected. Cognitive therapists believe that your present state is a direct consequence of what you

"Not AN EYE that sees you, but is a Physician to commit on your malady" (Eric W Shakespeare) (2 Gents of Verona)

"Fallar sem CUIDAR é Atirar sem Apontar" "To Speak without Thinking is to shoot without taking (Caring)

believe and think now. It follows that as you can control your beliefs and thoughts, if you can understand the basis of the errors in your thinking, you will be able to change them and thereby also alter the factors which produce psychological distress.

One example of the errors in thinking that cognitive therapists are concerned with are what I call 'ANTs' or Automatic Negative Thoughts. ANTs seem to come on involuntarily and therefore appear automatic, but where do our ANTs come from?

Researchers in America armed a group of three-year-olds with tape-recorders which ran continuously, in an attempt to record all the statements made by adults to these children over a two-week period. Eighty-five per cent of the messages were found to be negative, thereby communicating to the three-year-olds that they were not good enough and that they must not do this or that.[2] Psychologists and psychiatrists now believe these negative statements we hear repeatedly during our formative years are probably incorporated into our outlook on life, in the form of self-talk – what we say to ourselves during our continuous inner conversation.

Every thought you have affects your mood.

Therefore, if you want to improve your mood, energy and optimism, you have to start by analysing what you say to yourself. If, when things in your life go wrong, or are not as you would like them to be, your internal monologue is preoccupied with blaming yourself, and in particular with finding fault with yourself, then you may be suffering from a bad case of ANTs.

Say, for example, you try to chat up someone you fancy, or apply for a new job, or try a new project, and you are rebuffed. If you automatically assume that these setbacks occur because you are ugly, stupid, or inadequate, then you are clearly plagued with ANTs, which are over-judgemental of yourself and are probably an echo of your personal tape-recorder, still running from when you were three years old. The solution is to become aware of these negative judgements and labels you automatically use to describe yourself, and to replace each devaluing statement with a more objective description of yourself.

For example, if when you get rejected by someone you fancy, you put it down to being flabby, try instead describing your figure less judgementally using your actual height and weight. Wipe out your

ANTs problem by replacing them with a commitment to use realistic self-descriptions rather than negative labels in your internal monologue.

You are not dumpy, you are four feet five inches tall; you are not stupid, but your mind does periodically go blank, particularly when nervous and trying to make conversation. Also list five good points about yourself that you take pride in and five things you are not so happy about – but phrased in objective and non-judgemental ways. Next time you find your ANTs infestation is putting you off going over to that good-looking person to chat them up, or applying for that job, give yourself a dose of reality by recalling your five good points, and do not tolerate those ANTs running all over you.

Perhaps the most common species of ANT which plagues us is the thought based on the presumption 'I must be loved or liked and approved of by every significant person I meet'. Instead, replace this particularly vicious, irrational ANT with something more realistic like, 'I, like most people, want to be loved or liked by others, and when this does not happen I am bound to feel disappointed or lonely, but I can cope with these feelings, and I can take constructive steps to make and maintain better relationships.'[3]

Another ANT you should mercilessly hunt down and destroy is the 'I must be perfectly competent, make no mistakes, and achieve every goal set for me to be considered a worthwhile person' belief. The best pesticide for this ANT is 'I, like most people, want to do some things well, but, again like most people, I will occasionally make mistakes. Then I will feel bad, but I can cope with that, and I can take constructive steps to do better next time'.[4]

I can't stress enough how important it is to watch out for these phrases which have an insidious habit of creeping up on you. The following phrase is useful to remember! 'To stop my daily RANTS against myself, I must kill my ANTs.'

This is the theory behind the cognitive approach. How does it work in practice? Take a specific problem, such as insomnia, or sleeplessness. This is an extremely common problem which many of us face – even if only temporarily – and has been shown by recent research to be linked to worry.[5] Worries (in case you've never had any) are defined by psychiatrists as 'the persistent awareness of possible future dangers', which are repeatedly gone over without being resolved. One finding from psychological research suggests that worrying seems the most difficult thing to dismiss from your mind, in other words it is almost as if worry is the part of your mind you have least control over.[6] This, in itself, makes the subject of worry fascinating, if not a little, er, worrying.

Since control over your mind and thoughts is a cornerstone of positive mental health, worries are a crucial obstacle to achieving such mental health.

Times of stress are marked by an increase in worrying, so much so that worry could be considered one of the most unpleasant and intrusive features of our mental lives. For many, chronic worry becomes a feature of everyday life, until eventually it is difficult to distinguish days of high and low stress, as every day seems to bring with it a whole gamut of worries, some new but many old.

In fact, the most common anxiety disorder in the UK is not caused by a simple phobia like a fear of dogs, but one in which chronic worry is the main feature. It is three times as common as simple phobias. Around 22 per cent of people will at some time suffer from chronic worry, this being more common among women than men.[7]

People differ not only in how much they worry, but also in what they worry about, if their worries are realistic, and whether they think about their worries in such a way as to lead to their constructive resolution, rather than an endless cycle of anxiety-making thoughts. It may be that worry is simply what we afterwards label unsuccessful attempts at problem-solving, or could it be that worriers are actually trying to solve insoluble problems? Perhaps they are trying to achieve the kind of certainty about the future or about an ambiguous situation that it is simply not possible to attain in an uncertain and unpredictable world?

Psychologists term the things people worry about as 'problems'; and problems in their terms are situations where the possibility of something bad happening to you is bothering you. So, a problem might be a project your boss has asked you to do but which you cannot finish by the deadline requested. The negative consequence you fear is that your boss will be annoyed with you, and this may lead to you being sacked. See how one worry leads to another?

Psychologists believe the mentally healthy way to approach problems like this is to solve them (problem-solving) whereas the mentally unhealthy tactic is to worry. In chapter 8, on coping, I discuss what to do when faced with an insoluble problem and I also discuss this in the chapter on mood management (psychologists are not so naive or upbeat to ignore the fact that some problems cannot be so easily solved).

Successful problem-solving as a process can be broken down into separate stages. The first step is to define the problem. The mistake most people make here is not to be specific enough about the precise aspect of the problem that really bothers them. So, is the problem handing the project in late, or that your boss will be annoyed, or that you will be upset with yourself? After all, managing the project timetable might require a different problem-solving strategy to that of manipulating your boss's emotions.[8]

The second stage of problem-solving is to brainstorm as many different solutions to your problem as possible, and here what characterises the mentally unhealthy is a lack of creativity and imagination when it comes to generating solutions to their problems. (In my opinion the option of suicide is often tragically the product of an extreme lack of imagination over problem-solving when feeling too bleak to be creative about other options.) Possible solutions, some better than others, to your project timetable problem or worry might range from going off sick to delegating work, explaining why the project is late, getting it in on time at the expense of doing it properly, obtaining help to finish it, warning your boss about the lateness, and so on. The mentally healthy tend to be willing to consider a wide variety of possible solutions, before deciding which one to adopt.

The third stage of problem-solving is to narrow your choice of solutions to the one that is likely to work best, that is practicable, and that best meets your needs. For example, using your previous knowledge of your boss you may decide that getting it in on time but in a less than perfect state is the best of all possible options.

The last stage of problem-solving is to implement your solution. A further stage might be to monitor how your implementation is going, with a view to changing the solution or altering the way you implement it.

Now no one is suggesting that problem-solving really will provide the answer to life, the universe and everything and that you will live happily ever after. Problems are difficult to wrestle with and many solutions you try will be less than perfect. The solution of explaining to your boss why your project is late, might, for example, be rejected and you might be required to start again. The real point here is that problem-solving is an invaluable approach to difficult situations you find yourself in. Furthermore, problem-solving takes practice, particularly if you are not used to it, but if you keep trying you will get better at it.

In my view, problem-solving is mostly about an attitude to life and its hurdles, and it is this practical approach on which much mental health rests. It is certainly superior to simple worry in terms of maintaining mental health.

Going back to the problem-solving process, research[9] has found that although worriers tended to be able to complete the first step – identifying the problem and its potential dangers – they had great difficulty in moving on to the next steps, that of generating and implementing solutions. The most likely explanation is that our immediate reactions to problematic situations, such as panicking or getting upset, cause us to worry and this tends to delay our use of problem-solving skills, such as articulating goals, generating solutions, making decisions, and implementing and verifying solutions. Thus it may be that worriers' problem-solving difficulties lie in the area of problem orientation, that is, how they approach problems right at the beginning, rather than in an actual lack of problem-solving skills.

Put another way, worriers do not think about the things which threaten them as problems which might have solutions, or as situations which might be helped by responses from themselves, but are caught like rabbits in a car's headlights, so terrified by their situation that they are unable to react positively.

Worriers tend to deal with their lack of skills in seeking and implementing solutions by avoiding confronting their problems. This, of course, diminishes their problem-solving performance further. Worriers thus first of all worry about their problem, then they worry about the solution. Will it work? Was it the best one to choose? Did I implement it correctly? They then lose confidence in the solutions they come up with.

It seems that worriers are overly indecisive over choice and implementation of solutions. One theory about why they do this is that worriers are looking for something they can never have – certainty that the solution they try will work. In their pursuit of a guaranteed resolution, worriers fail to grasp at any answers which are available.

This is clearly counterproductive, as all you can do when faced with a problem is to follow the four steps and try out responses; if you don't, the only alternative is to be stuck with the problem and worry about it. Since all you can do is try to generate and implement solutions to the best of your ability, once you have done this it is legitimate to stop worrying. Research has shown that once people adopt a problem-solving attitude to their problems they do largely cure themselves of unnecessary worry.[10]

To take another example, let us say your loved one is back late from the office and you start to worry that something terrible might have happened to him. Possible solutions include ringing the office, checking the news bulletins for train crashes, going to the station, ringing work colleagues, and so on. After trying these solutions, worry no longer serves a useful purpose – you have done all you can and continuing to worry beyond this point only serves to upset. Focusing on a negative possibility (a car crash) serves no further function; there is nothing you can do to solve the problem now. So you might as well concentrate on more positive possibilities, such as there having been an entirely innocent commuting problem. I talk in greater detail later on in this chapter about the use of further strategies, like distraction, to be implemented once you have done your problem-solving to the best of your ability.

One possible good thing about worry is that it makes you aware of your problem and may also motivate you into doing something constructive about it.

Often worriers are unable to implement solutions because they are caught between two choices, both of which seem to have possible negative consequences. For example, I tend to worry about filling out my tax return. If I took a problem-solving approach, I would ask myself what exactly is worrying me and would then do something about it. Let's say I am worried that I don't have the expertise to do the return and wonder if I should hire an accountant. But then I worry about the expense of an accountant and whether he or she is going to rip me off. Taking a problem-solving approach, I would work out how I could decide whether I have the expertise to do the return myself, or whether I could obtain it (for example, by asking a friend or reading up about tax). I would then either do the return myself or hire an accountant to do it, rather than worrying about it. I might decide to try an accountant for a year and then re-evaluate. If my precise worry is about the quality of accountant, I might focus on how to reduce the chances of getting a useless one by asking a trusted friend to recommend one.

But what I would do instead, if a classic worrier, would be to look at the tax return, worry about how time-consuming or difficult it was to do and how expensive it was to hire an accountant, bury it at the bottom of the pile of things to do and put off taking a decision. Recognise the symptoms?

The key to this kind of conflict is to examine which negative consequence is the worst, and go for the other one. One way of deciding which negative consequence is the worst is asking yourself 'which outcome could I least cope with?'

As mentioned earlier, worriers are fearful about problems in themselves, rather than lacking problem-solving skills once they get beyond the initial stage. Once I had decided whether to go for an accountant or do the tax form myself, for example, implementing the solution usually turns out to be less of a problem than choosing it in the first place. What chronic worriers don't realise is that the cost of delaying the implementation of the solution is merely more worry.

Cognitive therapies focus on changing worriers' perceptions of their problems so that they feel less reluctant to confront them, as well as increasing their problem-solving orientation (taking a more welcoming approach to problems).

Given what a common problem worry is, it is surprising that scientists still do not know what possible useful function worry might serve. One theory is that by worrying about an anticipated event we prepare ourselves for it, and so become more able to deal with it when it finally arrives. Some worry achieves this, but people who worry excessively often end up dealing badly with the situations they worry about, precisely because their fears have made them more anxious, and extreme nervousness leads to poor performance.

Another way in which worry is often unhelpful is that it leads to a host of imagined scenarios, usually much worse than what is really likely to happen, and the common reaction to such self-generated fears is to avoid the situation altogether. Take public speaking, for example. If you imagine a scenario in which you stutter with nerves and your audience expresses visible disapproval, you may well decide to forgo the experience. In this case, your worry will have led you to avoid experiencing something which, if you had actually tried it, might have proved your worries groundless, or at least overblown.

That is why the great conundrum (or worry) about worry is that if you do not worry about something (like falling over the edge of a cliff) you will tend not to take adequate precautions, while if you worry too much your precautions will prevent you taking the necessary risks which lead to personal growth (you will never get to enjoy the view). Chronic worriers avoid risk and certainly thereby avoid mistakes. But sometimes the mistakes are not as bad as worriers think they will be.

The very unreasonableness of most people's worries means that their anticipation of a bad thing is usually much worse than the reality, so that life is one long series of reliefs, rather than the sequence of nasty surprises it is for those who do not worry enough. This, perhaps, explains the possible benefit of worrying, which in turn explains why so many people continue to worry excessively when, on the face of it, this seems an extremely unpleasant option.

So, how do you know when you are worrying too much or too little, and when should you worry more or less? A good general rule for identifying a tendency to worry too much is if, after discussing your worry with your friends, you feel a sense of relief. If your friends have been able to reassure you that some of your worry was unnecessary, this demonstrates your own inability to reassure yourself: a classic sign of a chronic worrier.

However, if they then appear more anxious about your problem than you do, then you are not worrying enough! If you are worried about this 'resolution by democracy' approach to establishing the right amount of worry, an alternative is to review issues you have worried over in the past. Have your worries usually been justified, or have your fears generally been worse than the events themselves? If the latter is the case, a cognitive clinician would appeal to you to stop your excessive worrying, as the evidence suggests that you have an unrealistic view of the future.

If worry is defined as a negative anticipation of the future, worriers spend a lot of time imagining all the terrible things which might happen to them soon. A bout of worry occurs when your mind generates more and more, worse and even worse possible scenarios of what terrible things could happen to you. Worriers persistently ask themselves 'what if?': 'What if my boss doesn't like my last project and sacks me?' 'What if my child fails his exam and never gets any qualifications and then languishes for years unemployed?' 'What if I lost my job and then my house?'

In particular, research has shown that worriers, being natural pessimists, have a tendency to take an ambiguous signal or situation and put a negative spin on it. So, for example, suppose you pass your boss in the corridor and, despite a cheery hello from you, he just passes by without any acknowledgement? The worrier would immediately assume that this was a harbinger of negative news. Many worriers I see in my practice would have imagined their sacking by the time they reached the end of the corridor! The cognitive approach would argue that this is an ambiguous situation as your boss may be preoccupied by a forthcoming meeting or simply hungover; ignoring you does not mean he will sack you.

To deal with this worry, the cognitive therapist would ask you what evidence there was that your boss really hated you and was planning your redundancy. If you had recently received a pay rise or been complimented on your work, the therapist would question how realistic your deduction was. A further strategy the cognitive therapist would advise would be to check in some more definitive way what your boss really thought of you before getting upset, for example, by a seemingly innocent chat with his secretary or your colleagues.

In other words, the cognitive therapist would challenge the assumptions that underlie your unease, rather than directly confronting the worry. He would try to help you see that the world is filled with ambiguity and that we spend our lives trying to discern what means what: 'Does my date being late for our meal mean she doesn't like me?', 'If my child doesn't talk so much about school any more, does this mean he is being bullied?', and so on. Given this barrage of ambiguity, it is important to work out what really can or cannot be deduced from the very wide range of often confusing evidence. If something is uncertain, then after you have done your best to reduce as much uncertainty as you can, you need to learn to tolerate indeterminacy without getting too upset, as getting distressed over something you can do nothing about is not helpful. This is, of course, easier to say than to do, but you can improve with practice. Essentially, cognitive therapy is about improving your skills at forming reasonable deductions from the evidence life throws at you.

The kind of mental 'holding on' referred to above, the worriers' tendency to find it difficult to dismiss a worry or thought from their mind and replace it with something more realistic or cheerful, is called rumination, and plays a pivotal role in determining people's ability to cope with stressful events. Ruminators focus on relatively small events and issues, and blow them up into major problems. The crucial difference between ruminators and non-ruminators is the tendency to link small events with major consequences.

Why do people ruminate in the first place? Three possible origins for this could be: children learning it from ruminating parents, parents failing to teach children a repertoire of more adaptive strategies for handling a low mood, or the influence of biological factors such as genes.

Recent research[11] suggests that the way we interpret how our long-term goals are threatened by everyday events underpins rumination. So, those who link occurrences of small, negative events – say, gaining weight – as threats to higher goals – say, attaining promotion or being happy – ruminate more and experience more depression than those who tend not to interpret things in this way. If we constantly link minor events with major ones, this suggests that our understanding of how major goals are achieved is too dominated by linking them with comparably unrelated events. If we constantly do this, then relatively minor everyday irritations can become negatively related to depression and illness.

This hypothesis argues that 'linkers', as we could describe such people, not only ruminate more than 'non-linkers', but also that they tend to interpret most minor irritations as having deeper personal implications than they really do. In other words, rumination also shows an excessive focus on your own feelings and a tendency to see drastic personal implications in relatively innocuous events. Ruminators tend to agree with statements in psychology questionnaires such as 'I isolate myself to think about how I am feeling', whereas non-ruminators agree with statements such as 'I did something fun to get my mind off how I was feeling'. Given that the ability to control your inner mental life is crucial to mental health, it follows that those who frequently find themselves in the grip of uncontrolled thoughts are prone to mental health problems.

This is why the cognitive therapist would hope to persuade you that getting upset over a particular incident is not warranted, and that only if there is sufficient evidence would it be appropriate to be worried if your boss ignores you in the corridor.

Notice that in the treatment of worry, the cognitive therapist does not ask you to talk a lot about how belittled you feel by your boss, or how this reminds you of some childhood experience. The therapist does not encourage you to vent your anger at being ignored by the boss. Instead, the therapist moves straight away to question whether your beliefs, which underpin your bad feeling, are justified and, if not, how they should be modified.

So, if you see worry as simply what fills up the space between realising you have a problem and implementing the solution, then worry will serve only to prolong your experience of living under the shadow of a problem, and must contribute to much unnecessary stress. This effect may explain the power of worry, for example, that those prone to excessive worry take longer to recover from operations.[12]

Worriers make mountains out of molehills; the treatment is to learn to make molehills out of mountains. To see which you are better at making, try the following quiz:

ARE YOU A WORRIER?[13]

Some people are so worried that they avoid filling out quizzes in case their worst fears are confirmed... It is at this point that worry becomes a real problem, when it prevents us doing things most others can do.

WORRY SCALE

Each statement is followed by two possible responses: agree or disagree. Read each statement carefully and decide which response best describes how you feel. Then put a tick over the corresponding response. Please respond to every statement. If you are not completely sure which response is more accurate, put the response which you feel is most appropriate. Do not read the scoring explanation before filling out the questionnaire. Do not spend too long on each statement. It is important that you answer each question as honestly as possible.

		AGREE	DISAGREE
1	I will never lose my close friends	A	B
2	I am unattractive to many of the opposite sex	B	A
3	I never appear stupid to others	A	B
4	My future job prospects are not secure	B	A
5	My work is up to date	A	B
6	This country is in serious trouble	B	A
7	I open bills immediately	A	B
8	I might be a lot less healthy than I realise	B	A
9	The future will be better than the past	A	B
10	Something terrible could be about to happen	B	A

Add up your score from summing the numbers of As and Bs in each box you have ticked. Your score and the interpretation given below should be treated with caution – this short test is by no means definitive, but may offer a guide to where you stand compared to others around you.

SCORE

8 or more Bs. You are scoring high on worrying and this may mean that, while you may worry about a very significant event in your life, as anyone else might, you tend to remain concerned about the same problem for much longer; in fact, months go by with your preoccupation dominating your life more days than not. A large source of your worry could be the conviction that you are unable to do much to change your fate, while at the same time dreading what that may be. One way of tackling your tendency to worry is to investigate what you can do practically to resolve the issue. Once you have attempted this, you will learn that chronic worry may be a worse fate than your current fears.

Between 5 and 7 Bs. You appear to be not quite as worried as higher scorers, but your possible tendency constantly to judge yourself, and your concern over time and your perfectionism, all combine to suggest chronic worry is a major part of your life. In fact, your performance in all spheres of life would probably improve if you worried less, which runs counter to your intuition that if you do not worry you will not do as well. Worry might be used by you as a strategy to achieve success because you feel you might be able to avoid problems by anticipating them. This is true to some extent, but only if your worries are realistic. Unrealistic worries are those you find that only you have and which none of your friends or family understand or share.

Between 3 and 5 Bs. While you appear to be fairly free from worry about the problems chronic worriers are preoccupied with, like their health and injury, on many days you are apprehensive about financial affairs and perhaps broader subjects like politics and current affairs. One possible aspect of your tendency to worry is your frequent avoidance of the opportunity to take control of your life, leading to worry about how things will turn out. You are probably already able to dismiss some worries, and so have already learnt the valuable lesson that you must control the worry and not let it control you.

> *Between 0 and 2 Bs.* You appear to be scoring low on worrying, which means you are probably a lot less anxious than higher scorers about issues like your health, money, relationships, employment, family. While this means that your life is more relaxed than higher scorers, you should be aware of one advantage of some degree of worry, which is that it leads to preoccupation with an issue, which in turn makes it more likely that some unforeseen problem will be anticipated and planned for. Because worriers fear the worst, they are over-cautious, but that means that, in reality, life will not produce anything more terrible than they have imagined. For those who do not worry enough, life contains more unpleasant surprises.

Worry is something we associate with the responsibilities of adulthood, and childhood is thought to be the one time in our lives when we are relatively free from worry. However, a MORI survey of over 4,000 11–16-year-olds, conducted in 1997, found that 79 per cent of boys and 92 per cent of girls were plagued by worry. The main concern of most of these young people was the surprisingly adult preoccupation with their appearance. Childhood is clearly no longer the carefree time we can look back on with nostalgia from the careworn preoccupations of adult life, and recent surveys even suggest that as many as 10 per cent of children suffer from depression.

The latest research into worry throughout our lifespan has come up with some surprising answers about precisely when in life we worry least. Childhood, for example, is not pinpointed as one of the 'seven ages' when we are at our most nonchalant. The fact that researchers have found that we now seem to be worrying more than ever before may explain why psychological problems are on the increase, despite our better material comforts compared to previous generations. The escalating speed with which the world is changing means we have to face more uncertainty about the future than any previous generation, and this may explain our current spate of worry.

What people worry about, and how much, does seem to change as we move through our lives. It also seems that just as we learn to solve one set of worries, a new assortment arises to preoccupy us.

THE FIRST AGE OF WORRY (0–7). So, when in our lives does all this worrying first start? As all worries are about anticipating something bad happening in the future, in order to worry a child must be capable of imagining a variety of possibilities and children do not develop this mental skill before the age of six to seven; so, theoretically, it is impossible really to worry before that age. However, psychologists have observed what appear to be the first signs of worry in some children as young as two. A typical worry might relate to threats to typical physical well-being ('What if I get bitten by animals?', for example).

THE SECOND AGE OF WORRY (8–12). Worry in earnest begins around the age of eight to nine because only then does the ability to imagine multiple possible outcomes to a problem develop. Before eight, the poorer imagination of the younger child saves him from speculating about truly awful possibilities. The variety of worries generated by those over eight is nearly twice that of five-to-six-year-olds. While children at this younger age may worry fleetingly, because they are not capable of imagining the plethora of terrible things eight-year-olds can, their worries never last longer than a few moments, not long enough to count as real worrying. Typical worries relate to being good at tasks and parental approval ('What if I do not get picked for the football team?').

By around the age of eight, children also start being able to compare themselves to others, and are now aware for the first time that others are judging them and making comparisons. So they start to worry about how well they compare to others, particularly in performances like playing games or school work.

THE THIRD AGE OF WORRY (13–17). The competitive instinct which is first aroused at this stage will continue to be a major source of worry throughout adolescence, as children compare themselves to others of their age in looks and skills. The other problem adolescence brings is the realisation for the first time that the number of possibilities in life is indeed huge, and therefore things in our future could be even worse than we ever imagined, which leads to even more worry. Typical worry areas relate to exams, appearance and lack of confidence ('What if I never get a date?' or 'What if I look uncool?').

THE FOURTH AGE OF WORRY (18–24). Having survived the worries of adolescence, the preoccupations of young adulthood await. Here the concern, as further education or first jobs beckon, is that bad choices now could permanently ruin a career. While worries about forming relationships are now less acute, as some social skills have developed by this age, worry areas include starting relationships, career and goals in life ('What if I never achieve my goals?' or 'What if the person I date dumps me?').

THE FIFTH AGE OF WORRY (25–44). By the time full adulthood has been attained, usually marriage will have been safely negotiated and the earlier worries over never finding someone to settle down with have abated, only to be replaced by a new set of worries over maintaining the spark in the relationship and pursuing a career, while juggling new worries over children as they arrive and strained financial security. At this age, money and security worries reach a peak, as well as those about keeping relationships ('What if I discover I chose the wrong marriage partner?' or 'What if I am spending too much money?')

THE SIXTH AGE OF WORRY (45–64). Just as your children are reaching an age where it is possible to see the end of the financial burden, and marital relations are returning to a happier state, with the attention-sapping children on the way out of the family home, middle adulthood brings new worries in the form of fears of beckoning old age, retirement and anxieties over whether youthful goals will now ever be realised. Worry about elderly parents begins to replace worries about your own children. ('What if I am not a good parent?' or 'What if my parents get ill?')

THE SEVENTH AGE OF WORRY (65 and on). After all these years of worry, just when many psychologists thought being elderly would be the time of greatest worry because of real problems like physical decline, loss of close relations and friends, as well as financial concerns, instead, of all the age groups, the elderly seem to worry the least (apart from early childhood when worry may be impossible), though worry areas such as health and loneliness still exist ('What if I am abandoned to cope by myself?' or 'What if I get ill?').

One reason why the elderly worry less than other groups is that they generally seem to focus on the positive aspects of being old; they describe it as a time to do enjoyable things they have had to put off all their lives until they have shed their responsibilities.

Another possible explanation is that after middle adulthood people start to spend more time thinking about the past and less about the future, and, as worries are always anticipations of the future, older adults may worry less simply because they are less focused on the future. This may also explain why children, with their whole future ahead of them, fret so much about it.

Remember as well that the elderly have decades of worry behind them and over time they have probably had more chance than younger people to learn how to cope with the kind of threatening events which cause worry. Over the years they have finally gained the experience that shows that most of their fears and worries were over-pessimistic. If only we could teach children that before they get to 65!

The cognitive revolution, which offers an effective way of dealing with worry – questioning your thoughts and beliefs – is an important advance because, for many people, feelings are very difficult to talk about. In some senses it may even be beyond our capacity to verbalise exactly how we really feel. Few people are ever really able to verbalise, or even think, coherently about strong emotions, because the paradox is that when in the grip of a powerful emotion we are probably least able to contemplate coolly exactly what we are feeling. Trying to talk about it when the emotional turbulence has passed often means that it is difficult to recall exactly how you felt. So getting patients to talk about feelings can be an uphill struggle, and the belief that they will have to go over and over emotionally upsetting material, or their childhood, probably puts many people off seeking professional help or advice.

However, if there is a close relationship between our thoughts and our feelings, and if changing the way we think about something helps us to change the way we feel about it, then our beliefs about the world and ourselves become crucial to mental health. This is because beliefs determine feelings, despite the fact that it is still controversial which comes first: thoughts or feelings. Going back to the example of the boss passing you in the corridor, maybe you were feeling pretty gloomy that day anyway, and therefore had low self-esteem, which meant you were already inclined to harbour negative beliefs about yourself and your relationship with your boss, and this is what prompted your worry. So the low mood is what led to the troubling beliefs.

Some would argue that in this situation you need to treat the low mood before you can get rid of the negative beliefs. However, it does seem that, in practice, trying to think dispassionately about whether our beliefs are reasonable does help lift unreasonably low moods, even if the low mood is what came first. It is always difficult for patients, and lay people in general, to accept that causes are not really of that much interest to psychiatrists, who are concerned with the here and now.

The majority of letters people write to me through my national newspaper or magazine columns are about asking why they are the way they are: why they stay in a poor relationship, for example, or why they can't stop gambling. They are often deeply puzzled by their self-damaging behaviour. But the search for causes often hampers the quest for change, as causes may be lost back in the mists of time, and change is something which needs to be done now. So, while psychoanalysis, with its focus on early relationships, may be best placed to uncover causes (as mentioned in the chapter on therapy), often, after spending many years elucidating why they are the way they are, patients still don't seem to change. This is because why you are the way you are has much to do with the past, but what you need to do to change now has more to do with the present.

Incidentally, it does seem to me that the patients I see who are eager to embrace the idea that change is difficult and takes a long time often seem to be the ones who are least interested in changing in the first place. Those who are eager and impatient to change are the ones who end up transforming fastest.

In the quest for fast change, improving the rationality and reasonableness of our thoughts and beliefs does help rapidly to improve our feelings. This is why psychologists have abandoned the search for causes and, instead, focus on what maintains our present state.

While it may be impossible to determine what originally caused a female patient of normal weight to become obsessed with her appearance and to believe she is excessively fat, we do know that if she can learn to challenge her belief that everyone is looking at her and thinking how fat she is, she will get over her eating disorder. The key point is that you don't need to know where the belief came from to change it.

Thus, an essential constituent of positive mental health, from the cognitive therapy perspective, is that it requires the ability to examine as dispassionately as possible your thoughts on an issue that is causing you problems. Are you fat or just over-sensitive? Is your boss busy or is he trying to avoid you? You have to be open to the idea that your beliefs may not be the only reasonable deductions about your situation. This is a huge stumbling block for cognitive therapy as, in my experience, many patients are not willing to accept that just because the boss ignored them in the corridor, there are other plausible explanations, other than that he hates them with every fibre of his body.

Therefore, a cornerstone of positive mental health is the ability to change your mind and to be open to new beliefs to replace your old ones about a situation. You have to be able to accept basic concepts, like what counts as reasonable evidence and that it is unreasonable to hold beliefs without adequate grounds, or indeed without any evidence at all. For many people the need for evidence is not something which holds much sway, partly because they are already in the grip of such strong emotion that evidence seems superfluous.

This is precisely why, when politicians or other skilled manipulators are trying to persuade us of something, they use emotive language; they know that a direct appeal to emotion can bypass our more rational side, which would demand evidence before being convinced. But if you ignore evidence, you are also disregarding reality. Trying to keep a distinction between, for example, the reality of what your boss really thinks of you, and what you feel is going on, is crucial to maintaining mental health. Cognitive therapists cannot work with clients who simply assume that if they feel the boss hates them, then the boss *must* hate them, and that there is no room for dispute in the matter.

You may have noticed the rather childish quality to this reasoning, and there is a sense in which poor mental health is based on immature judgements about the world. The more mentally healthy you are, the more interested you are in evidence, which you are willing to weigh up before coming to conclusions about the world.

If you put these cognitive therapy ideas into practice you will soon notice that the initial worries following your boss ignoring you as you pass him in the corridor have been replaced with thoughts like: 'It's understandable that I should err on the side of unpleasant feelings when my boss appears to ignore me, because I am anxious about my job, but assuming that being ignored means I will get the sack is a form of thinking known as worrying – I am 'what-iffing'. As worry is a negative anticipation about the future, let me examine whether this negative anticipation is realistic. What is the evidence for it? Does my boss ignoring me mean I am going to get the sack, or am I jumping to conclusions? Let me also review what concrete evidence there already is about what my boss thinks about me...' Thinking aloud is a useful device, as it helps demonstrate more clearly to yourself some of the illogical steps your thinking may be taking. In fact, thinking aloud is one of the techniques cognitive therapists encourage their clients to use in a session.

Another technique you can borrow from cognitive therapy is to allow yourself, say, half an hour of unbridled worry every day. The theory behind this is that, as worry is such an ingrained part of us, appealing to our rational side is unlikely to work immediately. However, after the allotted half hour, you are no longer permitted to worry. This seems reasonable; after all, if half an hour of worry hasn't got you anywhere positive, what's the point of devoting more time to this unproductive activity?

Furthermore, a cognitive therapist would not begin a session like the Hollywood analyst with the question, 'How are you feeling?', but would start, instead, with something along the lines of 'What would you like to focus on today?' The emphasis is always on 'What would you like to change?', and 'Let's get on with it straight away', without wasting time on discussing something that does not take you towards change. Instead of asking about feelings, the cognitive therapist will repeatedly ask 'What is going through your mind right now?' or 'What was going through your mind when you were feeling that?' and, again, this is something you can easily do for yourself when attempting to understand the thoughts which underlie your feelings.[14]

The next question a cognitive therapist moves on to in a typical session is 'What's the evidence?' for your beliefs or point of view. They then proceed to asking 'Is there any other way to look at the situation, or another possible interpretation of what is going on?' Given that there are always multiple interpretations of any situation, the next question, if you have adopted one explanation for what is going on, would be 'How can you test your view to check it really is the right one?'

To take an example, suppose you are attracted to a stranger at a party and you approach him with a view to getting to know him better, and are rebuffed immediately, perhaps even somewhat abruptly. Someone with low self-esteem, and perhaps a low mood, might deduce that this means they are abnormally repulsive to look at or extremely boring. The cognitive therapist, in contrast, would start by asking what you would like to focus on in this situation. For example, do you want to change your view of yourself as abnormally repulsive, or do you want to be cheered up despite believing that you are awful to look at? If the latter is the case, then you will be told by your cognitive therapist that as long as you believe you are horribly ugly, it will be difficult to lift your mood; it is your underlying beliefs which have to be tackled.

After clarifying that you would really like to work on your belief that you look grotesque, the therapist then asks for the evidence to support this belief. How have people reacted to your appearance in the past? Have you known members of the opposite sex who seemed to find you attractive? Is it reasonable to deduce from the fact that one person possibly does not find you physically attractive that you are therefore repulsive to all and sundry?

The next step would then be to ask if there is another possible interpretation of what was going on when you were rebuffed. Is it probable that your target was uninterested in forming a new relationship with anyone as he was already attached? Is it likely he was not in the mood? Is it feasible he misinterpreted your intentions? Is it conceivable he did not want to be distracted at that particular moment from his conversation with someone else?

Having gone through a multitude of credible alternative interpretations of what lay behind your rebuff, the therapist would then ask you to seek to test which perspective is the correct one. You could observe the person who rebuffed you to see how they react when others approach them. You could try another approach to someone else to see how they react.

The cognitive therapist would also ask you to consider the effect of your thinking on yourself; if you really do believe you are horrendous to look at, you are unlikely to continue trying to meet new people. This will constrain your social circle and add to your feelings of loneliness, which in turn make you feel worse about yourself. You will also feel self-conscious, be more likely to focus on yourself and be a less interesting person to talk to.

The cognitive therapist would also ask you to consider what is the worst that could happen. If you approach more people you might well get rebuffed again and again and this will not help you feel great about yourself in the short term but, other than that, would being slighted kill you?

Finally, the cognitive therapist would ask you to consider what positive action you can take to help yourself. If you are worried about your appearance you could seek some extra help to improve your looks and self-confidence by a change of wardrobe or a haircut, or you could ask for advice from close friends about how to enhance your image, or even pay for professional advice, if you can afford it.

Essential to the ability to use cognitive therapy to improve mental health is being able to think rationally.

Having a rational internal conversation requires holding all the worries in check while you look for evidence, and this involves controlling your mind.

In other words, you need to be able to control your thoughts. While a key component to positive mental health is the ability to examine as dispassionately as possible your thoughts on an issue that is causing you problems, linked to this ability is that of dismissing a thought and thinking about something else if needs be.

The most commonly used method of being able to think about something else, rather than focusing perpetually on a worry, is termed distraction. We all need to be able to distract ourselves from our anxious, depressive or upsetting thoughts in order to think constructively. Perhaps seeing a film or talking to someone can be therapeutic merely because it achieves this aim.

Many of the therapeutic claims for music, calming audiotapes or even hypnotherapy, are likely to rest on the simple ability of all of these to distract us from troubling thoughts. (See the previous chapter on managing your moods for more on the use of distraction when regulating your emotions.)

One example of such control or distraction is to be able to 'switch off' and, instead of focusing on a worry, to think about something more pleasant. This ability to switch off, or switch thoughts, is central to positive mental health. But it's not straightforward, and that's why we devote time and energy to expensive holidays or other leisure pursuits. Distracting ourselves from everyday worries is more difficult than you'd imagine, hence many of us need props to help us do it.

In some cases, the more extreme a distraction aid you need, such as drugs, heavy drinking or a dramatic spending spree, the more that tells you about your mind's inability to distract you; or the more upsetting the thoughts you need to distract yourself from.

Although it is important to be able to divert yourself from a thought which is making you more and more upset, distraction can be counterproductive if overused and if employed as a permanent escape from reality. Many people use hobbies or socialising to try to avoid worries and responsibilities and do not face up to problems they need to solve before their life can move on.

We have all had the experience, when faced with a looming problem like an exam or an interview, of spending more time doing things like watching TV or getting absorbed in a pastime – anything other than doing what is necessary to help ourselves. What is happening is that we are distracting ourselves from facing up to an unpleasant aspect of our reality – our foreboding of the exam or interview. However, if we do this too much we are not helping ourselves because, although distraction will make us feel better in the short run, diverting ourselves will stop us from preparing properly.

Research has also shown that feeling good helps our problem-solving ability.[15] According to a survey in 1987, it seems that people are more creative about finding solutions to problems when they have just been given a treat, or watched a comedy film which cheers them up. This means that if facing a problem is getting you down, distracting yourself with pleasant music is not a bad strategy, since if you then return your attention to your difficult problem, your enhanced mood will improve your chances of solving it. So the skilful combination of distraction (turning your attention away from your worry) and problem-solving (returning your attention on to your worry in an attempt constructively to resolve it), in other words flexibility, is thus the key to mental health.

Where many people go wrong is in employing distraction, but enjoying having their unpleasant problem removed from their attention so much that they are loath to return to it and simply continue with the distraction. This, of course, makes you feel good in the short term, but provides no long-term solutions to your undealt-with problem.

So, a key to positive mental health is to be able to distract yourself when worrying is going to serve no useful purpose, but also to focus on a problem and not be tempted to employ distraction when problem-solving is necessary.

Although distraction and problem-solving appear to be opposite approaches, positive mental health means having both available to you, and knowing when to switch your strategy as the situation demands.

The reason these cognitive approaches are central to positive mental health is that, whatever the particular psychiatric problem, there now appears to be a cognitive approach to it. In other words, it is probable that simply being more 'cognitive' in outlook reduces the likelihood of practically any psychiatric disorder developing. When patients come to a therapist with a particular problem, say, a marital difficulty or an addiction, these are often symptomatic of general difficulties with the way clients view – or, as psychologists put it, construe – the world and themselves. It is these more fundamental perspectives which need changing before long-term mental health can be guaranteed. 'We tell ourselves stories in order to live'[16] and cognitive therapies seek to rid us of our pervasive, self-defeating, irrational and unrealistic ways of interpreting our world.

Cognitive therapists have identified three basic ways of drawing conclusions from evidence which seem to recur in those with poor mental health. These are 'selective abstraction', 'over-generalisation' and 'dichotomous thinking'.[17]

Selective abstraction refers to drawing a conclusion from only one small aspect of an event and ignoring the whole picture. For example, you encounter your boss all week and on each occasion he smiles and acknowledges you, but you focus on the one incident when he doesn't and conclude you are about to get the sack. Your cognitive error here is to fail to take into account the whole week.

Over-generalisation refers to the tendency to assume that because an event occurs, this has ramifications for other unlinked incidents. For example, because you fail maths you assume you can never pass an exam in any subject again.

Finally, dichotomous thinking means that no middle ground seems possible. When the boss smiles at you, this means you are his favourite employee and a big bonus is on its way, but when you are ignored a few seconds later, this means you are about to get the sack.

The cognitive therapist's final goal is to teach clients to overcome these types of thinking or irrational beliefs (IBs) for themselves.[18] This approach lends itself naturally to self-improvement of positive mental health. The pioneers of cognitive approaches, such as the famous US doctors Albert Ellis and Aaron Beck, made enormous strides in suggesting a new way of approaching mental illness which is rapidly becoming the standard approach in treatment in academic centres worldwide. However, they held back from the logical next step, which I am now suggesting for the first time, of ensuring that these approaches are taught to the general population *before* they become ill, not after, as a way of ensuring they do not suffer psychological problems in the first place.

For example, cognitive therapists have found that people with poor mental health harbour a negative way of thinking about three crucial aspects of life, called the negative 'triad': self, world and future. In other words, they have negative views of themselves as incapable and unworthy, they see the world as full of insurmountable obstacles, and they see little hope in the future. Clearly, encouraging a population to adopt an opposite set of beliefs to these from an early stage in life is likely to improve positive mental health. Individuals aware of the link between this triad and poor mental health are likely consciously to check that they are not falling victim to the triad long before it takes grip.

Although it makes intuitive (and logical sense) to get rid of things like ANTs and triads if you want to improve your mental health, and although in my own work at the Bethlem Royal and Maudsley Hospitals I have seen numerous patients benefit from the use of cognitive therapies, the reason why cognitive approaches work is still controversial. One possible answer, I believe, is that it is important for most of us to regard ourselves as reasonable, and sensible people do not hang on to unrealistic ways of thinking. So, once the irrationality of

ANTs or the triad is pointed out, being reasonable people we will gracefully up give these ideas. This means that if we continue to cling to a set of beliefs which underpin an unpleasant or unhealthy emotional state, it is usually because we consider, at some level, that these beliefs are reasonable, or that their alternatives are not reasonable.

Some of the patients I see simply will not give up convictions for which there is little evidence in their favour and much data against, despite numerous sessions of cognitive therapy. Appearing highly irrational does not bother them at all. Given the choice of being rational or clinging to their view of the world, they opt for the latter. Therefore, making a rational approach to life a major social value which should be espoused by all, is a project that preventive mental health care should adopt.

Cognitive therapy is built on the assumption that, while external events may certainly contribute to our emotional problems, no external event is ever the only or direct cause. Instead, we are responsible for these feelings by the way we react to events.

This is known as the ABC theory of mental illness (not to be confused with the ABC of changing behaviour mentioned in the chapter on the self): the A is for activating events (losing your job, for example), B is for beliefs (what you think losing your job will mean for you), and C is for consequences (how upset you get about losing your job). Before cognitive therapy, most people believed A caused C, and left out the importance of B. They therefore believed that losing your job caused you to be upset. Cognitive therapy enabled them to see that the crucial link between A and C is B; it is your belief about losing your job which will really determine how upset you get.[19]

But, aha! you say, suppose I discover I have a terminal illness which will cause me to die painfully and slowly. Surely there is no possible way I can think positively about my problem? It must therefore be the case that there is no relevant B (belief) between the A (activating event) and the C (consequence) in this instance? Or, say I become a refugee and, as well as losing my country, lose my family, job and status. Well, I would still argue that you could think positively. Cognitive therapists are not arguing that you will always feel happy no matter what happens to you, they are simply pointing out that it is often your interpretation of events, rather than the situation itself, which determines your reaction.

The degree to which people fear pain or death also varies hugely and will determine how they accept this news. Unlikely as it seems, some people will respond more positively than others. There is a huge variation in the way each of us reacts to the external world. If everyone reacted in the same way to the corresponding reality, behaviour would be much more uniform.

At the core of the cognitive approach lies the principle that while our thinking controls us, we can also control our thinking. We can challenge the very things our mind tells us, precisely because we are always in a state of inner dialogue with ourselves – that never-ending internal conversation, which some people term consciousness. The fact that you can have an internal disagreement and argue with yourself means that you can enter a dialogue with your mind, and so change it.

I have noticed in my clinical practice that one factor separating the mentally ill from the healthy is the ability to have an internal debate about an important idea. The mentally ill do not do this. Whenever I suggest alternative views to them about a belief they hold, it is clear that arguing with themselves is something they have never really done. So, mental health involves the ability to dispute with yourself, and the more mentally healthy you are, the better the quality of the argument. You can develop this ability with increased practice.

For example, I was treating a patient who had suffered a car crash and, as a result, had become highly nervous about driving. This anxiety contributed to his feeling that, whenever he was driving, other drivers appeared to be steering in a threatening manner at him. I asked him why he believed this. He said that it seemed that whenever he took to the roads, other drivers behaved in a particularly dangerous manner. Did this mean, I asked, that they drove like this all the time, or only when he was on the road, for if they drove like this continuously, it seemed surprising there were not more accidents. He said it seemed to him that other drivers were indeed driving in a particularly dangerous manner whenever he appeared in his car. I suggested that this seemed to intimate that there were people driving cars around the local area, expressly lying in wait for him to appear, so as to drive in a threatening manner near him. Why should that be the case?

He could see that this last statement was ridiculous, but would not give up the idea that whenever he drove other drivers appeared to have it in for him in particular, and seemed to drive in a way designed to engineer a crash. Given this man's beliefs, his anxiety over driving is understandable, but he was unwilling to change or explore his beliefs, despite their irrationality having been exposed in our debate.

One aspect of the particular personal style I bring to the way I practise cognitive therapy, which is different to most others, is to accept the client's perspective on the world and then examine the implications of that view. Often the logical consequences of the patient's assumptions highlight more readily the implausibility of their point of view.

For example, if there really are people lying in wait to drive dangerously at my driving instructor, how do they pass their time when he is not on the road? How do they cope when he eludes them on the roads? Do they worry about their no-claims bonuses?

Often by following through patients' ideas and examining the inevitable conclusions that stem from them they are better able to see the flaws in their perspective. You can try this for yourself and it can be a most entertaining way of becoming aware of some of the problems in your thinking.

The quality of your debate with yourself is often revealed when discussing issues or problems with a friend. If you have good mental health, you will probably already have considered most, or all, of the alternative perspectives they suggest. If you have poor mental health, you will most likely have failed to consider the more obvious alternative points of view to your own, and these will come as new ideas. Friends often come up with a novel perspective, simply because they are less close to a problem and less emotionally involved, and positive mental health is about striving to attain that emotional distance for yourself, when required.

The less mentally healthy tend to focus instead on all the reasons for continuing to believe what they already believe. They do not contemplate alternatives, or seek to understand other points of view, or even consider opposing evidence. Most therapists struggle simply to try to persuade their patients to adopt another perspective on their current ways of thinking. If you can do that yourself, you will save yourself a lot of therapy!

I do not mean to make this sound simple. Changing your thought process can be tough and sometimes painful. For example, you may be unable to argue productively with yourself and therefore be unable to change your mind and emotions. The irrational or unreasonable part of your mind may appear to have the strongest arguments, or the ones you like best. Think of flight phobics who refuse to get on aeroplanes despite the urgent need to do overseas business. As they get near the airport, their increasingly agitated mind comes up with all sorts of arguments about how unsafe aeroplanes are, which the part of the phobic who needs to fly is unable to oppose. One simple reason why bad arguments win is that you don't see them for what they are. You may not understand what constitutes a good argument and what makes a particular line of reasoning fallacious. Also, arguments are based on beliefs, made up of peripheral thoughts such as 'my boss hates me', which in turn are based on more obscure but fundamental core beliefs such as 'I am no good at my job'. Often, these core beliefs need to change before the arguments in our heads change.

One reason you may find it difficult to change your thinking is that your basic attitudes may be problematic.

Albert Ellis has classified the attitudes which lead to poor mental health into four main types which he calls the 'four categories of irrational beliefs'. These are 'demand statements', 'catastrophising beliefs', 'intolerance statements' and 'rating statements'.[20]

Demand statements are characteristic of people who 'musterbate', people for whom 'musts' pepper their thinking and language. The world *must* be a certain way, we *must* have what we want, people *must* do as we tell them. The irrationality at the core of their thinking is to suppose that simply because you want something you must have it. Of course, there are many things which we might like but this does not mean we can demand them of the world around us.

If you are someone who peppers demands and musts in your speech, you will become frustrated, intolerant and angry, because you believe the world somehow owes you these things. Your real problem is a failure to come to terms with the world as it is, a less than perfect place. To be able to live in such a world, everyone needs to understand the difference between what would be preferable, and what they *must* have. Those who demand approval, recognition, perfection, success or comfort are behaving as if they are the rulers of the universe, rather than just temporary occupants.

This is not to say that you shouldn't push for what you want and make demands of yourself and others. However, in making these demands, it is helpful to understand that if they fail to be met, you will make yourself feel much worse if you believe the world owes them to you. 'Must' statements imply that if you do not get your way, something terrible will happen, yet you are the one who has set yourself up for dreadful consequences when your demands fail to be met.

Catastrophising is when people make 'mountains out of molehills'. Something goes wrong and catastrophisers see this as the end of the universe as they know it. In fact, it is the catastrophising attitude and irrational thinking which lead to more trouble than the original problem. For example, a recovering bulimic may break the three-meals-a-day treatment regime by having a bit of a binge and immediately feel that her treatment has been a complete failure, abandoning further efforts to stick to her eating plan. In fact, it is not the lapse but the catastrophising attitude and irrational thinking which is the problem, legitimising her failure simply to go back to her treatment. A good test of whether you are a catastrophiser is to recollect how you have taken bad news in the past. If you can now see that you overreacted and that things were not nearly as bad as you initially thought, you need to be able to use the sense of perspective you now have on your past problem, at the time a new problem is occurring.

The opposite of catastrophising is trying to see the positive side of every problem. The American self-empowerment guru, Anthony Robbins, puts this well in the phrase which typifies his reaction to bad news: 'How can I make this problem more perfect?'.[21] In other words, how can I make the best of this dreadful situation, or even better, turn this problem to my advantage? I do think this slogan, 'How do I make this problem more perfect?', is inspired as it captures an attitude to problems which is hugely positive and upbeat. In practice, we may not always be able to maintain this kind of relentless optimism in the face of bad news, but it is helpful in gaining perspective, particularly for those who tend to catastrophise.

Intolerance statements are self-explanatory; we may complain, for example, that we cannot 'stand' our boss, or our working conditions, or the situation in which we find ourselves. Rational-emotive therapy teaches us that a large part of the upset of a situation is simply the belief that we cannot stand it. A more realistic assessment is usually that we can adapt and learn to tolerate what appears too hard or difficult. We can see this when we look back at a previous episode in our lives and often marvel at our ability to come through something we are convinced we could not cope with if we had to face it again; well, how did we endure the first time around? Furthermore, we are astonished at the ability of others to handle things we are convinced are simply not copable with; well, how are they doing it? More realistically, intolerance statements tell us more about our tendency to make such statements, or about our fear of not being able to cope, and hence our frustration, than whether or not we can actually cope.

To assess more pragmatically whether you can cope with something, you need ask the following types of question: Have I coped with this kind of thing before? Do others cope with this kind of situation? Have I faced worse things in the past? Could I ask for help to cope? Could I take a break from coping? How much of the difficulty I appear to have coping is down to fears of failure, rather than objective evidence of failure to cope?

Rating statements attempt to rate someone's (yours, for example), or something's, entire worth on the basis of one or a few attributes, drawing all-encompassing conclusions from unrelated or little evidence. For example, we fail an exam and conclude we are worthless human beings, when all we should say is that we were not good in that particular exam situation. If our best friend is late for a date, we conclude they are a terrible friend, when all we should rationally conclude is that their punctuality was poor on this occasion.

No one is saying you cannot judge how good or bad people or things are against certain criteria; it is quite legitimate to conclude that you may well not be as intelligent as others, or your friend may not be punctual. However, just because you are not intelligent or good at exams does not mean you are not a worthwhile person, or that your unpunctual friend does not like you. It is especially important for your self-esteem to abandon the attempt constantly to evaluate yourself. Instead, everyone needs to accept themselves just as being, or existing, whatever their particular traits. You can certainly judge yourself as a good or bad spouse, or a good or bad parent, or a hopeless lover or hopeless at work, but none of these statements means that you are a hopeless person. Rating statements are crucially linked to self-esteem and are explained in greater detail in the chapter on self.

Such irrational beliefs are poor thought processes and must be overcome to achieve mental health.

Albert Ellis and those who embrace the cognitive approach have pointed out that in addition to the four fundamental core beliefs which underpin psychiatric problems, there are a set of common mistakes in thinking. These can be categorised as six most common mistakes which characterise those who end up with psychiatric or psychological problems. They are: over-generalising, thinking in terms of black and white, ignoring the evidence, focusing on the negative, imagining the worst, and taking things personally.

The first common mistake is over-generalising. This refers to the tendency to reach a general conclusion about the world, the future, or yourself from limited evidence, say from just one incident. For example, your boss gives you some negative feedback about your performance and you deduce she hates you. Does just one, or even a few incidents justify the conclusion you have come to? A good test is to consider other incidents which do not support your over-generalised deduction.

The second common mistake is the tendency to think everything is black and white. People who do this decide that if everything is not wonderful, it must be absolutely terrible. The truth is rarely black or white, but usually a shade of grey. For example, if your boss is not completely enthusiastic about your performance, you assume he hates you. Well, he may not consider your recent performance your best but does that mean he has gone to the extreme of now plotting your removal?

The third common mistake is ignoring the evidence. This refers to the tendency to draw conclusions which are not warranted by the evidence, taking an extreme position beyond what the evidence warrants, or holding a position for emotional reasons which actually ignore the evidence. In particular, it refers to not drawing conclusions after a dispassionate assessment of the evidence. For example, someone tells you they overheard someone else who had heard in passing that your boss did not like your last piece of work. Is this really good-quality evidence that you are about to get the sack, as you deduced? Before drawing conclusions, cognitive therapists urge clients also to consider the quality of the evidence and come to conclusions based only on factual evidence.

The fourth common mistake is focusing on the negative. This is a human tendency just to see what has gone wrong, or is not right, or is bad about a situation without also seeing what has gone well, is not so bad, or is generally working. Is your focus on the negative an objective appraisal of the situation? Are you ignoring all the positives?

The fifth common mistake is imagining the worst. Pessimism is rampant amongst the psychologically unwell and reflects a tendency always to assume that the worst possible thing is inevitable. This is the mistake which supports chronic worry.

Finally, the sixth common mistake is taking events personally. When things happen, you assume it is because of you, or that all are blaming you or that everyone notices your errors all the time and is staring at you, pondering negative thoughts about you. Do not put yourself at the centre of the universe, everyone else is too busy imagining they are at the centre of the universe to put you there.

On top of these common mistakes in thinking are popular irrational beliefs, as listed below, alongside their rational counterparts.[22, 23]

IRRATIONAL BELIEF	MORE RATIONAL REPLACEMENT
I must be loved or at least liked by every significant person I meet.	I want to be approved of by some of the people in my life. I will feel lonely when that doesn't happen, but I can endure these feelings, and take constructive steps to make and keep better relationships.
I must be completely competent to be worthwhile.	I want to do some things well, most of the time. But like everybody, I will occasionally fail and commit errors. Then I will feel bad, but I can handle this, and I can take productive steps to do better next time.

295

If things are not as I should like them, the world will come to an end.

It is disappointing when things aren't how I would like them to be, but I can survive that. Usually, I can take helpful steps to make things more as I would like them to be, but if I can't it doesn't help to exaggerate my frustration.

My unhappiness is outside of my control and there is nothing I can do about it.

My problems may be influenced by factors outside my power, but my thoughts and actions also influence my problems and they are under my command.

I should worry about bad things happening.

Worrying about something that might go wrong won't stop it from happening, it just makes me unhappy now! I can take valuable steps to prepare for possible problems, and that's as much as anyone can do. So I won't dwell on the future now.

It is better to put off unpleasant things than face them.

Facing difficult situations will make me feel bad at the time, but I can survive these feelings. Putting off problems doesn't make them any easier, it just gives me longer to obsess over them.

I need someone stronger than myself to depend on.

It's great to get support from others when I want it, but the only person I really need to rely on is myself.

| My problems are because of my past and that is why I suffer now. | My problems may have started in some past events, but what keeps them going now are my thoughts and actions, and they are under my control. |

It may take a while to get out of the habit of irrational thoughts, but once you have got into the habit of analysing your thought process, it will gradually become easier, until, hopefully, one day it is second nature! Whenever we indulge in irrational thinking we are being ruled by what has been called by Albert Ellis 'the tyranny of the three musts': (1) I must do well, (2) you must treat me kindly, fairly and considerately and (3) the world must make things easy for me.[24]

The basic logical flaw behind these 'musts' is that although we would like to perform well, others to treat us reasonably and the world to be as we would like it, there is no earthly reason why our preferences should be met. And when we demand things of ourselves, others and the world, insisting that we 'must' get our way, we get ourselves upset. We 'must' away at ourselves, the world and others, but all that 'musting' serves to do is trouble us. It doesn't change the logical reality around us.

Instead of suffering under the tyranny of the three 'musts', a more rational approach is to understand that we have preferences, and that it would be wonderful if these preferences were met, but that having them does not mean necessarily mean they will be: they are preferences, not musts. Understanding the likely gap between our preferences and harsh reality, and not allowing it to upset us, is a more rational response. Replace every must in your life with a preference and you will begin to feel better.

So, for example, when someone cuts you up on the road, you will upset yourself if you think to yourself 'others must always drive well' rather than the more logical, 'I would prefer it if people drove safely, but my preference won't necessarily be met.' Understanding that the world presents you with many unmet preferences will upset you less than finding yourself in a world full of unmet demands.

But while Albert Ellis's work has been profoundly useful in clarifying the way we think irrationally, this thinking is often difficult to put into practice, because to do so puts the emphasis on not doing something (that is, on not thinking irrationally) rather than spelling out clearly what a more healthy replacement would be; and rational thinking often feels more clumsy and awkward than the more familiar irrational thinking.

One solution to this problem is to see thinking more positively as a kind of game you can learn to play with yourself. This was first called the 'glad game', introduced in a famous novel *Pollyanna* by Eleanor Porter, published in 1913. Pollyanna is the main character, whose name has for ever been linked with unbridled optimism; indeed if you want to pour cold water over an enthusiast's schemes, you call them a 'Pollyanna'.

To everyone she meets Pollyanna teaches the 'glad game',[25] which is based on the idea that no matter what happens to you in life, and in particular no matter how apparently bad the event is, there is always something to be glad about. The idea of the 'glad game', therefore, is to learn the art of hunting for the positive aspect in seemingly bad experiences. In fact, the more dire the predicament, the more challenging and fun the glad game becomes.

In Eleanor Porter's story, Pollyanna appears plagued by misfortune. Her mother has been dead for some time and her father (a penniless minister) has just died too; as a result she has to live with an unwelcoming aunt. However, playing the glad game, Pollyanna admits to missing her father, but is glad he is dead because he can be in heaven with her mother. Although her aunt gives her an ugly attic room, Pollyanna is glad, because if she lived in a more pleasant room she probably wouldn't notice and appreciate the lovely view outside her window.

Pollyanna plays the game relentlessly, and it appears to be helpful to her as a useful mechanism for coping with misfortune. But, treading on more dangerous ground, she also inflicts her game on others. When she meets a man with a broken leg, she reminds him that he should at least be glad he didn't break both legs. She tells a gardener with a bent back that he should be glad because it must mean he finds bending over to weed easier. She tells a friend too sick to leave her bed that she should be glad no one else has her dreadful illness. When Pollyanna falls victim to a dreadful car accident, as a result of which both her legs are paralysed, she learns that it is always easier to see the positive side of a crisis when it is not your own predicament – and even she appears at first grief-stricken. But then her relentless optimism returns: her accident, she says, is a good thing because now her awful aunt feels obliged to start treating her well, and losing her legs means that for the first time she appreciates having had legs at all in the first place.

Although *Pollyanna* went on to become a massive bestseller and hugely influential – glad clubs were set up all over the world – the lasting legacy has been to see unbridled optimism as fundamentally heartless to victims. Today we feel we should sympathise rather than try to see the positive in a nightmare situation.

Yet although at one level Pollyanna went too far, at another she set an example of an important principle of mental health. This kind of optimism has been found to be markedly predictive of greater physical and mental health throughout a lifetime in those who have it than in those who do not.[25]

The criticism of optimism is that it is unrealistic. However, as I shall examine in the next chapter, surprisingly sometimes being unrealistic is the more mentally healthy strategy. There is no sense in which pessimism, or only seeing the worst implications of negative events, is the best strategy in life. And Pollyanna is on to an important point: while we cannot choose for bad things not to happen to us, we can select our reaction and our response.

The most productive approach is one that leads us to being active in helping ourselves as much as we can, no matter how awful our circumstance. Playing the glad game is more likely than pessimism to lead us to keep trying to overcome our problems. Of course some kinds of optimism can lead to complacency. But the kind of optimism that helps us to see that there are always solutions and ways of coping is available to the players of the glad game, and not to those who prefer the sad game.

Sensible optimism is about the way you explain negative events to yourself. If you see an unpleasant circumstance as being caused by something internal to yourself, rather than external, arising as a result of circumstances often beyond your control, then you are more pessimistic. If you assess these causes as circumstances that are likely to continue inevitably into the future, that is also a form of pessimism. And if you believe that these causes are pervasive, likely to apply to domains in your life other than the ones in which the bad fortune happened, then that too is a sign of pessimism – for example, if your spouse leaves you and you assume this means you are so useless in life that you are probably poor at your job as well.

Instead of this kind of pessimistic thinking, sensible optimism is about seeing negative events as caused by external circumstances (which might change), a result of a single moment and therefore not inevitably eternal, and down to a particular part of your life and so not likely to apply across the board.

So part of positive mental health is to maintain optimism even in the depths of disaster, and to do that we have something to learn from Pollyanna.

But many remain sceptical that this kind of more optimistic and 'rational' approach is really realistic and therefore helpful in the face of real life difficulties. However, recent research conducted on unemployed people in Britain has found that those given training in the cognitive therapy strategies we have discussed in this chapter were almost three times more likely to find work four months after their cognitive therapy training than a control group who were not trained to think this way.[26]

But our thoughts and feelings are particularly difficult to change when they are both very closely in synch with each other.

Earlier in this chapter, I argued that thinking determines feeling. However, the two can't always be separated so neatly, and attitudes may be made up both of thoughts and feelings. An example of a mental state that is part thought and part feeling is a defence mechanism. Researchers[27] have found a link between different styles of defence and those suffering from poor mental health.

Defence mechanisms are the way we reconcile what we would like if we could have our way with the external reality of the world as we find it. The explanation of defence mechanisms remains one of Freud's great contributions to the understanding of mind. For example, they include regression (where you appear to return to a more childish way of dealing with things: when faced with stress in a relationship with a sibling, you return to behaving how you did when you were five); displacement (where you express an emotion to someone other than who you really feel that emotion for: you come home from a bad day with your irritating boss, to whom you behaved impeccably, but get angry with your wife); and projection (where you see aspects of yourself in others: for example, chronic liars tend to assume they are always being lied to by others).

Defence mechanisms are important because of what they help us to understand about personality problems. Personality disorders are those mental health problems people seem to have had all their lives, even from early childhood.

It seems that our personality is characterised by the tendency to use certain defence mechanisms selectively.

There are three main types of disordered personality: those who seem to prefer fantasy to reality; those who are chronic novelty-seekers; and those who devote too much energy to avoiding harm and so are over-fearful and pessimistic. Quick recap test: can you work out in which category chronic worriers are most likely to end up?

The most immature personalities of all – those who seem to have done very little growing up – can fall into any of the three categories above. They tend to choose action-oriented defences such as withdrawal and aggressive behaviour. These indicate an inability to control impulses, which thus produces behaviour problems, like temper tantrums or hitting someone when angry, or refusing to come out of your room to talk to your family when upset.

Idealisation, where you see only the good side of someone or a situation, and devaluation, when you see only their bad side, are defences employed by slightly more mature personalities who can control themselves, so they do not assault people when upset, but they still have difficulty viewing themselves and others realistically. These people fall victim to the dichotomous thinking cognitive therapists warn about. The problem for these people is that their relationships are always torrid: one moment they have met Mr Perfect, but when he blots his copybook, the next day they think they are going out with the most awful man in the world.

More mature are those able to function relatively normally, yet who remain unable to fulfil their full creative potential due to self-sacrificing defences like 'pseudo-altruism in masochistic relationships'. This means that you keep putting others first over yourself, then wonder why they are getting ahead compared to you. The woman who tolerates her husband's alcoholism, or the man who keeps loaning his car to his reckless son who frequently damages it, fall into this category. The reason you do this is because you may fear putting yourself first, as you mistake this for being self-centred.

The most mature defences of all are humour and sublimation, which imply an ability to accept difficult situations, while taking the edge off pain by producing a creative response to anxiety. Sublimation occurs when your inner conflicts are diverted into creative energies, so your irritation with your boss may come out only in the kind of painting you produce in your art class.[28]

Researchers who followed up a group of men over a 45-year period to see which defence mechanisms were associated with best mental health found a link between the more immature defence mechanisms (such as withdrawal and aggressive behaviour) and aspects of character such as an inability to behave consistently in reaching for chosen goals, an inability to accept and work with other people; being chronically dependent on others, or being too self-involved. People with these character traits were highly likely to be diagnosed as having a personality disorder. Since much psychological distress arises from an interaction between stressful life events and the kind of people we are, achieving positive mental health involves examining the kind of defence mechanisms we tend to use, and trying to shift them towards the more mature end of the spectrum, that is sublimation and humour.

In this chapter I have argued that when we moan or think about how the world has done bad things to us, our focus is in the wrong place (assuming we want to stay emotionally healthy). We should, instead, concentrate on why we believe we can blame the world for our troubles. The fundamental problem with the idea that others, or external events, are the cause of the mental distress we are suffering, is that if this really is the case, our mental health is at the mercy of external events. In other words, we would have little power to influence it. But if this were true, why moan about something we can do nothing about? The very fact that you have got this far in the book means that a part of you believes you can do something about your mental health. I agree with you; you *can* examine yourself and your belief system whenever you feel your mental health slipping away from you. And you *can* change it to one which is more realistic and supportive of your mental health.

So, to summarise, to stay sane you need constantly to challenge your thoughts to see if the facts support them, and to check whether you are falling into any of the four classic traps: 'musterbation', catastrophising, rating yourself, or intolerance. You need to exterminate your ANTS, or Automatic Negative Thoughts, and replace them with more realistic and less judgemental self-statements. You should keep reminding yourself of your positive qualities, particularly at times of personal rejection.

You also need to identify you IBs, or Irrational Beliefs, such as the fact that you are a worthless person because of an isolated failure.

You need to beware of triads – negative views of self, the world and the future.

You need to cease 'what iffing' and eliminate worry by replacing it with problem-solving, interspersed with distraction so that you feel better before commencing your problem-solving.

Finally, preventive mental health rests on society valuing rationality and a rational approach to personal problems. Until this happens, it is desirable to embrace a rational perspective on emotional difficulties, despite the fact this may seem alien or unpopular with friends, because rationality is a key signpost on the pathway to staying sane.

The study which followed up the group of men for 45 years to investigate which personality characteristics predicted long-term mental health was really probing what makes one person resilient and another less hardy. The next chapter examines this issue in detail.

" The Mind CONTRIVES to hear Listening hosts where there are no visible LISTENING HOSTS "

GCHQ
THINK SHARKS

2017

8

I WILL SURVIVE

Building Resilience *in 1 yr..*

+ 29.8 %

'Life is hard, but so am I...
(Lyric from a pop song – 'Novocaine for the Soul'
by The Eels, Warner Records, 1997)

2017

INDESCRIBE/BABBLE

What makes one person able to withstand crisis after crisis and another fail to cope with the slightest set-back? Perhaps one clue lies in a recent – and rare – study of 40 'trauma survivors'. All 40 surveyed had gone through dreadfully traumatic experiences, such as rape at gunpoint, incest, sexual abuse, witnessing murder in their family, accidental injuries and political torture, yet without suffering any significant psychological problems such as Post-Traumatic Stress Disorder.

The following recurring themes were found.[1] First, they did not dwell on the trauma. Secondly, they lived a hard-working, productive life characterised by self-determination and self-reliance. Thirdly, they accepted and learned from the traumatic experience and faced life's future challenges, and finally, they had 'biological endurance' due to their physical health, which some have called stamina.[2]

It may sound straightforward, but the idea that you can survive terrible life events and emerge relatively unscathed is still extremely difficult for many clinicians to accept. Some even suggest that the refusal to assume the 'sick role' or to seek help for suffering is in itself a disorder – a kind of masochism.[3] But, gradually, interest is developing in the idea that if some can survive severe or traumatic events without suffering stress, perhaps a major part of the causes of psychiatric problems lie within the individual. In other words, the terrible event the individual has faced is not solely responsible.

If bad things happening to us was the sole cause of psychiatric problems, how would one account for the research finding that only 32 per cent of psychiatric cases were attributable to stressful life events?[4] In addition, we also need to take into account an inclination described as 'the search for meaning'. This refers to our tendency when we feel unwell to look back at our recent past to see if our negative feeling could be explained by a recent adverse event.[5] In other words, even if our bad feeling comes from within we look for, and possibly find, causes in our external environment.

Despite these factors, by the mid-1970s, academic psychologists and psychiatrists had acknowledged that stressful events certainly tended to lead to illness.

The technical definition of a life event as being when 'the environment changes but the individual does not' incorporates the individual and the response as being an important part of the impact of such events.[6] If a change occurs in your life which you had been anticipating and perhaps even been coached for, let's say a promotion at work, this probably would not count as a life event. This is because you would have encountered the transition with little disturbance.

Conversely, even if the transition was supposed to be positive, like getting married, if you did not change while your environment did, those supposedly positive life events would be likely to produce stress as you struggled to adapt to the alteration in your life.

The ability to change with your environment is a way of ensuring that life events do not pose problems to your mental health. One approach to achieving this is to ask questions like, 'In what way would I need to change, given that my environment has altered, to fit in with it better?' Or, 'How do people who cope well with this situation differ from me?'

To discover how stressful events could lead to illness, psychologists and psychiatrists have focused their research on those who do badly under stress and become ill. This focus has always puzzled me. Studying the sick is obviously an essential side of the research, but it only provides part of the story. The other group, those who seem relatively unperturbed by great stress, is the one that it seems equally, if not more important to explore.

Junior doctors or medical researchers at the various postgraduate hospitals at which I have worked often ask my advice about their research projects. A common area of study is the impact of a particular negative event or situation on the well-being of a population, for example, how being made homeless affects mental health. Their research, predictably, focuses on finding and studying those who have been made ill by

For thought the Slave of life; and Life Times.

homelessness. However, they ignore those who lose their homes and yet stay well! I believe we could learn a lot about staying sane if we could investigate how this group differs from those who do suffer from their negative experiences. Of course, research is often determined by practical issues: sick people will inevitably turn up at casualty departments, or GP practices, or become known to helpers in the field, while the healthy group will not. The healthy will, therefore, be more difficult for medical researchers to track down. But it is also true that psychiatrists as a group do not on the whole acknowledge the need for such studies. Psychiatrists see ill people all day, not those who stay healthy despite having the same problems. And psychologists, who, in contrast, usually deal with the well, don't pursue the link with mental illness. So, a crucial area of mental health research is largely ignored.

Eliot Benezra, the author of the study on 'trauma survivors', made the comment on one of the subjects in the study, who was a personal friend of the researcher, that, despite surviving extraordinary Nazi atrocities during the 1940s, including losing his home and family, this person exhibited feature number one on the list – not dwelling on the trauma – to the extent of being extremely reluctant to discuss his horrific ordeal. The surprising lack of bitterness displayed by Benezra's friend, given the terrible atrocities he had survived, fits in with various long-term (over several decades) follow-up studies aimed at uncovering the early practices of good long-term health.

For example, one study following up women physicians who completed medical school in the mid-1960s found that low hostility and anger under stress as measured in the 1960s, predicted better general health 22 years later.[7] The authors of this study suggested that displaying hostility when under stress may lead to low social support. In addition, they found that those with a cynical approach would tend to discount the advice of others, while generalised distrust would impair planning and decision-making. So, hostility reflects a pessimistic world view, and is bad for our health. Similarly, for Eliot Benezra's friend, whenever related subjects came up, like Germany or World War II, he tactfully evaded these subjects, clearly unwilling to bend his listeners' ears on his experiences.[8]

This points to another problem with studying the resilient, or survivors. Given that one characteristic of hardiness is the unwillingness

Rumour is a pipe, Blown by Surmises, Jealousys
that the Vast, discordat, wavering, multi-

to recall horrendous trauma, people who have survived shock might well be the least willing to volunteer to talk about themselves and their experiences to researchers. This then calls into question one of the basic tenets of much psychotherapeutic practice, that it is always good to talk.

Let me start with the last of the list of characteristics found in those who survive severe stress without professional help first: biological endurance.

Before considering the psychological aspects of resilience, it is important to ensure that your body, brain and nervous system are physically resilient. A physical health check is important for your mental health, as your brain and nervous system support your conscious self. Psychiatrists, who are first trained as doctors, are able to investigate the physical causes of psychological disturbance as well as the purely emotional ones. Many common coping techniques used to deal with psychological distress – drinking alcohol, smoking, over-eating and drug abuse, for example – all cause physical damage to the body, and this reduces psychological resilience in the long term.

Recent emphasis by family doctors on physical fitness is all about building up physical resistance to illness. Physicians want you to be physically fit, not so you can compete in the Olympics, but so that your body will be better able to withstand the negative effects of old age, viruses and other disease-causing agents in general. They are also concerned about the dangers (such as heart problems) of physical inactivity and a poor diet.

Some symptoms of mental disorders are physical, and include loss of weight, palpitations, tingling in the limbs and nausea. Take the anxiety disorder known as Post-Traumatic Stress Disorder, which follows the experience of extraordinary trauma. Symptoms can include the above list as well as hyper-alertness, sleeplessness, irritability and nervousness, and this has led some psychologists to speculate that these are all evidence of a hyperactive nervous system, which has been 'stirred up' by the trauma. In other words, those who suffer from Post-Traumatic Stress Disorder have less biological endurance than those who suffer similar stress but not the resulting trauma illness.[9]

Physical resilience has many components, including diet and exercise. In the case of exercise it is important not take it to extremes. For example, some female athletes are too thin to menstruate and a few male

307

body-builders abuse steroids in the pursuit of the appearance of 'physical perfection'. This can then cause physical disease and even precipitate severe mental illness, such as psychosis. This kind of physical fitness is obviously different from that pursued in order to ward off illness.

Physical fitness is associated with psychological health for many reasons, not least because physical illnesses are clearly unpleasant and make us feel miserable. Conversely, studies have demonstrated that exercise has a marked antidepressant effect due to the production of the body's own pain-relieving and energising chemicals. It is still puzzling, given this strong relationship between exercise and elevation of mood, why more people don't exercise regularly.

Psychologists interested in exercise have recently suggested that this reluctance might be because starting to exercise will probably lead to a short-term worsening of mood, particularly if you are not used to it, and that this is the stage at which most people give up. If they could only persist a little longer, they would begin to feel the mood-elevating effects.[10] Exercise is also healthy because it is a good distracter. In the next chapter on coping, I explain in greater detail the mental health benefits of being able to employ distraction.

So, regular exercise will help build physical resilience as well as help regulate your mood, and thus enhance psychological resilience. But what about that other favourite modern preoccupation – diet? Can you eat your way to mental health?

In 1968, chemistry Nobel Laureate, Linus Pauling, suggested that while the rest of the body may have adequate amounts of a particular vitamin or nutrient, the brain could still be deficient. He also argued that people's needs could vary considerably. In other words, you could not rely on the 'RDA' (Recommended Daily Allowances) so famously printed on vitamin tablet bottles as applying to you and your mental health in particular.[11]

This is a crucial issue, as most nutritionists would argue that as long as you eat a balanced diet there is no reason anyone in the comfortably well-off West should need to take vitamin or mineral supplements. Most nutritionists dismiss the view that vitamin and mineral supplements hold the key to both physical and mental fitness, as an attempt by certain vitamin and mineral bottlers to boost their profits. Nutritionists point out, for example, that taking minerals and vitamins to excess can itself cause health problems. For instance, taking large amounts of zinc will cause a lowering of body copper which will, in turn, cause mood changes such as irritability.

While most doctors do not believe that those without symptoms of illness need vitamin or mineral supplements, they would agree that there is a need to check carefully whether a poor diet may be contributing to psychiatric problems. This is due to the fact that many early or mild deficiencies in vitamins or minerals first manifest themselves through psychological problems.[12]

These checks for biological causes of psychological problems are extremely important as it is often not possible to tell simply from symptoms whether a depression is being caused by outside events or by a vitamin or mineral deficiency. On many occasions my clinical team has felt that the cause of a patient's poor mental health must be clearly attributable to their recent negative life events. Then their blood test results have come back showing a vitamin or mineral deficiency and when this was corrected their mental health improved, despite the adverse life situation not improving. It is routine at the Maudsley, as at all good psychiatric hospitals, for all client referrals from the family doctor to be initially screened with blood tests to check for such deficiencies.

A good example of where an apparently healthy diet could cause psychological problems is in the burgeoning rise in vegetarianism. While there are certainly some benefits – for example, many of the health problems associated with meat are avoided – in other respects, vegetarianism can sometimes lead to its own health problems. For instance, iron from plant sources is less well absorbed by the body than that which comes from meat, so vegetarians must be careful to take enough Vitamin C which improves iron uptake. A deficiency in iron can cause anaemia, or a lowered red cell blood count, which in turn can cause many symptoms of depression, including fatigue, lethargy and poor concentration. Good sources of iron include meat, offal, eggs, green vegetables, pulses and wholegrain cereals.

While world-wide iron deficiency is probably the most prevalent nutritional disorder, this should not be found so frequently or to such extremes in the well-nourished West. Yet a recent survey found that 52 per cent of women and 11 per cent of men in Britain had only marginal iron intake.[13] Women on the contraceptive pill need to be particularly careful that they are not low in iron, as recent research suggests that, for some women, taking the pill may cause depression if they are low in iron.

Another mineral which we should all ensure we are getting adequate amounts of is selenium, another mineral where deficiency may be widespread and also is linked to poor mental health. The average intake was recently calculated to be approaching only between half to two-thirds of the daily recommended intake. Varying levels of selenium in soils throughout the world explain its variability in the food chain, with New Zealand, United Kingdom, parts of China, Scandinavia and the United States being particularly vulnerable to low levels in food.[14] Selenium is needed by the body only in trace amounts, but is important as it has been found to be concentrated in parts of the brain. It is also needed in the manufacture of thyroxine, an important hormone which regulates our mood and metabolic rate and is made by the thyroid gland.[15]

One study researching the effects of selenium gave normal adults an added supplement of selenium (100 micrograms) and found that, in comparison to a control group, the supplement led to a marked improvement in mood. The findings were that the lower the levels of selenium had been in the diet before the experiment, the more anxiety, depression and tiredness decreased following five weeks of selenium therapy in the experiment.[16]

Most selenium is consumed either in grain or in meat. Wheat used for flour contains selenium and the decrease in bread intake has been implicated in the lower intake of selenium recently.[17–19] Exactly what proportion of the population may be selenium deficient – in the sense that taking more selenium would improve their mental health – is still unknown. However, selenium can be dangerous if taken in very large amounts and anyone taking supplements should ensure they do not exceed the recommended dose.

While exact statistics for selenium deficiency are hard to obtain, much research has been conducted regarding vitamin deficiency. A recent survey used blood tests to check vitamin status and found that as many as 37 per cent of young British adults did not have an adequate level of the Vitamin B2 group member riboflavin; 22 per cent did not have adequate levels of Vitamin B1 group member thiamine; and 43 per cent did not have adequate levels of Vitamin B6 pyridoxine. Other studies have found that specific nutritional deficiencies commonly occur in young adults, particularly of iron, zinc and Vitamins A, B and C.[20]

If you eat a diet without *any* vitamin B2 or riboflavin, depression and lethargy will result in as little as 50 days. Moreover, one study found that of those admitted to psychiatric hospital, around a third were riboflavin deficient.[21] Riboflavin is found in mild cheese, eggs, kidneys and liver.

Vitamin B1 or thiamine (found in pork, eggs, grains and cereals) is easily destroyed by boiling and, as the body has only small stores of thiamine, there is a risk of deficiency if the level of intake is reduced for even a few weeks. Doctors themselves debate what the minimum thiamine requirement is, as there are wide individual needs. A low-thiamine diet leads to an inability to concentrate, confusion, amnesia, anorexia, irritability, depression and insomnia.

One study done in the 1940s found that if people whose diet supplied them with enough thiamine were given twice the recommended daily allowance, they benefited by improved eyesight, quicker reaction times, and even by growing significantly taller and scoring better on tests of memory and intelligence. These findings have been replicated in more recent research published in the 1990s. Those who drink heavily, have a junk food diet, or eat a lot of carbohydrates need to be particularly careful, as all these use up the body's thiamine rapidly. Brain damage due to a lack of thiamine has been found in almost 3 per cent of the population of Australia, yet in only a fifth of these was the brain damage diagnosed while they were alive.

This evidence suggests that of all vitamins, thiamine should be given the highest priority for those concerned with staying sane, because the correct minimum levels of intake have yet to be agreed by doctors. A recent survey found that 22 per cent of young males and 20 per cent of young females had either marginal or deficient intake of thiamine.[22] This has particularly worrying consequences for mental health, given that a direct relationship has been found between the amount of thiamine in your body and how good your mood is – the more thiamine, the better.[23]

Another important vitamin is folic acid, which is found, for example, in offal and raw, green, leafy vegetables. A fifth of all admissions to one

British psychiatric hospital were found to have low levels of this vitamin.[24] Deficiency causes tiredness, depression and confusion. Folic acid is also an important factor in preventing handicaps such as spina bifida and, in the UK, is given as a supplement to pregnant women. Folic acid is concentrated in the fluid bathing the brain and is linked to the body's manufacture of serotonin, which is a chemical thought to be implicated in depression if levels in the brain are too low. The same study found that one-quarter of all admissions to a psychiatric hospital had low levels of Vitamin B12, which is found in liver, eggs, cheese, meat and fish. Deficiency is linked to memory impairment and serious mental illness, such as psychosis.[25]

Low levels of Vitamin B6 (found in meats, fish, eggs and cereal) have been implicated in autism, a psychiatric disorder which starts in childhood and which manifests itself in poor relationship-building abilities. And some have gone as far as suggesting that in some cases of autism Vitamin B6 may reverse the condition.[26] Deficiency also causes fatigue, irritability and insomnia. The problem with administering high doses of B6, though, is that these have been reported to cause nerve damage and skin blisters.

Given that the RDA for minerals and vitamins is controversial, and the benefits of having plentiful supplies of them are so pronounced, perhaps you do not have to be deficient in the accepted medical sense to need a top-up. This suggestion is reinforced by the finding that giving extra vitamins like thiamine to people who are not medically deficient in vitamins and minerals seems to improve their mood and mental functioning.[27] Remember that a mild vitamin or mineral deficiency seems to manifest itself first with psychological symptoms.[28] And there is startling research evidence that vitamins and minerals, in general, may be helpful to mental functioning, particularly for those on a poor diet. According to a study carried out in Belgium, multi-vitamin and mineral supplementation raised the IQs of teenage boys on a poor diet by six points over a period of only five months.[29–31]

A similar study of Welsh 12-year-old children found a parallel average rise of an IQ point every month after eight months of added vitamin and mineral supplements.[32] And yet another study in Wales of six-year-olds found an increase in IQ of over seven points after taking vitamin and mineral supplements for only two months. In those taking a placebo the IQ scores fell by almost two points over the same time.[33]

But you should not necessarily have to take vitamin or mineral pills to ensure your nutrient status is OK, as eating a healthy and varied diet will usually accomplish this. For example, a positive link has been found between the consumption of fresh fruit and vegetables and mental health in women[34] while the benefits of additional vitamins in tablet form may take a long time to come through. One study found that administering ten times the RDA of a range of vitamins led to improvement in mood after a year.[35] The improvement in mood was particularly linked with rising levels of riboflavin and Vitamin B6. Yet the levels of blood vitamins reached a plateau after three months, suggesting that the improvement in mood after a year cannot simply be explained by making good a previously deficient intake.

Scientists are still undecided as to whether the benefits to mood and the intellect of extra vitamins are due simply to reducing a deficiency in a poor diet or represent an added gain beyond just correcting a pre-existing deficiency.[36] For optimal psychological health the best advice seems to be to make sure you consume enough iron (especially if you are female), maintain adequate levels of selenium, make sure you are not deficient in vitamins, particularly those of the B group, and possibly even take additional thiamine supplements as well (given that the RDA of this vitamin is controversial and higher levels are linked with positive mood). The best current American nutritionist advice is that, unless you are extremely careful about eating a healthy food selection at every meal, you should take a daily recommended daily allowance multivitamin, as well as folic acid if you are female (because of the benefits in preventing nervous system disorders in babies).[37]

Nutritionists also recommend including oily fish such as herring, sardines, mackerel or salmon in your diet as these are a good source of essential fatty acids which play vital roles in the brain.[38] A fifth of the dry weight of the brain consists of fats[39] and these play an important role in the structure of membranes which lie between nerve cells, and are crucial in facilitating the transmission of nerve cell signals to each other.

Further evidence for the importance of an adequate diet on brain function comes from a study of the effect of a famine in Holland due to an imposed Nazi transport embargo. From October 1944 to May 1945 the average food intake in the affected areas fell to around 1,000 calories a day. As the duration of the famine is known, it was possible to follow up those who were in the womb at the time their mothers were on this severe diet. From 1978–89 it was found that women whose mothers had consumed less than 1,000 calories a day during the first three months of pregnancy had more than twice the rate of schizophrenia compared with those whose mothers had eaten more. The effect was similar for men with schizophrenia, though less pronounced.[40] Clearly this suggests that ensuring adequate maternal nutrition during pregnancy is implicated in preventing poor mental health in future offspring.

While exercising regularly and eating healthily will certainly improve your mental health, another important nutrient the brain appears to need to maintain mental health is high-intensity light. The emergence of research evidence in the 1980s that a significant minority of the population are extra-sensitive to sunlight and so become clinically depressed during winter, because of the shorter days and less light, led doctors to affirm that Seasonal Affective Disorder (SAD) is a real illness, unlike many other new diagnoses.

Interest in the effects of light on mental health started in the early 1980s when psychiatrists of the USA National Institute of Mental Health reviewed the history of a 29-year-old woman being treated for intermittent depression. They noticed not only that these bouts of depression occurred during winter, but that as this woman moved over the course of several years to a number of different cities in the US, the further north she moved, the earlier she became depressed in the autumn and the longer she remained depressed in the spring. When, on two occasions, she went to Jamaica in midwinter for a holiday, her depression disappeared within a couple of days of arrival.[41]

Why some people are so sensitive to light is still not known, but the treatment, which is highly effective, has traditionally been to advise sufferers to expose themselves to high-intensity artificial light for a few hours every day during the dark winter months. Usually this is white light of around 2,500 lux of intensity, a lux being a unit equivalent to the illumination cast on a surface by one candle one metre away. The patient is exposed to this for around two hours a day. Customary indoor lights range from 250 to 500 lux. In contrast, being outside on a cloudy day in

Northern Europe exposes us to around 10,000 lux, and on a sunny day close to the equator to the equivalent of 80,000 lux.

Exactly how such light has an effect on the brain is still unknown, other than that it is light which enters through the eyes which is important, not that absorbed via the skin. The advice to sufferers from SAD is to look at bright artificial light from time to time. However, given that the lights used for treatment are expensive because of the high intensity they must generate, recent research has suggested that exposing oneself to more outdoor light would be a simple and effective alternative.

The intensity of illumination outdoors, even in the depth of winter, is in the order of between ten and over a hundred times greater than artificial light indoors.[42] One recent study has suggested that a daily, one-hour morning walk could replace the standard artificial light treatment.[43] Hence, perhaps the real reason SAD exists is that in temperate countries people go out less during the cold winter months, leading to light starvation of the brain.

One study measured the amount of time per day that healthy elderly people in San Diego – quite a sunny place – were exposed to outdoor sunlight. Unexpectedly, the men were in sunlight for only 75 minutes a day and the women for only 20 minutes a day.[44] A survey of 200 subjects chosen at random from the New York City telephone directory found that around half exhibited various symptoms of SAD, that is, having low energy, gaining weight, sleeping more and socially withdrawing during winter months.[45]

So, while this daily hour's walk will undoubtedly help prevent psychological disturbance in those prone to SAD, what about the rest of us? There is evidence that even ordinary depression benefits to some extent from light.[46] One recent study looked at the speed of recovery rates for all depressed patients (not just those with SAD) who had been admitted to a psychiatric unit, and found that those randomly assigned bedrooms that were bright and sunny recovered significantly faster than those in dull rooms.[47]

Thus, there is some evidence that we could all benefit from an hour's walk outdoors every day. It also kills two birds with one stone, as it combines both exercise and light. To make it easier to fit into a busy lifestyle, such a walk could always be broken into two half-hour stints, for example at the beginning and end of the day, to and from work. Even if you cannot do this, and you are largely stuck indoors because of work or other reasons, you can try to be near windows, or spend more time in sunny rooms than darker ones.

The evidence is also that light exposure in the morning is more effective for enhancing mood than that in the rest of the day.[48] You will have noticed that one of the symptoms of SAD is weight gain during winter, which appears to be a result of carbohydrate cravings at that time. One theory is that eating high carbohydrate and very low-protein meals is the SAD sufferer's attempt to self-treat their low mood. Such a combination of foods will probably raise brain levels of a chemical called serotonin, which is precisely the nerve transmitter agent many antidepressants act on to elevate, and is one of the brain substances thought to be the key to improving mood.[49]

This has even led to the suggestion that changing your diet could alter your mood, indicating that there may be a dietary treatment of depression, and even a dietary prevention for low mood.[50]

The problem is that the kind of diet which would be needed reliably to enhance brain serotonin levels is one which would consist of less than 5 per cent protein and this is very difficult to achieve. In addition, the protein remaining in the stomach from a previous meal means that such a strange diet would have to be sustained for long periods to have an antidepressant effect, which has never been reliably demonstrated anyway.[51]

To complicate the issue further, some research has found that reducing the carbohydrate content of a diet by eliminating refined sucrose has led to improved mood, though this experiment included removing caffeine from the diet as well. So whether it was the sucrose or caffeine elimination which helped is still not known.[52]

But there is enough evidence to warrant the manipulation of caffeine and carbohydrates in your diet if you notice a link between the consumption of these and your mood, or if you are taking extremely large or small amounts of carbohydrate or huge daily doses of caffeine. Massively excessive caffeine consumption is certainly associated with anxiety and depression but even consuming just over five cups of coffee a day is linked to increased anxiety and depression.[53]

There is, however, one very common manipulation of diet which does reliably lead to poorer mental health, and this is the effect of dieting in an attempt to lose weight, a very common occurrence in women, particularly young women today. One estimate is that at any one time one-third of the British population is dieting.[54] The evidence is that losing just over two pounds because of dieting leads to poor concentration, memory problems and slower brain functioning[55] whilst longer-term dieting produces lethargy, depression and irritability.[56]

The two main explanations for the negative effects of dieting are that dieting results in a shortage of essential brain nutrients and that the emotional effort of maintaining a diet reduces mental capacity.

These negative effects of dieting on mood and intellectual performance may explain why some move from simple dieting to an irrational pursuit of weight loss beyond what is necessary, so producing the current epidemic of eating disorders.

The best positive mental health strategy is to diet only when advised to by a doctor, follow a sensible nutritious food plan, and combine dieting with exercise (as attempts at weight loss without increased exercise simply lead to more extreme dieting behaviour).

There are obviously different approaches to optimising your diet, exercise and exposure to sunlight. But however you do it, I believe that if you are interested in staying sane you will check you are getting enough brain nutrients in your regular diet, sufficient exercise and adequate exposure to light.

So, diet, sunlight and exercise all help to produce physical stamina, which in turn helps to build resilience to psychological difficulties. But what about the non-physical dimension?

I mentioned earlier the recurring themes found in the study of trauma victims. On the psychological side, these included not dwelling on the trauma, living a hard-working, productive life characterised by self-determination and self-reliance and, finally, accepting and learning from life's traumatic experiences and facing life's future challenges.

The few psychologists who were interested in this group defined the quality that distinguished them as 'hardiness', while others used the term 'resilience'. Whatever the word, this concept lies at the core of positive mental health. Resilience is a characteristic which lies dormant during good times, perhaps leaving that person indistinguishable from anyone else, but which becomes apparent once adversity strikes.

Psychologists who advocate the existence of a personality characteristic called hardiness, or resilience, suggest that you are either born hardy or that you achieve hardiness through fortunate early childhood experiences.[57] In other words, you cannot really *choose* to be hardy as an adult. If I believed that, this would be a very short chapter! I differ from these academics by believing that you can become hardy, even as an adult, so do not despair if you have not had particularly positive childhood experiences. Instead, I will look at the evidence for producing resilient children and then investigate whether it is possible to replicate it in adults who have not had such benefits.

The first interesting thing about resilient children is that, whatever problems they have faced, be they economic, maltreatment, or emergencies like fires, the same background themes seem to promote resilience.[58] They include a good, warm relationship with at least one care-giver, an absence of early separations or losses and a sense of humour. These children grow into resilient adults if they have good social support from spouse, family or other figures, a good network of informal relationships, and involvement with organised religious activity.

Of course, children are not in a position to choose their family circumstances, so their resilience is often beyond their control – something which either happens to them or not. Adults, on the other hand, have more power to determine their destiny, particularly in the light of information they have about what is of benefit to them. So I will now discuss how to build resilience *whatever* happened to you during childhood. The first step is, however, to establish that resilience clearly exists.

Research has shown that even among children exposed to the most serious disadvantages, such as physical, sexual or emotional abuse, it is unusual for more than half of them to succumb[59] to long-term psychological problems.[60] Psychiatrists investigating the mental health of children with a high genetic risk of serious mental illness such as psychosis – a psychiatric problem most likely to have a strong biological and genetic component – are often surprised at their resilience.[61]

Of those children who would have been expected to develop serious mental illness due to their genetic background (many close relatives suffering from psychosis), in a significant percentage of cases the psychiatrist investigating them declared that 'these children with psychotic parents were not simply escaping from whatever genetic transmission destiny had in store for them, and not merely surviving the milieu of irrationality generated by psychotic parenting; but were apparently thriving under conditions that sophisticated observers judged to be highly detrimental to a child's psychosocial development and well-being'.[62]

So, resilience and hardiness have been interpreted as factors which not only promote survival, but which also contribute to thriving when the going gets tough.[63] Another important point about resilience is that what is helpful under some circumstances may not be so under others. For example, while having a high IQ as a child seems to be of general benefit while the going is non-stressful, there is some evidence that, in the face of adversity, children with high IQs do worse in some circumstances than those with lower IQs.[64]

This may be because, if you are young when adversities strike, being less intelligent may help protect you because you do not have the intellectual capacity to realise the true implications, unlike brighter children. In this chapter I will define factors which promote resilience as those which are helpful *whatever* the circumstance you find yourself in.

Another example of the complexity of defining resilience is that, for reasons which are still not entirely clear, before adolescence girls are more protected from psychological problems than boys, while after adolescence the opposite is true.[65] One possible explanation might be that if you are a junior member of a family and live in close proximity to others who have authority over you, internalising your emotional upset (taking things out on yourself) as women tend to do will help you get on with others even when you are in distress.

So, before adolescence, when you are still living at home, this may be the practical approach. In contrast, externalising (taking things out on others) by behaving badly, as men tend to when upset, will provoke your family and so create a cycle of further upset when you are a child. However, when you leave your family and live by yourself, or begin to have more authority over those around you, externalising may be a better coping strategy than internalising.

As mentioned, protective factors for mental illness need to be selected to be useful whatever the situation you find yourself in, clearly a difficult enterprise. And given that psychologists and psychiatrists are at long last realising that there will never be enough professionals to treat the true level of psychological distress among the public, there has been an increasing interest in the idea of encouraging resilience, particularly in children, as a way of aiding preventive mental health care.[66]

This doesn't help much, since mental health professionals are still far from knowing how reliably to ensure that our personality absorbs healthy elements such as hardiness. However, there appears to be an interesting analogy with immunisation as a way of protecting positive physical health among children and adults.

Just as immunisation does not work by making you feel better (many people have minor adverse reactions), resilience is similarly not just about feeling good. Immunisation means exposure to, and successful coping with, a small, modified dose of a noxious infectious agent.[67] This helps the body mount a strong response should a more serious exposure to the dangerous agent occur in the future.

Research done as far back as the 1950s[68] found that rat pups subjected to electrical shocks showed an enhanced resistance to later stress. One[69] explanation for this effect seems to lie in the idea that the nervous and hormone system adapts to this early experience and so is better able to cope with later stress.

However, the 'steeling effect'[70] of previous stress depends on whether you emerged successfully from the first stress with improved coping mechanisms, enhanced self-esteem or a more effective biological response from your body's nerves and hormones. If you do so you are likely to become more stress-resistant. If, on the other hand, you are left distraught, unable to cope or biologically impaired by the first stress, this will not have a steeling effect, but rather a weakening one.[71]

So, a controlled exposure to stress in supportive circumstances will help promote successful coping or adaptation. For example, the children who have been shown to cope best with separation from their parents if they have to be admitted to hospital are those who endured some kind of controlled separation before,[72] such as staying the night with friends.

A good illustration of this principle is a recent study comparing Australian teenage students going away for the first time on an exchange scheme, with those who stayed at home.[73] The researchers found that although the students felt stress at being away from home, this was limited because these were supportive and controlled circumstances – the students could always be relocated if their placement did not work out and also had access to help from the exchange organisation. Despite the increased stress, on returning home the exchange students were measured to have decreased vulnerability to neurosis. It seems that being away had accelerated the maturity of their personality in terms of resilience.

So, exposing oneself to stress in a controlled and supportive manner helps foster resilience. I notice that many of my patients seem keen to avoid any stress under any circumstances and that this is probably because they have not had experiences earlier in life which have led them to feel what psychologists call successful at 'task accomplishment'.

The tasks referred to are interpreted widely to span taking positions of responsibility as well as success in non-academic pursuits. Engaging in tasks will inevitably bring stress. However, if you have had a previous positive experience of success, when encountering a similar strain, such as surviving giving your first talk, this will help build resilience, not just in childhood but throughout life, though obviously it is in childhood that such crucial experiences start.

Notice that exposing yourself to pressure is a strategy which fosters positive mental health while you are fairly well. However, once you become unwell, a temporary reduction in tension probably aids recovery. The kinds of stresses the well should expose themselves to are the sort of situations we tend to avoid at the moment because they might produce discomfort, but which would have no really terrible consequences if we were to fail. For example, this might be attending an evening class in ballroom dancing which we avoid because we fear the anxiety of public embarrassment. Or it might be trying to make friends with those whom we avoid at the moment because we fear we might be rebuffed. Or it could be enquiring about another job which we avoid because we fear rejection. Our lives are built up of many years spent avoiding stress, of a multitude of small and large avoidances. This bypassing of strain is perfectly understandable as a short-term attempt to reduce the tension in our lives. However, as mentioned, the best long-term approach is to build resistance so that we no longer find these issues a burden.

A good way of encouraging yourself to plunge into slightly stressful situations is to ask yourself what the worst consequences might be. Is it that you might die because of the stress? Or be driven mad? Or suffer permanent physical damage? If none of these things are likely outcomes then expose yourself to the new predicament. You have an added incentive now that you know there are long-term benefits from such graded and controlled exposure, whereas before there appeared to be only the negative cost of unpleasant feelings.

On 19 April 1993 the FBI attempted to end a siege at Mount Carmel, near Waco, Texas, where a cult called the Branch Davidians led by David Koresh were ensconced.[74] The resulting gun battle led to a fire which demolished the compound, killing 83 inhabitants. Dentists were needed to aid the identification of bodies from dental remains; and, at the same time, psychiatrists investigated the factors which could predict which dentists would cope best with the stress of such severe trauma as dealing with the dead and handling children's bodies.[75]

They found that a major factor predicting successful coping was previous experience of such disturbing experiences; the more inexperienced dentists coped less well.[76] This suggests that one of the best ways of becoming resilient is to have experienced perturbing events. In other words, trying to protect yourself from such experiences, which might be the instinctive response, is associated with less efficient coping. The authors of the study of the Waco dentists speculate that one reason previous exposure to such trauma may have been helpful is that this could have educated the experienced dentists in how better to use support from colleagues and spouses. They might also have been more aware of the strain on anyone having to deal with the aftermath.

But what, in more detail, do we mean by the term 'resilience'? Psychologists in the 1980s broke down hardiness into characteristic tendencies embedded in our personality, and which reflect the recurrent manner in which we approach and interpret our experience. Hardiness is usually seen as being made up of the three Cs: Commitment, Control and Challenge.[77]

First, commitment. This refers to a sense of meaning and purpose to one's existence. It implies that you are committed to some goal in life, a kind of mission which drives you forward and from which you will not be deflected. A term frequently used in the 1960s for mental good health was 'self-actualising': these people were seen as having a mission, or focus, outside themselves. In having a focus outside yourself, when a negative event does occur, you do not ruminate on how the event has hurt you or affected you; your attention remains directed externally and you concentrate on how to deal with it in terms of how it stops you from attaining your goal.

In this context, it is interesting to note that therapists dealing with couples have remarked that those who stay together despite difficulties are the ones who appear to share a common goal. Loving your partner is not about facing each other, but more about facing in the same direction.[78] So a couple is more likely to survive one partner being away for long periods of time if the purpose of being away is linked to a goal the couple both share, let's say building financial security. Being away from home begins to cause problems in a relationship only when this is for a purpose both do not shoulder equally.

The notion of commitment may explain how some people, such as the Beirut hostages, who were held for several years and endured incredible stresses, can emerge relatively unscathed psychiatrically. One characteristic of all the hostages was that they did not give up. They seemed committed to surviving for various reasons outside themselves – like for their families, girlfriends or careers.

Some of the relationships between the hostages and those in the outside world which sustained them during their incarceration did not survive once they were released. So it seems that whatever you are committed to which aids survival may simply be something that helps you during that crisis, and does not imply a life-long devotion. The stresses people such as these endure successfully usually also have some kind of meaning to them in terms of their life goals. In the case of the hostages, the jobs they did and the places they visited meant they had already accepted the possibility of such a thing happening to them and see it as a 'risk of the job'.

They may even have understood how, if they survived physically, they could turn the experience to their advantage. Many people who have undergone extremely stressful events say things like, 'I'm a better person for it', or, 'It has helped me be more sympathetic to other people'. Stress which the sufferer can see no meaning in whatsoever is naturally more difficult to deal with, as it is tough to integrate it into their lifeplan. Most of my patients have great difficulty understanding how their particular stress, which has contributed to their mental illness, can be understood as part of their life. They say things like 'Why did it happen to me?'

So, for example, if a negative event occurs to you while you are doing your job as a journalist, like being taken hostage in a basement in Beirut, you are more likely to survive successfully if you try to see the event as something which is an inevitable hazard of your job, something which you should expect to have to encounter if you want to pursue your career as a journalist. Moreover, if you also believe that coping with the event might help make you a better journalist, for example, or even try to see how you could get some journalistic coup from the bad circumstance, such an attitude is more likely to help you survive.

Often people who become particularly depressed because a partner has left act as if this has never happened to anyone ever before, and as though they have been singled out in some way for this unfair act. Or someone suffering badly from post-traumatic stress after a spectacular car accident seems oblivious to the fact that car accidents are unfortunate but do happen all the time. If you view a stressful event as unique and believe that somehow you as opposed to anyone else in the world have been targeted, you will inevitably find the disaster more difficult to deal with.

While this chapter focuses on the type of person, and the kind of attitude to life that will best best survive distress, the next chapter on coping ('Crisis, What Crisis?') looks at the specific responses in the face of crisis that are associated with positive mental health.

For example, in my clinical experience, the photocopier salesman who drives on a motorway every day to sell his copiers but who develops agoraphobia is driven to overcome his illness by his need to work to feed his family. Yet the housewife with agoraphobia who doesn't need to get out because the family does the shopping and any other tasks which involve the outside world is much less likely to recover. She seems to have little incentive to change and the illness does not appear to be preventing her from doing what she desperately needs to accomplish.

The reason why long-term goals are crucial to mental health is that ambitions drive you forward and so often put you in situations where you have to do things you would rather not do. You do them in order to attain your long-term aspirations. Moving towards a goal is a reward in itself which helps to compensate for the unpleasantness of the intermediate tasks.

The crucial difference between those who display personal initiative and those who don't is the presence of long-term goals in the former. Personal initiative is a pivotal concept in overcoming difficulty as it differentiates between those willing to do what is required to solve a problem, not just what is expected by peers or convention.[79]

I also believe that personal conflicts can bring about change. The copier salesman has a conflict between his need to get out and his qualms about the outside world. If there was nothing conflicting with his fears he would have more difficulty overcoming his ill-health. Another example is a journalist I have treated. She suffered from terrible temper tantrums, provoked by frustration when she could not get her way. She would throw things around the office – everything from paperclips to coffee mugs. Once, she even physically attacked a colleague. In the end, she was motivated to change because her inability to control her anger jeopardised her career, which she valued highly. She came to me, keen to change because her goal of career promotion was being jeopardised by her symptoms.

So I believe that a crucial component of positive mental health is to be committed to values and a lifestyle which require mental health. If what you want out of life does not require mental health, your ability to maintain it will be questionable. The more mental health required by your lifestyle the better.

I also like to think of commitment as 'stickiness'. How much do you stick to, or persist in, trying to solve the problem the stressful event presents you with? People who are low on commitment give up on devoting energy to solving a problem. They are the kind of people who say, 'This bad thing that happened to me is simply too unfair for me to have to try and cope' or 'No one should be expected to have to deal with this kind of mess, so I shan't.'

If you have commitment, negative events will not leave you confused, but you will see them as obstacles to be overcome on the way to your aspirations.

The second component of resilience is control. Control is a sense of autonomy and the ability to influence one's own destiny. Control refers to the belief that you have some capacity to influence the outcome of some horrible event; in other words, that you do not see the event as completely overwhelming.

My patients who are most curious about their symptoms and want to understand why this is happening to them, implicitly believe that these symptoms are things over which they should be able to gain some kind of control. For example, I have patients who are high-powered city brokers who develop panic symptoms while on the trading floor and are keen to get these resolved, as large sums of money are at stake. They bombard me with questions about the nature of panic and why they are experiencing these symptoms.

On the other hand, I have seen patients who develop a phobia of not being anywhere higher than the ground floor who find it difficult to explain exactly what terrible thing would happen to them if they climbed some stairs. These patients do not appear in the least bit interested in why they feel a need to avoid higher floors, they just accept it and prefer not talking about it; they are happy as long as they steer clear of higher floors.

The city broker wants to control himself; he realises he cannot control his environment, the trading floor. The housewife on the other hand wants to control her environment and not herself, and this leads to multiple avoidances. The likelihood is that dealing with stressful life events involves a bit of both, but the refusal to try and control oneself is linked to poor mental health.

Like the example of the housewife, my patients' phobia of stairs is partly because none of their long-term goals appear threatened by an inability to get above the ground floor, unlike the city brokers whose goal of becoming immensely wealthy is jeopardised by their panic attacks. This links back to commitment; by definition, if you have commitment to achieving a certain life goal you are likely also to subscribe to the belief that you have some control over your destiny. There are people who may be suffering distressing symptoms, but who approach their situation believing they can gain control and only need to know how to do so. They are often relentless in pursuing the information needed for the 'how'.

For example, being made redundant is highly likely to take away your sense of control over your life. Yet even when most people might feel powerless, the resilient are still aiming for some kind of control.

People who believe they can control outcomes say something like the following to themselves, 'First of all, I accept it is the position which has probably been made redundant, not me personally. I immediately have a new job, which is to find another job. If I devote myself to this new job, it will take my mind off this bad news. I'll ask my employer with help in printing out many copies of my cv now, as this can be expensive to do from home, and also ask if it is possible to be kept on nominally without pay as long as possible, so it appears to other employers that I am looking for a new job from a position of employment. This makes it more likely I will be offered a new position quickly. Once at home, I will organise a set routine, where I get up at the time I usually did while employed, and I shall devote a certain number of hours every day to looking for work. I will tell everyone I am looking for a new job, as up to one-quarter of redundant people obtain their next job by word of mouth. I will also get in touch with all the contacts I have in my line of work immediately, to let them know of my availability. I shall consider using my added spare time to do some voluntary work as this will make me feel needed, which is one of the major contributions work makes to my self-esteem. I will make a list of all my skills and achievements, which will again help my self-esteem and also enable me to see better what kind of work I am most suited for – it may not even be what I have been doing up until now! I should be prepared to see redundancy as an opportunity to take stock and head in the best direction for me in the future.'

People often avoid telling others they are unemployed because they are embarrassed, but telling others helps to demonstrate that you are facing up to your new situation. It is more positive than avoiding the subject, as it displays some attempt at controlling your future employment.

If you believe you have some control in your life, negative events will not leave you feeling helpless, and, as I have mentioned, helplessness is a recurrent theme running through much mental illness.

The third and final component of resilience is challenge. Challenge is a zest for life and living that leads you to perceive change as exciting and as providing opportunities for growth rather than threats to security or survival. If you strive continually to understand what is happening to you, no matter what the setbacks, you are demonstrating challenge. For example, if a bad event happens to you unexpectedly, instead of feeling

'I don't understand how this could possibly happen to me, I do not deserve such bad luck', the more resilient alternative is to accept that whatever happens to us in life is normal;[80] this is challenge. The very fact it has happened means we have to expect this kind of thing to occur. Once you see that, this helps you to become more flexible. When we find our circumstances have changed we need to alter our response. Not believing that this bad thing could ever have happened prevents adaptability, but we need to be adaptive because the reality is that nothing stays the same.

Challenge thus means that if something terrible happens to you, you can accept it as part of 'life's rich tapestry'. To survive unscathed mentally the event should somehow be of interest to you, and meaningful in some way; it arouses your curiosity about yourself and your environment because you now realise the world is not quite the way you had previously thought. Another way to look at it is that you do not just spend time wishing the event had not happened or trying to fathom how it could possibly have happened in the first place, instead you get involved in it.

Challenge is similar to commitment and control in that those who exhibit the last two will see life as a challenge. So, the hardy person understands and accepts that negative things are inevitable. People who exhibit challenge think about a negative event rather like this: 'This is part of life, so there is no point just wringing my hands and wailing about it. Bad events are there to be responded to, not just to be allowed to roll over me unhindered.' If you see someone or something as challenging, rather than just as an unexpected negative event, you are less likely to react in a hostile way. You will see the world as demanding an answer from you and will focus on the quality of that response, rather than seeing the event as completely negative.

You may even regard problems as opportunities for learning about yourself and life in general, as you are anxious to turn whatever happens to you into something you can use to achieve your goals. This is an extremely old idea, as embodied in the ancient Roman saying, '*quae nocent, docent*' ('those things that hurt, also teach').[81]

If only we could have control, commitment and challenge as our guaranteed response to problems, mental health would be relatively easy to preserve.

One problem with the three Cs is that they do not seem clearly different from each other. Are they not all saying more or less the same thing? Research into which of these three factors most protects individuals from blood pressure changes when under stress suggests that challenge may be the crucial factor, while control or commitment are less important.[82] However, this is disputed, with other experts suggesting that control and commitment play complementary roles. Commitment allows people to remain involved in the situation, confronting its demands and consequences, while control means that people also try actively to solve their problems.

But even psychologists have questioned whether it is possible to separate the three factors. Perhaps you stay involved and do not distance yourself from the problem because you believe you can stay in control? Perhaps these are really different ways of describing the same phenomenon?

How do the qualities of commitment, challenge and control lead to hardiness? They may do so in several ways. Hardy people may not only meet a new, stressful situation better equipped because they already have stress buffers in their lives, such as a good network of friends and relations to provide social support (in passing, people high on commitment, control and challenge probably make good friends), but feelings of control, commitment and challenge may also cause them to perceive the world in a different way. To them, a stressful event is not as stressful as it is to a less hardy individual. You could say they have a 'higher stress threshold'.

This stress threshold helps to explain why some people find inviting people for tea stressful, while others can cope with a broken leg and simultaneous house move, for example. It may also be that the person with high hardiness learns from previous stressful situations and seems to be hardened, in a positive sense, by the experience of stress. Each stressful event contributes to greater future hardiness. In contrast, less hardy individuals take nothing positive from stressful situations, perhaps, even being weakened by them.

Going back to the idea that the process of developing resilience in life is like immunisation, it is easy to see that as your resilience grows you see each bigger stress as more manageable. A positive cycle develops, whereby stress helps you to cope with more stress.

Research with a group of medical students lends support for this last idea. It found that those scoring high in hardiness tended to view stressful events retrospectively as positive and controllable.[83] If, no matter how bad things were at the time, you can look back at a negative event and see something positive has come from it, you will be less frightened by the possibility of future negative events, and less inclined to stop taking risks in order to avoid them. This learning component is crucial.

How can you learn something positive from discouraging experiences? I believe that learning how to control your own emotions and the world around you, learning how to persist with coping, and how to see what positive things may be derived from a negative event, are skills which contribute to positive mental health.

This is in contrast to what psychologists call 'regressive coping strategies', characterised by an avoidance or shrinking away from potentially stressful situations. For example, a person who finds preparing for a tea party stressful will restrict such occasions, thus also making each occasion more traumatic. Shrinking from situations does not take away the problem because the person still dwells on the stress in a pessimistic way. This is in contrast to the optimistic and active way in which resilient people deal with their problems.

A further example is the way we approach the treatment of fears in clinical practices. The very best treatment goes further than simply exposing yourself to your fear – as in the case of making the businessman who fears flying having to stop avoiding planes. To make sure his fear of flying never returns we would ask him not just to fly a lot, but to go further and do things most people would not, such as trying parachuting for a short while as a hobby. Having to deal with the stress of going beyond the usual when you face your fear seems to make it extremely unlikely you will suffer a relapse in the future.

Asking those who suffer from a fear of heights to demand an office on the top floor as part of their treatment seems an extreme thing to do but if it prevents serious psychiatric problems in the future, it is clearly worthwhile. The crucial point here is that once you have faced and coped with a large stress, anything less than this in the future is usually unproblematic. However, anything close to the worse kind of stress you have coped with will always trouble you.

It may also be that hardiness is not acquired so much through developing control, commitment and challenge, but merely through not resorting to regressive strategies like avoidance, rumination and pessimism. In other words, hardiness may not be about what people do, but more what they do *not* do. Hardy people may simply *not* do the bad things the mentally unhealthy do. Obviously, one way to ensure you do not do something is to replace it with something else, and whatever the things are that hardy people *do* may be effective simply because they ensure that they *don't* follow the negative strategies of the mentally unhealthy.

Some evidence for this comes from the fact that when psychologists have critically examined questionnaire results which claim to measure hardiness scientifically, several of the questions measure hardiness by the respondent denying using poor mental health strategies, rather than admitting to actively adopting good mental health strategies.[84]

But exactly why are poor mental health strategies, such as avoidance, so bad for us? One reason is that they exacerbate stress, for example, by heightening our appraisal of stress as threatening.

From an evolutionary standpoint, how threatening an organism finds a stressful event may determine how extreme its reaction is. Clearly, if you decide something in your environment is so awful that you face imminent death, your body could make such an extreme response that it might actually damage itself. You may release excessive concentrations of stress hormones or chemicals into your bloodstream which raise your blood pressure so high as to damage your cardiovascular system, or weaken the lining of your stomach so much as to cause ulcers. If you repeatedly over-react, the cumulative effect over many years will be damaging.

Through millions of years of evolution, it is likely that the small negative effect of an extreme stress response made sense. It is a fair trade-off to sustain some small, short-term damage to your body in exchange for saving your life. However, suppose there was never a real threat to your life in the first place? Then your extreme reaction becomes inappropriate, and even more so if you repeat the error often and over many years.

Learning to appraise a threat correctly is fundamental to hardiness. If you constantly see more threat than there really is, your body will produce extreme 'flight-and-fight' reactions. These lead to high levels of adrenaline and adrenaline-like substances being released in your body, which will cumulatively damage you physically, and lead to exhaustion emotionally. Research has demonstrated that hardy individuals react in less extreme ways than less hardy individuals[85] in terms of physical changes in their body, such as blood pressure being pushed up.

This does not mean mental health is all about staying calm, regardless of the circumstances. The ability to respond in an extreme way to an intense situation is also important, and that's why those genes prone to emotionally extreme reactions – neurotic genes – have survived.

To illustrate the benefit of extreme reactions to stressful stimuli I would like to borrow an anecdote told by Professor Isaac Marks, the world's leading authority on anxiety disorders, in his excellent textbook *Fears, Phobias and Rituals*. He recounts a true story of neurotic elephants. In 1914, at Addo Park in South Africa, a hunter was commissioned to exterminate a herd of around 140 elephants. By about a year later, he had shot all but 20. A hunter stalking a herd of elephants will usually pick off only one or two at a time. So it is possible to see that the first elephants to be wiped out would be the confident, cool ones who didn't mind straying from the safety of the herd, while the neurotic ones buried themselves in the centre of the herd, as far away from the dangerous world as possible.

At the slightest crack of a twig, the neurotic elephants would probably bolt, while the more relaxed ones would not bother too much about signs that someone was approaching. As the elephants got picked off one by one, the last few remaining were bound to be the most neurotic ones of all.

The hunter was called off from his mission before he could kill the rest, and the area became a preserve in 1930. Although they have not been shot at since, the fourth generation of this herd remain shy and strangely nocturnal to this day.

The point of the story, for me, is that being neurotic or over-reacting to innocuous stimuli sometimes has survival value. In this case, it was the neurotic genes which got passed on to future generations, while the stable genes did not.

The key point from a mental health point of view is that each individual's ability to react in an extreme way can be useful in a particular predicament. However, of even more benefit is the capacity to appraise the situation accurately so that the correct response can be given. The mentally unhealthy, or the less hardy, tend to mistake relatively innocuous events as terribly serious ones and so over-react, leading to extreme emotional and physical reactions which in the long run produce mental illness.

If you wish to be mentally healthy, you must judge your reactions carefully to make sure you are not over-reacting. This is easy to say in theory and much more difficult in practice. How do you know whether you are over-reacting? One pointer is to look at the past: do you feel you have tended to over-react when you review the way you responded to past stressful events? Did you tend to think things would turn out much worse than they eventually did? Another useful pointer is to compare your own reaction to other people's given the same stressful situation: is your reaction more exaggerated than theirs?

Paradoxically, psychologists now believe there is some link between being mildly neurotic and being hardy.[86] Perhaps this is because being mildly neurotic means you take early steps to protect yourself from really major future negative events. Mild neurotics are likely to be slightly more careful when it comes to keeping a job, passing exams, locking up the house when leaving for the evening, and so will probably protect themselves from many negative events which the less cautious leave themselves open to. Note that being slightly neurotic meant you lived longer if you were a hunted elephant.

A good example of this principle is one call I took on a live TV phone-in from a distressed 17-year-old. Her parents were holidaying abroad and had left her to look after their house, but only after they secured her promise not to hold any parties. Well, you can almost guess the rest: she not only held a large party, but friends of friends were invited, with the upshot that her parents' house was completely trashed. The carpets and walls were stained, furniture scratched and so on. She rang me in some distress as her parents were due back in a week's time.

I suspect that if she had been even mildly neurotic she would never have risked the party in the first place, but because she was more laid-back about negative consequences, she went ahead and took the risk, leading to more distress in the long term. While the mildly neurotic might err too much on the side of caution (in terms of the statistical probability of predicting the future) they avoid more stress in the long term.

Another way of considering how to appraise a bad event might be to see this as the ability to assess reality correctly. A hallmark of mental illness, particularly serious disturbance of mind, is a view of reality which begins to depart radically from that held by the rest of the population. For example, characteristic symptoms of serious mental illness include hallucinations (seeing or hearing things which no one else sees or hears) and delusions (believing things about the world which no one else believes).

That is why psychologists and psychiatrists have laid great store by the ability to perceive reality as it 'really' is. Some have even gone so far as to suggest that this accounts for 50 per cent of the basis of a healthy personality,[87] and an emphasis on the accurate perception of reality preoccupies the writings of most eminent psychologists and psychiatrists, from Allport and Erikson to Menninger and Fromm. In one of the few books to review positive mental health, called *Current Concepts of Positive Mental Health*, published in 1958, the distinguished psychologist Marie Jahoda states, 'The perception of reality is called mentally healthy when what the individual sees, corresponds to what is actually there'.[88]

Given that everyone's perception of reality is rarely unanimous, what reality 'really is' is clearly difficult to agree on; if it wasn't, all human disputes would end immediately! Critics of psychiatrists have tried to suggest that these doctors admit anyone to hospital who simply does not agree with them or share their particular view of reality. I do not believe the crucial issue in mental health is seeing reality clearly, given that there is no objective reality, only varying ways in which people perceive the world. The central issue in mental health, I believe, is a concern for others' views of reality, particularly when they begin to depart from yours.

Sometimes, of course, inspirational leaders and thinkers will find themselves isolated in this way. Churchill, for example, was for a long while one of the few voices against appeasement before the start of World War II. Finding everyone disagrees with you has a respectable intellectual history and you will find yourself, with Newton, Darwin and Galileo, in distinguished company indeed. Where intellectual heavyweights differ from the mentally ill is that, although both are frequently out on a limb in terms of their perception of reality, geniuses at least appreciate that their views depart from the accepted. They are concerned by that fact, and they seek to understand why, rather than expecting everyone else to take their point of view without any explanation.

I never get into disputes with my patients over reality; I simply ask them to nominate just one other person who shares their view of actuality before I will agree that there is no problem with their way of viewing the world. What is interesting is that not only do they usually have difficulty finding that one person, but, more importantly, they also seem unconcerned by that fact! This illustrates another key feature of mental illness: a preoccupation with internal states and issues above the external world. If you are wrapped up with yourself and your own view of reality, it gets very difficult to give others' views much weight.

The key feature that the seriously mentally ill share is not so much, therefore, that their view of reality differs radically from the rest of the population (which it does), but that they do not seem in the least concerned by this – indeed they usually do not even see the need to account for why they experience what they experience or believe what they believe, despite the fact that it is being made clear to them they are out on a limb. My experience of the seriously mentally ill is that they are flummoxed or dumbfounded that anyone could not understand or share their view of the world and cannot comprehend why any other view is even possible.

So, for example, the anorexic who is convinced everyone believes she is overweight is not particularly concerned about checking her presupposition with anyone. Indeed, if anyone was to disagree with her openly about her weight, she would immediately assume they were lying so as not to hurt her feelings. The overwhelming tendency is to try to get your understanding of reality to fit your internal states, not the other way around.

In the case of the anorexic, if your internal state is one of conviction that you are overweight, you interpret whatever happens to you to fit in with that theory. The more mentally healthy approach, in contrast, is to stay open-minded enough to be interested in letting what you actually see of the world shape your internal state.

This unconcern for other people's views of reality clearly reaches an extreme in those who are deluded or are hallucinating. But it is also possible to detect elements of this problem in most people not yet suffering from severe mental illness. Although it may not yet represent a major issue, within it lie the seeds of future serious problems.

Yet psychologists have found that distorted perceptions of reality are indeed the norm.[89] Most of us appear conveniently to ignore any evidence which goes against our views and concentrate on the evidence in favour of our perceptions. Truly dispassionate scientists or genuine seekers-after-truth do the precise opposite; they concentrate on any evidence which runs against their point of view as opposed to the data which supports it. The ability to do this is a key component of mental health and I discussed it in further detail in the previous chapter, 'So, You Think You Are Sane?'.

The mentally healthy are therefore constantly checking that their view of reality is indeed appropriate and not prone to bias. Several methods of corroboration exist: one might be to verify with others you know well their perception of the situation. Another is to investigate the views of those who have been in similar situations before. Perhaps the most rigorous approach is to check with experts on those situations. Furthermore, you can collect instances of where your appraisal of reality was definably incorrect in the past and bear them in mind as pointers to where and how your evaluation tends to be inaccurate.

It is most important not to feel you always need to conform to other people's viewpoints, but if you do find yourself out on a limb when it comes to your view of reality, at least make sure you know why your perception is different from everyone else's.

So, concern for how other people appraise reality, including stressful or negative events, and an ability to alter your appraisal, taking into account how others see the world, is another feature of mental health. If your perception differs from that of others you should at least be interested in why. You may still decide you are right and others are wrong.

A good illustration of this occurred recently when I visited New York for the BBC while making and presenting a series on hostage negotiation for Radio 4. For the programme I interviewed a bank manager who, along with several colleagues, had been held hostage for many hours before being released physically unharmed. The hostage-taker had several guns, and also claimed to be carrying a bomb, so the situation was very stressful indeed. The bank manager informed us that all the others who had been held up in the bank had not coped very well; some had lost all their hair and many had developed serious psychological problems. Interestingly, the manager himself seemed to have emerged completely unscathed psychiatrically.

Thinking about what was so different about him compared to the others, he illustrated several of the features of positive mental health and hardiness we discussed in this chapter. First, of all the people we interviewed in New York, he was the only one to show us any hospitality by giving us a small meal before our interview – an illustration of his relationship-building skills. Although the incident had become one of national celebrity, he had rarely talked about it since, only doing so on police training courses for the benefit of hostage-negotiation training. While he was able to talk about it if needed, he just tended not to. In other words he did not dwell on his previous stress.

But, perhaps of most significance was when we talked about what had happened to the original hostage-taker. This man had attracted some sympathy when it turned out he was not so much a criminal, but more someone suffering from psychological problems. Nevertheless the bank manager said that he still had no sympathy for this man because of all the suffering he had caused the manager's colleagues. The manager went as far as saying he thought the perpetrator should have been much more severely punished, perhaps even deserving the electric chair. Realising that this may have sounded vindictive, he immediately followed up by saying that he realised it might make him appear a horrible person but he still believed it, because he had lived through it, unlike most others.

Here is a good example of someone being aware that his views might be different from others', but being sensitive to this contrast. He is not going to change his viewpoint, but is concerned as to why the difference exists.

Getting back to the theory behind the hardy personality, I've already said that the less hardy fail accurately to appraise how bad a stressful event is and so usually over-react, or sometimes, under-react. Social support and how it influences our appraisal seems vital to this.

This was clearly demonstrated in a study of rescue workers carried out in 1989. These workers faced coping with death on a large scale. They were involved in removing bodies from the wreckage in one of North America's worst peacetime disasters, when a charter airline carrying 248 soldiers home from peacekeeping duties in the Sinai desert crashed killing all on board.[90] The study found that the extent to which social support was helpful in promoting mental health depended crucially on the workers' hardiness.[91]

The fact of having social support alone was not an indication of good mental health. It was only if the workers scored high on scales measuring hardiness that they did well in the long run, even with lots of social support. If they scored low on hardiness, despite having much social support, they did not cope robustly. It seems such support may have been of the wrong kind: pampering, encouraging avoidance coping ('Maybe you should take the day off') and real or imagined illness ('You are not looking well, maybe you should take the day off').[92] So, it appears that unless you are hardy, social support could have the unfortunate effect of hindering coping.

The researchers interpreted the power of hardiness in warding off psychological problems amongst rescue workers as being due to commitment, control and challenge. Helpers who regarded their assistance activities as highly meaningful were also more committed. As mentioned earlier, if you are more committed to having to do a stressful job you are likely to suffer less for doing it.

Additionally, the hardy are perhaps better-equipped to make sense of ambiguously defined roles, drawing upon a personal sense of control to formulate their own definitions and decisions. In the chaos of the rescue, with no external directives, believing you are in control, despite the uniqueness of the situation, might be particularly helpful.

Finally, seeing coping with disaster as a challenge rather than a burden is likely to have aided coping.

Despite this, one gets a sense that those who appear to cope best in the face of such extreme adversity may be the ones whose extraordinary coping abilities reveal a similarly remarkable way of looking at the world. In other words in some respects they have a view of the world which differs from most others.

Just to show how complicated positive mental health is, I am now going to seem to contradict much of what I have just said! So far, I have emphasised the importance of appraising reality accurately, and I have also suggested that even an ever-so-slightly neurotic view of the world might help to anticipate future negative events, hence avoiding them. I am now going to confuse you by suggesting that an inaccurate and overwhelmingly positive view of one aspect of reality might contribute to a hardy personality!

Resolving this apparent contradiction requires splitting reality into two parts: the external world and your self. Everything I have said up until now applies to your environment, where as close to an accurate perception of reality as possible is important, or at least an understanding of where your perception differs significantly from others, and being able to justify this difference in your own mind.

However, when it comes to your perception of yourself, a different set of principles applies. Indeed, so error-prone or biased is the view of self which seems most associated with positive mental health, that it has even been termed an illusion. These illusions are unrealistically positive self-evaluations, and exaggerated perceptions of control, and unrealistic optimism.[93]

The first illusion, that we tend to see ourselves as better people than we really are, is widespread and has been repeatedly demonstrated in experiments. It has been found that the majority of mentally healthy people believe themselves to be better than average in a variety of ways, like, for example, their driving ability. Given that it is simply not possible for a large majority to be better than average psychologists have labelled this tendency an 'unrealistically positive view of self'.

However, people suffering from symptoms of mental illness such as depression or low self-esteem have been found to be more accurate and realistic in their views of themselves. Their self-appraisals seem to coincide more closely with appraisals by objective observers.[94] For example, they may think of themselves as fat and indeed be overweight!

So, for instance, their view of their own abilities and skills were more realistic than those who were not depressed.

The most seriously mentally ill, such as those suffering from psychotic depression, tend to have more negative perceptions of themselves than is probably supported by objective evidence, as they suffer from delusions that they are evil, or feel excessive guilt over minor misdemeanours. But, to become seriously mentally ill you have to pass through minor mental illness first. So the question, 'Who are those who tend to view themselves most accurately, and what are they like?' becomes important.

Since researchers find that the people who see themselves most accurately, as attested by outside observers, are less psychologically well in terms of mental health than those who have unrealistically positive self-regard,[95] the notion that accurate perception of reality is a cornerstone of mental health is not true where self-perception is concerned. Here, the mentally healthier strategy is to be kind to yourself, rather than purely objective. But this shouldn't mean you should go overboard and have delusions of grandeur!

The way this is achieved is by tending to recall past successes and forget failures, to assume what you are good at is important and your incompetencies are inconsequential; to attribute any success to yourself and to your ability, but failure to external circumstances. So if you are successful at one job interview and fail another, the best way to maintain your mental health appears to be to assume your achievement in the first was down to your skills and attainment while your defeat in the second was due to the poor interviewing ability of the appointments panel.

Another possible mechanism goes beyond mere kindness. If you assume you did not get a job because the interview panel was in inadequate, rather than because you over-estimated your talents, it is easy to see how this protects you from getting down, because you always assume negative events are not telling you something bad about yourself. Again, a balance must be struck since, if you are completely blind to your own contribution to your failure, you will make the same mistake again and again. The positive mental health attitude appears to be to err a little on the side of over-estimating how good you are.

A second major illusion is a sense of personal control. It seems that many people believe they have control in situations where they have none; the whole gambling industry is based on this common human error. Yet, people who are most accurate and realistic in their assessment of their ability to control the environment seem to be less mentally healthy and more depressed than those who inaccurately over-estimate their sense of control.[96]

Perhaps this is because if you tend to believe you have more control than you really do, you will keep trying positively to affect your environment and eventually benefit from your own efforts[97] or at least from the cheering and distracting effect of trying.

INTENTIONALLY

. . . ,

There is, however, an important caveat. If you wildly over-estimate your ability to control your situation, you will persist long after there is any point. This is simply a waste of energy and will, in the end, lead to low spirits. So the best balance again seems to be to err on the side of slightly over-estimating rather than under-estimating your level of control.

For example, suppose you see that, realistically, your chances of getting a job in a high-unemployment area are pretty grim. You feel that employment is beyond your control and give up looking for a job more quickly than if you more unrealistically assume that landing a job has more to do with your efforts than the economic climate. Even if you do not find a job, your over-optimistic sense of control will help maintain your spirits; you will be actively seeking work and will, perhaps, be more likely find a job than those who give up.[98]

Another possible benefit of over-estimating control is that whenever good things happen to you by chance, you are likely to attribute this to your own efforts or talent, which will bolster your self-esteem.

Perhaps most amazing and important of all is that those who tend to over-estimate how much control they have may not even see where they are failing, because they do not label these experiences as failures.[99] This probably contributes to their tenacity when trying to overcome obstacles.

All depressed people, and certainly many of the mentally ill, entertain strong feelings of hopelessness about the future. These are often unrealistically pessimistic. However, of all groups of people, the mildly depressed tend to entertain the most balanced assessment of their likely future circumstances, whereas the non-mentally ill tend to entertain strictly unrealistic positive views of their future. For example, they estimate the likelihood of positive life events like gaining a good job or having gifted children as higher for them than for everyone else, and they also believe the chances of bad things happening to them in the future are less than for everyone else.

So, the mentally healthy hold unrealistically positive views of the future in general, and also as it pertains to them personally. This illusion of optimism about the future is clearly relevant to maintaining mental health. It seems that the more upbeat you are, the more it helps protect your mental health.

The idea that illusions, albeit positive, are protective of mental health, runs counter to the previous emphasis by psychologists and psychiatrists on mental health being founded on precisely accurate perceptions of reality. These illusions have been demonstrated by experiments to be at odds with reality, but are still firmly held by individuals, and are more predictive of positive mental health than the more realistic assessments of self, control and future held by the less mentally healthy.

If you see mental ill-health as being brought about by an accumulation of morale-sapping events, it is easy to see that those who have higher stores of this 'good stuff' (positive illusions) – even too much to be consistent with reality – have more reserves they can afford to lose before they hit ill-health. Such optimism could be seen as forming a 'self-esteem credit note'.

HOW GOOD IS YOUR MORALE?

The news is often dominated by reports of low morale among employees in various organisations, or among those who live in violent parts of the world. It is also possible to measure morale in individuals as well as groups; those with low morale cope poorly with stress and are prone to depression. Morale is a basic sense of satisfaction with yourself, a feeling that there is a place in the world for you and an acceptance of what cannot be changed in your life. By contrast, happiness is a transitory mood which is less likely to predict future mental good health than morale. High morale tends to indicate courage, discipline, confidence and enthusiasm.

As people live longer, morale is of growing importance as it appears that once we pass middle age it is difficult for morale to increase. Instead, it remains stable or suffers a slow decline, so part of the key to a happy old age would seem to be high morale during youth!

MORALE SCALE

Each statement is followed by two possible responses: agree or disagree. Read each statement carefully and decide which response best describes how you feel. Then put a tick over the corresponding response. Please respond to every statement. If you are not completely sure which response is more accurate, put the response which you feel is most appropriate. Do not read the scoring explanation before filling out the questionnaire. Do not spend too long on each statement. It is important that you answer each question as honestly as possible.

		AGREE	DISAGREE
1	These are not the best years of my life	A	B
2	I have been luckier than most people	B	A
3	I would change my past if I could	A	B
4	I feel things are going my way	B	A
5	I am less interested than before in what I do	A	B
6	In my life the future is very exciting	B	A
7	Life has been getting harder recently	A	B
8	I do some things better than anyone else	B	A
9	I do not cope well at times of stress	A	B
10	I play an important part at work and home	B	A

Add up your score from summing the numbers of As and Bs in each box you have ticked. Your score and the interpretation given below should be treated with caution – this short test is by no means definitive, but may offer a guide to where you stand compared to others around you.

SCORE

8 or more Bs. You are scoring high on morale. Either you have had some good news recently which is making you feel good temporarily, or you are normally optimistic about the future. You are likely to feel quite high at times but these may be accompanied by some crushing lows when things don't go as you would like. Your enthusiasm means you are fun to be with, but you probably get irritated with those whose morale is not as high as yours and who don't appear to help themselves as much as you do.

Between 5 and 7 Bs. Your morale is quite good but something is lowering it at times, it may be not getting your way at work or in your relationships. One of your problems is that, while you can strive effectively to better yourself and your situation, you have difficulty accepting that you may not be able to change everything. Try to resign yourself to the fact that some things in life will not turn out the way you would like.

Between 3 and 5 Bs. While your morale is good, it could be enhanced substantially if you had higher self-esteem and this means you are often pessimistic about yourself and your abilities. Your occasional low zest for life can turn into a self-fulfilling prophecy, leading you not to take risks and therefore not to explore your full potential. Don't forget that although those with higher morale may appear to have more fun than you, all they had at the beginning was simply more belief in themselves.

Between 0 and 2 Bs. You are scoring low in morale and this could be for two main reasons. You are either currently embroiled in a web of relationships which constantly undermine your confidence by providing negative feedback, or something unpleasant has happened recently which is undermining your confidence. Your morale will climb as you spend more time with those who believe in you. Focus on those parts of your life where you are good at what you do, and gradually expand your horizons into new projects – you will eventually succeed in these, too, given good enough morale.

Another benefit of morale is that it helps build relationships – you can also see how gathering social support is easier for those who are over-optimistic. Such people are more fun to be with and are likely to attract a wider and deeper social circle than those whose grasp on reality is more sobering. The overly optimistic are a great panacea to our worries and are also unlikely to burden us with theirs. Their upbeat, sanguine and enthusiastic attitude regardless of their own problems make them great companions, particularly at times of stress. So a positive cycle is set up: unrealistic positive illusions protect you directly from mental illness and also bolster your social support, which again contributes to your optimism.[100]

But how do mentally healthy people maintain positive illusions about themselves, if they have had negative or contradictory feedback, such as after getting the sack for incompetence or being dumped by their intimate partners? Several mechanisms may be at work, but it seems that the mentally healthy have a kind of mental filter which allows them to process incoming information in a way that helps maintain their positive illusions about self.

One such filter works by assuming that negative incidents are the fault of others; you got the sack because your boss was unreasonable, you were dumped because your partner had emotional problems. Another filter seems to be in the memory, and helps the mentally healthy retrieve positive memories about the self and forget negative ones.

But surely, many mental health professionals will protest, precise contact with reality in terms of your view of yourself is crucial to mental health, otherwise positive illusions about self could lead you to ignore dangers? However, the evidence is that the crucial combination for mental health seems to be an accurate, perhaps even slightly negative, view of the world, along with a positive view of self. Then, when the world presents dangers, like an obviously irritated boss, you do not ignore this or misperceive it as friendliness, but your view of self allows you to believe it's not your fault and that you can cope with the situation.

These filters may seem dangerous because they appear to represent a loss of contact with reality, but this need not necessarily be so. It may simply be that the mentally healthy can appreciate the same reality as the others, but tend not to put an interpretation on it which produces negative assessments of self. For example, doing badly at their job may be interpreted by the mentally healthy more as performing in an environment they do not like, or not being comfortable with their boss or fellow employees, so leading them to leave the job. This produces the same outcome – leaving the job – as the more accurate perception of reality that you are doing your job badly but with less of a negative impact on self-esteem.[101]

But how necessary is it to have these positive illusions of self in order to maintain high self-esteem? A recent study of over 100 mentally healthy university students found that only 10 per cent had high self-esteem in the absence of such illusions of self while a mere 11 per cent had low self-esteem in the presence of such illusions of self.[102] In other words, in almost 80 per cent of cases whether you had high or low self-esteem seemed to follow directly from whether you had positive illusions about yourself or not. This suggests that, although such illusions are not the only way to maintain good self-esteem, they are an important factor.

To sum up, at the core of hardiness and resilience lie two processes. First, the ability to appraise stressful events as not excessively threatening, which depends on your perception of the world. Secondly, a view of self which leads you to believe that you will cope with an event successfully. A positive illusion about self may help prevent you adopting regressive coping strategies, such as denial and withdrawal.

Perhaps hardiness is not so much a separate psychological characteristic, but more a reflection of your intellectual sophistication, how much education you have had and your income level. If all those are in your favour, no wonder you can be more hardy than those less fortunate! This has been termed the St Matthew Effect, 'For whoever hath, to him shall be given, and he that hath not, from him shall be taken away even that he hath.'[103, 104] However, research, for example into troops who survived the Persian Gulf War, found that hardiness was separate from education level, income and intellectual sophistication, and was also a much more powerful predictor of recovery from psychological problems like Post-Traumatic Stress Disorder than these other personal resources.[105]

Other research into the trauma of prisoners of war and concentration camp victims of wars such as the last World War, Korea and Vietnam, has persistently found a subset of victims free of significant psychological problems.[106] The inevitable conclusion must be that stress alone does not evoke psychopathology; it is more that illness is a product of a particular interaction between the vulnerable individual and the negative event.

Resilience does not mean you will be unchanged by an experience of severe trauma. Instead it seems when you have faced life-threatening events like cancer, no one ever really gets back to normal. However, the resilient usually conclude that their lives have benefited from the adverse experience. Women suffering from breast cancer, for example, said the illness had helped them re-order their priorities so they devoted more attention to important relationships and less to everyday tasks like housework.[107]

But the women who adjusted better to the stress of having breast cancer were definitely those who held illusions, albeit positive ones. For example, only two of the 72 women in the study believed they were doing worse than the average woman coping with breast cancer; in other words, the vast majority believed they were doing better than average – a logical impossibility. Many also believed they had personal control over the cancer (despite there being no objective evidence for this) and even went as far as declaring they had beaten it, although their medical chart records clearly indicated to the psychologist researchers that they were going to die soon.[108]

So these illusions appear associated with better coping under stress. But how is it that ignoring reality and simply always assuming that the best will happen does not just produce a laissez-faire attitude, and so reduce people's motivation to help themselves? Why does it not lead to the avoidant coping associated with poorer mental health?

One reason this doesn't happen is that better adjustment under stress seems linked more with active optimism (things will turn out OK because my own efforts and abilities will ensure this) rather than naive optimism (things will turn out OK).[109] Because this healthier active optimism is based on the conviction that you *can* do something about bad things in your environment, those with positive illusions about self are more likely than those without to attend to threatening information and make efforts to do something about it.[110] So, positive illusions do not lull their bearers into wishful inaction, rather they seem to stimulate active efforts to do what can be done to improve a terrible predicament. If anything, they seem linked to a more careful assessment of a bad situation with a view to targeting the aspect which is amenable to some personal control.[111]

But what happens when those with positive illusions eventually come face to face with harsh reality? In one study of HIV positive men, it seems that those who over-optimistically did not believe it likely they would develop AIDS, still did not end up with poorer psychological adjustment compared with those who had been more realistic.[112]

Instead, the persistent optimist appears able to adjust to setbacks, and to keep shifting their viewpoint to place the best possible light on even a worsening reality. A good example of this comes from research into those suffering from renal failure who decide to opt for a kidney transplant. When the transplant fails, how do they avoid not blaming themselves for their decision to opt for this procedure? It seems they sustain the tricky balancing act of not abrogating responsibility for having made the decision, yet not being able to view the failure in positive terms (some would die as a result and most would be worse off) by indicating to others they felt they had made the only decision they could given their circumstances. By not blaming the doctors they retained their own sense of personal control, and this is associated with better adjustment to trauma.

It seems that those expert at maintaining positive illusions carefully select the aspect of the situation most likely to produce an assured self-perception. For example, they compare their situation to a possible worse one ('I was so lucky it could have been much worse'), or they see a benefit in the midst of a predicament ('I would never have taken up reading again if I hadn't got this injury').

But if the ability to maintain positive illusions seems extraordinary and beyond most people's ability, remember that the evidence is that the vast majority of the population already 'suffer from' positive illusions of themselves, their personal control and the future. The resilient merely manage to maintain these illusions in the face of negative life-events. This is an important skill as what makes a life-event negative in the first place is its tendency to challenge positive assessments of self, the perception of personal control and optimism about the future. It seems that the resilient may achieve this partly because their positive illusions may just be mildly more positive than the norm. Any really unrealistic assessments are likely to be contradicted by those they know well, so bringing them down to earth.

Some psychologists have argued that the concept of hardiness is not that useful because it is basically the same thing as saying you feel good; – if you suffer from 'well-being' you will have commitment, challenge and control. However, research is beginning to demonstrate[113] that hardiness and resilience are different to mere well-being, and although the first can cause the second, many people experience the second without having the first. This suggests that their sensation of well-being will be just that – a sensation – and the lack of supporting hardiness means they will be more likely to suffer in the future 'the slings and arrows of outrageous fortune'.

One of the fundamental lessons to emerge from the concept of resilience is that resilient people's whole approach to life, not just to problems, is different. Just as if you enjoy your job you never have to do a day's work again; if you are hardy, then stress is not really a strain in the same sense that it is for the less resilient. Another way of looking at resilience has been termed a sense of coherence.[114] Simply put, this is a view that life makes sense (it is comprehensible), life will be bearable (it is manageable) and life is not a burden but a challenge (it is even helpful).

When we roamed the African savannah millions of years ago, it was bodily strength which determined who survived to fight another day. But today, the challenges at which many will fall and only a few survive come in the form of psychologically demanding predicaments. Having to stand up for yourself, dealing with rejection, coping with the breakdown of relationships, surviving radical changes at work, and having to perform unpleasant duties like telling someone off for poor performance or even sacking them, are just a few of the new ways our survival abilities are put to the test. So while you may work out in the gym every day, being physically fit won't guarantee you victory in your most crucial battles. Instead it is psychological resilience which now separates the truly tough from the weaklings.

Pressure? Don't talk to me about pressure!

Imagine the nerves of playing in a top sporting event, like a crucial rugby league game, watched by thousands of spectators and millions on TV where any mistake you might make could have devastating consequences for your club – and on top of that strain, then imagine the whole stadium starts to hurl abuse at you personally. Are you mentally tough enough to handle that kind of pressure? This is what used to happen regularly to Martin Offiah MBE, the most famous rugby league player the British game has ever produced; he is currently sixth in the all-time try scoring list with 438 tries, and he has played for Great Britain 34 times. Worse still, when he first moved north to play for famous clubs like Widnes and Wigan, a black face was rare on the pitch and off, and in the early days he often faced a barrage of racist abuse.

Elite athletes admit that at the highest levels of sport, it is mental toughness which separates the winners from the losers, not in fact physical fitness or skill, in which the differences between the best players are usually marginal. It took resilience of the highest order to produce Martin's extraordinary performances when under pressure.

The key to resilience appears to be what is going through his mind during a high-pressure situation. Martin seems to be using a technique called in psychology 'self-instructional training'[115], although he seems to have evolved it without ever having to be helped by a resilience expert. Again and again when I have interviewed those who distinguish themselves by their mental toughness in challenging times, whether they are even aware of it or not, self-instructional training keeps cropping up. It now seems to me that if you are not using self-instructional training, then you will be for ever mentally kicked around the rugby pitch of life.

Basically self-instructional training is about learning to control precisely what goes through your mind during high pressure. This is very important because it combats what appears to be a natural human tendency in such situations to flood your mind with uncontrolled thoughts which make failure more likely.

When a crowd used to start hurling abuse at Martin, what was his mental reaction? 'It used to inspire me – in fact I often played better then, I always thought the best way to exact revenge is to score, rather than standing around shouting back. You hurt your detractors most by playing well.'

Certainly 'standing around shouting back' appears to be what the mentally weak do, and probably would only have led to him getting more upset. A key point here is that Martin is staying 'task-focused' rather than allowing self-doubt or worry to distract him. He mentally uses the potential distraction of the crowd to keep him centred on his goal – to score. Again this is a common theme with winning performers:

an ability not to get discouraged when something bad happens but to use mentally whatever has just happened to raise their game.

Tennis professionals learn not to brood on bad mistakes, as this will interefere with performance during the next point. Their psyche coaches use the phrase 'clear your computer' as a way of teaching that you must erase from your memory bank a poor point, so that it will not affect the next one.

When his side is losing Martin says to himself, 'What are you going to do now? Are you going to let them score again or are you going to respond?' In fact Martin believes often top sportsmen produce their best performances if they commit an error early in the game, because they then say to themselves, 'I've got to make up for that mistake.' This helps them get more involved in the rest of the contest. Indeed Martin thinks a good strategy all the best players use is to try and 'do something' early in a match, because even if they make an error, it helps inspire more intense involvement afterwards. This explains the sporting cliché 'get an early touch' and, says Martin, accounts for why footballers pass the ball back to the goalie at the start of the match, so he can get involved right from the beginning.

But where does the confidence that you can make up for a mistake come from? Most of us, if we miss an open goal in life, shrivel up and hope the wind will blow us away. The Chicago Bulls Basketball superstar Michael Jordan always manages to stay calm and not choke in crucial high-pressure moments because instead of dwelling on his errors and deficiencies he mentally calls up images of past successes. 'OK, I've been here before,' he reminds himself. But what do you do if you can't ever recall performing well under pressure? In fact the mental memory image can be a past success of any kind, no matter how small. The real power of this technique is that it stops you clouding your mind with negative thoughts, which are damaging because they distract from your goal.

It's odd how easy it is for us to recall instantly past failures or embarrassments (they often enter our minds totally unprompted) and how difficult it is to remember our past triumphs and successes. It may be because this appears big-headed in everyday conversation and therefore we get into the habit of self-deprecation. But in the privacy of your own mind, keeping a ready list of past personal triumphs is absolutely vital to help you mentally rise to the occasion when under pressure.

Can you list ten previous successes in your life? The longer you take, the less likely you are to have the mental toughness to perform when pressure beckons. Certainly longer than one minute is a bad sign. Start mentally carrying this list around with you, and keep reminding yourself of things you have done well recently, no matter how apparently trivial.

This doesn't mean your life has to brim with success for mental toughness to develop. In fact, it is being exposed to problems and stresses, and gaining strength from them, that builds resilience. This process is termed by psychologists 'steeling', and partly derives from the saying 'a flame melts the wax, but tempers the steel'.

Those who lack mental toughness fear failure desperately, because flopping has such global implications for their self-esteem. One important element of steeling is the ability when you have not performed well not to take that particular performance as a global comment on your entire self-worth. Failing an exam may mean your revision skills need improving, but it does not imply you are an entirely worthless person.

Fear of failure leads the less resilient to avoid situations where failure is a possibility, but this means they are bypassing the chance of success. In other words, they avoid risk. This explains why those low in resilience have difficulty learning from their mistakes. All learning by necessity involves an openness to error. Whenever you start to learn any new skill you are going to make mistakes (if you don't then you don't need to learn). The mentally weak find it too painful to examine those times they failed, and so never learn the valuable lessons contained in their mistakes. But only by being open to understanding what went wrong in pressure situations in the past, can you improve for the next time.

Professor Daniel Dennett, Director of the Center for Cognitive Studies at Tufts University in the USA, delineates the very different attitude the mentally tough have to their mistakes: 'You must learn not to deny to yourself that you have made them or try to forget them. That is not easy. The natural human reaction to a mistake is embarrassment and anger, and you have to work hard to overcome these emotional reactions. Try to acquire the weird practice of savouring your mistakes, delighting in uncovering the strange quirks that led you astray. Then, once you have sucked out all the goodness to be gained from having made them, you can cheerfully forget them, and go on to the next big opportunity.'[116]

The ability to find something positive from your darkest hour is a defining characteristic of the resilient. Researchers at Washington University in St Louis, USA, recently found that survivors of three traumatic events – a tornado, a plane crash, and a mass shooting – were least likely to be psychologically damaged by these incidents if they had the habit of finding something good that came out of the experience soon after it happened[117] – for example, if they realised facing death had made them appreciate their family more or changed their priorities in life in a positive way.

The researchers also found that inhabitants of small towns tended to do better than those who lived in big cities, suggesting the social support found in closer-knit communities could be an important factor in mental toughness. In other words being mentally tough does not mean being aloof or detached from others; rather it includes being able to confide in friends and discuss personal stress. Repressing one's feelings of vulnerability by never sharing them with confidantes is a way of avoiding the stress of confronting your potential weaknesses. As we have seen already from their attitude to mistakes, the mentally tough face up to stress, they do not avoid it.

But how do you become resilient enough to deal with a stressful situation which you have never had to face before? The kind of hurdle where there has been no chance to practise and gain experience?

Chief Superintendent Michael Humberston was the chief police negotiator during the 1982 Air Tanzanian hijacking. The armed gunmen had already shot and injured one member of the air crew by the time the plane landed at Stansted airport and they claimed to have explosives all over the aeroplane and that they were prepared to blow it up. Humberston had to negotiate, despite the fact that he and the British police had never before had to wrestle with an aeroplane hijacking.

At one point while Humberston was negotiating, the gunmen's patience snapped and they drove the plane dangerously around Stansted airport, threatening to blow up the aircraft immediately if their demands were not met. Humberston and his fellow police officers and negotiators hit the deck of air traffic tower where they were negotiating from, as they expected the plane to detonate, but Humberston kept talking to the gunmen on the radio, trying to calm them down. The gunmen shouted that Humberston's attempts were too late and the police should arrange for a hundred coffins to be brought to the airport as they would be needed for the passengers.

The nerve and grit required by police officers like Humberston to call the bluff of people threatening to blow a plane up appears incredible, but while Humberston admits to being frightened, he was also outwardly calm in the dramatic circumstances. His mental toughness appears to come from a relative lack of self-doubt. While the rest of us would be cursing ourselves for having said the wrong thing, which might cause the plane to be blown up, this kind of negative thought never seems to enter the heads of professional negotiatiors, like Humberston – instead he had confidence his training and skills would resolve the situation.

In the end Humberston and his colleagues successfully negotiated the gunmen and their hostages out without the loss of a single life. It was his mental toughness which the British Government depended on when they declared that the Air Tanzanian flight was not leaving British soil, and the police negotiators would have to resolve the situation. Several previous countries had simply let the aircraft refuel and take off, as they were too frightened of dealing with this stressful situation.

Martin Offiah, Michael Jordan and Mike Humberston have in common their faith in their meticulous preparation for difficult situations. They take their training seriously and once they enter the arena of performance, they are calm because they know they have done all they possibly can to prepare themselves for the rigours to come.

A large part of the self-doubt which plagues the unresilient as they attempt to rise to a high-pressure occasion is their anticipation of failure, based on worry that their skills are not adequate to the task, or they have omitted some important training. But if you have trained rigorously and exhaustively, self-doubt is clearly not warranted – after all, what more can you do? So training properly is an important part of mental toughness because it aids self-confidence and staying task-focused during high-pressure situations.

Indeed your nerves before a high-pressure situation may be telling you something valuable about your preparation – that it's been inadequate! This is why the hoary old chestnut about relaxation before facing a high-tension scenario often doesn't work: you can't relax because the reason why you are tense is a perfectly good one – your fear of failure is a realistic appraisal of your inadequacy for the task ahead. It is only if you have done all you can to prepare for a demanding experience that relaxation becomes possible.

The main reason the mentally weak do not prepare properly for the calls which will be made on them by pressure is that they tend not to anticipate properly what these demands will be. Intelligent anticipation requires the ability to draw analogies with past situations, which may be in many ways different from the current one. There is a sense in which the ability to anticipate is the main advantage our complex nervous system gives us over lower life forms, and so it follows that those of us who have better anticipation skills are more evolved along the resilience dimension.

For example, if you have to perform the unpleasant task of sacking someone and you have never done so before, intelligent anticipation involves recalling particular difficulties you may have had giving bad news in the past, seeing what you can do to improve those skills, imagining how the employee is likely to react based on how he or she responded to difficulties in the past, and planning how you should behave depending on what they do.

Anticipation is absolutely crucial to mental toughness because the most destabilising events are those we did not anticipate.[118]

Psychologists have demonstrated a link between the tendency to anticipate the future and so plan for it, and resilience. Studying how those previously identified as very resilient coped, compared to those measured as less resilient, after Hurricane Iniki battered Hawaii in 1993, they found, oddly, that scoring high on resilience before the storm seemed to predict you would experience less property damage by the hurricane, and that you would feel less stress for the same level of destruction. This was in fact because the resilient had prepared more, boarding up windows and investing in good insurance[119]. So good anticipation and practical steps taken in the light of this foresight seem to be part of the benefits of resilience.

The first step towards becoming mentally tough is to start believing in yourself rather than others, as holding the solutions to your problems.

DO YOU BELIEVE IN YOURSELF?

While it is obvious that many entrepreneurs must have great belief in themselves in order to take the risks they do, when going it alone, it is less apparent that people who believe in themselves are often actually easier to work and live with. In fact, research has found a link between self-belief and helping others. Self-belief is part of what psychologists call a feeling of autonomy – a sense of personal power or self-empowerment. Self-empowered people accept their thoughts and feelings as being worthy; hence they are willing to honestly express their ideas to others even if these may be ridiculed. Because they believe in themselves they often stick to their point of view in the face of opposition, and are able to comfort themselves even when the going gets tough and it appears no one else believes in them. As they have true confidence in themselves, they do not manifest the arrogance of the basically insecure, and hence they are willing to learn from others.

Since people who believe in themselves believe others will eventually perceive their deep personal qualities, they don't try to manipulate others by deceit. Instead they rely on open, honest, communication. Previously, organisations were suspicious of people who had great self-belief as they wondered whether they would be really good team players or try to go it alone too often. But now it is being realised that people who believe in themselves often believe in others; their optimism about others generates a positive working environment; this means they are nicer to live with as well.

SELF-BELIEF SCALE

Each statement is followed by two possible responses: agree or disagree. Read each statement carefully and decide which response best describes how you feel. Then put a tick over the corresponding response. Please respond to every statement. If you are not completely sure which response is more accurate, put the response which you feel is most appropriate. Do not read the scoring explanation before filling out the questionnaire. Do not spend too long on each statement. It is important that you answer each question as honestly as possible.

		AGREE	DISAGREE
1	It's usually better to hide what you are thinking from others	A	B
2	I tend to act on what I believe in, rather than to wait for guidance	B	A
3	Many discussions get too intense for me	A	B
4	I tell my parents what I think even if they don't like it	B	A
5	My successes often come from good luck or a lot of help	A	B
6	I trust my own judgement even when others disagree	B	A
7	If others advise against it I would never take a risk	A	B
8	I think I am equal to anyone	B	A
9	Thinking deeply about myself is often painful	A	B
10	I have made a valuable contribution to others' lives	B	A

SCORE

Add up your score from summing the numbers of As and Bs in each box you have ticked.

8 or more Bs. You are scoring very high indeed on self-belief and this means you are close to being what psychologists call fully 'self-actualised' – a state of almost complete self-acceptance and lack of negativity towards yourself, combined with acceptance of others, leading you to spontaneous and open relationships with others. The only problem on the horizon is that your independence may need to be tempered a little when you are with others who may find your spontaneity a little intimidating. You may also find it puzzling how unreflective others are about themselves, compared to your own ability to examine your motivations in great detail (which you have because your belief in yourself makes it unlikely you would be threatened by any grisly discovery about yourself).

Between 5 and 7 Bs. You are scoring above average for self-belief, which explains why you have the courage to do what you think is right in the face of opposition, even if it is very difficult to do. You believe in action rather than too much waiting around to get everyone's agreement – hence your impatience with others who have less belief in themselves than you do. You may not realise actually how confident you are in yourself, and hence you may need to consider taking the plunge more seriously, and striking out on your own in your work or relationships – something you have been considering recently.

Between 3 and 5 Bs. You are scoring around average to just below average for self-belief, which explains why you often worry about being too helpful to your competitors. Your lack of self-belief compared to higher scorers means you don't have the confidence in yourself that you will succeed because of your talents and commitment. You are too self-critical and hence you ignore your achievements or tend to forget them quickly, and dwell instead on your failures, which is draining your belief in yourself. Your relative lack of self-belief explains why you often don't think too hard about yourself – you're worried about negative things coming up.

Between 0 and 2 Bs. You are scoring well below average in self-belief, which explains why external rewards are so important to you: if you do not get rewarded by others in some way for your actions or work, you have great difficulty in believing that any of it was at all worthwhile. You need to see that your lack of belief in yourself makes you too dependent on others' opinions. This also makes you less generous to others than higher scorers. Your lack of belief in yourself is reflected in cynicism about others' motivations – you believe others could easily damage you if they put their mind to it.

The careful balance necessary for positive mental health appears to be being overly positive about your self, confident when in the midst of a crisis, but before an emergency, to anticipate possible disaster so planning to cope in advance by preserving resources or taking precautions. This last strategy is called proactive coping and links to the mildly negative view of the world mentioned before, which helps anticipate future disaster.[120]

While the preservation of resources and extra vigilance underlie proactive coping, how do you cope when, despite your best efforts, a crisis hits? That is the subject of the next chapter.

TELEPHONE STRAINING THOUGHTS
9

CRISIS, WHAT CRISIS?

Essential Coping Skills

" Stealthy Thoughts, Steal thy thoughts "

'Living is a constant process of deciding what we are going to do.'
José Ortega Y Gasset

In my monthly column for *Cosmopolitan*, I interviewed a young female reader who had been happily married for several years – or so she thought... One night while she was reading quietly in bed, her husband, who had spent rather a long time pottering around in the bathroom, burst in. He was wearing women's clothes from head to toe – tights, a short skirt, a blouse, stilettos and garishly pasted-on make-up. At his wife's shocked expression, he ran out of the room shouting that it had just been a joke. A few days later she plucked up the courage to ask him if this really was the case. He replied haltingly that he had in fact been wearing women's clothes in secret since he'd been a young child.

So, what do you do when your partner of many years suddenly reveals that they are actually very different to the person you thought you knew? This is a good example of a crisis and, surely, no matter how mentally healthy you are, it is difficult to survive this kind of trauma without being destabilised in some fundamental way?

'Prevention is better than cure' has been the theme of this book so far. If you take measures now you will certainly benefit in the future, but what do you do right away, if crisis strikes? This chapter focuses on effective ways of coping in the short term. I look at precisely what you should do the minute you realise a disaster has struck.

Effective crisis coping skills are not just helpful in the short term, but are essential to preserve and enhance your long-term mental health. They lessen the impact of negative events in your life, such as a divorce or break-up, losing your job, being robbed or the death of a friend. Research has shown that being exposed to such a crisis can make you between six and fourteen times more likely to develop a major depressive illness

HUG YOUR THOUGHTEDDY'S

within a month of the event, depending on how vulnerable you are to depression genetically.[1] Good coping can reduce these probabilities.

Moreover, given that a large percentage of psychiatric patients are not simply people in crisis but more those who have coped badly with it – for example, with acts of self-harm like self-mutilation, suicide, heavy drinking, drug abuse, or violence to others – behaviours which then need treatment themselves, it is clear that learning effective coping skills is vital.

Half of the art of successful coping is not to make things worse than they already are.[2] Coping skills don't just help people to deal with negative events, they also help them make the most of life. Confidence in your coping skills lessens your feelings of personal vulnerability, so that you are less anxious about whatever the future may hold. It also widens your view of the kind of challenges you are prepared to undertake. If you are confident about your coping skills, you are more likely to leave unsuitable relationships, take the initiative in new situations and have a more adventurous attitude to life.

In this chapter I look at features which distinguish good copers from bad, and the many short-term devices which sometimes pass as coping but which are ultimately self-destructive – from ignoring or refusing to take any responsibility for your problems to drowning your sorrows with drink or drugs. I put forward proven ways of responding to a 'routine crisis', as well as advice on how to deal with the most serious crises of all, such as the death of a partner, close relation or friend.

Although much of the advice mentioned may seem almost too simple, I believe it is important to set out clearly that there are only ever one or two sensible ways to react to a crisis, and see what they are. Otherwise the tendency is to flail around, frantically searching for options that are of no real help.

Crises, great or small, are part of everyday life. For example, within a few minutes of arriving at my office every morning I am greeted by my indomitable secretary at the Maudsley with the latest crises involving my patients. No doubt the same applies to you whether at home or at work so I can guarantee that reading this chapter won't be time wasted!

A typical morning at my clinic might bring the following cases:

THEY'RE EVERYWHERE

- A couple will fight and the husband will have been thrown out. He turns up panic-stricken at our clinic.
- A wife will have discoverd her 'recovered' alcoholic husband's secret store of vodka in the garage and rings us for advice on what to do.
- A schizophrenic son will not have returned home the previous night.

Typically, community psychiatry in the British NHS revolves more around crisis management than the slow intensive long-term individual help which forms the media's stereotype of psychiatry. This suggests that there is a greater need for improvement of personal crisis management skills than for long-term psychotherapy.

To make the most of the advice given in this book, you will need to practise the stratagems until they become second nature – your reflex response to a crisis. To do this, however, you will need to *want* to cope, which is not as straightforward as it sounds. We have all come across people who seem not to want personally to deal with their problems. Often, these are the people who appear resilient in all other respects, leading to the supposition that, perhaps, they gain something from not coping? They are often the people who constantly seek the help of friends, colleagues, or professionals.

Perhaps not coping wins that person much-needed attention. For example, friends or relatives rally round when they hear someone saying they can't cope. If this proves the best – or only – way for someone to attract attention, it will be tempting to use it again and again. Constantly courting misfortune is also an effective way to ensure that no one else turns to you for help or support, or asks you for favours. A friend of mine commented on the coincidence that every time she experienced something bad – her husband losing his job or undergoing an operation – her mother-in-law developed pneumonia, or discovered some major house repair, which rendered her unavailable when needed most. Far from being a coincidence, this is a typical avoidance strategy.

There is a sense in which not coping can be a form of coping. People who don't cope claim that involving friends or relatives can be a good thing, so why should they learn self-reliance? What they do not realise is that their undue and one-sided dependence on others will corrode their relationships in the long run. Allowing people to cope for you may work as long as the lack of personal resources which others compensate for are never needed – and found wanting. But these people usually restrict their lives so that they face few challenges, as well as putting pressure on those on whom they depend not to leave them out of their life-plans, a form of emotional blackmail, perhaps.

The spouses or relatives of many patients I see have their lives grossly restricted by constantly having to weigh up whether a house move, change of job – or even where they go on holiday – might adversely affect the fragile stability of their dependants. Conversely, a sign of good mental health in yourself is that having a relationship with you does not entail your partner, friends or relatives having to restrict their activities.

I had an agoraphobic patient whose valiant friends would comply with his complicated demands to be first picked up and then only sit in certain seats at the end of rows near the exits of cinemas in case he had a panic and needed to flee instantly. He would eat only in restaurants where he was allowed to sit near the door. If you can't cope with a visit to the cinema, who is going to be able to rely on you for help with their lives?

All relationships require some reciprocity. I believe one of the most attractive aspects of potential partners or friends is their ability to act as a help and confidant when you are in crisis. Those who offer good advice, are good listeners and remain calm under pressure tend to form the relationships you end up valuing most. In contrast, people who always seem to need your help, but on whom you cannot rely when you are in a crisis, are much less appealing as friends.

One of the ways to assess your own mental health is to check whether others turn to you when in crisis. People have an intuitive feel for who is most resilient and to whom they can turn when they feel vulnerable. Even amongst psychiatrists, there are colleagues with whom a chat usually makes us feel better, while others can make us worse. It is also flattering to be asked for advice and support, yet this will be a rare experience for those with poor mental health. My own theory is that being able to handle crisis yourself, and provide good advice to others, is a marker of positive mental health. So those who aren't able to offer support are more likely to suffer poor mental health themselves in the future.

Think now about people you know who appear to cope well, and how they differ from those who seem to cope badly. For example, good copers don't whinge about the terrible things that have happened to them, or the ghastly people they have encountered. They don't use giveaway phrases like the one made famous by Victor Meldrew in the sitcom TV series *One Foot in the Grave*. His catchphrase when confronted with crisis was 'I don't believe it!' It is because he didn't believe it that he couldn't cope. Copers do not focus on problems, they concentrate on solutions. A good, long-term, positive mental health strategy is to surround yourself with good copers and try to keep away from poor copers.

So, not coping may bring short-term advantages, but is always counterproductive in the long run. There are several other so-called coping strategies which do not deal constructively with the source of the problem, and may even exacerbate the original difficulty. For example, transmitting your negative feelings on to someone else is one. Hitting your spouse may be a way of coping with a bad day at the office. However, this only produces more problems for you in the long run when your spouse leaves you or your children end up hating you, making you feel worse. The essence of this strategy is to involve others in dealing with your bad mood because you cannot cope with it yourself. You feel awful, so you then behave terribly towards someone close to you, who is left with no choice but to try and appease you as a way of ensuring that you do not carry on behaving unpleasantly towards them.

A typical short-term negative coping reasoning might be as follows: 'I feel terrible so no one else has the right to feel OK because my feelings are the most important thing in the universe. Only when they feel as bad as I do will I know that my feelings have been given the priority they deserve by those I know.' You feel miserable and, as a consequence, you make everyone around you feel as bad.

Another common example of poor coping is 'wishful thinking' of the type 'If only…' or 'I wish it were not true that…' or 'If only I could turn the clock back.'[3] This is a kind of fantasy or day-dream approach to coping which makes you feel better in the short run, while you muse that the crisis does not exist. But you always feel worse again when reminded of the reality of your situation.

In contrast, real coping occurs only when your response truly does lessen the impact of negative events. Real coping not only reduces the short-term pain of crisis and reduces the likelihood of serious or long-term psychiatric problems, it also ensures you do not destroy relationships by drawing on them too much, and, as mentioned, marks you out as someone others will turn to when they need help.

However, before learning about effective coping, you need to be honest with yourself and rule out the possibility that you have something to gain, at least in the short term, from not coping effectively. In my clinical practice I see many couples, and even families, where the very basis of the relationship is founded upon poor coping – what binds many of them together is their dependency on each other because they are unable to cope by themselves. But when one party learns more effective coping skills and grows more confident in their own ability to manage by themselves, the relationship no longer has an underpinning and falls apart!

It may be that you feel you cope effectively at the moment anyway and wonder why you should need to improve your coping skills. Ask yourself whether your coping is reliant on others, or whether there are circumstances in which you cope less well? In my clinical experience, much mental illness is precipitated by a change in circumstance, which coping skills that are honed to adapt to the previous circumstances cannot now accommodate. For example, the sudden arrival of a new manager with a new way of working has precipitated psychological problems in patients of mine who had coped perfectly well with the same job for several decades.

A good test of future ability to cope, even if you think your current coping repertoire needs no embellishment, is to try imagining future possible situations which might pose coping difficulties. It could be losing a close relationship, or having a disturbed neighbour move in next door. The more complicated or unlikely the scenario you have to construct before you begin to become concerned about your coping adequacy, the more mentally healthy you are. Indeed, this simple exercise of anticipating possible future disaster and planning how you might cope beforehand is a vital part of good long-term coping.

We all evolve lifestyles which reflect our current coping repertoire, which mean that we can cope as long as our situations do not alter. However, we live in an increasingly changing world, where jobs are no longer 'for life' and where we no longer expect to live within a few miles of the place we were born. The key to survival is having coping skills which can adapt to whatever comes our way, whether a change of relationship, job or location.

If this is beginning to sound rather daunting, the fascinating thing about coping skills is that psychologists and psychiatrists now teach more or less the same form of coping techniques to their clients, whatever the predicament the patient faces. The importance of the advice in this chapter is not only that this reflects the widespread consensus amongst psychologists and psychiatrists that these are the most positive responses to crisis currently available, but also that they apply under all circumstances.

Knowing that there are only really one or two simple ways that preserve our mental health is invaluable at a time when it is difficult to think clearly or calmly. But if with each crisis you get different advice from whoever is around at the time, you may be failing to see the basic principles that lie behind all forms of effective coping.

Coping is a skill which can be continually refined and improved. Merely thinking about a crisis in terms of coping, rather than focusing on the worst aspect of the problem for you, is a first step towards effective coping. One intriguing question is why there is so much poor coping? If all our lives we have been wrestling with crises, surely we should have learned which coping strategies are effective and which are not?

There are several possible explanations for our ignorance. First, as pain tends to lessen over time, you may assume that your method of coping has been responsible for this, whereas it may even have slowed down recovery.

Secondly, as coping is not something which is formally taught (and I believe firmly that it ought to be on the school curriculum, as the only way to make a real impact on preventive mental health care), you tend simply to muddle through. You probably adopt the coping strategies of those around you, particularly your parents. According to this theory, your coping tactics are limited by the examples you see around you, which are usually not extensive.

As I've said, another reason for poor coping is that people think about it only when in the grip of crisis, when they are not at their most rational. Ideally, of course, you should plan how to greet crisis before it happens so you have some strategies to call on when the storm hits. But, of course, given the choice between relaxing in the garden with a glass of wine and a book, or reviewing our latest coping strategies, how many of us would choose the latter? Instead we resort to the most common method of dealing with future problems: hoping that they won't happen.

Finally, for many of us, the top priority is simply to get rid of our pain as quickly as possible. So we do whatever achieves this most effectively, regardless of the long-term costs. The alcoholic probably began by turning to drink as an anaesthetic when in crisis, and found that alcohol was his most effective coping strategy for rapid pain relief. In the short term this works but over a longer period it will destroy your mental health.

These less-than-useful strategies are probably adopted simply because of a lack of awareness of any other ways to cope. Having a variety of ways to respond, or several positive avenues to bring to mind, will prevent you from having to resort to destructive methods.

So, how can you find out about better ways of coping? You might think it would be common to gain advice from a professional. But, in fact, of those experiencing significant psychological distress, only around a quarter seek such help, whether from a psychologist, psychiatrist or other professional helping body.[4] This figure may be a little misleading, in that priests and family doctors are said to see more people suffering from emotional distress than psychologists and psychiatrists.[5]

It is a shame that effective help is not sought, as a recent study shows that people whose depression had been detected by a family doctor before really serious problems arose had a better record of recovery than those whose depression had not been diagnosed earlier.[6] One form of poor coping is not even recognising when your own coping repertoire is no longer adequate and needs enhancement.

Sometimes, they aren't even aware that they're not coping. While feeling bad is one of the major signs of stress, the two other main signs psychologists look for are changes in daily routine (like eating and sleeping in a different pattern, or not socialising as much) and preoccupation with the body or its symptoms (skin problems, sore muscles, nausea). These two main symptoms can occur without the sufferer fully realising they are suffering from strain. In fact the commonest sign of distress reported by the general public[7] is not, as you might expect, feeling bad (which is the fourth commonest sign), but (in descending order) irritability, lack of concentration, a sore neck and sore body muscles. As each person shows stress in different ways the key thing to look for is a change in some aspect of yourself, even if it is as subtle as leaving your home more messy than it usually is. It is vital to recognise signs of stress as otherwise, untreated, even subtle clues could be harbingers of future serious psychological disturbance. The earlier you deal with such problems the better, hence the importance of recognising as early as possible your own personal signs of tension.

But it's not even as straightforward as deciding you need to seek professional advice. Waiting times are long and the complexity of the referral process means that by the time you get to see a mental health professional, the acute stage of your crisis might long be over.

While, of course, some people will manage to implement some form of coping without the aid of professional psychological expertise, exactly how well they are coping is open to conjecture. Because of the absence of training in coping at school, and the paucity of information available to the public, much distress is being inadequately coped with. So, here is the advice these experts would give you, in plenty of time for your next crisis, I hope.

The acid test for coping skills is how you react when you are up against devastating and unexpected crisis. If you feel you have done badly in exams, you have time to prepare yourself for the result and think of ways to cope. But being suddenly made redundant is a different matter.

Good coping starts with assuming that bad things, which commonly happen to others, are also likely to befall you and to start considering how to react when they do.

In these instances it is useful to memorise a 'mantra', or coping statement, to repeat to yourself when the storm hits. A good example is something like the one shown below, based on my clinical experience and a synthesis of what all good coping advice usually boils down to. You may want to adapt its sentiments (which are in three parts) to fit your own perspective and approach to life.

STEP 1:
'Because of this awful thing which has happened to me I am bound to feel terrible, indeed I should absolutely expect to feel bad, and it would be even more surprising if I did not. So the pain I feel now, given my

circumstances, is completely understandable. However, let me just ask myself exactly how bad I should feel about this? I should not try to deny or repress my feelings, but I should also not exaggerate them by getting how awful this is out of proportion.'

STEP 2:
'Even if this is the worst possible thing that could happen to me, the best way of dealing with it is to see what constructive thing I can do right now to improve this situation as much as possible.'

STEP 3:
'If there really is nothing productive I can do right now, there is absolutely no point in worsening my morale by dwelling on a problem I can do nothing about. After I have checked I really can do nothing more immediately, I will occupy myself by doing something distracting which will improve my mood and hence my morale, for if I am feeling a little better I will be in a stronger position to help myself. In this crisis I need all the help I can get, so I shall try to help myself and not make things worse for myself.'[8]

The first step involves accepting upset as an inevitable part of crisis. Often people seek help to alleviate distress which is completely understandable in the circumstances. Do not make your problem worse by adding more pressure on yourself – coping with your emotions, as well as coping with your problem. Allowing yourself to be unnerved is something many people have difficulty doing and they seek therapy merely to obtain permission to be upset.

A good example of an acceptable emotion at a time of crisis is crying. Many people, perhaps especially men, try to avoid crying at all costs, no matter how upset they may feel. However, the evidence suggests that crying usually makes us feel a little better. Crying reduces tension and has even been theorised by psychologists to be part of a biological response to stress that we are genetically programmed for to help to restore our equilibrium.[9] Indeed, one of the features of very serious clinical depressions is a relative lack of crying compared to milder forms of low mood. This suggests that being able to cry may even help prevent a low mood worsening.[10] Exactly why crying achieves this is still unknown, although there is some evidence[11] that tears shed from grief have a different chemical make-up than tears shed for other reasons. One theory is that crying relieves distress because it allows the body to shed some kind of toxin which builds up as a result of distress.

A more psychological explanation is that crying signals to others our upset and need for help or comfort. However, as even crying in private seems to help relieve pain, it may be that the physical acknowledgement of our misery to ourselves, by releasing our emotions, takes away some of our tension. Although crying often signals a complete collapse of our ability to fight our distress, trying to stop ourselves feeling bad is not a good form of coping in the initial stage of upset – as long as we then move on to the next stage.

This next stage is to check that your emotional reaction is based on a sound rational evaluation of your situation. Ask yourself what is the worst possible thing that could happen to you, and then, what the evidence is for your appraisal? Do you need more information before you can evaluate how bad things are? If so, try to postpone your evaluation until you obtain the relevant information. For example, if you lose your job your first instinct might be to panic and think 'we'll have to sell the house'. A rational appraisal would involve going through your finances, seeing if you could agree a mortgage holiday and so on. This will lead to a clearer assessment of what the more immediate problems will be and whether you really will have to sell the house soon.

A good way of coping is to seek the guidance of people who have been in the same situation themselves. Trying to introduce some rational assessment of your situation is crucial in limiting your stress when in crisis. Think back to any bad times you experienced in the past and ask whether you tended to imagine things would be worse than they eventually turned out.

When I give this advice at the Maudsley, my patients often ask why you need to interfere so consciously, even artificially, with your natural reaction to a crisis? Why has nature not evolved for us over millions of years of natural selection a more helpful instinctive response to stress?

I suspect this is because, in the animal kingdom, surviving a crisis hinges on immediate response. If a gazelle, aware of a lion bearing down on it, stopped to go through my suggested coping mantra, it would be dead meat before it got to Step 2. So, from the world of the jungle, nature has built into our bodies and brains a tendency to respond first and think later. This works fine in the world our biology evolved to cope with, but is no longer appropriate in modern civilisation, when crisis is not generally of the kind which requires quick physical action to save our lives.

Instead, we have consciously to fight our instincts, which tell us to react emotionally to crisis by assuming that the very worst has happened and we should act immediately. From a survival standpoint, it makes sense for nature to build into a gazelle the tendency to assume the worst. Such a gazelle is more likely to survive than one who tends to underestimate the gravity of a lion bounding towards it – or even one who stops to check it has appraised the situation correctly, as it has learnt from its cognitive therapist! But such instincts are not helpful to humans today. In my clinical experience, the instinct to act in the midst of a crisis usually compounds the original problem.

One of the common themes of poor coping is a tendency to avoid dealing directly with the crisis. One of the reasons this happens is that the less confident you feel about coping with stressful events, the more stressful you will find them. A recent study showed that a 'negative life event of the same severity' was twice as likely to cause major depression in people who felt they would be unable to cope with the resulting stress as in those who were more confident about coping.[12, 13] This probably goes a long way towards explaining why small stresses seem to destabilise some people, while others are unaffected by quite large stresses.

So, developing good coping skills will help you with much more than simply coping with an immediate crisis. If you learn the coping mantra by heart and get used to using it, your confidence will increase, and this in itself will improve your reaction to stress.

The coping mantra works because it focuses on what you can do to help yourself and implicitly encourages a positive and optimistic approach to solving your problems. The opposite of this is to 'wallow in self-pity', or 'self-focus', as psychologists put it. Research into how the clinically depressed respond to crisis shows that they tend to self-focus at times of stress. This means that instead of attending to the environment around them, they are inward-looking. They think a lot about themselves and how bad they are feeling. Whereas a person with good coping skills will use phrases like 'It's happened – now what's the best response from me?' someone who 'self-focuses' uses ones like 'How unfair it is that this has happened – why is the world so terrible? Look how bad this has made me feel.'

Interestingly, when psychologists set up experiments in which the depressed experienced success, the depressed switched to being outward-looking, becoming more aware of their environment than of themselves.[14, 15] Yet any emotion is intensified by self-focusing. If you do not self-focus when feeling positive, but only when feeling negative like the people in the experiments, you are continually enhancing your experience of negative states, and diminishing your appreciation of positive ones.[16, 17]

This is taken to extremes by the really severely depressed I treat as in-patients on my ward. These people become so inward-dwelling that it becomes very difficult indeed even to engage them in conversation. They stare into the middle distance with their eyes lowered, obsessing only on their thoughts. Nothing going on around them holds any interest for them. Eventually they lose interest even in eating or any other aspect of life. This is just one of the ways in which a serious depressive illness can be life-threatening.

Another positive benefit of the coping statement is that it helps make you less self-focusing at times of distress by shifting your attention from your misery on to the outside world. It does this by getting you to focus on solving your problem, or then distracting yourself from an unpleasant situation.

In the longer term, however, these research findings suggest that it is important to be self-focused when enjoying success and positive states. After all, if you think a lot about yourself only when feeling bad or in crisis, you will tend to learn to think of yourself in negative terms.

When we think about ourselves, one of the things we do automatically is check if we are where we want to be in terms of our values, expectations and standards.[18] Clearly, if you self-focus when upset or in crisis you are likely to be disappointed. However, when good things happen and you self-focus, you should find that you have exceeded your expectations, values and standards, which may help you feel even better.

Since the psychologically unhealthy tend to self-focus when down and not when up, the message is clear for preservation of positive mental health – self-focus more when up and less when down.

One example of controlling self-focus is embodied in the advice given to social phobics over social encounters. Social phobics avoid socialising, partly because they harbour deep fears about the possible negative consequences of meeting others. They are nervous to begin with and then, as they are also inward-focused, they imagine everyone else is aware of how terrified they feel. This makes them even more nervous, as their deepest fear is that others will notice how anxious they are, and evaluate them negatively because of their nervousness. In fact, at a party, no one is really observing anyone that closely – they are too busy trying to have a good time. Instead of being so self-focused during a social encounter, social phobics would be better off distracting themselves from their anxiety by focusing more on their environment. They should soak up the atmosphere, notice what others are up to and become involved in that, rather than staying wrapped up in themselves. Helping to serve drinks, or looking to see if there is anyone else to talk to who is also standing alone are just two ways of doing this. This will distract you from your inner state and in so doing defuse your tension.

This is an example of positive coping, whilst the more common negative, or poor coping, is to react to crisis by assuming that you will not cope because you are weak or a terrible person. One of the reasons good coping is so difficult is that a crisis usually comes as a double whammy. A terrible thing happens to you, which requires you to mobilise all your resources. However, as you are not feeling well, you are less likely to be able to do so. In addition, you may also blame yourself for the bad thing that has happened. The bad event seems further evidence that you are no good and this also makes it unlikely that you will feel strong enough to cope. Precisely when you need it most, you have least confidence in yourself and your abilities. This can lead to a negative self-image, because you feel you are weak or a terrible person for not coping.[19]

The coping mantra helps you to refocus on what is needed to cope now, so you are not distracted by undermining thoughts. The coping mantra is also general enough so that, as long as you are making some steps in the direction suggested, you have started positive coping.

This advice on self-focusing when in a positive mood may at first glance seem distasteful or self-centred. However, if it preserves your self-esteem and so saves your mental health, you can see that it is a helpful thing to do.

Although concluding that you cannot cope represents an immediate saving of energy and time, in the long term it is linked with a tendency to severe psychiatric illness. This is because those who start by assuming they cannot cope with a major crisis gradually get into the habit of not coping with more and more things. Eventually they become unable to cope with even the smallest aspect of their lives. Coping is like a muscle, the more you use it, the stronger it becomes, whereas if you determine not to use it, it atrophies.

The coping mantra probably works for many reasons, but one powerful effect is in stopping the knee-jerk 'I can't cope' reaction and allowing you to move on to the next step. 'Even if this is the most horrendous thing that could happen to me, the best way of dealing with it is to see what I can do constructively right now to improve the situation as much as possible.'

Easier said than done! One way to help you think constructively is to discuss the situation with someone supportive as soon as you can. By supportive I mean someone who will implement or help you to implement the ideas behind the coping mantra, not someone who will encourage you to over-react and only get you more agitated. In the thick of a crisis it is natural to try to contact your closest friend. However, it may be better, when not in crisis, calmly to review who is the most appropriate person to contact – for example, who has been of most assistance in the past?

Different friends may have contrasting coping skills, depending on the particular crisis. Having a set of your own personal crisis lines to ring at the drop of a hat will work only if your friends do not feel put upon, so go out of your way to ensure you are in emotional credit with them by helping them out whenever they need it. Then they will – or should – be only too pleased to repay the favour when you ring for assistance.

The first crucial quality of a good confidant is discretion – you must be able to trust them to keep confidential, sensitive or negative information about yourself. This can be particularly difficult, given that a good friend may have conflicting loyalties. The second important quality is the capacity to be non-judgemental, as you will undoubtedly be revealing negative aspects of yourself or your behaviour. You want them to be as objective as possible about your situation and not let their own personal prejudices or experience interfere with their view of your situation. Finally, you also need them to be able to offer new insights into your situation.

An important initial step in coping with crisis is obtaining more information about the situation you find yourself in. Your friends and relatives may generally be helpful but you might also need to seek out those who have gone through something similar, have particular specialist knowledge, or even a self-help group of people who have faced similar difficulties in the past and are now organising to help others. Arming yourself with information aids coping with crisis.[20]

I would argue that discretion, non-judgementalism and insight are essential criteria to look for when selecting those suitable to be close friends, who can help in a crisis. Incidentally, these are also characteristics which, if we develop them ourselves and become known for them, will ensure we are attractive to others as confidants. This, in turn, will help build and deepen our own social network. But such qualities are not as common as you would expect, and perhaps one reason many seek a professional therapist rather than using a friend or relative is that the ideal combination of requirements is difficult to find informally.[21]

Your confidante should not only have these qualities, but should be someone who will be encouraging and boost your self-respect. Just as the most positive effect of psychological treatment is that it enhances clients' self-esteem,[22] the friend or relative you turn to for help should be able to boost this at a time of crisis.

To cope you need to be persistent in trying to cope. However, you can only persist as long as you expect to succeed. Getting the support of someone who will motivate you to keep up your positive coping strategies[23] is therefore crucial. This is not just a sophisticated brainwashing exercise, as research shows that one of the key indicators of success is your expectation to succeed. A breakdown in motivation not only becomes self-fulfilling, but can also lead to severe psychological problems,[24] if it leads to hopelessness and the feeling that things are not going to get better in the future.

What if you don't have friends who can encourage you? Most of the people who ring me on my TV phone-ins do not seem to have been able to consult with very many, if any, significant others in their lives about their problem. But you probably have more friends than you think – give it some thought. A reluctance to trust others can result in no friends at all.

An alternative is to seek professional psychotherapeutic help. If you really feel you are desperate for someone to talk to, this may be an option, but I believe it should be treated as a last resort. In chapter 2, on counselling and therapy, I explained my scepticism regarding this choice and I set out the research evidence which raises questions over the methods and benefits of therapy. That's why the emphasis in this chapter, as throughout the book, is what you can do for yourself without turning to professionals.

However, it is interesting to note that while some studies have found that some clients do benefit from professional therapy, what is often forgotten is that half the 'control' group (a group which receives no formal psychotherapeutic help, but is set up for comparison purposes only) usually experience a substantial degree of positive change.[25] This has been explained by notions of spontaneous remission and the idea that the natural course of most emotional distress is for it to get better anyway. However, another possible explanation is that informal help and social support may explain why those who receive no formal help still improve so much.[26]

Furthermore, of those who receive formal help, the fact that they all seem to improve by roughly the same amount, regardless of the particular treatment they receive, has led many researchers to suggest that these studies are unable to point to any specific benefit from formal treatment, but rather that seeing someone supportive is what is proving useful. Given that we know those who enter formal therapy also seem actively to seek more informal help alongside their pursuit of formal help,[27] this raises the question of whether the research finding that formal therapy helps people has merely been measuring the benefit of all that informal help those people are also getting.

All coping represents an attempt to master the painful consequences of negative events, which threaten your sense of control and mastery of your life.[28] Effective coping helps restore your sense of control over your destiny.

There is much evidence that you do not even need to be in complete control of the situation, but just have to feel you have *some* control. Even if that feeling is erroneous, this mere perception of control is sufficient to reduce stress.[29]

Just how important control is for health in general, not just mental health, is demonstrated by the recent research findings from thousands of British Whitehall civil servants, which found that those who reported feeling low control at work (in the form of low levels of autonomy and decision-making responsibility) were more at risk of future coronary heart disease.[30]

In fact, measures like cholesterol levels do not explain why people of a higher social class are less susceptible to heart disease than those from lower social classes. Instead, the evidence points to feelings of being in control of one's life as being a more important factor.[31]

Why should control, or feeling in control, be so important? Perhaps the most plausible explanation is that a fundamental aspect of human nature is a drive to master the environment. We are motivated to interact successfully with the world and this motivation to be competent is called a feeling of efficacy. This, perhaps, explains why we often end up doing the things we feel we are good at and are reluctant to learn new skills which, to begin with anyway, will produce feelings of low self-efficacy. If mastering our environment is a fundamental drive, thwarting this desire for mastery inevitably leads to poor functioning.[32]

Psychiatrists have termed the link between poor mental health – depression, in particular – and a diminished sense of personal control as 'learned helplessness'.[33] This describes the situation where people act in an inappropriately passive way towards the world and, especially, to negative events. It accounts for why they fail to cope with the demands of a situation that seems fully within their competence. The man who reacts to losing his job by pretending it never happened or the woman who falls to pieces when her husband has left her, are examples of such learned helplessness.

Given the importance of a sense of personal control, a key question is, how can more personal control be nurtured? It seems that the central issue in developing personal control is how we explain to ourselves what happens to us, termed our 'causal interpretation of events'. If, whenever a bad thing happens to us, we automatically assume this is because of our actions – 'it's me' – this is more likely to lead to a long-term diminishment of self-esteem. So the better mental health strategy is to seek causes that lie outside ourselves. For example, take the following reactions to losing your job. If you assume it is because of something you did, you will have more difficulty coping and it will have a longer-term impact on your feelings of employability than if you see the problem as to do with your boss or the company.

Another causal interpretation of events which leads to poor mental health is to assume that a situation is not going to change. If you assume, for example, that you lost your job because of a long-term problem in the economy, this is more likely to foster passivity in the face of unemployment than if you assume your job problems are due to a short-term issue with the company.

Further, a 'global' explanation is worse than a 'specific' one. Taking the view that losing your job means you are hopeless at everything you attempt in life is likely to lead to more helplessness than assuming you simply went through a brief spate of bad luck. Conversely, 'global' explanations are precisely the kind you should go for when good things happen to you! Again, you can see the all-important balancing act on which positive mental health seems to rely: learning reflexively to use the right explanatory strategies for negative and positive life events aids mental health.

These explanations are in crucial in enhancing mental health. They will determine how much you believe you can control your future and this, in turn, leads to a positive sense of self-efficacy, or personal control. People with positive self-efficacy believe they succeed in the end, no matter how often they have failed in the past. This is also linked to a central concept in psychology: the notion of 'locus of control'. Your locus of control is either internal or external: 'internals' believe that what happens to them is down to them; 'externals' believe it's down to the world and they can do little to determine their future.[34]

No matter what precautions you take, though, and however much you try to maintain a sense of control, many negative life events are beyond your control. Accidents and catastrophes still happen, and realising that you are not invulnerable to disaster is one of the first steps to positive coping. This is because of what psychologists call the 'myth of personal invulnerability'. Some people persistently underestimate their susceptibility to life crises and therefore have more difficulty adjusting to them, should they occur.[35] For example, psychologists have demonstrated a persistent tendency for many people to overestimate how long they are going to live, despite being given information about the average lifespan.[36] This seems to be part of an inclination, even when you know about the likelihood of negative events, to assume you are somehow immune from them.[37] If you go through life *not* expecting to deal with the crises which the average person has to contend with, you are more likely to cope poorly when they happen to you.[38]

A positive mental health strategy is to be realistic about the likelihood of suffering and the many unfortunate and unpredictable negative life events which beset the average citizen. Be grateful if you have so far not experienced these – but do not assume they will never happen to you. Once bad things do happen, the accuracy of your assessment of your ability to control or prevent further negative events will determine how well you cope. Obviously you should make every attempt to prevent even those negative events you can control, but it is poor coping to assume you have control in situations where you do not.

For example, one study examined those who believed they could prevent disaster and took steps to do so but who, in the event, did not avert the feared catastrophe. They were shown to cope much worse than those who did not take steps to control the largely uncontrollable.[39] You see this most starkly among the terminally ill, where those who are used to controlling their lives have much more difficulty coping with the prospect of death (the ultimate event beyond their control) than more passive people.[40]

The best strategy is to learn to distinguish between situations in which you have control, and those in which you do not. Exaggerating your ability to control or alter outcomes may just prove you are not adapting to reality. When an outcome is truly uncontrollable or unavoidable, the most sane response may be to give up and accept the situation.[41]

ARE YOU COMPETENT?

One of the enduring mysteries of life is that those who are successful are those who expect to be successful, which is precisely why they continue to strive in the face of failure, until they achieve success; on the other hand, those who fail frequently do so precisely because they expect to fail, and do not persist with tasks until success is achieved. How optimistic you are about your chances of success plays a large part in determining whether or not you actually will succeed. This may have something to do with your previous experience of personal success.

It may be that therapy works simply to alter individual expectations of personal mastery and success. Try this quiz to see how your levels of confidence stand at the moment.

HOW WELL DO YOU COPE?[42]

Each of the following statements is followed by two possible responses: agree or disagree. Read each statement carefully and decide which response best describes how you feel. Then put a tick over the corresponding response. Please respond to every statement. If you are not completely sure which response is more accurate, put the response which you feel is most appropriate. Do not read the scoring explanation before filling out the questionnaire. Do not spend too long on each statement. It is important that you answer each question as honestly as possible.

		AGREE	DISAGREE
1	My friends like me because they are friendly to most people	A	B
2	Once something needs doing I start on it straight away	B	A
3	I prefer to wait to be noticed by those I want to meet	A	B
4	I rarely leave any project unfinished	B	A
5	I often start things before realising they are too difficult	A	B

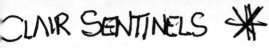

		AGREE	DISAGREE
6	Failure usually just makes me try harder	B	A
7	Things can be divided into those I can do, and those I can't.	A	B
8	I persist with unpleasant tasks until they are finished	B	A
9	I often make plans feeling they are not going to work	A	B
10	I usually can get down to work when I should	B	A

Add up your score from summing the numbers of As and Bs in each box you have ticked. Your score and the interpretation given below should be treated with caution – this short test is by no means definitive, but may offer a guide to where you stand compared to others around you.

SCORE

8 or more Bs. You are scoring very highly indeed for feelings of self-competence and this perhaps explains why gaining mastery over your environment and those around you may seem to be one of the most important aims in your life. The possible problem for you is that your tendency to feel that you control the world around you through sheer hard work and ability is actually slightly unrealistic; life is too unpredictable for anyone to control it all the time. Maybe you need to learn to accept a more whimsical approach to life, which acknowledges that people are the erratic and inconsistent beings which you find so hard to accept, as they contrast sharply with your own dependability.

Between 5 and 7 Bs. You are scoring above average for feelings of self-competence and this means that, for most of the time, you seem to have a great deal of confidence in your own ability to achieve the goals you have set yourself in life. You may also believe that you can solve most of the problems life throws your way. However, your confidence in your own ability is most shaken possibly when dealing with the unexpected, and contemplating possibilities that are outside what you consider to lie within your own view of what you are good at. To enhance further your feelings of confidence, you may need to open your mind to the possibility that you have talents you have yet to uncover.

Between 3 and 5 Bs. You are scoring between average and just below average for feelings of self-competence and this may be explained by the mixed picture of past successes and failures you have experienced during your attempts to change your life. Perhaps the reason for your moderate feeling of self-competence is that you tend to remember the failures more than the successes and these make you very pessimistic about your ability to change your future. This means you stop trying after only a few attempts if you do not feel you are getting anywhere quickly. You might need to learn that persistence is more likely to be rewarded than giving up.

Between 0 and 2 Bs. You are scoring very low on feelings of self-competence and this explains why you may tend to avoid new situations and new relationships. Your fears and anxieties inhibit you from exploring new environments and so prevent you learning about new things that life has to offer and new aspects of yourself, and thus developing the kind of confidence in yourself and your abilities that higher scorers have.

Low feelings of confidence may also arise when extremely negative events include a sense of shock. For example, when someone we are close to dies unexpectedly this is more traumatic than if they die slowly and predictably from a chronic illness. This may seem odd, given that the loss is exactly the same. Yet, there is good evidence that the first kind of loss has a more severe negative impact on our mental health than the second.

Psychologists argue that unpredictable shocks threaten the assumptions on which we base our lives, about the predictability and continuity of the universe which we inhabit. If you really had no idea what was going to happen to you tomorrow or next month, it would be impossible to plan your life. We tend to walk around full of assumptions, usually right, about what will happen next week, based, quite reasonably, on what happened last week. But people who have experienced a disaster such as a train crash or hurricane have their view of what they can anticipate happening to them threatened. Recovering a sense of understanding of the world takes time and energy.

The most traumatic experiences are the ones which threaten our most basic assumptions, such as the belief that we are invulnerable, that the world is on the whole a benevolent place, that events make sense in some way (bad random events do not happen to good people) and that we have a self-worth which is recognised by others.[43]

However, when a boat sinks or a plane goes down or you find you have cancer, these assumptions all get turned on their heads. At first, this can be difficult to accept, hence perhaps the oft-repeated phrase, 'I never thought it would happen to me' or, 'I always thought this stuff happened to others, not people like us'. In fact, after people have suffered an unexpected disaster, such as a car crash, they often go too far in the other direction and are reluctant to get in a car ever again, because they now feel that no vehicle is safe.

Perhaps there is even a biological mechanism wired into our brains, whereby we are genetically programmed to be very cautious indeed about trying something again where a disaster occurred. That is, after all, nature's way of ensuring that an animal that has experienced a close shave does not inadvertently repeat the error.

Clearly, the person who has survived a traumatic traffic accident and refuses to drive ever again or is extremely anxious when next in a car does not see himself as over-cautious. Instead, he believes the correct evaluation of driving on the roads today is that it is extremely dangerous, and perhaps it is everyone else who is wrong when they drive without anxiety.

Everyone has a different view of the reality of how dangerous driving is and it is difficult to say whose view is the correct one, or whether there is, in fact, even such a thing as an exact view of actuality. What we can say is that everyone's view of reality is a sum of their experiences and thoughts and of advice taken from others. But a lot of coping hinges on how we deal with threats to this view. So, as well as the immediate shock of a traumatic event, such as a car crash, there is the added shock of adapting our view to accommodate new information.

In cases of people who are too frightened ever to drive again, the central problem is that they do not appreciate that it is their view of reality which has changed, not the reality of how dangerous driving is in itself.

Thus, a central sign of poor mental health is an inability to adapt to and incorporate new information into your view of reality. For example, the person whose view of the roads changes after a crash to the perspective that it is now too dangerous to drive at all has adapted their understanding of life to the new information, but in a way which means that their new assessment of reality will prove very disabling to them in terms of getting around.

In my experience, underlying people's difficulty in coping with any traumatic event is either a reluctance to give up a previous view of reality, or an inability to integrate the new information into a rational new sense of reality, in other words, to understand what this new information is telling us.

One client who rang my phone-in, for example – a mother who discovered her son had not been at medical school as he had claimed, but instead was unemployed, may have difficulty coping with this shock because she cannot alter her view of her son. If she continues to trust him, a reflection of her view that he is honest, no matter how many lies he tells her, she is clearly having difficulty adjusting her view of reality to her son's real personality. She will then get upset every time her son violates her trust and may even ask to see someone like me to help her cope with her upset, or appeal to me to change her son. The more realistic view would be that her son is not the trustworthy person she imagined and that until he regains her trust she simply cannot trust him as much as she would dearly love to.

Another example of people who have problems in adapting their view of reality are the pushy parents who want their child to succeed academically. I see a lot of these! Often the child continually fails to perform at the level they would like, no matter what help she is given or how much she is pushed. A sensible reformulation might be that some children are not as academically gifted as their parents would like. But all too often these parents cannot accept this and instead blame the teachers or their child for not trying hard enough. This failure to accept what the new information is telling you and to adjust your sense of reality leads to poor coping.

Instead of resisting bad news, a more positive approach is to welcome it as valuable information about reality and as a sign that your understanding of the world may have to change. If you can do this, coping with the event becomes much easier.

In contrast to the pushy parents, the mentally healthy are always open to changing their view of reality. So, well-adjusted parents would greet their child's poor exam performance as sad news, but important news none the less. It may be their child really has not been working hard enough; or that he is just never going to make it; or that the teachers are not putting in enough effort. Whatever the reason, those mentally healthy parents will consider the evidence to see which aspect of their understanding needs to change and use this to guide them as to how to respond.

If parents treat a disappointing event as 'news', they will be able to turn it to a constructive use, rather than simply getting terribly upset with their child or their situation. This does not mean they should not still strive for better results for their child, but it does mean that they may have to start questioning some of their original assumptions. Poor coping would be just to get terribly upset because of the clear mismatch between the world as it really is and how they had hoped it might be. The only viable response if the world is not as you would like it is either to (a) change the world or (b) change what you like. Much psychiatric treatment is actually about helping people to come to terms with unpalatable truths they would rather ignore.

Once you can take a step back and start evaluating a crisis more rationally and calmly, you can usually see that behind it is a 'message' about a long-standing personal difficulty, and what is needed to resolve it. The exam failure of the child of pushy parents may suddenly precipitate a crisis in their relationship. The hidden message, however, is that the connection between child and parent had probably been problematic for some time, if affection by the parents for the child was contingent on exam success. Maybe the parents' own frustration with their lives was being displaced too much on to their children.

So, to summarise, 'bad news' may be bad – and those who cope badly focus on the 'bad' – but it is also 'news'; in other words, information about what is really going on out there, to which you must adapt. Better to incorporate this information into your understanding of the world and adapt to it than to ignore the news and simply feel bad. If you react to the 'news' rather than just the 'bad' part, your view of reality will be more accurate, and you will be better placed to avoid more bad news hitting you so hard in the future. If your child gets poor exam results next time, if you have assimilated the earlier news this will not be such a shock. Crisis occurs when our theories about ourselves in relation to the outside world go fundamentally wrong. The problem is compounded by our own reluctance to change our theories.[44]

A central element to shock is denial, which is traditionally considered a bad thing. Denial occurs because the news is not something you want to hear. You do not want to believe that your child is not as bright as you had hoped, or that your son may be a compulsive liar. The tendency to bend reality to fit wishful thinking, rather than to face unpalatable truths about yourself and the world around you, in itself is a form of denial.

Research has shown that once the average person develops a view of the world, or a personal theory about what is going on, they are loath to change it to accommodate new evidence, no matter how strong.[45] This is partly because most people seek evidence which supports their point of view, and ignore or belittle evidence that runs against it.

That is why the mother who discovers her son has been lying to her will focus on evidence from his early childhood that he was trustworthy and ignore indications of more recent deceit.

Denial is a good example of how complicated the problem of maintaining mental health can be. Most psychiatrists would consider denial a refusal to accept external reality as it really is and, as such, consider it an unsuccessful strategy. The phrase 'she's in denial' is used, for example, to describe an abandoned partner who refuses to accept, or denies, that he or she has really been left, and who still vainly believes the beloved will return. Victims of serious crime may manifest denial by throwing themselves into work or some other activity and appear busy all the time.[46] Newcomers at the Nazi concentration camps appeared to deny, or did not behave in a way which showed acceptance of how dangerous their situation was.[47] Anna Freud, Sigmund's daughter, saw denial as a defence mechanism, or the way the mind tries to reduce the stress of an external threat.[48] Her father defined denial as a disavowal of external reality[49] and went as far as linking this strategy with very serious mental illness, basically of a psychotic nature.

Inability to accept reality is certainly a symptom of poor mental health, because if your understanding of actuality is out of step with everyone else's, or is just basically wrong, apart from not coping you are destined to waste your resources on projects which will never be of any use, such as trying to get someone back into your life who is clearly never intending to return. Also, the refusal to accept external reality as others do would suggest that strong internal emotional issues (obsessive love, for example) are taking precedence over external reality.[50]

None the less, denial is now seen to have some advantages. For example, 'positive self-illusions' – thinking more positively about yourself than may strictly be warranted – are now seen as a feature of positive mental health. Some would say this is a form of denial, in that you deny the evidence that you should *not* think as well of yourself as you do. And the process of denial, where you initially refuse to accept the reality of what has happened, is one mechanism which may be helpful when you find your view of yourself and your world has been undermined by some shocking event.

For example, disagreeing with the doctors who say you have a fatal disease may buy you time to get used to a particularly bad piece of news. By denial you may be letting the reality sink in gradually rather than all at once, giving you time to mobilise your resources and get help from others before accepting the reality of the bad news.[51]

Another example suggests that denial may even save lives. One study found that 40 per cent of heart attack patients claimed not to experience any feeling of fear or apprehension during their hospital stay. This group was classified as denyers, in contrast to those who admitted to feeling some fear. But the group who did admit to feeling frightened suffered more deaths while in hospital than the denying group.[52] One explanation for this is that denial minimises discomfort, and as high anxiety can affect the heartbeat, denial may protect the heart from stress and so may even aid recovery from heart attacks.[53]

Denial is an 'avoidance strategy', in that it diverts attention away from the problem. This is in contrast to 'attention strategies' which concentrate on the source of stress or on your feelings about it. Perhaps one advantage of not trying to focus on the crisis at the beginning is that, as is the nature of emergencies, an awful lot is happening very quickly and the brain may suffer from information overload. This may be why it switches to denial.

The evidence suggests that in the early stages of stress, the initial shock is best dealt with by avoidance or denial, but that once this has bought the individual time to mobilise resources to cope, the best strategy is to deal with the problem.[54] The issue is no longer as simple as whether denial is good or bad for you, but rather at what point denial becomes counterproductive. Persistent denial over a long period is likely to be unhelpful, so the natural tendency for denial to start off strongly and abate with time may make it not such a bad way of dealing with stress.

It is important not to confuse denial with something which may appear at first glance similar: hope. Hope involves concentrating on whatever positive features there are in your otherwise dire situation. Hope is not based on a false illusion and so acknowledges the reality of what is happening to you. It is, rather, a realistic appraisal of what positive aspects there might be in a generally negative situation. Denial is more like a kind of false hope, an unrealistic attempt to see the positive.

But what about crisis where there really does appear to be no hope?

The most major crisis of all is usually the loss of someone or something central to your life, your sense of self-esteem or your sense of identity. This may be the loss of a job, your partner or a parent, for example through death.

At these times, the 'problem-solving' approach mentioned earlier is not going to work – after all, how do you 'problem-solve' the death of a spouse? 'Coming to terms with loss' is the catchphrase for the treatment of bereavement and grief. Put another way, when a loss is irreplaceable, 'There is no arguing with life, there is only acceptance'.[55] Coping with these crises involves an entirely different approach, usually centred around some form of grieving.

Coping with such severe losses or traumas will never be easy. However, to simplify how it can be achieved, psychiatrists divide this coping into four main tasks of grieving or successful bereavement. This model includes both the idea of the work a person must do in order to cope with their loss, as well as the sequence in which the activity should be carried out, the first task being completed before moving on to the second, and so on. The model also helps you to pinpoint the stage where someone may have become stuck, which explains why they are now having difficulty coping. Although these tasks of grieving are usually discussed in the context of death, the same principles apply when dealing with less profound loss.

The first task of grieving is to accept the reality of the loss. Many of the recently bereaved behave as if their loved one is still alive. They may lay a place at the table for them, or even hallucinate that they are still alive. Or, like Dickens's Miss Havisham, they keep their rotting wedding dress on show. In the early stages of a loss, this behaviour is so common as to be considered almost a normal part of grieving. But if it is still going on many months after the death, it shows that the loss has not been fully accepted.

The term 'reality of the loss' applies to many situations other than just the loss of a person. It applies, for example, to the pushy parents whose child fails at exams, and who need to accept the loss of their ambitions for their child to excel at school. And if Victor Meldrew ever started to say, 'I do believe it', it would show that he had begun to accept the deprivation.

After accepting intellectually the reality of the loss, the second task of grieving is to release and deal with the emotions that follow from it. These may range from anger to frustration or despair. Whatever they are, acknowledging and expressing them is extremely important.

In my experience those who make a poor recovery from deep loss often appear on the outside to have coped magnificently, organising the funeral or busying themselves with a hobby, despite the loss of their partner. Yet, because they have never articulated what they feel, be it despair, anger or even relief, these emotions will never have been dealt with. They will therefore contribute to longer-lasting problems which may not emerge until years later. If we do not express how we feel, particularly with disturbing emotions, an important part of us is unacknowledged. This disregard contributes to a growing feeling of alienation between us and others or even between us and our true selves.

Once this second task has been completed, the third task can be attempted, that of learning new skills. Whenever we suffer a fundamental loss, it usually means we will have to adapt to it and this may require additional competencies. Those who have lost a partner may have to learn how to manage the finances or how to cook. The parents of our hapless child may have to learn how to play with their child rather than constantly push her academically, and so on.

If you have become unemployed, coping with the loss of a job may mean learning the new skills of occupying yourself during the day, budgeting and facing up to the loss of status when socialising. Those who have not accepted the reality of the loss – task number one – may have particular difficulty seeing the need for new skills as they feel the latest situation is probably more temporary than it really is. It is difficult to start the onerous task of learning new skills if you are still bogged down with the need to articulate emotions produced by the loss, or are struggling to accept the reality of the loss. But once tasks one and two are completed, new skills need to be acquired, otherwise coping will be stuck here.

Once the third task has been completed, the fourth and final task beckons. This is to reinvest into some new project the emotional energy that was allotted to the person or thing that has been lost. Those who have lost a partner may have to reinvest their feelings into someone else – another partner, friend or relative – or perhaps become engaged in charity work.

Of course, if a loss is fundamental enough there is no way you can replace it but there has to be some attempt to fill the emotional hole left.

When one of Freud's children split up from a suitor whom she had hoped to marry, the astute psychiatrist, aware of the need to complete task four to recover from a loss, bought his 'mourning' child a pet dog. Having someone to look after and dote on, and which in turn reciprocated her feelings of affection clearly cured the forlorn child of lovesickness. Nowadays pets are even formally recommended as part of the treatment for grief.

One problem in dealing with losses such as bereavement is that we often lack the social skills to help others cope with such a misfortune. Because death is not an event we encounter frequently in modern society – unlike 100 years ago, when death was an everyday occurrence and not so taboo – it is important to remember that it is natural when faced with a new situation to have to *learn* how to behave. It is impossible to become an expert on a particular human problem if you have never faced it before.

One difficulty is that there are no rules about what bereaved people want from others at this time; they themselves will not know what they want, so it is acceptable to take the initiative. They will usually give off signals about whether they appreciate your efforts to comfort them or not.

Another key difficulty is whether to talk about the person who has recently died. Many people have confided to me that they fear bringing this subject up as they dread that this will merely 'set the bereaved person off' and upset them even more. In fact, it is those who do not talk enough who are most likely to end up suffering more in the long term. Often a bereaved person will be interested in hearing your thoughts on the recently departed and how you have reacted to the death.

In fact, many experts dealing with abnormally severe reactions to bereavement advise talking as much as possible about the relationship with the person who has died. Going through an old photograph album with the bereaved and reminiscing about the past is not a bad way of helping them deal with their feelings. Remember that it is natural for the bereaved to feel devastated, so if they appear upset don't blame yourself.

The bereaved often look to others to take control of conversation as they are too exhausted to take charge. As long as you are sensitive to any signals that they want to change the subject, just take the initiative in determining what the conversation should be about. It is fine to be light-hearted or talk about apparently trivial things, even though, at first glance, these may seem inappropriate, given the enormity of death. In fact, the trivial or light-hearted may well be a welcome distraction for the bereaved, precisely because they want to escape from the enormity of death.

Many people avoid inviting the bereaved to social gatherings, just when they need company most, thinking they want to be left alone. In reality, this is just a way of helping us avoid an awkward situation. We should give the bereaved the choice.

Activities to distract them from their loss are also helpful, such as a shopping expedition, or helping you with the gardening or an errand. Any activity which involves contact with children is particularly good, as children do not understand bereavement and will treat the recently bereaved more normally than adults do. Children also act as a reminder that life goes on.

Finally, even when the bereaved seem to get over their loss, they will need support from family and friends long after the bereavement, especially on anniversaries.

While it is easy to see major events like death as representing the main challenge to our coping skills, there may in fact be other more demanding tests.

Throughout this chapter I have looked at both major life crises and the minor ones. I have referred to 'negative life events' as the things you have to cope with. This is because we find it relatively easy to grasp the idea that when bad things happen to us, like losing our job, the stress of the event requires effective coping in order to prevent psychological problems. While these major events have been shown to be a significant contributing factor to psychiatric difficulties, some researchers have found an even stronger relationship with the kind of daily situations which I will call 'micro-stressors'. Although these are relatively small units of stress, acting cumulatively they seem to account for as much, if not more, distress than major life events such as job losses and bereavements.[56]

Such everyday hassles include the stress of commuting to work, arguments with spouses, losing things and being caught in the rain. Indeed, it may even be that major life events like a divorce lead to psychological problems more because of the new batch of daily irritations this presents – having to reschedule your life to fit in with picking up the children, preparing your own meals and keeping house and so on – than the event itself. So niggles may be the mediator by which major life events impact on our psychological health.

Irritations can sap mental health because they may be so small and familiar that they can easily get taken for granted, while you focus your coping resources on the more major life events. But the evidence suggests that effective coping skills need to be mobilised on a daily basis to tackle everyday irritations if psychological problems are to be prevented.

And maybe as we observe ourselves coping poorly this gradually leads to a view of the world as a frightening and daunting place. In fact I believe that our fears are not about the objects we dread, like spiders, heights or the boss. It is more that the feared object highlights your concern about your ability to handle the situation. So if you have a fear of flying you do not dread planes so much as have misgivings about your ability to handle an aircraft journey.

The point of this distinction is that the flight phobic often appreciates at some level that millions of people fly perfectly safely every day, so their lack of faith is not so much in the structure of aircraft, but more towards themselves. They fear having a panic on the aircraft and so doing something embarrassing in front of the other passengers. Or they worry that if the aeroplane is going down in trouble they will be unable to follow safety procedures because of their blind panic. It is not so much what the environment will do to us that we most fear, but rather whether we can respond adequately.

If instead we could become confident that we would act in a way which would be the best possible response given the difficulties of the situation, in other words that we would not let ourselves down, then what could we have to fear of the world?

We have shown that the common response to most feared situations is to avoid them. But in so doing, you prevent yourself learning to handle them. Put another way, if you have fears about your ability to cope, you will avoid putting your coping skills to the test. Once you can recognise this, improving your coping skills becomes the only effective way of dealing with your fears.

As you brood about the negative things which could happen to you if you choose various options in life, underlying your pessimism is the nagging doubt as to whether you would be able to handle the scenarios you find yourself in. Of course, many situations, such as unemployment or bereavement, are difficult to cope with, but the fact is that many people do learn, eventually, to endure. All that separates them from us is that they have learnt the relevant coping skills.

Learning to deal effectively with difficult events may be unpleasant, but is usually possible. Anyone can acquire the necessary skills; they do not reside in your genes or in the experiences of your early childhood.

So, the next time you contemplate a particularly unsavoury possibility for your future, instead of worrying about your ability to cope with it, replace your negative view of your coping skills with a more realistic and positive assessment.

Now that you know a bit about coping skills, let's go back to the example at the very beginning of this chapter. What would you now do if your spouse suddenly burst into your bedroom wearing clothes of the opposite sex?

Recall that my client was probably in a bit of shock or denial and ignored the incident at first, not bringing up the subject until a few days later. Not such a bad approach. It gave her time to recover so she could then discuss it more calmly. Then she did not avoid the problem, though it must have been embarrassing and fraught, but raised the issue with him. She also sought fully to comprehend the reality of this and did not revert to wishful thinking – it was just a one-off – but instead checked exactly how long he had been doing this.

The fact that she consulted me because she was concerned about what this behaviour might indicate, meant she was seeking more information about her new situation. Obviously this was such an embarrassing area that she could not talk about it with her friends so she sought out a professional with whom to discuss it.

Finally, she kept focused on what positive response she could make to help their relationship survive this revelation. She was not prepared to make love to her husband while he wore women's clothes (as he later said he wanted) all the time, so they tried to negotiate a compromise. Her attempt at positive coping may not have rescued her marriage, but it did possibly save her from a nervous breakdown.

What her story illustrates, and I hope this chapter has shown, is that, when it comes to coping, all our psychiatric and psychological expertise, research and experience can be boiled down to only two bits of advice. This includes the entire work of Freud, Jung and all the biggest names in the field. Basically the sum total of our knowledge suggests you have just two options. You can either change your environment and therefore start to solve the problems causing you stress, or change yourself and adjust to the new circumstances so they do not bother you so much. So either change the world, or change yourself. Often you have to do a bit of both. But if you are not doing either, you are not coping.

Changing the environment is otherwise known as problem-solving, a strategy we have tackled in detail before. It is possible, though, that you discover you have a problem that is unsolvable, in which case further attempts at problem-solving or trying to change an unchangeable environment will result in a waste of your resources. It is then time to switch strategy and instead focus on changing yourself.

Problem-solving has always been an easy approach to teach as it appears vigorous and helpful. Adopting a strategy of changing yourself instead, which may involve resigning yourself to a problem, may appear to most to be a defeatist, fatalistic and all in all less sexy and assertive way of dealing with life's problems.

However, since much that life has to throw at us is in the form of unsolvable problems, learning to change yourself – to adjust and not get too upset by these – is a vital life skill. Many people try to problem-solve death for example, at the moment a clearly unsolvable problem. When they discover they have a terminal incurable disease they devote themselves to pursuing any and every possible cure in the attempt to prevent or reverse the inevitable. But while one should certainly fight as long as victory is possible, sometimes trying to change the world when it is not possible to do so simply serves to upset you more as you try harder and harder to achieve the impossible.

Learning to adjust yourself to difficult situations so they do not upset you so much is a valuable technique which, once mastered, you will find yourself using several times a day. Often you will use it more than problem-solving. However, beware of adjusting yourself to an apparently unsolvable problem when in fact the problem was solvable all along. This is an ineffective strategy. The first step in all coping is to decide how solvable your problem is. If it is at all solvable, you should try to solve it, to the extent that it is solvable. If it is unsolvable, or to the extent it is unsolvable, you should learn to adjust your emotional state.

There are several useful techniques you can use when it comes to learning to adjust and resign yourself to difficulty. I have already discussed some of these in the chapter on managing your moods titled, 'Crying is Good for You'. I present some more here.

Retaining a sense of humour and being able to apply it when facing a fraught situation have been shown repeatedly by research to be extremely helpful coping skills.[57] However, a sense of humour is only really useful when your problem is not solvable. Tasks requiring more active problem-solving behaviour are less amenable to the beneficial effects of humour.[58] For if a problem is solvable, making light or fun of the situation probably distracts you from seriously applying yourself to solving your problem. This explains why people who have a good sense of humour and keep applying it all the time are not good in a crisis where action and problem-solving are required. But when there is nothing practical you can do to help yourself, keeping your spirits up and distracting yourself from your misery with a sense of humour is a vital coping skill.

At the core of a sense of humour is the ability to tolerate paradox. Central to all jokes or comic situations is tragedy which has been turned upside down to appear funny. The ability therefore to see the funny in the tragic is an essential coping skill. The capacity to sustain a sense of paradox was seen as a defining characteristic of one of the most mature minds, by researcher George Valliant in his long-term follow-up of Harvard graduates to identify which factors predicted future mental health and resilience.[59]

Of the other techniques you need in order to cope with unsolvable problems, the first is not to awfulise (see the chapter 'So, You Think You are Sane?), that is, exaggerate how truly awful your predicament is. Instead, imagine how much worse things could have been. There is nothing terrible which happens to you which could not in fact have been worse. Instead of focusing on how bad things are, get used to reflexively considering how much worse things could have been.[60] This will help you to count your blessings, even when there appear to be none around at all.

A second tip is when dealing with difficult people who have upset you, instead of reflexively losing your temper with them, and so further upsetting yourself, 'see the innocence in their actions'.[61] Often they have done something to hurt you, but without targeting you personally. Their upset was usually caused to you inadvertently, and not on purpose. Thinking like this avoids personalising the distress others cause us, which merely serves to upset us further and often damages our relationships with these people irreparably.

A third tip is to try imagining that everyone else but you is perfectly enlightened and that by their inexplicably difficult and frustrating behaviour they are trying to teach you something. This technique helps you stay in a learning frame of mind when people appear to behave badly to you. It keeps you trying to understand what is going on, which is more useful than immediately getting upset and retaliating. So when you receive poor service at a restaurant, one coping skill is to try to imagine what your waiter might be trying to teach you about life, as if in fact he was not performing poorly because of being an awful waiter but was perfectly enlightened and trying to teach you to learn to be more patient in life.

A similar technique to this is to reverse our usual thinking pattern when someone behaves disgracefully towards us. When this happens we usually immediately try working out exactly what is wrong with our adversary – are they stupid, mad or both? The problem with this approach is it inevitably leads to an antagonistic response from you. Instead try the opposite: try to see what is right in their actions. For example, when someone says something that appears irritating, instead of focusing on what is wrong with what they have said, assume that something about what this person has said to you is in fact true and the problem is just that you can't immediately see the truth. Concentrate on what might be true. Supposing it is true, what would it be true of? If, for example, your work has been dealt with in a very critical way by a colleague, imagine what they are saying has some kernel of truth in it. The trick for you is to grasp that particular aspect.[62]

Trying to see the truth in even hurtful things people have said to us keeps us from dismissing out of hand those who say them. This usually leads to a more positive response from us, and one where we have learnt what needs to change within us to get a better response from others.

One of the key techniques that helps us adjust to crisis comes from Zen Buddhism. Central to Buddhist teaching is an acceptance that the central reality of our universe is change. An inability to accept the inevitability of change seems to lie at the heart of Western difficulty in adjusting to crisis. This is because at the heart of all crisis is a change. Since change is inevitable, things can only come as unexpected shocks to us if we refuse to accept that all aspects of our life will change. For example, all your current relationships, no matter how strong and important they are to you, will inevitably end at some point in the future. At the last they will be terminated by death. When we grieve that we lose people, perhaps part of the deep distress we face is resistance to the fact that loss was inevitable all along. This leads us not to cherish the relationship as we should if we fully accepted its temporary nature.

The catchphrase to sum up this attitude is 'think of the glass as already broken'.[63] In this analogy the breaking of a glass is used to represent when things go wrong in our life, or the loss of things we treasure, be they relationships or possessions. It refers to the situation when a nice glass you own gets broken in your house by a guest, which upsets you. But you would get very distressed if you somehow didn't accept in the first place that all your glasses, no matter how well you look after them, will eventually break. They may not even smash in your lifetime, or not in the next thousand years, but all glasses eventually break, sooner or later. To avoid extreme distress, then, we must accept that glasses will always break: everything changes and change is inevitable. Because the Zen Buddhist master realises that his contact with the intact glass is merely transitory, when he hears the tinkle of his glass breaking, he doesn't get upset or shocked; instead, he simply says, 'Ah, there it goes.'

Follow the coping mantra and advice I have set out in this book, plan to cope, believe you can cope, learn to cope – and you will find that you *can* cope. As Allan Night Chalmers said, 'Crises refine life. In them you discover what you are.'

10

IS PREVENTION POSSIBLE?

A Life Without Breakdowns

'Life is seldom as unendurable as, to judge by the facts, it ought to be.'
Brooks Atkinson[1]

The chapters up to now have dealt with individual components of building mental health. This chapter looks at the most fundamental question of all – is prevention possible? Apart from all the intuitive reasons, a new and pressing incentive for emphasising such prevention has emerged recently. In the past psychiatrists investigated whether mental illness was caused by a disturbed brain function or structure. The latest research suggests that it may in fact be the other way around and that experiencing the severe distress which is associated with mental illness could then produce physical brain damage.[2]

One study involved soldiers who had seen military combat. Researchers measured their part of the brain linked to memory (the hippocampus) and found this to be significantly smaller than that of control groups (matched as precisely as possible to the soldiers on age, race, sex, years of education, socio-economic status, body size and years of alcohol abuse).[3] The length of time the soldiers had been exposed to the stressful conditions of combat correlated with the reduction in this part of the brain's volume. In other words, the more combat you saw, the smaller your hippocampus became.[4]

The theory that the hippocampus may be damaged by mental illness might explain why memory problems underlie many psychiatric symptoms, such as the flashbacks and intrusive memories of Post-Traumatic Stress Disorder, the tendency of the depressed to recall only negative memories, and the difficulty the psychiatrically unwell have in learning they can do something about their situation.

The researchers speculated that under conditions of extreme strain an exceptional amount of stress hormones are released in our bodies, which cause brain damage. They reached this conclusion because of the finding that patients who were not exposed to stressful situations, but who had a hormone disorder producing increased stress hormones also suffered similar brain injury.[5]

While the above study dealt with people who had been exposed to extreme situations, a more worrying finding is that this reduction in hippocampal volume has also been found in depressed people who had been exposed to less extreme situations and had never been in war. Again, the length of time they were seriously depressed for, predicted how small their hippocampi became.[6]

While nothing has been conclusively proven, these preliminary findings raise the concern that poor mental health might produce brain changes, which in turn could make an individual more prone to psychological problems in the future. This cycle invokes the notion of 'kindling', whereby the more psychiatric disorder you experience, the more brain damage you sustain and the more vulnerable you become to future disorder.

This is why I have emphasised throughout this book that the sooner you deal with a psychological problem, the better your chances of recovery.

If prolonged psychological disorder can cause brain damage, rather than the other way round, this is an overriding argument for prevention to be given priority in psychiatry. Why, then, does there appear to be so much resistance to it?

One frequently used argument against prevention is that as genetic factors underpin many psychiatric problems, there is not much you can do to prevent them in the first place. The problem with this argument is that the influence of genetic factors is in itself determined by the environmental consideration. So if prevention strategies are not used, the role of genes is likely to be exaggerated, just as if you took a group of people with no previous training and investigated how fast they ran the 100-metres race, their genes are likely to explain – in the absence of training – a large part of the final result. However, if you then took half this group away and trained them intensively, and then reunited them with the untrained half to re-run the race, genetic factors would now be found to be much less important to the final result.

As long as we delay putting prevention at the core of our mental health services, mental illness will be a growing problem. The World

Health Organisation predicts that severe depression, which in 1990 was fourth in the world-wide league table of causes of disability, will rise to second place by 2020.[7] Even now, one in four of the population in any one year consult their family doctor because of psychiatric difficulties,[8] while more than one in seven women and one in sixteen men in inner city areas are affected by the kind of severe psychiatric disturbance treated in specialist clinics during any one month.[9]

The sheer scale of the mental health problem means that, logically, prevention should be at the top of the agenda. But, acknowledging this is one thing; implementing it another. Even the experts acknowledge that there could never be enough clinicians to treat everyone who requires help[10] and some have even advocated the idea that non-clinicans such as teachers and the clergy should be recruited to fill the gap. I believe, instead, that it is the general public who should be recruited to assist themselves. This seems much more likely to achieve the aim of prevention, for the simple reason that no matter how dedicated the professional, no one has as much interest in your own mental health as yourself.

There is also the more fundamental point of control. If, instead of prevention, the received wisdom is to suggest that people should always seek external advice, you are implicitly wresting control from them. I believe that the very act of helping often reduces, rather than enhances, the client's sense of control and self-esteem.[11] Given that feelings of helplessness, an inability to control oneself and a lack of self-determination underlie much mental ill health, I would argue that enhancing an individual's feelings of control is crucial to developing positive mental health.

Some of my colleagues would argue against my view by saying that, because we do not know what causes mental illness, prevention is bound to be elusive, a hit-and-miss affair at best. However, throughout history successful public health campaigns have reduced the incidence of disease without consciously understanding their causes.[12] For example, cleaning nearby swamps responsible for marsh gases helped prevent malaria (which means bad air), although campaigners did not discover until later that malaria is not caused by the bad smell from swamps, but by mosquitoes which breed there. If they had waited until they ascertained the precise cause of malaria rather than acting against what they knew was linked to malaria, many would have died.[13]

Modern public health medicine is often said to have started when John Snow reduced cholera in 19th-century London by stopping people from using a particular pump. Again he saved lives despite having no idea of what the specific cause of cholera was.

So, while academic doctors may devote a lifetime to finding precise causes – and this is clearly valuable work – the public need to know what they can do *now* to help themselves. They cannot afford to wait for medical discoveries which may come after an illness has started and when it is too late.

While these same academic doctors might scoff at those who adopt positive mental health strategies on the grounds that no one knows what causes most mental illness, they themselves are busy prescribing treatments such as antidepressants, even though they do not know exactly how antidepressants work. Yet this does not, and should not, stop us using these highly effective medicines.[14]

I believe that instead of needing to know the precise causes of illness – whether physical or mental – to bring about change, we simply need to know the associations between factors. For example, if certain cognitive therapy strategies are associated with good mental health, and have proved effective in the treatment of mental illness, it makes sense to teach these to the public.

My view is that we need a radical rethink of the whole subject of mental health so that strategies to enhance positive mental health become part of our culture. Society needs to embrace values such as discouraging dependency on counsellors, encouraging people to react rationally rather than emotionally, advocating self-control and seeing psychological problems as eminently treatable.

Some might question why everyone should take up these values when only those prone to psychiatric disorder would benefit?[15] Perhaps they are really confusing mental health prevention with physical health prevention, where the majority do not usually benefit much from a particular health promotion. Public health experts advise that it is only those at high risk who need to take active steps to prevent themselves from getting ill. So the smoker and heavy eater will benefit much more from a 'healthy heart' campaign than the average person, although the average person will have made the effort to improve diet and take more exercise. This has been called the 'prevention paradox', where a measure may bring benefit to a community overall (because they don't have to shoulder the burden of care for people who might otherwise have become ill) but offers little to the majority of individuals in that group who have also worked hard to improve their health.[16] And clearly, we are less likely to follow the advice of a public health campaign if we cannot see a direct personal benefit.

However, I would argue that mental health campaigns are entirely different. The number of people who suffer from psychological difficulties is huge, much larger than those prone to illnesses such as heart disease, for which traditional prevention strategies have evolved. Certainly I do not believe that anyone reading this book will never have experienced distressing worries or moods. Involving the public in positive mental health enhancement would therefore not run up against the prevention paradox, in that promotion would usually be as beneficial to the individual as the community. So, although the chronic worrier or the manic depressive will benefit most from the strategies I have suggested, everyone will experience some advantage.

While most mental illnesses are treatable, once you get one you tend to become more dependent on others for help with recovery than would be the case for most physical illnesses. This is because your mind is unable to function properly when suffering psychological problems and your ability to make decisions about whether to go for help and how to follow medical advice is weakened. This is obviously not the case for gallstones or a hernia. With a mental illness you will also often need others to tell you that you are becoming unwell – again, more so than with physical illnesses. With such illnesses, you will be the one who has to signal you are not feeling well, for example, to your boss before asking for time off, whereas with psychiatric problems, particularly severe ones, it is often your boss who will have a quiet word with you.

This loss of insight (which I covered in the chapter 'Me, Me, Me') is a feature of psychological problems. It is possible for you to behave in a manner worrying to others for quite a long time before you realise the damage you have been doing to your reputation. As I argued earlier, self-deception is widespread and we are all vulnerable to it in varying degrees, so we often display some loss of insight long before we experience serious problems.

Often a major reason I am involved in committing the severely unwell to hospital against their will is because their bizarre behaviour is destroying their standing in their community. Some of my depressed patients become so withdrawn that neighbours notice that they have not been seen for weeks. They may be heard crying loudly inside their homes and then not respond to the doorbell, so that the police are called to break in. Even after having successfully recovered from serious psychological problems, it is very difficult to recover your status in the eyes of others, and this is in itself a strong argument for prevention, even for disorders that are eminently treatable.

Another argument in favour of preventive strategies is the precariousness of funding for mental health services and the wide variability in standards of mental health care throughout the world. Not only can you not rely on getting professional help when you need it, but psychiatric and psychological services tend not to be as good as the facilities used by the mentally healthy. The mentally ill are clearly less able to be effective advocates for improvements in mental health services than, say, members of the Parkinson's Disease Society or the British Diabetic Association. And because of the associated stigma, those who have recovered from psychiatric problems are not likely to draw attention to their illness by becoming active campaigners. These facts mean it is even more vital to be able to help yourself.

Usually one way of ensuring that good practitioners flourish and poor ones are discouraged from practising is word-of-mouth. Again, the same fear of stigma applies. While you may feel happy to recommend a good dentist to a friend, are you likely to mention the excellent psychologist who brought you back from suicidal depression? Clients of mental health services have always had more difficulty finding good practitioners, the problem being particularly acute in the unregulated field of private practice counselling.

Prevention in its truest sense – what doctors call primary prevention – means stopping healthy people from becoming ill. This is opposed to secondary prevention, which means halting an illness from progressing. The small amount of preventive work in psychiatry has tended to focus on educating parents who are either already in dysfunctional families or in those at risk of being so. These parents are taught practices designed to prevent the production of disturbed children. One example is the STEEP programme – Steps Toward Effective Enjoyable Parenting.[17, 18, 19] In this intensive programme, psychologists visited the homes of high-risk mothers (for example those whose experience of being abused as children put them at high risk of developing problems in their relationships with their babies). During these home visits psychologists videotaped the mother and baby in a variety of situations such as feeding, playing and bathing. They then watched the tapes with the mother, discussing them in a non-judgemental manner to enhance the mothers' understanding of their relationship with their baby. For example, they might discuss how to recognise what the baby's behaviour might be signalling (i.e. that crying doesn't mean that a baby is being naughty). Helping parents recognise and understand that the way they respond to and approach their child helps determine the child's behaviour as a key goal.

Certainly, good parenting and positive childhood experiences have an important place in the prevention of adult psychiatric problems. I mentioned, for example, in the chapter I Will Survive how a controlled exposure to stress helps to build resilient children. And in the chapter on thinking your way to sanity I stressed the importance of the precise form of words parents use in scolding children .

Research has found that poor parenting in childhood is linked to an increased risk of depression as well as, to a lesser extent, anxiety, in adult life. This might appear to reinforce the argument that the best prevention strategies for disorders where there are strong continuities between childhood and adult problems are those which target parenting practices. I still disagree. Of course, acquiring good parenting skills is important but I firmly believe that the best kind of prevention tactics are those which anyone with an interest in improving their mental health can adopt. Moreover, while it remains a controversial area, it does seem possible that vulnerability to poor mental health operates through poor coping skills in dealing with life stress. If this is the case the techniques described in 'Crisis, What Crisis?' should help prevent psychiatric problems, even in those who have had unfortunate childhood experiences of parenting. I believe that the message that it is never too late to improve mental health is much more helpful than that which says that if you've had poor childhood experiences there's little you can do. But the problem with prevention is that people keep putting off taking actions now which will provide benefits in the future.

DO YOU PUT THINGS OFF?

Procrastinators are people who keep putting off tasks they need to do. These may be a variety of things from filling out your tax-return to tidying the house or revising for an exam. Dawdlers procrastinate as an approach to life. They keep postponing what they need to do to achieve their goals, which explains why they either don't achieve their goals at all, or end up getting into a panic just before a deadline and doing too much in a rush, with added stress and often poorer results. Studies have suggested that up to 50 per cent of people may suffer from problems through constantly postponing vital things they need to do now. The essential enigma of procrastination is that it is irrational. Procrastinators persistently harm themselves by putting off doing something indefinitely which, if they were to do it today, would benefit them greatly.

To see if you suffer from chronic procrastination problems, try the quiz below.

PUTTING-OFF SCALE

Each statement is followed by two possible responses: agree or disagree. Read each statement carefully and decide which response best describes how you feel. Then put a tick over the corresponding response. Please respond to every statement. If you are not completely sure which response is more accurate, put the response which you feel is most appropriate. Do not read the scoring explanation before filling out the questionnaire. Do not spend too long on each statement. It is important that you answer each question as honestly as possible.

		AGREE	DISAGREE
1	I find it easy to be early for appointments	A	B
2	Shopping for presents is usually a last-minute rush	B	A
3	I plan what I am going to do on holiday before I get there	A	B
4	I rarely go to events where tickets sell out quickly	B	A
5	I usually pay bills before the reminder comes	A	B
6	My desk or room where I do paperwork is rarely tidy	B	A
7	I check my diary for up-coming events every day	A	B
8	When packing for holidays I usually forget at least one thing	B	A
9	I prefer to finish a project before moving on to something else	A	B
10	I usually spent the night before an exam revising until late	B	A

Add up your score from summing the numbers of As and Bs in each box you have ticked. Your score and the interpretation given below should be treated with caution – this short test is by no means definitive, but may offer a guide to where you stand compared to others around you.

SCORES

8 or more Bs. You are scoring very high indeed for procrastination, which means you tend to avoid doing things you don't enjoy or find boring for as long as possible. What you may not realise is that your frequent feelings of anxiety or depression may be linked to this tendency. You may be getting depressed thinking of the growing number of things which need doing, and you are putting them off because thinking about doing them makes you anxious. You should try the 'Swiss-cheese' approach to all those activities – don't try to do them all at once. Instead, attack your mountain of undone activities by burrowing into them at random, in a small way, whenever you have a spare moment – thus making small holes in your workload.

Between 5 and 7 Bs. You are scoring above average for tendencies to procrastinate, which probably means that just before you settle down to do the things you need to, your dawdling self finds lots of excuses to put off work until later. You need to learn to anticipate the excuses you tend to come up with and firmly dispel them with rational argument. In particular, you must rehearse this rebuttal of your usual excuses long before you get ready to do the job which needs doing. At the moment you may be relying too much on others, and on ultimatums, to provide the motivation to get things done. Ask yourself how much you really want the goals you have set yourself, or are they, instead, goals others have set up for you?

Between 3 and 5 Bs. You are scoring around average to below average for a tendency to dawdle and this means that although you do get projects finished before deadlines, the last few weeks are still more hectic than you had planned. It may be there are many things which distract you from your goals, which means you rarely concentrate purely on one project for long enough before moving on to something else. Your ambition means you may attempt too much at once, which ends up slowing you down in the long run. Work only on one project at a time and in a place which is devoid of distractions.

> *Between 0 and 2 Bs.* Congratulations! You are scoring very low
> indeed for a tendency to dawdle and this means you
> instinctively already know that golden time management rule –
> never have to be told about a deadline twice. Do tasks the
> minute you become aware they need doing without any delay
> at all. In the office, never touch the same piece of paper twice –
> do paperwork the minute it lands on your desk. The problem
> for you is that others will have noticed that because of your
> efficiency you always have spare capacity to do more, and you
> may be exploited by others who dawdle. While being firm with
> dawdlers, you need to be more understanding of the emotional
> reasons which lead them never to seem to do things until the
> last moment.

Another reason for putting off taking action is that many people still
believe that early childhood experiences are so crucial that prevention is
not possible – they argue that our predisposition to psychological
problems will have already been determined. This view is reinforced by
many therapists, particularly with a Freudian or psychoanalytic
background. I have shown how these therapists believe that much
therapeutic work in clinical practice relies heavily on us reappraising
our childhood, with a view to trying to understand the roots of present
psychological disturbance. They believe that the key to solving present
problems is to release clients from the impact of negative childhood
experiences.

So, despite the hippy aphorism, 'It's never too late to have a happy
childhood', according to them it may indeed be too late to do anything
about your past. If you agree with their view, prevention strategies after
terrible childhood experience would be redundant. Indeed, research
suggests that depression in childhood or adolescence is associated with
a fourfold increase in the risk of major depression in adult life.[20]

The validity of this view becomes particularly crucial if, as the facts
might suggest, an unhappy childhood is more common than realised.
Research is now documenting that children are perhaps as vulnerable to
psychiatric problems as adults are. Previously the thinking was that
although children could get miserable it was, for example, impossible for
them to suffer the serious kind of depression which adults get.

Psychiatrists held this view until a few decades ago. Yet recent research suggests that 10 per cent of children will suffer from serious clinical depression,[21] and the suicide rate in some parts of the Western world for children aged between 10 and 14 has doubled since the 1980s.[22]

One explanation for this is that we underestimated the rate of suicide amongst the very young both because these acts are often disguised as accidents and because depressed children sometimes seem to be the most well-behaved and quiet ones, their depression being overlooked.[23]

That said, the idea that infancy and early years of childhood have a special importance in personality development and psychological problems is now widely attacked by the new generation of research psychiatrists and psychologists.[24] The current view is the *whole* of development is important in terms of the cause of psychological problems, with infancy no less nor more so than the years of middle and later childhood or even the rest of adult life.

But surely as a young child I am vulnerable to what my parents or family did to me, you might argue. The answer is not quite as straightforward as you might think. The new concept of 'sensitive responsiveness' reflects the shift in the view of parenting as doing things to the baby to it as a process of mutual interaction – an active dialogue between parent and child. For example, there are many different types of babies' cry – one for hunger, one for teething, one for needing comfort, and so on – and it may be that it is the parents' ability to discriminate between these and to respond appropriately which is important. Then again, the temperament of the baby also affects the situation, as different babies will react to their parents' attitudes to their crying in different ways. So, with the exception of extreme cases such as parents who are violent abusers, the kind of baby you are may be as important in moulding your parents as they are in shaping you.

So the chain of causality becomes complicated. For example, take the idea that your parents were too punitive to you as a child. Perhaps your particular temperament in relation to that of your parents meant that you were more likely to provoke punishment than another child might have been. This idea of interactivity in human relationships – even between a child and its parents – means that to blame the way you are on something someone did to you appears overly simplistic. Of course, that is not to excuse parents who are brutal to children, but merely to suggest that several factors are at work.

Books such as John Bowlby's *Can I leave my Baby?*, published in 1958, shaped the way a generation of parents related to their offspring. This book was interpreted as insisting that continuity and closeness of maternal care were the only certain ways of preventing adolescent and adult psychological disorders. The inevitable conclusion was that mothers should not go out to work, and day nurseries and creches became viewed as dangerous to children's mental health. All mothers who wanted a career or a life outside of childcare worried about comments like Bowlby's 'Mother-love in infancy and childhood is as important for mental health as are vitamins and proteins for physical health.'

Yet again, the reality is slightly more complex. Bowlby identified the important fact that a child needed a close, continuous relationship. Recent research, however, suggests that the primary care-giver need not necessarily be the mother, nor that her absences are always hazardous.[25]

John Bowlby was the psychoanalysist who was most influential in the 1960s and 1970s in emphasising the importance of early attachment between child and mother as determining future mental health. Yet he felt that positive change could occur despite previous poor relationships with parents if you had emotionally 'corrective' experiences in current or future relationships. So even if you felt abandoned by your mother, a secure long-term relationship afterwards could break the cycle of mistrust in relationships.

Another simplistic notion, that the early hours of birth are critical because parental bonding affects later mental health, is incompatible with observations that fathers and adoptive parents both develop close ties to their children in spite of not having had much contact in the neonatal period.

I would argue that the idea that early childhood trauma can have irreversible long-term consequences is fixed in society's psyche simply because it is rare to suffer severe deprivation during infancy followed by a marvellous environment throughout the rest of childhood or life. So adults with problems are often shown to have had bad childhoods, and people immediately assume cause and effect. But the things which cause problems in childhood, like severe poverty or poor parenting, often

411

continue throughout a person's life. Their effects will therefore be long term. If, in contrast, you have suffered from a traumatic childhood but experience a reasonably good environment after that, there is little evidence that the trauma should determine the future of your mental health.

An example of how undetermined our destiny is by the past is that children who have suffered appalling deprivation up to the age of six or seven, and are then rescued, can more than double their IQ within seven years from the time they are helped. In the chapter on resilience I also discussed how correcting vitamin deficiency can dramatically help brain function in children. It seems that as the brain is still developing throughout childhood (for example, which side of the brain responsible for talking only becomes designated at around puberty), it is more able at this stage to rearrange itself to cope with possible early bad experiences.

So, for example, brain lesions are often less likely to lead to permanent language impairment if they occur during early childhood than later in life. While this does not mean that early childhood deprivation or abuse should be ignored, it does suggest that the assumption that bad events in your childhood are somehow more damaging than similar negative experiences later in life is probably an argument still waiting to be proven.

There are, however, a few important exceptions to this. For example, foetal damage, which might occur if a mother gets flu[26] during a particular stage of her pregnancy, or if the baby suffers from obstetric complications during delivery, may be responsible for a proportion of those who get schizophrenia in later life.

Some schizophrenics appear to have widened spaces in their brains and this is predicted by severe delivery complications, for example lack of oxygen and trauma during birth.[27] This cause of schizophrenia probably only accounts for a small proportion of all schizophrenics, yet does raise the importance of good antenatal and obstetric care for pregnant mothers to prevent this severe mental illness. Also relevant in preventing later schizophrenia, as mentioned in the chapter on resilience ('I Will Survive'), is a good maternal diet during pregnancy.

I have argued that infancy and the early years of childhood do not have an all-encompassing influence on personality development. That said, although childhood is not somehow biologically critical, happenings during infancy do matter because of the way early experiences may influence later vulnerability by increasing or decreasing sensitivity to later stresses.[28]

Apart from this, damage due to severe early trauma or deprivation is childhood can be reversed to a considerable extent later in life if the environmental change is sufficiently great and if later experiences are sufficiently good.

But how can a person change his or her environment and so ward off future mental health problems? A good example of how it is possible to alter one's destiny can be found in the example of antisocial personality disorder, which has one of the strongest links between childhood and adult problems in psychiatry. Here a strong continuity has been found between badly behaved children, later juvenile delinquency, subsequent adult criminal behaviour and the inability to fit in later in life. This leads, amongst other problems, to a poor work record, such as an inability to keep a job. Psychiatrists term bad behaviour in children conduct disorder and this is strongly linked to family discord. Well, you may ask, 'What can I do about it if I am born into a dysfunctional family – after all I cannot choose my parents!'

Even if you are heading down this apparently fixed path, if, by early adulthood, you choose a supportive, non-deviant partner who provides you with a harmonious marital relationship, this will be a highly protective influence, preventing a downward spiral into more villainous behaviour.[29] Avoiding deviant peers has also been found to help steer young people away from a destiny of social maladjustment, even if they had already started not fitting in. Agreeable family ties seem to protect the young from falling into the hands and influence of aberrant peer groups. The common theme here is the shielding effect of positive relationships, which is why I have devoted a whole chapter on relationships and how these keep you sane.[30]

Studies have also found that the ability to plan for the future specifically protects girls from later personality problems such as antisocial personality disorders. This may be because it is linked with the avoidance of unplanned teenage pregnancy.[31] Avoiding pregnancy is probably helpful to girls' long-term mental health because it protects them from deviant peer groups and partners. If a girl allows herself to settle with a child's father 'for the sake of the baby' when she would not otherwise have chosen to do so, she is highly likely to become depressed in the future. So, choice and care in relationship selection are clearly crucial in mental health prevention. For boys, a commitment to work has shown to be similarly helpful, while, compared with housewives, studies show that employed women have a greater sense of self-esteem and personal satisfaction. Employment clearly serves as a factor protecting, in particular, working-class women from depression.[32]

In the chapters on mood and resilience, I discussed the importance of goals and how striving towards various kinds of goal protects mental health.

The critical point here is that, regardless of how things started out, you can still improve your mental health. It is never too late to prevent psychiatric disturbance. 'Staying sane' strategies are appropriate for all of us, whatever our vulnerability. However, as I have tried to demonstrate in this book, you need to adopt several different strategies at the same time to ward off mental illness. Each chapter has highlighted different ones – from ways to preserve self-esteem (in the 'Me, Me, Me' chapter) to tactics to deal with worry in 'So, You Think You Are Sane?'. This may begin to seem rather complicated, and now you could be asking 'Is there not just one thing I need to do to enhance my mental health rather than have to take up all these many different strategies?'

Although many self-help books attempt to sell readers the one simple path to mental health, perhaps the oldest approach of this type should not be dismissed so easily – religion.

In 1968, the atheist philosopher Ernst Bloch wrote: 'Where people have hope, there is religion.'[33] In addition to being a core concept in religion, hope is a central notion in psychiatry.[34, 35] When psychiatrists see it as one of their tasks to substitute hope for hopelessness, rather than simply confronting negative thinking they may be able to learn something from religion, which, after all, has many centuries of experience in this particular area.

Although not formally religious myself, I consider one neglected cause of the recent rise in psychiatric disorders is the declining role of religion in people's lives. I believe that any comprehensive attempt to prevent psychological problems should take account of religion (which evolved over millenia) as a coherent and effective way of dealing with – and preventing – suffering. The non-religious who wonder how anyone could believe in religious phenomena in the absence of adequate scientific proof have, in my opinion, missed the point.

Religion exists because it is a powerful way of dealing with important human needs. It is a comfort in times of stress to such a powerful extent that it often reduces the need to seek formal psychological help. I do not believe religion exists because the evidence for a deity is overwhelming, but rather that it is pervasive because its effect is to offer a solution to human problems which otherwise would result in deteriorating mental health.

One historic role of religion was to enhance people's capacity to deal with natural or environmental factors beyond their control or management.[36] Since this need was universal, religious attitudes and orientations were integral to all societies. But in modern times, science has appeared to be able to take over this mantle, and as psychiatry sought to hook its fortunes to this rising star, it has increasingly scorned the religious domain.

The conclusion that religion is no longer necessary was perhaps premature. For example, one review of research in this area, including[37] 57 studies which examined the link between mental health and being religious, concluded that there was by and large a positive relationship. It appears that the consequence of religosity most aligned with mental health[38] is that of bringing meaning and direction to life. And some psychiatrists have noted[39] that 'the therapeutic potency of religious phenomena compared with psychotherapy's therapeutic potency seems like atomic power compared to dynamite'. With a few exceptions,[40] there continues to be a dearth of serious psychiatric research on the protective aspects of religious beliefs.

Perhaps it is something about religious faith which makes it an uneasy research topic for psychiatrists. Those working in the behavioural sciences tend to be less religious than those in other sciences[41] perhaps because the attempt to approach private feelings objectively may reduce personal commitment to phenomena like religion.[42] So non-religious people who want to help the distressed may choose to enter psychiatry, while the religious with comparable interests opt for the ministry.[43]

One survey from North America found that 56 per cent of psychiatrists are agnostic or atheist, as opposed to only 5 per cent of the general public.[44] If behavioural scientists and clinicians find religion irrelevant to their own lives, they are likely to assume that religion is similarly extraneous to their subjects and patients as well.[45]

Surveys of Christian psychiatrists have found that, as might be expected, their religious beliefs are linked to increased sensitivity to religiosity. For example, they rated the Bible and prayer higher than psychiatric medication as treatment for suicidal intent, grief reaction, sociopathy and alcoholism.[46]

The positive effect of religious beliefs on mental health may be accounted for by their ability to provide a basis for the positive framing of any event, either external or internal.[47] It provides a method of perpetually discerning positive, benevolent and promising aspects of the self, others and the world. If you have sinned, redemption is possible; if a disaster befalls you, it is all part of God's purpose.

Even though Freud, 'an unrepentant atheist',[48] viewed religion as a regressive illusion and an obsessive neurosis, and unambiguously asserts that religion is associated with mental illness, he did argue in his book *The Future of an Illusion* that if religion genuinely helped in the search for happiness, in comforting and reconciling us to life, no one should dream of interfering with this.[49] To the extent that religion performed a civilizing function and kept instinctual chaos at bay, Freud could approve of it. In other words, if religion helped us behave ourselves according to social or moral codes by fearing the consequences if we just did what our animal urges or instincts drove us to do, Freud agreed that was a good thing.

For Carl Jung, religion was even necessary for mental health. A religious outlook cured psychological problems because it brought meaning to life, providing reasons for withstanding the severest hardships.[50, 51] Jung felt that psychotherapy should go beyond recovering suppressed parts of the individual personality and also explore universal aspects of human nature, such as the collective unconscious, which was often expressed through shared religious ideas. One of the points he made was that one advantage of religion is that it brought people together, while the individualist focus of psychotherapy may drive them apart.

Freud, in contrast, assumed atheism was the norm and that religion was simply a vestige of the childhood of humankind. He felt that while infantile needs for protection, comfort, compensation and the assuaging of guilt are common in the world of the child, they are destined to be outgrown.[52] Freud suggested that, through fantasy, religion reduces the terror of uncaring Nature by personalising the natural order (you believe a personality is at work directing nature); removes the fear of death by providing an illusion of immortality; and reconciles us to the social necessity of self-denial by promising to reward us for it in the hereafter.[53]

Although Freud was anti-religion, in fact some of the problems he pointed out and what he advocated may be answered by religion. He believed that even with the benefits of psychoanalysis or therapy, the price of civilization is neurosis.[54] We have to learn to subjugate what we would really like to do because of social mores and constraints, and this tension produces psychological problems. This may in fact be the problem to which religion offers a solution. Controlling the passions and channelling (sublimating) them into higher mental functions was important to Freud. His solution was 'where id is, let ego be' – where instincts exist, let rational self control rather than irrational repression reign.[55] Taking responsibility for oneself and voluntarily choosing the path of self-control is at the core of the moral code. And Christianity, like other religions, offers personal fulfilment and happiness to the person who renounces egoistic goals in favour of the community, which is another way of putting into practice what Freud advocated.

Furthermore, aspects of worship like prayer yield perspective (your problems seem minor compared to those God must be wrestling with; prayer also helps you think of others and know you're not alone) and the capacity to distinguish between values (why should your problems take priority over other important problems?), as well as a reduction of tensions by catharsis (you set up an internal dialogue and ventilate your most fervent wishes when you pray) which is a way of describing what much of psychotherapy is about.[56]

Another reason why it was perhaps premature to replace religion with science is that, despite the technological advances of the twentieth century, for many of us life can still appear beyond our control, unexplained, and rich with danger. As mentioned, historically religion was seen to deal with these anxieties and psychiatry does not appear to have a well-developed alternative. There are certainly psychological issues for which psychiatry has proved to be an effective solution (such as many severe mental illnesses), but there are other areas where a religious approach may be more suitable.

Indeed, I would argue that technological advances have made religion more, not less, necessary. While labour-saving devices reduce stress, psychological problems do not seem to be alleviated by helpful gadgets. If anything, technology has contributed to the increasing pace of modern times, and heightened efficiency and competitiveness only means our lives are more cluttered.

This is partly due to our economic growth being founded on increased consumption, so that after a while the only way to ensure we consume more and more products and services is for consumption to take up more and more of our time. As we have only a finite amount of time, consumption within that time becomes more frenetic. This partly explains the increased portability of gadgets (such as the mobile phone) – the easier for us to take them around with us, the better to ensure they occupy our time. If you can't take something with you, that period away from it is dangerous, as you can't then be consuming it!

As we only buy things we feel we lack, needs have to be created, through advertising, for example. A well-established way of making us want something is to trade on our insecurities and fears. So you feel you must buy a particular car because it will signal potency to members of the opposite sex, or buy a particular watch to show your sophistication. But by constantly preying on our insecurities, by making us anxious about our appearance or our sexuality, capitalism is also producing neurosis as a by-product.

For example, today, when women are at their most free to pursue their lives as they wish (though that is not to say that all sexism has been eradicated) mental health problems in the form of eating disorders are also reaching epidemic proportions.

My own explanation for this is that the very hard-won freedom has, via capitalism, produced the problem. Women's greater independence meant they could work outside the home and this produced more female economic power than ever before. To exploit this new group with disposable income, capitalists came up with goods such as fashion, cosmetics and women's magazines, creating whole new markets which simply did not exist 50 to 100 years ago.

But the only way to sell these products to women was to make them insecure and anxious about themselves. If they felt anxious about their appearance, for example, they then had to rush out and buy this cosmetic or that dress. This greater insecurity about appearance has led to eating disorders on a huge scale.

The final capitalist triumph is to flog a product which does not work – diets, for instance – but then get the consumer to blame themselves for its failure. They are told, for example, that it is their lack of willpower which explains why the diet failed, even though research has shown that most diets are likely to falter for several reasons.

I make no apology for going into detail on this subject as it is thought that over 90 per cent of women will diet at some time in their lives. The dieting industry is now worth over a billion pounds a year (from just 34 million pounds a year in 1969) and ensures that three-quarters of 17-year-old women are on a diet. In doing so it is busy creating an epidemic of eating disorders, and it is psychiatrists like me who have to deal with the consequences.

The first reason a diet is likely to fail is that your body has a genetically programmed sense of what weight it thinks it ought to be and if it detects it falling below that, it simply reduces its metabolic rate to slow down or stop any weight loss.

Research has demonstrated the one certainty about restricting your intake of food, even for only a few days, is that you will become preoccupied by it. Again, this is probably genetically built in to our systems from tens of thousands of years ago, when any restriction in food intake meant we were in the midst or a famine or that food supplies had otherwise become uncertain.

As a survival mechanism our bodies are programmed under such conditions to become obsessed with food to ensure we devote all our efforts to searching it out. This absorption of the mind with food when on a diet makes it difficult to sustain for very long. The body is also programmed to lay down any food it now comes across as long-term stores – in other words, fat. The body reasons that as regular food supplies have clearly become uncertain it had better take a cautious strategy when it comes to what it does with any calories now taken in.

These mechanisms explain how a common outcome of embarking on a diet is weight-gain. After all, if diets worked, why would there be a need for so many of them, and a constant stream of new ones?

The only way to lose weight is, first, have a sensible target, not the unrealistic aspirations conveyed by the media. The second crucial thing to do is to exercise more. Finally, ensure your exercise and diet balance are sustainable as part of a new lifestyle – and not just a temporary change.

The dieting industry is one specific example of how modern commercial interests can contribute to mental health problems. There is an increasing awareness that our technological and materialistic society as a whole poses problems to long-term mental health.

Although there might appear on one level to be a decline in interest in religion, at another level religious interest is reaching new heights, as shown by the growth of extreme religions and cults.

One reason for the apparent rejection of religions is an apprehension among many that the religious conception of life is simplistic and flawed, and that its response to suffering was therefore sometimes weak. For example Freud noted: '…it is by no means the rule that virtue is rewarded and wickedness punished, but it happens often enough that the violent, the crafty, and the unprincipled seize the desirable goods of the earth for themselves, while the pious go empty away…'[57] Perhaps for these reasons religions have sprung up which take a more active approach to changing the world than the more passive approach of traditional religions.

Since World War II there has been an unprecedented growth in the number of new religions and cults and there are now estimated to be over one thousand. As these are usually secretive organisations, some researchers speculate that there may even currently be as many as three to five thousand 'New Religious Movements' (NRMs), to use the buzz term of cult investigators.[58]

Some, like the Unification Church, the International Society of Krishna Consciousness (ISKCON), the Church of Scientology, or the Divine Light Mission, Rajneeshism and Rastafarianism, are famous. They are often in the news, usually as the result of 'brainwashing' scares. Others are more obscure, but it is precisely the lesser known which are perhaps the most worrying.

For example, David Koresh's obscure cult, Waco, dominated headlines for weeks, and was full of people willing to die dramatically for a cause. This is by no means the most sensational event in the history of NRMs. In 1978, for example, 900 members of the cult 'People's Temple' in Guyana, followers of Jim Jones, committed mass suicide through voluntary ingestion of cyanide. This followed their murder of four US Congress officials who were visiting the enclave. Over 200 were children, while another 200 were over the age of 65. Babies had cyanide squirted into their mouths while the adults queued up to drink theirs mixed into Kool-Aid.

The tape of the last hours of the cult survived – currently residing in University of Washington and FBI archives. Labelled 'The Death Tape' it reveals a macabre debate between members of the cult over whether they should commit mass suicide.[59] Someone is heard to argue that the act of mass suicide was unprecedented, to which Jones responded that mass suicide had been chosen by many cults in history. In fact he was right.

The last recorded occasion of mass suicide in the world occurred about one hundred years previously, only four hundred miles south of Jonestown in a native South American Indian community called Bekeranta.[60] Their leader declared they would have to kill each other so that they could be reborn as white people and enjoy all the subsequent benefits. Immediately after this speech, he turned to a follower and split his head open with a club. So started an orgy of killing leading to the death of 400 men, women and children. Although this was mass suicide, it was different from Jonestown, and also perhaps Waco, in that most did not take their own lives, but set out to kill each other.

There have been other cases in history which have left their mark on modern life. In 73 AD a group of religious Jews were besieged by the Romans at Masada. When they realised defeat was inevitable, they committed mass suicide. This event influences Jewish thought even today, in fact, the modern state of Israel is sometimes described as having a 'Masada complex'.[61]

Perhaps the most dramatic examples of those willing to gamble with the highest stakes was an obscure Russian religious sect called the 'Old Believers'. During the late seventeenth and early eighteenth century, at least 20,000 burned themselves to death rather than accept the state's religious orthodoxy, although the doctrinal differences were relatively trivial.[62]

But this willingness to sacrifice life or devote your self to a cause for often trivial reasons is part of the enigma of NRMs. The depth of philosophy involved seems scarcely to justify the attachment of members to cults.

Another example the Hare Krishna movement, founded in the USA in 1965 by an enterprising Indian businessman, A C Bhaktivedanta Swami Prabhupada, who devoted the latter part of his life to exporting to the west a form of low Hinduism that had been practised for hundreds of years in Bengal. A central belief of the movement is that 'time has no beginning and no end', a truism which hardly seems worth shaving your hair off and dancing in the streets about.

Or take the Children of God movement – a weird cocktail of fire-and-brimstone Christian evangelism combined with hippyism and radical free enterprise – founded by David Berg in 1967. This had as its central theme that communism would take over the world in the 1980s.[63]

Scientology, founded some years after his book *Dianetics – The Modern Science of Mental Health* had begun to sell in large numbers in the early 1950s, was developed by Lafayette Ron Hubbard from the sub-plot of his science fiction stories. Dianetics is founded on the highly original and earth-shattering principles that repressing traumatic memories leads to neurosis, and that most world problems are a result of breakdowns of communication.

Apart from being based on trivial or simply wrong ideas, like the firm 'end of the world' predictions of 1967 by Sun Myung Moon, head of the Unification Church, and in 1975 by the Jehovah's Witnesses, another cause for concern is how organisations appear able to juggle being religious and spiritual associations with all the trappings of modern multinational corporations, benefiting from the tax exemptions of charitable bodies.

Most successful NRMs seem too commercially viable to be religious movements. The real mystic, after all, gives up a better life for an impoverished one.

This prompts the question of how it is possible for adult men and women, many of whom are well-educated, to agree to follow or even take their own lives at the behest of the leaders of these cults. Research by psychologists trying to understand the power of cults suggests that, far from cult members being mad, as the FBI concluded about WACO, most people could easily fall victim to the spell of a charismatic leader, and end up succumbing to a Waco-type of scenario!

Studies show that most who join cults are not particularly stupid or weak-willed. In fact, on the basis of any psychological testing, they are remarkable similar to most of the population. However, they appear more concerned than 'normal' people over the lack of spiritual and family values in contemporary society. The demographic breakdown of people joining NRMs is dominated by single young adults aged 18-25, drawn from the upper half of the population economically and educationally. University campuses are a favourite recruiting ground.

Cults therefore seem to arise because of the ability of charismatic leaders to exploit the genuine concerns of those who are sane and intelligent, but perhaps alienated from the superficial values of modern society. Cults like Jim Jones' People's Temple were built on the debris of the sixties, on its frustrations and failures, argued Shiva Naipaul in 1980.[64]

It may be that Waco tells us something similar about the 1990s, that suicide happens when energies and resources become exhausted producing a crisis felt to be insoluble. What seems common to all mass suicides is a deep pessimism about the future, about adversaries and about life in general.

What is worrying about the 1990s is the prevalence of such pessimism. We have become cynical about the possibility of solutions to major problems such as homelessness, pollution and unemployment. This gloom seems to spring from our doubts about each other: we distrust our opponents and colleagues, we question their motives and their abilities to make a positive contribution. The end result is paranoia and despair all round, to which NRMs appear to many to be the only groups vigorously attempting to provide solutions.

Contrary to popular belief, cult leaders are entirely sane in the medical sense – they do not hear voices or genuinely believe they are God. What they suffer from is megalomania, self-centredness and the sophisticated ability to manipulate the vulnerable.

The first thing the charismatic leader does is set up a community isolated from the real world. His followers come to depend more and more on him for their basic material needs – food and shelter – so they become grateful to him and more willing to follow his orders. Their isolation from family and friends means they have no way of discussing the ideas they are exposed to with others, and so they never encounter an alternative viewpoint.

The leader then points to all the bad things in the outside world, rising crime, moral degeneracy, lack of spiritual values and paints his enclave as a haven from the emerging tide of social breakdown outside. He will then go on to elaborate an apocalyptic vision of the future outside the enclave – one which foresees the final breakdown of the world order – ready to be replaced by an elite, emerging from havens like his own, prepared to take over and run a better world. Subtly the promise of future rewards is thus woven into the prize for following the leader.

And if you come to believe in a soon to be future of armageddon, you are more likely to entertain violent measures as a way of life. If there may be no future for the whole world anyway, suicide becomes more rational.

Furthermore, like the Japanese kamikaze pilots, who were willing to die for their nation, the suppression of individuality and the encouragement of collectivism, makes dying for your group more legitimate. In a long siege situation, the sacrifices of the others builds obligations on to yourself to make similar responses. Thinking of yourself rather than the group becomes viewed as selfishness.

Jim Jones even prepared his followers for mass suicide by setting up several false suicides, where everyone was asked to drink poison, although they were then told the poison had not been real. He reminded them that they would have to do the real thing at some time. But this suicide rehearsal makes the actual act more likely, as it may be that when it comes to the actual event many do not believe that there really is going to be a suicidal act, because of all the false starts. The speed at which fire spread through the enclave at Waco suggests they were well prepared for such a combustion, and so the cult may have been subject to similar rehearsals – even being duped into thinking this was also not the real event.[65]

Because members are conditioned into seeing the cult as an ark for survival in an apocalyptic future, any attack on this will be seen as leaving no options for any cult member. So, those who threaten the ark will be met with severe violence. Finally if the ark is lost, suicide becomes the only rational response.

So cults depend for their existence and their constituents' obedience on a carefully constructed view of the outside world, whereby it is those on the outside who have been brainwashed into accepting an increasingly degenerate way of life. This topsy-turvy thinking leads gradually to an unbridgeable gap between the cult and everyone else, making negotiations in a siege situation, such as at Waco extremely difficult.

Perhaps most worrying of all about cults is that their basic features are endemic in most mainstream political, business and public bodies today, whether it is members placing their allegiance in a powerful leader in whom they impute great abilities to solve their problems, or members tending to surround themselves with others holding similar perspectives, or that contact with alternative viewpoints is discouraged.

This leads to the inevitable conclusion that cults succeed because they are merely exploiting to an extreme degree forces to which we are all already subject and vulnerable. From membership of childhood gangs to adult concerns about getting into 'the' tennis club, being a member of the right group is something we all have a weakness for. Because we all want to be different, and we all want to belong.

However, Freud's account of the religious outlook is vastly over-simplified. All religions which have survived for centuries with large numbers of adherents take a more sophisticated account of suffering than psychiatrists might realise. Indeed it is often said that suffering is an important cause of religion, since the promises held out by religion represent a way in which men can feel reassured in the face of catastrophe or death.[66] The possible decline in traditional religion may in part be explained as paralleling our lessened anxiety about death and reduced contact with it due to the longer lives we lead these days. Indeed as we get older and death seems closer, our interest in religions increases.

Yet even if our anxiety is no longer so much about facing death but confronting suffering, it may still be that any attempt to devise a viable long-term mental health strategy needs to draw on the lessons of the main religions of the world. You can see this if you inspect the response to suffering in Judaism, Christianity, Islam, Buddism and Hinduism.

While it is beyond the scope of this book to explore the different religions in detail, I will briefly summarise the main stance of each in relation to suffering.

In Judaism it was recognised that the righteous also suffer, which meant that a more positive view of the point of suffering was needed – the most common was that suffering is a test of faith. This appears in classic form in Abraham's willingness to sacrifice Issac (Genesis 22, 1-19) which shows how suffering can be made purposeful. If people retain their trust and confidence in God in the face of suffering, he will restore them to their land. But God also does not test a man more than he is able, or as Ishmael put it, according to a camel's strength, so is its load.[67]

A second vital theme in Judaism is that, as God has a central role in creation of the universe, any individual problem must be set in the far greater context of creation as a whole, and so the community as a whole. The individual is such a tiny part of the whole pattern that he cannot possibly comprehend the total design: '...where were you when I laid the earth's foundations? Tell me, since you are so well-informed! Who decided the dimensions of it, do you know? Or who stretched the measuring line across it?' Job 38, 4.

Given the enormity of God's plan, suffering should be put in perspective for if you do so his plan might them become apparent. This is the key to the Jewish response to suffering and persecution – 'he who gladly bears the sufferings that befall him brings salvation to the world'.[68]

Whereas, in Christianity the question of suffering is a problem principally because it conflicts with the assertion that God is love, in Islam the problem is that it conflicts with the belief that God is omnipotent. In both cases it begs the question, is the universe out of God's control? But if God is all-powerful, and if the universe is not out of control, then suffering must in some sense come from God. The Koran[69] puts it briefly – 'there is no kind of blow except by the leave of God'.

But the Koran has an explanation for why God may produce suffering – namely that suffering is a trial or test: 'Did you reckon that you would enter the garden without God knowing those of you who make an effort, and without knowing those who are patient?'.[70] Thus suffering becomes a necessary part of the purposes of God in that it helps to create a faithful disposition and also helps to discriminate the sincere from the insincere. What this means in effect is that suffering not only forms character, but it also exposes it. It reveals a man's true nature as only under pressure will a man reveal what he is really worth.

Faithfully accepted, suffering helps to produce an equal and balanced character and conversely fear of suffering is a mark of inadequate trust.

While Judaism, Christianity and Islam contain sophisticated responses to suffering, of all religions, Buddhism is the one which concentrates most immediately and directly on it.[71] The Buddha's insight in essence is found in the 'noble truths' concerning the existence of suffering – the causes of suffering – the cessation of suffering and the path that leads to the arrest of suffering. The first sermon of the Buddha at Benares[72] argues the noble truth of the halting of suffering is in essence this: it is the complete giving up of every thirst (craving), renouncing it, emancipating oneself from it, detaching oneself from it.

According to the Hindu Vedas suffering is the essence of the universe, since the universe is a chain of killing and being killed, of devouring and being devoured – 'the whole world is just food and the eater of food'.[73] Hence the central affirmation of the Upanishads about suffering is that to create duality or the possibility of not suffering is to create suffering. Suffering is a result of introducing duality into a non-dualistic situation. In other words suffering is all around us and so implicit in the very idea of existence. Existence is a unity, to break down that unity is to introduce tension and conflict and strife. It is the attempt to live without suffering which produces it. To regard the apparently different forms of the universe as being always and irreconcilably differentiated is to have only the most primitive and inadequate conception. True perception is to see the unity behind the manifest forms.[74] Those individuals who have an adequate grasp of this ultimate truth will find that suffering falls away in significance.

But besides helping us endure suffering, the major religions of the world may help mental health for other reasons. Religious beliefs can be seen as providing for certain key needs in human relationships. We all have a need for closeness to others, and meditation and prayer lead people to feel close to their particular deity, and so God remains a profound source of closeness.[75]

Furthermore, the adoring relationship is satisfying for a number of reasons. One is that being in the presence of someone who is imagined as mighty creates a sense of security. Just as a child is accustomed to having someone to look up to and rely upon, it is conceivable that religious belief is an expression of man's continuing need for an upwardly directed relationship.[76]

But the tension here is that psychiatrists and the non-religious observing the bizarre behaviour which periodically hits the headlines surrounding cults, and the injunctions of various religions over abortion, sex before marriage or homosexuality, find the religious outlook difficult to adopt, despite the mental health benefits of the religious account of suffering.

Without religion, hope in the face of terrible suffering is difficult to sustain, but hope is clearly essential for maintaining a positive mental health when we face adversity. Ironically, while psychiatrists and psychologists are suspicious of religious ideas and dismiss them as illusions, research into resilience finds that positive illusions over ourselves, our personal control and our futures is beneficial for our mental health.

One possible reconciliation is the notion that religion helps cope with suffering because it make a contribution towards what could be described as personal competencies or life skills which help positive mental health. It is not the religion in itself which helps (many religious people still become mentally unwell), but the way it bolsters the individual. For some people religion simply would not provide the succour it does for others. Whether you are religious or not, the kind of life skills we have discussed in this book will be equally helpful.

An important consequence of a religious outlook is the sustenance of hope even when things appear hopeless. As hope is vital to maintaining mental health, how you arrive at hope is less important than simply getting there. Perhaps one avenue for the non-religious is simply the knowledge that hope is an important ingredient in positive mental health and maybe the lesson of new religious movements is that as each generation faces what it believes are new causes for despair so it turns to new religions. Possibly in the modern secular world counselling is fast becoming a new religion. After all, the main thing it seems to offer is hope.

And just as religion is an investment of faith in an entity external to oneself to help, like a priest, a church or a God, so counselling is a belief in the power of the therapist to produce salvation. Like with religion, this involves a relationship with an authority figure which explains why so many people find it difficult to leave counselling. But, being able to cope without an authority figure is my model of positive mental health.[77]

However, at first glance, even within religions, those that appear to emphasise the authority of God appear to have lower suicide rates than those which do not. It was this finding which launched the whole subject of sociology around a century ago.

In his classic text, *Suicide*, Emile Durkheim, often considered the 'father of sociology', observed that Protestant areas of Europe during the nineteenth century experienced higher suicide rates than predominantly Catholic regions.[78] For Catholics, suicide is a much more serious sin than for Protestants, and perhaps what religion you follow may therefore determine partially whether suicide is an option you consider. But Durkheim discounted the role of differential church disapproval regarding suicide as explaining this finding. Instead he contrasted Protestant free enquiry with Catholic emphasis on unquestioning acceptance of beliefs and rituals – 'the Catholic accepts his faith ready made', whereas 'the Protestant is far more the author of his faith'. In other words Protestantism is a much more individualistic religion, while Catholicism emphasises belonging to a community.

Durkheim thus linked what appears the most individualistic of acts, suicide, with wider social forces. He argued that Catholicism has a tendency to promote integration of the individual into his society through ritual and community. In contrast he noted that Protestantism places less emphasis on unifying rituals, and typically affords far greater opportunity for theological individualism. According to Durkheim's view, since suicide is the final product of alienation and disaffection from those around you, different religions provide varying protection from suicide depending on how they promote shared values and strong social bonds.

But since Durkheim, the evidence in favour of sociology's supposed one law has been decidedly mixed and, marking the 100th anniversary of *Suicide*, a spate of recent research has sought to evaluate its current status. For example, one study found that high concentrations of Catholics in some areas are actually linked to increased suicide rates.[79] Data from the Netherlands gathered by the Netherlands Demographic Institute for the beginning of the twentieth century, and so roughly contemporaneous with Durkheim's original study, has recently come to light.[80] This suggests his observed Catholic–Protestant differential in suicide rates is explicable entirely in terms of the practice of categorising as sudden deaths, or deaths from ill-defined or unspecified causes, a large proportion of fatalities among Catholics which would have been categorised as suicides had they occurred among Protestants.

It seems there is a stronger tendency among Roman Catholics to conceal the fact that suicide is the cause of death, than among religious groups which do not punish suicide with religious sanctions. By pretending ignorance, or even blatantly telling the family doctor that the death was accidental, relatives try to avoid the scandal of having the deceased buried in unconsecrated soil. This is an understandable reaction among groups who seem to fear the judgement of the priest, neighbours and acquaintances even more than they fear the wrath of God. Even though this evidence might appear to disprove sociology's one law, it still shows the power of social forces to influence human action.

But Durkheim's basic idea, that religion is an important factor in suicide for sociological rather than religious reasons, stubbornly refused to die. Other research has found some faith groups, particularly Baptists, Catholics and Jews, exert protective effects on suicide in their regions of historical strength, but have aggravating effects in other parts of a country.[81] In other words being a Catholic where Catholicism is a minority religion seems to make suicide more likely.

This seemed to turn the issue into one not of the effect of a particular religion, but more of the mix of religions in a society. The very latest research published in 1998, by a group headed by Christopher Ellison at the University of Texas, has found a strong inverse association between religious homogeneity in a community – the extent to which community residents adhere to a single religion, or a small number of faiths – and its level of suicide.[82] In other words, the fewer the religions represented in your neighbourhood, the lower the suicide rate.

The finding has been explained by sociologists as religious homogeneity increasing the likelihood that social interaction with neighbours and co-workers, as well as unplanned contact with strangers, will occur among persons of similar rather than disparate faith backgrounds. Social bonds form most readily among persons who share beliefs, interests and activities; individuals who share faith commitments also tend to share other values and assumptions about morality, family, community affairs and so forth. Studies of who is found most supportive at times of stress emphasise that support attempts are most valuable when provider and recipient share customs over the language, practice and meaning of supportive conduct. It would seem that the less likely your neighbour is to subscribe to the same religious outlook as yourself, the less likely you are to feel bonded to him or able to find support from him. This might have an effect on alienation, as it would make you more likely to feel disaffected or alienated from your neighbourhood, and alienation has an effect on suicide.

Perhaps it was inevitable that sociology's one law would require tinkering with for it to withstand the passage of time, for religion no longer enjoys the cultural hegemony once forged between Roman Catholicism and the medieval state, or between the Anglican church and the Georgian British state. If anything we live in an increasingly religiously pluralistic society. Given the negative implications of this for a community's sense of integration, why should this process appear so inexorable in the latter half of the twentieth century, partly fuelled by the relentless rise of so many new religions, sects and cults?

In fact this effect, that religions would multiply even though this had a negative effect on a community's sense of togetherness, was predicted a full hundred years before Durkheim's *Suicide*, in a largely ignored chapter from another social science classic, Adam Smith's *The Wealth of Nations*. Smith argued that market forces constrain churches just as they do secular firms, and that the benefits of competition plus the burdens of monopoly are as real in religion as in any other sector of the economy. Smith believed self-interest motivates the clergy just as it does secular producers. In the past you were prohibited from following any religion other than that sanctioned by the state. In other words until quite recently state religions enjoyed a kind of monopoly over religious practices in most countries. Established churches, insulated from competitive pressures and the preferences of those they served, tended to provide suboptimal effort and so lower quality of service. The twentieth century has seen the equivalent of a deregulation of the religious market in the West, with religious freedom of expression enshrined in law.

Given that 'consumers' are now more than ever free to choose what religion they will participate in, a particular religion can flourish only if it provides a commodity that is at least as attractive as its competitors. According to economic theory, in times of monopoly of state religion there would be a poorer consumer take-up of religious services, compared to that when there is a freely competitive market place, where a wider variety of religions would compete to serve the different tastes of consumers. The theory has been supported from recent research from Santa Clara University in the USA. Laurence Iannaccone found in a study of seventeen developed Western countries that levels of religious belief and participation are lower in monopolised religious markets than in competitive ones.[83] Competition among doctrines encourages greater consumption of religious services as faiths compete to best satisfy consumer demand. This explains why the growth in numbers of religions is inevitable in an unregulated market.

Once societies liberalised the practice of religion, so that you were no longer constrained to having to follow the state religion in order, say, to get on with your career or to get married, a kind of free market naturally arose among religions, just as it does among companies. Just as a free market leads to more competition, so the unregulated market in religions leads to more competition amongst religious groups. In order to cater for the great variety of religious tastes, new and small 'companies' or religions naturally spring up to capture these 'markets'. Also because of this competition, religions work harder at providing religious services – perhaps they have a tendency to escalate their fervour – in order to capture the market of those looking for religion to play a greater part in their lives. In contrast more docile religions will also exist, as long as there is a market for those who want their religion provided in a 'quieter' form.

While for Adam Smith the advantage of the free market is a more efficient provision of religious services, it seems that for Durkheim the price of the freedom to choose your faith is inevitably a less strong sense of community. The more different we choose to be, the more we sacrifice the opportunity for closeness with our neighbours.

Perhaps another reason therefore we have poorer mental health in modern society is that our greater religious – as well as other lifestyle –

pluralism leaves us freer to exercise our individuality but also renders us feeling less connected to each other. While our greater freedom of individual expression is something worthwhile in terms of all sorts of benefits to us, there is a hidden cost to our mental health. I believe this simply means that a society where individuality is encouraged and conformity discouraged needs to work harder to maintain its mental health, and so needs to implement prevention strategies even more vigorously than one where conformity is encouraged.

Although I have used the word 'prevention' thoughout this book to refer to strategies anyone can adopt, the correct academic term is not in fact prevention – which, in its technical sense, means help targeted on the vulnerable or those at high risk – but health promotion.[84] I believe such mental health promotion is more powerful as a way of alleviating poor mental health than what is currently termed prevention.

This is because your sanity is not just a long-term benefit to you, but also a resource to others – both those who might turn to you for help now, as well as future generations. So, because of their recognised stability, the mentally healthy become focal points in their local social circle. Sane people also evolve into rational parents who produce lucid children, who will then grow up to perpetuate this positive cycle. So, it is vitally important to us all to become absorbed in positive mental health promotion – not just to reduce mental illness today and help those around us, but also to prevent it long into the future, so aiding the spread of sanity.

The mental health characteristics of competent parents include maintaining their own self-esteem and personal development; being there when needed; protecting children from harm; providing affection, emotional support, comfort, food, shelter and information; using their authority so they are in charge of their children; respecting their children's emotional status and judging it accurately; keeping adult business (sex, marital conflict etc) away from their children; setting reasonable limits of tolerance on their children's behaviour; establishing a moderate amount of justifiable household rules; having their own lives and not living through their children.[85] These all relate to themes already discussed in this book – self-control, personal goals, accurate appraisal of your environment, relationship building, mood management and problem-solving, amongst many others.

Indeed, my view of psychiatry is not that each mental illness should be viewed discretely from each other but that they all share certain themes. They are all exaggerations of the more normal mind, often as a result of poor coping with a difficult environment. So, instead of trying to prevent each mental illness seperately, we should aim to promote personal competencies which will reduce mental disorders across the board.[86]

Underlying all the arguments in this book has been the basic theme that the best approach for mental health is to invest your belief in yourself – that you *can* help yourself.

This is not an isolationist manifesto. I am not saying we do not need each other, but rather that poor mental health produces insecurity, fear and pessimism, all of which will shake your belief in yourself and will naturally lead you to turn to others for support.

There is nothing wrong with that, but do not let your poor mental health blind you as well to your greatest resource – yourself.

Just as being more physically fit makes it less likely we will develop a plethora of different discrete physical illness, so I argue by becoming generally more mentally healthy you are less likely to go down with individual mental illnesses.

The publication of the first edition of this book was greeted with a storm of controversy, in particular surrounding the central arguments I assert about the need for modern psychiatry to emphasise prevention rather than just treatment. That this should cause controversy at first appeared odd to me. Prevention has long been a central pillar of the practice of physical medicine, so why should it not be so of psychiatry? However, I now realise that many reviewers and mental health professionals have had principal difficulty grasping the fact that *Staying Sane* is about true prevention and not treatment because the idea is so new that anyone writing about mental health is still presumed to be writing (as everyone else still does) primarily about mental illness, and not genuinely about mental health. For example, even within the field, prevention programmes are still often perceived as targeted at young children already identified as exhibiting signs of psychiatric disorder.[87] This is laudable, but not the kind of genuine prevention I have been writing about in this book, which concerns well people and keeping them well.

Perhaps one reason it is difficult to get people to take prevention seriously is that it seems to many that anything that reduces our distress, from lowering unemployment rates to improved international relations, are steps towards the promotion of mental health. Therefore the subject appears too massive when examined cursorily from the outside.[88] I have tried to demonstrate that any attempt to improve our mental health by reducing our problems is doomed to failure – instead we have to increase the tools we have at our disposal for dealing with problems. Returning to the catchphrase I employed in the chapter 'How to be Happy', we don't need fewer problems, we need more solutions.

Criticism was levelled at the book as providing inadequate suggestions for the treatment of mental illness, and in particular serious psychiatric disorder. But as I have repeatedly stated throughout, this volume is not about treatment: if you are seriously disordered you will have to seek help elsewhere. I am writing for ordinary people, as well as clinicians and academics, who want to seriously investigate the science of how to prevent illness before it has ever started.

Perhaps one reason for the difficulty in accepting some of the ideas in this book is because they are radical. A world in which people actively attempt with effective strategies to prevent themselves developing psychological problems would look very different from ours, in often undreamed of ways.

Public policy too rarely considers personal mental health implications. For example, the USA's high homicide rate was in the news again because of the Jonesboro spree shooting by boys aged thirteen and eleven in March 1998. This was widely seen as another strong case for gun control.

Psychiatrists, however, have long been aware that America loses more people from suicide with guns (7.35 per 100,000 population) than from homicide (5.85 per 100,000 population).[89] If guns are not easily available, the suicidal resort to other methods, like overdoses, where you have longer during the act in which to change your mind as to whether you really want to kill yourself – longer than the time it takes for a bullet to travel down a barrel. Recent cross-national research (including the USA) published in the *European Journal of Psychiatry*[90] supported this by finding that in countries where guns are more available people switch to firearms from other 'safer' suicide methods.

But greater gun availability in a country is also correlated with higher homicide rates by other non-firearm methods. It seems gun accessibility affects the choice of methods chosen for suicide, but maybe not so much the selection of tools for homicide. Countries which have high homicide rates by guns, also have high murder rates where other methods are used. It may therefore be that gun availability is a reflection of general bloodthirstiness in a nation, rather than being a cause of it. The stronger argument for tighter gun control is that it will save more lives by reducing the suicide rate than it will via any impact on homicide rates. This is relevant to spree shootings, which are in fact usually a form of 'extended suicide' by the perpetrator – as in Dunblane, Scotland, where Thomas Hamilton shot a classroom full of schoolchildren before killing himself.

The reason I believe you hear less about suicide than homicide statistics is that most people probably fear being shot by another more than being shot by themselves, yet statistically speaking, in practically every Western nation (except interestingly the UK), you have more to fear from yourself when it comes to guns. The difference in the UK may be due to the relatively low penetration of guns into the general community compared to the criminal fraternity. This tendency to believe we have more to fear from others than ourselves is part of a widespread denial of the role of psychological problems in our own lives that I referred to earlier, and it is this which partly hinders the adoption of proper prevention strategies.

Until quite recently prevention and health promotion in psychiatry and primary mental health care were not even of interest to academics. This began to change with the publication of a book entitled *Preventing Mental Illness: Mental Health Promotion in Primary Care*, edited by Jenkins and Ustun and published in 1998.[91] The chapters are individual contributions from the first collaborative conference, held in 1995, between the British Department of Health, the World Health Organization, the Royal Institute of Public Health and Hygiene and the British Health Education Authority, on preventing mental illness.

While the book is to date clearly the most comprehensive academic evaluation of where the field stands at present, unfortunately basic conceptual confusion still persists in its pages (as elsewhere) about the difference between primary prevention, which necessarily targets those not yet ill, and the treatment of those already symptomatic.

For example, John Bowis, formerly the British minister with responsibility for mental health, introduces the book with the announcement of a mental health research initiative within the Department of Health's policy programme. For the first time, he claims, substantial funds have been ring-fenced specifically for work on 'mental health': £2.4 million over the next five years. But the seven priority themes in which the money will be invested include the management of challenging behaviour and how to detect minor mental illness. There is no mention of anything to do with real primary prevention. Yet again, the term mental health is really a disguise for talking about mental illness.

Perhaps because psychiatrists have only relatively recently, in terms of the long history of the profession, reached international agreement on definitions of mental illness, it will be some time before a similar coherent consensus on mental health arrives, as work in this area is only just developing. At the moment the working meaning of mental health still appears to be the absence of mental illness. This explains why so-called psychiatric prevention textbooks appear to discuss health promotion and primary prevention, but in the end merely return to focusing on mental illness. This perpetually locks the debate into addressing treatment and case detection but not proper primary prevention.

In fact the definitive literature in this area remains Jahoda's 1958 book *Current Concepts of Positive Mental Health*. How to properly define mental health, as the first step towards measuring it, while clearly central to research on health promotion, is still only briefly touched on by current academic psychiatric works. (I discussed this in detail in the chapter 'Am I Insane – or is it Everyone Else?')

A problem with prevention that receives little discussion in the field is that doctors' interventions may sometimes make the targeted group worse. For example, a recent primary prevention study from the Oxford University Department of Psychiatry found that educating healthy adolescent girls about eating disorders actually increased dietary restraint at six month follow-up in the intervention group, compared to the controls.[92] This effect could be explained as being because psychiatric illness usually has multifactorial aetiology: each individual suffers from the results of many factors in their circumstances combining to produce their disease. So prevention targeting one or a few risk factors is unlikely to be so successful. Indeed the high levels of co-morbidity (most have

437

more than one thing wrong with their mental health) amongst psychiatric patients suggests general mental health promotion is likely to be more effective than specific primary prevention targeted at preventing particular illnesses. Health promotion directs itself at common, global or non-specific factors, that play a role in many diseases.

So if you inform healthy young girls about eating disorders without also trying to improve their general mental health, for instance by helping them prevent depression and relationship problems, you may merely be educating them on how to take up eating disorders as a response to distress produced by other areas of their lives not working well. Proper prevention must therefore be holistic – we need to know how to maintain all areas of our psychology healthily, not just aim to prevent one or two specific diseases.

My theory is backed up by research into which prevention programmes are most effective in delinquency prevention. Strategies that specifically target the prevention of delinquent behaviour are less successful than those which take a more comprehensive view of what needs to change in the child's whole life to improve his or her general well-being.[93]

Even when successful primary prevention work on those yet to develop an illness is discussed in psychiatric textbooks and programmes, the models used are clumsily transplanted from an illness-management perspective. For example, a New York selective prevention intervention targeted a group of women pregnant for the first time and who were predicted to be at high-risk for infant health and development problems. This programme is praised by a contributor to Jenkins and Ustan's book as the gold standard in primary prevention. But the intervention involved nine nurse home visits during pregnancy, and continued visits until the child was two years of age. Although the measured outcomes included clear benefits to both physical and emotional well-being for the child as well as the mother, this prevention intervention did not look that different, from the health services standpoint, to what the treatment might have been for mothers with already developed infant health problems. If the nurse just saw ill people, effort would always be invested in those who definitely need it. But given that primary prevention often means you devote resources to those who would not have become ill, this approach necessarily meant some of this nurse's time was spent on people who wouldn't really benefit. The inappropriate employment of professionals is a central problem with most current prevention interventions, and may explain why clinicians often find prevention unrewarding work. Instead I advocate a self-help approach where the individual takes responsibility for improving their own health and so avoids possible contact with professionals.

These are issues pertinent not just to psychiatry but to medicine and public health in general. After all, the main contributions to improved public health this century have probably come not from medicine, but from economic growth, which financed better housing, sewage, working conditions and nutrition. Even the anti-smoking public health campaigns only began to have an impact when smoking became an issue embedded in wider culture – determining with whom you might share a flat or date.

Healthy behaviour cannot always be seen as a matter of individual choice: it is mainly shaped by socio-cultural realities. For example, urbanisation and modernisation have often been accompanied by increased rates of violence, alcohol and drug use. But my self-help approach suggests that, while we endeavour to change society, in the meantime we learn to adapt to whatever our environment throws at us.

Wider society seems, from the amount of time and space devoted to health in the media, very concerned indeed about health promotion, yet doctors constantly struggle to get pertinent information across. Perhaps this is partly because too much time is spent telling people what they should be doing, and not how they should be doing it: that is to say, we make the mistake of disseminating knowledge rather than skills. *Staying Sane* has instead attempted not only to inform about what needs to be done, but also to give guidance on how to achieve this.

This is not to deny the importance of getting mental health promotion and primary prevention on to the agenda of schools and workplaces. Ironically this means that just when attempts are being made to introduce prevention into the clinic, it is being ushered out again into wider society. But that is where it belongs – if it is to be effective. What this suggests is that doctors in general, and psychiatrists in particular, themselves have to emerge (blinking while their eyes adjust to the light) from their clinics, and become actively involved in the wider cultural life of our society. That is the important issue I have been hoping to encourage doctors to take up, and which they are only just beginning to tackle.

But while the evidence is that doctors have on average better physical health than the lay population, which certainly suggests physicians are following their own prevention advice (like not smoking), it seems that doctors in general, and psychiatrists in particular, often have worse mental health than the general public.[94, 95] Perhaps until we have some personal zeal for our own prevention advice, and demonstrate it to be effective, the public will be understandably reluctant to follow our lead. It seems that the profession itself needs educating on how to prevent psychological disorder. This may explain its scepticism over some of the prevention strategies I have been describing in this book.

Maybe the success of this book will be measured by the extent to which it is able to infect others with enthusiasm for prevention. But we can take the first major step forward in encouraging clinicians to engage in prevention by demonstrating that prevention of the serious illnesses psychiatrists treat even on in-patient units is definitely possible.

While it is currently certainly true that there is little definite evidence from medical research that any specific mental disorder can be prevented, there is now considerable information about certain risk factors which have been clearly identified. This book has attempted to be the first to explore comprehensively the scientifically proven risk factors for mental illness. When we attempt to prevent physical illness we act to reduce risk factors – so while the precise cause of cancer remains unknown, smoking is a clear risk factor and public health campaigns designed to help us give up smoking will reduce cancer rates. Preventive interventions rarely wait for complete scientific knowledge about causation and treatment. There is a distinction between knowing how to treat a disorder and knowing how to prevent it. An effective treatment is not always necessary for potent prevention. For example, treatments for AIDS and Fetal Alcohol Syndrome (the name of the disorder where a baby is born damaged by its mother's high alcohol intake) remain under active investigation. Yet successful prevention is already possible, by safer sex and getting women to give up or cut down alcohol while pregnant respectively. Although there isn't today satisfactory treatment of lung cancer, smoking cessation interventions have proved effective.[96]

Using this model found effective in the prevention of physical disorders, where precise causes of disorders and effective treatments often remain elusive, it seems sensible and appropriate to intervene to reduce those identified risk factors for mental illness, and also to enhance known protective factors for mental health in our lives.[97]

For example, some of the risk factors we have looked at for poor mental health include poor relationship quality and a proneness to irrational thinking. If you seek to reduce or eliminate these risk factors you will certainly reduce your chances of psychological problems like depression, even though the precise causes of these illnesses remain to be properly elucidated and treatments remain problematic.

Some physicians have argued in response to this volume that patients should receive their preventive health advice directly from their doctor, not from a book. Yet recent evidence suggests smokers get annoyed by repeated anti-smoking advice from their GPs, probably negatively affecting their doctor-patient relationship and so if anything reducing the impact of health prevention advice.[98] An examination of the success of anti-smoking campaigns suggests family doctors lecturing each patient about the dangers of smoking was not nearly as effective as when the anti-smoking sentiment started to become part of our everyday culture – large areas in restaurants, aircraft, trains and offices became designated non-smoking areas, and smokers risked public opprobrium whenever they lit up, making smoking a culturally sanctioned activity.

So it is clear to me that for prevention to really work in the arena of mental health, we have to take the issues beyond the narrow limits of the clinic and make them part of our everyday culture. Mental health issues have to be discussed in everyday conversation and be part of our newspaper columns and broadcast programmes for mental health promotion to really have an impact.

Doctors and academics are suspicious of attempts to popularise their subjects but the sober fact is individual doctors intervening in our lives have had less impact on the general health of the population than the activities of engineers, planners, farmers and economists who have improved our housing, clean water supply, standard of living, diet and waste disposal. Through the history of medicine the main improvements in our health have come from the activity of those who were not simply preoccupied with the treatment of disease. Even psychologists agree that their profession has in fact contributed little to helping people directly prevent future mental illness.[99]

It is as likely that the prevention of mental illness and enhancement of mental health in a population will come from the development of a new understanding of the biological mechanism of schizophrenia, as from changes in our lifestyle that reduce the risk factors for psychosis. A reason for the antagonism to the central message in this book from some clinicians may be, then, that mental health specialists find it uncomfortable to be reminded that doctors' interventions might be less effective in promoting the mental health of populations than making the issues in this volume a part of our popular culture.

Important though preventive intervention is, the risk to an individual of getting a disease must be weighed against the cost, risk and discomfort of the intervention. I have been careful to always suggest prevention strategies that are unlikely to be costly, or have unwelcome health side-effects or be painful.

Another issue to bear in mind is that universal prevention measures are those that are desirable for everybody in the eligible population. This contrasts with selective preventive measures for which the identification of those few whom the indicated preventive measure would benefit is the objective of screening programmes.[100] The measures I have suggested would be of positive benefit whoever takes them up.

Some will argue that for those who inherit a high genetic predisposition for mental illness, or who already have several risk factors loaded against them, it is naïve to suggest that these people's prognosis can be altered by prevention strategies. It is certainly true that heritability estimates for most mental disorders tend to be in the 30–60 per cent range, so the genetic component, although not overwhelming, is by no means trivial in psychological problems.[101] But while these statistics might put off those whose parents or siblings already have mental disorder from trying to reduce the risk in themselves, in fact heritability estimates are not particularly useful because they carry no information about the mechanisms involved in genetic risk. So while we know genetic factors play a role in alcohol dependence, depressive disorders, neurosis and temperamental characteristics amongst much else, we still don't know how the genes produce their effects. The implication of work investigating genetic risk mechanisms in other disorders like cardiovascular disease is that for most mental conditions we must move from thinking about a single cause of a disease (genetic or environmental) to considering the possible risk mechanisms. What this suggests is that if you already have a genetic predisposition for a mental disorder, it is even more important for you in particular to implement prevention strategies than it is for those suffering from lesser genetic risk.

For example, the recent identification of the gene encoding an enzyme crucial to heart functioning has led to the understanding that this is a risk factor for myocardial infarction, or heart attacks, in a specific subgroup of individuals.[102] The people missing this gene need to take more particular care over their cardiovascular health than those who have it. This will improve their prognosis.

Unlike physical illnesses, the diagnosis of mental disorders is still made on the basis of signs and symptoms of aberrant thoughts, words and behaviours. As yet there are no laboratory tests to diagnose these disorders. At the present state of our knowledge of the onset of mental disorders, there are few or no signs and symptoms that predict onset with certainty. Nevertheless precursor signs and symptoms can be helpful in identifying groups at much higher risk for onset than the general population: for instance, the two weeks of continuous absence of happiness we mentioned as one possible predictor of future clinical depression in the first chapter of this book, 'How to be Happy'.

It seems that in some people, experiencing two weeks or more of sad mood increases the risk 5.5 times of a first onset of major clinical depressive disorder during the next year compared to those who have not had this precursor symptom.[103] In the general population the one-year prevalence of a two-week period of sad mood is about 5 per cent[104] but clearly many will go through this risk factor but not develop full-blown clinical depression. As long as the preventive strategies they vigorously implement in response to the realisation they are at increased risk of major mental illness in themselves pose no risks, then a prevention approach makes perfect sense.

But any strategy which merely targets depression and doesn't also aim to improve general mental health is likely to be doomed to failure. Depressive disorders have a high rate of co-morbidity – that is, they are associated with a number of other serious mental disorders, in particular substance abuse, anxiety disorders and schizophrenia. They frequently accompany severe life stress such as divorce, job loss or bereavement. They are strongly associated with suicide, one of the leading causes of death: as mentioned earlier, more individuals in the United States die as a result of suicide than as a result of homicide.[105] The risk of suicide among depressed persons of all ages is thirty times higher than in the general population.[106] The cost of depression and and anxiety (including lost production) was estimated to be at least £5.6 billion a year in the UK in the 1980s.[107]

But is depression really preventable? Surely, one might ask, the kind of clinical depression which follows from a job loss or bereavement isn't?

Whereas negative life circumstances predispose to depression, the presence of close intimate supportive relationships appears to protect against it. However the nature of these relationships is complex. It seems that an early loss of a significant relationship while a child predisposes to future depression, but that is not a sufficient event. Researchers have shown[108] that adults who lost a parent in childhood and have become depressed not only have that risk factor but also have experienced a provoking agent in adulthood, like a stressful life event, and the absence of good social support. In studies of inner-city women in London who had lost a parent in childhood, researchers have demonstrated[109] that those who did not have a close confiding relationship in adulthood had unusually strong stressor-developed depression. Those who had lost a parent in childhood but had good relationships and no such stressors did not develop depression.

These studies also showed that the loss of care in childhood following loss of a mother is associated with mood disturbance in adulthood. Inadequate care in the childhood of a girl increases the risk of her early premarital pregnancy, which in turn increases the risk of marriage to an undependable partner. Marriage to such a man, in addition to being low in intimacy, increases the risk of serious life events like trouble with the law, threats of eviction and poverty, and hence the risk of depression. So it seems that a combination of events are required for women to develop depression, not just one.

This was proved by a famous study[110] of 303 women living in Islington, London, selected because although they were free of depression at the start of the research, they were thought to be at high risk for developing future mental health problems. Their risk factors included long-term life difficulties like being single parents. In the next year of the research, 130 of these women experienced a severe life event of the kind known to present a high risk for the precipitation of clinical depression. These events include a loss or rejection in important family or personal relationships, and failures or disappointments, like a job loss. Yet of these 130 women, only 29 actually became clinically depressed.

The researchers investigated what it was that protected the other 101 women from developing clinical depression despite experiencing such severe life events. They found that the crucial protective factor was the effectiveness of support in the form of another person in the stressed woman's life. This effective crisis support had three key characteristics: firstly the simple presence of someone close in whom the person at risk could confide about the severe event; secondly that the person gave active and ongoing emotional support; thirdly that the person did not make negative comments about the person seeking help during the period where they needed support.

Of the women who said they could confide in their male partners when first interviewed by researchers before the major life event, and who later confirmed that during their stressful time their partners were indeed supportive, only 4 per cent of these got depressed. But of those who said before the major life event they could not confide in their partners, and who confirmed that indeed they got no emotional support during their crisis, 26 per cent got depressed. Of the women who thought they would be supported by their partners, but when the crunch came, they were not – in other words these women experienced being let down by their partners – 37 per cent got depressed. Of the women who before the major life event declared they had no one to confide in and indeed during their crisis no one materialised to support them, 25 per cent of these became depressed.

This research suggests you are at particular risk for depression if you confide in someone at an earlier point but then do not receive emotional support when you most expect and need it, during an actual crisis. This means being let down by those you turn to for support when you most need them is highly predictive of the development of future depression.

It also shows clearly that serious clinical depression can be prevented because having a supportive and confiding relationship definitely protected many women from depression despite facing a major stress on top of ongoing life difficulties.

The study also illustrates an important aspect of positive mental health we first discussed in the chapter on relationships, 'Hell is Other People'. Often we do not select those with whom we forge significant relationships because of their ability to provide emotional succour at times of crisis. Yet if our mental health is a priority in our lives, then we should, as those who provide empathetic support at times of crisis are crucial to our future mental health.

This kind of work suggests that if you do indeed ensure you have emotionally supportive relationships in your life which you can rely on even when in crisis, you have reduced your chances of developing serious clinical depression between six- and ninefold.

Another serious set of psychiatric problems which are preventable are those often linked closely to depression, like alcoholism. Alcohol is involved in over 100,000 deaths annually in the United States from motor vehicle crashes, intentional injuries, suicides and the medical effects of alcohol dependence, and this plays a major role in numerous medical and social problems.[111] Motor vehicle crashes are the Western world's leading cause of injury deaths, and appproximately half of all crash fatalities are alcohol-related.[112] Motor vehicle accidents are the major cause of death in Britain in those aged under forty. Alcohol is estimated to be involved in approximately 30 per cent of all suicides and plays a particularly significant role in adolescent suicide and in suicide with the use of firearms; and it is highly associated with homicides.[113] Alcohol even reaches across generations by causing fetal alcohol syndrome, or damage to the babies of mothers who drink during pregnancy.

So preventing yourself developing alcohol problems is a major mental health preservation issue. We have talked already in the 'Me, Me, Me' chapter about how to break bad habits which are developing, like alcohol dependence. You should be constantly vigilant to the possibility your drinking is reaching a level where you could be vulnerable to alcohol dependence. One way of avoiding this is ensuring at least two to three days a week are completely alcohol free. Another useful indicator of alcohol problems is if you answer yes to any of these four questions: (1) Have you ever tried to cut down on your drinking? (2) Have you ever got annoyed because someone mentioned your drinking? (3) Have you ever had a drink in the morning? (4) Have you ever felt guilty about your drinking?

But it is not only alcohol one should be wary of in the attempt to preserve your mental health, but also drugs like cannabis, cocaine, amphetamines, heroin, ecstasy and LSD. Besides their dependency potential, psychotic or schizophrenia-like illnesses may be precipitated by heavy drug abuse, in particular with cannabis, amphetamines and hallucinogens (hallucination-inducing drugs) like ecstasy and LSD. By psychotic and schizophrenia I mean those mental illnesses characterised by a radical loss of grip on reality, so that you end up believing you are the next messiah or hear voices.

It is possible that individuals who develop psychotic illnesses with drugs had precursor symptoms of schizophrenia and were self-medicating with these drugs, which then led to an exacerbation of the symptoms and the acute onset of schizophrenia.[114] In other words they began to feel unwell but then tried cannabis as a 'treatment' for their disturbed mental state, which of course only makes things worse.

In the US patients with schizophrenia occupy over 30 per cent of the nation's mental hospital beds on any given day.[115] The treatment costs in the US alone exceed $7 billion annually, and indirect costs of, for example, social services, loss of productivity and premature mortality account for at least double that figure, making the financial burden of schizophrenia in the United States approximately equal to that of all cancers combined.[116]

Schizophrenia and psychotic illnesses like it appear to many to be the kind of mental illness which is too severe or problematic to treat. However it is an illogical error to deduce that just because an illness is serious this somehow makes its prevention more difficult than that of a milder disease. The analogy I would draw is one where if I leave a cigarette burning on my sofa eventually my house will burn down, but if I simply stub the cigarette out before putting it anywhere near the sofa I can prevent a cataclysm fairly simply. The point is it gets easier to prevent something the earlier you start your prevention strategy. Once my living room is on fire it gets more difficult to stop my whole house going up in flames. But when the fire is just at the cigarette-stub stage averting disaster is much easier. So prevention of psychiatric illness for many people appears difficult but that is partly because they are not imagining starting early enough.

Schizophrenia is difficult to prevent for the same reason most mental illnesses are, which is that they rarely occur as just single diseases in an individual. Instead research suggests over 90 per cent of schizophrenic patients have at least one other mental disorder at some time.[117] This reinforces the point I have made before that in order to prevent psychological problems effectively we probably have to enhance our overall mental health, not just one part of it.

But can we predict who is most likely to develop a psychotic illness, before it happens? The earlier we can see the predictors of psychosis in someone, the easier it might be to prevent that psychosis eventually occurring.

A study following up 2,000 students first assessed to be normal, over ten years, at the University of Wisconsin found that those most likely to develop a psychotic illness after ten years were those who a decade earlier scored high on scales measuring irrational thinking and poor relationship skills.[118] Remember the emphasis I placed on both these areas of life in the chapters on relationships and thinking? This research on the psychosis-prone individual would suggest that if irrational thinking and poor relationship skills could be reduced early enough, even psychotic illnesses might be preventable.

But what about disorders thought to be secondary to brain damage, like dementias? Dementia is the deterioration in memory produced by the kind of brain shrinkage which occurs with advancing age. Surely, many argue, dementia is not preventable?

Well, a history of head trauma is a risk factor for Alzheimer's dementia in several studies.[119] A clinical syndrome called *Dementia Pugilistica*, which has long been described in the clinical literature,[120] in which brain degenerative changes are distributed more widely than in Alzheimer's dementia; it is most likely to occur among those who sustain repeated closed head injuries, especially boxers. Dementia typically begins several years after exposure to trauma and it is most common among those who also have a history of vascular disease (atherosclerosis), alcoholism or a low IQ.[121] All these other risk factors heighten vulnerability to the effects of brain damage.

So if you want to minimise your chances of dementia later in life, ensure your alcohol use is low and take care to avoid banging your head. Head trauma can be reduced by use of seat belts and air bags in automobiles, wearing helmets while riding motorcycles or bicycles and reducing exposure to events likely to result in trauma such as boxing.

An even weaker association was found between Alzheimer's dementia and maternal age at time of birth, with the prevalence of Alzheimer's dementia increased among those born to either unusually young or unusually old mothers.[122]

Several studies have shown a higher prevalence of dementia among those with less education.[123] If schooling has the effect of increasing synaptic density (the number of connections between brain cells) in some brain regions and if it is indeed loss of cells in these regions that predisposes to clinical dementia, then the epidemological and biological data could be integrated into a plausible theory.

The effect of education would not be to alter the underlying biological cause of cell loss, but rather to delay its clinically detectable effects so that dementia does not ensue for an additional five or so years. In other words, you may not be able to stop losing brain cell connections if that is part of the inevitable process of old age, but having more connections in the first place means you can afford to lose a lot more, before the effects of dementia become apparent.

But there may be a more controversial way of preventing dementia than simply trying to keep pursuing education all your life, and not just while you are at school. Recent research has found that those who smoked more were less likely to have Alzheimer's dementia[124] This has some biological plausibility because nicotine is an active agent in tobacco products which binds to the acetylcholine receptors whose loss on nerve cells is associated with Alzheimer's dementia. It is thus not unreasonable to postulate that smoking might delay the onset of dementia symptoms. For example, one study from the Netherlands found that when two or more family members developed Alzheimer's dementia, one of whom smoked and the others not, the onset was later for the smokers.

This does not suggest that smoking all your life protects you from Alzheimer's dementia, as the long-term damage of smoking is such that it is more likely to lead to reduced blood and oxygen perfusion of the brain,[125] which is another cause of dementia. However, what it does suggest, perhaps controversially, and one should await further evidence, is that taking up smoking in advanced old age might contribute a protective effect against the development of dementia.

There is also evidence that family size and child timing protects the mental health of offspring. Smaller family structure, that is not more than four children in the family, and spacing of more than two years between siblings has been found to be protective.[126] In early childhood, having a close relationship with a parent who is responsive and accepting is very important. For older children, supportive parents, good sibling relationships and adequate rule-setting by parents have been found to be protective. A supportive relationship with one parent was found to provide a substantial protective effect for children living in severely discordant unhappy homes.[127]

The tendency of poor mental health to be passed on through generations even without genetic mechanisms emphasises the importance of preventive strategies. For instance, about 10 per cent of post-partum women develop a depressive disorder severe enough that it interferes with daily functioning,[128] and these problems are eventually reflected in the mother-infant relationship. In one study the infants of depressed mothers received less appropriate and responsive attention and more negative and rejecting care than the comparison group at two months.[129] The impact of maternal depression on the infants' development can be seen quite early. These infants can develop a 'depressed mood style' as early as three months and this mood state lasts over the first year of life if the mother's depression persists.[130] By the end of the first year this mood has influenced physical growth and more general infant development.

There is also some evidence that by eleven to seventeen months of age infants of depressed mothers exhibit reduced activity in the right frontal area of the brain.[131] This finding raises the possibility that maternal behaviour can influence not only an infant's developing psychosocial areas of functioning, but also the development of the central nervous system.

So we can see how poor mental health becomes easily promulgated through generations once it is generated. Preventive strategies to promote mental health are therefore important not just for ourselves but also for our children.

One of the crucial aspects of the mind, often reflected in trying to understand mental illness is its essential continuity. Your mind even when angry or upset is in a real sense continuous with that same mind when calm or happy. Your mind also shares some essential continuity with the minds of others, otherwise we would not be able to understand or empathise with each other. Your mind also has some continuity with your mind as it was as a child, years ago. Given this, your mind's ability to embrace change and yet remain intact remains, to my view, its most remarkable feature, and the key to its resilience.

You may wonder how I can be so confident about everyone's ability to help themselves stay sane, given that my job ensures I encounter daily a fair degree of what is widely regarded as the most profound insanity.

Yet it is my patients who have given me most cause for faith in the human predicament. I have seen people face the most extraordinary hardships yet emerge, often after severe psychological distress, with a return to sanity. In my experience healing is the consequence of mental illness – no matter how severe – not persistent despair.

Seeing my patients have the gift to recover from insanity gave me the conviction they also have the strength to prevent it.

But this feature is not accidental. We have evolved over millions of years through the process of natural selection and the survival of the fittest to have the characteristics we display now, precisely because these features aid survival. Over millions of years we have taken what nature has to throw at us, via epidemics, hurricane and famine, and survived. Certainly some did not make it – so their genes did not get passed on to future generations. Indeed, the DNA you have now remained in the gene pool because these were the tougher genes. We are therefore designed and built to be survival machines. You are one of those survival machines. You have the power to cope with life and to keep in optimum shape mentally.

I hope I have helped you to understand how positive mental health works, and given you some skills to keep psychologically fit. Use them – and help yourself stay sane.

Given you are a survival machine, I have every confidence you will.

451

Introduction

1. K. Hawton (1994) 'Suicide'. In E.S. Paykel and R. Jenkins (1994) *Prevention in Psychiatry* (Gaskell, Royal College of Psychiatrists, London).
2. Ibid.
3. J. Scott and E.S. Paykel (1994) 'Affective disorders'. In E.S. Paykel and R. Jenkins (1994) *Prevention in Psychiatry* (Gaskell, Royal College of Psychiatrists, London).
4. B.A. Rorsman, A. Grasbeck and P. Hagnell (1990) 'A prospective study of first-incidence depression. The Lundby Study 1957–1972. *British Journal of Psychiatry*, 156, 336–42.
5. T. Davies (1997) 'ABC of mental health', *British Medical Journal*, 314, 24 May 1997, 1536–9.
6. R.C. Kessler, K.A. McGonagle, Zhao Shanyang, C.B. Nelson, M. Hughes, S. Eshleman, H. Wittchen, K. Kendler (1994) 'Lifetime and 12 month prevalence of DSMIIIR psychiatric disorders in the United States', *Archives of General Psychiatry*, 51, Jan 1994, 8–19.
7. Davies, 'ABC of mental health'.
8. Ibid.
9. Ibid.
10. Ibid.
11. Kessler et al., 'Lifetime and 12 month prevalence'.
12. Ibid.
13. World Bank. World Development Report (1995): Investing in health. (Oxford University Press, New York).
14. R. Doll (1983) 'Prospects for prevention', *British Medical Journal*, 286, 445–53.
15. E.S. Paykel and R. Jenkins (1994) *Prevention in Psychiatry* (Gaskell, Royal College of Psychiatrists, London).
16. F. Post (1994) 'Creativity and psychopathology: a study of 291 world-famous men', *British Journal of Psychiatry*, 165, 22–34.
17. N.C. Andreasen (1987) 'Creativity and mental illness: prevalence rates in writers and their first-degree relatives', *American Journal of Psychiatry*, 144, 1288–96.
18. K.R. Jamison (1989) 'Mood disorders and patterns of creativity in British writers and artists', *Psychiatry*, 32, 125–34.
19. H.J. Eysenck (1983) 'The roots of creativity: cognitive ability or personality trait?', *Roeper Review*, (May) 10–12.
20. F. Post (1996) 'Verbal creativity, depression and alcoholism. An investigation of 100 American and British writers', *British Journal of Psychiatry*, 545–55, Vol 168.
21. Andreasen 'Creativity and mental illness'.
22. J.D. Mayer and P. Salovey (1993) 'The intelligence of emotional intelligence', *Intelligence*, 17, 433–42.
23. J.D. Mayer, P. Salovey, S. Gomberg-Kaufman and K. Blainey (1991) 'A broader conception of mood experience', *Journal of Personality and Social Psychology*, 60, 1, 100–11.
24. M.E. Ford, and M.S. Tisak (1983) 'A further search for social intelligence', *Journal of Educational Psychology*, 75, 2, 196–206.
25. D.P. Keating.(1978) 'A search for social intelligence', *Journal of Educational Psychology*, 70, 2, 218–23.
26. H.G. Gough (1966) 'Appraisal of social maturity by means of the CPI', *Journal of Abnormal Psychology*, 71, 3, 189–95.
27. P. Warr, J. Barter and G. Brownbridge (1983) 'On the independence of positive and negative affect', *Journal of Personality and Social Psychology*, 44, 644–51.
28. Ibid.
29. M. Eysenck (1994) *Happiness: Facts and Myths* (Lawrence Erlbaum Associates Ltd, East Sussex, UK).
30. M. Argyle (1986) *The Psychology of Happiness* (Methuen and Co. Ltd, London and New York).
31. D. Goldberg (1996) 'A dimensional model for common mental disorders', *British Journal of Psychiatry*, 168 (suppl), 44–9.
32. C. Dowrick (1996) Medicine and books section. 'Book review – The prevention of mental illness in primary care', *British Medical Journal*, 313, 24, 501.
33. L. Schlessinger (1996) *How could you do that?* (Harper Collins, New York).
34. M. Gagnon, J.F. Dartigues, L. Latenneur and P.G. Barberger (1990) 'Identification des facteurs de risque de la maladie d'Alzheimer. Resultats preliminaires de Programme de Recherche PAQUID' (Risk factors in Alzheimer's disease. Results of an epidemiological study in the area of Bordeaux, France), *Psychologie Medicale*, 22, 12, 1248–51.
35. Ibid.
36. J.L. Eaves, H.J. Eysenck and N.G. Martin (1988) *Genes Culture and Personality: An Empirical Approach* (Academic Press, New York).
37. T.J. Boutchard, D.T. Lykken, M. McGue, N.L. Segal and A. Tellegen (1990) 'Sources of human psychological differences: the Minnesota study of twins reared apart', *Science*, 250, 223–8.
38. K.S. Kendler, R.C. Kessler, E.E. Walters, C. MacLean, M.C. Neale, A.C. Heath amd L.J. Eaves (1995) 'Stressful Life events, genetic liability and onset of an episode of major depression in women', *American Journal of Psychiatry*, 152, 833–42.
39. D.R. Hannay (1979) *The Symptom Iceberg* (Routelege and Kegan Paul, London and Boston).

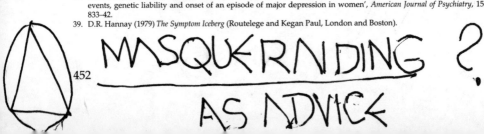

40. R.E. Thayer (1970) 'Activation states as assessed by verbal report and four psychophysiological measures', *Psychophysiology*, 7, 86–94.
41. D. Payne (1998) 'Male suicide rate rises as Irish Troubles cease', *British Medical Journal*, 316, 20 June, 1850.
42. D. Lester (1996) 'Gun ownership and rates of homicide and suicide', *European Journal of Psychiatry*, Vol 10, No. 2, 83–5.
43. M. Taylor, and H. Ryan (1988) 'Fanaticism, political suicide and terrorism', *Terrorism*, 11, 91–111.
44. T. Foster, K. Gillespie, and R. McClelland (1997) 'Mental disorders and suicide in Nothern Ireland', *British Journal of Psychiatry*, 170, 453–5.
45. Ibid.
46. D. Lester (1994) 'Suicide rates before, during and after the world wars', *European Psychiatry*, 9, 262–4.
47. D. Lester (1991) 'The association between involvement in war and rates of suicide and homicide,' *The Journal of Social Psychology*, 131, 6, 893–5.
48. D. Lester (1994) 'Involvement in war and suicide rates in Great Britain, 1901–65', *Psychological Reports*, 75, 1154.
49. D. Lester and B. Yang (1992) 'The influence of war on suicide rates', *The Journal of Social Psychology*, 132, 1, 135–7.
50. D. Lester (1994) 'Suicide rates before, during and after the world wars', op. cit.
51. J.R. Marshall (1981) 'Political integration and the effect of war on suicide: United States, 1933–76', *Social Forces*, 59, 3, 771–85.
52. P. O'Malley (1975) 'Suicide and war', *British Journal of Criminology*, 15, 4, 348–59.
53. D.J. Somasundaram and S. Rajadurai (1995) 'War and suicide in northern Sri Lanka', *Acta Psychiatrica Scand*, 91, 1–4.
54. D. Lester (1970) 'Suicidal behaviour and external constraints', *Psychological Reports*, 27, 777–8.
55. D. Lester (1972) 'Suicide after restoration of sight', *Journal of the American Medical Association*, 219, 6, 757.
56. B. Yang, and D. Lester (1997) 'War and rates of personal violence', *The Journal of Social Psychology*, 137, 1, 131–2.

1 How to be Happy

1. W.M. Rahn, R. Kroeger, and C.M. Kite (1996) 'A framework for the study of public mood', *Political Psychology*, 17, 1.
2. G.L. Klerman and M.M. Weissman (1989) 'Increasing rates of depression', *Journal of the American Medical Association*, 261, 15, 2229–35.
3. P.M. Lewinsohn, P. Rohde, J.R. Seeley and S.A. Fischer (1993) 'Age-cohort changes in the lifetime occurrence of depression and other mental disorders', *Journal of Abnormal Psychology*, 102, 1, 110–20.
4. J.J. Schwab, R.A. Bell, G.J. Warheit and R.B. Schwab (1979) *Social Order and Mental Health* (Brunner/Mazel, New York).
5. K.C. Burke, J.D. Burke, D.S. Rae and D.A. Regier (1991) 'Comparing age at onset of major depression and other psychiatric disorders by birth cohorts in five US community populations', *Archives of General Psychiatry*, 44, 727–735.
6. N.M. Weissman, M.L. Bruce, P.J. Leaf *et al* (1991) 'Affective Disorders'. In L.N. Robbins and D.A. Regier (eds), *Psychiatric Disorders in America: the Epidemiologic Catchment Area Study* (Free Press, New York).
7. G.L. Klerman (1988) 'The current age of youthful melancholia: evidence for increase in depression among adolescents and young adults', *British Journal of Psychiatry*, 152, 4–14.
8. P.M. Lewinsohn, P. Rohde, J.R. Seeley and S.A. Fischer (1993) op. cit.
9. Ibid.
10. Cross-national Collaborative Group (1992) 'The changing rate of major depression', *Journal of the American Medical Association*, 268, 21, 3098–3105.
11. O. Hagnell, J. Lanke, B. Rorsman and L. Ojesjo (1989) 'Are we entering an age of melancholy? Depressive illness in a prospective epidemiologic study over 25 years: the Lundby study, Sweden', *Psychological Medicine*, 12, 279–89.
12. B.L. Neugarten (1975) 'Adult personality: toward a psychology of the life cycle'. In W.C. Sze (ed), *Human Life Cycle* (James Aronson, New York).
13. L.N. Robins, J. Tipp and T. Przybeck (1991) 'An overview of psychiatric disorders in America'. In L.N. Robins and D.A. Regier (eds) *Psychiatric Disorders in America: the Epidemiologic Catchment Area Study* (Free Press, New York), 328–66.
14. N.M. Weissman, M.L. Bruce, P.J. Leaf *et al* (1991) op. cit.
15. G.A. Carlson, C.L. Rich, P. Grayson, and R.C. Fowler (1991) 'Secular trends in psychiatric diagnoses of suicide victims', *Journal of Affective Disorders*, 21, 127–32.
16. K.C. Lee, Y.S. Kovak and H. Rhee (1987) 'The national epidemiological study of mental disorders in Korea', *Journal of Korean Medical Science*, 2, 19–34.
17. G.J. Canino, H.R. Bird, P.E. Shrout and M. Bravo (1987) 'The prevalence of specific psychiatric disorders in Puerto Rico', *Archives of General Psychiatry*, 44, 727–735.
18. G.L. Klerman and M.M. Weissman (1989) op. cit.
19. O. Hagnell, J. Lanke, B. Rorsman and L. Ojesjo (1989) op. cit.
20. G.L. Klerman (1988) op. cit.
21. P.M. Lewinsohn, P. Rohde, J.R. Seeley and S.A. Fischer (1993) op. cit.
22. G.L. Klerman, P. Lavori, J. Rice, T. Reich, J. Endicott, N.C. Andreasen, M.B. Keller and R.M.A. Hirschfield (1985) 'Birth cohort trends in rates of major depressive disorder among relatives of patients with affective disorder', *Archives of General Psychiatry*, 42, 689–695.
23. P. Lavori, G.L. Klerman, M. Keller, T. Reich, J. Rice and J. Endicott (1987) 'Age period cohort analyses of secular trends in onset of major depression: findings in siblings of patients with major affective disorder', *Journal of Psychiatric Research*, 21, 23–35.
24. L.N. Robins, J. Tipp and T. Przybeck (1991) op. cit.
25. P.M. Lewinsohn, P. Rohde, J.R. Seeley and S.A. Fischer (1993) op. cit.
26. D.D. Ryan, D.E. Williamson, S. Iyengar, H. Orvaschel, T. Reich, R.E. Dahl and J. Puig-Antich (1992) 'A secular increase in child and adolescent onset affective disorder', *Journal of the American Academy of Child and Adolescent Psychiatry*, 1992, 31, 4: 600–5.
27. E.S. Gershon, J.H. Hamovit, J.J. Guroff, J.I. Nurnberger (1987) 'Birth cohort changes in manic and depressive disorders in relatives of bipolar and schizoaffective affective disorders', *Archives of General Psychiatry*, 44, 314–19.
28. N. Sartorius, J.A. Nielsen and E. Stromgren (1989) 'Changes in frequency of mental disorder over time: results of repeated surveys of mental disorders in the general population', *Acta Psychiatrica Scandinavica*, 79, 248, 5–6.
29. G.L. Klerman (1988) op. cit.

30. Ibid.
31. P.M. Lewinsohn, P. Rohde, J.R. Seeley and S.A. Fischer (1993) op. cit.
32. D.D. Ryan, D.E. Williamson, S. Iyengar, H. Orvaschel, T. Reich, R.E. Dahl and J. Puig-Antich, (1992) op. cit.
33. M. Rutter, and D. J. Smith (1995) 'Towards causal explanations of time trends in psychosocial disorders of young people'. In Michael Rutter and David Smith (eds), *Psychosocial Disorders in Young People: Time Trends and Causes* (John Wiley and Sons, Chichester).
34. Ibid.
35. M. Jahoda (1979) 'The impact of unemployment in the 1930s and the 1970s', *Bulletin of the British Psychological Society*, 32, 309–14.
36. E. Fombonne (1995) 'Depressive disorders: time trends and possible explanatory mechanisms'. In Michael Rutter, and David Smith (eds) *Psychosocial Disorders in Young People: Time Trends and Causes* (John Wiley and Sons, Chichester).
37. R.A. Easterlin (1980) *Birth and Fortune* (Basic Books, New York).
38. L. Srole and A.K. Fischer (1980) 'The midtown Manhattan longitudinal study vs the mental paradise lost doctrine', *Archives of General Psychiatry*, 37, 209–21.
39. J. Bowlby (1973) *Attachment and Loss, Vol 2, Separation: Anxiety and Anger* (Hogarth Press and the Institute of Psychoanalysis, London).
40. M. Rutter and D. J. Smith (1995) op. cit.
41. J.S. Price, and L. Sloman (1987) 'Depression as yielding behaviour: an animal model based upon Schjelderup-Ebbe's pecking order', *Ethology and Sociobiology*, 8, 85–98
42. P. Gilbert (1992) *Depression: the Evolution of Powerlessness* (Lawrence Erlbaum Associates, Hove and London; Hillsdale, NJ).
43. N. Allen (1995) 'Towards a computational theory of depression', *ASCAP: Newsletter of the Society for Sociophysiological Integration*, 8, 7, 3–12.
44. M.E.P Seligman (1975) *Helplessness: On Depression Development and Death* (W.H. Freeman, San Francisco).
45. E. Fombonne (1995) op. cit.
46. W. Rodgers (1982) 'Trends in reported happiness within demographically defined subgroups, 1957–78', *Social Forces*, 60, 826–42.
47. R. Veenhoven (1991), op. cit.
48. B. Headey and A. Wearing (1988) 'The sense of relative superiority – central to well-being', *Social Indicators Research*, 20, 1988, 497–516.
49. R. Veenhoven (1984) *Conditions of Happiness* (University of Rotterdam, Netherlands).
50. Ibid.
51. Ibid.
52. Ibid.
53. R. Veenhoven (1991) 'Questions on happiness: classical topics, modern answers, blind spots'. In F. Strack, M. Argyle and N. Schwartz (eds) *Subjective Well-Being: an Interdisciplinary Perspective* (Pergamon Press, Oxford).
54. B. Headey, and A. Wearing (1988) op. cit.
55. L.B. Alloy and L.Y. Abramson (1979) 'Judgment of contingency in depressed and non-depressed students: sadder but wiser?' *Journal of Experimental Psychology*: General 108, 441–85.
56. W. Glatzer and W. Zapf (1984) *Lebensqualität in der Bundesrepublik: Objektive Lebensbedingungen und subjektives Wohlbefinden* (Campus Verlag, Frankfurt).
57. F. Fujita, E. Diener and E. Sandvik (1991) 'Gender differences in negative affect and well-being: the case for emotional intensity', *Journal of Personality and Social Psychology*, 61, 3, 427–34.
58. R. Veenhoven (1984) op. cit.
59. R. Veenhoven (1984) op. cit.
60. S.C. Bhatia, M.H. Khan, R.P. Mediratta and A. Sharma (1987) *The International Journal of Social Psychiatry*, 33, 3, 226–36.
61. K. Oatley and E. Duncan 'Incidents of emotion in daily life'. In K.T. Strongman (ed) *International Review of Studies on Emotion, Vol. 2* (John Wiley and Sons, Chichester).
62. N.M. Bradburn (1969) *The Structure of Psychological Well-being* (Aldine Publishing, Chicago).
63. M.S. Goerge, T.A. Ketter, P.I. Parekh, B. Horwitz, P. Herscovitch and R.M. Post (1995) 'Brain activity during transient sadness and happiness in healthy women', *American Journal of Psychiatry*, 152, 341–51.
64. E. Diener and R.A. Emmons (1984) 'The independence of positive and negative affect', *Journal of Personality and Social Psychology*, 47, 1105–1117.
65. N.M. Bradburn and D. Caplovitz (eds) (1969) *Reports on Happiness* (Aldine Publishing, Chicago).
66. R.A. Emmons and E. Diener 'Personality correlates of subjective well-being', *Personality and Social Psychology Bulletin*, 1985, 11, 89–97.
67. S.D. Harding (1982) 'Psychological well-being in Great Britain: an evaluation of the Bradburn Affect Balance Scale,' *Personality and Individual Differences*, 3, 167–75.
68. G. Perry and P. Warr (1980) 'The measurement of mothers' work attitudes', *Journal of Occupational Psychology*, 1980, 53, 245–252.
69. P.B. Warr (1978) 'A study of psychological well-being', *British Journal of Psychology*, 69, 111–21.
70. D. Watson and A. Tellegen (1985) 'Toward a consensual structure of mood', *Psychological Bulletin*, 98, 2, 219–35.
71. R.J. Wheeler (1991) 'The theoretical and empirical structure of general well-being', *Social Indicators Research*, 24, 71–9.
72. D.P. Green, S.L. Goldman and P. Salovey (1993) 'Measurement error masks bipolarity in affect ratings', *Journal of Personality and Social Psychology*, 64, 1029–41.
73. E. Diener and R.A. Emmons (1984) op. cit.
74. E. Diener, R.J. Larsen, S. Levine and R.A. Emmons (1985) 'Intensity and Frequency: dimensions underlying positive and negative affect', *Journal of Personality and Social Psychology*, 48, 5, 1253–65.
75. S. Epstein (1983) 'A research paradigm for the study of personality and emotions'. In H. Howe and R. Dienstbier (eds) *Nebraska Symposium on Motivation: 1982* (Nebraska University Press, Lincoln) 91–154.
76. R. J. Larsen and E. Diener (1987) 'Affect intensity as an individual difference characteristic: a review', *Journal of Research in Personality*, 21, 1–39.

77. E. Diener, R.J. Larsen, S. Levine and R.A. Emmons (1985) op. cit.
78. R. J. Larsen and E. Diener (1987) op. cit.
79. M. J. Stones and A. Kozma (1994) 'The relationships of affect intensity to happiness', *Social Indicators Research*, 31, 159–73, 1994.
80. E. Diener, R.J. Larsen, S. Levine and R.A. Emmons (1985) op. cit.
81. R.J. Larsen, E. Diener and R.S. Cropanzano (1987) 'Cognitive operations associated with individual differences in affect intensity,' *Journal of Personality and Social Psychology*, 53, 4, 767–74.
82. M. Martin and D.M. Clark (1985) 'Cognitive mediation of depressed mood and neuroticism', *IRCS Medical Science*, 13, 252–3.
83. M. Martin, M. Argyle and J. Crossland (1988) 'On the measurement of happiness', *The Psychologist*, 1, 8, 33.
84. A.T. Beck (1976) *Cognitive Therapy and the Emotional Disorders* (International Universities Press, New York).
85. Ibid.
86. R. J. Larsen and E. Diener (1987) op. cit.
87. Ibid.
88. F. Fujita, E. Diener and E. Sandvik (1991) op. cit.
89. S. Nolen-Hoeksema (1987) 'Sex differences in unipolar depression: evidence and theory', *Psychological Bulletin*, 101, 259–82.
90. R.J. Larsen, E. Diener and R.S. Cropanzano (1987) op. cit.
91. E. Diener, E. Sandvik and W. Pavot (1990) 'Happiness is the frequency, not the intensity, of positive versus negative affect'. In F. Strack, M. Argyle and N. Schwarz (eds), *Subjective Well-Being: an Interdisciplinary Perspective* (Pergamon Press, Oxford), 119–36.
92. Ibid.
93. Ibid.
94. S. Freud (1930) *Civilization and its Discontents* (Hogarth Press, London).
95. C.R. Rogers (1961) *On Becoming a Person* (Houghton Mifflin, Boston).
96. E. Diener, R.J. Larsen, S. Levine and R.A. Emmons (1985) op. cit.
97. P.W. Linville (1982) 'Affective consequences of complexity regarding the self and others'. In M. Clark and S. Fiske (eds) *Affect and Cognition: Seventeenth Annual Symposium of Cognition* (Erlbaum, Hillsdale, NJ), 79–109.
98. M. Argyle (1987) *The Psychology of Happiness* (Methuen, London).
99. E. Diener, E. Sandvik and R.J. Larsen (1985) 'Age and sex effects for emotional intensity', *Developmental Psychology*, 1985, 21, 542–46.
100. M. Csikszentimihalyi and R. Larsen (1984) *Being Adolescent: Conflict and Growth in the Teenage Years* (Basic Books, New York).
101. P.M. Lewinsohn, J.E. Redner and J.R. Seeley (1991) 'The relationship between life satisfaction and psychosical variables: new perspectives'. In F. Strack, M. Argyle and N. Schwartz (eds), *Subjective Well-Being: an Interdisciplinary Perspective* (Pergamon Press, Oxford).
102. Ibid.
103. A. Dryman and W.W. Eaton (1991) 'Affective symptoms associated with the onset of major depression in the community: findings from the US National Institute of Mental Health Epidemiologic Catchment Area Program', *Acta Psychiatrica Scandinavica* 84, 1, 1–5.
104. W.W. Eaton, M. Badawi and B. Melton (1993) 'Prodromes and precursors for four DIS/DSM-III disorders: epidemiologic data for prevention of disorders with slow onset', unpublished manuscript.
105. D. Watson and L.A. Clark (1988) 'Positive and negative affectivity and their relation to anxiety and depressive disorders', *Journal of Abnormal Psychology*, 97, 3, 346–53.
106. Ibid.
107. R. Veenhoven (1988) 'The utility of happiness', *Social Indicators Research*, 20, 333–54.
108. R.A. Easterlin (1974) 'Does economic growth improve the human lot? Some empirical evidence'. In P.A. David and W.R. Melvin (eds) *Nations and Households in Economic Growth* (Stanford University Press, Palo Alto, CA), 98–125.
109. R. Veenhoven (1991) 'Is happiness relative?' *Social Indicators Research*, 24, 1–34, 1991.
110. Ibid.
111. R. Veenhoven (1984) op. cit.
112. M. Rutter and D. J. Smith (1995) op. cit.
113. A.C. Michalos (1985) 'Multiple discrepancies theory (MDT)', *Social Indicators Research*, 16, 347–413.
114. E. Diener (1994) 'Assessing subjective well-being: progress and opportunities', *Social Indicators Research*, 31, 103–57.
115. A.C. Michalos (1985) op. cit.
116. W. Schulz (1995) 'Multiple-discrepancies theory versus resource theory,' *Social Indicators Research*, 34, 153–69, 1995.
117. M.A. Stassen and A.R. Staats (1986) 'Hope and happiness: a comparison of some discrepancies', *Social Indicators Research*, 20, 1988, 45–58.
118. G.H. Elder (1974) *Children of the Great Depression* (Chicago University Press, Chicago).
119. F. Strack, N. Schwarz and E. Gschneideinger (1985) 'Happiness and reminiscing: the role of time perspective, affect and mode of thinking', *Journal of Personality and Social Psychology*, 49.
120. A. Campbell, P.E. Converse and W.L. Rodgers (1976) *The Quality of American Life* (Sage, New York).
121. W. Glatzer (1991) 'Quality of life in advanced industrialised countries'. In F. Strack, M. Argyle and N. Schwarz (eds), *Subjective Well-Being: an Interdisciplinary Perspective* (Pergamon Press, Oxford).
122. W.G. Runciman (1966) *Relative Deprivation and Social Justice* (Routledge and Kegan Paul, London).
123. C. Fraser (1984) 'Pay comparisons and pay satisfaction'. Paper to conference of European Association for Experimental Social Psychology, Tilburg.
124. W. James (1892) *Psychology* (Holt, New York).
125. V.H. Medvec, S.F. Madey and T. Gilovich (1995) 'When less is more: counterfactual thinking and satisfaction among Olympic medallists', *Journal of Personality and Social Psychology*, 69, 4, 603–10.
126. D. Kahneman and A. Tversky (1982) 'The simulation heuristic'. In D. Kahneman, P. Slovic and A. Tversky (eds), *Judgement Under Uncertainty: Heuristics and Biases* (Cambridge University Press, New York) 201–8.
127. V.H. Medvec, S.F. Madey and T. Gilovich (1995) op. cit.

128. P. Brickman, D. Coates, and R. Janoff-Bulman (1978) 'Lottery winners and accident victims: is happiness relative?', *Journal of Personality and Social Psychology*, 36, 8, 917–27.
129. Ibid.
130. H.E. Unger (1970) 'The feeling of happiness', *Psychology*, 7, 27–33.
131. S. Freud (1961) *Civilization and its Discontents*, J. Strachey (ed and translator) (Hogarth Press, London).
132. C.N. Mitchell (1987) 'Legal restraint, happiness and anxiety – parallels between utilitarianism and psychiatry', *International Journal of Law and Psychiatry*, 10, 265–81.
133. R.L. Solomon (1980) 'The opponent process theory of acquired motivation', *American Psychologist*, 35, 8, 691–712.
134. M. Argyle and A. Furnham (1982) 'The ecology of relationships: choice of situation as a function of relationships', *British Journal of Social Psychology*, 21, 259–62.
135. W. Stroebe and M.S. Stroebe (1987) *Bereavement and Health* (Cambridge University Press, Cambridge).
136. A. Kozma and M.J. Stones 'Predictors of happiness', *Journal of Gerontology*, 1983, 38, 5, 626–628.
137. N. Bolger, A. Delongis, R.C. Kesiler and E.A. Schilling (1989) 'Effects of daily stress on mood', *Journal of Personality and Social Psychology*, 57, 808–818.
138. D. Zillman (1984) 'Transfer of excitation in emotional behaviour'. In J.T. Cacioppo and R.E. Petty (eds), *Social Psychophysiology: a Source-book* (Guilford Press, New York), 215–40.
139. B. Zilbergeld (1983) *The Shrinking of America: Myths of Psychological Change* (Little Brown, Boston).
140. M. Csikszentmihalyi (1975) *Beyond Boredom and Anxiety* (Jossey-Bass, San Francisco).
141. M. Csikszentmihalyi and J. Nakamura (1989) 'The dynamics of intrinsic motivation'. In R. Ames and C. Ames (eds), *Handbook of Motivation Theory and Research, Vol. 3: Goals and Cognition* (Academic Press, New York).
142. A. Tversky and D. Griffin (1991) 'Endowment and contrast in judgments of well-being'. In F. Strack, M. Argyle and N. Schwarz (eds) *Subjective Well-being: an Interdisciplinary Perspective* (Pergamon Press, Oxford).
143. The European Commission 'Satisfaction with life', *Eurobarometer*, 46, May, 34–35.
144. M.C. Robbins, B.R. DeWalt and P.J. Pelto (1972) 'Climate and behaviour: a biocultural study', *Journal of Cross-cultural Psychology*, 3, 4, December, 331–344.

2 Am I Insane – or is it Everyone Else?

1. P.D. Slade and R.P. Bentall (1988) *Sensory Deception: Towards a Scienific Analysis of Hallucinations* (Croom Helm, London).
2. T.B. Posey and M.E. Losch (1983) 'Auditory hallucinations of hearing voices in 375 normal subjects', *Imagination, Cognition and Personality*, 2, 99–113.
3. T.R. Barrett and J.B. Etheridge (1992) Verbal hallucinations in normals. 1: People who hear 'voices'. *Applied Cognitive Psychology*, 6, 379–87.
4. I. al-Issa (1995) 'The illusion of reality or the reality of illusion. Hallucinations and culture', *British Journal of Psychiatry*, 166, 368–73.
5. N. Tarrier, R. Beckett, S. Harwood et al. (1993a) 'A trial of two cognitive-behavioural methods of treating drug-resistant residual psychotic symptoms in schizophrenic patients: 1. Outcome', *British Journal of Psychiatry*, 162, 524–32.
6. N. Tarrier, L. Sharpe, R. Beckett et al. (1993b) 'A trial of two cognitive-behavioural methods of treating drug-resistant residual psychotic symptoms in schizophrenic patients', *Social Psychiatry and Psychiatric Epidemiology*, 28, 5–10.
7. Tarrier, Beckett et al., 'A trial of two cognitive-behavioural methods'.
8. Tarrier, Sharpe et al., 'A trial of two cognitive-behavioural methods'.
9. R. Persaud and I. Marks (1995) 'A pilot study of exposure treatment for chronic auditory hallucinations', *British Journal of Psychiatry*, 167, 45–50.
10. B. Farid and E. Alapont (1993) 'Patients who fail to attend their first psychiatric out-patient appointment: Non-attendance or inappropriate referral?', *Journal of Mental Health*, 2, 81–3.
11. A. Robin (1976) 'Rationing out-patients: a defence of the waiting list', *British Journal of Psychiatry*, 128, 138–41.
12. D. Beecher (1988) 'The lover's body: the somatogenesis of love in renaissance medical treatises', *Renaissance and Reformation*, 12, 1, 1–11.
13. S.A. Cartwright (1851) 'Report on the diseases and physical peculiarities of the negro race', *The New Orleans Medical and Surgical Journal*, May, 691–715.
14. G. Engel (1961) 'Is grief a disease? A challenge for medical research', *Psychosomatic Medicine*, 23, 18.
15. M.L. Elks (1996) 'Popular press diagnoses and psychiatric diagnoses', *Medical Hypotheses*, 1996, 46, 331–6.
16. Dr Charles (1997) On Call. Style Section. *The Sunday Times*, 6 July 1997, 41.
17. D.S. Leathar and G.B. Hastings (1984) 'Evaluation of the Scottish Health Education Group's 1981–1982 environmental health campaign', *Journal of the Royal Society of Health*, 104, 4, 140–3
18. World Health Organisation (1984) Health Promotion: a discussion document on the concept and principles. Copenhagen, WHO Regional Office for Europe.
19. Anonymous (1986) Ottawa Charter for Health Promotion, *Canadian Journal of Public Health/Revue Canadienne de Sante Publique*, 77, 6, 425–30.
20. A. Lewis (1953) 'Health as a social concept', *British Journal of Sociology*, 4, 109–24.
21. A. Bandura (1969) *Principles of Behaviour Modification* (Holt Rhinehart and Winston, New York).
22. M. Jahoda (1958) *Current Concepts of Positive Mental Health* (Basic Books, New York).
23. H. Hartmann (1947) 'On rational and irrational action'. In Geza Rohein (ed) *Psychoanalysis and the Social Sciences 1* (International Universities Press).
24. H. Hartmann (1939) 'Psychoanalysis and the concept of health', *International Journal of Psychoanalysis*, 20, 308–318.
25. L.S. Kubie (1954) 'The fundamental nature of the distinction between normality and neurosis', *Psychoanal Quart.*, 23, 187–8.
26. I.D. Yallom and M.A. Lieberman (1991) 'Bereavement and heightened existential awareness', *Psychiatry*, November 54 (4) 334–45.
27. A.H. Maslow (1956) 'Personality problems and personality growth'. In C. Moustakas (ed) *The Self.* (Harpers).
28. M. Jahoda (1953) 'The meaning of psychological health', *Social Casework*, 34, 349.
29. S.W. Ginsburg (1955) 'The mental health movement and its theoretical assumptions'. In Ruth Kotinsky and Helen Witmer (eds) *Community Programs for Mental Health* (Harvard University Press).

30. M. Jahoda (1958) *Current Concepts of Positive Mental Health* (Basic Books, New York) p3.
31. R. Dubos (1959) *Mirage of Health: Utopias, Progress, and Biological Change* (Harper, New York).
32. H. Hafner (1985) 'Are mental disorders increasing over time?', *Psychopathology*, 18, 66–81.
33. G.L. Klerman, P.W. Lavori, J. Rice, T. Reich, J. Endicott, N.C. Andreasen, M.B. Keller, and R.M. Hirschfield (1985) 'Birth cohort trends in rates of major depressive disorder among relatives of patients with affective disorder', *Archives of General Psychiatry*, 42 (7), 689–93.
34. K.L. Lamb, S. Dench, D.A. Brodie and K. Roberts (1988) 'Sports participation and health status: a preliminary analysis', *Social Science and Medicine*, 27 (12) 1309–16.
35. J.E. Ware jr (1986) 'The assessment of health status'. In L.H. Aiken and D. Mechanic (eds) *Applications of Social Science to Clinical Medicine and Social Policy*, 204–28 (Rutgers University Press, New Brunswick); J.E. Ware jr, S.A. Johnston, A.A. Davies and R. Brook (1979) 'Conceptualisation and measurement of health for adults in the health insurance study', *Mental Health* (Rand Corporation, Santa Monica, California) R-1987/3-HEW; J.E. Ware jr, W.G. Manning jr, N. Duan, K.B. Wells and J.P. Newhouse (1984) 'Health status and the use of ambulatory mental health services', *American Psychologist*, 39, 1090–100.
36. A. LaRue, L. Bank, L. Jarvik and M. Hetland (1979) 'Health in old age: how do physicians' ratings and self-ratings compare?' *Journal of Gerontology*, 34, 687–961.
37. M. Eisen, C.A. Donald, J.E. Ware and R.H. Brook (1980) 'Conceptualisation and measurement of health for children in the health insurance study', *Mental Health* (Rand Corporation, Santa Monica) R2312-HEW.
38. G.G. Fillenbaum (1979) 'Social context and self-assessment of health among the elderly', *Journal of Health and Social Behaviour*, 20, 45–51.
39. J.M. Mossey and E. Shapiro (1982) 'Self-rated health: a predictor of mortality among the elderly', *American Journal of Public Health*, 72, 800–8.
40. G.A. Kaplan and T. Camacho (1983) 'Perceived health and mortality: a nine-year follow-up of the human population laboratory cohort', *American Journal of Epidemiology*, 117, 292–304.
41. K.F. Ferraro (1980) 'Self-ratings of health among the old and the old old', *Journal of Health and Social Behaviour*, 21, 377–83.
42. L. Luborsky and H. Bachrach (1974) 'Factors influencing clinician judgments of mental health', *Archives of General Psychiatry*, 31, 292–9.
43. M. Monk (1981) 'Blood pressure awareness and psychological well-being in the health and nutrition examination survey', *Clinical Investigations in Medicine*, 4, 183–9.
44. L. Luborsky (1975) 'Clinicians' judgments of mental health', *Bulletin of the Menninger Clinic*, 39, 5, 448–81.
45. S. Freud (1933) 'Anxiety and the Instinctual Life'. In J. Strachey (ed) *The Complete Psychological Works* (standard edn) (Hogarth Press, London) p22.
46. K. Horney (1951) *Neurosis and Human Growth* (Routeledge and Kegan Paul, London).
47. A.H. Maslow (1968) *Toward a Psychology of Being* (2nd edn) (Van Nostrand Reinhold, New York).
48. G.W. Allport (1955) *Becoming* (Yale University Press).
49. A.H. Maslow (1955) 'Deficiency, motivation and growth motivation'. In M.R. Jones (ed) *Nebraska Symposium on Motivation* (University of Nebraska Press, Nebraska).
50. P. Fonagy, M. Steele, H. Steele, G. Moran and A. Higgitt (1991) 'The capacity for understanding mental states: the reflexive self in parent and child and its significance for security attachment', *Infant Mental Health Journal*, 12, 201–17.
51. G.W. Allport (1937) *Personality* (Holt).
52. J.C. Crumbagh and L.T. Maholick (1964) 'An experimental study in existentialism; the psychometric approach to Frankl's concept of noogenic neurosis', *Journal of Clinical Psychology*, 20, 200–214.
53. E.L. Shoestrom (1964) 'An inventory for the measurement of self-actualization', *Educational and Psychological Measurement*, 24, 2, 207–218.
54. J. Condry (1977) 'Enemies of exploration: self-initiated versus other initiated learning', *Journal of Personality and Social Psychology*, 35, 459–77.
55. D. Cervone (1989) 'Effects on envisioning future activities on self-efficacy, judgements and motivation: an availability heuristic interpretation', *Cognitive Therapy and Research*, 13, 247–62.
56. Allport, *Becoming*.
57. Ibid.
58. Ibid.

3 Anyone Who Goes to See a Therapist Needs His Head Examined

1. L. Hodgkinson, (1992) *Counselling* (Simon and Schuster Ltd, London).
2. W. Dryden (1984) *Individual Therapy in Britain* (Harper and Row, London).
3. B. Sibbald, J. Addington-Hall, D. Brenneman and P. Freeling (1993) 'Counsellors in English and Welsh general practices: their nature and distribution', *British Medical Journal*, 306, 29–33.
4. C. Feltham (1995) *What is Counselling? The Promise and Problem of the Talking Therapies* (Sage Publications Inc, London).
5. H. Bourne (1993) 'A billion pounds of psychotherapy', *Psychiatric Bulletin*, 17, 295–6.
6. Ibid.
7. C. Feltham and W. Dryden (1993) *Dictionary of Counselling* (Whurr Publishers, London) Xii p216.
8. British Association for Counselling (1979) *Counselling: definition of terms in use with expansion and rationale* (British Association for Counselling, (Rugby).
9. D. Brown and J. Pedder (1979) 2nd edition. *Introduction to Psychotherapy: An Outline of Psychodynamic Principles and Practice* (Tavistock/Routledge, London).
10. Feltham *What is Counselling?*
11. S. Quillam and I. Grove-Stephenson (1990) *The Best Counselling Guide* (Thorsons, London).
12. N. Timms and R. Timms (1982) *Dictionary of Social Welfare* (Routledge and Kegan Paul, London).
13. P. Lomas (1981) *The Limits of Interpretation* (Penguin, London).
14. J. Sayers (1991) *Mothering Psychoanalysis* (Penguin, London).
15. E. Mahler (1995) 'Von der Gruppenpsychoanalyse zu einer psychoanalytischen Soziotherapie' ('From group analysis to psychoanalytic sociotherapy'), *Zeitschrift-fur-Psychoanalytishce-Theorie-und-Praxis*, 10 (1) 93–118.
16. T. Zeldin (1994) *An Intimate History of Humanity* (Sinclair-Stephenson, London).

"He who is not FREE is not an AGENT but a Patient..." (Charles Wesley)

457

17. B. Sibbald, J. Addington-Hall, D. Brenneman and P. Freeling (1993) 'Counsellors in English and Welsh general practices: their nature and distribution', *British Medical Journal*, 306, 1993, 29–33.
18. S. Freud (1978) *The Question of Lay Analysis* (W.W. Norton, New York).
19. H.J. Eysenck (1992) 'The effects of psychotherapy: an evaluation', *Journal of Consulting and Clinical Psychology*, 60 (5) 659–63.
20. H.J. Eysenck (1952) 'The effects of psychotherapy: an evaluation', *Journal of Consulting and Clinical Psychology*, 16, 1952, 319–24.
21. G. Andrews (1993) 'The essential psychotherapies', *British Journal of Psychiatry*, 162, 447–51.
22. British Psychology Society (1980) 'Statement on the statutory registration of psychotherapists', *Bulletin of the BPS*, 33, 353–6.
23. N. Symington (1986) *The Analytic Experience: Lectures from the Tavistock* (Free Association Books, London).
24. J. Masson (1990) *Against Therapy* (Fontana, London).
25. D. Kramer, R. Ber and M. Moore (1989) 'Increasing empathy among medical students', *Medical Education*, Mar 23 (2) 168–73.
    P.J. Kramer (1989) *Moments of Engagement* (W.W. Norton, New York).
26. Feltham *What is Counselling?*
27. H.H. Mozak (1989) 'Adlerian Psychotherapy'. In R. Corsini and D. Wedding (eds) *Current Psychotherapies*, 4th edn (Peacock, Itasca, Illinois).
28. Dryden *Individual Therapy in Britain*.
29. N. Pesechkian (1986) *The Psychotherapy of Everyday Life* (Springer-Verlag, Berlin).
30. G. Wood (1983) *The Myth of Neurosis* (Macmillan, London).
31. D. Cohen (1990) *Challenging the Therapeutic State: Critical Perspectives on Psychiatry and the Mental Health System* (Institute of Mind and Behaviour, New York).
32. Wood *The Myth of Neurosis*.
33. T. Parsons (1978) 'Health and Disease: A Sociological and Action Perspective'. In W.T. Reich (ed) *Encyclopedia of Bioethics* (The Free Press, New York) pp 590–9.
34. H. Winthrop (1969) 'Bad faith in counseling and therapy', *Mental Hygiene*, 53, 415–21.
35. J. Green and T. Davey (1992) 'Counselling with the worried well', *Counselling Psychology Quarterly*, 5, 2, 213–20.
36. B. Raphael, L. Meldrum and A.C. McFarlane (1995) 'Does debriefing after psychological trauma work?', *British Medical Journal*, 310, 1479–80.
37. D.P. Goldberg and V.E. Hillies (1979) 'A scaled version of the GHQ', *Psychological Medicine*, 9, 139–45.
38. Raphael et al, 'Does debriefing after psychological trauma work?'
40. Wood, *The Myth of Neurosis*.
41. H.H. Strupp (1974) 'On the basic ingredients of psychotherapy', *Psychotherapy and Psychosomatics*, 24, 249–60.
42. J. Holmes and R. Lindley (1991) *The Values of Psychotherapy* (Oxford University Press, Oxford, New York).
43. British Association of Counselling (1988) *The Directory of Training Courses in Counselling and Psychotherapy* (British Association for Counselling, Rugby).
44. Ibid.
45. R.B. Sloane, E.R. Staples, A.H. Cristol, N.J. Yorkston and K. Whipple (1975) *Psychotherapy vs Behaviour Therapy* (Harvard University Press, Cambridge).
46. N.R. Simonson and S. Bahr (1974) 'Self disclosure by the professional and paraprofessional therapist', *Journal of Consulting and Clinical Psychology*, 42, 359–63.
47. D. Faust and C. Zlotnick (1995) 'Another dodo bird verdict? Revisiting the comparative effectiveness of professional and paraprofessional therapists', *Clinical Psychology and Psychotherapy*, 2, no 3, 157–67.
48. G. Alberts and B. Edelstein (1990) 'Therapist training: a critical review of skill training studies', *Clinical Psychology Review*, 10, 497–511.
49. I. Owen (1992) 'The tower of babel: searching for core clinical, theoretical and technical issues in psychotherapy', *Counselling Psychology Quarterly*, 5, 1, 67–78.
50. M.B. Maskin(1974) 'Differential impact of student counsellors self-concept on clients perceptions of therapeutic effectiveness', *Psychological Reports*, 34, 967–9.
51. G. Alberts and B. Edelstein (1990) 'Therapist training: a critical review of skill training studies', *Clinical Psychology Review*, 10, 497–511.
52. T.H. Peake and J.D. Ball (1991) *Psychotherapy Training* (The Haworth Press, New York and London).
53. J. Mcleod (1992) 'What do we know about how to best assess counsellor competence?' *Counselling Psychology Quarterly*, 5, 4, 359–72.
54. J. S. Berman and N.C. Norton (1985) 'Does professional training make therapists more effective?' *Psychological Bulletin*, 98, 401–7.
55. J.A. Durlak (1979) 'Comparative effectiveness of paraprofessional and professional helpers', Jan 86 (1) 80–92.
56. A. MacIntyre (1958) *The Unconscious* (Routeledge and Kegan Paul, London).
57. H.G. Pope and J.I. Hudson (1995) 'Can memories of childhood sexual abuse be repressed?', *Psychological Medicine*, 25, 121–6.
58. M. Lakin (1988) *Ethical Issues in the Psychotherapies* (Oxford University Press, New York).
59. L. Power and D. Pilgrim (1990) 'The fee is psychotherapy: practioners' accounts', *Counselling Psychology Quarterly*, 3 (2) 153–70.
60. Masson *Against Therapy*.
61. J. Holmes and R. Lindley (1991) *The Values of Psychotherapy* (Oxford University Press, Oxford, New York) p166.
62. Lakin *Ethical Issues in the Psychotherapies*.
63. Dryden *Individual Therapy in Britain*.
64. M.B. Parloff, P. London and B. Wolfe, B (1986) 'Individual psychotherapy and behaviour change', *Annual Review of Psychology*, 37, 321–49.
65. Andrews 'The essential psychotherapies'.
66. G. McGrath and K. Lowson (1986) 'Assessing the benefits of psychotherapy: the economic approach', *British Journal of Psychiatry*, 150, 65–71.

458

67. A. France (1988) *Consuming Psychotherapy* (Free Association Books, London).
68. Lakin *Ethical Issues in the Psychotherapies*.
69. Ibid.
70. B. Furrow (1980) *Malpractice in Psychotherapy* (Lexington Books, Lexington, MA).
71. N. Gartrell, J. Herman, S. Olarte, M. Feldstein and R. Localio (1986) 'Psychiatrist patient sexual contact: results of a national survey, 1: prevalence', *American Journal of Psychiatry*, 143, 1126–31.
72. V. Davidson (1977) 'Psychiatry's problem with no name: therapist-patient sex', *American Journal of Psychoanalysis*, 37, 43–50.
73. R.Z. Folman (1991) 'Therapist-patient sex: attraction and boundary problems', *Psychotherapy*, 28, 168–73.
74. Ibid.
75. Masson *Against Therapy*.
76. C.J. Robins and A.M. Hayes (1993) 'An appraisal of cognitive therapy', *Journal of Consulting and Clinical Psychology*, 48, 205–14.
77. France *Consuming Psychotherapy*.
78. D.I. Templer (1971) 'Analyzing the psychotherapist', *Mental-Hygiene*, 55 (2), 234–6.
79. J.S. Phillips and K.L. Bierman (1981) 'Clinical psychology: individual methods', *Annual Review of Psychology*, 32, 1981, 405–38.
80. P. Crits-Cristoph (1992) 'The efficacy of brief dynamic psychotherapy: a meta-analysis', *American Journal of Psychiatry*, 149, 151–8.
81. N. Symington (1986) *The Analytic Experience: Lectures from the Tavistock* (Free Association Books, London).
82. M. Harty and L. Horowitz (1976) 'Therapeutic outcome as rated by patients, therapists and judges', *Archives of General Psychiatry*, 33, 957–61.
83. Ibid.
84. I.E. Waskow and M.B. Parloff (1975) *Psychotherapy Change Measures* (GPO, Washington DC).
85. C.G. Jung (1966) *The Practice of Psychotherapy* (Pantheon, New York).
86. E.F. Torrey (1986) *Witchdoctors and Psychiatrists: The Common Roots of Psychotherapy and Tts Future* (Jason Aronson, New York).
87. G. Goleman (1986) 'Psychiatry: guide to therapy is fiercely opposed', *New York Times*, 23 Sept, C1, 2.
88. F. Cioffi (1970) 'Freud and the Ideas of a Pseudo–Science'. In R. Borger and F. Cioffi (eds) *Explanation in the Behavioural Sciences* (Cambridge University Press, Cambridge).
89. I. Owen (1992) 'The tower of babel: searching for core clinical, theoretical and technical issues in psychotherapy', *Counselling Psychology Quarterly*, 5, 1, 67–78.
90. Dryden *Individual Therapy in Britain*.
91. Lakin *Ethical Issues in the Psychotherapies*.
92. H.H. Strupp, S.W. Hadley and B. Gomes-Schwartz (1977) *Psychotherapy for Better or Worse* (Aronson, New York).
93. M.J. Lambert, A.E. Bergin and J.L. Collins (1977) 'Therapist-Induced Deterioration in Psychotherapy'. In A.S. Gurman and A.M. Rogers (eds) *The Therapist's Contributions to Effective Treatment* (Pergamon, New York).
94. D.T. Mays and C.M. Franks (1985) *Negative Outcome in Psychotherapy and What To Do About It* (Springer Publishing Company, New York).
95. Ibid.
96. M. Lambert and A.E. Bergin (1994) 'The Effectiveness of Psychotherapy'. In A.E. Bergin and S.L. Garfield (eds) *Handbook of Psychotherapy and Behavior Change* (4th edn) (John Wiley & Sons, New York) xvi, 864.
97. M.J. Lambert, A.E. Bergin and J.L. Collins (1977) 'Therapist-induced Deterioration in Psychotherapy'. In A.S. Gurman and A.M. Razin *Effective Psychotherapy: A Handbook of Research* (Pergamon Press, Oxford).
98. D. Gray (1988) 'Counsellors in general practice', *Journal of the Royal College of General Practitioners*, 38, 50–1.
99. M.B. King (1994) 'Counselling services in general practice: the need for evaluation', *Psychiatric Bulletin*, 18, 65–7.
100. Lambert et al. 'Therapist-Induced Deterioration in Psychotherapy'.
101. R.N. Bellah, R. Madsen, W.M. Sullivan, A. Swidler and S. Tipton (1985) *Habits of the Heart* (University of California Press, Berkely, CA).
102. A. MacIntyre (1981) *After Virtue* (Notre Dame Press, Notre Dame).
103. A. Ryle (1982) *Psychotherapy: A Cognitive Integration of Theory and Practice* (Academic Press, London).
104. D. Bakan (1966) *The Duality of Human Existence* (Rand McNally, Chicago).
105. Bellah et al. *Habits of the Heart*.
106. MacIntyre, *After Virtue*.
107. Ryle *Psychotherapy: A Cognitive Integration of Theory and Practice*.
108. Lakin *Ethical Issues in the Psychotherapies*.
109. Ibid.
110. G. Straker and F. Moosa (1988) 'Post traumatic stress disorder; a reaction to state-supported child abuse and neglect', *Child Abuse and Neglect*, 12, 383–95.
111. G. Margolin (1982) 'Ethical and legal considerations in marital and family therapy', *American Psychologist*, 37, 788–801.
112. H. Marcuse (1966) *Eros and Civilisation* (Beacon Press, Boston).
113. G.C. Murphy and J.A. Athanasou (1987) 'School to work transition: behavioral counselling approaches to the problem of finding jobs for unemployed adolescents', *Behaviour Change*, 4, 41–4.
114. G. Wood (1983: *The Myth of Neurosis* (Macmillan, London).
115. London *The Modes and Morals of Psychotherapy*.
116. M. Sherwood (1969) *The Logic of Explanation in Psychoanalysis* (Academic Press, New York and London).
117. R.B. Sloane, F.R. Staples, A.H. Cristol, N.J. Yorkston and K. Whipple (1975) *Psychotheray vs Behaviour Therapy* (Harvard University Press, Cambridge).
118. London *The Modes and Morals of Psychotherapy*.
119. P. Lomas (1973) *True and False Experience* (Allen Lane, London).
120. L. Taylor (1993) 'Good grief blues', *New Statesman and Society*, 16, July 23, 15–16.
121. Lomas *True and False Experience*.

459

122. London *The Modes and Morals of Psychotherapy*.
123. R. Rosenthal (1955) 'Changes in some moral values following psychotherapy', *Journal of Counselling Psychology*, 19, 431–4.
124. M.B. Parloff (1956) 'Some factors affecting the quality of therapeutic relationships', *Journal of Abnormal and Social Psychology*, 52, 5–10.
125. G. Halliday (1991) 'Psychological self-help books – how dangerous are they?' *Psychotherapy*, 28, 678–80.
126. A. Bandura (1977) *Social Learning Theory* (Prentice Hall, Englewood Cliffs, NJ).
127. B. Gomes-Schwartz, S.W. Hadley. and H.H. Strupp (1978) 'Individual psychotherapy and behaviour therapy', *Annual Review of Psychology*, 29, 435–71.
128. M. Hersen and A.S. Bellack (1976) 'Social skills training for chronic psychiatric patients: rationale, research findings and future directions', *Comprehensive Psychiatry*, 17, 559–80.
129. G.M. Rosen (1976) 'The development and use of nonprescription behaviour therapies', *American Psychologist*, 31, 139–41.
130. J. Griffin (1979) 'Is unhappiness morally more important than happiness?' *Philosophical Quarterly*, 29, 47–55.
131. K. Popper (1966) *The Open Society and Its Enemies* (Routledge & Kegan Paul, London).
132. Griffin, 'Is unhappiness morally more important than happiness?'.
133. Ibid.
134. S. James (1982) 'The duty to relieve suffering', *Ethics*, 93, 4–21.
135. W. Tseng and J.F. McDermott (1975) 'Psychotherapy: historical roots, universal elements and cultural variations', *American Journal of Psychiatry*, 132, 378–84.
136. J. Leff, N. Sartorius, A. Jalbensky, A. Korten, and G. Ernberg (1992) The international pilot study of schizophrenia: five year follow up findings', *Psychological Medicine*, 22, 131–45.
137. R. Persaud (1993) 'The "career" of counselling: careering out of control?', *Journal of Mental Health*, 2, 283–5.
138. M. Natale, C.C. Dahlberg, J. Jaffe (1978) 'The relationship of defensive language behaviour in patient monologues in the course of psychoanalysis', *Journal of Clinical Psychology*, 34, 466–70.
139. R.E. Ingram (1990) 'Self-focused attention in clinical disorders: review and conceptual model', *Psychological Bulletin*, 107, 2, 156–76.
140. R.G. Priest, C. Vize, A. Roberts, M. Roberts and A. Tylee (1996) 'Lay people's attitudes to treatment of depression: results of opinion poll for Defeat Depression Campaign just before its launch', *British Medical Journal*, 1996, 313, 858–9.
141. A. Tylee (1997) 'Counselling in primary care', *Lancet*, 1997, 350: 1643–4.
142. K. Friedli, M. King, M. Lloyd and J. Horder (1997) 'Randomised controlled assessment of non-directive psychotherapy versus general-practitioner care', *Lancet*, 1997, 350, 1662–5.
143. J. McLennan, K. Culkin and P. Courtney (1994) 'Telephone counsellors' conceptualising abilities and counselling skills', *British Journal of Guidance and Counselling*, 1994, 22, 183–95.
144. I. Bobevski, A.M. Holgate and J. McLennan (1997) 'Characteristics of effective telephone counselling skills', *British Journal of Guidance and Counselling*, 1997, 25, 2, 239–49.
145. Ibid.
146. Ibid.
147. Ibid.
148. D.C. Fowles (1980) 'The three arousal model: implications of Gray's two-factor theory for heart rate, electrodermal activity, and psychopathy', *Psychophysiology*, 1980, 17, 87–104.
149. J.W. Pennebaker, J.K. Kiecolt-Glaser and R. Glaser (1988) 'Disclosure of traumas and immune function: health implications for psychotherapy', *Journal of Consulting and Clinical Psychology*, 1988, 56, 2, 239–45.
150. Ibid.

4 Hell is Other People

1. J.M. Gottman (1993) 'The roles of conflict engagement, escalation and avoidance in marital interaction: a longitudinal study of five types of couples', *Journal of Consulting and Clinical Psychology*, 61, 6–15.
2. J. Hall, D. Roter and N. Katz (1988) 'Meta-analysis of correlates of provider behaviour in medical encounters', *Medical Care*, 26, 657–73.
3. E. Aronson(1984) *The Social Animal* (W.H. Freeman, New York).
4. C. Orpen (1996) 'The effects of ingratiation and self promotion tactics on employee career success', *Social Behaviour and Personality*, 24, 3, 213–14.
5. W. Hartin (1988) *Why Did I Marry You?* (Hill Of Content, Melbourne).
6. S. Brehm (1987) 'Coping After a Relationship Ends'. In C.R. Snyder and C.E. Ford (eds) *Coping With Everyday Negative Life Events: Clinical and Social Psychological Perspectives* (Plenum Press, New York).
7. B.S. Frey and R. Eichenberger (1996) 'Marriage paradoxes', *Rationality and Society*, 8, 2, 187–206.
8. J.D. Baldwin and J.I. Baldwin (1981) *Behaviour Principles of Everyday Life* (2nd edn) (Prentice Hall, Englewood Cliffs, NJ).
9. H.T. Reis (1984). 'Social Interaction and Well-being'. In S. Duck (ed) *Personal relationships, 5: Repairing Personal Relationships* (Academic Press, London).
10. W.W. Hartup and N. Stevens (1997) 'Friendships and adaption in the life course', *Psychological Bulletin*, 121, 3, 355–70.
11. M. Argyle and A. Furnham (1983) 'Sources of satisfaction and conflict in long-term relationships', *Journal of Marriage and the Family*, 45, 481–93.
12. G.W. Brown and T. Harris (1978) *Social Origins of Depression*.
13. Argyle and Furnham, 'Sources of satisfaction and conflict in long-term relationships'.
14. A.E. Kelly and K.J. McKillop (1996) 'Consequences of revealing personal secrets', *Psychological Bulletin*, Nov, 120 (3) 450–65.
15. J.S. House, C. Robbins and H.L. Metzner (1982) 'The association of social relationships and activities with mortality: prospective evidence from the Tecumseh Community Health Study', *American Journal of Epidemiology*, 116, 123–40.
16 R. Larson and M. Lee (1996) 'The capacity to be alone as a stress buffer', *Journal of Social Psychology*, 136 (1), 5–16.

17. R. Larson and M. Csikszentmihalyi (1980) 'The significance of time alone in adolescent development', *Journal of Current Adolescent Medicine*, 2, 33–40.
18. J.J. Rousseau (1979) *Reveries of the Solitary Walker* (P. France, trans) (Penguin Books, Harmondsworth, UK) (original work published in 1778).
19. D.W. Winnicott (1958) 'The capacity to be alone', *International Journal of Psychoanalysis*, 39, 416–20.
20. R. Larson (1990) 'The solitary side of life: an examination of the time people spend alone from childhood to old age', *Developmental Review*, 10, 155–83.
21. C. Johnson and R. Larson (1982) 'Bulimia, an analysis of moods and behaviour', *Psychosomatic Medicine*, 44, 341–51.
22. M.W. De Vries, P. Delespaul and C.I.M Dijkman-Caes (1987) 'Affect and Anxiety in Daily Life'. In G. Racagni and E Smeralid (eds) *Anxious Depression Assessment and Treatment* (Raven Press, New York) pp21–32).
23. W.W. Hartup and N. Stevens (1997) 'Friendships and adaption in the life course', *Psychological Bulletin*, 121, 3, 355–70.
24. S. Cohen and T.A. Wills (1985) 'Stress, social support, and the buffering hypothesis', *Psychological Bulletin*, 98, 310–57.
25. C. Tolsdorf (1976) 'Social networks, social support, and coping', *Family Process*, 15, 407–17.
26. T.A. Wills (1985) 'Supporting Functions of Interpersonal Relationships'. In S. Cohen and S.L. Syme (eds) *Social Support and Health* (Academic, New York) 61–82.
27. Tolsdorf 'Social networks, social support, and coping'.
28. G.H. Wills (1987) 'A community role for counselling psychologist', *Australian Psychologist*, 1992, Jul, 27 (2), 96–8.
29. B.M. DePaulo (1982) 'Social Psychological Processes in Informal Help-Seeking'. In T.A. Wills (ed) *Basic Processes in Helping Relationships* (Academic Press New York) 255–79.
30. C.B. Truax and R.R. Carkhuff (1967) *Towards Effective Counselling and Psychotherapy* (Aldine Publishing Company, Chicago).
31. S. Brehm (1987) 'Coping After a Relationship Ends'. In C.R. Snyder and C.E. Ford (eds) *Coping With Negative Life Events* (Plenum Press, New York and London).
32. G.B. Spanier and R.F. Castro (1979) 'Adjustment to Separation and Divorce: A Qualitative analysis'. In G. Levinger and O.C. Moles (eds) *Divorce and Separation* (Basic Books, New York) pp211–27.
33. T.D. Stephen. (1984) 'Symbolic interdependence and post-break-up distress: a reformulation of the attachment construct', *Journal of Divorce*, 8 (Fall), 1–16.
34. S. Brehm (1985) *Intimate Relationships* (Random House, New York).
35. H.M. Newman and E.J. Langer (1981) 'Post divorce adaption and the attribution or responsibility', *Sex Roles*, 7, 223–32.
36. W.W. Hartup and N. Stevens (1997) 'Friendships and adaption in the life course', *Psychological Bulletin*, 121, 3, 355–70.

5 Me, Me, Me

1. L.Y. Abramson and H.A. Sackheim (1977) 'A paradox in depression: uncontrollability and self-blame', *Psychological Bulletin*, 84, 838–51.
2. J.R. Ferrari and W.T. Mautz. (1997) 'Predicting perfectionsism: applying tests of rigidity', *Journal of Clinical Psychology*, 53 (1), 1–6.
3. M. McKay and P. Fanning (1992) *Self Esteem* (New Harbinger Publications Inc, California).
4. A. Robbins (1995) *Notes From a Friend* (Fireside, New York).
5. M. Nadich, M. Gargan and L. Michael (1975) 'Denial, anxiety locus of control and the discrepancy between aspirations and achievements as components of depression', *Journal of Abnormal Psychology*, 84, 1–9.
6. S. Blatt and D.C. Zuroff (1992) Interpersonal relatedness and self-definition: two prototypes for depression', *Clinical Psychology Review*, 12 (5) 527–62.
7. T.O. Harris (1988) 'Psychosocial Vulnerability to Depression'. In S. Henderson and G. Burrows (ed) *Handbook of Social Psychiatry* (Elsevier, Amsterdam).
8. Ibid.
9. J. Dent and J.D. Teasdale (1988) 'Negative cognition and the persistence of depression', *Journal of Abnormal Psychology*, 97, 29–34.
10. D.C. Zuroff, R. Koestner and T.A. Powers (1994) 'Self-criticism at age 12: longitudinal study of adjustment'.
11. McKay and Fanning *Self Esteem*.
12. C.S. Carver and R.J. Ganellen (1983) 'Depression and components of self-punitiveness: high standards, self-concept and overgeneralisation', *Journal of Abnormal Psychology*, 92, 330–7.
13. L. Ashner and M. Meyerson (1997) *When is Enough, Enough?* (Element, Dorset).
14. C.S. Carver and M.F. Scheier (1981) *Attention and Self-Regulation: A Control-Theory Approach to Human Behaviour* (Springer, New York).
15. P. Linville (1985) 'Self-complexity and affective extremity: don't put all your eggs in one cognitive basket', *Social Cognition*, 3, 94–120.
16. Ibid.
17. R.A. Witter, W.A. Stock and M.A. Okun (1985) 'Religion and subjective well-being in adulthood: a quantative synthesis', *Review of Religious Research*, 26, 332–41.
18. Ibid.
19. F.H. Kanfer and L. Gaelick-Buys (1991) 'Self-Management Methods'. In F. Kanfer and A.P. Goldstein (eds) *Helping People Change* (Pergamon Press, New York).
20. A.W. Logue. (1995) *Self-Control: Waiting Until Tomorrow for What You Want Today* (Prentice Hall, New Jersey).
21. C.C. DiClemente and J.O. Prochaska (1982) 'Self-change and therapy change of smoking behaviour: a comparison of processes of change in cessation and maintenance', *Addictive Behaviours*, 7 (2) 133–42.
22. R.G. Smith and B.A. Iwata (1997) 'Antecedent influences on behaviour disorders', *Journal of Applied Behaviour Analysis*, 30, 343–75.
23. W. Mischel and N. Baker (1975) 'Cognitive appraisals and transformations in delay behaviour', *Journal of Personality and Social Psychology*, 31, 254–61.
24. G. Ainslie (1975) 'Specious reward: a behavoural theory or impulsiveness and impulse control', *Psychological Bulletin*, 82, 463–96.
25. R. Audi (1988) 'Self-Deception, Rationalization, and Reasons for Acting. In Brian P McLaughlin and Melie Oksenberg Rorty (eds) *Perspectives on Self Deception* (University of California Press, Berkeley and Los Angeles, California).

26. M. Schaller (1997) 'The psychological consequences of fame: three tests of the self-consciousness hypothesis', *Journal of Personality*, 65, 2, 291–309.
27. J. Bybee, S. Luthar, E. Sigler and R. Merisca (1997) 'The fantasy, ideal, and ought selves: content, relationships to mental health and functions', *Social Cognition*, 15, 1, 37–53.

6 Crying is Good for You

1. T. Strentz and S.M. Auerbach (1988) 'Adjustment to the stress of simulated captivity: effects of emotion-focused versus problem-focused preparation on hostages differing in locus of control', *Journal of Personality and Social Psychology*, Oct, 55 (4) 652–60.
2. R.S. Lazarus and R. Launier (1978) 'Stress Related Transactions Between Person and Environment'. In L.A. Pervin and M. Lewis (eds) *Perspectives in Interactional Psychology* (Plenum Press, New York) pp 287–327.
3. Strentz and Auerbach 'Adjustment to the stress of simulated captivity'.
4. K.J. Mearn and S.J. Catanzaro (1994) 'Mood regulation expectancies as determinants of dysphoria in college students', *Journal of Counselling Psychology*, 37, 306–12.
5. R. De Sousa (1994) 'Emotions'. In Samuel Guttenplan (ed) *A Companion to the Philosophy of Mind* (Blackwell Publishers, Oxford).
6. R.E. Thayer (1996) *The Origin of Everyday Moods* (Oxford University Press, Oxford).
7. K. Kendler, A. Heath, N. Martin and L. Eaves (1987) 'Symptoms of anxiety and symptoms of depression', *Archives of General Psychiatry*, 122, 451–7.
8. D. Goldberg and P. Huxley (1992) *Common Mental Disorders – A Biosocial Model* (Routledge, London).
9. R. Finlay-Jones and G.W. Brown (1981) 'Types of stressful life event and the onset of anxiety and depressive disorders', *Psychological Medicine*, 11, 803–16.
10. T.O. Harris and G.W. Brown (1989) 'The LEDS Findings in the Context of Other Research: An Overview'. In G.W. Brown and T.O. Harris (eds) *Life Events and Illness* (Hyman Unwin, London).
11. P. McGuffin, R. Katz, J. Aldrich and P. Bebbington (1988a) 'The Camberwell Collaborative Depression Study. II. Investigation of family members', *British Journal of Psychiatry*, 152, 766–74.
12. P. McGuffin, R. Katz and P. Bebbington (1988b) 'The Camberwell Collaborative Depression Study. III. Depression and adversity in the relatives of depressed probands', *British Journal of Psychiatry*, 152, 775–82.
13. P. McGuffin et al. 'The Camberwell Collaborative Depression Study. II'.
14. P. McGuffin et al. 'The Camberwell Collaborative Depression Study. III'.
15. G.W. Brown. and T.O. Harris (1978a) *Social Origins of Depression* (Tavistock, London).
16. G.W. Brown and T.O. Harris (1978b) 'Social Origins of Depression: a reply', *Psychological Medicine*, 8, 577–88.
17. M. Rutter (1985) 'Reslience in the face of adversity' *British Journal of Psychiatry*, 147, 598–611.
18. D. Goldberg and P. Huxley (1992) *Common Mental Disorders – A Biosocial Model* (Routledge, London).
19. M. Argyle (1987) *The Psychology of Happiness* (Methuen and Co, London).
20. P.M. Lewinsohn and M. Graf (1973) 'Pleasant activities and depression', *Journal of Consulting and Clinical Psychology*, 41, 261–8.
21. P.M. Lewinsohn, J.M. Sullivan and S.J. Grosscup (1982) 'Behavioral Therapy: Clinical Applications. In A.J. Rush (ed) *Short Term Therapies for Depression* (Guilford, New York).
22. R.J. Turner, M.F. Ward and D.J. Turner (1979) 'Behavioural treatment for depression: an evaluation of therapeutic components', *Journal of Clinical Psychology*, 35, 166–75.
23. P.H. Blaney (1981) 'The Effectiveness of Cognitive and Behavioural Therapies'. In L.P. Rehm (ed) *Behavioural Therapy for Depression* (Academic Press, New York).
24. R.C. Miller and J.S. Berman (1983) 'The efficacy of cognitive behaviour therapies: a quantitative review of the research evidence', *Psychological Bulletin*, 94, 39–53.
25. J.M.G. Williams (1984) *The Psychological Treatment of Depression* (Croom Helm, London).
26. C.Z. Fuchs and L.P. Rehm (1977) 'A self-control behaviour therapy program for depression', *Journal of Consulting and Clinical Psychology*, 45, 206–15.
27. E.M. Heiby, M. Ozaki and P.E. Campos (1984) 'The effects of training in self-reinforcement and reward: implications for depression' *Behaviour Therapy*, 15, 544–9.
28. P. Ekman and W.V. Friesen. (1989) 'The Argument and Evidence about Universals in Facial Expressions of Emotion. In H. Wagner and A. Manstead (eds) *Handbook of Social Psychophysiology* (John Wiley and Sons Ltd, Chichester, England) xvi, 447.
29. W. Gaylin (1979) *Feelings, Our Vital Signs* (Harper and Row, New York).
30. H. Benson and G.S. Everly (1989) 'Disorders of arousal and the relaxation response: speculations on the nature and treatment of stress-related diseases', *Int J Psychosom* 36 (1–4): 15–21.
31. D.W. Woods and R.G. Miltenberg (1996) 'Are people with nervous habits nervous? A preliminary examination of habit function in a nonreferred population', *Journal of Applied Behavior Analysis*, 29, 259–61.
32. D.W. Woods, R.G. Miltenberger and A.D. Flach (1996) 'Habits, tics and stuttering', *Behavior Modification*, 20, 2, 216–25.
33. D.J. Hansen, A.C. Tishelman, R.P. Hawkins and K.J. Doepke (1990) 'Habits with potential as disorders', *Behavior Modification*, 14, 1, 66–80.
34. M.A. Stanley, J.W. Borden, S.G. Mouton and J.K. Breckenridge (1995) 'Nonclinical hair-pulling: affective correlates and comparison with clinical samples', *Behaviour Research and Therapy*, 33, 2, 179–86.
35. Woods and Miltenberg 'Are people with nervous habits nervous?'.
36. D.W. Woods and R.G. Miltenberger (1995) 'Habit reversal: a review of applications and variations', *Journal of Behavior Therapy and Experimental Psychiatry*, 26, 2, 123–31.
37. S.R. Rachman and R.J. Hodgson (1980) *Obsessions and Compulsions* (Prentice-Hall, New Jersey).
38. Ibid.
39. P. Victor (1996) 'Exams make teenagers suicidal', *The Independent*, 23 April, 1.
40. C.D. Spielberger and P.R. Vagg (1995) *Test Anxiety: Theory, Assessment and Treatment* (Taylor and Francis, Washington, USA).
41. Ibid.

42. C.D. Fisher (1993) 'Boredom at work: a neglected concept', *Human Relations*, 46, 3, 395–417.
43. W.N. McBain (1970) 'Arousal, monotony, and accidents in line driving', *Journal of Applied Psychology*, 54, 509–19.
44. V.L. Grose (1989) 'Coping with boredom in the cockpit before it's too late', *Professional Safety*, 1989, 34, 7, 24–6.
45. Fisher 'Boredom at work: a neglected concept'.
46. J.F. O'Hanlon (1981) 'Boredom: practical consequences and a theory', *Acta Psychologica*, 49, 53–82.
47. Fisher 'Boredom at work: a neglected concept'.
48. Ibid.
49. R. Farmer and N. Sundberg (1986) 'Boredom proneness – the development of a new scale', *Journal of Personality Assessment*, 50, 1, 4–17.
50. Fisher 'Boredom at work: a neglected concept'.
51. R.P. Smith (1981) 'Boredom: a review', *Human Factors*, 23, 3, 329–40.
52. Fisher 'Boredom at work: a neglected concept'.
53. Ibid.
54. Ibid.
55. Ibid.
56. Ibid.
57. Ibid.
58. Ibid.
59. E.A. Locke and G.P. Latham (1990) *A Theory of Goal Setting and Task Performance* (Prentice Hall, Englewood Cliffs, New Jersey).
60. D.E. Berlyne (1960) *Conflict, Arousal, and Curiosity* (McGraw-Hill, New York).
61. O. Fenichel (1951) 'On the Psychology of Boredom'. In D. Rapaport (ed) *Organisation and Pathology of Thought* (Columbia University Press, New York) 349–61.
62. J.E. Barmack (1938) 'The effect of benzidrine sulphate upon the report of boredom and other factors', *Journal of Psychology*, 5, 125–33.
63. M.R. Leary, P.A. Rogers, R.W. Canfield and C. Coe (1986) 'Boredom in interpersonal encounters: antecedents and social implications', *Journal of Personality and Social Psychology*, 51, 968–75.
64. R.W. Frick (1992) 'Interestingness', *British Journal of Psychology*, 83, 113–28.
65. R.E. Thayer (1996) *The Origin of Everyday Moods* (Oxford University Press).
66. N.H. Frijda (1988) 'The laws of emotion', *American Psychologist*, 43, 349–58.
67. M. Seligman (1975) *Helplessness: On Depression, Development and Death* (W.H. Freeman, San Francisco).
68. Thayer *The Origin of Everyday Moods*.
69. D. Watson and A. Tellengren (1985) 'Toward a consensual structure of mood', *Psychological Bulletin*, 98, 219–35.
70. W.P. Morgan and M.L. Pollock (1978) 'Psychologic characterisation of the elite distance runner', *Annals of the New York Academy of Science*, 301, 1978, 382–403.
71. T.A. Wehr, D.A. Sack and N.E. Rosenthal (1987) 'Seasonal affective disorder with summer depression and winter hypomania', 140th Annual Meeting of the American Psychiatric Association, Chicago, Illinois, *American Journal of Psychiatry*, 144 (12), 1602–3.
72. Thayer *The Origin of Everyday Moods*.
73. Ibid.
74. Ibid. V. Rippere (1977) 'What's the thing to do when you're depressed – a pilot study', *Behaviour Research and Therapy*, 15, 185–91.
75. G.B. Parker and L.B. Brown (1982) 'Coping behaviours that mediate between life events and depression'. *Archives of General Psychiatry*, 39, 1386–91.
76. Thayer *The Origin of Everyday Moods*.
77. Ibid.
78. Ibid.
79. C.S. Pomerleau, H.H. Scherzer, N.E. Grunberg, J. Judge, J.B. Fertig and J. Burleson (1987) 'The effect of acute exercise on subsequent cigarette smoking', *Journal of Behavioural Medicine*, 10, 117–27.
80. J.R. Grove, A. Wilkinson and B.T. Dawson (1993) 'Effects of exercise on selected correlates of smoking withdrawal', *International Journal of Sports Psychology*, 24, 217–36.
81. R.A. Faulkner, D.A. Bailer and R.L. Mirwarld (1987) 'The relationship of physical activity to smoking characteristic in Canadian men and women', *Canadian Journal of Public Health*, 78, 155–60.
82. S. Sethi and M.E. Seligman (1993) 'Optimism and fundamentalism', *Psychological Science*, 4, 256–9.
83. S.K. Nolen-Hoeksema (1987) 'Sex differences in unipolar depression: evidence and theory', *Psychological Bulletin*, 101, 259–82.
84. W.G. Parrott (1993) 'Beyond Hedonism: Motives for Inhibiting Good Moods and for Maintaining Bad Moods'. In D.M. Wegner and J.W. Pennebaker (eds) *Handbook of Mental Control* (Prentice Hall, Englewood Cliffs, New Jersey) 278–305.
85. M.W. Fordyce (1977) 'Development of a program to increase personal happiness', *Journal of Counselling Psychology*, 24, 511–21.

7 So, You Think You are Sane?

1. A. Ellis (1983) 'Failures in Rational-Emotive Therapy'. In E.Foa and P.M.G. Emmelgamp (eds) *Failures in Behaviour Therapy* (John Wiley and Sons, New York) pp 159–71.
2. K. Pollack (1994) *No Chance Encounter* (Findhorn Press, Scotland).
3. A. Ellis and R. Grieger (eds) (1977) *Handbook of Rational-Emotive Therapy* (Springer, New York).
4. Ibid.
5. F. Tallis (1997) *How to Stop Worrying* (Sheldon Press, London).
6. G. Davey and F. Tallis (1994) *Worrying. Perspectives on Theory, Assessment and Treatment*, Wiley Series in Clinical Psychology (Wiley, Chicester).
7. E. Lindal and J.G. Stefansson (1993) 'The lifetime prevalence of anxiety disorders in Iceland as estimated by the US National Institute of Mental Health Diagnostic Interview Schedule', *Acta Psychiatrica-Scandinavica* Jul, 88 (1), 29–34.

8. P. Salovey and J.A. Singer (1991) 'Cognitive Behaviour Modification'. In F.H. Kanfer and A.P. Goldstein (eds) *Helping People Change* (Pergaman, New York).
9. G. Davey and F. Tallis (1994) *Worrying. Perspectives on Theory, Assessment and Treatment*, Wiley Series in Clinical Psychology (Wiley, Chicester).
10. Tallis *How to Stop Worrying*.
11. W.D. McIntosh, T.F. Harlow and L.L. Martin (1995) 'Linkers and nonlinkers: goal beliefs as a moderator of the effects of everyday hassles on rumination, depression and physical complaints'. Special Issue: Rumination and intrusive thoughts. *Journal of Applied Social Psychology*, 25, 1231–44.
12. Tallis *How to Stop Worrying*.
13. F. Tallis, M. Eysenck and A. Matthew, 'A questionnaire for the measurement of nonpathological worry', *Personality and Individual Differences*, 13, 2, 161–8.
14. Salovey and Singer 'Cognitive Behaviour Modification'.
15. A.M. Isen, K.A. Daubman and G.P. Nowicki (1987) 'Positive affect facilitates creative problem solving', *Journal of Personality and Social Psychology*, 1987, 52, 6, 1122–31.
16. D.A. Haaga and G.C. Davison (1991) 'Cognitive Change'. In F.H. Kanfer and A.P. Goldstein (eds) *Methods in Helping People Change* (Pergamon Press, New York, Oxford).
17. A.T. Beck, A.J. Rush, B.F. Shaw and G. Emery (1979) *Cognitive Therapy of Depression: A Treatment Manual* (Guilford Press, New York).
18. W. Dryden. and J. Gordon (1990) *Think Your Way to Happiness* (Sheldon Press, London).
19. Ibid.
20. A. Ellis and R. Grieger (eds) (1977) *Handbook of Rational-Emotive Therapy* (Springer, New York).
21. A. Robbins (1995) *Notes from a Friend* (Fireside Books, Simon and Shuster, New York).
22. B. Montgomery and L. Morris (1988) *Getting On With The Oldies* (Lothian, Pt Melbourne).
23. A. Ellis and R. Harper (1985) *A New Guide to Rational Living* (Wilshire Books, California).
24. A. Ellis (1994) *Reason and Emotion in Psychotherapy: a Comprehensive Method of Treating Human Disturbances* (Carol, New York).
25. C. Peterson and L. M. Bossio (1991) *Health and Optimism* (Free Press, New York).
26. J. Proudfoot, D. Guest, J. Carson, D. Graham and J. Gray (1997) 'Effect of cognitive-behavioural training on job-finding among long-term unemployed people', *Lancet*, 12 July, 350, 96–100.
27. G.E. Valliant and C.O. Valliant (1990) 'Natural history of male psychological health, X11: a 45 year study of predictors of successful aging at age 65', *American Journal of Psychiatry*, 147: 31–7.
28. Ibid.

8 I Will Survive

1. E.E. Benezra (1996) 'Personality factors of individuals who survive traumatic experiences without professional help', *International Journal of Stress Management*, 3, 3, 147–54.
2. L.K. Cartwright, P. Wink and C. Kravetz (1995). 'What leads to good health in midlife women physicians?', *Psychosomatic Medicine*, 57, 284–92.
3. R.H. Rahe (1993) 'Acute versus chronic post-traumatic stress disorder', *Integrative Psychological and Behavioural Science*, 28, 45–6.
4. D.J. Cooke and D.J. Hole (1983) 'The aetiological importance of stressful life events', *British Journal of Psychiatry*, 143, 397–400.
5. J.G. Andrews and C. Tennant (1978) 'Life events and psychological illness', *Psychological Medicine*, 8, 545–9.
6. T.W. Miller (1988) 'Advances in understanding the impact of stressful life events on health', *Hospital and Community Psychiatry*, 39, 6, 615–22.
7. L.K. Cartwright, P. Wink and C. Kravetz (1995) 'What leads to good health in midlife women physicians?' *Psychosomatic Medicine*, 57, 284–92.
8. Ibid.
9. R.H. Rahe (1993) 'Acute versus chronic post-traumatic stress disorder', *Integrative Psychological and Behavioural Science*, 28, 45–6.
10. R.R. Yeung (1996) 'The acute effects of exercise on mood state', *Journal of Psychosomatic Research*, 40, 2, 123–41.
11. D. Benton (1996) *Food for Thought* (Penguin Books, London).
12. Ibid.
13. Ibid.
14. M.I. Barclay and A. MacPherson (1986) 'Selenium content of wheat flour used in the UK', *Journal of Science of Food and Agriculture*, 37, 1133–8.
15. J.R. Arthur, F. Nicol and J. Beckett (1990) 'Hepatic iodothyronine 5-deiodinase', *Biochemical Journal*, 272, 537–40.
16. D. Benton and R. Cook (1991) 'The impact of selenium supplementation on mood', *Biological Psychiatry*, 29, 1092–8.
17. J. Thorn, Robertson and D.H. Buss (1978) 'Trace nutrients: selenium in British food', *British Journal of Nutrition*, 39, 391–6.
18. M.I. Barclay and A. MacPherson, (1986) 'Selenium content of wheat flour used in the UK', *Journal of Science of Food and Agriculture*, 37, 1133–8.
19. C.T. Short, G.G. Duthie, J.D. Robertson, P.C. Morrice, F. Nichol and J.R. Arthur (1997) 'Selenium status of a group of Scottish adults', *European Journal of Clinical Nutrition*', 51, 400–4.
20. Benton, *Food for Thought*.
21. M.W.P. Carney (1990) 'Vitamin deficiency and mental symptoms', *British Journal of Psychiatry*, 156, 878–82.
22. D. Benton, R. Griffiths and J. Haller (1997) 'Thiamine supplementation mood and cognitive functioning', *Psychopharmacology*, 129, 66–71.
23. D. Benton, J. Haller and J. Fordy (1995b) 'Vitamin supplementation for one year improves mood', *Neuropsychobiology*, 32: 98–105.
24. M.W.P. Carney and B.F. Sheffield (1978) 'Serum folic acid and B12 in 272 psychiatric in-patients', *Psychological Medicine*, 8, 139–44.
25. Ibid.

26. J. Martineau, C. Barthlomew, B. Garreau and G. LeLard (1985) 'Vitamin B6, magnesium and combined B6-Mg: therapeutic effects in childhood autism', *Biological Psychiatry*, 462–75.
27. Benton et al., 'Thiamine supplementation mood and cognitive functioning'.
28. Ibid.
29 D. Benton and R. Cook (1991) 'Vitamin and mineral supplements improved intelligence scores and concentration of six-year-old children', *Personality and Individual Differences*, 12, 1151–8.
30. D. Benton and J.P. Buts (1990) 'Vitamin / mineral supplementation and intelligence', *The Lancet*, May 12, 335, 1159–60.
31. D. Benton and G. Roberts (1988) 'Effect of vitamin and mineral supplementation on intelligence of a sample of school children', *The Lancet*, Jan 23, 140–1.
32. Ibid.
33. Benton and Cook, 'Vitamin and mineral supplements'.
34. R. Cook and D. Benton (1993) 'The relationship between diet and mental health', *Personality and Individual Differences*, 14, 3, 397–403.
35. D. Benton, J. Haller and J. Fordy (1995b) 'Vitamin supplementation for one year improves mood', *Neuropsychobiology*, 32: 98–105.
36. J.T. Ussher, C. Dewberry, H. Melson and J. Noakes (1995) 'The relationship between health related quality of life and dietary supplementation in British Middle Managers: a double blind placebo study', *Psychology and Health*, 10, 97–111.
37. W.C. Willett (1997) 'Potential Benefits of Preventive Nutrition Strategies. In A. Bendich and R.J. Dedelbaum (eds) *Preventive Nutrition* (Humane Press, Totowa, New Jersey).
38. Benton. *Food for Thought*.
39. R. Doug-Dagech, P. Mena, and P. Periano (1997) 'Dietary Polyunsaturated Fatty Acids for Optimal Neurodevelopment. In A. Bendich and R.J. Dedelbaum (eds), *Preventive Nutrition, the Comprehensive Guide for Health Professionals* (Humane Press, Totowa, New Jersey).
40. E.S. Susser, P.H. Shang and P. Lin. (1992) 'Schizophrenia after prenatal exposure to the Dutch Hunger Winter of 1944–1945', *Archives of General Psychiatry*, 49, 1992, 983–8.
41. N.E. Rosenthal, D.A. Seck, C. Gillin, A.J. Lewn, F.K. Goodwin, Y. Davenporte, P.S. Mueller, D.A. Newsome and A.T. Wher (1984) 'Seasonal Affective Disorder: a description of the syndrome and preliminary findings with light therapy', *Archives of General Psychiatry*, 41, 1, 72–80.
42. A. Wirz-Justice, P. Graw, K. Krauchi, A. Sarrafzadeh, A., J. English, J. Arendt and L. Sand (1996) 'Natural light treatment of seasonal affective disorder', *Journal of Affective Disorders*, 37, 109–20.
43. Ibid.
44. R.J. Wurtman and J.J. Wurtman (1994) 'Carbohydrates and Depression'. In R.D. Masters and M.T. McGuire (eds) *The Neurotransmitter Revolution: Serotonin, Social Behaviour and the Law* (Southern Illinois University Press, Carbondale).
45. Ibid.
46. D.F. Kripke, J.C. Gillan, D.J. Mullaney, S.C. Risch and D.S. Janowski (1987) 'Treatment of Major Depressive Disorders by Bright White Light for Five Days'. In A. Halaris (ed) *Chronobiology and Psychiatric Disorders* (Elsevier, New York).
47. K.M. Beauchemin and P. Hays (1996) 'Sunny hospital rooms expedite recovery from severe and refractory depressions', *Journal of Affective Disorders*, 40, 49–51.
48. Wurtman and Wurtman 'Carbohydrates and Depression'.
49. Ibid.
50. B. Spring, J. Chiodo, and D.J. Bowen (1987) 'Carbohydrates, tryptophan and behaviour: a methodological review', *Psychological Bulletin*, 102, 2, 234–56.
51. Ibid.
52. L. Christensen and R. Burrows (1990) 'Dietary treatment of depression', *Behaviour Therapy*, 21, 183–93.
53. J.F. Gredan, P. Fontaine, M. Lubetsky and K. Chamberlain (1978) 'Anxiety and depression associated with caffeinism and academic performance', *American Journal of Psychiatry*, 138, 512–14.
   K. Gilliland and D. Andress (1981) 'Ad lib caffeine consumption, symptoms of caffeinism and academic performance', *American Journal of Psychiatry*, 138, 512–14.
54. Benton, *Food For Thought*.
55. M.W. Green, P.J. Rogers, N.A. Elliman and S.J. Gatenby (1994) 'Impairment of cognitive performance associated with dieting and high levels of dietary restraint', *Physiology and Behaviour*, 55, 447–52.
56. A. Keys, J. Brozek, A. Herschel, O. Mikelson, and H.L. Taylor (1950) *The Biology of Human Starvation, vol 2* (University of Minnesota Press, Minneapolis).
57. S.R. Maddi and S.C. Kobasa, (1984) *The Hardy Executive: Health Under Stress* (Dow-Jones-Irwin, Homewood, Illinois).
58. P. Fonagy, M. Steele, H. Steele, A. Higgitt and M. Target (1994) 'The theory and practice of resilience', *Journal of Child Psychology and Psychiatry*, 35, 2, 231–57.
59. M. Rutter (1985) 'Resilience in the face of adversity: protective factors and resistance to psychiatric disorder', *British Journal of Psychiatry*, 147, 598–611.
60. S. Wolff (1995) 'The concept of resilience', *Australian and New Zealand Journal of Psychiatry*, 29, 565–74.
61. E.J. Anthony (1987) *The Invulnerable Child* (The Guildford Press) p147.
62. Ibid.
63. S.S. Luthar (1993) 'Methodological and conceptual issues in research on childhood resilience', *Journal of Child Psychology and Psychiatry*, 34, 4, 441–53.
64. Wolff, 'The concept of resilience'.
65. M. Rutter (1987) 'Psychosocial resilience and protective mechanisms', *American Journal of Orthopsychiatry*, 57, 3, 316–31.
66. Fonagy et al., 'The theory and practice of resilience'.
67. Rutter, 'Psychosocial resilience and protective mechanisms'.
68. S. Levine, J.A. Chevalier, S.J. Korchin(1956) 'The effects of early shock and handling on later avoidance learning', *Journals of Personality*, 24, 475–93.
69. J. Hunt (1979) 'Psychological development: early experience', *Annual Review of Psychology*, 30, 103–43.
70. H. Ursin, E. Baade and S. Elvine (1978) *Psychobiology of Stress – A Study of Coping Men* (Academic Press, New York).

465

71. M. Stacey, R. Dearden, R. Pill and D. Robinson (1970) *Hospitals, Children and their Families: The Report of a Pilot Study* (Routledge and Kegan Paul, London).
72. Rutter, 'Psychosocial resilience and protective mechanisms'.
73. G. Andrews, A.C. Page, M. Neilson (1993) 'Sending your teenagers away', *Archives of General Psychiatry*, 50, July, 585–9.
74. J.E. McCarroll, C.S. Fullerton, R.J. Ursana and J.M. Hermsen (1996) 'Post-traumatic stress symptoms following forensic dental identification, Mt Carmel, Waco, Texas', *American Journal of Psychiatry*, 153:6, June 1996, 778–82.
75. Ibid.
76. Ibid.
77. Maddi and Kobasa, *The Hardy Executive*.
78. W. Hartin (1988) *Why Did I Marry You?* (Hill of Content, Melbourne, Australia).
79. M. Frese, D. Fay, T. Hilburger, K. Leng and A. Tag (1997) 'The concept of personal initiative', *Journal of Occupational and Organisational Psychology*, 70, 139–61.
80. Sanborn (1996) *Sanborn on Success* (Griffin Publishing, California).
81. Benezra, 'Personality Factors of Individuals'.
82. R. Contrada (1989) 'Type A behaviour, personality, hardiness and cardiovascular responses to stress', *Journal of Personality and Social Psychology*, 57, 895–903.
83. K.D. Pagana (1990). 'The relationship of hardiness and social support of student appraisal of stress in an initial clinical nursing situation', *Nursing Education*, 29, 255–61.
84. S.C. Funk and B.K. Houston (1987) 'A critical analysis of the hardiness scales validity and utility', *Journal of Personality and Social Psychology*, 53, 572–8.
85. D.J. Wiebe (1991) 'Hardiness and stress moderation: a test of proposed mechanisms', *Journal of Personality and Social Psychology*, Jan 60 (1) 89–99.
L.A. Schmied (1987) 'The relationship of stress. Type A behaviour and powerlessness to physiological responses in female clerical workers', *Journal of Psychosomatic Research*, 31 (5) 555–66.
86. S.C. Funk, (1992) 'Hardiness: a review of theory and research', *Health and Psychology*, 11, 5, 335–45.
87. S.M. Jourard and T. Landsman (1980) *Healthy Personality: An Approach from the Viewpoint of Humanistic Psychology* (4th edn) (Macmillan, New York).
88. M. Jahoda (1958) *Current Concepts of Positive Mental Health* (Basic Books, New York).
89. S.T. Fiske and S.E. Taylor (1991) *Social Cognition* (2nd edn) (McGraw Hill Book Company, New York) xviii, pp717.
90. P.T. Bartone, R. J. Ursano, K. Wright, L.H. Ingraham (1989) 'The impact of a military air disaster on the health of assistance workers', *Journal of Nervous and Mental Disease*, 177, 6, 317–27.
91. Ibid.
92. Ibid.
93. S. Taylor and J.D. Brown (1988) 'Illusion and well-being: a social psychological perpective on mental health', *Psychological Bulletin*, 103, 2, 193–210.
94. P.M. Lewinsohn, W. Mischel, W. Chaplin and R. Barton (1980) 'The role of illusory self-perceptions', *Journal of Abnormal Psychology*, 89 (2), 203–12.
95. L.B. Alloy, L.Y .Abrahamson and D. Viscusi (1981) 'Induced mood and the illusion of control', *Journal of Personality and Social Psychology*, 41, 1129–40.
96. B. Felson (1984) 'The effect of self-appraisals of ability on academice performance', *Journal of Personality and Social Psychology*, Nov, 47 (5) 944–52.
97. K. Underlid (1996) 'Activity during unemployment and mental health', *Scandinavian Journal of Psychology*, 37, 269–81.
98. C.I. Diener and C.S. Dweck (1978) 'An analysis of learned helplessness: continuous changes in performance, strategy and achievement cognitions following failure', *Journal of Personality and Social Psychology*, 36 (5) 451–62.
99. A.M. Isen, and B. Means (1983) 'The influence of positive affect on decision-making strategy', *Social Cognition*, 2 (1) 18–31.
100. S.E. Taylor, and J.D. Brown (1988) 'Illusion and well-being: a social psychological perspective on mental health', *Psychological Bulletin*, Mar 103 (2) 193–210.
101. Ibid.
102. W.C. Compton (1992) 'Are positive illusions necessary for self-esteem?' *Personality and Individual Differences*, 13, 12, 1343–44.
103. St Matthew 13:12.
104. E. Kringlen (1994) 'Theory of schizophrenia: comments', *British Journal of Psychiatry*, 164, S1:62–4.
105. P.B. Sutker, J.M. Davis, M. Uddo and S.R. Ditta (1995), 'War zone stress, personal resources, and PTSD in Persian Gulf war returnees', *Journal of Abnormal Psychology*, 104, 3, 444–52.
106. Ibid.
107. S.E. Taylor, R.R. Lichtman and J.V. Wood (1984) 'Attributions, beliefs about control and breast cancer', *Journal of Personality and Social Psychology*, 46, 489–502.
108. S.E. Taylor and D.A. Armor (1996) 'Positive illusions and coping with adversity', *Journal of Personality*, 64, 4, 873–98.
109. S. Epstein and P. Meier (1989) 'Constructive thinking: A broad coping variable with specific components', *Journal of Personality and Social Psychology*, 57, 332–50.
110. S.E. Taylor and D.A. Armor (1996) 'Positive illusions and coping with adversity', *Journal of Personality*, 64, 4, 873–98.
111. Ibid.
112. Ibid.
113. S. Kravetz, Y. Drory and V. Florian (1993) 'Hardiness and sense of coherence and their relation to negative effect', *European Journal of Personality*, Oct, 7 (4) 233–44.
114. B.J. Bowman (1997) 'Cultural pathways toward Antonovsky's sense of coherence', *Journal of Clinical Psychology*, 53, 2, 139–42.
115. D. Meichenbaum (1977) *Cognitive Behaviour Modification* (Plenum Press, New York).
116. D. Dennett (1995) 'How to make mistakes'. In J. Brockman and K. Matson (eds) *How Things Are* (Weidenfeld and Nicolson, London).
117. A. Murphy Paul (1998) 'The flip side of disaster', *Psychology Today*, March/April, 18.

118. 'Anticipation entry'. In R.L. Gregory and O.L. Zangwill (eds) *The Oxford Companion to the Mind* (Oxford University Press, Oxford).
119. D. Blum (1998) 'Finding strength: how to overcome anything', *Psychology Today*, June, 32–8.
120. L.G. Aspinwall and S.E. Taylor (1997) 'A stitch in time: self-regulation and proactive coping', *Psychological Bulletin*, 121, 3, 417–36.

9 Crisis, What Crisis?
1. K.S. Kendler, R.C. Kessler, E.E. Walters, C. MacLean, A.C. Heath and L.J. Eaves (1995) 'Stressful life events, genetic liability, and onset of an episode of major depression in women', *American Journal of Psychiatry*, 152, 6, 1995, June 833–42.
2. G. Parry (1990) *Coping With Crisis* (Routledge, London).
3. Ibid.
4. T.A. Wills (ed) (1987) *Basic Processes in Helping Relationships* (Academic Press, New York) pp255–79.
5. R.A. Schurman, P.D. Kramer and J.B. Mitchell (1985) 'Treatment of mental illness by nonpsychiatrist physicians', *Archives of General Adult Psychiatry*, 42, 89–94.
6. P. Freeling, B. Rao, B., E. Paykel, L. Sireling and R. Burton (1985) 'Unrecognised depression in general practice', *British Medical Journal*, 290, 1880–3.
7. H. Hinds and W.J. Burroughs (1997) 'How you know when you are stressed: self-evaluations of stress', *Journal of General Psychology*, 124, 1, 105–11.
8. B. Montgomery and Morris (1988) *Getting on with the Oldies* (Lothan, Port Melbourne, Australia).
9. D. Bindra (1972) 'Weeping: a problem of many facets', *Bulletin of British Psychological Society*, 1972, 25, 281–4.
10. V. Patel (1993) 'Crying behaviour and psychiatric disorders in adults: a review', *Comprehensive Psychiatry*, 34, 3 (May/June), 206–11.
11. W.H. Frey, C. Hoffman-Ahern, R.A. Johnson, D.T. Lykken and U.B. Tuason (1983) 'Crying behaviour in the human adult', *Integrative Psychiatry*, Sept–Oct: 94–100.
12. Kendler et al. 'Stressful life events'.
13. S.D. Hollon, R.J. DeRubeis and M.E.P. Seligman (1992) 'Cognitive therapy and the prevention of depression', *Applied and Preventive Psychology*, 1, 89–95.
14. M.F. Schier and C.S. Carver (1977) 'Self-focused attention and the experience of emotion: attraction, repulsion, elation, and depression', *Journal of Personality and Social Psychology*, 35, 625–36.
15. T. Pyszczynski and J. Greenberg (1987) 'Depression, Self-Focused Attention and Self-Regulatory Preservation'. In C.R. Snyder and C.E. Ford (eds) *Coping with Negative Life Events: Clinical and Social Psychological Perspectives* (Plenum Press, New York and London).
16. Schier and Carver, 'Self-focused attention'.
17. Pyszczynski and Greenberg 'Depression, Self-Focused Attention and Self-Regulatory Preservation'.
18. M.L. Smith, G.V. Glass and T.I. Miller, 1980. *The Benefits of Psychotherapy* (John Hopkins University Press, Baltimore, Maryland).
19. G. Parry (1990) *Coping With Crisis* (Routledge, London).
20. A.E. Kelly and McKillop (1996) 'Consequences of revealing personal secrets', *Psychological Bulletin*, 120, 3, 450–65.
21. T.A. Wills (1985) 'Supportive Functions of Interpersonal Relationships. In S. Cohen and S.L. Syme (eds) *Social Support and Health* (Academic, New York) pp 61–82.
22. B.P. Dohrenwend, P.E. Shrout, G. Egris and F.S. Mendelsohn (1980) 'Nonspecific psychological distress and other dimensions of psychopathology', *Archives of General Psychiatry*, 37, 1229–36.
23. L. Luborsky, B. Singer and L. Luborsky (1975) 'Comparative studies of psychotherapies', *Archives of General Adult Psychiatry*, 32, 995–1008.
24. P.M. Lewinsohn, H. Hoberman, L. Teri and M. Hautzinger (1985) 'An Integrative Theory of Depression'. In S. Reiss and R. Bootzin (eds) *Theoretical Issues in Behaviour Therapy* (Academic Press, New York) pp331–59).
25. D.G. Cross, P.W. Sheehan and J.A. Khan (1980) 'Alternative advice and counsel in psychotherapy', *Journal of Consulting and Clinical Psychology*, 48, 615–25.
26. C.R. Snyder and C.E. Ford (eds) (1987) *Coping With Everyday Negative Life Events: Clinical and Social Psychological Perspectives* (Plenum Press, New York) xv p420.
27. Cross et al., 'Alternative advice'.
28. C. Peterson and A.J. Stunkard (1992) 'Cognates of personal control: focus of control, self-efficacy, and explanatory style', *Applied and Preventive Psychology*, 1:111–17.
29. Snyder and Ford, *Coping With Everyday Negative Life Events*.
30. H. Bosma, M.G. Marmot, H. Hemingway, A. Nicholson, E.J. Brunner and S. Stansfield (1997) 'Low job control and risk of coronary heart disease in the Whitehall II (prospective cohort) study', *British Medical Journal* 314: 558–65.
31. E. Brunne, (1997) 'Stress and the biology of inequality' *British Medical Journal* 314, 1472–6.
32. R.W. White (1959) 'Motivation reconsidered: the concept of competence', *Psychological Review*, 66, 297–333.
33. M.E.P. Seligman (1975) *Helplessness: On Depression, Development and Death* (Freeman, San Francisco).
34. J.B. Rotter (1966) 'Generalised expectancies for internal versus external control of reinforcement', *Psychological Monographs*, 80, 1, 609.
35. C.R. Snyder (1978) 'The illusion of uniqueness', *Journal of Humanistic Psychology*, 18, 3–41.
36. L.S. Perloff and P. Brickman (1982) 'False consensus and false uniqueness: biases in perceptions of similarity', *Academic Psychology Bulletin*, 4, 3, 475–94.
    L.S. Perloff (1987) 'Illusions of Invulnerability'. In C.R. Snyder and C.E. Ford (eds) *Coping with Negative Life Events* (Plenum Press, New York).
37. Ibid.
38. R. Janoff-Bulman and D. Golden (1984) 'Attributions and adjustment to abortion'. Paper presented at the annual meeting of the American Psychological Association, Toronto.
39. C.B. Wortman and J.W. Brehm (1975) 'Responses to Uncontrollable Outcomes: An Integration of Reactance Theory and the Learned Helplessness Model'. In L. Berkowitz (ed) *Advances in Experimental Social Psychology* (vol 8) (Academic Press, New York).
40. E. Kubler-Ross (1969) *On Death and Dying* (Macmillan, New York).

41. Parry, *Coping With Crisis*.
42. R.L. Williams, J.S. Verble, D.E. Price and B.H. Layne (1995) 'Relationship of self management to personality types and indices', *Journal of Personality Assessment*, 1995, 64, 3, 494–506.
43. R. Janoff-Bulman (1985) 'The Aftermath of Victimisation: Rebuilding Shattered Assumptions'. In C.R. Figley (ed) *Trauma and its Wake* (Brunner/Mazel, New York) 15–35.
44. C.A. Anderson, M.R. Lepper and L. Ross (1980). 'Perseverance of social theories: the role of explanation in the persistence of discredited information', *Journal of Personality and Social Psychology*, 39, 1037–49.
45. Ibid.
46. M. Bard, and D. Sangrey (1979) *The Crime Victims Book* (Basic Books, New York).
47. L. Etinger (1983) 'Denial in Concentration Camps: Some Personal Observations on the Positive and Negative Functions of Denial in Extreme Life Situations'. In S. Breznitz (ed) *The Denial of Stress* (International Universities Press, New York) 199–212.
48. A. Freud (1936) *The Ego and the Mechanisms of Defense* (International Universities Press, New York).
49. S. Freud (1961) *The Loss of Reality in Neurosis and Psychosis* (standard edn) (Hogarth, London) (Originally published, 1924.) 23, 271–8).
50. R.S. Lazarus (1983) 'The Costs and Benefits of Denial'. In S. Reznitz (ed) *The Denial of Stress* (International Universities Press, New York) 1–30.
51. Ibid.
52. T.P. Hackett, N.H. Cassem and H.A. Wishnie(1968) 'The coronary care unit: an appraisal of its psychological hazards', *New England Journal of Medicine*, 279, 1365–70.
53. Ibid.
54. J. Suls and B. Fletcher (1985) 'The relative efficacy of avoidant and nonavoidant coping strategies: a meta-analysis', *Health Psychology*, 4, 249–88.
55. L. Pinkus (1997) *Death and the Family: The Importance of Mourning* (Faber and Faber, London, Boston).
56. A.D. Kanner and J.C. Coyne (1981) 'Comparison of two modes of stress management: daily hassles and uplifts versus major life events', *Journal of Behavioural Medicine*, 4, 1, 1–39.
57. S.M. Skevington and A. White (1998) 'Is laughter the best medicine?' *Psychology and Health*, 13, 157–69.
58. H.M. Lefcourt, K. Davidson, K.M. Prkachin and D.E. Mills (1997) 'Humour as a stress moderator in the prediction of blood pressure obtained during five stressful tasks', *Journal of Research in Personality*, 31, 523–542.
59. G.E. Valliant (1993) *The Wisdom of the Ego* (Harvard University Press, Cambridge, Massachusetts).
60. R. Carlsson (1997) *Don't Sweat the Small Stuff* (Hodder and Stoughton, London).
61. Ibid.
62. S.H. Elgin (1995) *You Can't Say That to Me* (John Wiley and Sons, Chichester).
63. R. Carlsson (1997) op. cit.

10 Is Prevention Possible?

1. S.E. Taylor and D.A. Armour (1996) 'Positive Illusions and coping with adversity', *Journal of Personality*, 64, 4, 873–98.
2. R.M. Sapolsky (1996) 'Why stress is bad for you', *Science*, 273, 9, 749–50.
3. J.D. Bremmer, P. Randall, T.M. Scott, R.A. Bronen, J.P. Seibyl, S.M. Southwick, R.C. Delaney, G. McCarthy, D.S. Charney and R.B. Innis 'MRI-based measurement of hippocampal volume in patients with combat-related post-traumatic stress disorder', *American Journal of Psychiatry*, 152, 7, 973–81.
4. Sapolsky,. 'Why stress is bad for you'.
5. M.N. Starkman, S.S. Gebarski, S. Berent and D.E. Schteingart, D.E. (1992) 'Hippocampal formation volume, memory dysfunction and cortisol levels in patients with Cushings Syndrome', *Biological Psychiatry*, 32, 756–65.
6. Sapolsky, 'Why stress is bad for you'.
7. A. Derrington (1997) 'The unsolved case of the old grey matter', *Financial Times*, March 1, section 3, 1.
8. D. Goldberg and P. Huxley (1980) *Mental Illness in the Community: The Pathway to Psychiatric Care* (Tavistock, London).
9. P. Bebbington, J. Hurry, C. Tennant, E. Sturt and J.K. Wing (1981) 'Epidemiology of mental disorders in Camberwell', *Psychological Medicine*, 11, 561–79.
10. J. Newton (1992) *Preventing Mental Illness in Practice* (Tavistock/Routledge, London).
11. J. Rodin, C. Cashman and L. Desiderato (1987) 'Psychosocial Interventions in Ageing and Focusing on Enrichment and Prevention'. In M. Riley, A. Baum and J. Matarazzo (eds) *Perspectives on Behavioural Medicine IV* (Academic Press, New York).
12. B.L. Bloom (1965) 'The medical model, miasma theory, and community mental health', *Community Mental Health Journal*, 1, 333–8.
13. R.F. Munoz (1987) 'Depression Prevention Research in Depression Prevention'. In Ricardo F Munoz (ed) *Research Directions* (Hemisphere Publishing Corporation, New York).
14. R.J. Baldessarini (1983) *Biomedical Aspects of Depression and its Treatment* (American Psychiatric Press, Washington DC).
15. G. Rose (1981) 'Strategy of prevention: lessons from cardiovascular disease', *British Medical Journal*, 282, 1847–51.
16. Ibid.
17. H. Heath, S. Scattergood and S. Meyer (1983) *Learning About Parenting* (Educating and Parenting, Philadelphia, PA) revised 1988.
18. H. Parens (1988) 'A Psychoanalytic Contribution Toward Rearing Emotionally Healthy Children: Education for Parenting. In J.M. Ross and W.A. Myers (eds) *New Concepts in Psychoanalytic Psychotherapy* (American Psychiatric Press, Washington DC) 120–138.
19. S. Provence and A. Naylor (1983) *Working with Disadvantaged Parents and their Children* (Yale University Press, New Haven, USA).
20. M. Rutter, (1995) 'Relationships between mental disorders in childhood and adulthood', *Acta Psychiatrica Scandinavica*, 91, 73–85.
21. J.E. Fleming and D.R. Offord (1990) 'Epidemiology of childhood depressive disorders: a critical review', *Journal of American Academy of Child and Adolescent Psychiatry*, 29: 571–80.
22. L. Cytryn and D. McKnew (1996) *Growing up Sad: Childhood Depression and its Treatment* (Norton, New York).
23. Ibid.

24. A.M. Clarke and S.D.B. Clarke (1976) *Early Experience: Myth and Evidence* (Open Books, London).
25. M. Rutter (1972) *Maternal Deprivation Reassessed* (Penguin, London).
26. N. Takei, R.M. Murray, P.O. Sham and E. Callaghan (1995) 'Schizophrenia risk for women from in utero exposure to influenza', *American Journal of Psychiatry*, 152, 1, 150–1.
27. T.D. Cannon, S.A. Mednick, J. Parnas, F. Schulsinger et al. (1994) 'Developmental brain abnormalities in the offspring of schizophrenic mothers: II. Structural brain characteristics of schizophrenia and schizotypal personality disorder', *Archives of General Psychiatry*, 51 (12) 955–62.
28. L.A. Sroufe (1977) 'Early experience evidence and myth', *Contemporary Psychology*, 22, pp878–80.
29. Rutter 'Relationships between mental disorders in childhood and adulthood'.
30. D. Quinton, A. Pickles, B. Maughan and M. Rutter (1993) 'Partners, peers and pathways: assortative pairing and continuities in conduct disorder', *Development Psychopathology*, 5, 763–83.
31. Ibid.
32. G.W. Brown and T. Harris (1978) *Social Originals of Depression a Study of Psychiatric Disorders in Women* (Tavistock).
33. E. Bloch (1968) 'Atheismus im Christentum. Zur Religion des Exodus und des Reichs', *Frankfurt am Main: Taschenbuecherausgabe* (1978), 13.
34. L.Y Abrahamson, L.B. Alloy and G.I. Metalsky (1989) 'Hopelessness depression: a theory-based subtype of depression', *Psychological Review* 96, 358–72.
35. N.C. Andreasen (1972) 'The role of religion in depression', *Journal of Religion and Health*, 11, 153–66.
36. D. Allen, (1966) 'Motives, rationales, and religious beliefs', *American Philosophical Quarterly*, 3, 2, 111–27.
37. C.D. Batson and W.L. Ventis (1982) *The Religious Experience: A Sociological Perspective* (Oxford University Press, New York).
38. Ibid.
39. I.M. Marks, (1978) 'Behavioural Psychotherapy of Adult Neurosis. In Garfield and E. Bergin (eds) *Handbook of Psychotherapy and Behaviour Change* (Wiley, New York).
40. P. Pressman, J.S. Lyons, D.B. Larson et al. (1990) 'Religious belief, depression and ambulation status in elderly women with broken hips', *American Journal of Psychiatry*, 147, 758–60.
41. M. Galanter, D. Larson and E. Rubenstone (1991) 'Christian psychiatry: the impact of evangelical belief on clinical practice'. *American Journal of Psychiatry*, 148, 1, 90–5.
42. B. Spilka, B. Beit-Hallahmi and H.N. Malony (1991) 'Personality, Theory and Religion'. In H. N. Malony (ed) *Psychology of Religion: Personalities, Problems, Possibilities. Psychology and Christianity, 5* (Baker Book House, Grand Rapids, MI, US) 141–210.
43. R.L. Gorsuch (1988) 'The psychology of religion', *Annual Review of Psychology*, 39, 201–21.
44. American Psychiatric Association (1975) Psychiatrists' viewpoints on religion and their services to religious institutions and the ministry. A report of a survey conducted by the task force on Religion and Psychiatry. Washington DC, American Psychiatric Association.
45. J. Neeleman and R. Persaud (1995) 'Why do psychiatrists neglect religion?', *British Journal of Medical Psychology*, 68, (2), 169–78.
46. M. Galanter, D. Larson and E. Rubenstone (1991) 'Christian psychiatry: the impact of evangelical belief on clinical practice', *American Journal of Psychiatry*, 148, 1, 90–5.
47. M. Pollner (1989) 'Divine relations, social relations, and well-being', *Journal of Health and Social Behaviour*, 30, 92–104.
48. J. Forsyth (1989) *Freud, Jung and Christianity* (University of Ottawa Press, Ottawa).
49. S. Freud (1927) *The Future of an Illusion* (Anchor Books, Garden City, New York) (trans J. Sterachey 1961; rev edn 1964).
50. C.G. Jung (1958) *The Undiscovered Self* (Little, Brown and Co, Boston).
51. C.G. Jung (1993) *Memories, Dreams, Reflections* (recorded and edited by Aniela Jaffe) (Fontana, London).
52. Freud, *The Future of an Illusion*.
53. Neeleman and Persaud, 'Why do psychiatrists neglect religion?'.
54. S. Freud (1963) *Civilization and its Discontents* (translated from German by Joan Riviere; revised and newly edited by James Strachey) (Hogarth Press, London).
55. Ibid.
56. W.H. Clark, (1968) *The Psychology of Religion* (MacMillan, New York).
57. S. Freud (1974) *Introductory Lectures on Psychoanalysis* (Pelican, Harmondsworth).
58. T. Robbins and D. Anthony (1979) 'The sociology of contemporary religious movements', *Annual Review of Sociology*, 5, 75–89.
59. J.T. Richardson (1980) 'People's temple and Jonestown: a corrective comparison and critique', *Journal for the Study of Religion*, 19, 3, 239–55.
60. L. Drummond (1983) 'Jonestown: a study in ethnographic discourse', *Semiotica*, 2, 4, 46, 167–209.
61. M. Schwartz and K.J. Kaplan (1992) 'Judaism, Masada, and suicide: a critical analysis', *Omega*, 25, 2, 127–32.
62. R. Crummey (1970) *The Old Believers and the World of the Antichrist* (University of Wisconsin, Madison, Wisconsin).
63. E. Barker (1986) 'Religious movements: cult and anticult since Jonestown', *Annual Review of Sociology*, 12, 329–46.
64. S. Naipaul (1981) *Journey to Nowhere: A New World Tragedy* (Simon and Schuster, New York).
65. B. Allen (1990) 'Jonestown – two faces of suicide: a Durkheimian analysis', *Suicide and Life Threatening Behaviour*, 20, 4, 285–306.
66. J. Bowker (1970) *Problems of Suffering in Religions of the World* (Cambridge University Press, London and New York).
67. Ibid.
68. Tanhuma, 101a, b. In J. Bowker (1970) *Problems of Suffering in Religions of the World* (Cambridge University Press, London and New York).
69. The Koran (lxiv, 11) In J. Bowker (1970) *Problems of Suffering in Religions of the World* (Cambridge University Press, London and New York).
70. The Koran (iii, 134, 140) In J. Bowker (1970) *Problems of Suffering in Religions of the World* (Cambridge University Press, London and New York).
71. J. Bowker (1970) *Problems of Suffering in Religions of the World* (Cambridge University Press, London and New York).
72. Samyutta-nikaya, lvi, 11 In J. Bowker (1970) *Problems of Suffering in Religions of the World* (Cambridge University Press, London and New York).

469

73. Brihad-aranyka Upanishad, i 4.6. In J. Bowker (1970) *Problems of Suffering in Religions of the World* (Cambridge University Press, London and New York).

74. Ibid.

75. J. Birtchnell, (1993) *How Humans Relate: A New Interpersonal Theory* (Praeger, London).

76. Ibid.

77. R.D. Persaud and C.J. Meux (1994) 'The psychopathology of authority and its loss: the effect on a ward of losing a consultant psychiatrist', *British Journal of Medical Psychology*, 67, 1–11.

78. K.D. Breault (1986) 'Suicide in America: a test of Durkheim's theory of religious and family integration, 1933–80', *American Journal of Sociology*, 92, 3, 628–56.

79. W.B. Bankston, D.H. Allen and D.S. Cunningham (1983) 'Religion and suicide: a research note on sociology's one law', *Social Forces*, 62, 2, 521–8.

80. F. Van Poppel and L.H. Day (1996) 'A test of Durkheim's theory of suicide – without committing the "Ecological Fallacy"', *American Sociological Review*, 61, 500–7.

81. C.G. Ellison, J.A. Burr and P.L. McCall (1997) 'Religious homogeneity and metropolitan suicide rates', *Social Forces*, 76, 1, 273–99.

82. Ibid.

83. L.R. Iannaccone (1991) 'The consequences of religious market structure', *Rationality and Society*, 3, 2, 156–177.

84. E.S. Paykel (1994) 'Introduction'. In E.S. Paykel and R. Jenkins (eds) *Prevention in Psychiatry* (Gaskell Press, Royal College of Psychiatrists, London).

85. Q. Spender and P. Hill (1996) 'Primary Prevention of Childhood Mental Health Problems'. In T. Kendrick, A. Tylee and P. Freeling (eds) *The Prevention of Mental Illness in Primary Care* (Cambridge University Press, Cambridge).

86. G. Albee and M. Perry (1996) 'Are we preventing diseases or promoting competencies?', *Journal of Mental Health*, 5, 4, 421–2.

87. E.L. Cowen (1996) 'The ontogenesis of primary prevention: lengthy strides and stubbed toes', *American Journal of Community Psychology*, 24, 2, 235–249.

88. Ibid.

89. D. Lester (1996) 'Gun ownership and rates of homicide and suicide', *European Journal of Psychiatry*, 1996, Vol 10, No. 2, 83–5.

90. Ibid.

91. Rachel Jenkins and T. Bedirhan Ustun (eds) (1998) *Preventing Mental Illness: Mental Health Promotion in Primary Care* (John Wiley and Sons, Chichester).

92. J.C. Carter, A.D. Stewart, V.J. Dunn and C.G. Fairburn (1997) 'Primary prevention of eating disorders: might it do more harm than good?' *International Journal of Eating Disorders*, 22, 167–72.

93. E.L. Cowen (1996) op. cit.

94. I.J. Deary, R.M. Agius and A. Sadler (1996) 'Personality and stress in consultant psychiatrists', *International Journal of Social Psychiatry*, 42, 4, 112–13.

95. A. J. Krakowski (1982) 'Stress and the practice of medicine – the myth and reality', *Journal of Psychosomatic Research*, 26, 1, 91–8.

96. R. Gordon (1987) 'An operational classification of disease prevention'. In J.A. Steinberg and M.M. Silverman (eds), *Preventing Mental Disorders* (Rockville, MD: dept of health and human services), 20–6.

97. P. J. Mrazek, and R. J. Haggerty (eds) (1994) 'The frontiers of preventive intervention research', in *Reducing Risks for Mental Disorders* (Institute of Medicine National Academy Press, Washington DC) vii.

98. C.C. Butler, P. Roisin, N.C.H. Stott (1998) 'Qualitative study of patients' perceptions of doctors' advice to quit smoking: implications for opportunistic health promotion', *British Medical Journal*, 316, 1878–81.

99. E.L. Cowen (1996) op. cit.

100. R. Gordon (1983) 'An operational classification of disease prevention', *Public Health Reports*, 98, 107–9.

101. M. Rutter, J. Silberg, and E. Simonoff (1993) 'Whither behaviour genetics? A developmental psychopathology perspective'. In R. Plomin and G.E. McClearn (eds), *Nature, Nurture and Psychology* (Amercian Psychiatric Association, Washington, DC).

102. F. Cambien, O. Poirer, L. Lecerf, A. Evans, J.P. Cambou, D. Arveiler, G. Luc, J.M. Bard, L. Bara, S. Richards, L. Tiret, P. Amouyel, F. Alhenc-Gelas and F. Soubrier (1992) 'Deletion polymorphism in the gene for angiotensin-converting enzyme is a potent risk for myocardial infarction', *Nature*, 359, 641–4

103. A. Dryman and W.W. Eaton (1991) 'Affective symptoms associated with the onset of major depression in the community: findings from the US National Institute of Mental Health Epidemiologic Catchment Area Program', *Acta Psychiatrica Scandinavica*, 84, 1, 1–5.

104. W.W. Eaton, M. Badawi, and B. Melton (1993) 'Prodromes and precursors for four DSM-III disorders: epidemiologic data for prevention of disorders with slow onset', unpublished manuscript.

105. National Center for Health Statistics (1993) 'Advance report of final mortality statistics, 1990: monthly vital statistics report', 41, (7) suppl., 1–52.

106. S. Guze and E. Robins (1970) 'Suicide and primary affective disorders', *British Journal of Psychiatry*, 117, 437–8.

107. C. Croft-Jeffreys and G. Wilkinson (1989) 'Estimated costs of neurotic disorders in UK general practice in 1985', *Psychological Medicine*, 19, 549–58.

108. G.W. Brown and T.O. Harris (1989) 'Depression'. In G.W. Brown and T.O. Harris (eds), *Life Events and Illness* (Guilford Press, New York, NY), 49–94.

109. G.W. Brown and T.O. Harris (1989) op. cit.

110. G.W. Brown (1992) 'Life events and social support: possibilities for primary prevention'. In Rachel Jenkins, Jennifer Newton and Robyn Young (eds), *The Prevention of Anxiety and Depression: the role of the primary care team* (London: HMSO).

111. National Institute on Alcohol Abuse and Alcoholism (1991) 'Alcohol research, promise for the decade' (DHHS).

112. Department of Health and Human Services (1990) 'Seventh Special report to the US congress on alcohol and health' (Rockville, MD) DHHS Pub no (ADM) 90–1656.

113. National Institute on Alcohol Abuse and Alcoholism (1991) op. cit.

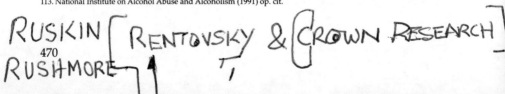

"Primus in Orbe Deos fecit amor (Statius)
'Fear was the first creator of Gods in this World,

114. A.Y. Tien, and J.C. Anthony (1990) 'Epidemiological analysis of alcohol and drug use as risk factors for psychotic experiences', *Journal of Nervous and Mental Disease*, 178: 473–80.

115. R. W. Manderscheid and S.A. Barrett (eds) (1987) *Mental Health, United States* (Government Printing Office Washington, DC) DHHS Publication No. (ADM) 87–1518:79.

116. W. Hall, G. Goldstein, G. Andrews, H. Lapsley, R. Bartel, and D. Silove (1985) 'Estimating the economic costs of schizophrenia', *Schizophrenia Bulletin*, 11, 598–611.

117. L.N. Robins and D.A. Regier (1991) *Psychiatric Disorders in America: the Epidemiologic Catchment Area Study* (The Free Press, New York, NY).

118. T.R. Kwapil, M.B. Miller, M.C. Zinser, J. Chapman and L.J. Chapman (1997) 'Magical ideation and social anhedonia as predictors of psychosis proneness: a partial replication', *Journal of Abnormal Psychology*, 106, 3, 491–5.

119. A.S. Henderson, A.F. Jorm, A.E. Korten, H. Creasey, E. McCusker, G.A. Broe, W. Longley and J.C. Anthony (1992) 'Environmental risk factors for Alzheimer's disease: their relationship to age of onset and to familial or sporadic types', *Psychological Medicine*, 22, 429–36.

120. M. F. Mendez (1993) 'Miscellaneous causes of dementia'. In P. J. Whitehouse (ed), *Dementia* (F.A. Davis, Philadelphia, PA), 343–6.

121. Ibid.

122. W.A. Rocca, C.M. van Duijn, V. Chandra, L. Fratiglioni, A.B. Graves, A. Heyman, A.F. Jorm, E.M. Kokmen, K. Kondo, J.A. Mortimer, S. Shalat, H. Soininen and A. Hofman (1991) 'Alcohol and Alzheimer's disease: a collaborative re-analysis of case-control studies', *International Journal of Epidemiology*, 20, s21–s27.

123. R. Katzman (1993) 'Views and reviews: education and the prevalence of dementia and Alzheimer's disease', *Neurology*, 43, 13–20.

124. A.B. Graves *et al* (1991) 'Alcohol and tobacco consumption as risk factors for Alzheimer's disease: a collaborative reanalysis of case-control studies', *International Journal of Epidemiology* 20, suppl. 2, s48–s57.

125. A. Ott, A.J.C. Slooter, A. Hofman, F. van Harskamp, J.C.M. Witteman, C. Van Broeckhoven, C.M. van Duijn and M.M.B. Breteler (1998) 'Smoking and risk of dementia and Alzheimer's disease in a population-based cohort study: the Rotterdam Study', *Lancet*, 351, 20 June, 1840–3.

126. E.E. Werner and R.S. Smith (1992) *Overcoming the Odds: High-risk Children from Birth to Adulthood* (Cornell University Press, New York).

127. M. Rutter (1985) 'Resilience in the face of adversity: protective factors and resistance to psychiatric disorder', *British Journal of Psychiatry*, 147, 598–611.

128. S.B. Campbell and J.F. Cohn (1991) 'Prevalence and correlates of post partum depression in first-time mothers', *Journal of Abnormal Psychology*, 100, 594–599.

129. S.B. Campbell, J.F. Cohn, C. Flanagan, S. Popper, T. Meyers (1992) 'Course and correlates of postpartum depression during the transition to parenthood', *Development and Psychopathology*, 4, 29–47.

130. T. Field (1992) 'Infants of depressed mothers', *Development and Psychopathology*, 4: 49–66.

131. G. Dawson, L.G. Klinger, H. Panagiotides, S. Spieker and K. Frey (1992) 'Infants of mothers with depressive symptoms: electroencephalographic and behavioural findings related to attachment status', *Development and Psychopathology*, 4: 67–80.

INFORMATIFF
TELE THERAPY
PLATO THOUGHTS
MINDSET & MINDSNET THOUGHTS
A Line hath its begining from a point
MIND > THE MONKEY
EDWARD BESTELLER & MORTIMMER MOUTH..
BOUNZING THOUGHTS

471
2015

INDEX

For thoughts the Slave of life; and life's
times fool; and time which has this measure of all the things

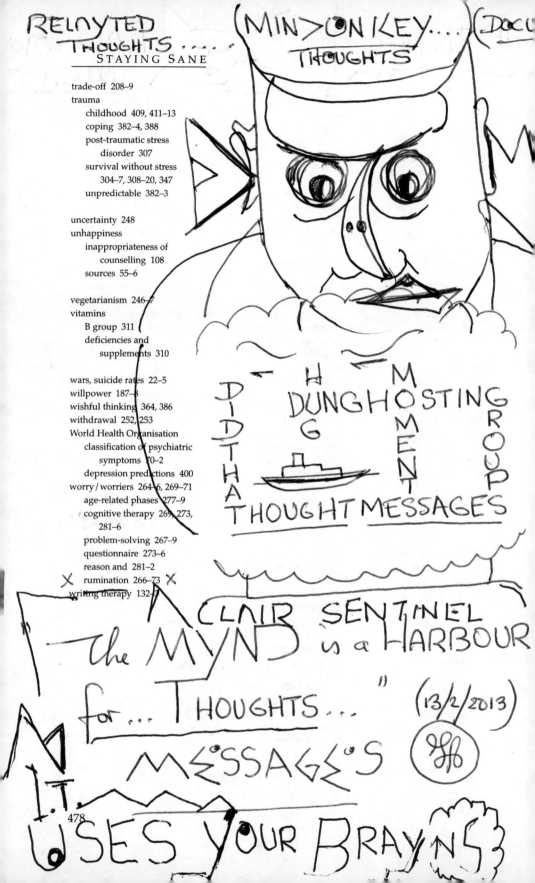

DID THAT HUGG MOMENT DUNGHOSTING GROUP
THOUGHT MESSAGES

"the MYND CLAIR SENTINEL is a HARBOUR
for ... THOUGHTS ... "   (13/2/2013)
MESSAGE'S
I.T.
USES YOUR BRAYNS

478

NTRYS... (... STEALTHY THOUGHTS, that
STEAL THY THOUGHTS
(26/Oct/2013)

MENTARY

"...Alone and warming his five wits
the White Owl in the Belfrey sits"

(Tennyson)

A THINKINGHOST... OWLS THOUGHTS...
ASA... DOCOMMENTARY

SPO (17/4/2013)

OWLS... A THOUGHT DIVINER/MINDREADER

SPO 26/10/2013

"WEBASTO" MYN MONKEY

WEBHASTO

RYTON...O MONITOR

THOUGHTS

TELL TALES

"The Fear of GOD, furthers every enterprise, that Governments do undertake..." (Machieavellie)

"FRIGHTENED by certain non-persons called GHOSTS (Fielding

"For THOUGHTS....can
    FRIGHTEN...
"UNLESS; they are Righton. → FORETHOUGHT
we are
RYTON, (LA) 2000   FOM RE
RIGHTON

2016

LA 2010 For Thought
    "HAS the Language "Watch Dogs/Monitor."

"This inward state of mind, calme region once and full of peace; now tost and turbulent".

John Milton (1573)

MINDS with S HHHHREWD GR E ⃨⃨⃨⃨ by ... THOUGH, T$ ...

(2011)(2013)

"Rumour is a Pipe; blown by surmises, jealousies, Conjectures, of so many and so varied stop, that the vast discordant, wavering multitude, may play upon it" (William Shakespeare)

SUBAUDITIONS ...

" PROPHETS RECHTS, PROPHETS LINKS ... DER WELTKIND IN DER MITTEN. "

GOETHE

SUBAUDITOURS
SUBAID.

The GHOSTS intent on Haunting You...
Goods To Intent...
ITS GOD to KNOW

ABBOT EADWINE'S

© HfB 2012

...ORACLES ADYTON to Thoughts...

SOMETHING
HEARD within
JUNG HOSTING...
THOUGHT MESSAGES

HfB 2013 THOUGH

AN INARTIFICIAL... THINK BALLOONS 4U
ARGUMENT IS THE
TESTIMONY OF ANOTHER.
* ✓ (Watts)

MEIKLE PHOINEAS

PRIMUS IN ORBE; DEOS FECIT IMOR (Statius)
"Fear, was the first creator of GODS, in this world."

THE MINDONKEY FORAGING FOR

THOUGHTMESSAGES *sary*

H E A R D   I N D R U M   H O N T H   > U G G E S T   G H O S T I N G

...INTERNALLY... (ʒʃʒ)

TOTEM UP
IN MIN> POLE

HEAR,WITHIN,THE,
THOUGHTS   > (ʒʃʒ) 2013

O15

"Yea, I will be thy priest and build a fane,
in some forgotten region of ~~mind~~ thy brain,
where branched thoughts instead of pines;
shall murmur in the wind "

(Rewritten Poem;) Milton? + ʒʃʒ

Thought messages heard Mindrum suggest...
>UNGHOSTING doth hon un..
(honour one)

FOOD FOR THOUGH

MYNDER RE

* "No Thought can be valuable of which good sense is not the GROUNDWORK..." (Jo Addison)

" The Dimensions of this MERCY are above my thoughts — it is for aught I know a crowning mercy..." (Oliver Cromwell)

MUSES

① DISTRAUGHT
② DUNGHOSTING
③ DUMPHONE
④ THOUGHTMESSAGES

2012

" There is a breathings space in Thoughts between Innate and acquired Ideas "

2013